MODERN MICROECONOMICS

A. KOUTSOYIANNIS

Professor of Economics
University of Waterloo, Ontario

M

First edition 1975
Reprinted 1976 (twice), 1977 (twice)

Published by
THE MACMILLAN PRESS LTD

London and Basingstoke
Associated companies in Delhi Dublin
Hong Kong Johannesburg Lagos Melbourne
New York Singapore and Tokyo

ISBN 0 333 18285 5

Printed in Great Britain at
THE PITMAN PRESS
Bath

By the same author

THEORY OF ECONOMETRICS
(*Second Edition*)

To Charles F. Carter

and

Janet Carter

Contents

Preface   xi

PART ONE

THE BASIC TOOLS OF ANALYSIS

1 INTRODUCTION   3
   I   Economic Models   3
  II Classification of Markets   4
 III The Concept of an 'Industry'   7
     A. The Importance of the Concept of an 'Industry'   7
     B. Criteria for the Classification of Firms into Industries   8

2 THEORY OF DEMAND   13
   I Theory of Consumer Behaviour   13
     A. The Cardinal Utility Theory   14
     B. The Indifference Curves Theory   17
     C. The Revealed Preference Hypothesis   28
     D. The Consumers' Surplus   32
     E. Some Applications of Indifference Curves Analysis   35
  II The Market Demand   44
     A. Derivation of the Market Demand   44
     B. Determinants of Demand   45
     C. Elasticities of Demand   46
     D. Market Demand, Total Revenue and Marginal Revenue   50
 III Recent Developments in the Theory of Market Demand   53
     A. The Pragmatic Approach to Demand Analysis   53
     B. Linear Expenditure Systems   58
 IV The Demand for the Product of a Firm   60

3 THEORY OF PRODUCTION   67
   I The Production Function for a Single Product   67
  II Laws of Production   76
     A. Laws of Returns to Scale   76
     B. The Law of Variable Proportions   82
 III Technological Progress and the Production Function   85
 IV Equilibrium of the Firm: Choice of Optimal Combination of Factors
    of Production   86
     A. Single Decision of the Firm   86
     B. Choice of Optimal Expansion Path   92

    V Derivation of Cost Functions from Production Functions   95
        A. Graphical Derivation of Cost Curves from the Production   95
            Function
        B. Formal Derivation of Cost Curves from a Production Function   97
   VI The Production Function of a Multiproduct Firm   99
        A. The Production Possibility Curve of the Firm   99
        B. The Isorevenue Curve of the Multiproduct Firm   102
        C. Equilibrium of the Multiproduct Firm   104

4 THEORY OF COSTS   105
    I General Notes   105
   II The Traditional Theory of Cost   106
        A. Short-Run Costs   107
        B. Long-Run Costs: The 'Envelope Curve'   111
   III Modern Theory of Costs   114
        A. Short-Run Costs   115
        B. Long-Run Costs: The 'L-Shaped' Scale Curve   120
   IV Engineering Cost Curves   122
        A. Short-Run Engineering Costs   124
        B. Long-Run Engineering Costs   125
    V The Analysis of Economies of Scale   126
        A. Real Economies of Scale   128
        B. Pecuniary Economies of Scale   137
   VI Empirical Evidence on the Shape of Costs   137
        A. Statistical Cost Studies   138
        B. Studies Based on Questionnaires   143
        C. Engineering Cost Studies   143
        D. Statistical Production Functions   146
        E. The 'Survivor Technique'   146
   VII The Relevance of the Shape of Costs in Decision-making   148

PART TWO

THEORY OF THE FIRM

SECTION A: PERFECT COMPETITION, MONOPOLY,
MONOPOLISTIC COMPETITION

5 PERFECT COMPETITION   154
    I Assumptions   154
   II Short-Run Equilibrium   155
        A. Equilibrium of the Firm in the Short Run   155
        B. The Supply Curve of the Firm and the Industry   159
        C. Short-Run Equilibrium of the Industry   160
   III Long-Run Equilibrium   160
        A. Equilibrium of the Firm in the Long Run   160
        B. Equilibrium of the Industry in the Long Run   161
        C. Optimal Resource Allocation   163
   IV Dynamic Changes and Industry Equilibrium   164
        A. Shift in the Market Demand   164
        B. Predictions of the Perfect Competition Model when Costs
            Change   167
        C. Effects of Imposition of a Tax   168

6 MONOPOLY 171
   I   Definition 171
   II   Demand and Revenue 171
   III   Costs 174
   IV   Equilibrium of the Monopolist 174
      A.   Short-Run Equilibrium 174
      B.   Long-Run Equilibrium 177
   V   Predictions in Dynamic Changes 179
      A.   Shift in the Market Demand 179
      B.   An Increase in the Costs of the Monopolist 181
      C.   Imposition of a Tax 182
   VI   Comparison of Pure Competition and Monopoly 183
   VII   The Multiplant Firm 186
   VIII   Bilateral Monopoly 189

7 PRICE DISCRIMINATION 192
   I   Assumptions 192
   II   The Model 192
   III   Effects of Price Discrimination 195
   IV   Price Discrimination and Elasticity of Demand 198
   V   Price Discrimination and the Existence of the Industry 199
   VI   Government-Regulated Monopoly 200

8 MONOPOLISTIC COMPETITION 202
   I   Assumptions 203
   II   Costs 203
   III   Product Differentiation and the Demand Curve 204
   IV   The Concepts of the 'Industry' and the 'Group' 204
   V   Equilibrium of the Firm 205
   VI   Critique 209
   VII   Comparison with Pure Competition 212

SECTION B: CLASSICAL OLIGOPOLY

9 NON-COLLUSIVE OLIGOPOLY 216
   I   Cournot's Duopoly Model 216
   II   Bertrand's Duopoly Model 225
   III   Chamberlin's Oligopoly Model 228
   IV   The 'Kinked-Demand' Model 230
   V   Stackelberg's Duopoly Model 233

10 COLLUSIVE OLIGOPOLY 237
   I   Cartels 237
      A.   Cartels aiming at Joint Profit Maximisation 237
      B.   Market-Sharing Cartels 242
   II   Price Leadership 244
      A.   The Model of the Low-Cost Price Leader 245
      B.   The Model of the Dominant-Firm Price Leader 246
      C.   Critique of the Traditional Price Leadership Models 247
      D.   Barometric Price Leadership 248
   III   The Basing-Point Price System 252
      A.   The Single Basing-Point System 252
      B.   Multiple Basing-Point System 253

SECTION C: AVERAGE-COST PRICING

11 A CRITIQUE OF THE NEOCLASSICAL THEORY OF THE
    FIRM: THE MARGINALIST CONTROVERSY   256
    I   The Basic Assumptions of the Neoclassical Theory   256
    II   The Hall and Hitch Report and the 'Full-Cost' Pricing Principle 263
    III Gordon's Attack on Marginalism   265
    IV   In Defence of Marginalism   267

12 A REPRESENTATIVE MODEL OF AVERAGE-COST PRICING   271
    I   Goals of the Firm   271
    II   Demand and Cost Schedules   272
    III Price Determination: The 'Mark-Up' Rule   273
    IV   Comparison with Pure Competition   275
    V   Predictions of Average-Cost Pricing Theory in Changing Market
         Conditions   276
    VI   Critique of Average-Cost Pricing   277

SECTION D: LIMIT-PRICING (or ENTRY-PREVENTING PRICING) 283

13 BAIN'S LIMIT-PRICING THEORY   284
    I   Bain's Early Model   284
    II   Barriers to New Competition   287
         A.   Bain's Concepts of 'Competition' and 'Entry'   288
         B.   Barriers to Entry   289
    III Summary of Bain's Empirical Findings   301
    IV   Industry Equilibrium   301
    V   Some Comments   304

14 RECENT DEVELOPMENTS IN THE THEORY OF LIMIT-
    PRICING   305
    I   The Model of Sylos-Labini   305
    II   The Model of Franco Modigliani   313
    III The Model of Bhagwati   319
    IV   The Model of Pashigian   320

SECTION E: MANAGERIAL THEORIES OF THE FIRM 323

15 BAUMOL'S THEORY OF SALES REVENUE MAXIMISATION   325
    I   Rationalisation of the Sales Maximisation Hypothesis   325
    II   Interdependence and Oligopolistic Behaviour   326
    III Baumol's Static Models   327
    IV   Baumol's Dynamic Model   342
    V   Empirical Evidence   346
    VI   Some Comments   348

16 MARRIS'S MODEL OF THE MANAGERIAL ENTERPRISE   352
    I   Goals of the Firm   352
    II   Constraints   354
    III The Model: Equilibrium of the Firm   356
    IV   Maximum Rate of Growth and Profits   364
    V   Comparison with Baumol's Model   366
    VI   Comparison with a Profit Maximiser   367
    VII Critique of Marris's Model   368

17 O. WILLIAMSON'S MODEL OF MANAGERIAL DISCRETION 371
    I   The Managerial Utility Function 371
    II   Basic Relationships and Definitions 372
    III The Model 373
         A. A Simplified Model of Managerial Discretion 373
         B. The General Model of Managerial Discretion 376
    IV   Implications of the Model 378
    V   Comparative Static Properties 379
    VI   Empirical Evidence 381

SECTION F: BEHAVIOURAL THEORY OF THE FIRM

18 THE BEHAVIOURAL MODEL OF CYERT AND MARCH 386
    I   The Firm as a Coalition of Groups with Conflicting Goals 386
    II   The Process of Goal-Formation: the Concept of the 'Aspiration
          Level' 387
    III   Goals of the Firm: Satisficing Behaviour 388
    IV   Means for the Resolution of the Conflict 390
    V   The Process of Decision-making 393
    VI   Uncertainty and the Environment of the Firm 395
    VII   A Simple Model of Behaviourism 396
    VIII A Comparison with the Traditional Theory 398
    IX   Critique 400

SECTION G: THEORY OF GAMES
LINEAR PROGRAMMING

19 THEORY OF GAMES 404
    I   Some Definitions 404
    II   Two-Person Zero-Sum Game 406
         A. Certainty Model 406
         B. Uncertainty Model 408
    III Non-Zero-Sum Game 410
    IV   The 'Prisoner's Dilemma': A Digression 412

20 LINEAR PROGRAMMING
    I   General Notes 414
    II   Statement of the Linear Programming Problem 415
    III Graphical Solution 416
         A. Graphical Determination of the Region of Feasible Solutions 416
         B. Graphical Determination of the Objective Function 420
         C. Determination of the Optimal Solution 420
    IV   The Simplex Method 423
         A. The Iterative Procedure 424
    V   The Dual Problem and Shadow Prices 434

21 CONCLUDING REMARKS 435

Select Bibliography 437

Index 453

Preface

This is an attempt to present a contemporary microeconomics textbook at an intermediate level. In teaching microeconomic theory at all levels and in various countries the author became increasingly aware of a twofold gap in the established textbooks in this field. Most of these texts use obsolete tools of analysis, namely smooth U-shaped cost curves and steeply sloping demand curves for the individual firms. Such cost and demand curves bear little resemblance to the real world cost and demand conditions, and hence are not suitable for the analysis of the behaviour of the modern large enterprise. Furthermore, it is a fact that in market economies oligopoly is the main market structure. Mixed and capitalistic economies continue to be characterised by increasing concentration in the industrial sector; still most micro-texts continue to do this fact scant justice, by devoting only a few pages to the analysis of oligopolistic behaviour. The impressive new developments in the oligopoly front over the last two decades are either being ignored or treated superficially in established textbooks. In this book we make an attempt to fill this gap.

The author has adopted the verbal method of presenting the material covered, with extensive use of diagrams to illustrate the verbal exposition. Mathematical proofs, where necessary, are presented in footnotes, or, when in the text, they are printed in small print so as not to interrupt the main theme.

The book is written at an intermediate level and is designed for undergraduate micro-theory courses. In addition, post-graduate courses in which micro-theory is taught not at too specialised a level, could make use of the text.

The approach adopted in this book is that of *partial equilibrium analysis*. We will be examining the behaviour of buyers and sellers in a particular industry in isolation from the conditions prevailing in other industries (markets). The interaction of industries as studied by various *general equilibrium methods* will not be discussed in this book.

The book is divided in two parts. In Part One (Chapters 1–4) we examine the behaviour of the consumer and of other buyers, and we develop the basic tools of analysis of the behaviour of the firm, its revenue and cost curves. These curves determine the equilibrium output of the firm. The market demand and the market supply define the equilibrium of the industry. The revenue curve of the firms is closely related to market demand, while the cost curves of the firms determine the market supply. Thus the equilibrium of the firm defines and is defined by the equilibrium conditions of the industry. The revenue and costs of the firm and the demand and supply of the market determine the market price and the output of both the firm and the industry. Chapter 1 contains some definitions and a classification of the main market structures traditionally adopted in micro-economic theory. In Chapter 2 we develop the theory of consumer behaviour and market demand, paying special attention to the recent developments in this field of microeconomics. In particular, we examine the attempts to abandon the non-operational concept of utility and to render the demand function dynamic by incorporating into it appropriate time lags. In Chapter 3 we develop the theory of production, stressing again the recent developments in this field. In Chapter 4 we examine the traditional and modern theories of cost, and we attempt a systematic analysis of the various types of economies of scale. We also present the available empirical evidence regarding the shape of cost curves, which refutes the smooth U-shaped costs of the traditional theory. The main emphasis in Part One is on equipping the student with a 'kit of modern tools' of economic analysis, which will help him understand and analyse the complexities of the real business world.

Part Two of the book is divided in six sections. In Section A (Chapters 5–8) we examine the traditional theories of perfect competition, monopoly and monopolistic competition. In Chapters 5 and 6 we examine the behaviour of the firm in the basic market structures of perfect competition and monopoly. In Chapter 7 we discuss price discrimination, a practice widely used by firms in the modern business world. In Chapter 8 we examine the equilibrium of the firm and the industry in the market structure of monopolistic competition. The remaining five Sections of Part Two are devoted to the examination of the behaviour of the firm in oligopolistic market structures. Thus the greatest part of this book deals with oligopoly. There are several reasons for this. Firstly, oligopoly, as we said, is the main form of market structure in the modern industry. Secondly, there are many theories of oligopolistic behaviour, and each of them needs careful examination. Thirdly, theories of oligopoly developed since 1950 have mostly been omitted from textbooks. Almost all textbooks on microeconomics stop at the 'theory' of the kinked-demand curve. Even the classical oligopoly models of collusion and price leadership are dealt with inadequately in most textbooks. In this book we attempt a detailed examination of the main *classical* and *modern* theories of oligopoly. In Section B (Chapters 9–10) we examine the classical models of oligopoly (duopoly, cartels, price leadership). In Section C (Chapters 11–12) we examine the attack on marginalism and the abortive attempts to develop a theory of *average-cost pricing* as a substitute for the traditional marginalistic pricing models. In Section D (Chapters 13–14) we review the basic models of *limit-pricing* (or *entry-preventing pricing*). We discuss in detail the theories of J. Bain and subsequently we examine the recent developments in the limit-price theory (Sylos's model; Modigliani's formalisation of the entry-preventing models; Bhagwati's extensions of earlier models; Pashigian's 'mixed strategy'). In Section E (Chapters 15–17) we examine the *managerial theories* of the firm. We discuss in detail Baumol's 'sales maximisation' hypothesis, Marris's model of 'managerial enterprise', and Williamson's model of 'managerial discretion'. In Section F (Chapter 18) we examine the *behavioural theory* of the firm as developed by Cyert and March. Finally in Section G (Chapters 19–20) we discuss briefly the *theory of games* and the *linear programming* model of optimal decision-making. The models of entry-forstalling, of managerialism and behaviourism are largely ignored in textbooks or are mentioned briefly as 'experiments' in the theory of the firm. In this book we attempt to give these theories their due position in the theory of microeconomics.

Three important topics (factor pricing, general equilibrium, welfare theory) usually included in textbooks on price theory, are omitted from this text. The exclusion was dictated by financial cost considerations: the length of the text had to be kept within such limits that would make it possible to offer the book to students at a reasonable price. Given these length limitations and faced with the choice of either omitting part of the new material in this volume or excluding the above three topics, we felt that the second alternative was preferable. Thus we decided to bring up to date the major areas of micro-theory rather than rehash the material of the existing textbooks on price theory. It is hoped that the comprehensive treatment of the material covered and the inclusion of the main 'recent' developments in the theory of the firm will provide the student with the necessary modern tools and general theoretical framework with which to approach and analyse with more realism the complex phenomena of the contemporary business world.

I am greatly indebted to Professor Charles F. Carter, Vice-Chancellor of the University of Lancaster and former Editor of the *Economic Journal*, who gave me the opportunity to write this book and made many constructive criticisms and valuable suggestions. I am also indebted to Professor Harry Townsend of the University of Lancaster who read through the typescript and made many helpful suggestions. From Professor Kenneth Alexander of the University of Strathclyde, Professor R. Barback of the University of Hull, Professor Robert Kerton and Professor Stanley Kardasz of the University of Waterloo, Mr. George McGregor-Reid, Mr. Len Skerrat, Mr. Ronald Akehurst, Mr. Geoffrey Dixon and Miss Susan Charles of the University of Lancaster I received helpful comments on particular sections of the book. Mr. Tin Nguyen of the University of Lancaster checked the examples and helped with various suggestions.

I am thankful to my students at the University of Lancaster and the University of Waterloo, Ontario, who with their comments and general reactions helped me improve the exposition of several parts of the book. Katherine Kossentos, Stuart James, Paul Pezaros, John Andrew, Antony Akeroyd and Ian Horgan deserve special mention. I have also benefited from the detailed comments of two anonymous referees. Any mistakes and defects, however, are my responsibility.

I would like to dedicate this book to Charles F. Carter, who taught me the real meaning of economics, and to Janet Carter, who taught me, in her own way, 'what the Ithakas mean'.[1]

Waterloo, Ontario, 1975   A. KOUTSOYIANNIS

---

[1] C. P. Cavafy, 'Ithaka', in *Four Greek Poets* (Penguin, 1966).

PART ONE

BASIC TOOLS OF ANALYSIS

1. Introduction

I. ECONOMIC MODELS

In this chapter we will introduce some definitions which will be needed throughout the book, and we will examine the classification of the main market structures traditionally adopted in microeconomic theory.

Economic theory aims at the construction of models which describe the economic behaviour of individual units (consumers, firms, government agencies) and their interactions which create the economic system of a region, a country or the world as a whole.

A model is a simplified representation of a real situation. It includes the main features of the real situation which it represents. A model implies abstraction from reality which is achieved by a set of meaningful and consistent assumptions, which aim at the simplification of the phenomenon or behavioural pattern that the model is designed to study. The degree of abstraction from reality depends on the purpose for which the model is constructed. The series of assumptions in any particular case are chosen carefully so as to be consistent, to retain as much realism as possible and attain a 'reasonable' degree of generality. Abstraction is necessary, given that the real economic world is extremely complex and any attempt to study it in its *true* form would lead to an analysis of unmanageable dimensions. Thus models do not describe the *true* economic world since by their nature they are constructed as abstractions from the 'truth'. However, abstraction does not imply unrealism, but is a simplification of reality. It is the beginning of understanding the great complexity of the real economic world.

A model can be constructed at different levels of aggregation, detail and sophistication depending on its purpose. There are two main purposes for which a model is built – *analysis* and *prediction*.

Analysis implies the explanation of the behaviour of economic units, consumers or producers. From a set of assumptions we derive certain 'laws' which describe and explain with an adequate degree of generality the behaviour of consumers and producers.

Prediction implies the possibility of forecasting the effects of changes in some magnitudes in the economy. For example, a model of supply might be used to predict the effects of imposition of a tax on the sales of firms.

The validity of a model may be judged on several criteria. Its predictive power, the consistency and realism of its assumptions, the extent of information it provides, its generality (that is, the range of cases to which it applies) and its simplicity.

There is no general agreement regarding which of the above attributes of a model is more important. The views of economists range from Milton Friedman's position[1] that the most important criterion of the validity of the model is its predictive performance,

[1] See M. Friedman, *Essays in Positive Economics* (Chicago University Press, 1953).

to Paul Samuelson's position[1] that realism of assumptions and power of the model in explaining the behaviour of the economic agents, producers or consumers, is the most important attribute of a model.

Most economists take the position that what is the most important attribute of a model depends on its purpose, the use to which one puts the model. Predictive performance is important when the purpose of the model is forecasting the effects of a certain change in a variable. Realism of assumptions and explanatory power are important features of a model if the purpose of the model is the explanation of why a system behaves as it does. Ideally a model should fulfil both criteria: it should be the best predictor of the behaviour of the system *and* provide the most complete explanation of this behaviour. However, this ideal is rarely met in practice, one reason being that the relationships in a model change continuously over time. Another reason is the skills of model-builders. A person that gives the best forecasts does not necessarily also provide the most accurate explanations. The model-builder must define the primary purpose of his model before constructing it. He should then build the model in such a way as to best attain its primary objective, even if this course of action means that the model will not be suitable for other secondary objectives. In particular, the number and nature of the assumptions of the model, its degree of detail (or level of aggregation) and the amount of information it can yield will depend on the purpose of building the model.

The purpose of the theory of the firm is to provide models for the analysis of the decision-making in the firm in various market structures. A theory of the firm should explain how the decisions of the firm are taken: how the firms set their price, decide the level and style of their output, the level of advertising expenses and other selling activities, the level of research and development expenditures, their financial policies, their investment decisions and so on.

A theory of the firm must have a minimum degree of generality so as to be applicable to the explanation of the behaviour of a 'group' of firms rather than to the explanation of the behaviour of a particular firm. Individual case studies are of interest to the particular firms to which they refer, but several case studies are required before a theoretical model of the behaviour of firms may be constructed.

We finally note that a model should be constructed in such a way so as to be *testable*, that is, to be capable of being verified or refuted when confronted (compared) with the true economic facts.

II. CLASSIFICATION OF MARKETS

Various criteria have been suggested for the classification of markets. The basic criteria are the existence and closeness of substitutes (*substitutability of products criterion*) and the extent to which firms in the industry take into account the reactions of competitors (*interdependence criterion*). The latter criterion is closely related to the number of firms in the industry and the degree of differentiation of the product. If there are many firms in the industry each one of them will tend to ignore its competitors and act atomistically. If there are few firms in the industry each one will be conscious of its interdependence with the others and will take into account their reactions. Bain[2] has suggested a third criterion for market classification, namely the 'condition of entry' which measures the 'ease of entry' in the various markets (see below).

---

[1] See P. Samuelson, *Foundations of Economic Analysis* (Harvard University Press, 1947).

[2] See J. S. Bain, 'Chamberlin's Impact on Microeconomic Theory', in R. E. Kuenne (ed.), *Studies in Impact of Monopolistic Competition Theory* (Wiley, 1967); reprinted in H. Townsend (ed.), *Readings in Price Theory* (Penguin, 1971).

Traditionally the following market structures are distinguished.

Perfect competition

In perfect competition there is a very large number of firms in the industry and the product is homogeneous. Competition is perfect in the sense that every firm considers that it can sell any amount of output it wishes at the going market price, which cannot be affected by the individual producer whose share in the market is very small. Thus although *competition* is perfect, there is no *rivalry* among the individual firms. Each one firm acts atomistically, that is, it decides its level of output ignoring the others in the industry. The products of the firms are perfect substitutes for one another so that the price-elasticity of the demand curve of the individual firm is infinite. Entry is free and easy.

Monopoly

In a monopoly situation there is only one firm in the industry and there are no close substitutes for the product of the monopolist. The demand of the monopolist coincides with the industry demand, which has a finite price elasticity. Entry is blockaded.

Monopolistic competition

In a market of monopolistic competition there is a very large number of firms, but their product is somewhat differentiated. Hence the demand of the individual firm has a negative slope, but its price elasticity is high due to the existence of the close substitutes produced by the other firms in the industry. Despite the existence of close substitutes each firm acts atomistically, ignoring the competitors' reactions, because there are too many of them and each one would be very little affected by the actions of any other competitor. Thus each seller thinks that he would keep some of his customers if he raised his price, and he could increase his sales, but not much, if he lowered his price: his demand curve has a high price elasticity, but is not perfectly elastic because of the attachment of customers to the slightly differentiated product he offers. Entry is free and easy in the industry.

Oligopoly

In an oligopolistic market there is a small number of firms, so that sellers are conscious of their interdependence. Thus each firm must take into account the rivals' reactions. The competition is not perfect, yet the rivalry among firms is high, unless they make a collusive agreement. The products that the oligopolists produce may be homogeneous (pure oligopoly) or differentiated (differentiated oligopoly). In the latter case the elasticity of the individual market demand is smaller than in the case of the homogeneous oligopoly. The sellers must 'guess' at the rivals' reactions (as well as at the consumers' reactions). Their decisions depend on the ease of entry and the time lag which they forecast to intervene between their own action and the rivals' reactions. Given that there is a very large number of possible reactions of competitors, the behaviour of firms may assume various forms. Thus there are various models of oligopolistic behaviour, each based on different reaction patterns of rivals.

From the above brief description of the characteristics of the various markets we may present a scheme of market classification using the following measures for the degree of product substitutability, sellers' interdependence and ease of entry.

The degree of substitutability of products may be measured by the conventional *price cross-elasticity* (e_p) for the commodities produced by any two firms[1]

$$e_{P,ji} = \frac{dq_j}{dp_i} \cdot \frac{p_i}{q_j}$$

This measures the degree to which the sales of the *j*th firm are affected by changes in the price charged by the *i*th firm in the industry. If this elasticity is high, the products of the *j*th and the *i*th firms are close substitutes. If the substitutability of products in a market is perfect (homogeneous products) the price cross-elasticity between every pair of producers approaches infinity, irrespective of the number of sellers in the market. If the products are differentiated but can be substituted for one another the price cross-elasticity will be finite and positive (will have a value between zero and infinity). If the products are not substitutes their price cross-elasticity will tend to zero.

The degree of interdependence of firms may be measured by an unconventional *quantity cross-elasticity* for the products of any two firms[1]

$$e_{q,ji} = \frac{dp_j}{dq_i} \cdot \frac{q_i}{p_j}$$

This measures the proportionate change in the price of the *j*th firm resulting from an infinitesimally small change in the quantity produced by the *i*th firm. The higher the value of this elasticity is, the stronger the interdependence of the firms will be. If the number of sellers in a market is very large, each one will tend to ignore the reactions of competitors, irrespective of whether their products are close substitutes; in this case the quantity cross-elasticity between every pair of producers will tend to zero. If the number of firms is small in a market (oligopoly), interdependence will be noticeable even when products are strongly differentiated; in this case the quantity cross-elasticity will be finite.[2]

For a monopolist both cross-elasticities will approach zero, since *ex hypothesi* there are no other firms in the industry and there are no close substitutes for the product of the monopolist.

The ease of entry may be measured by Bain's concept of the '*condition of entry*', which is defined by the expression

$$E = \frac{P_a - P_c}{P_c}$$

where E = condition of entry
        P_c = price under pure competition
        P_a = price actually charged by firms.

The condition of entry is a measure of the amount by which the established firms in an industry can raise their price above P_c without attracting entry (see Chapter 13).

[1] See R. L. Bishop, 'Elasticities, Cross-Elasticities, and Market Relationships', *American Economic Review* (1952); comments by W. Fellner and E. Chamberlin and reply by Bishop *American Economic Review* (1953) pp. 898–924; comment by R. Hieser and reply by Bishop, *American Economic Review* (1955) pp. 373–86. Also see R. L. Bishop, 'Market Classification Again', *Southern Economic Journal* (1961).

[2] Alternatively, one might use the number of firms in a market as a measure of the degree of interdependence. This measure, however, may be misleading when the number of firms is large, but the market is dominated by one (or a few) large seller(s). Under these conditions interdependence would obviously be strong despite the large number of firms in the industry.

The market classification which emerges from the application of the above three criteria is shown in table 1.1.

It should be noted that the dividing lines between the different market structures are to a great extent arbitrary. However, markets should be classified in one way or another for analytical purposes.

Table 1.1 Classification of markets[1]

Type of market	Substitutability-of-product criterion $e_{P,ji} = \dfrac{dq_j}{dp_i}\dfrac{p_i}{q_j}$	Interdependence-of-sellers criterion $e_{Q,ji} = \dfrac{dp_j}{dq_i}\dfrac{q_i}{p_j}$	Ease-of-entry criterion $E = \dfrac{P_a - P_c}{P_c}$
Pure competition	$\to \infty$	$\to 0$	$\to 0$
Monopolistic competition	$0 < e_{P,ji} < \infty$	$\to 0$	$\to 0$
Pure oligopoly	$\to \infty$	$0 < e_{Q,ji} < \infty$	$E > 0$
Heterogeneous oligopoly	$0 < e_{P,ji} < \infty$	$0 < e_{Q,ji} < \infty$	$E > 0$
Monopoly*	$\to 0$	$\to 0$	blockaded entry

* For the monopolist the price and quantity cross-elasticities refer to products and sellers in other industries.

III. THE CONCEPT OF AN 'INDUSTRY'

In this book we will adopt the partial equilibrium approach. The basis of this approach is the study of *the industry*. In this section we will attempt to define this concept and show its usefulness in economic theory.

A. THE IMPORTANCE OF THE CONCEPT OF AN 'INDUSTRY'

The concept of an industry is important for economic analysis. It is also important to the businessman, to the government, to those involved in the collection and processing of economic data, and to all research investigators.

In economic analysis the concept of an industry is very important in the study of competition. Firstly, it reduces the complex interrelationships of all firms of an economy to manageable dimensions. In a broad sense each firm is competing with any other firm in the economy. This might lead one to think that a general equilibrium approach in which the behaviour of each firm would be depicted by an equation (the Walrasian-type analysis) is more appropriate for the study of the economic reality. However, the general equilibrium has not as yet yielded a satisfactory framework for the analysis of the individual economic units, consumers or firms. The general equilibrium approach and its current applications (input–output analysis and aggregate econometric models) are designed to deal with a different range of problems than the partial equilibrium approach. The aggregate econometric models (and the input–output models) are relevant for the study and the prediction of aggregate magnitudes, such as total output of any economy, total employment, consumption, investment, etc. By their nature they cannot include the

[1] See J. Bain, 'Chamberlin's Impact on Microeconomic Theory', in R. E. Kuenne (ed.), *Studies in Impact of Monopolistic Competition Theory* (Wiley, 1967) pp. 147–76; reprinted in H. Townsend (ed.), *Readings in Price Theory* (Penguin, 1971).

detailed information required for the study and the prediction of the behaviour of individual economic units. The study of the behaviour of firms makes it necessary to demarcate areas of close interaction of firms in order to gain some insight into their decision-making process. The concept of *an industry* has been developed to include the firms which are in some form of close relationship with one another. Irrespective of the criterion used in order to draw the borderlines between the various groups, the firms in each group are behaviourally interdependent. Secondly, the concept of the industry makes it possible to derive a set of general rules from which we can predict the behaviour of the competing members of the group that constitute the industry. Thirdly, the concept of the industry provides the framework for the analysis of the effects of entry on the behaviour of the firm and on the equilibrium price and output.

Empirical research would be unmanageable if one had to work with data of the individual firms of all the economy simultaneously. Even Triffin, who argued in favour of the abandonment of the concept of the industry as a tool of analysis, recognised its importance for empirical research. He argued that the concept is useful in concrete empirical investigations after the industry's 'content' has been empirically determined to suit the purpose of the research.[1]

The businessmen act with the consciousness of belonging to an industry, which they perceive as comprising those firms more closely linked with them. All decisions are taken under some assumptions about probable reactions of those firms which the businessman thinks will be influenced in some way by his actions. The businessman perceives that the industry comprises the firms which will be affected by his decisions and hence will react in one way or another.

Published data are grouped on the basis of standard industrial classifications. The grouping is based on some criteria which may change over time. The compatibility of the data of different sources which publish data 'by industry' is one of the main concerns of any empirical investigator.

The government policy is designed with regard to 'industries'. Government measures aim in general at the regulation of the activity and performance of industries rather than of individual firms.

B. CRITERIA FOR THE CLASSIFICATION OF FIRMS INTO INDUSTRIES

Two criteria are commonly used for the definition of an industry, *the product* being produced (market criterion), and *the methods of production* (technological criterion). According to the first criterion firms are grouped in an industry if their products are close substitutes. According to the second criterion firms are grouped in an industry on the basis of similarity of processes and/or of raw materials being used.

Which classification is more meaningful depends on the market structure and on the purpose for which the classification is chosen. For example, if the government wants to impose excise taxes on some industries the most meaningful classification of firms would be the one based on the product they produce. If, on the other hand, the government wants to restrict the imports of some raw material (e.g. leather), the classification of firms according to similarity of processes might be more relevant.

Market criterion: similarity of products

Using this criterion we include in an industry those firms whose products are sufficiently similar so as to be close substitutes in the eyes of the buyer. The degree of similarity

---

[1] See R. Triffin, *Monopolistic Competition and General Equilibrium Theory* (Harvard University Press, Cambridge, Mass., 1939).

is measured by the cross-elasticity of demand, which we defined as

$$e_c = \frac{dq_j}{dp_i} \cdot \frac{p_i}{q_j}$$

where $\quad q_j$ = quantity produced by the jth firm
$\qquad p_i$ = price charged by the ith firm.

What is the required value of the cross-elasticity in order to classify the ith and jth firms in the same industry? The answer to this question cannot be based on *a priori* theoretical grounds if the products are differentiated. In this event the degree of closeness or similarity is defined on an empirical basis, depending on the purpose of the study in each particular case. For some purposes a broad definition of products is more appropriate, while for other purposes a narrower definition based not only on the *technical substitutability* but also on the *economic substitutability* (in the sense of similar price ranges) of commodities, may be more desirable. For example, the motor-car industry would include all types of motor-cars, from the cheapest Mini to the most expensive Rolls-Royce and the specialised sports cars. This classification is used by the tax authorities in Britain where car taxation is uniform for all types of cars. However, this classification is not appropriate if one wants to analyse the pricing decisions of the car manufacturers. For this purpose one should use a narrower definition of an industry, for example the 'popular' models, the 'luxury' models and the 'sports' models.[1] In each such 'group' the products are both technical and economic substitutes.

It is useful to examine the concept of an industry as applied in the different traditional market structures, so as to illustrate the importance of substitutability.

In pure competition the application of the product criterion for the definition of an industry is straightforward. In this market structure the product is assumed to be homogeneous and the number of sellers is large. Under these conditions the cross-elasticity of demand for the product of each firm is infinite. There is perfect substitutability between the products of the various firms and this leads to a unique price in the market, since no buyer would be prepared to pay a higher price for a product technically identical with that of other firms.

In monopolistic competition products are differentiated by design, quality, services associated with its supply, trade marks, etc. Thus the products are not perfect substitutes in the eyes of the buyer, and the question arises of how close substitutes the commodities must be if they are to be grouped in the same 'industry'. Both Chamberlin and Joan Robinson recognised that with differentiated products each firm has its own market, and hence some degree of monopoly power in setting its own price. However, they both recognised the necessity of retaining the concept of an industry in order to give their theory the required degree of generality, and develop it within the partial-equilibrium framework. Joan Robinson[2] defined the product as 'a consumable good, arbitrarily demarcated from other kinds of goods, but which may be regarded for practical purposes as homogeneous within itself'. Thus, she views products as forming a chain of substitutes, the continuity of which is broken by gaps between successive products along the chain. Products thus isolated by such gaps can be classified in an industry despite their minor differences. Basically this definition of the industry uses the measure of price cross-elasticity. An industry includes the firms whose demand curves exhibit high price cross-elasticity. She brushed aside the problem of how high this cross-elasticity should be by *assuming* that there would be gaps in the values of cross-elasticity and these gaps would demarcate the industrial groups.

[1] See H. R. Edwards, *Monopoly and Competition in the British Soap Industry* (Oxford University Press, 1964).
[2] Joan Robinson, *Theory of Imperfect Competition* (Macmillan, 1933).

A similar definition was adopted by Kaldor.[1] He views products as occupying a given position on a scale, with products on either side being more close substitutes as compared with products further away on this scale:

> Each 'product' can be conceived as occupying a certain position on a 'scale'; the scale being so constructed that those products are neighbouring each other between which the consumer's elasticity of substitution is the greatest (a 'product' itself can be defined as a collection of objects between which the elasticity of substitution of all relevant consumers is infinite). Each producer then is faced on each side with his nearest rivals; the demand for his own product will be most sensitive with respect to the prices of these; less and less sensitive as one moves further away from him.

Chamberlin, in his original formulation of the *Theory of Monopolistic Competition* (Harvard University Press, 1933) defined his large 'group' as comprising firms which produce very similar although differentiated commodities: '... The difference between (the varieties of products) are not such as to give rise to differences in cost. This might be approximately true where say similar products are differentiated by trade marks' (p. 83). The conceptual and empirical difficulties implied in the above definition of an industry lead Triffin[2] to preach the abandonment of the concept of the industry as being inconsistent with the notion of 'product differentiation' and the unique character of each firm's product:

> The monopolistic competition writers resorted to the limping device of keeping intact, for the purpose of analysis, that concept of an industry, which their study of differentiation showed to be untenable.

Triffin argued that all goods are to some degree substitutable for one another in that they compete for a part of the income of the consumer. Every firm competes with all the other firms in the economy, but with different degrees of closeness. Thus, he concluded, the concept of an industry is irrelevant as a tool of analysis. The best way for analysing the economic relationships of firms is to adopt a general equilibrium approach. This view was later adopted by Chamberlin.[3]

Andrews[4] has severely criticised the abandonment of the concept of an industry. He argued that the rejection of the concept of the industry is both unnecessary and undesirable. The concept is of great importance both in economic analysis and in real-world situations (see above, pp. 7–8). Andrews advocated the classification of industries on the basis of similarity of processes, arguing that this classification is more relevant for analysing the pricing decisions of the firm (see below).

Edwards[5] in dealing with oligopolistic markets, has attempted to retain the definition of an industry in terms of the product. He argues that the retention of the concept of an industry as a tool of analysis is essential to the economist as well as to the businessman and the government. He says that product differentiation does not necessitate the abandonment of the concept of an industry. He accepts Chamberlin's view that a 'group' or 'industry' is not a *definite* economic entity (with definite edges) like the Marshallian concept of an industry, but an analytical tool which should be used with all degrees of generality. In a broad definition an industry includes all the range of products which are

[1] N. Kaldor, 'Market Imperfection and Excess Capacity', *Economica* (1935) pp. 38–9.

[2] R. Triffin, *Monopolistic Competition and General Equilibrium Theory* (Harvard University Press, Cambridge, Mass., 1939) pp. 88–9.

[3] E. Chamberlin, 'Monopolistic Competition Revisited', *Economica* (1951).

[4] P. W. S. Andrews 'Industrial Analysis in Economics', in P. W. S. Andrews and T. Wilson (eds.), *Oxford Studies in the Price Mechanism* (1951) pp. 143.

[5] H. R. Edwards, *Monopoly and Competition in the British Soap Industry* (Oxford University Press, 1964).

technical substitutes in that they satisfy the same need (for example the motor-car industry includes all firms which produce all types of cars). Within this broad group of products there are definite subgroups (popular models, luxury models, sports cars) which tend to have very similar technical characteristics. Thus, for each subgroup there will be a unique price in the long run (because the products are technically identical or very similar and there will be no cost differences), but consumers' preferences create a separate market for each firm. For the broad group of products there will be *a cluster of prices* in the long term reflecting the differences in the technical characteristics and therefore the differences in costs of the different varieties. Edwards argues that there is a tendency in British manufacturing for the pattern of production within an industry (in the broad definition) to stabilise (in normal conditions) into a conventional product-pattern with a corresponding conventional price-pattern (Edwards, *Monopoly and Competition in the British Soap Industry* pp. 54–5). If the price–quality pattern is strictly stable then the various subgroups of products can be treated as one for demand purposes.[1] Edwards recognises that in the real world the price–quality pattern does not in fact remain strictly stable. However, he argues that the degree of stability is sufficient to justify the assumption that the price–quality is approximately constant and can be treated as such for all practical purposes.

The technological criterion: similarity of processes

According to this criterion, an industry is defined so as to include firms which use similar processes of production. The similarity may lie in the methods of production, the raw materials used, or the channels of distribution.

Chamberlin, before Triffin's attack on his 'large group' model, attempted the extension of the concept of the industry to cover the supply aspects of a market. He said that the 'group' need not necessarily be defined on the basis of the substitutability between products. Industry classifications based upon technological criteria rather than upon the possibility of market substitution were perfectly legitimate for all purposes.[2]

Andrews[3] also advocated the definition of an industry on the basis of similarity of processes.

Joan Robinson[4] in her later writings recognised that her original definition of the industry was not adequate for oligopolistic market structures and suggested a redefinition of the industry based on the technological criterion of similarity of processes:

> The concept of an industry, though amorphous and impossible to demarcate sharply at the edges, is of importance for the theory of competition. It represents the area within which a firm finds it relatively easy to expand as it grows. There are often certain basic processes required for the production of the most diverse commodities (tennis balls, motor tyres and mattresses) and economies in the utilisation of by-products under one roof. The know-how and trade connections established for one range of products make it easier to add different commodities of the same technical nature to a firm's output than it is to add mutually substitutable commodities made of different materials, or made or marketed by radically different methods.

[1] See J. R. Hicks, *Value and Capital* (Oxford University Press, 1946) pp. 311–12. Also P. A. Samuelson, *Foundations of Economic Analysis* (Harvard University Press, Cambridge, Mass., 1947) pp. 141–3.

[2] E. Chamberlin, 'Monopolistic or Imperfect Competition?', *Quarterly Journal of Economics* (1937) p. 574.

[3] See P. W. S. Andrews, 'Industrial Analysis in Economics' in T. Wilson and P. W. S. Andrews (eds.), *Oxford Studies in the Price Mechanism* (Oxford University Press, 1951). Also Andrews, *On Competition in Economic Theory* (Macmillan, 1964) and Andrews, *Manufacturing Business* (Macmillan, 1949).

[4] Joan Robinson, 'Imperfect Competition Revisited', *The Economic Journal* (1953).

It should be noted that the technological criterion of similarity of processes suffers from the same defects as the product-substitutability criterion. How similar should the processes employed by various firms be in order to group them in the same industry? The advocates of the technological criterion do not discuss such problems.

In conclusion we can say that in markets where the product is differentiated the 'industry' concept cannot be as definite as in markets where the product is homogeneous. The definition of the borderlines between industries will be to some extent arbitrary, irrespective of the criterion used for the classification of firms into industries.

Regarding the two criteria traditionally used for industrial classifications, no general conclusion can be drawn as to which is better. The choice depends on the purpose of the classification. It seems, however, that the integration of the two criteria (substitutability of products and technological similarity of processes) is most desirable in analysing the behaviour of the firm in oligopolistic market structures which are typical of the modern business world. It is generally accepted that entry considerations are important in explaining the observed behaviour of firms. (See Part Two, Chapters 13–14.) Entry cannot be satisfactorily analysed unless both the demand substitutability and the supply conditions are simultaneously considered. It is via substitutability of the products that the entry of additional firms can affect the demand of established firms. Thus the effects of entry cannot be analysed on the basis of technological similarity alone.

In general all decisions of firms (pricing, level of output, changes in style, selling activities, financial policies, investment decisions) are taken in the light of actual as well as of potential competition by new entrants. This suggests that product considerations as well as technological similarities of processes should be integrated in analysing the behaviour of firms.

2. Theory of Demand

The purpose of the theory of demand is to determine the various factors that affect demand. One often reads that the *raison d'être* of the theory of demand is the establishment of the 'law of demand' (that the market demand is negatively related to the price) but this is misleading in that it concentrates on price as the sole determinant of demand, *ceteris paribus*.

Demand is a multivariate relationship, that is, it is determined by many factors simultaneously. Some of the most important determinants of the market demand for a particular product are its own price, consumers' income, prices of other commodities, consumers' tastes, income distribution, total population, consumers' wealth, credit availability, government policy, past levels of demand, and past levels of income.

The traditional theory of demand has concentrated on four of the above determinants, the price of the commodity, other prices, income and tastes. Some of the other factors have been introduced in the theory of demand recently. We will first examine the traditional static theory of demand and subsequently we will briefly discuss some recent developments in this field.

It should be noted that the traditional theory of demand examines only the final consumers' demand for durables and non-durables. It is partial in its approach in that it examines the demand in one market in isolation from the conditions of demand in other markets. An important implicit assumption of the theory of demand is that firms sell their products directly to the final consumers. This is not the general case in the modern business world (as we will see in section IV), and this has serious implications for the determination of prices. Another shortcoming of the traditional theory is that it does not deal with the demand for investment goods, nor with the demand for intermediate products. Total demand includes final demand and intermediate demand. Final demand is subdivided into consumers' demand and demand for investment goods. Traditional theory of demand deals only with consumers' demand, which is only a fraction[1] of the total demand in the economy as a whole. In this section we examine the traditional theory of consumers' demand. In section IV we look at the demand of the individual firm, and we discuss the various sources of demand for the product of manufacturing firms in particular. This analysis will cover some aspects of the demand for intermediate commodities and for investment goods.

I. THEORY OF CONSUMER BEHAVIOUR

The traditional theory of demand starts with the examination of the behaviour of the consumer, since the market demand is assumed to be the summation of the demands of

[1] Consumers' demand ranges between 30 and 40 per cent of total demand in developed economies.

individual consumers. Thus we will first examine the derivation of demand for an individual consumer.

The consumer is assumed to be rational. Given his income and the market prices of the various commodities, he plans the spending of his income so as to attain the highest possible satisfaction or utility. This is the *axiom of utility maximisation*. In the traditional theory it is assumed that the consumer has full knowledge of all the information relevant to his decision, that is he has complete knowledge of all the available commodities, their prices and his income. In order to attain this objective the consumer must be able to compare the utility (satisfaction) of the various 'baskets of goods' which he can buy with his income. There are two basic approaches to the problem of comparison of utilities, the *cardinalist approach* and the *ordinalist approach*.

The cardinalist school postulated that utility can be measured. Various suggestions have been made for the measurement of utility. Under certainty (complete knowledge of market conditions and income levels over the planning period) some economists have suggested that utility can be measured in monetary units, by the amount of money the consumer is willing to sacrifice for another unit of a commodity. Others suggested the measurement of utility in subjective units, called *utils*.

The ordinalist school postulated that utility is not measurable, but is an ordinal magnitude. The consumer need not know in specific units the utility of various commodities to make his choice. It suffices for him to be able to *rank* the various 'baskets of goods' according to the satisfaction that each bundle gives him. He must be able to determine his *order of preference* among the different bundles of goods. The main ordinal theories are the *indifference-curves approach* and the *revealed preference hypothesis*.

In examining the above approaches we will first state the assumptions underlying each approach, derive the equilibrium of the consumer, and from this determine his demand for the individual products. Finally we point out the weaknesses of each approach.

A. THE CARDINAL UTILITY THEORY[1]

Assumptions

1. *Rationality*. The consumer is rational. He aims at the maximisation of his utility subject to the constraint imposed by his given income.

2. *Cardinal utility*. The utility of each commodity is measurable. Utility is a cardinal concept. The most convenient measure is money: the utility is measured by the monetary units that the consumer is prepared to pay for another unit of the commodity.

3. *Constant marginal utility of money*. This assumption is necessary if the monetary unit is used as the measure of utility. The essential feature of a standard unit of measurement is that it be constant. If the marginal utility of money changes as income increases (or decreases) the measuring-rod for utility becomes like an elastic ruler, inappropriate for measurement.

4. *Diminishing marginal utility*. The utility gained from successive units of a commodity diminishes. In other words, the marginal utility of a commodity diminishes as the consumer acquires larger quantities of it. This is the *axiom of diminishing marginal utility*.

---

[1] The concept of subjective, measurable utility is attributed to Gossen (1854), Jevons (1871) and Walras (1874). Marshall (1890) also assumed independent and additive utilities, but his position on utility is not clear in several aspects.

5. The total utility of a 'basket of goods' depends on the quantities of the individual commodities. If there are n commodities in the bundle with quantities $x_1, x_2, \ldots, x_n$, the total utility is

$$U = f(x_1, x_2, \ldots, x_n)$$

In very early versions of the theory of consumer behaviour it was assumed that the total utility is *additive*,

$$U = U_1(x_1) + U_2(x_2) + \cdots + U_n(x_n)$$

The additivity assumption was dropped in later versions of the cardinal utility theory. Additivity implies independent utilities of the various commodities in the bundle, an assumption clearly unrealistic, and unnecessary for the cardinal theory.

Equilibrium of the consumer

We begin with the simple model of a single commodity x. The consumer can either buy x or retain his money income Y. Under these conditions the consumer is in equilibrium when the marginal utility of x is equated to its market price (P_x). Symbolically we have

$$MU_x = P_x$$

If the marginal utility of x is greater than its price, the consumer can increase his welfare by purchasing more units of x. Similarly if the marginal utility of x is less than its price the consumer can increase his total satisfaction by cutting down the quantity of x and keeping more of his income unspent. Therefore, he attains the maximisation of his utility when $MU_x = P_x$.[1]

If there are more commodities, the condition for the equilibrium of the consumer is the equality of the ratios of the marginal utilities of the individual commodities to their prices

$$\frac{MU_x}{P_x} = \frac{MU_y}{P_y} = \cdots = \frac{MU_n}{P_n}$$

[1] *Mathematical derivation of the equilibrium of the consumer*
The utility function is

$$U = f(q_x)$$

where utility is measured in monetary units. If the consumer buys q_x his expenditure is $q_x P_x$. Presumably the consumer seeks to maximise the difference between his utility and his expenditure

$$U - P_x q_x$$

The necessary condition for a maximum is that the partial derivative of the function with respect to q_x be equal to zero. Thus

$$\frac{\partial U}{\partial q_x} - \frac{\partial (P_x q_x)}{\partial q_x} = 0$$

Rearranging we obtain

$$\frac{\partial U}{\partial q_x} = P_x \quad \text{or} \quad MU_x = P_x$$

The utility derived from spending an additional unit of money must be the same for all commodities. If the consumer derives greater utility from any one commodity, he can increase his welfare by spending more on that commodity and less on the others, until the above equilibrium condition is fulfilled.

Derivation of the demand of the consumer

The derivation of demand is based on the axiom of diminishing marginal utility. The marginal utility of commodity x may be depicted by a line with a negative slope (figure 2.2). Mathematically the marginal utility of x is the slope of the total utility function $U = f(q_x)$. The total utility increases, but at a decreasing rate, up to quantity x, and then starts

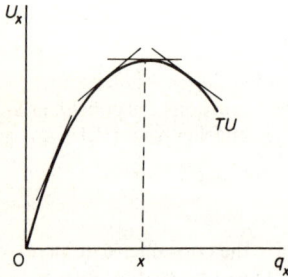
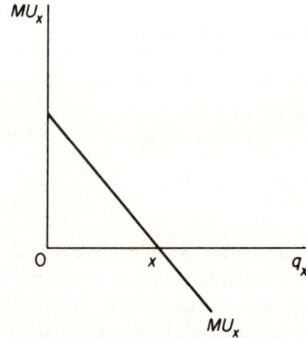

Figure 2.1   Figure 2.2

declining (figure 2.1). Accordingly the marginal utility of x declines continuously, and becomes negative beyond quantity x. If the marginal utility is measured in monetary units the demand curve for x is identical to the positive segment of the marginal utility curve. At x_1 the marginal utility is MU_1 (figure 2.3). This is equal to P_1, by definition. Hence at P_1 the consumer demands x_1 quantity (figure 2.4). Similarly at x_2 the marginal utility is MU_2, which is equal to P_2. Hence at P_2 the consumer will buy x_2, and so on. The negative section of the MU curve does not form part of the demand curve, since negative quantities do not make sense in economics.

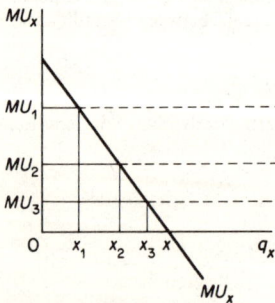
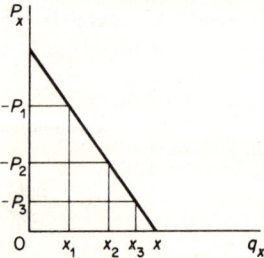

Figure 2.3   Figure 2.4

Critique of the cardinal approach

There are three basic weaknesses in the cardinalist approach. The assumption of cardinal utility is extremely doubtful. The satisfaction derived from various commodities cannot be measured objectively. The attempt by Walras to use subjective units (*utils*) for the measurement of utility does not provide any satisfactory solution. The assumption of constant utility of money is also unrealistic. As income increases the marginal utility of money changes. Thus money cannot be used as a measuring-rod since its own utility changes. Finally, the axiom of diminishing marginal utility has been 'established' from introspection, it is a psychological law which must be taken for granted.

B. THE INDIFFERENCE-CURVES THEORY[1]

Assumptions

1. *Rationality.* The consumer is assumed to be rational – he aims at the maximisation of his utility, given his income and market prices. It is assumed he has full knowledge (certainty) of all relevant information.

2. *Utility is ordinal.* It is taken as axiomatically true that the consumer can rank his preferences (order the various 'baskets of goods') according to the satisfaction of each basket. He need not know precisely the amount of satisfaction. It suffices that he expresses his preference for the various bundles of commodities. It is not necessary to assume that utility is *cardinally measurable*. Only *ordinal measurement* is required.

3. *Diminishing marginal rate of substitution.* Preferences are ranked in terms of indifference curves, which *are assumed to be convex* to the origin. This implies that the slope of the indifference curves increases. The slope of the indifference curve is called the marginal rate of substitution of the commodities. The indifference-curve theory is based, thus, on *the axiom of diminishing marginal rate of substitution* (see below).

4. The total utility of the consumer depends on the quantities of the commodities consumed

$$U = f(q_1, q_2, \ldots, q_x, q_y, \ldots, q_n)$$

5. *Consistency and transitivity of choice.* It is assumed that the consumer is consistent in his choice, that is, if in one period he chooses bundle *A* over *B*, he will not choose *B* over *A* in another period if both bundles are available to him. The consistency assumption may be symbolically written as follows:

$$\text{If } A > B, \text{ then } B \not> A$$

Similarly, it is assumed that consumer's choices are characterised by transitivity: if bundle *A* is preferred to *B*, and *B* is preferred to *C*, then bundle *A*, is preferred to *C*. Symbolically we may write the transitivity assumption as follows:

$$\text{If } A > B, \text{ and } B > C, \text{ then } A > C$$

---

[1] See J. Hicks and R. J. Allen, 'A Reconsideration of the Theory of Value', *Economica* (1934). See also Hicks, *Value and Capital* (Oxford University Press, 1939).

Equilibrium of the consumer

To define the equilibrium of the consumer (that is, his choice of the bundle that maximises his utility) we must introduce the concept of indifference curves and of their slope (the marginal rate of substitution), and the concept of the budget line. These are the basic tools of the indifference curves approach.

Indifference curves. An *indifference curve* is the locus of points – particular combinations or bundles of goods – which yield the same utility (level of satisfaction) to the consumer, so that he is indifferent as to the particular combination he consumes.[1]

An *indifference map* shows all the indifference curves which rank the preferences of the consumer. Combinations of goods situated on an indifference curve yield the same utility. Combinations of goods lying on a higher indifference curve yield higher level of satisfaction and are preferred. Combinations of goods on a lower indifference curve yield a lower utility.[2]

An indifference curve is shown in figure 2.5 and a partial indifference map is depicted in figure 2.6. It is assumed that the commodities y and x can substitute one another to a

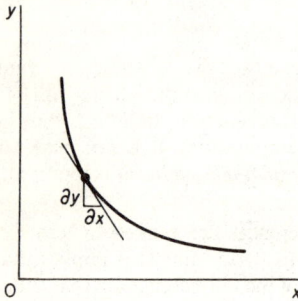

Figure 2.5

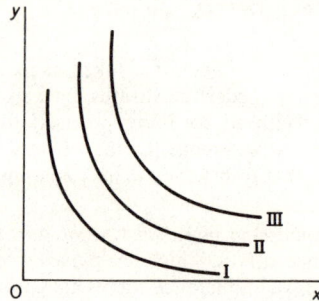

Figure 2.6

certain extent but are not perfect substitutes (see footnote, p. 20). The slope of an indifference curve at any one point is called the marginal rate of substitution of the two commodities, x and y, and is given by the slope of the tangent at that point:

$$\begin{bmatrix} \text{slope of} \\ \text{indifference} \\ \text{curve} \end{bmatrix} = -\frac{dy}{dx} = MRS_{x,y}$$

The marginal rate of substitution of x for y is defined as the number of units of commodity y that must be given up in exchange for an extra unit of commodity x so that the consumer maintains the same level of satisfaction. With this definition the proponents of the indifference-curves approach thought that they could avoid the non-operational concept of marginal utility. In fact, what they avoid is the assumption of diminishing

---

[1] Symbolically an indifference curve is given by the equation

$$U = f(x_1, x_2, \ldots, x_n) = k$$

where k is a constant.

[2] An indifference map may be derived by assigning to k every possible value.

individual marginal utilities and the need for their measurement. The concept of marginal utility is implicit in the definition of the *MRS*, since it can be proved[1] that the marginal rate of substitution (the slope of the indifference curve) is equal to the ratio of the marginal utilities of the commodities involved in the utility function:

$$MRS_{x,y} = \frac{MU_x}{MU_y} \quad \text{or} \quad MRS_{y,x} = \frac{MU_y}{MU_x}$$

Furthermore, the indifference-curves theorists substitute the assumption of diminishing marginal utility with another which may also be questioned, namely the assumption that the indifference curves are convex to the origin, which implies diminishing *MRS* of the commodities.

Properties of the indifference curves. An indifference curve has a negative slope, which denotes that if the quantity of one commodity (y) decreases, the quantity of the other (x) must increase, if the consumer is to stay on the same level of satisfaction.

The further away from the origin an indifference curve lies, the higher the level of utility it denotes: bundles of goods on a higher indifference curve are preferred by the rational consumer.

Indifference curves do not intersect. If they did, the point of their intersection would imply two different levels of satisfaction, which is impossible.

[1] Proof: The slope of a curve at any one point is measured by the slope of the tangent at that point. The equation of a tangent is given by the total derivative or total differential, which shows the total change of the function as all its determinants change.

The total utility function in the case of two commodities x and y is

$$U = f(x, y)$$

The equation of an indifference curve is

$$U = f(x, y) = k$$

where k is a constant. The total differential of the utility function is

$$dU = \frac{\partial U}{\partial y} dy + \frac{\partial U}{\partial x} dx = (MU_y) dy + (MU_x) dx$$

It shows the total change in utility as the quantities of both commodities change. The total change in U caused by changes in y and x is (approximately) equal to the change in y multiplied by its marginal utility, plus the change in x multiplied by its marginal utility.

Along any particular indifference curve the total differential is by definition equal to zero. Thus for any indifference curve

$$dU = (MU_y) dy + (MU_x) dx = 0$$

Rearranging we obtain

$$\text{either} \quad -\frac{dy}{dx} = \frac{MU_x}{MU_y} = MRS_{x,y} \quad \text{or} \quad -\frac{dx}{dy} = \frac{MU_y}{MU_x} = MRS_{y,x}$$

Note that the slope of the indifference curve at any one point is

$$MRS_{x,y} = MRS_{y,x}$$

The indifference curves are convex to the origin.[1] This implies that the slope of an indifference curve decreases (in absolute terms) as we move along the curve from the left downwards to the right: the marginal rate of substitution of the commodities is diminishing. This axiom is derived from introspection, like the 'law of diminishing marginal utility' of the cardinalist school. The *axiom of decreasing marginal rate of substitution* expresses the observed behavioural rule that the number of units of y the consumer is willing to sacrifice in order to obtain an additional unit of x decreases as the quantity of x increases. It becomes increasingly difficult to substitute x for y as we move along the indifference curve. In figure 2.9 the fifth unit of y can be substituted for x by the consumer giving up x_1x_2 of x; but to substitute the second unit of y and still retain the same satisfaction the consumer must give up a much greater quantity of x, namely x_3x_4.

The budget constraint of the consumer. The consumer has a given income which sets limits to his maximising behaviour. Income acts as a constraint in the attempt for maximising utility. The income constraint, in the case of two commodities, may be written

$$Y = p_x q_x + p_y q_y \qquad (2.1)$$

We may present the income constraint graphically by the budget line, whose equation is derived from expression 2.1, by solving for q_y:

$$q_y = \frac{1}{P_y} Y - \frac{P_x}{P_y} q_x$$

Assigning successive values to q_x (given the income, Y and the commodity prices, P_x, P_y, we may find the corresponding values of q_y. Thus, if $q_x = 0$ (that is, if the consumer spends all his income on y) the consumer can buy Y/P_y units of y. Similarly, if $q_y = 0$ (that is, if the consumer spends all his income on x) the consumer can buy Y/P_x units of x. In figure 2.10 these results are shown by points A and B. If we join these points

---

[1] This assumption implies that the commodities can substitute one another, but are not perfect substitutes. If the commodities are perfect substitutes the indifference curve becomes a straight line with negative slope (figure 2.7). If the commodities are complements the indifference curve takes the shape of a right angle (figure 2.8).

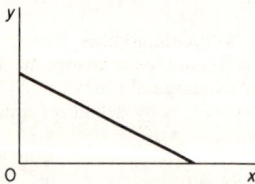

Figure 2.7   Perfect substitutes   Figure 2.8   Complementary goods

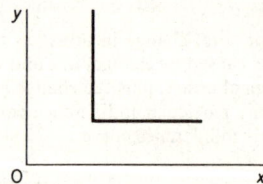

In the first case the equilibrium of the consumer may be a corner solution, that is, a situation in which the consumer spends all his income on one commodity. This is sometimes called 'monomania'. Situations of 'monomania' are not observed in the real world and are usually ruled out from the analysis of the behaviour of the consumer. In the case of complementary goods, indifference-curves analysis breaks down, since there is no possibility of substitution between the commodities.

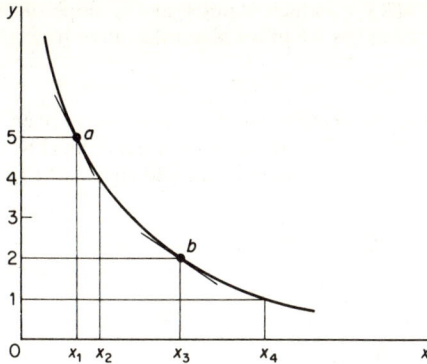

Figure 2.9

with a line we obtain the budget line, whose slope is the ratio of the prices of the two commodities. Geometrically the slope of the budget line is

$$\frac{OA}{OB} = \frac{Y/P_y}{Y/P_x} = -\frac{P_x}{P_y}$$

Mathematically the slope of the budget line is the derivative

$$\frac{\partial q_y}{\partial q_x} = -\frac{P_x}{P_y}$$

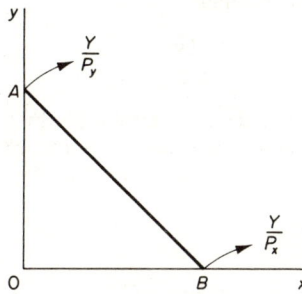

Figure 2.10

Derivation of the equilibrium of the consumer. The consumer is in equilibrium when he maximises his utility, given his income and the market prices. Two conditions must be fulfilled for the consumer to be in equilibrium.

The first condition is that the marginal rate of substitution be equal to the ratio of commodity prices

$$MRS_{x,y} = \frac{MU_x}{MU_y} = \frac{P_x}{P_y}$$

This is a necessary but not sufficient condition for equilibrium. The second condition is that the indifference curves be convex to the origin. This condition is fulfilled by the axiom of diminishing $MRS_{x,y}$, which states that the slope of the indifference curve decreases (in absolute terms) as we move along the curve from the left downwards to the right.

Graphical presentation of the equilibrium of the consumer. Given the indifference map of the consumer and his budget line, the equilibrium is defined by the point of tangency of the budget line with the highest possible indifference curve (point e in figure 2.11).

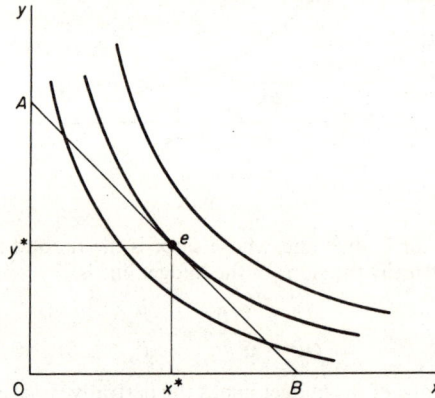

Figure 2.11

At the point of tangency the slopes of the budget line (P_x/P_y) and of the indifference curve $(MRS_{x,y} = MU_x/MU_y)$ are equal:

$$\frac{MU_x}{MU_y} = \frac{P_x}{P_y}$$

Thus the first-order condition is denoted graphically by the point of tangency of the two relevant curves. The second-order condition is implied by the convex shape of the indifference curves. The consumer maximises his utility by buying x^* and y^* of the two commodities.

Mathematical derivation of the equilibrium. Given the market prices and his income, the consumer aims at the maximisation of his utility. Assume that there are n commodities available to the consumer, with given market prices $P_1, P_2, \ldots, P_n$. The consumer has a money income (Y), which he spends on the available commodities.

Formally the problem may be stated as follows.

Maximise $\qquad\qquad\qquad U = f(q_1, q_2, \ldots, q_n)$

subject to $\qquad\qquad\sum_{i=1}^{n} q_i P_i = q_1 P_1 + q_2 P_2 + \cdots + q_n P_n = Y$

We use the 'Lagrangian multipliers' method for the solution of this constrained maximum. The steps involved in this method may be outlined as follows:

(a) Rewrite the constraint in the form

$$(q_1 P_1 + q_2 P_2 + \cdots + q_n P_n - Y) = 0$$

(b) Multiply the constraint by a constant λ, which is the Lagrangian multiplier

$$\lambda(q_1 P_1 + q_2 P_2 + \cdots + q_n P_n - Y) = 0$$

(c) Subtract the above constraint from the utility function and obtain the 'composite function'

$$\phi = U - \lambda(q_1 P_1 + q_2 P_2 + \cdots + q_n P_n - Y)$$

It can be shown that maximisation of the 'composite' function implies maximisation of the utility function.

The first condition for the maximisation of a function is that its partial derivatives be equal to zero. Differentiating ϕ with respect to $q_1, \ldots, q_n$ and λ, and equating to zero we find

$$\frac{\partial \phi}{\partial q_1} = \frac{\partial U}{\partial q_1} - \lambda(P_1) = 0$$

$$\frac{\partial \phi}{\partial q_2} = \frac{\partial U}{\partial q_2} - \lambda(P_2) = 0$$

$$\vdots \quad \vdots \quad \vdots \quad \vdots$$

$$\frac{\partial \phi}{\partial q_n} = \frac{\partial U}{\partial q_n} - \lambda(P_n) = 0$$

$$\frac{\partial \phi}{\partial \lambda} = -(q_1 P_1 + q_2 P_2 + \cdots + q_n P_n - Y) = 0$$

From these equations we obtain

$$\frac{\partial U}{\partial q_1} = \lambda P_1$$

$$\frac{\partial U}{\partial q_2} = \lambda P_2$$

$$\vdots \quad \vdots \quad \vdots$$

$$\frac{\partial U}{\partial q_n} = \lambda P_n$$

But

$$\frac{\partial U}{\partial q_1} = MU_1, \qquad \frac{\partial U}{\partial q_2} = MU_2, \ldots, \frac{\partial U}{\partial q_n} = MU_n.$$

Substituting and solving for λ we find

$$\lambda = \frac{MU_1}{P_1} = \frac{MU_2}{P_2} = \cdots = \frac{MU_n}{P_n}$$

Alternatively, we may divide the preceding equation corresponding to commodity x, by the equation which refers to commodity y, and obtain

$$\frac{MU_x}{MU_y} = \frac{P_x}{P_y} = MRS_{x,y}$$

We observe that the equilibrium conditions are identical in the cardinalist approach and in the indifference-curves approach. In both theories we have

$$\frac{MU_1}{P_1} = \frac{MU_2}{P_2} = \cdots = \frac{MU_x}{P_x} = \frac{MU_y}{P_y} = \cdots = \frac{MU_n}{P_n}$$

Thus, although in the indifference-curves approach cardinality of utility is not required, the *MRS* requires knowledge of the ratio of the marginal utilities, given that the first-order condition for any two commodities may be written as

$$\frac{MU_x}{MU_y} = \frac{P_x}{P_y} = MRS_{x,y}$$

Hence the concept of marginal utility is implicit in the definition of the slope of the indifference curves, although its measurement is not required by this approach. What is needed is a diminishing marginal rate of substitution, which of course does not require diminishing marginal utilities of the commodities involved in the utility function.

Derivation of the demand curve using the indifference-curves approach

Graphical derivation of the demand curve. As the price of a commodity, for example of *x*, falls, the budget line of the consumer shifts to the right, from its initial position (*AB*) to a new position (*AB'*), due to the increase in the purchasing power of the given money income of the consumer. With more purchasing power in his possession the consumer can buy more of *x* (and more of *y*). The new budget line is tangent to a higher indifference curve (e.g. curve II). The new equilibrium occurs to the right of the original equilibrium (for normal goods) showing that as price falls more of the commodity will be bought. If we allow the price of *x* to fall continuously and we join the points of tangency of successive budget lines and higher indifference curves we form the so-called price–consumption line (figure 2.12), from which we derive the demand curve for commodity *x*. At point e_1 the consumer buys quantity x_1 at price y_1. At point e_2 the price, y_2, is lower than y_1, and the quantity demanded has increased to x_2, and so on. We may plot the price–quantity pairs defined by the points of equilibrium (on the price–consumption line) to obtain a demand curve, as shown in figure 2.13.

The demand curve for normal commodities[1] will always have a negative slope, denoting the 'law of demand,' (the quantity bought increases as the price falls).

In the indifference-curves approach the 'law of demand' is derived from what is known as *Slutsky's theorem*, which states that *the substitution effect of a price change is always negative*. The formal proof of Slutsky's theorem involves sophisticated mathematics. However, we may show graphically the implications of this theorem.

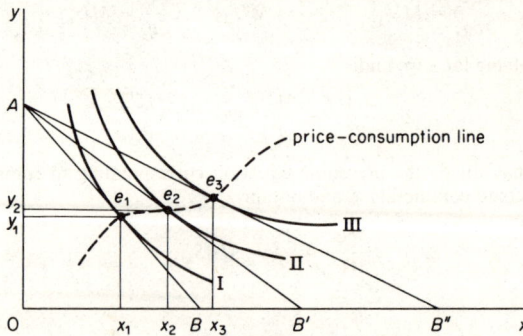

Figure 2.12

[1] A commodity is defined as 'normal' when its demand changes in the same direction as income. If the demand of a commodity decreases when income increases, the commodity is called 'inferior'.

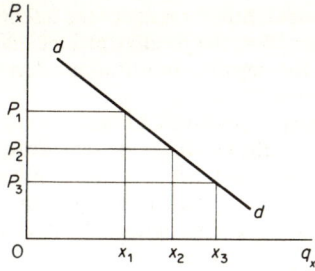

Figure 2.13

We saw that a fall in the price of x from P_1 to P_2 resulted in an increase in the quantity demanded from x_1 to x_2. This is the *total price effect* which may be split into two separate effects, a *substitution effect* and an *income effect*. The substitution effect is the increase in the quantity bought as the price of the commodity falls, after 'adjusting' income so as to keep the real purchasing power of the consumer the same as before. This adjustment in income is called *compensating variation* and is shown graphically by a parallel shift of the new budget line until it becomes tangent to the initial indifference curve (figure 2.14). The purpose of the compensating variation is to allow the consumer to remain on the same level of satisfaction as before the price change. The compensated-budget line will be tangent to the original indifference curve (I) at a point (e_1') to the right of the original tangency (e_1), because this line is parallel to the new budget line which is less steep than the original one when the price of x falls. The movement from point e_1 to e_1' shows the substitution effect of the price change: the consumer buys more of x now that it is cheaper, substituting y for x. However, the compensating variation is a device which enables the isolation of the substitution effect, but does not show the new equilibrium of the consumer. This is defined by point e_2 on the higher indifference curve II. The consumer has in fact a higher purchasing power, and, if the commodity is normal, he will spend some of his increased real income on x, thus moving from x_1' to x_2. This is the income effect of the price change. The income effect of a price change is negative for normal goods and it reinforces the negative substitution effect (figure 2.14). If, however, the commodity is *inferior*, the income effect will be positive: as the purchasing power

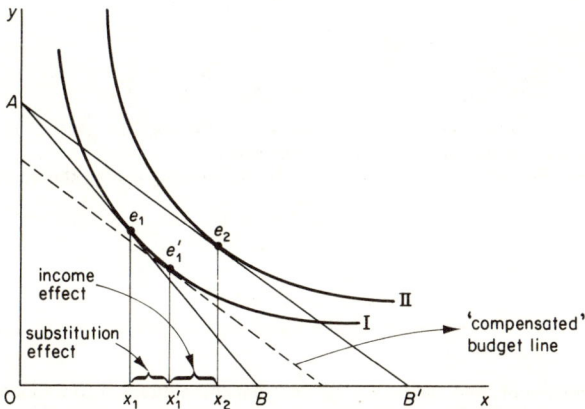

Figure 2.14

increases, less of x will be bought. Still for most of the inferior goods the negative substitution effect will more than offset the positive income effect, so that the total price effect will be negative. Thus the negative substitution effect is in most cases adequate for establishing the law of demand.

(It is when the income effect is positive and very strong that the 'law of demand' does not hold. This is the case of the Giffen goods, which are inferior and their demand curve has a positive slope. Giffen goods are very rare in practice.)[1]

It should be noted that although Slutsky's theorem can be proved mathematically, its proof is based on the axiomatic assumption of the convexity of the indifference curves.

Mathematical derivation of the demand curve. The demand curve may be derived from the equilibrium condition

$$\frac{MU_x}{P_x} = \frac{MU_y}{P_y} = \cdots = \frac{MU_n}{P_n}$$

and the budget constraint

$$Y = \sum_{i=1}^{n} p_i q_i$$

For example, assume that there are only two commodities and that the total utility function is multiplicative of the form

$$U = \tfrac{1}{4} q_x q_y$$

The marginal utilities of x and y are

$$MU_x = \frac{\partial U}{\partial q_x} = \tfrac{1}{4} q_y$$

and

$$MU_y = \frac{\partial U}{\partial q_y} = \tfrac{1}{4} q_x$$

Substituting the marginal utilities in the equilibrium condition we obtain

$$\frac{(\tfrac{1}{4}) q_y}{P_x} = \frac{(\tfrac{1}{4}) q_x}{P_y}$$

or

$$q_y P_y = q_x P_x$$

(Note that the equality of expenditures of the two commodities is not a general rule; the expenditures depend on the specific form of the utility function.)

We may derive the demand for commodity x by substituting $q_y P_y$ in the budget constraint:

$$q_y P_y + q_x P_x = Y$$

$$2 q_x P_x = Y$$

$$q_x = \frac{1}{2 p_x} Y$$

[1] For a discussion of other cases of 'irregular' demand patterns see H. Leibenstein, 'Bandwagon, Snob and Veblen Effects in the Theory of Consumers' Demand', *Quarterly Journal of Economics* (1950) pp. 183–207.

Thus the demand for x is negatively related to its own price p_x and positively to income Y.

Similarly the demand for y is obtained by substituting $q_x p_x$ in the budget constraint:

$$q_y = \frac{1}{2p_y} Y$$

In our particular example the demand curves are symmetric due to the particular multiplicative form of the consumer's utility function which we assumed.

Critique of the indifference-curves approach

The indifference-curves analysis has been a major advance in the field of consumer's demand. The assumptions of this theory are less stringent than for the cardinal utility approach. Only ordinality of preferences is required, and the assumption of constant utility of money has been dropped.

The methodology of indifference curves has provided a framework for the measurement of the 'consumer's surplus', which is important in welfare economics and in designing government policy. The measurement of the consumers' surplus is discussed in section D below (p. 32).

Perhaps the most important theoretical contribution of this approach is the establishment of a better criterion for the classification of goods into substitutes and complements. Earlier theorists were using the total effect of a price change for this purpose, without compensating for the change in real income. The classification was based on the sign of the cross-elasticity of demand

$$e_{yx} = \frac{\partial q_y}{\partial p_x} \cdot \frac{p_x}{q_y}$$

where the total change in the quantity of y was considered as a result of a change in the price of x. A positive sign of the cross-elasticity implies that x and y are substitutes; a negative sign implies that the commodities are complements. This approach may easily lead to absurd classifications if the change in the price of x is substantial. For example, if the price of beef is halved it is almost certain that both the consumption of beef and of pork will be increased, due to the increase of the real income of the consumer. This would imply a negative cross-elasticity for pork, and hence pork would be classified as a complementary commodity to beef!

Hicks[1] suggested measuring the cross-elasticity after compensating for changes in real income. Thus, according to Hicks, goods x and y are substitutes if, after compensating for the change in real income (arising from the change in the price of x) a decrease in the price of x leads to a decrease in the quantity demanded of y.

Although this criterion is theoretically more correct than the usual approach based on the total change in the quantity of y as a result of a change in the price of x, in practice its application is impossible because it requires knowledge of the individual preference functions, which cannot be statistically estimated. On the other hand, the usual approach of the total price effect is feasible because it requires knowledge of the market demand functions which can be empirically estimated.

Although the advantages of the indifference-curves approach are important, the theory has indeed its own severe limitations. The main weakness of this theory is its axiomatic assumption of the existence and the convexity of the indifference curves. The theory does not establish either the existence or the shape of the indifference curves. It assumes that they exist and have the required shape of convexity. Furthermore, it is

---

[1] J. Hicks, *Value and Capital* (Oxford Universiy Press, 1946) 2nd edn, pp. 42–52.

questionable whether the consumer is able to order his preferences as precisely and rationally as the theory implies. Also the preferences of the consumers change continuously under the influence of various factors, so that any ordering of these preferences, even if possible, should be considered as valid for the very short run. Finally, this theory has retained most of the weaknesses of the cardinalist school with the strong assumption of rationality and the concept of the marginal utility implicit in the definition of the marginal rate of substitution.

Another defect of the indifference curves approach is that it does not analyse the effects of advertising, of past behaviour (habit persistence), of stocks, of the interdependence of the preferences of the consumers, which lead to behaviour that would be considered as irrational, and hence is ruled out by the theory.[1] Furthermore speculative demand and random behaviour are ruled out. Yet these factors are very important for the pricing and output decisions of the firm.[2]

C. THE REVEALED PREFERENCE HYPOTHESIS[3]

Samuelson introduced the term 'revealed preference' into economics in 1938. Since then the literature in this field has proliferated.

The revealed preference hypothesis is considered as a major breakthrough in the theory of demand, because it has made possible the establishment of the 'law of demand' directly (on the basis of the *revealed preference axiom*) without the use of indifference curves and all their restrictive assumptions. Regarding the ordering of consumers' preferences, the revealed preference hypothesis has the advantage over the Hicks–Allen approach of *establishing* the existence and the convexity of the indifference curves (it does not accept them axiomatically). However, the indifference curves are redundant in the derivation of the demand curve. We will first examine the derivation of the 'law of demand'; we will then show how indifference curves can be established.

Assumptions

1. *Rationality.* The consumer is assumed to behave rationally, in that he prefers bundles of goods that include more quantities of the commodities.

2. *Consistency.* The consumer behaves consistently, that is, if he chooses bundle A in a situation in which bundle B was also available to him he will not choose B in any other situation in which A is also available. Symbolically

$$\text{if } A > B, \text{ then } B \ngtr A$$

3. *Transitivity.* If in any particular situation $A > B$ and $B > C$, then $A > C$.

4. *The revealed preference axiom.* The consumer, by choosing a collection of goods in any one budget situation, *reveals his preference* for that particular collection. The chosen bundle is revealed to be preferred among all other alternative bundles available under

---

[1] See H. Leibenstein, 'Bandwagon, Snob, and Weblen Effects in the Theory of Consumers' Demand', *Quarterly Journal of Economics* (1950) pp. 183–207.

[2] For a summary discussion of indifference-curves analysis and its limitations see E. J. Mishan, 'Theories of Consumers' Behaviour: A Cynical View', *Economica* (1961) pp. 1–11; reprinted in *Readings in Microeconomics*, ed. D. R. Kamerschen (John Wiley, 1969).

[3] P. Samuelson, *Foundations of Economic Analysis* (Harvard University Press, Cambridge, Mass., 1947).

the budget constraint. The chosen 'basket of goods' maximises the utility of the consumer. The revealed preference for a particular collection of goods implies (axiomatically) the maximisation of the utility of the consumer.

Derivation of the demand curve

Assume that the consumer has the budget line AB in figure 2.15 and chooses the collection of goods denoted by point Z, thus revealing his preference for this batch. Suppose that the price of x falls so that the new budget line facing the consumer is AC. We will show that the new batch will include a larger quantity of x.

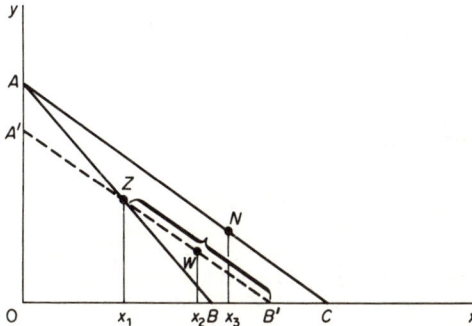

Figure 2.15

Firstly, we make a 'compensating variation' of the income, which consists in the reduction of income so that the consumer has just enough income to enable him to continue purchasing Z if he so wishes. The compensating variation is shown in figure 2.15 by a parallel shift of the new budget line so that the 'compensated' budget line $A'B'$ passes through Z. Since the collection Z is still available to him, the consumer will not choose any bundle to the left of Z on the segment $A'Z$, because his choice would be inconsistent, given that in the original situation all the batches on $A'Z$ were revealed inferior to Z. Hence the consumer will either continue to buy Z (in which case the substitution effect is zero) or he will choose a batch on the segment ZB', such as W, which includes a larger quantity of x (namely x_2). Secondly, if we remove the (fictitious) reduction in income and allow the consumer to move on the new budget line AC, he will choose a batch (such as N) to the right of W (if the commodity x is normal with a positive income effect). The new revealed equilibrium position (N) includes a larger quantity of x (i.e. x_3) resulting from the fall in its price. Thus the revealed preference axiom and the implied consistency of choice open a direct way to the derivation of the demand curve: as price falls, more of x is purchased.

Derivation of the indifference curves

Although not needed for establishing the law of demand, indifference curves can be derived and their convexity proved by the revealed preference hypothesis.

The indifference-curves approach requires less information than the neoclassical cardinal utility theory. But still it requires a lot from the consumer, since the theory expects him to be able to rank rationally and consistently *all possible* collections of commodities.

Samuelson's revealed preference theory does not require the consumer to rank his preferences or to give any other information about his tastes. The revealed preference permits us to construct the indifference map of the consumer just by observing his behaviour (his choice) at various market prices, provided that (a) his choice is consistent, (b) his tastes are independent of his choices over time and do not change, (c) that the consumer is rational in the Pareto sense, that is, he prefers more goods to less.

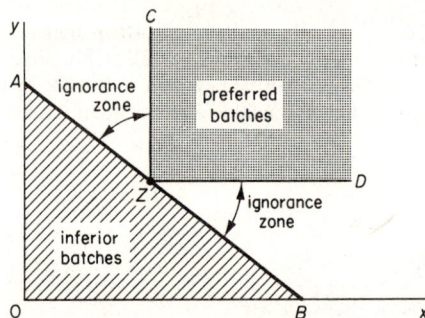

Figure 2.16

Assume that the initial budget line of the consumer is AB in figure 2.16 and he chooses the batch Z. All the other points on the budget line and below it denote inferior batches to Z. If we draw perpendiculars through Z, CZ and ZD, all the batches on these lines, and in the area defined by them to the right of Z, are preferred to Z because they contain more quantity of at least one commodity. Batches of goods in the remaining area (below CZD and above the budget line) are still not ordered. However, we may rank them relative to Z by adopting the following procedure. Let the price of x fall so that the new budget line EF passes below Z (figure 2.17).

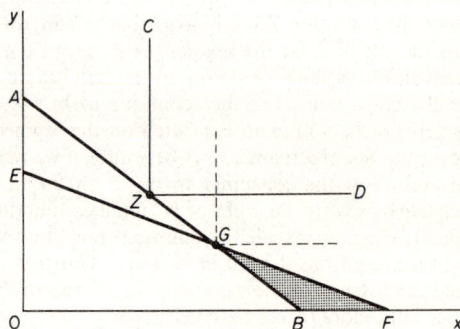

Figure 2.17

The consumer will choose either G or a point to the right of G (on GF), since points on EG would imply inconsistent choice, being below the original budget line and hence inferior to G. Assume that the consumer chooses G. Using the transitivity assumption we have

$$Z > G \qquad \text{(in the original situation)}$$
$$G > (GBF) \quad \text{(in the new budget situation)}$$
$$\text{hence} \quad Z > (GBF)$$

In this way we managed to rank all the batches in *GBF* relative to *Z*. We may repeat this procedure by drawing budget lines below *Z* and defining gradually all the batches of the 'lower ignorance zone' that are inferior to *Z*. Similarly we may rank (relative to *Z*) all the batches of the 'upper ignorance zone.' For example, assume that the price of *x* increases and the new budget line *KL* passes through *Z*. The consumer will either stay

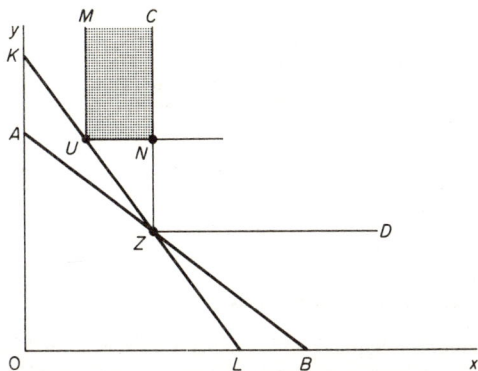

Figure 2.18

at *Z* or choose a point such as *U* on *KL* (figure 2.18). Using the rationality assumption we find

$$(MUN) > U$$

From the revealed preference principle

$$U > Z$$

and from the transitivity postulate

$$(MUN) > Z$$

Thus we managed to rank the batches in (*MUN*) as preferred to *Z*. Repeating this procedure we may gradually narrow down the 'ignorance zone' until we locate the indifference curve within as narrow a range as we wish. Hence the revealed preference axiom permits us to derive the indifference curve from the behaviour (actual choice) of the consumer in various market situations.

The convexity of the indifference curve may be established graphically as follows. Let us redraw the original budget situation (figure 2.19). We observe that the indifference curve through *Z* must be somewhere in the ignorance zone and must be convex, because it cannot have any other shape. The indifference curve cannot be the straight line *AB* because the choice of *Z* shows that all the other points on *AB* are inferior to *Z* (hence the consumer cannot be at the same time indifferent between them). It cannot be a curve or line cutting *AB* at *Z*, because the points below *Z* would imply indifference of the consumer, while he has already revealed his preference for *Z*. Finally, the indifference curve cannot be concave through *Z*, because all its points have already been ranked as inferior to *Z* (they contain less goods). Hence the only possible shape of the indifference curve is to be convex to the origin.

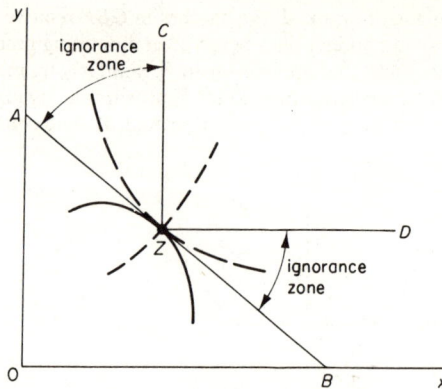

Figure 2.19

Critique of the revealed preference hypothesis[1]

We have already said that Samuelson's revealed preference theory is a major advancement to the theory of demand. It provides a direct way to the derivation of the demand curve, which does not require the use of the concept of utility. The theory can prove the existence and convexity of the indifference curves under weaker assumptions than the earlier theories. It has also provided the basis for the construction of index numbers of the cost of living and their use for judging changes in consumer welfare in situations where prices change. This topic is discussed in section E below.

D. THE CONSUMERS' SURPLUS

The Marshallian surplus

The consumers' surplus is a concept introduced by Marshall, who maintained that it can be measured in monetary units, and is equal to the difference between the amount of money that a consumer actually pays to buy a certain quantity of a commodity x, and the amount that he would be willing to pay for this quantity rather than do without it.

Graphically the consumers' surplus may be found by his demand curve for commodity x and the current market price, which (it is assumed) he cannot affect by his purchases of this commodity. Assume that the consumer's demand for x is a straight line (AB in figure 2.20) and the market price is P. At this price the consumer buys q units of x and pays an amount $(q) \cdot (P)$ for it. However, he would be willing to pay P_1 for q_1, P_2 for q_2, P_3 for q_3 and so on. The fact that the price in the market is lower than the price he would be willing to pay for the initial units of x implies that his actual expenditure is less than he would be willing to spend to acquire the quantity q. This difference is the consumer's surplus, and is the area of the triangle PAC in figure 2.20.

The Marshallian consumers' surplus can also be measured by using indifference-curves analysis.

---

[1] For an interesting review of the various theories of consumers' behaviour see E. J. Mishan, 'Theories of Consumers' Behaviour: A Cynical View', loc. cit.

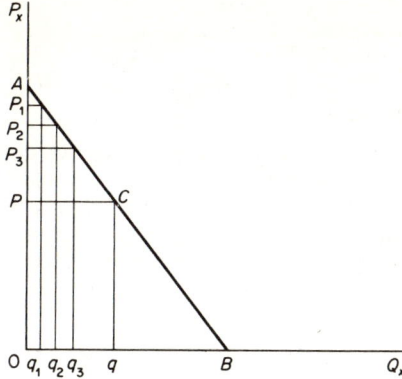

Figure 2.20

In figure 2.21 the good measured on the horizontal axis is x, while on the vertical axis we measure the consumer's money income. The budget line of the consumer is MM' and its slope is equal to the price of commodity x (since the price of one unit of monetary income is 1). Given P_x, the consumer is in equilibrium at E: he buys $0Q$ quantity of x and pays AM of his income for it, being left with $0A$ amount of money to spend on all other commodities.

We next must find the amount of money which the consumer would be willing to pay for the $0Q$ quantity of x rather than do without it. This is attained by drawing an indifference curve passing through M. Under the Marshallian assumption that the MU of money income is constant, this indifference curve (and any other of the indifference map) will be *vertically parallel* to the indifference curve I_1; the indifference curves will have the same slope at any given quantity of x. For example, at Q the slope of I_1 is the same as the slope of I_0

$$\begin{bmatrix} \text{slope } I_1 \\ \text{for } Q \\ \text{units of } x \end{bmatrix} = MRS_{x, M} = \frac{MU_x}{1} = MU_x$$

(given that $MU_M = 1$)

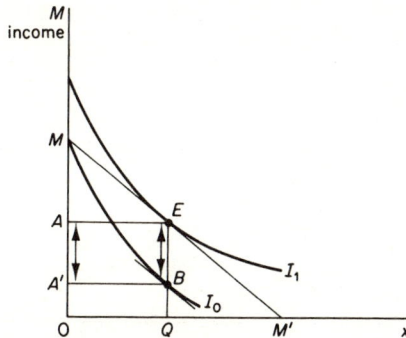

Figure 2.21

Similarly

$$\begin{bmatrix} \text{slope } I_0 \\ \text{for } Q \\ \text{units of } x \end{bmatrix} = MRS_{x, M} = \frac{MU_x}{1} = MU_x$$

Given that the quantity of x is the same at E and B, the two slopes are equal.

The indifference curve I_0 shows that the consumer would be willing to pay $A'M$ for the quantity $0Q$, since point B shows indifference of the consumer between having $0Q$ of x and $0A'$ of income to spend on other goods, or having none of x and spending all his income M on other goods. In other words $A'M$ is the amount of money that the consumer would be willing to pay for $0Q$ rather than do without it.

The difference

$$A'M - AM = AA' = EB$$

is the difference between what the consumer actually pays (AM, given P_x) and what he would be willing to pay for $0Q$ of x. That is, this difference is the Marshallian consumers' surplus.

An alternative measure of the consumer's surplus

In the above analysis it was assumed that the marginal utility of money is constant. Clearly this assumption is very strong. If we relax this assumption, the size of the consumer's surplus is smaller than the Marshallian theory of cardinal utility implies. To see this, in figure 2.22 we start from an initial equilibrium E, defined by the tangency of the budget line MM' to the highest possible indifference curve I_1. Here the consumer buys $0Q_1$ of x at the market price P_1, which is the slope of indifference curve I_1 at point E, since at this point

$$MRS_{x, M} = \frac{P_x}{P_M} = P_x$$

given $P_M = 1$. The actual expenditure of the consumer for $0Q_1$ is $P \cdot Q_1 = AM$.

To find the maximum amount of money the consumer would be willing to pay for the same quantity ($0Q_1$) rather than do without, we draw an indifference curve I_0 through M, in figure 2.22. This indifference curve is flatter than I_1, for any given quantity of x,

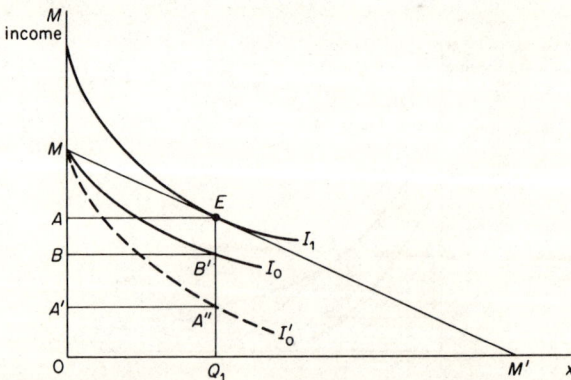

Figure 2.22

showing that the marginal utility of money changes inversely with the amount of money income. Thus the consumer would be willing to pay BM for Q_1 rather than do without, and the consumers' surplus is the difference

$$BM - AM = BA = B'E$$

To compare this measurement of the consumer's surplus with the Marshallian measure we draw through M the indifference curve I_0' vertically parallel to I_1, implying constant MU of money. Under this assumption the (Marshallian) consumer surplus is EA'' which is clearly larger than EB', the surplus under the assumption of decreasing MU of money income.

Note: Both at E and B' the quantity of x is the same $(0Q_1)$, so that the MU_x is constant at these two points. However, the income left to be spent on other goods $(0A)$ is larger at E as compared with B' (where the remainder income is $0B$). Hence at B' the MU of money income is higher than at E. Thus, comparing the slopes of I_1 at E and of I_0 at B' we see that

$$\left[\begin{array}{c} \text{slope } I_0 \\ \text{at } B' \end{array} \right] = \frac{MU_x}{MU_{M_B}} < \frac{MU_x}{MU_{M_A}} = \left[\begin{array}{c} \text{slope } I_1 \\ \text{at } E \end{array} \right]$$

that is, the slope of I_0 is smaller than I_1 for any given quantity of x.

E. SOME APPLICATIONS OF INDIFFERENCE-CURVES ANALYSIS

The leisure–income trade-off and the need for overtime rates higher than the normal wage rate

Indifference-curves analysis may be used to explain why firms must pay higher rates for overtime work.

We first derive the income–leisure curve of an individual consumer. This curve shows different combinations of income, earned by working, and leisure time. Assume that we measure money income on the vertical axis and leisure time on the horizontal axis. Assume further that the maximum time available for either leisure or work is $0Z$ hours a day. The individual can either use all the $0Z$ hours for leisure, in which case he earns zero income, or he can choose to work all the $0Z$ hours and earn a maximum money income $0M$ (given the current market wage rate w) or he can use part of the $0Z$ hours for leisure (e.g. $0A$) and the remaining (AZ) hours for work, in which case he would earn

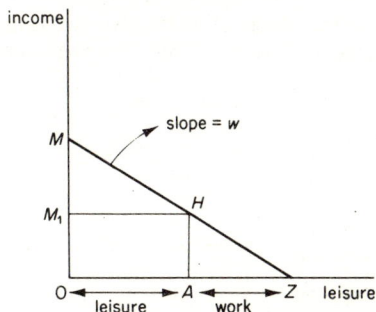

Figure 2.23   Income–leisure constraint.

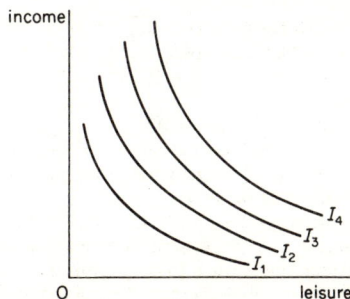

Figure 2.24   Income–leisure trade-off

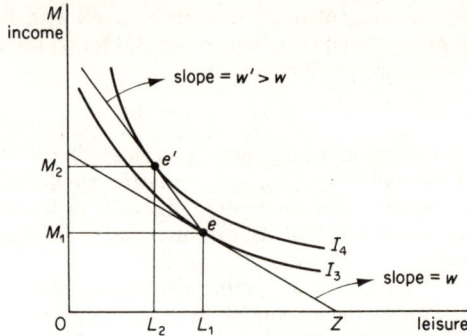

Figure 2.25

$0M_1$ income. The line MZ is the income–leisure curve, which shows how much time of his leisure an individual must give up if he wants to earn a certain income.

The slope of the income–leisure line is equal to the market wage rate.[1]

We may next construct the indifference map of the individual, which shows the ranking of his preferences as between income and leisure. Each indifference curve shows various combinations of income and leisure which yield the same level of satisfaction (utility) to the individual. The indifference curves have the usual properties: they are convex to the origin, they do not intersect and they show a higher level of satisfaction the further away from the origin they are.

The individual's equilibrium is determined by the point of tangency of his income–leisure line with the highest possible trade-off curve (point e in figure 2.25). Given the wage rate w, the individual maximises his utlity by working L_1Z hours, earning income $0M_1$ and using the remaining time ($0L_1$) for leisure.

If firms want more hours of work they will have to pay a higher hourly rate than the normal w in order to give an incentive to the individual to reduce his leisure time. An increase in the overtime rate is depicted by a leisure–income line which is steeper to the left of e (figure 2.25). With higher overtime payment the individual will be induced to give up some of his leisure time because in this way he will reach a higher indifference curve. The income–leisure line becomes kinked at e, and the new equilibrium of the individual is at e' on indifference curve I_4, showing that he will increase his working hours (by L_1L_2) and earn a higher income ($0M_2 > 0M_1$).

Evaluation of alternative government policies using indifference-curves analysis

Indifference curves may be used to evaluate the effects of alternative government policies. For example, assume that the government considers either the adoption of a

[1] *Proof*:
The slope of MZ is $0M/0Z$
But $0M$ = total income earned for working $0Z$ hours
    $0Z$ = total hours worked to obtain $0M$ income
Therefore $0M/0Z = w$
Another way to establish this relation is the following:
    (a) $0M$ is the maximum income obtainable given the market wage rate w. The hours that the individual must work to obtain this income are $0M/w$.
    (b) $0Z$ are *ex hypothesi* the maximum hours available for either work or leisure (or any combination of both).
    (c) Therefore $0M/w = 0Z$ or $0M/0Z = w$.

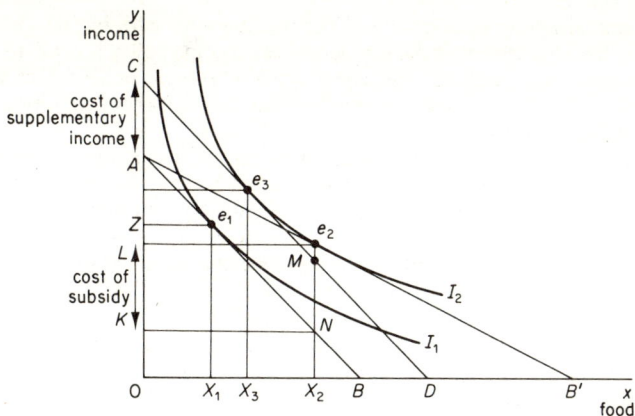

Figure 2.26

food subsidisation policy for pensioners or granting a supplementary income to them. Which of these measures costs less to the government (and hence to the tax payer)? What are the effects of these policies on the demand patterns of a pensioner? Such questions may be answered by using indifference-curves analysis. We will illustrate the way in which the above information may be obtained, assuming for simplicity that there is a single pensioner and two commodities, x (food) and y (money income).

The initial equilibrium of the pensioner is at point e_1, where his budget line, AB, is tangent to indifference curve I_1: he consumes $0X_1$, units of food, paying ZA of his income, and having $0Z$ income left over to spend on other commodities. The goal of the government is to make it possible for the pensioner to move to the higher level of welfare (satisfaction) denoted by the indifference curve I_2.

The effects of the food subsidy. Assume that the government gives food coupons to the pensioner which allow him to buy food at half the market price. Following this measure the budget line of the pensioner shifts to AB', which is tangent to I_2 at point e_2. At his new equilibrium position the pensioner buys $0X_2$ units of food, paying for this quantity AL of his income. If there were no food subsidy the pensioner would have to spend AK of his income to buy $0X_2$ units of food. Since he pays only AL, the difference $LK = (AK - AL)$ must be paid to the food producers by the government. Thus, if the government adopts the food subsidy policy we have the following effects: (*a*) The cost to the government (and to the taxpayer) is LK. (*b*) the market price of food is not affected by this policy, so that other consumers continue to pay the original price. (*c*) the government is certain that the pensioners will consume more food. This effect may be particularly desirable (as a subsidiary goal of the government) if there are surpluses of food. Actually it is often the case that food subsidies are designed in such a way as to benefit not only the consumers but also the producers of foodstuff. (*d*) the assistance to pensioners via the food subsidy imposes a certain pattern of consumption, a certain choice of spending their income.

The effects of a supplementary income policy. Assume that the government considers granting to the pensioner a supplementary income which will enable him to reach the higher welfare level implied by indifference curve I_2. To find the amount of such a supplementary income we simply draw a budget line (CD), parallel to the original budget line (AB) and tangent to I_2 (at point e_3). The pensioner will now buy $0X_3$ units of food. The cost to the government of the supplementary income policy is equal to CA, which (in our example) is smaller than the cost of the food subsidy policy.[1] Furthermore the quantity of food in this case ($0X_3$) is smaller than the quantity which would be bought under a food subsidy programme ($0X_2$).

Comparing the two alternative policies we observe that both policies achieve the government's goal of enabling the pensioner to reach the higher welfare state implied by I_2. But the food subsidy programme is more costly (in our example) than the supplementary income policy. In fact if the government were to give to the pensioner the cost of the subsidy in the form of supplementary income, the pensioner would attain a higher level of satisfaction (an indifference curve above I_2). However, the consumption of food will be greater in the case of the food subsidy policy.

Which one of these alternative policies the government will adopt depends not only on the above considerations, but also on the other goals of the government and the indirect effects of each policy. For example, if there is a surplus food production, the government may adopt the more costly subsidisation policy, which, apart from increasing the welfare of the consumer, also benefits the producers by reducing or even eliminating the surplus. Furthermore, supplementary incomes policies are in general more inflationary than price subsidies to specific individuals (especially if there is a surplus of the subsidised commodities). Increasing the incomes of some groups of 'needy' consumers may lead to increases of the market prices of commodities for all consumers, thus decreasing their welfare.

The above discussion illustrates how indifference-curves analysis may give insight into the implications of selective government measures, and thus help efficient policy formulation.

Indifference-curve analysis and the theory of exchange

Indifference-curves analysis may be used to explain why exchange of commodities among individuals (or groups of individuals, countries, regions, and so on) takes place. We will show that, under certain conditions, exchange of commodities leads to an increase in the welfare of at least one individual without any reduction in the welfare of the other, so that the overall welfare which can be enjoyed from a given bundle of commodities is increased.

We will use the device of the *Edgeworth box*.[2] We assume that there are only two individuals, A and B, and two commodities, x and y, whose quantities are given. These quantities are measured along the sides of the Edgeworth box. Any point of the Edgeworth box shows a certain distribution of the available quantities of x and y between individuals A and B.

The preferences of consumer A are represented by a set of indifference curves (denoted by A with an appropriate subscript) which are convex to the origin 0_A. The preferences

---

[1] From figure 2.26 we see that $CA = MN$, since these lines are opposite sides of the parallelogram $ANMC$. Also $LK = e_2N$. But $e_2N = e_2M + MN = LK$. Therefore

$$MN < LK$$

or

$$CA < LK$$

that is

$$\begin{bmatrix} \text{cost of} \\ \text{income} \\ \text{policy} \end{bmatrix} < \begin{bmatrix} \text{cost of} \\ \text{food} \\ \text{subsidy} \end{bmatrix}$$

[2] Named after Edgeworth, who first used this construction.

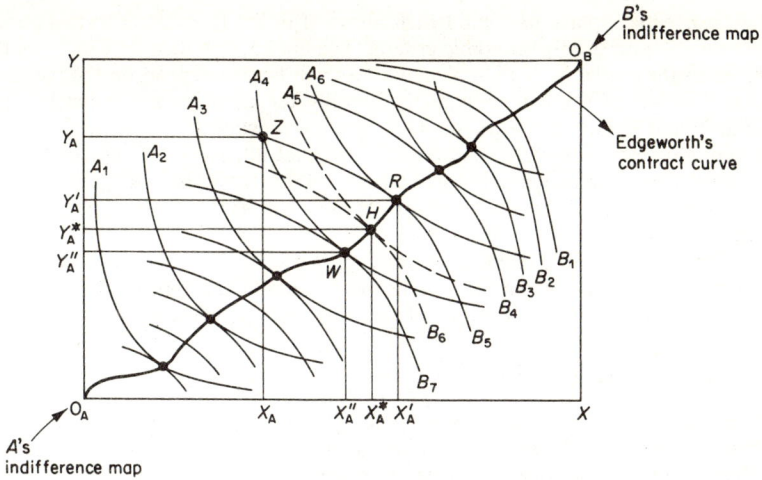

Figure 2.27

of consumer B are represented by the set of indifference curves (denoted by B with an appropriate subscript) which are convex to 0_B. The indifference maps have the usual properties. For example, the further down an indifference curve of B lies, the greater is the satisfaction. The two sets of indifference curves, being of opposite curvature, have points of tangency which form the so-called *Edgeworth's contract curve* $(0_A 0_B$ in figure 2.27). In other words the contract curve is the locus of points of tangency of the indifference curves of A and B, and therefore the locus of points at which the *MRS* of the two commodities is the same for both consumers

$$MRS^A_{y,x} = MRS^B_{y,x}$$

Only points lying on the contract curve represent optimal distribution of the available quantities of x and y between the two consumers, in the sense that any divergence from this curve implies a lower level of satisfaction for at least one individual. For example, consider point Z off the contract curve. At this point consumer A owns $0X_A$ of commodity x and $0Y_A$ of commodity y, with the remaining quantities $(X_A X$ and $Y_A Y)$ owned by consumer B. With this distribution of the two commodities consumer A is on indifference curve A_4 while consumer B is on indifference curve B_5. We will show that point Z represents a suboptimal distribution of x and y, because if A and B exchange some of the quantities of the two commodities so as to move to any point on the section WR of the contract curve at least one (and probably both) of them will be better off (on a higher indifference curve) without the other being worse off.

If the consumers exchange x for y so that they arrive at the distribution denoted by R (consumer A giving away $Y_A Y'_A$ of commodity y in exchange for $X_A X'_A$ of commodity x), consumer A will reach a higher welfare situation (moving from indifference curve A_4 to the higher one A_6) while consumer B retains his initial level of satisfaction (both Z and R lying on the same indifference curve B_5).

If the consumers reach, via exchanging commodity x for y, to the distribution denoted by W the opposite situation will obtain: consumer A will retain his initial level of satisfaction (since Z and W lie on the initial indifference curve A_4) while consumer B will attain a higher indifference curve (B_7).

If the consumers reach any other distribution between W and R, e.g. the one denoted by H, they will both be better off, reaching higher indifference curves (A_5 and B_6 respectively) as compared to their initial positions at Z.

If exchange takes place who will benefit more, *A* or *B*? The answer to this question cannot be given on purely economic criteria. The final distribution of *x* and *y* and the 'gains' from the exchange of these commodities will largely depend on the bargaining skills and power of the two individuals. Usually the consumers will reach a point between *W* and *R*, both gaining some welfare in the process.

In summary: the contract curve includes optimal allocation of the commodities, in the sense that if the individuals are at a point off this curve they will gain by moving to a point on it, since at least one (or both) of them will be better off without the other becoming worse off.[1]

It is implicit in the above elementary analysis of exchange that the tastes of *A* and *B* do not change and that the quantities of the two commodities are given. If these assumptions do not hold, the result of the act of exchange may be different.

Indifference-curves analysis of the cost of living

Indifference-curve analysis and the theory of revealed preference can be used to establish whether, over a period of time during which both money incomes and prices have been changing, the consumer is better or worse off.

The assumption underlying the following discussion is that the consumer spends all his money income in all time periods, that is, he chooses a point *on* his budget line in any particular period.[2]

In the initial (base) period the consumer's income and expenditure is:

$$Y_0 = \sum q_0 p_0$$

and in the current period

$$Y_t = \sum q_t p_t$$

Assuming that both prices and money income changed between the base and the current periods, how can we decide whether the consumer is better off? To answer this question we require index numbers of income and prices.

An index of income changes is given by the expression

$$I_Y = \left(\frac{Y_t}{Y_0}\right) \cdot 100$$

where Y_0 = money income in the base period
         Y_t = money income in the current period

The index number of the income in the base period is 100. If in period *t* the index number is 125 we conclude that money income has increased by 25 per cent in period *t* as compared with the base period.

Changes in the price level are measured by two traditional price indexes, the Laspèyres price index, defined by

$$L = \left(\frac{\sum q_0 p_t}{\sum q_0 p_0}\right) \cdot 100$$

[1] An interesting illustration of the above type of analysis may be found in S. Enke, 'Using Costs to Select Weapons', *American Economic Review* (1965); and S. Enke, 'Some Economic Aspects of Fissionable Materials', *Quarterly Journal of Economics* (1954).

[2] Savings can be treated as one commodity in the bundle of goods selected by the consumer at any time.

and the Paasche index, defined by

$$P = \left(\frac{\sum q_t p_t}{\sum q_t p_0} \right) \cdot 100$$

where q_0 = quantities of the commodities bought in the base period
p_0 = prices of the commodities in the base period
q_t = quantities of the commodities bought in period t
p_t = prices of the commodities in period t

Given the above index numbers we will prove that:
(i) the consumer is better off in period t as compared with the base period if the index number of income is greater than the Laspèyres price index, that is, if

$$\left(\frac{Y_t}{Y_0} \right) \cdot 100 > L$$

(ii) the consumer is worse off in period t as compared with the base period if the index number of income is smaller than the Paasche price index, that is, if

$$\left(\frac{Y_t}{Y_0} \right) \cdot 100 < P$$

The use of the Laspèyres price index. Assume that the initial income and expenditure of the consumer is

$$Y_0 = \sum q_0 p_0$$

In period t prices have changed to p_t, and if we estimate the cost of the 'basket q_0' at the new prices we find

$$\sum q_0 p_t$$

If $\sum q_0 p_t \leq Y_t$, the initial 'basket q_0' is available to the consumer in the current price (and income) situation. That is, with his current income (Y_t) the consumer can still purchase the original basket of goods if he so wishes. If he actually makes this choice in period t then

$$\sum q_0 p_0 = \sum q_0 p_t = Y_t$$

and the consumer retains the same level of satisfaction in period t as in the base period (he remains on the same indifference curve). However, if the consumer chooses in period t another basket of goods q_t (while q_0 continues to be available) then two situations may occur:

either $\quad \sum q_0 p_t < \sum q_t p_t$ \hfill (2.2)

which implies that q_0 is below the new budget line of the consumer, who, buying q_t, is better off (because he can buy basket q_t which was beyond his means in the base period)

or $\quad \sum q_0 p_t = \sum q_t p_t$

which implies that both baskets are equally expensive (q_0 and q_t both lie on the new budget line), but the consumer reveals his preference for q_t presumably because q_t gives him more satisfaction (lies on a higher indifference curve).

Dividing equation (2.2) through by $\sum q_0 p_0$ (the initial income) and multiplying by 100 we obtain

$$\left[\frac{\sum q_0 p_t}{\sum q_0 p_0} \cdot 100 \right] < \left[\frac{\sum q_t p_t}{\sum q_0 p_0} \cdot 100 \right]$$

The left-hand side of this inequality is the Laspèyres price index, while the right-hand side is the income index number ($\sum q_t p_t$ being the current income and $\sum q_0 p_0$ being the income of the base period). Thus we may write

$$L < \left[\frac{Y_t}{Y_0} \cdot 100 \right]$$

which shows that the consumer is better off if the Laspèyres price index is smaller than the income index. This conclusion may be illustrated diagrammatically by using indifference curves.

In figure 2.28 the initial budget line is MM, defined by the equation

$$Y_0 = \sum q_0 p_0 = (q_{x,0})(p_{x,0}) + (q_{y,0})(p_{y,0})$$

The consumer is in equilibrium at point A, buying $q_{x,0}$ and $q_{y,0}$ of the two commodities.

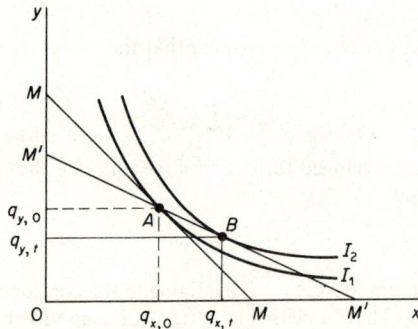

Figure 2.28

The new budget line is $M'M'$ defined by the expression

$$Y_t = \sum q_t p_t = (q_{x,t})(p_{x,t}) + (q_{y,t})(p_{y,t})$$

The new budget line passes through the initial equilibrium point A,[1] showing that 'basket q_0' is still available to the consumer at the new set of prices (p_t). The consumer can, therefore, continue to purchase q_0, thus remaining on the initial indifference curve I_1. But he can reach a higher indifference curve (I_2) by choosing basket q_t shown by point B in figure 2.28. This point was above the initial budget line, and hence beyond the reach of the consumer (given Y_0 and p_0). In other words the cost of bundle q_t (= point B) estimated at the original prices (p_0) was higher than the cost of bundle q_0 (at p_0). In the new price situation both bundles have the same cost since they lie on the new

[1] If A lies below $M'M'$, although available, it will not be chosen, because part of the income Y_t would be unspent, contrary to our assumption. If A lies above $M'M'$, the consumer is worse off in period t. This case is examined in the next section.

budget line ($M'M'$). Yet q_t is chosen because it lies on a higher indifference curve: the consumer is better off with the new income (Y_t) and the new set of prices (p_t).

The use of the Paasche price index. Assume, as before, that in the base period the consumer has income Y_0 and chooses basket q_0, spending on it all his income $\sum q_0 p_0 = Y_0$.

In the period t the consumer chooses a new basket q_t, spending all his income $\sum q_t p_t = Y_t$.

The cost of basket q_t, estimated at the prices of the base period, is $\sum q_t p_0$.

If
$$\sum q_0 p_0 > \sum q_t p_0 \qquad (2.3)$$

then the basket chosen in period t (q_t) was available in the base period, but was not chosen by the consumer, because presumably it was lying on a lower indifference curve than q_0.

Given that in period t the consumer does actually choose q_t, spending all his income ($\sum q_t p_t$) on it, it follows that basket q_0 is now beyond his means (i.e. q_0 is above the new budget line of the consumer). Hence the consumer is worse off in period t.

Dividing equation (2.3) through by $\sum q_t p_t$ and multiplying by 100 we obtain

$$\left[\frac{\sum q_0 p_0}{\sum q_t p_t} \cdot 100 \right] > \left[\frac{\sum q_t p_0}{\sum q_t p_t} \cdot 100 \right]$$

Taking the inverse of each side we find

$$\left[\frac{\sum q_t p_t}{\sum q_0 p_0} \cdot 100 \right] < \left[\frac{\sum q_t p_t}{\sum q_t p_0} \cdot 100 \right]$$

The left-hand side is the income index number and the right-hand side is the Paasche price index. Hence we may write

$$\left[\frac{Y_t}{Y_0} \cdot 100 \right] < P$$

that is, the consumer is worse off in period t as compared with the base period if the income index is smaller than the Paasche price index. We may show this result on a graph using indifference-curves analysis.

In figure 2.29 the equilibrium of the consumer in the base period is defined by C. Although basket D (including $q_{x,t}$ and $q_{y,t}$) was on his original budget line, the consumer did not choose it, because it was lying on the lower indifference curve I_1.

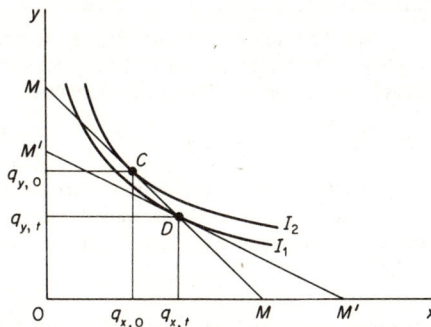

Figure 2.29

In period t the new budget line $(M'M')$ defined by the expression

$$Y_t = \sum q_t p_t = (q_{x,t})(p_{x,t}) + (q_{y,t})(p_{y,t})$$

lies below basket q_0: the consumer cannot afford to buy the original bundle at the new prices (p_t). Thus the consumer chooses basket q_t, that is, he is worse off as compared to the base period. (If q_0 was available in period t and the consumer chose q_t, he would be inconsistent, since in the base period he had preferred q_0 to q_t).

It should be noted that comparisons of the above type are valid only if tastes and quality of the commodities have not changed in the two periods.

II. THE MARKET DEMAND

A. DERIVATION OF THE MARKET DEMAND

The market demand for a given commodity is the horizontal summation of the demands of the individual consumers. In other words, the quantity demanded in the market at each price is the sum of the individual demands of all consumers at that price. In table 2.1 we show the demands of four consumers at various prices of a certain commodity and the total market demand. These data are presented graphically in figure 2.30. We observe that although for consumer B commodity x is a Giffen good, the market demand has the normal negative slope, because the demands of other consumers more than offset the Giffen effect.

Table 2.1   Individual and market demand

Price	Quantity demanded by consumer A	Quantity demanded by consumer B	Quantity demanded by consumer C	Quantity demanded by consumer D	Market demand
2	40	4	45	18	107
4	30	2	35	16	83
6	24	5	30	13	72
8	18	7	20	12	57
10	14	10	15	11	50
12	10	7	13	8	38
14	8	5	10	6	29
16	6	3	8	4	21
18	4	2	0	0	6
20	3	0	0	0	3

Economic theory does not define any particular form of the demand curve. Market demand is sometimes shown in textbooks as a straight line (linear-demand curve) and sometimes as a curve convex to the origin. The linear-demand curve (figure 2.31) may be written in the form

$$Q = b_0 - b_1 P$$

and implies a constant slope, but a changing elasticity at various prices. The most common form of a non-linear-demand curve is the so-called 'constant-elasticity-demand curve', which implies constant elasticity at all prices; its mathematical form is

$$Q = b_0 \cdot P^{b_1}$$

where b_1 is the constant price elasticity (see section III). The concept of elasticity is discussed in the following section.

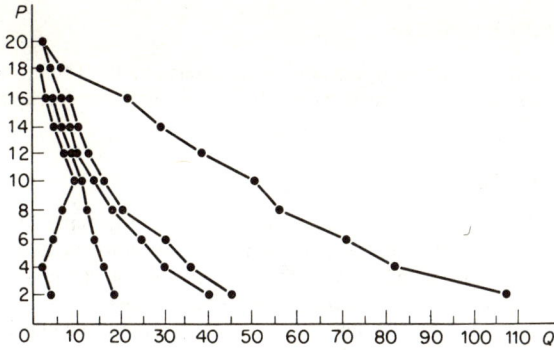

Figure 2.30

B. DETERMINANTS OF DEMAND

We said at the beginning of this chapter that demand is a multivariate function; it is determined by many variables. Traditionally the most important determinants of the market demand are considered to be the price of the commodity in question, the prices of other commodities, consumers' income and tastes. The result of a change in the price of the commodity is shown by a movement from one point to another on the *same* demand curve, while the effect of changes in other determinants is shown by a shift of the demand curve. Thus these factors are called *shift factors*, and the demand curve is drawn under the *ceteris paribus* assumption, that the shift factors (prices of other commodities, incomes and tastes) are constant. The distinction between movements along the curve and shifts of the curve is convenient for the graphical presentation of the demand function. Conceptually, however, demand should be thought of as being determined by various factors (is multivariate) and the change in any one of these factors changes the quantity demanded.

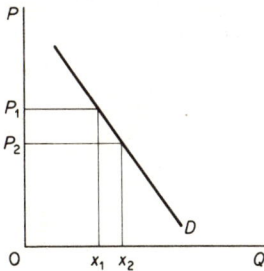

Figure 2.31 Movement along the demand curve as the price of x changes.

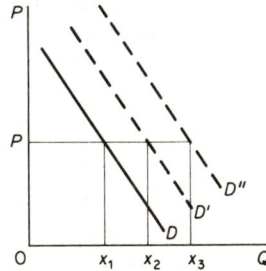

Figure 2.32 Shifts of the demand curve as, for example, income increases.

Apart from the above determinants, demand is affected by numerous other factors, such as the distribution of income, total population and its composition, wealth, credit availability, stocks and habits. The last two factors allow for the influence of past behaviour on the present, thus rendering demand analysis dynamic. The incorporation of the latter factors into the demand function will be examined in section III.

C. ELASTICITIES OF DEMAND

There are as many elasticities of demand as its determinants. The most important of these elasticities are (*a*) the price elasticity, (*b*) the income elasticity, (*c*) the cross-elasticity of demand.

The price elasticity of demand

The price elasticity is a measure of the responsiveness of demand to changes in the commodity's own price. If the changes in price are very small we use as a measure of the responsiveness of demand the *point elasticity of demand*. If the changes in price are not small we use the *arc elasticity of demand* as the relevant measure.

The point elasticity of demand is defined as the proportionate change in the quantity demanded resulting from a very small proportionate change in price. Symbolically we may write

$$e_p = \frac{dQ}{Q} \bigg/ \frac{dP}{P} \tag{2.4}$$

or

$$e_p = \frac{dQ}{dP} \cdot \frac{P}{Q}$$

If the demand curve is linear

$$Q = b_0 - b_1 P$$

its slope is $dQ/dP = -b_1$. Substituting in the elasticity formula we obtain

$$e_p = -b_1 \cdot \frac{P}{Q}$$

which implies that the elasticity changes at the various points of the linear-demand curve. Graphically the point elasticity of a *linear-demand* curve is shown by the ratio of the segments of the line to the right and to the left of the particular point. In figure 2.33 the elasticity of the linear-demand curve at point F is the ratio

$$\frac{FD'}{FD}$$

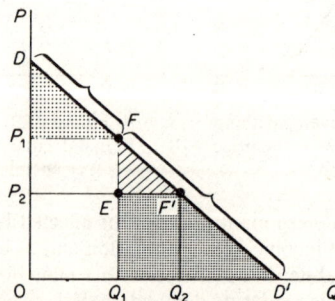

Figure 2.33

Proof

From figure 2.33 we see that

$$\Delta P = P_1 P_2 = EF$$
$$\Delta Q = Q_1 Q_2 = EF'$$
$$P = 0P_1$$
$$Q = 0Q_1$$

If we consider very small changes in P and Q, then $\Delta P \approx dP$ and $\Delta Q \approx dQ$. Thus, substituting in the formula for the point elasticity, we obtain

$$e_p = \frac{dQ}{dP} \cdot \frac{P}{Q} = \frac{Q_1 Q_2}{P_1 P_2} \cdot \frac{0P_1}{0Q_1} = \frac{EF'}{EF} \cdot \frac{0P_1}{0Q_1}$$

From the figure we can also see that the triangles FEF' and $FQ_1 D'$ are similar (because each corresponding angle is equal). Hence

$$\frac{EF'}{EF} = \frac{Q_1 D'}{FQ_1} = \frac{Q_1 D'}{0P_1}$$

Thus

$$e_p = \frac{Q_1 D'}{0P_1} \cdot \frac{0P_1}{0Q_1} = \frac{Q_1 D'}{0Q_1}$$

Furthermore the triangles $DP_1 F$ and $FQ_1 D'$ are similar, so that

$$\frac{Q_1 D'}{FD'} = \frac{P_1 F}{FD} = \frac{0Q_1}{FD}$$

Rearranging we obtain

$$\frac{Q_1 D'}{0Q_1} = \frac{FD'}{FD}$$

Thus the price elasticity at point F is

$$e_p = \frac{Q_1 D'}{0Q_1} = \frac{FD'}{FD}$$

Given this graphical measurement of point elasticity it is obvious that at the mid-point of a linear-demand curve $e_p = 1$ (point M in figure 2.34). At any point to the right of M

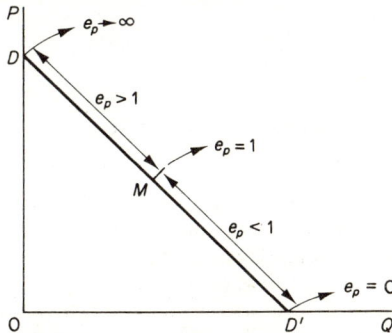

Figure 2.34

the point elasticity is less than unity ($e_p < 1$); finally at any point to the left of M, $e_p > 1$. At point D the $e_p \to \infty$, while at point D' the $e_p = 0$. The price elasticity is always negative because of the inverse relationship between Q and P implied by the 'law of demand'. However, traditionally the negative sign is omitted when writing the formula of the elasticity.

The range of values of the elasticity are

$$0 \le e_p \le \infty$$

If $e_p = 0$, the demand is perfectly inelastic (figure 2.35)
If $e_p = 1$, the demand has unitary elasticity (figure 2.36)
If $e_p = \infty$, the demand is perfectly elastic (figure 2.37)
If $0 < e < 1$, we say that the demand is inelastic.
If $1 < e < \infty$, we say that the demand is elastic.

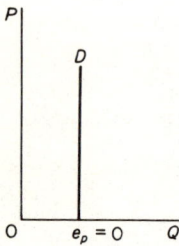
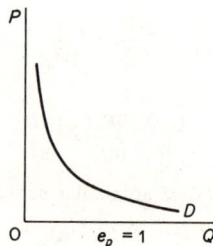
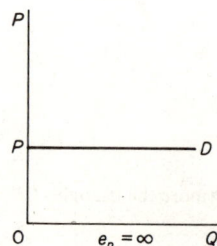

Figure 2.35   Figure 2.36   Figure 2.37

The basic determinants of the elasticity of demand of a commodity with respect to its own price are:

(1) The availability of substitutes; the demand for a commodity is more elastic if there are close substitutes for it.

(2) The nature of the need that the commodity satisfies. In general, luxury goods are price elastic, while necessities are price inelastic.

(3) The time period. Demand is more elastic in the long run.

(4) The number of uses to which a commodity can be put. The more the possible uses of a commodity the greater its price elasticity will be.

(5) The proportion of income spent on the particular commodity.
The above formula for the price elasticity is applicable only for infinitesimal changes in the price. If the price changes appreciably we use the following formula, which measures the *arc elasticity* of demand:

$$e_p = \frac{\Delta Q}{\Delta P} \cdot \frac{\dfrac{P_1 + P_2}{2}}{\dfrac{Q_1 + Q_2}{2}} = \frac{\Delta Q}{\Delta P} \cdot \frac{(P_1 + P_2)}{(Q_1 + Q_2)} \tag{2.5}$$

The arc elasticity is a measure of the *average* elasticity, that is, the elasticity at the mid-point of the chord that connects the two points (A and B) on the demand curve defined by the initial and the new price levels (figure 2.38). It should be clear that the measure of the arc elasticity is an approximation of the true elasticity of the section AB of the demand curve, which is used when we know only the two points A and B from the demand curve, but not the intermediate ones. Clearly the more convex to the origin the demand curve is, the poorer the linear approximation attained by the arc elasticity formula.

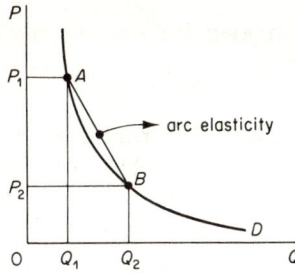

Figure 2.38

The income elasticity of demand

The income elasticity is defined as the proportionate change in the quantity demanded resulting from a proportionate change in income. Symbolically we may write

$$e_Y = \frac{dQ}{Q} \Big/ \frac{dY}{Y} = \frac{dQ}{dY} \cdot \frac{Y}{Q} \tag{2.6}$$

The income elasticity is positive for normal goods. Some writers have used income elasticity in order to classify goods into 'luxuries' and 'necessities'. A commodity is considered to be a 'luxury' if its income elasticity is greater than unity. A commodity is a 'necessity' if its income elasticity is small (less than unity, usually).

The main determinants of income elasticity are:

1. The nature of the need that the commodity covers: the percentage of income spent on food declines as income increases (this is known as *Engel's Law* and has some-times been used as a measure of welfare and of the development stage of an economy).

2. The initial level of income of a country. For example, a TV set is a luxury in an underdeveloped, poor country while it is a 'necessity' in a country with high *per capita* income.

3. The time period, because consumption patterns adjust with a time-lag to changes in income.

The cross-elasticity of demand

We have already talked about the price cross-elasticity with connection to the classific-ation of commodities into substitutes and complements (see section I).

The cross-elasticity of demand is defined as the proportionate change in the quantity demanded of x resulting from a proportionate change in the price of y. Symbolically we have

$$e_{xy} = \frac{dQ_x}{Q_x} \frac{dP_y}{P_y} = \frac{dQ_x}{dP_y} \cdot \frac{P_y}{Q_x} \tag{2.7}$$

The sign of the cross-elasticity is negative if x and y are complementary goods, and positive if x and y are substitutes. The higher the value of the cross-elasticity the stronger will be the degree of substitutability or complementarity of x and y.

The main determinant of the cross-elasticity is the nature of the commodities relative to their uses. If two commodities can satisfy equally well the same need, the cross-elasticity is high, and vice versa.

The cross-elasticity has been used for the definition of the firms which form an in-dustry (see Chapter 1).

D. MARKET DEMAND, TOTAL REVENUE AND MARGINAL REVENUE

Demand and total revenue

From the market-demand curve we can derive the total expenditure of the consumers, which forms the total revenue of the firms selling the particular commodity.

The total revenue is the product of the quantity sold and the price

$$TR = P \cdot Q$$

If the market demand is linear the total-revenue curve will be a curve which initially slopes upwards, reaches a maximum point and then starts declining (figure 2.40).

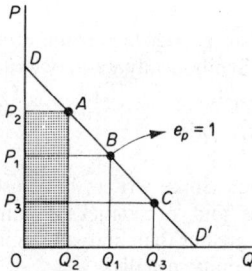
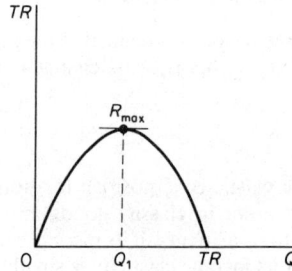

Figure 2.39   Figure 2.40

At any one price the total revenue is the area of the rectangle defined by drawing perpendiculars from that price and the corresponding quantity to the demand curve. For example, in figure 2.39, the total revenue at price P_2 is the area of the rectangle $P_2 A Q_2 O$.

Of particular interest to the theory of the firm is the concept of *marginal revenue*. The marginal revenue is the change in total revenue resulting from selling an additional unit of the commodity.

Graphically the marginal revenue is the slope of the total-revenue curve at any one level of output. If the demand curve is linear, it is obvious that in order to sell an additional unit of x its price must fall. Since the whole quantity will be sold at the new lower price, the marginal revenue will be equal to the price of the extra unit sold minus the loss from selling all previous units at the new lower price:

$$MR = P_{n+1} - (P_n - P_{n+1})Q_n$$

where Q_n is the quantity sold before the fall in price. Clearly at all prices the MR is smaller than the price, given that $(P_n - P_{n+1})(=\Delta P)$ is positive and Q_n is positive.

Graphically the marginal revenue can be derived from the demand curve as follows. Choose any point of the demand curve (such as point A) and draw perpendiculars from it on the price and the quantity axes (AP and AQ respectively). Next find the mid-point of the perpendicular PA. In figure 2.41 the mid-point of PA is C. Draw a straight line from D through C and extend it until it cuts the perpendicular AQ (at point B in figure 2.41). This line is the marginal-revenue curve. To see that, we first note that the total revenue at price $P(= OPAQ)$ is the sum of the marginal revenues of all individual units $(= ODBQ)$ The two areas, $OPAQ$ and $ODBQ$, are in fact equal because they have in common the area $OPCBQ$, and the triangles DPC and CAB are equal (they have the corresponding

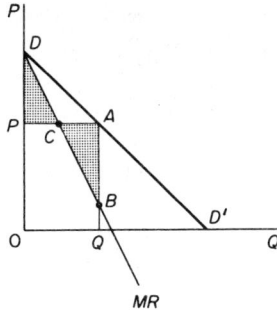

Figure 2.41

angles equal and one side equal: by construction $PC = CA$). Hence the MR curve is the line DCB, and may be derived by joining the midpoints of perpendiculars drawn from the demand curve to the price-axis. In other words, the MR curve cuts any such perpendicular at its midpoint.

Mathematically the MR is the derivative of the TR function:

$$MR = \frac{d(TR)}{dQ} = \frac{d(PQ)}{dQ}$$

or

$$MR = P + Q \cdot \frac{dP}{dQ} \tag{2.8}$$

If the demand curve is linear its equation is

$$Q = b_0 - b_1 P$$

or, solving for P,

$$P = a_0 - a_1 Q$$

where

$$a_0 = \frac{b_0}{b_1} \quad \text{and} \quad a_1 = \frac{1}{b_1}$$

Substituting P in the total revenue function we find

$$TR = PQ = a_0 Q - a_1 Q^2$$

The MR is then

$$MR = \frac{d(TR)}{dQ} = a_0 - 2a_1 Q$$

This proves that the MR curve starts from the same point (a_0) as the demand curve, and that the MR is a straight line with a negative slope twice as steep as the slope of the demand curve. This is the same result that we established above using simple geometry.

The relationship between marginal revenue and price elasticity

The marginal revenue is related to the price elasticity of demand with the formula

$$MR = P\left(1 - \frac{1}{e}\right) \qquad (2.9)$$

This is a crucial relationship for the theory of pricing.

Proof

Assume that the demand function is

$$P = f(Q)$$

The total revenue is

$$TR = PQ = [f(Q)]Q$$

The *MR* is

$$MR = \frac{d(PQ)}{dQ} = P\frac{dQ}{dQ} + Q\frac{dP}{dQ} = P + Q\frac{dP}{dQ}$$

The price elasticity of demand is defined as

$$e = -\frac{dQ}{dP} \cdot \frac{P}{Q}$$

Rearranging we obtain

$$-e\frac{Q}{P} = \frac{dQ}{dP}$$

$$-\frac{P}{eQ} = \frac{dP}{dQ}$$

Substituting dP/dQ in the expression of the *MR* we find

$$MR = P + Q\frac{dP}{dQ} = P - Q\frac{P}{eQ} = P - \frac{P}{e}$$

or

$$MR = P\left(1 - \frac{1}{e}\right)$$

Total revenue, marginal revenue and elasticity

We said that if the demand curve is falling the *TR* curve initially increases, reaches a maximum, and then starts declining. We can use the earlier derived relationship between *MR*, *P* and *e* to establish the shape of the total-revenue curve.

The total-revenue curve reaches its maximum level at the point where $e = 1$, because at this point its slope, the marginal revenue, is equal to zero:

$$MR = P\left(1 - \frac{1}{1}\right) = 0$$

If $e > 1$ the total-revenue curve has a positive slope, that is, it is still increasing, and hence has not reached its maximum point given that

$$P > 0 \quad \text{and} \quad \left(1 - \frac{1}{e}\right) > 0; \quad \text{hence} \quad MR > 0$$

If $e < 1$ the total-revenue curve has a negative slope, that is, it is falling, given

$$P > 0 \quad \text{and} \quad \left(1 - \frac{1}{e}\right) < 0; \quad \text{hence} \quad MR < 0$$

We may summarise these results as follows:

If the demand is inelastic ($e < 1$), an increase in price leads to an increase in total revenue, and a decrease in price leads to a fall in total revenue.

If the demand is elastic ($e > 1$), an increase in price will result in a decrease of the total revenue, while a decrease in price will result in an increase in the total revenue.

If the demand has unitary elasticity, total revenue is not affected by changes in price, since if $e = 1$, then $MR = 0$.

III. RECENT DEVELOPMENTS IN THE THEORY OF MARKET DEMAND

A. THE PRAGMATIC APPROACH TO DEMAND ANALYSIS

Many writers have questioned the usefulness of the various theories of consumers' behaviour. There has been an increasing awareness that although the various approaches to utility are theoretically impressive, there is very little an applied economist can use to explain the complexity of the real world. Thus many writers have followed a pragmatic approach to the theory of demand. They accepted the fundamental 'law of demand' on trust, and formulated demand functions directly on the basis of market data without reference to the theory of utility and the behaviour of the individual consumer. Demand is expressed as a multivariate function, and is estimated with various econometric methods. Such demand functions refer obviously to the market behaviour of the consumers, that is, to the behaviour of all consumers as a group, and not to the behaviour of single individuals. Furthermore, in most cases the demand functions refer to a group of commodities, e.g. demand for food, demand for consumer durables, etc.

Serious difficulties arise in estimating demand functions. The aggregation of demand over individuals and over commodities makes the use of index numbers inevitable, but the problems associated with such indexes are numerous. Furthermore, there are various other estimation problems which impair the reliability of the statistically-estimated demand functions. The most important of these difficulties arise from the simultaneous change of all the determinants, which makes it extremely difficult to assess the influence of each individual factor separately. However, there has been a continuous improvement in the econometric techniques and currently demand functions are fairly easy to estimate statistically.

The constant-elasticity demand function

The most commonly used form of demand function in applied research has been the 'constant-elasticity' type

$$Q_x = b_0 \cdot P_x^{b_1} \cdot P_0^{b_2} \cdot Y^{b_3} \cdot e^{b_4 t}$$

where Q_x = quantity demanded of commodity x
P_x = price of x
P_0 = prices of other commodities
Y = consumers' aggregate income
$e^{b_4 t}$ = a trend factor for 'tastes' (e = base of natural logarithms)
b_1 = price elasticity of demand
b_2 = cross-elasticity of demand
b_3 = income elasticity of demand

The term 'constant elasticity demand function' is due to the fact that in this form the coefficients b_1, b_2, b_3 are elasticities of demand which are assumed to remain constant.

Proof

It will be proved that b_1 is the (constant) price elasticity of demand. Expressing the above demand function in the logarithms of the variables we obtain:

$$\log Q_x = \log b_0 + b_1 \log P_x + b_2 \log P_0 + b_3 \log Y$$

(The term for the trend is ignored for simplicity.)
The partial derivative of the function with respect to the price P_x is

$$\frac{\partial \log Q_x}{\partial \log P_x} = b_1$$

From a basic property of logarithms it is known that the change of the logarithm of a variable is equal to the proportionate change of the variable. Applying this property to the above partial derivative we obtain

$$\partial \log Q_x = \frac{\partial Q_x}{Q_x} \quad \text{and} \quad \partial \log P_x = \frac{\partial P_x}{P_x}$$

and by substituting we have

$$\frac{\partial Q_x / Q_x}{\partial P_x / P_x} = b_1$$

Clearly b_1 is the price elasticity of demand:

$$e_p = \frac{\partial Q_x / Q_x}{\partial P_x / P_x} = \frac{\partial Q_x}{\partial P_x} \cdot \frac{P_x}{Q_x} = b_1$$

Since b_1 is constant in the above formulation of the demand function, the price elasticity (and the other elasticities) is constant.

Usually the followers of the pragmatic approach, although not adhering to utility functions, express the demand function in such a way as to incorporate the assumption of 'no money illusion' postulated by the traditional theory of the consumer. In technical jargon they express the demand as a *homogeneous function of degree zero*. This has been (most commonly) effected by introducing real income and relative prices in the function, that is

$$Q_x = b_0 \left(\frac{P_x}{P}\right)^{b_1} \cdot \left(\frac{P_0}{P}\right)^{b_2} \cdot \left(\frac{Y}{P}\right)^{b_3}$$

where P is a general price index. In this formulation it is obvious that if prices and income change by the same proportion, for example by k per cent, the quantity demanded of x

will not change, because k will appear in both the numerator and the denominator of the relative prices and real income, and hence will cancel out. The new quantity demanded will be the same as the initial one: there is no money illusion in the behaviour of the consumer.[1]

Dynamic versions of demand functions: Distributed-lag models of demand

A recent development in demand studies is the expression of demand functions in dynamic form.

Dynamic demand functions include lagged values of the quantity demanded and of income as separate variables influencing the demand in any particular period. Dynamisation of the demand functions expresses the generally accepted idea that current purchasing decisions are influenced by past behaviour.

To express the idea that current decisions are influenced by past behaviour we must postulate a particular type of relationship between the past and the present. The most common assumption in this respect is that current behaviour depends on past levels of income and past levels of demand. If the commodity is a durable past purchases constitute a 'stock' of this commodity which clearly affects the current (and future) purchases of such durable. If the commodity is non-durable (for example, tobacco, food, etc.), past purchases reflect a habit which is acquired by buying and consuming the commodity in the past, so that the level of purchases in previous periods influences the current (and future) patterns of demand. Incorporating the influence of past decisions and experiences in the demand function is a way for rendering it dynamic. Another usual assumption concerning the way in which past behaviour affects the present is that the more recent of past levels of income or demand have a greater influence on present consumption patterns than the more remote ones (for example, we are more influenced by our income in the last year than by the income we earned five or ten years ago).

Models (functions), including lagged values of demand, of income (or of other variables) are called '*distributed-lag models*'. In general form a distributed-lag model may be expressed as

$$Q_{x(t)} = f\{P_{x(t)}, P_{x(t-1)}, \ldots, Q_{x(t-1)}, Q_{x(t-2)}, \ldots, Y_{(t)}, Y_{(t-1)}, \ldots\}$$

The number of lags depends on the particular relationship being studied.

The necessity of a dynamic approach has long been recognised for the study of the demand of certain commodities (consumer durables). R. Stone[2] extended the dynamic

---

[1] The assumption of 'no money illusion' is called assumption of 'zero homogeneity' because the coefficients of prices and income must add to zero if the consumer is not to suffer from money illusion. Thus the initial quantity demanded is

$$Q_x = b_0 \cdot P_x^{b_1} \cdot P_0^{b_2} \cdot Y^{b_3}$$

If prices and income change by k per cent the new quantity demanded will be

$$Q_x^* = b_0(kP_x)^{b_1}(kP_0)^{b_2}(kY)^{b_3}$$

or

$$Q_x^* = (b_0 P_x^{b_1} P_0^{b_2} Y^{b_3})k^{(b_1 + b_2 + b_3)}$$

The new quantity differs from the initial one by the term $k^{(b_1 + b_2 + b_3)}$. For the two quantities to be the same (i.e., for the consumer not to suffer from money illusion) this term must be equal to unity, which occurs if the sum of the coefficients is equal to zero: $(b_1 + b_2 + b_3) = 0$.

[2] R. Stone and D. A. Rowe, 'The Durability of Consumers Durable Goods', *Econometrica* (1960).

formulation to a wider range of commodities. Houthakker and Taylor[1] generalised the dynamisation of demand functions.

A widely used model, both in demand functions and in investment functions, is the model based on the '*stock-adjustment principle*' ,which has been developed by Nerlove. This model has initially been applied to the study of demand functions for consumer durables. Recently Houthakker and Taylor have extended the 'stock-adjustment principle' to non-durables, giving it the name '*habit-creation principle*'.

Nerlove's 'stock-adjustment principle'. The model as applied to consumer durables results in a demand function of the form

$$Q_{(t)} = a_1 Y_{(t)} + a_2 Q_{(t-1)}$$

The model is derived as follows. There is a desired level of durables $Q_{(t)}^*$, which is determined by the current level of income:

$$Q_{(t)}^* = b Y_{(t)}$$

However, the consumer cannot immediately acquire the desired level of durables due to limited income, credit limitations, etc. Thus in each period the consumer acquires only a part of the desired level. In other words, the acquisition of the desired level of durables is gradual; in each period we come closer to $Q_{(t)}^*$.

In each period we purchase a certain quantity $Q_{(t)}$. There is an actual change from the quantity bought in the previous period denoted by the difference $Q_{(t)} - Q_{(t-1)}$. This change in actual purchases is only a fraction k of the desired change, $Q_{(t)}^* - Q_{(t-1)}$. Thus

$$\underset{\text{actual change}}{[Q_{(t)} - Q_{(t-1)}]} = \underset{\text{desired change}}{k[Q_{(t)}^* - Q_{(t-1)}]}$$

where *k is the coefficient of stock adjustment.* (The value of k lies between zero and one.) If in this expression of stock adjustment we substitute for $Q_{(t)}^*$ we obtain

$$Q_{(t)} - Q_{(t-1)} = k(b Y_{(t)} - Q_{(t-1)})$$

Rearranging we have

$$Q_{(t)} = (kb) Y_{(t)} + (1 - k) Q_{(t-1)}$$

Setting $kb = a_1$ and $(1 - k) = a_2$ we obtain the final form of the stock-adjustment model

$$Q_{(t)} = a_1 Y_{(t)} + a_2 Q_{(t-1)}$$

Houthakker's and Taylor's dynamic model. Their model is based on Nerlove's formulation. They extended the idea of stock adjustment to non-durables. The current demand for durables depends on, among other things, the stock of such commodities (stock-adjustment process). The current demand for non-durables depends on, among other things, the purchases of the commodities in the past, because by consuming a certain commodity we get accustomed to it (habit-formation process). The demand function is of the form

$$Q_t = a_0 + a_1 P_t + a_2 \Delta P_t + a_3 Y_t + a_4 \Delta Y_t + a_5 Q_{t-1}$$

[1] H. S. Houthakker and L. D. Taylor, *Consumer Demand in the United States* (Harvard University Press, Cambridge, Mass., 1966).

where ΔY_t is the change in income and ΔP_t is the change in price between period t and $t - 1$. The demand function is derived as follows.

Demand in any particular period depends on price, on stocks of the commodity and on the current level of income

$$Q_t = b_0 + b_1 P_t + b_2 S_t + b_3 Y_t \tag{2.10}$$

where S_t = stocks of durables, if the function refers to such goods
S_t = 'stocks of habits', if the function refers to non-durables

The sign of the coefficient of S will be negative for durables: the more we have of furniture, electrical appliances, etc., the less our demand for such commodities will be.

The sign of the coefficient of S will be positive for non-durables: the higher our purchases of non-durables the stronger our habit becomes.

Stocks S, however, cannot be measured: (i) The stock of durables is composed of heterogeneous items of various ages – the electrical equipment we have is not of the same age, some items may be very old and need scrapping and replacing, some others are new. Their heterogeneity also makes direct measurement difficult. What we ideally want for stocks is the sum of depreciated inventories of durables; but the appropriate depreciation rates are not known. (ii) The 'stock of habits' is a psychological variable and cannot be quantified.

However, we can eliminate algebraically stocks, S_t, from the demand function and replace it with other measurable variables by making some 'reasonable' assumptions.

For durables the elimination process may be outlined as follows:

(1) The net change in stocks realised in any period $(S_t - S_{t-1})$ is equal to our purchases in that period minus the depreciation of our old possessions:

$$S_t - S_{t-1} = Q_t - \text{depreciation}$$

(2) Assume that depreciation is equal in all the periods of the life of the durable, i.e.,

$$\text{Depreciation} = \delta S_t$$

where δ is a constant depreciation rate (for example, if the life of the durable is ten years, we assume that the yearly depreciation is 10 per cent of the value of the durable). Thus

$$(S_t - S_{t-1}) = Q_t - \delta S_t \tag{2.11}$$

(3) From the demand function

$$Q_t = b_0 + b_1 P_t + b_2 S_t + b_3 Y_t$$

solving for S_t we obtain

$$S_t = \frac{1}{b_2}(Q_t - b_0 - b_1 P_t - b_3 Y_t) \tag{2.12}$$

Substituting this value in the right-hand side of equation 2.11 we have

$$(S_t - S_{t-1}) = Q_t - \delta \frac{1}{b_2}(Q_t - b_0 - b_1 P_t - b_3 Y_t) \tag{2.13}$$

(4) Since the relation $Q_t = b_0 + b_1 P_t + b_2 S_t + b_3 Y_t$ holds for period t, the relationship

$$Q_{t-1} = b_0 + b_1 P_{t-1} + b_2 S_{t-1} + b_3 Y_{t-1}$$

will hold for period $t - 1$.
Subtracting these two equations we have

$$Q_t - Q_{t-1} = b_1(P_t - P_{t-1}) + b_2(S_t - S_{t-1}) + b_3(Y_t - Y_{t-1}) \tag{2.14}$$

(5) Substituting equation 2.13 in equation 2.14 we find

$$Q_t - Q_{t-1} = b_1(P_t - P_{t-1}) + b_2\left[Q_t - \frac{\delta}{b_2}(Q_t - b_0 - b_1 P_t - b_3 Y_t\right] + b_3(Y_t - Y_{t-1})$$

Rearranging this expression we obtain

$$Q_t = Q_{t-1} + b_1(P_t - P_{t-1}) + b_2 Q_t - \delta(Q_t - b_0 - b_1 P_t - b_3 Y_t) + b_3(Y_t - Y_{t-1})$$

$$Q_t(1 - b_2 + \delta) = (\delta b_0) + (\delta b_1)P_t + b_1(\Delta P_t) + (\delta b_3)Y_t + b_3(\Delta Y_t) + Q_{t-1}$$

$$Q = \frac{\delta b_0}{1 - b_2 + \delta} + \frac{\delta b_1}{1 - b_2 + \delta} P_t + \frac{b_1}{1 - b_2 + \delta}(\Delta P_t)$$

$$+ \frac{\delta b_3}{1 - b_2 + \delta} Y_t + \frac{b_3}{1 - b_2 + \delta}(\Delta Y_t) + \frac{1}{1 - b_2 + \delta}(Q_{t-1})$$

Setting a_0, a_1, a_2, a_3, a_4 and a_5 for the coefficients of this equation we arrive at the final form of Houthakker's and Taylor's formulation

$$Q_t = a_0 + a_1 P_t + a_2(\Delta P_t) + a_3 Y_t + a_4(\Delta Y_t) + a_5 Q_{t-1}$$

Note: The above exposition is an approximation to Houthakker's version. The basic procedure and the final form of the demand function are the same, but some of the intermediate steps have been simplified to facilitate the exposition.

B. LINEAR EXPENDITURE SYSTEMS

These are models which deal with groups of commodities rather than individual commodities. Such groups, when added, yield total consumer expenditure. Linear expenditure systems are thus of great interest in aggregate econometric models, where they provide desirable disaggregation of the consumption function. One of the earliest linear expenditure models was suggested by R. Stone (*Economic Journal*, 1954). The linear expenditure systems (*LES*) are usually formulated on the basis of a utility function, from which demand functions are derived in the normal way (by maximisation of the utility function subject to a budget constraint). In this respect the approach of *LES* is the same as that of models based on indifference curves. However, *LES* differ in that they are applied to 'groups of commodities' between which no substitution is possible, while the indifference-curves approach is basically designed for handling commodities which are substitutes. The very notion of an indifference curve is the substitutability of the commodities concerned. Actually the indifference map of a *LES* would appear as in figure 2.42, implying the non-substitutability of groups of commodities. The utility function is additive, that is, total utility (U) is the sum of the utilities derived from the

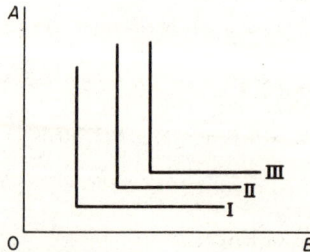

Figure 2.42   Indifference map for complementary goods

various groups of commodities. For example, assume that all the commodities bought by the consumers are grouped in five categories:

A Food and beverages
B Clothing
C Consumers' durables
D Household-operation expenses
E Services (transport, entertainment, etc.).

The total utility is

$$U = \sum U_i$$

or

$$U = U_{(A)} + U_{(B)} + U_{(C)} + U_{(D)} + U_{(E)}$$

Additivity implies that the utilities of the various groups are independent, that is, that there is no possibility of substitution (or complementarity) between the groups A, B, C, D and E.

In linear expenditure systems the commodities bought by the consumers are grouped in broad categories, so as to be compatible with the additivity postulate of the utility function. Thus each group must include all substitutes, and complements. In this way substitution between groups is ruled out, but substitution can occur within each group.

The consumers buy some minimum quantity from each group, irrespective of prices. The minimum quantities are called 'subsistence quantities' because they are the minimum requirements for keeping the consumer alive. The income left (after the expenditure on the minimum quantities is covered) is allocated among the various groups on the basis of prices.

The income of the consumer is, therefore, split into two parts: the 'subsistence income', which is spent for the acquisition of the minimum quantities of the various commodities, and the 'supernumerary income', the income left after the minimum expenditures are covered.

A simple linear expenditure system

The utility function may take any additive form. Stone's utility function, for example, is additive in the logarithms of the group utilities:

$$U = \sum_{i=1}^{n} b_i \log(q_i - \gamma_i)$$

i.e.,

$$U^* = (q_1 - \gamma_1)^{b_1} \cdot (q_2 - \gamma_2)^{b_2} \cdots (q_n - \gamma_n)^{b_n}$$

or

$$U = b_1 \log(q_1 - \gamma_1) + b_2 \log(q_2 - \gamma_2) + \cdots + b_n \log(q_n - \gamma_n)$$

where γ_i = minimum quantity of group i
       b_i = marginal budget shares; that is, each b_i shows by how much the expenditure on group i will increase if total income changes by one unit (see below)

It is obvious that $\sum b_i = 1$, since the changes of expenditures must be equal to the change in income (by the budget constraint).

The crucial assumptions of this model are:

(1)   Rationality of the consumers
(2)   Additivity of utilities
(3) $0 < b_i < 1$

$$\gamma_i \geq 0 \quad \text{(there is no negative minimum quantity)}$$
$$(q_i - \gamma_i) > 0 \quad \text{(some quantity above the minimum is purchased)}$$

The consumers maximise their total utility, subject to the (total) income constraint. In the case of Stone's utility function we have:

Maximise $\qquad\qquad U = b_1 \log(q_1 - \gamma_1) + \cdots + b_n \log(q_n - \gamma_n)$

subject to $\qquad\qquad Y = \sum p_i q_i + \sum p_i \gamma_i$

Maximisation of the constrained utility function yields the following demand functions:

$$q_i = \gamma_i + \frac{b_i}{p_i}\left(Y - \sum p_i \gamma_i\right)$$

where q_i = quantity demanded of group i
$\qquad\quad \gamma_i$ = minimum quantity of group i
$\qquad\quad b_i$ = marginal budget share
$\qquad\quad Y$ = consumers' total income
$\qquad\quad p_i$ = price index of group i
$\quad \sum p_i \gamma_i$ = subsistence income
$(Y - \sum p_i \gamma_i)$ = supernumerary income

The demand function may be written in the slightly different form:

$$p_i q_i \quad = \quad \gamma_i p_i \quad + \quad b_i\left(Y - \sum p_i \gamma_i\right)$$

or

$$\begin{bmatrix} \text{expenditure} \\ \text{on group } i \end{bmatrix} = \begin{bmatrix} \text{subsistence} \\ \text{expenditure} \end{bmatrix} + \begin{bmatrix} \text{supernumerary} \\ \text{expenditure} \end{bmatrix}$$

From this form it is easy to see why the coefficients b_i are marginal budget shares. It is clear that b_i is the partial derivative of the expenditure on i with respect to the supernumerary income:

$$b_i = \frac{\partial(q_i p_i)}{\partial(Y - \sum p_i \gamma_i)}$$

There are various versions of the linear expenditure model, depending on the form of the utility function. Various writers assume a different form of the utility function and hence they derive a different formulation of the demand functions. The examination of more complicated *LES* models goes beyond the scope of this book.

IV. THE DEMAND FOR THE PRODUCT OF A FIRM

The shape of the individual firm's demand curve

The analysis of the previous section was concentrated on the aggregate demand for consumers' goods. However, for the theory of the firm and the understanding of the decision-making process of the firm we must look at the demand for the product of the individual firm. Consumers' demand is a small fraction of the aggregate demand for manufacturing products. The majority of manufacturing commodities is sold to other businesses, other firms for further processing, or to traders (wholesalers and retailers).[1]

---

[1] For a detailed discussion of this topic see P. W. S. Andrews, *Manufacturing Business* (Macmillan, 1949).

Even if the firm produces final consumers' goods, it seldom sells them directly to the consumers. Most products reach the consumer through a retailer. Traditional economic theory has ignored the distribution methods of the commodities produced and their effect on the pricing policy of the firm. Furthermore, traditional theory has ignored the distinction between short-run and long-run demand. The long run is not defined from the standpoint of demand, as it is from the standpoint of production and costs. It is usually stated that in the long run demand is more elastic than in the short run, but the time periods involved in this statement are left in obscurity.

In traditional economic theory the shape of the demand curve of the firm is different in various market structures.

In *pure competition* the demand of the individual firm is perfectly elastic (figure 2.43). This shape is the consequence of the assumptions of the purely competitive model, the assumptions of an homogeneous product and of large numbers of sellers. In pure competition the firm, however large, offers a small part of the total quantity in the market and hence it cannot affect the price. The firm is a price-taker. The market price is determined by the market supply and demand functions (see Chapter 5) and at this price the firm can sell any quantity it wishes.

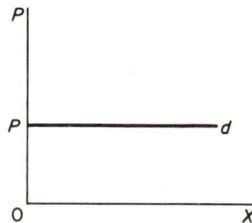

Figure 2.43   Demand of the firm in pure competition

In *monopoly* the firm's demand is the demand of the industry (see Chapter 6), and the monopolist decides his price and output on the basis of the market demand which is downward-sloping, obeying the general 'law of demand' (figure 2.44).

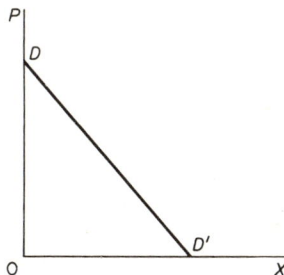

Figure 2.44   Demand of the monopolist

In *monopolistic competition* (see Chapter 8) the demand of the individual firm is downward-sloping, as is the market demand. Chamberlin was the first economist who stressed the multivariate nature of the demand of the individual firm. He postulated that as a consequence of product differentiation the firm has some freedom in setting its own price. Each firm has its own customers, who have a preference for the firm's products.

To strengthen the preferences of consumers and secure its market the firm pays particular attention to the style and quality of its product. Furthermore the firm undertakes
advertising and other selling activities in an attempt to enlarge its market (shift its
demand outwards) and make its demand more inelastic. Thus the demand for the product
of a firm is multivariate

$$d_i = f(P_i, P_0, P, A_i, A_0, S_i, S_0, Y, t, \ldots)$$

where d_i = demand of the ith firm
$\quad\quad P_i$ = price of the ith firm
$\quad\quad P_0$ = price of competitors
$\quad\quad P$ = price of other commodities
$\quad\quad A_i$ = advertising and other selling expenses of the ith firm
$\quad\quad A_0$ = advertising and other selling activities of competitors
$\quad\quad S_i$ = style of the product of the ith firm
$\quad\quad S_0$ = style of the product of other competitors
$\quad\quad Y$ = consumers' income
$\quad\quad t$ = consumers' tastes

The firm's demand curve (figure 2.45) is drawn under the usual *ceteris paribus* assumption: it shows the quantity demanded of the product of the ith firm at different prices
charged by the firm given the style of the product, the selling activities, and so on. If any
one of these factors changes, the demand for the product of the firm will shift (figure 2.46).

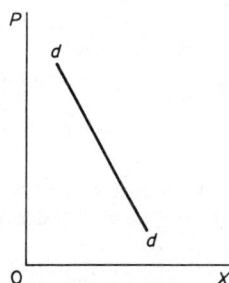

Figure 2.45   Demand of
the firm in monopolistic
competition

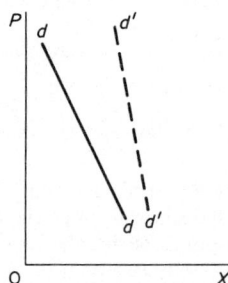

Figure 2.46   Shift in the
firm's demand curve due,
say, to an improvement in
style of its product

The main criticism against Chamberlin's demand function is that it refers only to the
demand of final consumers, thus ignoring the other buyers of the product of a manufacturing business, as well as the channels of distribution of the commodities.[1]

Some writers have argued that Chamberlin's demand curve is valid only for the short
run; in the long run the demand curve cannot have a negative slope, because this would
imply irrational preferences of the consumers.[1] We think that this criticism implies a
special definition of rational behaviour. In particular it is implicitly assumed that
consumers are irrational if they pay a higher price for technically identical or very similar
products. This definition of rationality is too narrow.[2] The rational consumer aims

[1] See P. W. S. Andrews, *Competition in Economic Theory* (Macmillan, 1964).
[2] See W. J. Baumol, *Business Behaviour, Value and Growth*, Harcourt, Brace, revised edition
1967, pp. 46–7.

at the maximisation of his utility or satisfaction. What gives him a higher satisfaction is a purely subjective matter. If the shopping from a 'trendy' shop gives the consumer a 'conspicuous' satisfaction despite his having to pay a higher price for the same (or very similar) commodities, surely one cannot say that the consumer behaves irrationally. He would be irrational if he adopted a course of action inconsistent with his preferences.

In *oligopolistic models* various shapes of the firm's demand curve have been adopted. It is generally agreed that there is great uncertainty regarding the demand curve of the oligopolist, due to the interdependence of competitors and the uncertainty as to their reaction to any particular decision of a firm within the group.

Some writers have made specific assumptions about the competitors' reactions and have drawn a downward-sloping demand curve for the firm based on the assumptions they made (see Chapter 9).

Other writers have based their analysis on a market-share demand curve. This individual demand curve is derived from the market demand curve (which is assumed to be known) on the assumption that the firm keeps a constant share of the market at all price levels. The constant-share demand curve has the same elasticity as the market-demand curve at all prices (see Chapter 13).

Some economists have assumed a 'kinked' shape of the firm's demand curve (see Chapter 9). The kink implies that the firm expects that its competitors will follow suit with price cuts, but not price rises. Thus to the left of the kink the demand curve has a greater elasticity than at points to the right of the kink.

Other economists have developed their models using a long-run demand curve which is very elastic without, however, attempting to define the determinants of this demand, or the time dimensions of their analysis.[1]

It has been argued in economic literature that the uncertainty surrounding the demand curve of the individual firm is so great that it has little or no relevance as a tool of analysis in the decision-making process in a firm.[2]

Finally, several modern theorists have taken the firm's demand as given, on the grounds that interdependence is largely ignored in the day-to-day decisions of the firm.[3]

The widely differing views stem from a widespread confusion between the *demand curve* and the *demand function*. The demand curve depicts the relationship between the quantity demanded and the price of the product of the particular firm under the *ceteris paribus* clause, while the demand function includes *all* the determinants of the demand which may change simultaneously. The fact that prices in some oligopolistic markets are sticky (except when rising costs render price increases inevitable) has been interpreted mistakenly as implying the non-existence of the individual demand curve. Yet the fluctuation of sales at the prevailing (sticky) market prices suggests that some of the other determinants of the *demand function* caused the *demand curve* to shift. The observed constancy of price implies that we cannot measure the price elasticity of the firm's curve, and the changes in sales must be attributed to the change in some of the other determinants of demand. These determinants will be better understood if we examine the sources of demand of the firm, that is, the buyers of the typical manufacturing business.

Sources of demand for the product of a firm

In the modern business world the typical buyer of a firm is another firm and not the consumer as the traditional theory accepted. Even in the case of a firm producing

[1] See, for example, R. Harrod, *Economic Essays*, (Macmillan, 1952).
[2] See P. W. S. Andrews, *Manufacturing Business*, (Macmillan, 1949).
[3] See, for example, W. J. Baumol, *Business Behaviour, Value and Growth* (1967).

consumer goods, the firm markets its products through wholesalers and retailers (in most cases). These intermediaries are profit-seeking enterprises and hence behave in a different way than the consumer.[1]

Let us examine in detail the probable shape of the demand of the various types of buyers of a manufacturing firm.

The final consumers. It has been argued by some writers that in the long run the demand of consumers (for the product of a firm) will not be downward sloping for technically identical or very similar products, because this would imply irrational preferences.[2] Consumers' preferences, they argue, are not sticky in the long run. Consumers' tastes change continuously over time, and even the same person, if he is rational, will try the cheaper products and change his supplier in the long run. We do not agree with this reasoning. It is an observed fact that different brands of commodities are sold at different prices and still keep their market share over periods that may by any standard be considered long (ten or twenty years). This may be due to habit persistence, inertia, incomplete knowledge, conspicuous-consumption effects, and other reasons. Whatever the cause, it remains a fact that very similar commodities are sold over long periods of time at different prices. Thus consumers' preferences for particular brands are persistent and give rise to a demand curve with a negative slope. This is more so for consumer durables, where the amounts of money involved in each item are substantial for the household. In these cases the choice of the consumer is mostly based on brand names and on information of friends and relatives who have already tried the products and have acquired experience about their quality.

Other manufacturing firms. Here we must distinguish between investment goods and intermediate goods which will be used as parts of the product of the buying firm.

Regarding investment goods, brand names play an important role. Machinery and other equipment involve large expenditures and are to be used for a considerable time period. Thus the investing firms will be expected to have a strong preference for the machinery supplied by well-established firms even if they have to pay a higher price. This behaviour will give rise to a negatively-sloping demand curve for investment goods. For intermediate commodities, however, which are often standardised, no firm will be prepared to pay a higher price if it can buy them from another supplier at a lower price. Thus, for firms who produce standardised intermediate products the demand curve will be infinitely elastic, not only in the long run but also in the short run. The market share of such firm-suppliers will be determined by factors other than the price, such as prompt delivery and 'good service' in general.

Wholesalers. Wholesalers are profit-seeking businessmen and can affect to a certain extent their customers' demand by their stock policy. They will prefer to buy and stock (in order to resell) commodities on which their profit margins are larger, that is, products which, though similar to others, can be bought at a lower price. However, we believe that their discretion is limited. If they are wholesalers of final commodities, surely they can pass on to their customers a higher price if they have a strong demand for a product, thus keeping their profit margins at the desired level. If they are wholesalers of inter- mediate goods which are of standard specifications, they will not be prepared to pay a higher price for goods technically identical, because they can influence their buyers by offering the cheaper products, even if the brand is not as yet long-established. If the

[1] For many industrial firms the government is an important buyer. However, the analysis of the purchasing policies of public agencies will not be attempted here.

[2] See, for example, P. W. S. Andrews, *Manufacturing Business* (1949).

wholesaler deals in spare parts, naturally he has no power on the price that the manufacturing firm will supply him at, except if he is a very big dealer in such spare parts and stocks parts of products of other producers (e.g. spare parts of cars). Thus the demand of wholesalers for the product of a manufacturing firm will have in most cases a negative slope.

Retailers. Here also we must distinguish between two types of action of the retailer: he may resell the manufactured product branded, or he may sell it under his own brand name. Large supermarkets sell an increasing number of products with their own brand name (Spar, St Michael, Co-op, Tesco), but they also sell other brands. They can influence to a certain degree the final consumer by not stocking a particular brand. The effectiveness of such policy depends on whether they have a locational monopoly, and in any case their discretion can only be important in the short run. The locational advantage can easily be lost, by a new retailer establishing a new shop close to them. Furthermore, retailers are interested in their profit margin, and there is no reason why they should not pay a higher price for a certain branded commodity if they can pass it on to the consumers who have a preference (rational or irrational) for this particular brand. It is only if they buy goods to resell under their own brand name that they will not be prepared to pay a higher price for a 'raw material' they can obtain cheaper from another supplier. In summary, if the retailer buys a commodity already branded in order to resell it, his demand (from the manufacturer of the branded product) will be downward sloping, reflecting the preferences of the final consumers; if, however, he buys the commodity as a 'raw material,' to resell it under his own brand name, then his demand will be infinitely elastic.

The conclusion of the above discussion is that the shape of the *demand curve* of an oligopolist will depend on the nature of his product and his distribution channels. The *demand function* of the oligopolist is multivariate. Thus even if prices are sticky, there are other factors that influence the demand to the firm. In principle, the demand for the product of a firm can be estimated statistically from historical observations of sales, prices charged by the firm and its competitors, advertising expenditures, and other relevant factors. However, the difficulties involved in this process are so great that very few firms attempt to estimate statistically their own demand function. Even if the estimation difficulties are overcome, the environment of the firm in the real world changes so fast that any statistical (historical) demand function becomes inappropriate for future decision unless continuously revised. Given the uncertainties of the environment (and the scarcity of good econometricians), firms tend to avoid price competition

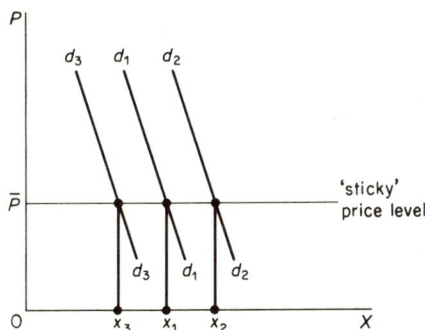

Figure 2.47 Changing market share of an oligopolist

and to rely on other competitive weapons. The predominance of non-price competition in the modern highly competitive oligopolistic world suggests that the demand curve is often a subjective concept in the decision-making process of businessmen: because they are uncertain about the effects of price changes, businessmen prefer to use other instruments, such as style of the product, advertising, research and development programmes, which they consider as less dangerous. Their market share at the given price will be determined by the effectiveness of such policies, as well as by the dynamic changes in the market conditions. In oligopolistic markets the determinants of the *market share* (at the given price) are the determinants of the demand function of the firm, and their effect is shown graphically by shifts of the (subjective) demand curve at the going price (figure 2.47). If sales, and hence market-share, change at a given price one must look at the other determinants of demand in order to explain the change.

We will discuss in detail the determinants of demand (and of the market share) of the individual firm in various market structures in several chapters of this book.

3. Theory of Production

I. THE PRODUCTION FUNCTION FOR A SINGLE PRODUCT

The production function is a purely technical relation which connects factor inputs and outputs. It describes the laws of proportion, that is, the transformation of factor inputs into products (outputs) at any particular time period.[1] The production function represents the technology of a firm of an industry, or of the economy as a whole. The production function includes all the technically efficient methods of production (see below).

A method of production (*process, activity*) is a combination of factor inputs required for the production of one unit of output. Usually a commodity may be produced by various methods of production. For example, a unit of commodity x may be produced by the following processes:

	Process P_1	*Process P_2*	*Process P_3*
Labour units	$\begin{bmatrix} 2 \end{bmatrix}$	$\begin{bmatrix} 3 \end{bmatrix}$	$\begin{bmatrix} 1 \end{bmatrix}$
Capital units	$\begin{bmatrix} 3 \end{bmatrix}$	$\begin{bmatrix} 2 \end{bmatrix}$	$\begin{bmatrix} 4 \end{bmatrix}$

Activities may be presented graphically by the length of lines from the origin to the point determined by the labour and capital inputs. The three processes above are shown in figure 3.1. A method of production A is technically efficient relative to any other

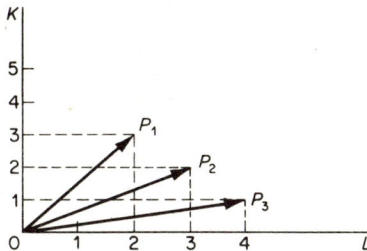

Figure 3.1

---

[1] If the technology changes we have technological progress. See section (III).

method B, if A uses less of at least one factor and no more from the other factors as compared with B. For example, commodity y can be produced by two methods:

$$
\begin{array}{ccc}
 & A & B \\
\text{Labour} & \begin{bmatrix} 2 \\ 3 \end{bmatrix} & \begin{bmatrix} 3 \\ 3 \end{bmatrix} \\
\text{Capital} & &
\end{array}
$$

Method B is technically inefficient as compared with A. The basic theory of production concentrates only on efficient methods. Inefficient methods will not be used by rational entrepreneurs.

If a process A uses less of some factor(s) and more of some other(s) as compared with any other process B, then A and B cannot be directly compared on the criterion of technical efficiency. For example, the activities

$$
\begin{array}{ccc}
 & A & B \\
\text{Labour} & \begin{bmatrix} 2 \\ 3 \end{bmatrix} & \begin{bmatrix} 1 \\ 4 \end{bmatrix} \\
\text{Capital} & &
\end{array}
$$

are not directly comparable. Both processes are considered as technically efficient and are included in the production function (the technology). Which one of them will be chosen at any particular time depends on the prices of factors. The theory of production describes the laws of production. The choice of any particular technique (among the set of technically efficient processes) is an economic one, based on prices, and not a technical one. The choice of technique by a firm is discussed in Section IV below. We note here that a technically efficient method is not necessarily economically efficient. There is a difference between technical and economic efficiency.

An *isoquant* includes (is the locus of) all the technically efficient methods (or all the combinations of factors of production) for producing a given level of output.

The production isoquant may assume various shapes depending on the degree of substitutability of factors.

Linear isoquant. This type assumes perfect substitutability of factors of production: a given commodity may be produced by using only capital, or only labour, or by an infinite combination of K and L (figure 3.2).

Input–output isoquant. This assumes strict complementarity (that is, zero substitutability) of the factors of production. There is only one method of production for any one commodity. The isoquant takes the shape of a right angle (figure 3.3). This type of isoquant is also called 'Leontief isoquant' after Leontief, who invented the input–output analysis.

Kinked isoquant. This assumes limited substitutability of K and L. There are only a few processes for producing any one commodity. Substitutability of the factors is possible only at the kinks (figure 3.4). This form is also called 'activity analysis-isoquant' or 'linear-programming isoquant', because it is basically used in linear programming.

Smooth, convex isoquant. This form assumes continuous substitutability of K and L only over a certain range, beyond which factors cannot substitute each other. The isoquant appears as a smooth curve convex to the origin (figure 3.5).

It should be noted that the kinked isoquants are more realistic. Engineers, managers, and production executives consider the production processes as discrete rather than

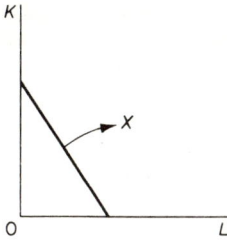

Figure 3.2 Linear iso-
quant

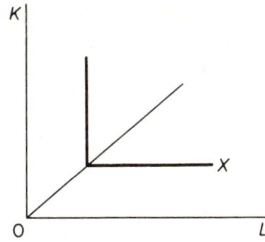

Figure 3.3 Input–output
isoquant

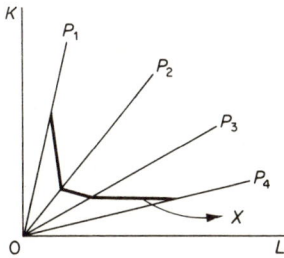

Figure 3.4 Linear programming-
isoquant

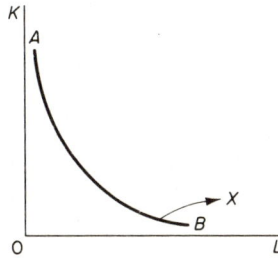

Figure 3.5 Convex isoquant

in a continuous array. However, traditional economic theory has mostly adopted the continuous isoquants, because they are mathematically simpler to handle by the simple rules of calculus. We may consider the continuous isoquant as an approximation to the more realistic form of a kinked isoquant: as we increase the number of processes the kinks come closer and closer, until at the limit (as the number of processes becomes infinite) the isoquant becomes a smooth curve.

The production function describes not only a single isoquant, but the whole array of isoquants, each of which shows a different level of output. It shows how output varies as the factor inputs change.

Production functions involve (and can provide measurements of) concepts which are useful tools in all fields of economics. The main concepts are:

1. The marginal productivity of the factors of production.
2. The marginal rate of substitution and the elasticity of substitution.
3. Factor intensity.
4. The efficiency of production.
5. The returns to scale.

These concepts will be discussed below.

The general mathematical form of the production function is

$$Y = f(L, K, R, S, v, \gamma)$$

where Y = output
L = labour input
K = capital input
R = raw materials
S = land input
v = returns to scale
γ = efficiency parameter.

All variables are flows, that is, they are measured per unit of time. In its general form the production function is a purely technological relationship between *quantities* of inputs and *quantities* of output. Prices of factors or of the product do not enter into the production function. They are used only for the production decision of the firm or other economic entities. (See section IV.) However, in practice it has been observed that raw materials bear a constant relation to output at all levels of production. For example, the number of bricks for a given type of house is constant, irrespective of the number of houses built; similarly the metal required for a certain type of car is constant, irrespective of the number of cars produced. This allows the subtraction of the *value* of raw materials from the *value* of output, and the measurement of output in terms of *value added* (X)

$$X = Y - R$$

Of course, in this way we destroy the pure technological nature of the production function, since the prices of raw materials and of the output are utilised: value added is measured, by necessity, in monetary units.

The input of land, S, is constant for the economy as a whole, and hence does not enter into an aggregate production function. However, S is not constant for individual sectors or for individual firms. In these cases land-inputs are lumped together with machinery and equipment, in the factor K.

Thus the production function in traditional economic theory assumes the form

$$X = f(L, K, v, \gamma)$$

The factor v, 'returns to scale', refers to the long-run analysis of the laws of production, since it assumes change in the plant. It will be discussed in detail in a subsequent section.

The efficiency parameter, γ, refers to the entrepreneurial-organisational aspects of production. Two firms with identical factor inputs (and the same returns to scale) may have different levels of output due to differences in their entrepreneurial and organisational efficiency.

Graphically, the production function is usually presented as a curve on two-dimensional graphs. Changes of the relevant variables are shown either by movements along the curve that depicts the production function, or by shifts of this curve. The most commonly used diagrams for the production function of a single commodity[1] are shown in figures 3.6 and 3.7. In figure 3.6 each curve shows the relation between X and L for given K, v and γ. As labour increases, *ceteris paribus*, output increases: we

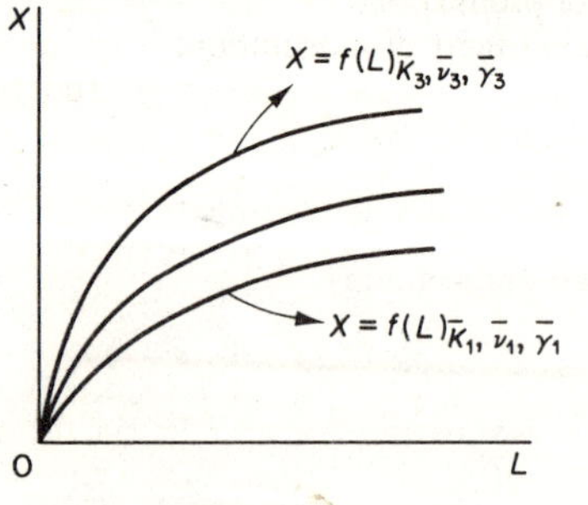

Figure 3.6 $K_1 < K_2 < K_3$ Figure 3.7 $L_1 < L_2 < L_3$

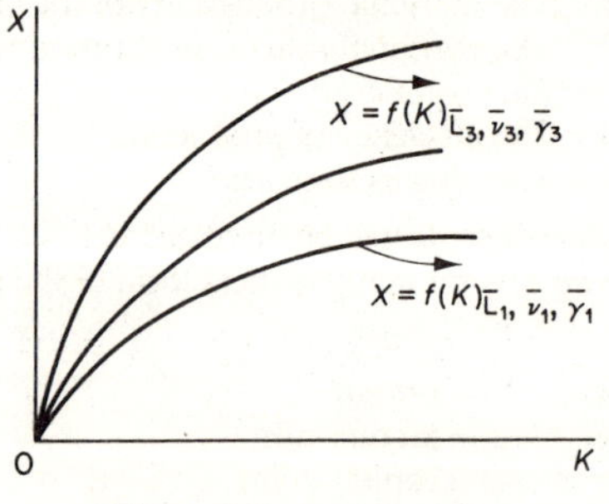

[1] For the production function of jointly produced commodities (multiproduct case) see section VI.

move along the curve depicting the production function. If capital (and/or v, and/or γ) increase, the production function $X = f(L)$ shifts upwards.

In figure 3.7 each curve shows the relation between X and K for given L, v and γ. As capital increases, *ceteris paribus*, output increases: we move along the curve. If L (and/or v, and/or γ) increase the production function $X = f(K)$ shifts upwards.

The slopes of the curves in figures 3.6 and 3.7 are the marginal products of the factors of production. The *marginal product* of a factor is defined as the change in output resulting from a (very small) change of this factor, keeping all other factors constant.

Mathematically the marginal product of each factor is the partial derivative of the production function with respect to this factor. Thus

$$MP_L = \frac{\partial X}{\partial L} \quad \text{and} \quad MP_K = \frac{\partial X}{\partial K}$$

Graphically the marginal product of labour is shown by the slope of the production function

$$X = f_1(L)_{\bar{K}, \bar{v}, \bar{\gamma}}$$

and the marginal product of capital is shown by the slope of the production function

$$X = f_2(K)_{\bar{L}, \bar{v}, \bar{\gamma}}$$

In principle the marginal product of a factor may assume any value, positive, zero or negative. However, basic production theory concentrates only on the efficient part of the production function, that is, on the range of output over which the marginal products of the factors are positive. No rational firm would employ labour beyond $0B$, or capital beyond $0D$, since an increase in the factors beyond these levels would result in the reduction of the total output of the firm. Ranges of output over which the marginal products of the factors would be negative (ranges beyond $0B'$ in figure 3.8, and $0D'$ in figure 3.9) imply irrational behaviour of the firm, and are not considered by the theory of production.

Furthermore, the basic theory of production usually concentrates on the range of output over which the marginal products of factors, although positive, decrease, that is, over the range of diminishing (but non-negative) productivity of the factors of production: the ranges of output considered by the traditional theory are $A'B'$ in figure 3.8 and $C'D'$ in figure 3.9. These ranges of output have been shown in figures 3.6 and 3.7.

Alternatively we may say that the theory of production concentrates on levels of employment of the factors over which their marginal products are positive but decrease: in figure 3.10 the range of employment of L examined by the theory of production is AB; over that range

$$MP_L > 0 \quad \text{but} \quad \frac{\partial (MP)_L}{\partial L} < 0$$

Similarly, in figure 3.11 the range of employment of capital examined by the theory of production is CD; over that range

$$MP_K > 0 \quad \text{but} \quad \frac{\partial (MP)_K}{\partial K} < 0$$

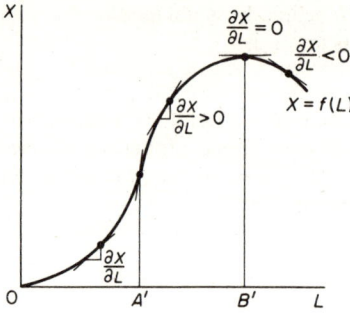

Figure 3.8

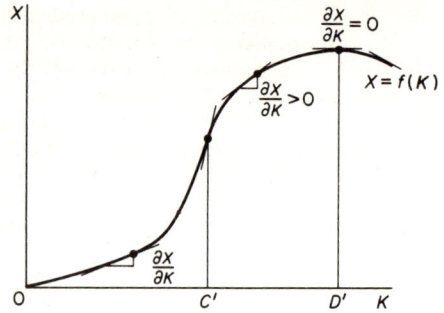

Figure 3.9

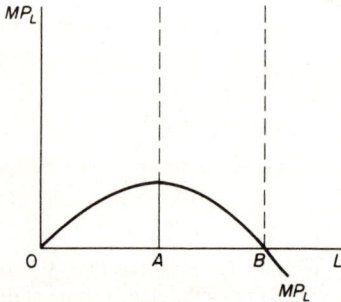

Figure 3.10

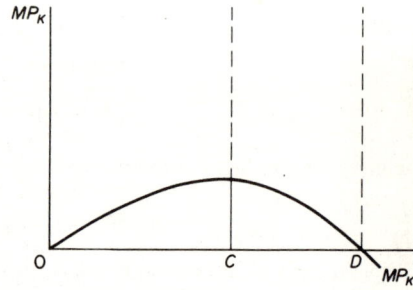

Figure 3.11

Formally the above discussion may be stated as follows:

$$X = f(L, K, v, \gamma)$$

$$\left.\begin{array}{l} \dfrac{\partial X}{\partial L} > 0 \\[2mm] \dfrac{\partial X}{\partial K} > 0 \end{array}\right\} \begin{array}{l} \text{positive} \\ \text{marginal} \\ \text{products} \end{array} \qquad \left.\begin{array}{l} \dfrac{\partial^2 X}{\partial L^2} < 0 \\[2mm] \dfrac{\partial^2 X}{\partial K^2} < 0 \end{array}\right\} \begin{array}{l} \text{the slope} \\ \text{of marginal} \\ \text{product curves} \\ \text{is negative} \end{array}$$

These conditions imply that the traditional theory of production concentrates on the range of isoquants over which their slope is negative and convex to the origin.

In figure 3.12 the production function is depicted in the form of a set of isoquants. By construction the higher to the right an isoquant, the higher the level of output it depicts. Clearly isoquants cannot intersect, by their construction. We said that traditional economic theory concentrates on efficient ranges of output, that is, ranges over which the marginal products of factors are diminishing but positive. The locus of points of isoquants where the marginal products of the factors are zero form the *ridge lines*. The upper ridge line implies that the *MP* of capital is zero. The lower ridge line implies that the *MP* of labour is zero. Production techniques are only (technically) efficient inside the ridge lines. Outside the ridge lines the marginal products of factors are negative and the methods of production are inefficient, since they require more quantity of both factors for producing a given level of output. Such inefficient methods are not considered by the theory of production, since they imply irrational behaviour of the firm. The

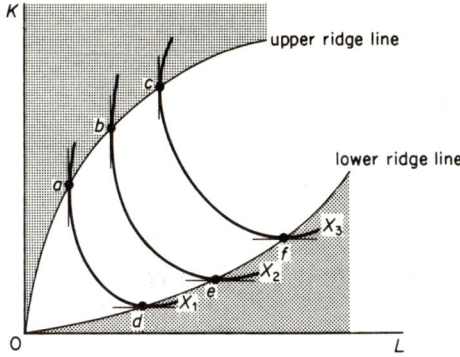

Figure 3.12

condition of positive but declining marginal products of the factors defines the range of efficient production (the range of isoquants over which they are convex to the origin).

The slope of the isoquant $(-\partial K/\partial L)$ defines the degree of substitutability of the factors of production (figure 3.13).

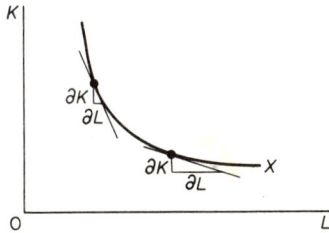

Figure 3.13

The slope of the isoquant decreases (in absolute terms) as we move downwards along the isoquant, showing the increasing difficulty in substituting K for L. The slope of the isoquant is called the *rate of technical substitution*, or the marginal rate of substitution (MRS) of the factors:

$$-\frac{\partial K}{\partial L} = MRS_{L, K}$$

It can be proved that the MRS is equal to the ratio of the marginal products of the factors

$$MRS_{L, K} = -\frac{\partial K}{\partial L} = \frac{\partial X/\partial L}{\partial X/\partial K} = \frac{MP_L}{MP_K}$$

Proof

The slope of a curve is the slope of the tangent at any point of the curve. The slope of the tangent is defined by the total differential. In the case of the isoquant the total differential is the total change in X resulting from small changes in both factors K and L. Clearly if we change K by ∂K, the output X will change by the product ∂K times the marginal product of capital

$$(\partial K)\left(\frac{\partial X}{\partial K}\right)$$

Similarly, if we change labour by an infinitesimal amount ∂L, the resulting change in X is

$$(\partial L)\left(\frac{\partial X}{\partial L}\right)$$

Now along any isoquant the quantity X is constant, so that the total change in X (the total differential) must be equal to zero. Thus

$$dX = (\partial K)\left(\frac{\partial X}{\partial K}\right) + (\partial L)\left(\frac{\partial X}{\partial L}\right) = 0$$

Solving for $\partial K/\partial L$ we obtain

$$-\frac{\partial K}{\partial L} = \frac{\partial X/\partial L}{\partial X/\partial K} = \frac{MP_L}{MP_K}$$

Along the ridge lines the $MRS = 0$. In particular along the upper ridge we have

$$MRS_{K,L} = \frac{\partial X/\partial K}{\partial X/\partial L} = \frac{0}{\partial X/\partial L} = 0$$

and along the lower ridge

$$MPS_{L,K} = \frac{\partial X/\partial L}{\partial X/\partial K} = \frac{0}{\partial X/\partial K} = 0$$

The marginal rate of substitution as a measure of the degree of substitutability of factors has a serious defect: it depends on the units of measurement of the factors. A better measure of the ease of factor substitution is provided by the elasticity of substitution. The *elasticity of substitution* is defined as the percentage change in the capital–labour ratio, divided by the percentage change in the rate of technical substitution

$$\sigma = \frac{\text{percentage change in } K/L}{\text{percentage change in } MRS}$$

or

$$\sigma = \frac{d(K/L)/(K/L)}{d(MRS)/(MRS)}$$

The elasticity of substitution is a pure number independent of the units of measurement of K and L, since both the numerator and the denominator are measured in the same units.

The *factor intensity* of any process is measured by the slope of the line through the origin representing the particular process. Thus the factor intensity is the capital–labour ratio. In figure 3.14 process P_1 is more capital intensive than process P_2. Clearly

$$\frac{K_1}{L_1} > \frac{K_2}{L_2}$$

The upper part of the isoquant includes more capital-intensive processes. The lower part of the isoquant includes more labour-intensive techniques.

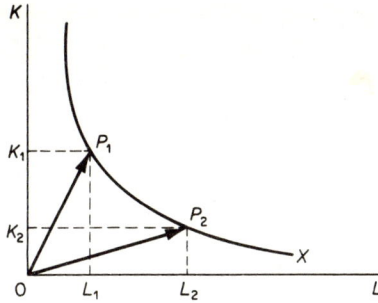

Figure 3.14

Example

Let us illustrate the above concepts with a specific form of production function, namely the Cobb–Douglas production function. This form is the most popular in applied research, because it is easiest to handle mathematically.

The Cobb–Douglas function is of the form

$$X = b_0 \cdot L^{b_1} \cdot K^{b_2}$$

1. *The marginal product of factors*
   (a) The MP_L

$$MP_L = \frac{\partial X}{\partial L} = b_1 \cdot b_0 \cdot L^{b_1-1} \cdot K^{b_2}$$

$$= b_1(b_0 L^{b_1} K^{b_2})L^{-1}$$

$$= b_1 \cdot \frac{X}{L} = b_1(AP_L)$$

where AP_L = the average product of labour
(b) Similarly

$$MP_K = b_2 \cdot \frac{X}{K} = b_2(AP_K)$$

2. *The marginal rate of substitution*

$$MRS_{L,K} = \frac{\partial X/\partial L}{\partial X/\partial K} = \frac{b_1\left(\dfrac{X}{L}\right)}{b_2\left(\dfrac{X}{K}\right)} = \frac{b_1}{b_2} \cdot \frac{K}{L}$$

3. *The elasticity of substitution*

$$\sigma = \frac{d(K/L)/(K/L)}{d(MRS)/(MRS)} = 1$$

Proof

Substitute the *MRS* and obtain

$$\sigma = \frac{d(K/L)/(K/L)}{d\left(\frac{b_1}{b_2}\cdot\frac{K}{L}\right)\Big/\left(\frac{b_1}{b_2}\right)\left(\frac{K}{L}\right)}$$

$$= \frac{d\left(\frac{K}{L}\right)\left(\frac{b_1}{b_2}\right)}{\left(\frac{b_1}{b_2}\right)d\left(\frac{K}{L}\right)} = 1$$

given that b_1/b_2 is constant and does not affect the derivative.

4. *Factor intensity.* In a Cobb–Douglas function factor intensity is measured by the ratio b_1/b_2. The higher this ratio the more labour intensive the technique. Similarly the lower the ratio b_1/b_2 the more capital intensive the technique.

5. *The efficiency of production.* The efficiency in the organisation of the factors of production is measured by the coefficient b_0. Intuitively it is clear that if two firms have the same K, L, b_1 and b_2 and still produce different quantities of output, the difference can be due to the superior organisation and entrepreneurship of one of the firms, which results in different efficiencies. The more efficient firm will have a larger b_0 than the less efficient one.

6. *The returns to scale.* This concept will be developed in the next section, since it refers to the long-run analysis of production. We state here that in a Cobb–Douglas function the returns to scale are measured by the sum of the coefficients $b_1 + b_2$. The proof is given on page 78.

II. LAWS OF PRODUCTION

The laws of production describe the technically possible ways of increasing the level of production. Output may increase in various ways.

Output can be increased by changing all factors of production. Clearly this is possible only in the long run. Thus the *laws of returns to scale* refer to the long-run analysis of production.

In the short run output may be increased by using more of the variable factor(s), while capital (and possibly other factors as well) are kept constant. The marginal product of the variable factor(s) will decline eventually as more and more quantities of this factor are combined with the other constant factors. The expansion of output with one factor (at least) constant is described by the *law of (eventually) diminishing returns* of the variable factor, which is often referred to as the *law of variable proportions*.

We will first examine the long-run laws of returns of scale.

A. LAWS OF RETURNS TO SCALE: LONG-RUN ANALYSIS OF PRODUCTION

In the long run expansion of output may be achieved by varying all factors. In the long run all factors are variable. The *laws of returns to scale* refer to the effects of *scale* relationships.

In the long run output may be increased by changing *all factors by the same proportion,* or by *different proportions*. Traditional theory of production concentrates on the first case, that is, the study of output as *all* inputs change *by the same proportion*. The term *'returns to scale'* refers to the changes in output as all factors change by the same proportion.[1]

Suppose we start from an initial level of inputs and output

$$X_0 = f(L, K)$$

and we increase all the factors by the same proportion k. We will clearly obtain a new level of output X^*, higher than the original level X_0,

$$X^* = f(kL, kK)$$

If X^* increases by the same proportion k as the inputs, we say that there are *constant returns to scale*.

If X^* increases less than proportionally with the increase in the factors, we have *decreasing returns to scale*.

If X^* increases more than proportionally with the increase in the factors, we have *increasing returns to scale*.

Returns to scale and homogeneity of the production function

Suppose we increase both factors of the function

$$X_0 = f(L, K)$$

by the same proportion k, and we observe the resulting new level of output X^*

$$X^* = f(kL, kK)$$

If k can be factored out (that is, may be taken out of the brackets as a common factor), then the new level of output X^* can be expressed as a function of k (to any power v) and the initial level of output

$$X^* = k^v f(L, K)$$

or

$$X^* = k^v X_0$$

and the production function is called *homogeneous*. If k cannot be factored out, the production function is *non-homogeneous*. Thus:

A *homogeneous function* is a function such that if each of the inputs is multiplied by k, then k can be completely factored out of the function. The power v of k is called the *degree of homogeneity* of the function and is a measure of the returns to scale:

If $v = 1$ we have constant returns to scale. This production function is sometimes called *linear homogeneous*.

If $v < 1$ we have decreasing returns to scale.

If $v > 1$ we have increasing returns to scale.

---

[1] 'Returns to scale' are only one part of the 'economies of scale'. Returns to scale are technical, while economies of scale include the technical as well as monetary economies. See Chapter 4, section V.

Returns to scale are measured mathematically by the coefficients of the production function. For example, in a Cobb–Douglas function

$$X = b_0 L^{b_1} K^{b_2}$$

the returns to scale are measured by the sum $(b_1 + b_2) = v$.

Proof

Let L and K increase by k. The new level of output is

$$X^* = b_0(kL)^{b_1}(kK)^{b_2}$$
$$= (b_0 L^{b_1} K^{b_2})k^{(b_1 + b_2)}$$

or

$$X^* = k^{(b_1 + b_2)}X$$

Thus $v = (b_1 + b_2)$.

For a homogeneous production function the returns to scale may be represented graphically in an easy way. Before explaining the graphical presentation of the returns to scale it is useful to introduce the concepts of *product line* and *isocline*.

Product lines

   To analyse the expansion of output we need a third dimension, since along the two-dimensional diagram we can depict only the isoquant along which the level of output is constant. Instead of introducing a third dimension it is easier to show the change of output by *shifts* of the isoquant and use the concept of *product lines* to describe the expansion of output.
   A product line shows the (physical) movement from one isoquant to another as we change both factors or a single factor. A product curve is drawn independently of the prices of factors of production. It does not imply any actual *choice* of expansion, which is based on the prices of factors and is shown by the expansion path (see section IV). The product line describes the technically possible alternative paths of expanding output. What path will actually be chosen by the firm will depend on the prices of factors.
   The product curve passes through the origin if all factors are variable. If only one factor is variable (the other being kept constant) the product line is a straight line parallel to the axis of the variable factor (figure 3.15). The K/L ratio diminishes along the product line.

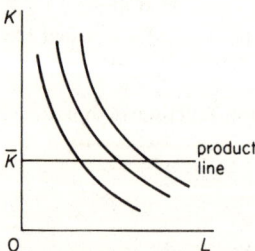

Figure 3.15 Product line for $\bar{K}$ given.

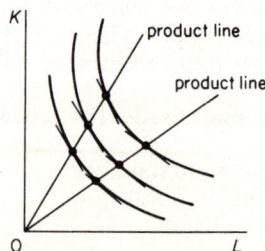

Figure 3.16 Homogeneous production function.

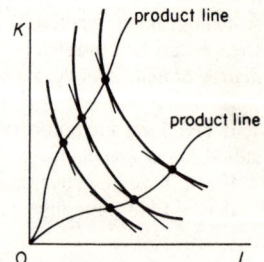

Figure 3.17 Non-homogeneous production function.

Among all possible product lines of particular interest are the so-called *isoclines*.[1] An isocline is the locus of points of different isoquants at which the *MRS* of factors is constant.

If the production function is homogeneous the isoclines are straight lines through the origin. Along any one isocline the K/L ratio is constant (as is the *MRS* of the factors). Of course the K/L ratio (and the *MRS*) is different for different isoclines (figure 3.16).

If the production function is non-homogeneous the isoclines will not be straight lines, but their shape will be twiddly. The K/L ratio changes along each isocline (as well as on different isoclines) (figure 3.17).

Graphical presentation of the returns to scale for a homogeneous production function

The returns to scale may be shown graphically by the distance (on an isocline) between successive 'multiple-level-of-output' isoquants, that is, isoquants that show levels of output which are multiples of some base level of output, e.g., X, $2X$, $3X$, etc.

Constant returns to scale. Along any isocline the distance between successive multiple-isoquants is constant. Doubling the factor inputs achieves double the level of the initial output; trebling inputs achieves treble output, and so on (figure 3.18).

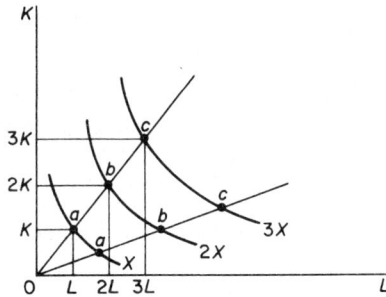

Figure 3.18   Constant returns to scale: $0a = ab = bc$

Decreasing returns to scale. The distance between consecutive multiple-isoquants increases. By doubling the inputs, output increases by less than twice its original level. In figure 3.19 the point a', defined by $2K$ and $2L$, lies on an isoquant below the one showing $2X$.

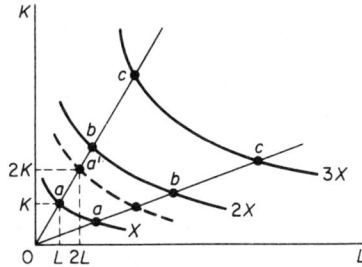

Figure 3.19   Decreasing returns to scale: $0a < ab < bc$

[1] The 'isocline' is useful for the *choice* of the firm. See section IV below.

Increasing returns to scale. The distance between consecutive multiple-isoquants decreases. By doubling the inputs, output is more than doubled. In figure 3.20 doubling K and L leads to point b' which lies on an isoquant above the one denoting $2X$.

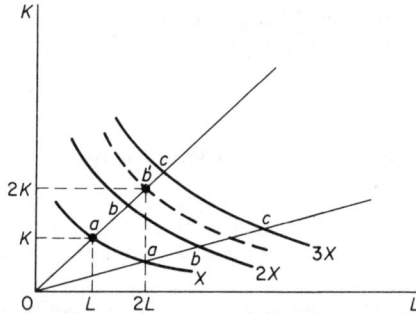

Figure 3.20   Increasing returns to scale: $0a > ab > bc$

Returns to scale are usually assumed to be the same *everywhere* on the production surface, that is, the same along all the expansion-product lines. All processes are assumed to show the same returns over all ranges of output: either constant returns everywhere, decreasing returns everywhere, or increasing returns everywhere. However, the technological conditions of production may be such that returns to scale may vary over different ranges of output. Over some range we may have constant returns to scale, while over another range we may have increasing or decreasing returns to scale. In figure 3.21 we see that up to the level of output $4X$ returns to scale are constant; beyond that level of output returns to scale are decreasing. Production functions with varying returns to scale are difficult to handle and economists usually ignore them for the analysis of production.

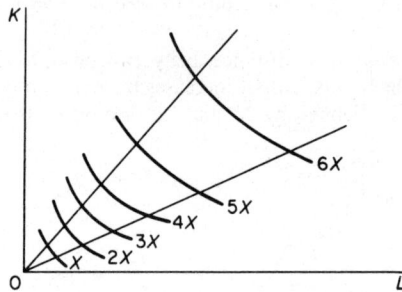

Figure 3.21   Varying returns to scale

With a non-homogeneous production function returns to scale may be increasing, constant or decreasing, but their measurement and graphical presentation is not as straightforward as in the case of the homogeneous production function. The isoclines will be curves over the production surface and along each one of them the K/L ratio varies. In most empirical studies of the laws of returns homogeneity is assumed in order to simplify the statistical work. Homogeneity, however, is a special assumption, in some cases a very restrictive one. When the technology shows increasing or decreasing returns to scale it may or may not imply a homogeneous production function.

Causes of increasing returns to scale. The increasing returns to scale are due to *technical and/or managerial indivisibilities.* Usually most processes can be duplicated, but it may not be possible to halve them.

One of the basic characteristics of advanced industrial technology is the existence of 'mass-production' methods over large sections of manufacturing industry. 'Mass-production' methods (like the assembly line in the motor-car industry) are processes available only when the level of output is large. They are more efficient than the best available processes for producing small levels of output. For example, assume that we have three processes:

	L (*men*)	K (*machines*)	X (*in tons*)
A: small-scale process:	1	1	1
B: medium-scale process:	50	50	100
C: large-scale process:	100	100	400

The K/L ratio is the same for all processes and each process can be duplicated (but not halved). Each process has a different 'unit'-level. The larger-scale processes are technically more productive than the smaller-scale processes. Clearly if the larger-scale processes were equally productive as the smaller-scale methods, no firm would use them: the firm would prefer to duplicate the smaller scale already used, with which it is already familiar. Although each process shows, taken by itself, constant returns to scale, the indivisibilities will tend to lead to increasing returns to scale.

For $X < 50$ the small-scale process would be used, and we would have constant returns to scale. For $50 < X < 100$ the medium-scale process would be used. The switch from the smaller scale to the medium-scale process gives a discontinuous increase in output (from 49 tons produced with 49 units of L and 49 units of K, to 100 tons produced with 50 men and 50 machines). If the demand in the market required only 80 tons, the firm would still use the medium-scale process, producing 100 units of X, selling 80 units, and throwing away 20 units (assuming zero disposal costs). This is one of the cases in which a process might be used inefficiently, because this process operated inefficiently is still *relatively efficient* compared with the small-scale process. Similarly, the switch from the medium-scale to the large-scale process gives a discontinuous increase in output from 99 tons (produced with 99 men and 99 machines) to 400 tons (produced with 100 men and 100 machines). If the demand absorbs only 350 tons, the firm would use the large-scale process inefficiently (producing only 350 units, or pro-ducing 400 units and throwing away the 50 units). This is because the large-scale process, even though inefficiently used, is still more productive (relatively efficient) compared with the medium-scale process.

The various types of economies of scale and their sources are discussed in detail in Chapter 4.

Causes of decreasing returns to scale. The most common causes are 'diminishing returns to management'. The 'management' is responsible for the co-ordination of the activities of the various sections of the firm. Even when authority is delegated to individual managers (production manager, sales manager, etc.) the final decisions have to be taken from the final 'centre of top management' (Board of Directors). As the output grows, top management becomes eventually overburdened and hence less efficient in its role as co-ordinator and ultimate decision-maker. Although advances in management science have developed 'plateaux' of management techniques, it is still a commonly observed fact that as firms grow beyond the appropriate optimal 'plateaux', management diseconomies creep in.

Another cause for decreasing returns may be found in the exhaustible natural resources: doubling the fishing fleet may not lead to a doubling of the catch of fish; or doubling the plant in mining or on an oil-extraction field may not lead to a doubling of output.

The sources of diseconomies of large-scale production are further discussed in Chapter 4.

B. THE LAW OF VARIABLE PROPORTIONS: SHORT-RUN ANALYSIS OF PRODUCTION

We said above that if one factor is variable while the other(s) is kept constant, the product line will be a straight line parallel to the axis of the variable factor (figure 3.14).

In general if one of the factors of production (usually capital K) is fixed, the marginal product of the variable factor (labour) will diminish after a certain range of production. We said that the traditional theory of production concentrates on the ranges of output over which the marginal products of the factors are positive but diminishing. The ranges of increasing returns (to a factor) and the range of negative productivity are not equilibrium ranges of output.

If the production function is homogeneous with constant or decreasing returns to scale everywhere on the production surface, the productivity of the variable factor will necessarily be diminishing. If, however, the production function exhibits increasing returns to scale, the diminishing returns arising from the decreasing marginal product of the variable factor (labour) may be offset, if the returns to scale are considerable. This, however, is rare. In general the productivity of a single-variable factor (*ceteris paribus*) is diminishing.

Let us examine the law of variable proportions or the law of diminishing productivity (returns) in some detail.

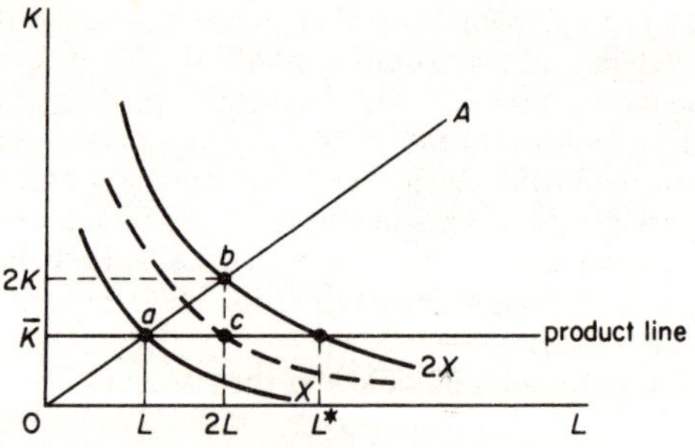

Figure 3.22

If the production function is homogeneous with constant returns to scale everywhere, the returns to a single-variable factor will be diminishing. This is implied by the negative slope and the convexity of the isoquants. With *constant returns to scale* everywhere on the production surface, doubling *both* factors ($2K$, $2L$) leads to a doubling of output. In figure 3.22 point b on the isocline $0A$ lies on the isoquant $2X$. However, if we keep K

constant (at the level $\bar{K}$) and we double only the amount of L, we reach point c, which clearly lies on a lower isoquant than $2X$. If we wanted to double output with the initial capital $\bar{K}$, we would require L^* units of labour. Clearly $L^* > 2L$. Hence doubling L, with K constant, less than doubles output. The variable factor L exhibits diminishing productivity (diminishing returns).

If the production function is homogeneous with decreasing returns to scale, the returns to a single-variable factor will be, *a fortiori*, diminishing. Since *returns to scale* are decreasing, doubling *both* factors will less than double output. In figure 3.23 we see that with $2L$ and $2K$ output reaches the level d which is on a lower isoquant than $2X$. If we double only labour while keeping capital constant, output reaches the level c, which lies on a still lower isoquant.

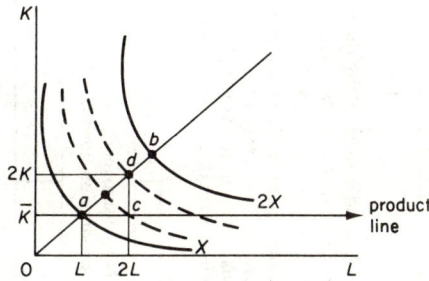

Figure 3.23

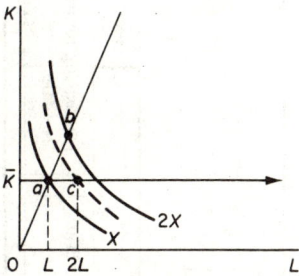

Figure 3.24

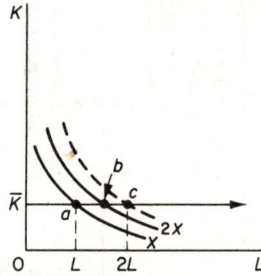

Figure 3.25

If the production function shows increasing returns to scale, the returns to the single-variable factor L will in general be diminishing (figure 3.24), unless the *positive returns to scale* are so strong as to offset the diminishing marginal productivity of the single-variable factor. Figure 3.25 shows the rare case of strong returns to scale which offset the diminishing productivity of L.

Summary

We may summarise the above analysis of the long-run and short-run laws of production schematically as in figure 3.26.

Expansion of output

A single-variable factor (other factors constant)
Short-run analysis
Law of variable proportions or *Law of (eventually) diminishing productivity* of the variable factor

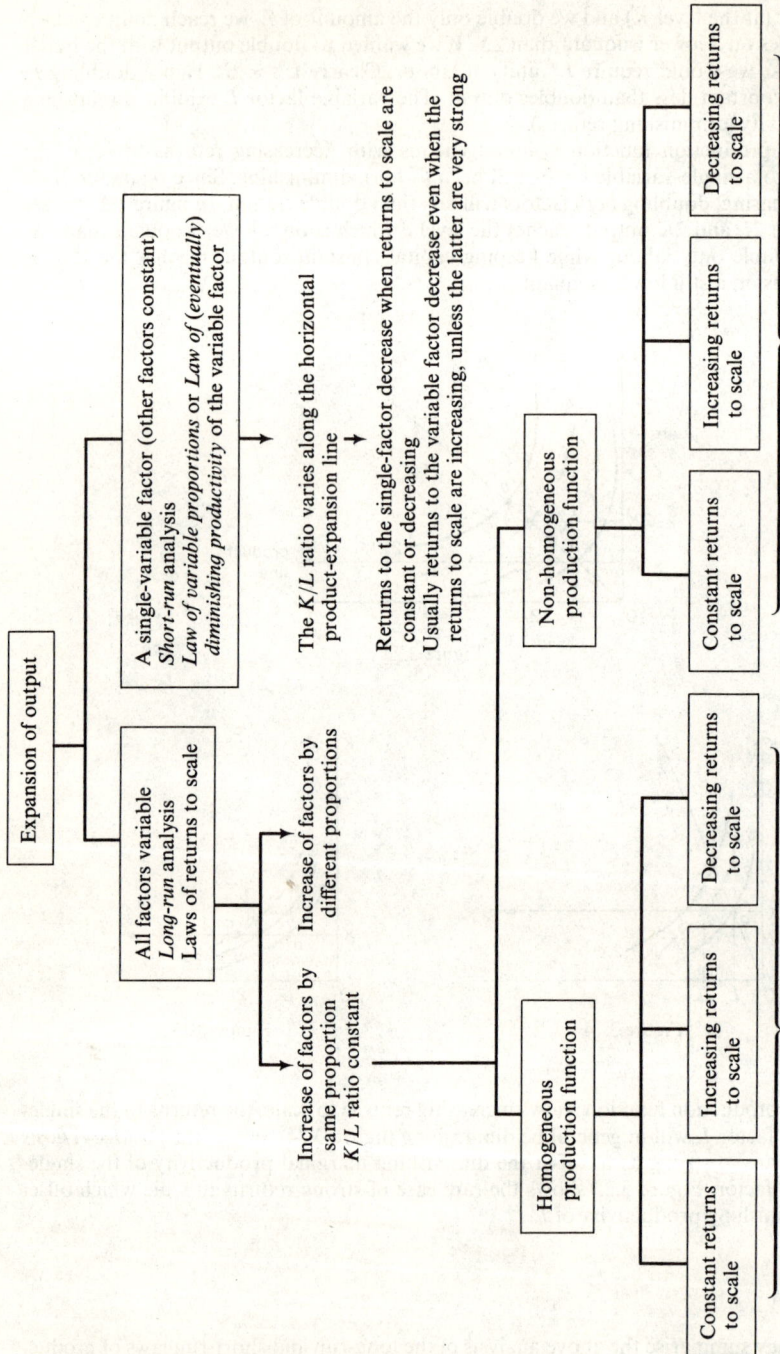

The K/L ratio varies along the horizontal product-expansion line

Returns to the single-factor decrease when returns to scale are constant or decreasing
Usually returns to the variable factor decrease even when the returns to scale are increasing, unless the latter are very strong

All factors variable
Long-run analysis
Laws of returns to scale

Increase of factors by same proportion
K/L ratio constant

Increase of factors by different proportions

Homogeneous production function

Constant returns to scale

Increasing returns to scale

Decreasing returns to scale

Isoclines are straight lines through the origin: along each isocline the K/L is constant

Non-homogeneous production function

Constant returns to scale

Increasing returns to scale

Decreasing returns to scale

Isoclines are curves through the origin: along each isocline the K/L ratio changes

Figure 3.26

III. TECHNOLOGICAL PROGRESS AND THE PRODUCTION FUNCTION

As knowledge of new and more efficient methods of production becomes available, technology changes. Furthermore new inventions may result in the increase of the efficiency of all methods of production. At the same time some techniques may become inefficient and drop out from the production function. These changes in technology constitute technological progress.[1]

Graphically the effect of *innovation in processes* is shown with an upward shift of the production function (figure 3.27), or a downward movement of the production isoquant (figure 3.28). This shift shows that the same output may be produced by less factor inputs, or more output may be obtained with the same inputs.

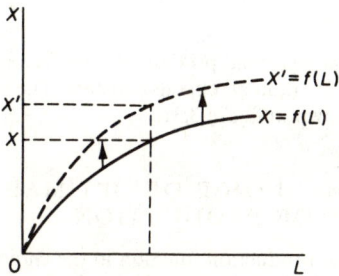
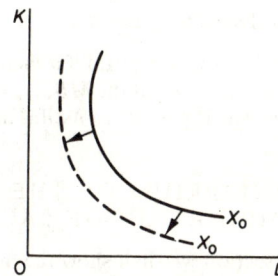

Figure 3.27   Figure 3.28

Technical progress may also change the shape (as well as produce a shift) of the isoquant. Hicks[2] has distinguished three types of technical progress, depending on its effect on the rate of substitution of the factors of production.

Capital-deepening technical progress

Technical progress is capital-deepening (or capital-using) if, along a line on which the K/L ratio is constant, the $MRS_{L,K}$ increases. This implies that technical progress increases the marginal product of capital by more than the marginal product of labour. The ratio of marginal products (which is the $MRS_{L,K}$) decreases in absolute value; but taking into account that the slope of the isoquant is negative, this sort of technical progress increases the $MRS_{L,K}$. The slope of the shifting isoquant becomes less steep along any given radius. The capital-deepening technical progress is shown in figure 3.29.

Labour-deepening technical progress

Technical progress is labour-deepening if, along a radius through the origin (with constant K/L ratio), the $MRS_{L,K}$ increases. This implies that the technical progress increases the MP_L faster than the MP_K. Thus the $MRS_{L,K}$, being the ratio of the marginal products $[(\partial X/\partial L)]/[(\partial X/\partial K)]$, increases in absolute value (but decreases if the minus sign is taken into account). The downwards-shifting isoquant becomes steeper along any given radius through the origin. This is shown in figure 3.30.

[1] Technical progress may also be due to *product innovation*. In this section we deal only with *process innovation*.

[2] See J. Hicks, *Value and Capital* (Oxford: Clarendon Press, 1946).

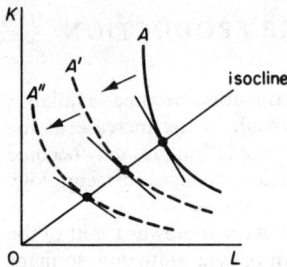
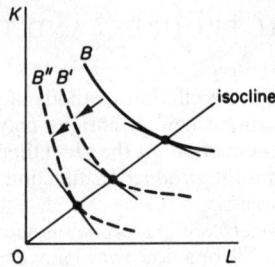
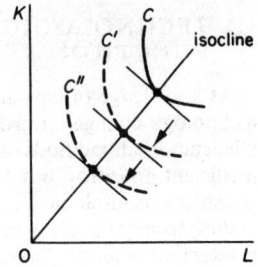

Figure 3.29 Capital-deepening   Figure 3.30 Labour-deepen-   Figure 3.31 Neutral tech-
      technical progress   ing technical progress   nical progress

Neutral-technical progress

Technical progress is neutral if it increases the marginal product of both factors by the same percentage, so that the $MRS_{L,K}$ (along any radius) remains constant. The isoquant shifts downwards parallel to itself. This is shown in figure 3.31.

IV. EQUILIBRIUM OF THE FIRM: CHOICE OF OPTIMAL COMBINATION OF FACTORS OF PRODUCTION

In this section we shall show the use of the production function in the choice of the optimal combination of factors by the firm. In Part A we will examine two cases in which the firm is faced with a single decision, namely maximising output for a given cost, and minimising cost subject to a given output. Both these decisions comprise cases of constrained profit maximisation in a single period.

In Part B we will consider the case of unconstrained profit maximisation, by the expansion of output over time.

In all the above cases it is assumed that the firm can choose the optimal combination of factors, that it can employ any amount of any factor in order to maximise its profits. This assumption is valid if the firm is new, or if the firm is in the long-run. However, an existing firm may be coerced, due to pressure of demand, to expand its output in the short-run, when at least one factor, usually capital, is constant. We will examine this case separately.

In all cases we make the following assumptions:

1.   The goal of the firm is profit maximisation – that is, the maximisation of the difference $\Pi = R - C$ where

$$\Pi = \text{profits}$$
$$R = \text{revenue}$$
$$C = \text{cost}$$

2.   The price of output is given, $\bar{P}_x$.
3.   The prices of factors are given:
$\bar{w}$ is the given wage rate
$\bar{r}$ is the given price of capital services (rental price of machinery).

A. SINGLE DECISION OF THE FIRM

The problem facing the firm is that of a constrained profit maximisation, which may take one of the following forms:

(a) Maximise profit Π, subject to a cost constraint. In this case total cost and prices are given ($\bar{C}, \bar{w}, \bar{r}, \bar{P}_x$), and the problem may be stated as follows

$$\max \Pi = R - \bar{C}$$
$$\Pi = \bar{P}_x X - \bar{C}$$

Clearly maximisation of Π is achieved in this case if X is maximised, since $\bar{C}$ and $\bar{P}_x$ are given constants by assumption.

(b) Maximise profit Π, for a given level of output. For example, a contractor wants to build a bridge (X is given) with the maximum profit. In this case we have

$$\max \Pi = R - C$$
$$\Pi = \bar{P}_x \bar{X} - C$$

Clearly maximisation of Π is achieved in this case if cost C is minimised, given that X and P_x are given constants by assumption.

The analysis will be carried out first by using diagrams and subsequently by applying calculus.

For a graphical presentation of the equilibrium of the firm (its profit-maximising position) we will use the isoquant map (figure 3.32) and the isocost-line(s) (figure 3.33).

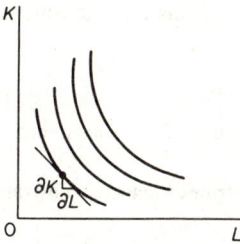
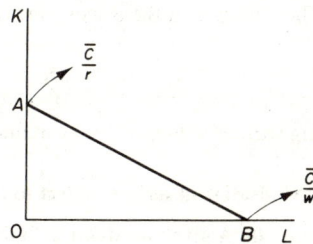

Figure 3.32   Figure 3.33

The isoquants have been explained in section I, where it was shown that the slope of an isoquant is

$$-\frac{\partial K}{\partial L} = MRS_{L,K} = \frac{MP_L}{MP_K} = \frac{\partial X/\partial L}{\partial X/\partial K}$$

The *isocost line* is defined by the cost equation

$$C = (r)(K) + (w)(L)$$

where w = wage rate, and r = price of capital services.

The isocost line is the locus of all combinations of factors the firm can purchase with a given monetary cost outlay.[1]

The slope of the isocost line is equal to the ratio of the prices of the factors of production:

$$\text{slope of isocost line} = \frac{w}{r}$$

---

[1] There is a close analogy between the consumer's budget line (Chapter 2, figure 2.10) and the firm's isocost line.

Proof

Assume that the total cost outlay the firm undertakes is $\bar{C}$. If the entrepreneur spends all the amount $\bar{C}$ on capital equipment, the maximum amount he can buy from this factor is

$$0A = \frac{\bar{C}}{r}$$

If all cost outlay is spent on labour the maximum amount of this factor that the firm can purchase is

$$0B = \frac{\bar{C}}{w}$$

The slope of the isocost line is

$$\frac{0A}{0B} = \frac{\bar{C}/r}{\bar{C}/w} = \frac{w}{r}$$

It can be shown that any point on the line AB satisfies the cost equation $(C = r \cdot K + w \cdot L)$, so that, for given prices of the factors and for given expenditure on them, the isocost line shows the alternative combinations of K and L that can be purchased by the firm. The equation of the isocost line is found by solving the cost equation for K:

$$K = \frac{\bar{C}}{r} - \frac{w}{r} L$$

By assigning various values to L we can find all the points of the isocost line.

Case 1: maximisation of output subject to a cost constraint (financial constraint)

We assume: (*a*) A given production function

$$X = f(L, K, v, \gamma)$$

and (*b*) given factor prices, w, r, for labour and capital respectively.

The firm is in equilibrium when it maximizes its output given its total cost outlay and the prices of the factors, w and r.

In figure 3.34 we see that the maximum level of output the firm can produce, given the cost constraint, is X_2 defined by the tangency of the isocost line, and the highest isoquant. The optimal combination of factors of production is K_2 and L_2, for prices w and r. Higher levels of output (to the right of e) are desirable but not attainable due

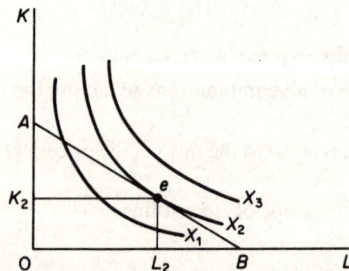

Figure 3.34

to the cost constraint. Other points on AB or below it lie on a lower isoquant than X_2. Hence X_2 is the maximum output possible under the above assumptions (of given cost outlay, given production function, and given factor prices). At the point of tangency (e) the slope of the isocost line (w/r) is equal to the slope of the isoquant (MP_L/MP_K). This constitutes the first condition for equilibrium. The second condition is that the isoquants be convex to the origin. In summary: the conditions for equilibrium of the firm are:

(*a*) Slope of isoquant = Slope of isocost

or
$$\frac{w}{r} = \frac{MP_L}{MP_K} = \frac{\partial X/\partial L}{\partial X/\partial K} = MRS_{L,K}$$

(*b*) The isoquants must be convex to the origin. If the isoquant is concave the point of tangency of the isocost and the isoquant curves does not define an equilibrium position (figure 3.35).

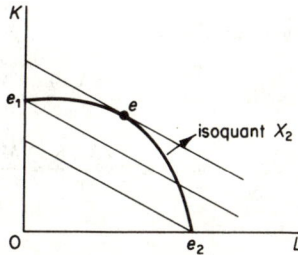

Figure 3.35

Output X_2 (depicted by the concave isoquant) can be produced with lower cost at e_2, which lies on a lower isocost curve than e. (With a concave isoquant we have a 'corner' solution.)

Formal derivation of the equilibrium conditions

The equilibrium conditions may be obtained by applying calculus and solving a 'constrained maximum' problem which may be stated as follows. The rational entrepreneur seeks the maximisation of his output, given his total-cost outlay and the prices of factors. Formally:

Maximise $X = f(L, K)$

subject to $\bar{C} = wL + rK$ (cost constraint)

This is a problem of constrained maximum and the above conditions for the equilibrium of the firm may be obtained from its solution.

We can solve this problem by using Lagrangian multipliers. The solution involves the following steps:

Rewrite the constraint in the form

$$\bar{C} - wL - rK = 0$$

Multiply the constraint by a constant λ which is the Lagrangian multiplier:

$$\lambda(\bar{C} - wL - rK) = 0$$

The Lagrangian multipliers are undefined constants which are used for solving constrained maxima or minima. Their value is determined simultaneously with the values of the other unknowns (L and K in our example). There will be as many Lagrangian multipliers as there are constraints in the problem.

Form the 'composite' function

$$\phi = X + \lambda(\bar{C} - wL - rK)$$

It can be shown that maximisation of the ϕ function implies maximisation of the output.

The first condition for the maximisation of a function is that its partial derivatives be equal to zero. The partial derivatives of the above function with respect to L, K and λ are:

$$\frac{\partial \phi}{\partial L} = \frac{\partial X}{\partial L} + \lambda(-w) = 0 \tag{3.1}$$

$$\frac{\partial \phi}{\partial K} = \frac{\partial X}{\partial K} + \lambda(-r) = 0 \tag{3.2}$$

$$\frac{\partial \phi}{\partial \lambda} = \bar{C} - wL - rK = 0 \tag{3.3}$$

Solving the first two equations for λ we obtain

$$\frac{\partial X}{\partial L} = \lambda w \quad \text{or} \quad \lambda = \frac{\partial X/\partial L}{w} = \frac{MP_L}{w}$$

$$\frac{\partial X}{\partial K} = \lambda r \quad \text{or} \quad \lambda = \frac{\partial X/\partial K}{r} = \frac{MP_K}{r}$$

The two expressions must be equal; thus

$$\frac{\partial X/\partial L}{w} = \frac{\partial X/\partial K}{r} \quad \text{or} \quad \frac{MP_L}{MP_K} = \frac{\partial X/\partial L}{\partial X/\partial K} = \frac{w}{r}$$

This firm is in equilibrium when it equates the ratio of the marginal productivities of factors to the ratio of their prices.

It can be shown[1] that the second-order conditions for equilibrium of the firm require that the marginal product curves of the two factors have a negative slope.

The slope of the marginal product curve of labour is the second derivative of the production function:

$$\text{slope of } MP_L \text{ curve} = \frac{\partial^2 X}{\partial L^2}$$

Similarly for capital:

$$\text{slope of } MP_K \text{ curve} = \frac{\partial^2 X}{\partial K^2}$$

The second-order conditions are

$$\frac{\partial^2 X}{\partial L^2} < 0 \quad \text{and} \quad \frac{\partial^2 X}{\partial K^2} < 0$$

and

$$\left(\frac{\partial^2 X}{\partial L^2}\right)\left(\frac{\partial^2 X}{\partial K^2}\right) > \left(\frac{\partial^2 X}{\partial L \, \partial K}\right)^2$$

These conditions are sufficient for establishing the convexity of the isoquants.

[1] See Henderson and Quandt, *Microeconomic Theory* (McGraw-Hill, 1958) pp. 49–54.

Case 2: minimisation of cost for a given level of output

The conditions for equilibrium of the firm are formally the same as in Case 1. That is, there must be tangency of the (given) isoquant and the lowest possible isocost curve, and the isoquant must be convex. However, the problem is conceptually different in the case of cost minimisation. The entrepreneur wants to produce a given output (for example, a bridge, a building, or $\bar{X}$ tons of a commodity) with the minimum cost outlay.

In this case we have a single isoquant (figure 3.36) which denotes the desired level of output, but we have a set of isocost curves (figure 3.37). Curves closer to the origin show a lower total-cost outlay. The isocost lines are parallel because they are drawn on the assumption of constant prices of factors: since w and r do not change, all the isocost curves have the same slope w/r.

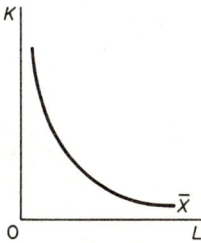 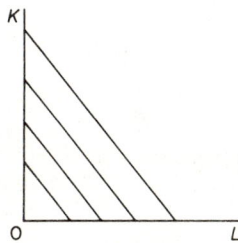

Figure 3.36   Figure 3.37

The firm minimises its costs by employing the combination of K and L determined by the point of tangency of the $\bar{X}$ isoquant with the lowest isocost line (figure 3.38). Points below e are desirable because they show lower cost but are not attainable for output $\bar{X}$. Points above e show higher costs. Hence point e is the least-cost point, the point denoting the least-cost combination of the factors K and L for producing $\bar{X}$.

Clearly the conditions for equilibrium (least cost) are the same as in Case 1, that is, equality of the slopes of the isoquant and the isocost curves, and convexity of the isoquant.

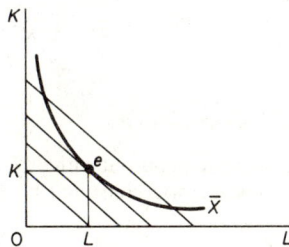

Figure 3.38

Formally:

Minimise

$$C = f(X) = wL + rK$$

subject to

$$\bar{X} = f(L, K)$$

Rewrite the constraint in the form

$$\bar{X} - f(L, K) = 0$$

Premultiply the constraint by the Lagrangian multiplier λ

$$\lambda(\overline{X} - f(L, K)) = 0$$

Form the 'composite' function

$$\phi = C - \lambda[\overline{X} - f(L, K)]$$

or

$$\phi = (wL + rK) - \lambda[\overline{X} - f(L, K)]$$

Take the partial derivatives of ϕ with respect to L, K and λ and equate to zero:

$$\frac{\partial \phi}{\partial L} = w - \lambda \frac{\partial f(L, K)}{\partial L} = 0 = w - \lambda \frac{\partial X}{\partial L}$$

$$\frac{\partial \phi}{K} = r - \lambda \frac{\partial f(L, K)}{\partial K} = 0 = r - \lambda \frac{\partial X}{\partial K}$$

$$\frac{\partial \phi}{\partial \lambda} = - [\overline{X} - f(L, K)] = 0$$

From the first two expressions we obtain

$$w = \lambda \frac{\partial X}{\partial L}$$

$$r = \lambda \frac{\partial X}{\partial K}$$

Dividing through these expressions we find

$$\frac{w}{r} = \frac{\partial X/\partial L}{\partial X/\partial K} = MRS_{L, K}$$

This condition is the same as in Case 1 above. The second (sufficient) condition, concerning the convexity of the isoquant, is fulfilled by the assumption of negative slopes of the marginal product of factors as in Case 1, that is

$$\frac{\partial^2 X}{\partial L^2} < 0, \quad \frac{\partial^2 X}{\partial K^2} < 0 \quad \text{and} \quad \left(\frac{\partial^2 X}{\partial L^2}\right)\left(\frac{\partial^2 X}{\partial K^2}\right) > \left(\frac{\partial^2 X}{\partial L \, \partial K}\right)^2$$

B. CHOICE OF OPTIMAL EXPANSION PATH

We distinguish two cases: expansion of output with all factors variable (the long run), and expansion of output with some factor(s) constant (the short run).

Optimal expansion path in the long run

In the long run all factors of production are variable. There is no limitation (technical or financial) to the expansion of output. The firm's objective is the choice of the optimal way of expanding its output, so as to maximise its profits. With given factor prices (w, r) and given production function, the optimal expansion path is determined by the points of tangency of successive isocost lines and successive isoquants.

If the production function is homogeneous the expansion path will be a straight line through the origin, whose slope (which determines the optimal K/L ratio) depends on the ratio of the factor prices. In figure 3.39 the optimal expansion path will be $0A$,

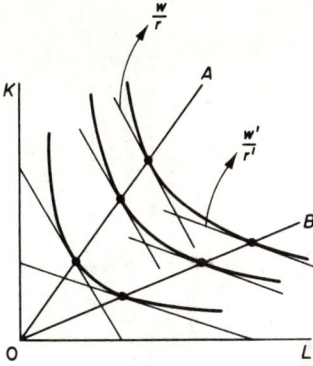

Figure 3.39

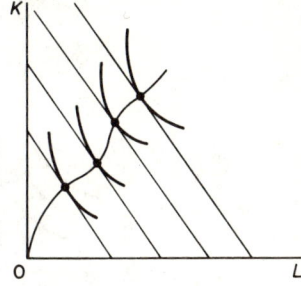

Figure 3.40

defined by the locus of points of tangency of the isoquants with successive parallel isocost lines with a slope of w/r. If the ratio of the prices increases the isocost lines become flatter (for example, with a slope of w'/r'), and the optimal expansion path will be the straight line $0B$. Of course, if the ratio of prices of factors was initially w/r and subsequently changes to w'/r', the expansion path changes: initially the firm moves along $0A$, but after the change in the factor prices it moves along $0B$.

If the production function is non-homogeneous the optimal expansion path will not be a straight line, even if the ratio of prices of factors remains constant. This is shown in figure 3.40. It is due to the fact that in equilibrium we must equate the (constant) w/r ratio with the $MRS_{L,K}$, which is the same on a curved isocline (see section II).

Optimal expansion path in the short run

In the short run, capital is constant and the firm is coerced to expand along a straight line parallel to the axis on which we measure the variable factor L. With the prices of factors constant the firm does not maximise its profits in the short run, due to the constraint of the given capital. This situation is shown in figure 3.41. The optimal expansion path would be $0A$ were it possible to increase K. Given the capital equipment, the firm can expand only along $\overline{K}\overline{K}$ in the short run.

The above discussion of the choice of optimal combination of the factors of production is schematically summarised on p. 94.

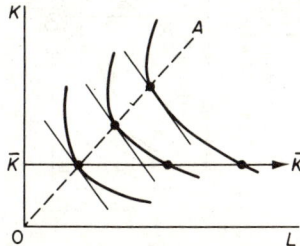

Figure 3.41

CHOICE BY THE FIRM (single product x)

1 Given: (a) the price of the product P_x
(b) the prices of factors, w, r.

2 Goal: Profit maximisation:
max $\Pi = R - C$

A SINGLE VARIABLE FACTOR
Short-run analysis
Law of diminishing marginal
product of the variable factor
Homogeneous P.F.

ALL FACTORS VARIABLE
Long-run analysis
Law of (technical) returns to scale

Either with homogeneous P.F. or with non-homogeneous P.F.

EXPANSION OF OUTPUT
(Output decisions over time)
UNCONSTRAINED PROFIT MAXIMISATION

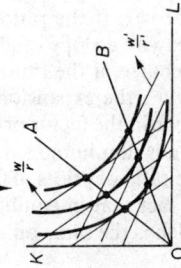

Homogeneous P.F.
The choice of the expansion
path depends on the ratio of
factor prices: with prices w
and r the firm will choose A;
with prices w and r' the firm
will choose B

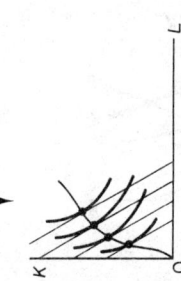

Non-homogeneous P.F.
The choice of the expansion path
depends on the ratio of factor prices.
Note that with a non-homogeneous P.F.
the expansion path will not be a
straight line even if the factor
prices remain constant over time,
because for equilibrium we must
equate the (constant) w/r to the
$MRS_{L,K}$

A SINGLE DECISION
CONSTRAINED PROFIT MAXIMISATION

Case 1: maximise profit $\Pi = R - \bar{C}$ (maximise X)
subject to a cost constraint $\bar{C}$

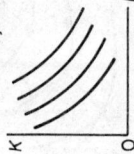

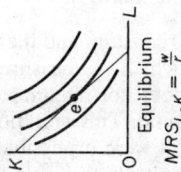

Isoquants   The isocost   Equilibrium
The condition for equilibrium: $MRS_{L,K} = \dfrac{w}{r}$

Case 2: maximise profit $\Pi = R - C$ (minimise cost)
subject to an output constraint $\bar{X}$

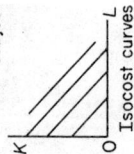

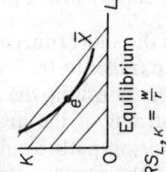

Isocost curves   The isoquant   Equilibrium
The condition for equilibrium: $MRS_{L,K} = \dfrac{w}{r}$

V. DERIVATION OF COST FUNCTIONS FROM PRODUCTION FUNCTIONS

Costs are derived functions. They are derived from the technological relationships implied by the production function. We will first show how to derive graphically the cost curves from the production function. Subsequently we will derive mathematically the total-cost function from a Cobb–Douglas production function.

A. GRAPHICAL DERIVATION OF COST CURVES FROM THE PRODUCTION FUNCTION

The total cost curve is determined by the locus of points of tangency of successive isocost lines with higher isoquants.

Assumptions for our example:

(a) given production function (that is, constant technology) with constant returns to scale;

(b) given prices of factors:

$$w = 20\text{p per man hour}$$
$$r = 20\text{p per machine hour}$$

The following methods of production are part of the available technology of the firm. They refer to the quantities of L and K required for the production of one ton of output which is the 'unit' level.

	P_1	P_2	P_3	P_4	P_5	P_6	P_7	P_8
Labour: hours	2	3·0	4·0	5·0	6·0	7·0	8·0	9
Capital: hours	6	4·5	4·0	3·7	3·5	3·3	3·1	3

The cost of each method for the production of one 'unit' of output (given the above factor prices) is as follows:

	Cost P_1	Cost P_2	Cost P_3	Cost P_4	Cost P_5	Cost P_6	Cost P_7	Cost P_8
Labour cost	40	60	80	100	120	140	160	180
Capital cost	120	90	80	74	70	66	62	60
Total cost	160	150	160	174	190	206	222	240

Clearly the least-cost method of production, given our assumptions, is the second method (P_2). This method will be chosen by the rational entrepreneur for all levels of output (given the assumption of constant returns to scale). Table 3.1 includes some levels of output and their respective total costs (for the chosen least-cost method of production, P_2). The product expansion path is shown in figure 3.42. It is formed from the points of tangency of the isocosts and the isoquants. The TC curve may be drawn from the information (on output and costs) provided by the points of tangency. For example,

at point a,	$X = 5$	$TC = 750$
at point b	$X = 10$	$TC = 1,500$
at point d	$X = 20$	$TC = 3,000$ etc.

Table 3.1   Output levels and TC (for activity P_2)

Output X (in tons)	Total cost (in pence)	AC (pence per ton)
0	0	–
5	750	150
10	1,500	150
15	2,250	150
20	3,000	150
25	3,750	150
30	4,500	150
35	5,250	150
40	6,000	150
45	6,750	150
50	7,500	150
55	8,250	150
60	9,000	150
65	9,750	150
70	10,500	150

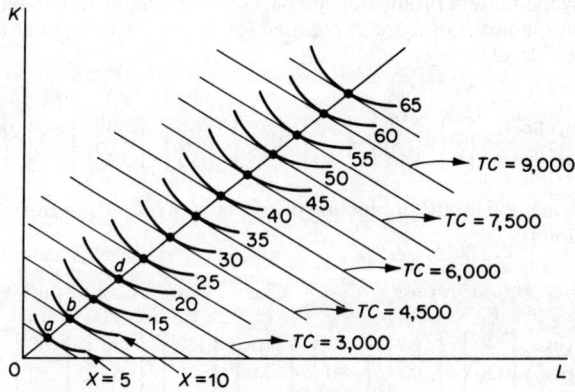

Figure 3.42

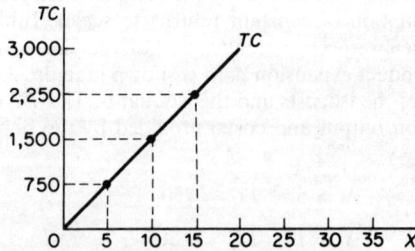

Figure 3.43

Plotting these points on a two-dimensional diagram with TC on the vertical axis and output (X) on the horizontal axis, we obtain the total-cost curve (figure 3.43). With our assumption (of constant returns to scale and of constant factor prices) the AC is constant (£1.50 per 'unit' of output), hence the AC will be a straight line, parallel to the horizontal axis (figure 3.44). It is important to remember that the cost curves assume that the problem of choice of the optimal (least-cost) technique has been solved at a previous stage. In other words, the complex problem of finding the cheapest combination of factor inputs must be solved before the cost curve is defined.

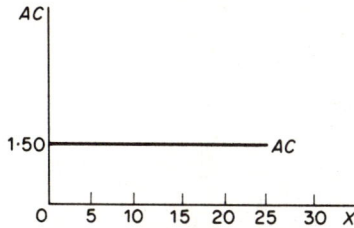

Figure 3.44

B. FORMAL DERIVATION OF COST CURVES FROM A PRODUCTION FUNCTION

In applied research one of the most commonly used forms of production function is the Cobb–Douglas form

$$X = b_0 L^{b_1} K^{b_2}$$

Given this production function and the cost equation

$$C = wL + rK$$

we want to derive the cost function, that is, the total cost as a function of output

$$C = f(X)$$

We begin by solving the constrained output maximisation problem:

Maximise
$$X = b_0 L^{b_1} K^{b_2}$$

subject to
$$\bar{C} = wL + rK \quad \text{(cost constraint)}$$

(The bar on top of C has the meaning that the firm has a *given* amount of money to spend on both factors of production.)
We form the 'composite' function

$$\phi = X + \lambda(\bar{C} - wL - rK)$$

where $\lambda =$ Lagrangian multiplier

The first condition for maximisation is that the first derivatives of the function with respect to L, K and λ be equal to zero:

$$\frac{\partial \phi}{\partial L} = b_1 \frac{X}{L} - \lambda w = 0 \tag{3.4}$$

$$\frac{\partial \phi}{\partial K} = b_2 \frac{X}{K} - \lambda r = 0 \tag{3.5}$$

$$\frac{\partial \phi}{\partial \lambda} = (C - wL - rK) = 0 \tag{3.6}$$

From equations 3.4 and 3.5 we obtain

$$b_1 \frac{X}{L} = \lambda w \quad \text{and} \quad b_2 \frac{X}{K} = \lambda r$$

Dividing these expressions we obtain

$$\frac{b_1}{b_2} \cdot \frac{K}{L} = \frac{w}{r}$$

Solving for K

$$K = \frac{w}{r} \cdot \frac{b_2}{b_1} L \tag{3.7}$$

Substituting K into the production function we obtain

$$X = b_0 L^{b_1} K^{b_2}$$

$$X = b_0 L^{b_1} \left[\frac{w}{r} \frac{b_2}{b_1} L \right]^{b_2}$$

$$X = b_0 \left[\left(\frac{w}{r} \right) \left(\frac{b_2}{b_1} \right) \right]^{b_2} L^{(b_1 + b_2)}$$

The term in brackets is the constant term of the function: it includes the three coefficients of the production function, b_0, b_1, b_2, and the prices of the factors of production.

Solving the above form of the production function for L, we find

$$\frac{1}{b_0 \left(\dfrac{w}{r} \dfrac{b_2}{b_1} \right)^{b_2}} X = L^{(b_1 + b_2)}$$

or

$$\left[\frac{1}{b_0 \left(\dfrac{w}{r} \dfrac{b_2}{b_1} \right)^{b_2}} \cdot X \right]^{1/(b_1 + b_2)} = L$$

or

$$L = \left(\frac{r b_1}{w b_2} \right)^{b_2/(b_1 + b_2)} \left(\frac{X}{b_0} \right)^{1/(b_1 + b_2)} \tag{3.8}$$

Substituting the value of L from expression 3.8 into expression 3.7 for capital we obtain

$$K = \frac{w}{r} \cdot \frac{b_2}{b_1} L$$

$$K = \left(\frac{w b_2}{r b_1} \right)^{1/(b_1 + b_2)} \left(\frac{X}{b_0} \right)^{1/(b_1 + b_2)} \tag{3.9}$$

Substituting expression 3.8 and 3.9 into the cost equation $C = wL + rK$ we find

$$C = \left(\frac{1}{b_0} \right)^{1/(b_1 + b_2)} \cdot \left[w \left(\frac{r b_1}{w b_2} \right)^{b_2/(b_1 + b_2)} + r \left(\frac{w b_2}{r b_1} \right)^{b_1/(b_1 + b_2)} \right] \cdot X^{1/(b_1 + b_2)}$$

Rearranging the expression above we obtain

$$C = \left\{ \left(\frac{1}{b_0}\right) \left[\left(\frac{b_1}{b_2}\right)^{b_2} + \left(\frac{b_2}{b_1}\right)^{b_1} \right] \right\}^{1/(b_1 + b_2)} \cdot \left\{ w^{b_1/(b_1 + b_2)} \cdot r^{b_2/(b_1 + b_2)} \right\} \cdot X^{1/(b_1 + b_2)}$$

This is the cost function, that is, the cost expressed as a function of
  (i) output, X;
  (ii) the production function coefficients, b_0, b_1, b_2; (clearly the sum $b_1 + b_2$ is a measure of the returns to scale);
  (iii) the prices of factors, w, r.
If prices of factors are given (the usual assumption in the theory of the firm), cost depends only on output X, and we can draw the usual diagrams of cost curves, which express graphically the cost function

$$C = f(X) \; \textit{ceteris paribus}$$

'*Ceteris paribus*' implies that all other determinants of costs, that is, the production technology and the prices of factors, remain unchanged. If these factors change, the cost curve will shift upwards or downwards (see Chapter 4).

VI. THE PRODUCTION FUNCTION OF A MULTIPRODUCT FIRM

In this section we will extend the analysis to the multiproduct firm. We simplify the exposition by assuming that the firm produces two products, X and Y. The analysis can easily be extended to any number of products.

A. THE PRODUCTION-POSSIBILITY CURVE OF THE FIRM

Each product is assumed to be produced by two factors, L and K. For each product we have a production function

$$X = f_1(L, K)$$
$$Y = f_2(L, K)$$

Each production function may be presented by a set of isoquants with the usual properties. We may now obtain the production-possibility curve of the firm by using the device of the *Edgeworth box*. We assume that the firm has total quantities of factors $0L$ and $0K$ (figure 3.45) measured along the sides of the Edgeworth box. Any point of the Edgeworth box shows a certain combination of quantities of x and y produced by the available factors of production. The production function for commodity x is represented by the set of isoquants denoted by A which are convex to the origin 0_x. The production function for commodity y is represented by the set of isoquants denoted by B which are convex to the origin 0_y. The further down an isoquant B lies, the higher the quantity of y it represents. The two sets of isoquants have points of tangency, which form the *contract curve*. Only points lying on the contract curve are efficient, in the sense that any other point shows the use of all resources for producing a combination of outputs which includes less quantity of at least one commodity. For example, assume that initially the firm produces at point Z, at which the quantity of x is A_3 and the quantity of y is B_6. The production of the level A_3 of x absorbs $0_x L_1$ of labour and $0_x K_1$ of capital. The remaining resources, $L_1 L$ and $K_1 K$, are used in the production of commodity y.

It can be shown that the firm can produce more of either x or y or of both commodities by reallocating its resources so as to move to any point between V and W on the contract

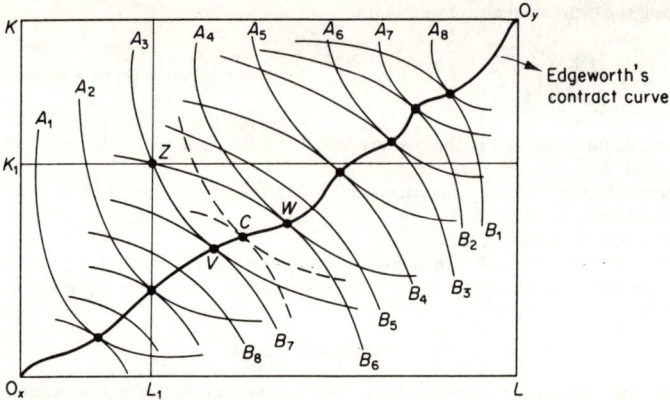

Figure 3.45

curve. If the firm moves to W it will be producing the same level of $y(B_6)$, but a higher level of $x(A_4)$. If the firm chooses to produce at V, it will produce the same quantity of $x(A_3)$, but more of $y(B_7)$. Finally, if the firm produces at any intermediate point between V and W, for example at point C, it will attain higher levels of production of both x and y. Thus points on the contract curve are efficient in that any other point *off* this curve implies a smaller level of output of at least one product. The choice of the actual point on the contract curve depends on the ratio of the prices of the two commodities (see below).

To determine the choice of levels of x and y we need to derive the *production-possibility curve* (or product-transformation curve) of the firm. This shows the locus of points of levels of x and y which use up all the available resources of the firm. The production-possibility curve is derived from the contract curve. Each point of tangency between isoquants, that is, any one point of the contract curve, defines a combination of x and y levels of output which lies on the production-possibility curve. For example, point V, representing the output pair A_3 from x and B_7 from y, is point V' on figure 3.46. Similarly point W of the contract curve is point W' on the production-possibility curve.

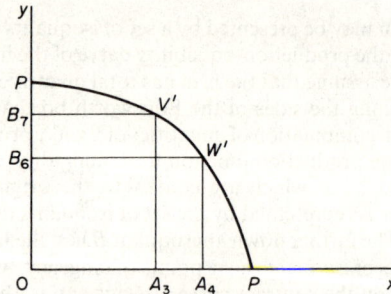

Figure 3.46

Formal derivation of the production-possibility curve

The slope of isoquant A is

$$-\frac{\partial K}{\partial L} = \frac{MP_{L,x}}{MP_{K,x}} = MRTS^x_{L,K}$$

where $MRTS_{L.K}^{x}$ = marginal rate of technical substitution of the factors K and L in the production of commodity x.

Similarly, the slope of isoquant B is

$$-\frac{\partial K}{\partial L} = \frac{MP_{L,y}}{MP_{K,y}} = MRTS_{L,K}^{y}$$

where $MRTS_{L.K}^{y}$ = marginal rate of technical substitution of the factors K and L in the production of commodity y.

At the points of tangency of isoquants on the contract curve the two slopes are equal

$$-\frac{\partial K}{\partial L} = \frac{MP_{L,x}}{MP_{K,x}} = \frac{MP_{L,y}}{MP_{K,y}}$$

The slope of the contract curve, say from V to W, can be represented also by the slope of the production-possibility curve PP, from V' to W' (in discrete terms).

The slope of the production-possibility curve is

$$-\frac{\partial y}{\partial x} = MRPT_{x,y}$$

where $MRPT_{x,y}$ = marginal rate of product transformation.

A reduction in the level of y releases factors of production

$$\partial L_y(MP_{L,y}) + \partial K_y(MP_{K,y})$$

An increase in the level of x requires additional factors

$$\partial L_x(MP_{L,x}) + \partial K_x(MP_{K,x})$$

If the factors are to be fully employed, then the quantities released from the decrease in y must be equal to the quantities used in increasing x. Thus

$$-\partial L_y = +\partial L_x$$
$$-\partial K_y = +\partial K_x$$

Now the total differential of the production-possibility curve, its slope, is

$$-\frac{\partial y}{\partial x} = \frac{\partial L_y(MP_{L,y}) + \partial K_y(MP_{K,y})}{\partial L_x(MP_{L,x}) + \partial K_x(MP_{K,x})} \tag{3.10}$$

For efficient production the firm must stay *on* the curve, not inside it. This implies that

$$\begin{bmatrix} \text{Slope of} \\ \text{isoquant } A \end{bmatrix} = \frac{MP_{L,x}}{MP_{K,x}} = \frac{MP_{L,y}}{MP_{K,y}} = \begin{bmatrix} \text{Slope of} \\ \text{isoquant } B \end{bmatrix} \tag{3.11}$$

This yields

$$MP_{L,x} = MP_{K,x}\left(\frac{MP_{L,y}}{MP_{K,y}}\right) \tag{3.12}$$

and

$$MP_{L,y} = MP_{K,y}\left(\frac{MP_{L,x}}{MP_{K,x}}\right) \tag{3.13}$$

Dividing the total differential by $\partial L_y (= -\partial L_x)$ we find

$$-\frac{\partial y}{\partial x} = \frac{MP_{L,y} + MP_{K,y}\left(\dfrac{\partial K_y}{\partial L_y}\right)}{-MP_{L,x} - MP_{K,x}\left(\dfrac{\partial K_x}{\partial L_y}\right)} \tag{3.14}$$

Substituting expressions 3.12 and 3.13 in expression 3.14 we obtain

$$-\frac{\partial y}{\partial x} = \frac{MP_{K,y}\left(\dfrac{MP_{L,x}}{MP_{K,x}} + \dfrac{\partial K_y}{\partial L_y}\right)}{-MP_{K,x}\left(\dfrac{MP_{L,y}}{MP_{K,y}} + \dfrac{\partial K_x}{\partial L_y}\right)}$$

The first terms in the brackets are equal by expression (3.11). The second terms in the brackets are also equal by the condition that $\partial K_y = \partial K_x$.
Consequently the bracketed terms cancel out and we have

$$[\text{slope of production-possibility curve}] = -\frac{\partial y}{\partial x} = \frac{MP_{K,y}}{MP_{K,x}}$$

Similarly, we may derive

$$-\frac{\partial y}{\partial x} = \frac{MP_{L,y}}{MP_{L,x}}$$

Thus the slope of the production-possibility curve (or product-transformation curve) is

$$-\frac{\partial y}{\partial x} = \frac{MP_{L,y}}{MP_{L,x}} = \frac{MP_{K,y}}{MP_{K,x}}$$

The optimal combination of the output pair is the one which yields the highest revenue, given the production-possibility curve, that is, given the total quantities of factors which define this curve. To find the equilibrium of the firm we need an additional tool, the isorevenue curve.

B. THE ISOREVENUE CURVE OF THE MULTIPRODUCT FIRM

An isorevenue curve is the locus of points of various combinations of quantities of y and x whose sale yields the same revenue to the firm (figure 3.47). The slope of the isorevenue curve is equal to the ratio of the prices of the commodities:

$$\begin{bmatrix}\text{slope of} \\ \text{isorevenue}\end{bmatrix} = \frac{0A}{0B} = \frac{P_x}{P_y}$$

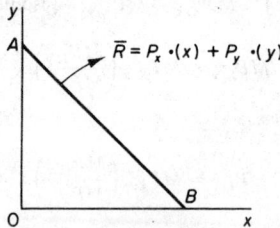

Figure 3.47

Proof Assume that we want an isorevenue depicting $\bar{R}$ total revenue.
   (a) If we sell only y the total revenue is $(0A)$. $P_y = \bar{R}$, that is, the quantity of y which yields $\bar{R}$ is $(0A) = \bar{R}/P_y$.

(*b*) Similarly the quantity of *x* that yields $\bar{R}$ is $0B = \bar{R}/Px$. Dividing $0A$ by $0B$ we obtain

$$\begin{bmatrix} \text{Slope of} \\ \text{isorevenue} \end{bmatrix} = \frac{0A}{0B} = \frac{\dfrac{\bar{R}}{Py}}{\dfrac{\bar{R}}{Px}} = \frac{Px}{Py}$$

Formally the $\bar{R}$ isorevenue curve may be obtained from the equation

$$\bar{R} = P_x \cdot (x) + P_y \cdot (y)$$

Solving for *y* we obtain

$$y = \frac{\bar{R}}{P_y} - \frac{P_x}{P_y} \cdot (x)$$

Given the prices of the two commodities and any value for $\bar{R}$, we may compute the points of the $\bar{R}$ line by assigning successive values to $x(x = 0, 1, 2, \ldots)$. For example:

if $\qquad\qquad x = 0, \qquad\qquad y = \dfrac{\bar{R}}{P_y} = 0A$

if $\qquad\qquad x = 1, \qquad\qquad y = \dfrac{\bar{R}}{P_y} - \dfrac{P_x}{P_y}$

if $\qquad\qquad x = 2, \qquad\qquad y = \dfrac{\bar{R}}{P_y} - 2\dfrac{P_x}{P_y}$

$\vdots \qquad\qquad\qquad \vdots \qquad\qquad\qquad \vdots$

if $\qquad x = 0B = \dfrac{\bar{R}}{P_x}, \qquad y = \dfrac{\bar{R}}{P_y} - \dfrac{P_x}{P_y}\dfrac{\bar{R}}{P_x} = 0$

We may in the same way define the whole set of isorevenue curves by assigning to $\bar{R}$ various values. The further away from the origin an isorevenue curve is, the larger the revenue of the firm will be.

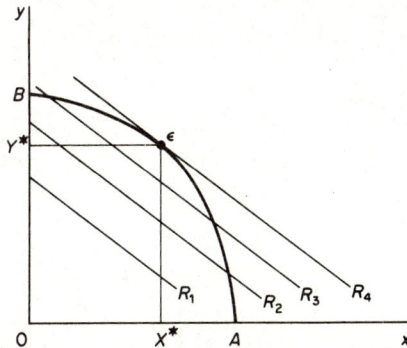

Figure 3.48

C. EQUILIBRIUM OF THE MULTIPRODUCT FIRM

The firm wants to maximise its profit given (i) the constraint set by the factors of production, (ii) the transformation curve, and (iii) the prices of the commodities (P_x, P_y) and of the factors of production (w, r).

Assuming that the quantity of the factors and their prices are given, then maximisation of Π is achieved by maximising the revenue, R.

Graphically the equilibrium of the firm is defined by the point of tangency of the given product-transformation curve and the highest isorevenue curve (figure 3.48). At the point of tangency the slopes of the isorevenue and the product-transformation curves are equal. Thus the condition for equilibrium is that these slopes be equal:

$$-\frac{dy}{dx} = \frac{MP_{L,y}}{MP_{L,x}} = \frac{MP_{K,y}}{MP_{K,x}} = \frac{P_x}{P_y}$$

4. Theory of Costs

I. GENERAL NOTES

Cost functions are derived functions. They are derived from the production function, which describes the available efficient methods of production at any one time.

Economic theory distinguishes between short-run costs and long-run costs. *Short-run costs* are the costs over a period during which some factors of production (usually capital equipment and management) are fixed. The *long-run costs* are the costs over a period long enough to permit the change of all factors of production. In the long run all factors become variable.

Both in the short run and in the long run, total cost is a multivariable function, that is, total cost is determined by many factors. Symbolically we may write the long-run cost function as

$$C = f(X, T, P_f)$$

and the short-run cost function as

$$C = f(X, T, P_f, \bar{K})$$

where C = total cost
  X = output
  T = technology
  P_f = prices of factors
  $\bar{K}$ = fixed factor(s)

Graphically, costs are shown on two-dimensional diagrams. Such curves imply that cost is a function of output, $C = f(X)$, *ceteris paribus*. The clause *ceteris paribus* implies that all other factors which determine costs are constant. If these factors do change, their effect on costs is shown graphically by a shift of the cost curve. This is the reason why determinants of cost, other than output, are called *shift factors*. Mathematically there is no difference between the various determinants of costs. The distinction between movements along the cost curve (when output changes) and shifts of the curve (when the other determinants change) is convenient only pedagogically, because it allows the use of two-dimensional diagrams. But it can be misleading when studying the determinants of costs. It is important to remember that if the cost curve shifts, this does not imply that the cost function is indeterminate.

The factor 'technology' is itself a multidimensional factor, determined by the physical quantities of factor inputs, the quality of the factor inputs, the efficiency of the entrepreneur, both in organising the physical side of the production (technical efficiency of the entrepreneur), and in making the correct economic choice of techniques (economic efficiency of the entrepreneur). Thus, any change in these determinants (e.g., the introduction of a better method of organisation of production, the application of an educational programme to the existing labour) will shift the production function, and hence will result in a shift of the cost curve. Similarly the improvement of raw materials, or the improvement in the use of the same raw materials will lead to a shift downwards of the cost function.

The short-run costs are the costs at which the firm operates in any one period. The long-run costs are *planning costs* or *ex ante costs*, in that they present the optimal possibilities for expansion of the output and thus help the entrepreneur *plan* his future activities. Before an investment is decided the entrepreneur is in a long-run situation, in the sense that he can choose any one of a wide range of alternative investments, defined by the state of technology. After the investment decision is taken and funds are tied up in fixed-capital equipment, the entrepreneur operates under short-run conditions: he is on a short-run cost curve.

A distinction is necessary between *internal (to the firm) economies of scale* and *external economies*. The internal economies are built into the shape of the long-run cost curve, because they accrue to the firm from its own action as it expands the level of its output. (See section II below.) The external economies arise outside the firm, from improvement (or deterioration) of the environment in which the firm operates. Such economies external to the firm may be realised from actions of other firms in the same or in another industry. The important characteristic of such economies is that they are independent of the actions of the firm, they are *external* to it. Their effect is a change in the prices of the factors employed by the firm (or in a reduction in the amount of inputs per unit of output), and thus cause a shift of the cost curves, both the short-run and the long-run.

In summary, while the internal economies of scale relate only to the long-run and are built into the shape of the long-run cost curve, the external economies affect the position of the cost curves: both the short-run and the long-run cost curves will shift if external economies affect the prices of the factors and/or the production function.

Any point on a cost curve shows the minimum cost at which a certain level of output may be produced. This is the *optimality* implied by the points of a cost curve. Usually the above optimality is associated with the long-run cost curve. However, a similar concept may be applied to the short-run, given the plant of the firm in any one period.

In the section II of this chapter we examine the traditional theory of U-shaped costs. In section III we examine some recent developments in the theory of costs which reject the strict U shape of the short-run cost curves on the grounds that its assumptions are not realistic, and question the 'envelope' long-run cost curve on the grounds that diseconomies are not a necessary consequence of large-scale operations.[1] In section V we examine the main types and sources of economies of scale. In section VI we summarise the available empirical evidence on the shape of the long-run and the short-run cost curves. Finally, in section VII we discuss briefly the relevance of the shape of cost curves in decision-making.

II. THE TRADITIONAL THEORY OF COST

Traditional theory distinguishes between the short run and the long run. The short run is the period during which some factor(s) is fixed; usually capital equipment and entrepreneurship are considered as fixed in the short run. The long run is the period over which all factors become variable.

---

[1] In section IV we discuss the engineering cost curves.

A. SHORT-RUN COSTS OF THE TRADITIONAL THEORY

In the traditional theory of the firm total costs are split into two groups: total fixed costs and total variable costs:

$$TC = TFC + TVC$$

The fixed costs include:
- (*a*) salaries of administrative staff
- (*b*) depreciation (wear and tear) of machinery
- (*c*) expenses for building depreciation and repairs
- (*d*) expenses for land maintenance and depreciation (if any).

Another element that may be treated in the same way as fixed costs is the normal profit, which is a lump sum including a percentage return on fixed capital and allowance for risk.

The variable costs include:
- (*a*) the raw materials
- (*b*) the cost of direct labour
- (*c*) the running expenses of fixed capital, such as fuel, ordinary repairs and routine maintenance.

The total fixed cost is graphically denoted by a straight line parallel to the output axis (figure 4.1). The total variable cost in the traditional theory of the firm has broadly an inverse-S shape (figure 4.2) which reflects the law of variable proportions. According to this law, at the initial stages of production with a given plant, as more of the variable factor(s) is employed, its productivity increases and the average variable cost falls.

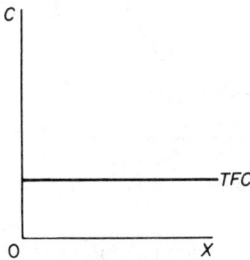

Figure 4.1

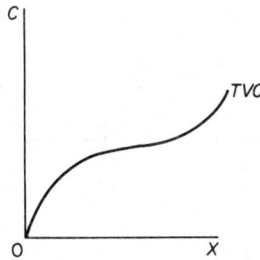

Figure 4.2

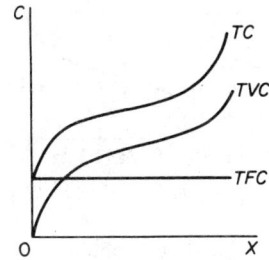

Figure 4.3

This continues until the optimal combination of the fixed and variable factors is reached. Beyond this point as increased quantities of the variable factor(s) are combined with the fixed factor(s) the productivity of the variable factor(s) declines (and the AVC rises). By adding the TFC and TVC we obtain the TC of the firm (figure 4.3). From the total-cost curves we obtain average-cost curves. The average fixed cost is found by dividing TFC by the level of output:

$$AFC = \frac{TFC}{X}$$

Graphically the AFC is a rectangular hyperbola, showing at all its points the same magnitude, that is, the level of TFC (figure 4.4). The average variable cost is similarly obtained by dividing the TVC with the corresponding level of output:

$$AVC = \frac{TVC}{X}$$

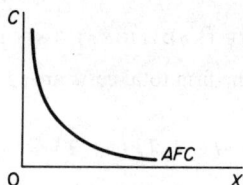

Figure 4.4

Graphically the *AVC* at each level of output is derived from the slope of a line drawn from the origin to the point on the *TVC* curve corresponding to the particular level of output. For example, in figure 4.5 the *AVC* at X_1 is the slope of the ray 0a, the *AVC* at X_2 is the slope of the ray 0b, and so on. It is clear from figure 4.5 that the slope of a ray through the origin declines continuously until the ray becomes tangent to the *TVC* curve at *c*. To the right of this point the slope of rays through the origin starts increasing. Thus the *SAVC* curve falls initially as the productivity of the variable factor(s) increases, reaches a minimum when the plant is operated optimally (with the optimal combination of fixed and variable factors), and rises beyond that point (figure 4.6).

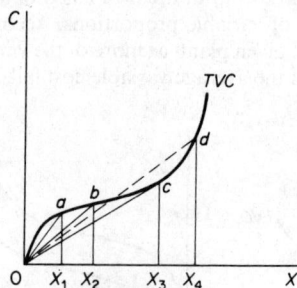

Figure 4.5

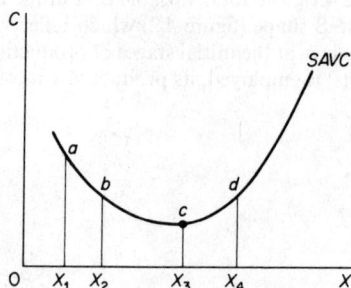

Figure 4.6

The *ATC* is obtained by dividing the *TC* by the corresponding level of output:

$$ATC = \frac{TC}{X} = \frac{TFC + TVC}{X} = AFC + AVC$$

Graphically the *ATC* curve is derived in the same way as the *SAVC*. The *ATC* at any level of output is the slope of the straight line from the origin to the point on the *TC* curve corresponding to that particular level of output (figure 4.7). The shape of the *ATC* is similar to that of the *AVC* (both being U-shaped). Initially the *ATC* declines, it reaches a minimum at the level of optimal operation of the plant (X_M) and subsequently rises again (figure 4.8). The U shape of both the *AVC* and the *ATC* reflects the *law of variable proportions* or *law of eventually decreasing returns* to the variable factor(s) of production (see Chapter 3). The marginal cost is defined as the change in *TC* which results from a unit change in output. Mathematically the marginal cost is the first derivative of the *TC* function. Denoting total cost by *C* and output by *X* we have

$$MC = \frac{\partial C}{\partial X}$$

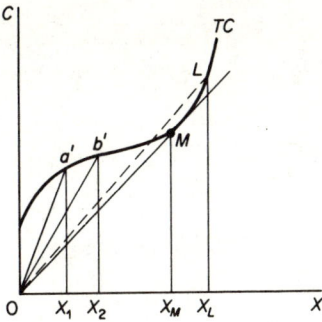

Figure 4.7

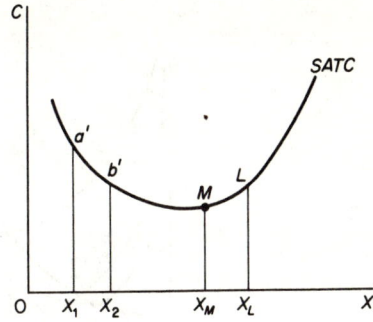

Figure 4.8

Graphically the MC is the slope of the TC curve (which of course is the same at any point as the slope of the TVC). The slope of a curve at any one of its points is the slope of the tangent at that point. With an inverse-S shape of the TC (and TVC) the MC curve will be U-shaped. In figure 4.9 we observe that the slope of the tangent to the total-cost curve declines gradually, until it becomes parallel to the X-axis (with its slope being equal to zero at this point), and then starts rising. Accordingly we picture the MC curve in figure 4.10 as U-shaped.

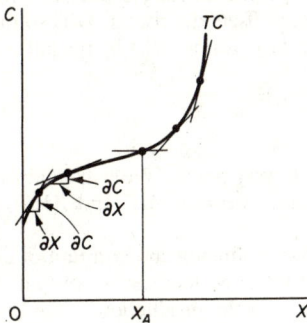

Figure 4.9

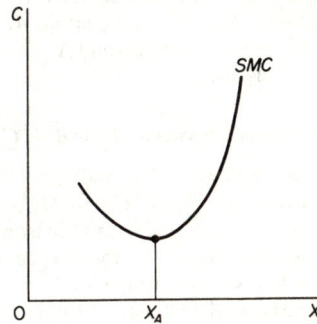

Figure 4.10

In summary: the traditional theory of costs postulates that in the short run the cost curves (AVC, ATC and MC) are U-shaped, reflecting the law of variable proportions. In the short run with a fixed plant there is a phase of increasing productivity (falling unit costs) and a phase of decreasing productivity (increasing unit costs) of the variable factor(s). Between these two phases of plant operation there is a *single point* at which unit costs are at a minimum. When this point on the $SATC$ is reached the plant is utilised optimally, that is, with the optimal combination (proportions) of fixed and variable factors.

The relationship between ATC and AVC

The AVC is a part of the ATC, given $ATC = AFC + AVC$. Both AVC and ATC are U-shaped, reflecting the law of variable proportions. However, the minimum point of the ATC occurs to the right of the minimum point of the AVC (figure 4.11). This is

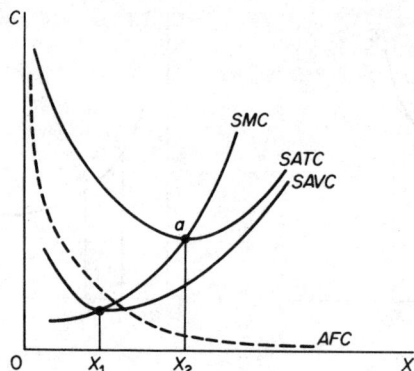

Figure 4.11

due to the fact that ATC includes AFC, and the latter falls continuously with increases in output. After the AVC has reached its lowest point and starts rising, its rise is over a certain range offset by the fall in the AFC, so that the ATC continues to fall (over that range) despite the increase in AVC. However, the rise in AVC eventually becomes greater than the fall in the AFC so that the ATC starts increasing. The AVC approaches the ATC asymptotically as X increases.

In figure 4.11 the minimum AVC is reached at X_1 while the ATC is at its minimum at X_2. Between X_1 and X_2 the fall in AFC more than offsets the rise in AVC so that the ATC continues to fall. Beyond X_2 the increase in AVC is not offset by the fall in AFC, so that ATC rises.

The relationship between MC and ATC

The MC cuts the ATC and the AVC at their lowest points. We will establish this relation only for the ATC and MC, but the relation between MC and AVC can be established on the same lines of reasoning.

We said that the MC is the change in the TC for producing an extra unit of output. Assume that we start from a level of n units of output. If we increase the output by one unit the MC is the change in total cost resulting from the production of the $(n + 1)^{th}$ unit.

The AC at each level of output is found by dividing TC by X. Thus the AC at the level of X_n is

$$AC_n = \frac{TC_n}{X_n}$$

and the AC at the level X_{n+1} is

$$AC_{n+1} = \frac{TC_{n+1}}{X_{n+1}}$$

Clearly

$$TC_{n+1} = TC_n + MC$$

Thus:

(a) If the MC of the $(n + 1)^{th}$ unit is less than AC_n (the AC of the previous n units) the AC_{n+1} will be smaller than the AC_n.

(b) If the MC of the $(n + 1)^{th}$ unit is higher than AC_n (the AC of the previous n units) the AC_{n+1} will be higher than the AC_n.

So long as the MC lies below the AC curve, it pulls the latter downwards; when the MC rises above the AC, it pulls the latter upwards. In figure 4.11 to the left of a the MC lies below the AC curve, and hence the latter falls downwards. To the right of a the MC curve lie above the AC curve, so that AC rises. It follows that at point a, where the intersection of the MC and AC occurs, the AC has reached its minimum level.[1]

B. LONG-RUN COSTS OF THE TRADITIONAL THEORY: THE 'ENVELOPE' CURVE

In the long run all factors are assumed to become variable. We said that the long-run cost curve is a *planning curve*, in the sense that it is a guide to the entrepreneur in his decision to plan the future expansion of his output.

The long-run average-cost curve is derived from short-run cost curves. Each point on the LAC corresponds to a point on a short-run cost curve, which is tangent to the LAC at that point. Let us examine in detail how the LAC is derived from the SRC curves.

Assume, as a first approximation, that the available technology to the firm at a particular point of time includes three methods of production, each with a different plant size: a small plant, medium plant and large plant. The small plant operates with costs denoted by the curve SAC_1, the medium-size plant operates with the costs on SAC_2 and the large-size plant gives rise to the costs shown on SAC_3 (figure 4.12). If the firm plans to produce output X_1 it will choose the small plant. If it plans to produce X_2 it will choose the medium plant. If it wishes to produce X_3 it will choose the large-size plant. If the firm starts with the small plant and its demand gradually increases, it will produce at lower costs (up to level X_1'). Beyond that point costs start increasing. If its demand reaches the level X_1'' the firm can either continue to produce with the small plant or it can install the medium-size plant. The decision at this point depends not on costs but on the firm's expectations about its future demand. If the firm expects that the demand will expand further than X_1'' it will install the medium plant, because

---

[1] The relationship between the MC and AC curves becomes clearer with the use of simple calculus. Given $C = zX$, where $z = AC$. Clearly $z = f(X)$. The MC is

$$\frac{\partial C}{\partial X} = \frac{\partial(zX)}{\partial X}$$

Applying the rule of differentiation of 'a function of a function' (which states that if $y = uv$, where $u = f_1(x)$ and $v = f_2(x)$, then $dy/dx = dy/du \cdot du/dx$), we obtain

$$MC = \frac{\partial C}{\partial X} = z\frac{\partial X}{\partial X} + X\frac{\partial z}{\partial X}$$

or

$$MC = AC + (X)(\text{slope of } AC)$$

Given that $AC > 0$ and $X > 0$, the following results emerge:
    (a) if (slope of AC) < 0, then $MC < AC$
    (b) if (slope of AC) > 0, then $MC > AC$
    (c) if (slope of AC) $= 0$, then $MC = AC$
The slope of the AC becomes zero at the minimum point of this curve (given that on theoretical grounds the AC curve is U-shaped). Hence $MC = AC$ at the minimum point of the average-cost curve.

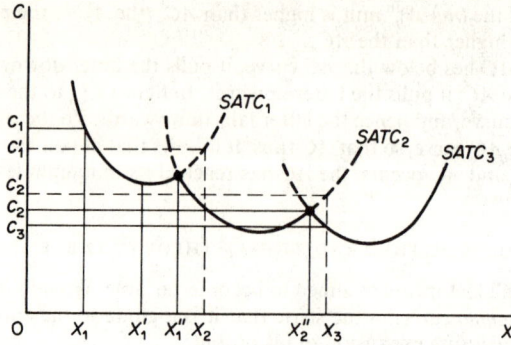

Figure 4.12

with this plant outputs larger than X_1'' are produced with a lower cost. Similar considerations hold for the decision of the firm when it reaches the level X_2''. If it expects its demand to stay constant at this level, the firm will not install the large plant, given that it involves a larger investment which is profitable only if demand expands beyond X_2''. For example, the level of output X_3 is produced at a cost c_3 with the large plant, while it costs c_2' if produced with the medium-size plant $(c_2' > c_3)$.

Now if we relax the assumption of the existence of only three plants and assume that the available technology includes many plant sizes, each suitable for a certain level of output, the points of intersection of consecutive plants (which are the crucial points for the decision of whether to switch to a larger plant) are more numerous. In the limit, if we assume that there is a very large number (infinite number) of plants, we obtain a continuous curve, which is the planning LAC curve of the firm. Each point of this curve shows the minimum (optimal) cost for producing the corresponding level of output. The LAC curve is the locus of points denoting the least cost of producing the corresponding output. It is a planning curve because on the basis of this curve the firm decides what plant to set up in order to produce optimally (at minimum cost) the expected level of output. The firm chooses the short-run plant which allows it to produce the anticipated (in the long run) output at the least possible cost. In the traditional theory of the firm the LAC curve is U-shaped and it is often called the 'envelope curve' because it 'envelopes' the SRC curves (figure 4.13).

Let us examine the U shape of the LAC. This shape reflects the *laws of returns to scale* (see Chapter 3). According to these laws the unit costs of production decrease as plant

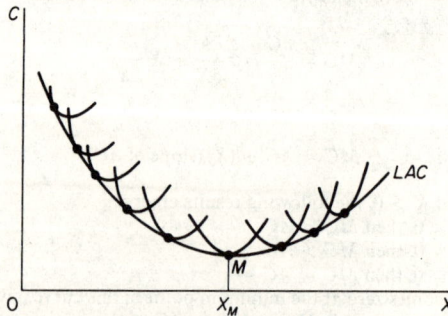

Figure 4.13

size increases, due to the economies of scale which the larger plant sizes make possible. The nature of economies of scale is discussed in section V below. The traditional theory of the firm assumes that economies of scale exist only up to a certain size of plant, which is known as the *optimum plant size*, because with this plant size all possible economies of scale are fully exploited. If the plant increases further than this optimum size there are diseconomies of scale, arising from managerial inefficiencies. It is argued that management becomes highly complex, managers are overworked and the decision-making process becomes less efficient. The turning-up of the *LAC* curve is due to managerial diseconomies of scale, since the technical diseconomies can be avoided by duplicating the optimum technical plant size (see section V).

A serious implicit assumption of the traditional U-shaped cost curves is that each plant size is designed *to produce optimally a single level of output* (e.g. 1000 units of X). Any departure from that X, no matter how small (e.g. an increase by 1 unit of X) leads to increased costs. The plant is completely inflexible. There is no reserve capacity, not even to meet seasonal variations in demand. As a consequence of this assumption the *LAC* curve 'envelopes' the *SRAC*. Each point of the *LAC* is a point of tangency with the corresponding *SRAC* curve. The point of tangency occurs to the falling part of the *SRAC* curves for points lying to the left of the minimum point of the *LAC*: since the slope of the *LAC* is negative up to M (figure 4.13) the slope of the *SRAC* curves must also be negative, since at the point of their tangency the two curves have the same slope. The point of tangency for outputs larger than X_M occurs to the rising part of the *SRAC* curves: since the *LAC* rises, the *SAC* must rise at the point of their tangency with the *LAC*. Only at the minimum point M of the *LAC* is the corresponding *SAC* also at a minimum. Thus at the falling part of the *LAC* the plants are not worked to full capacity; to the rising part of the *LAC* the plants are overworked; only at the minimum point M is the (short-run) plant optimally employed.

We stress once more the optimality implied by the *LAC* planning curve: each point represents the least unit-cost for producing the corresponding level of output. Any point above the *LAC* is inefficient in that it shows a higher cost for producing the corresponding level of output. Any point below the *LAC* is economically desirable because it implies a lower unit-cost, but it is not attainable in the current state of technology and with the prevailing market prices of factors of production. (Recall that each cost curve is drawn under a *ceteris paribus* clause, which implies given state of technology and given factor prices.)

The long-run marginal cost is derived from the *SRMC* curves, but does not 'envelope' them. The *LRMC* is formed from points of intersection of the *SRMC* curves with vertical lines (to the X-axis) drawn from the points of tangency of the corresponding *SAC* curves and the *LRA* cost curve (figure 4.14). The *LMC* must be equal to the *SMC* for the output at which the corresponding *SAC* is tangent to the *LAC*. For levels of X to the left of tangency a the $SAC > LAC$. At the point of tangency $SAC = LAC$. As we move from point a' to a, we actually move from a position of inequality of *SRAC* and *LRAC* to a position of equality. Hence the change in total cost (i.e. the *MC*) must be smaller for the short-run curve than for the long-run curve. Thus $LMC > SMC$ to the left of a. For an increase in output beyond X_1 (e.g. X_1'') the $SAC > LAC$. That is, we move from the position a of equality of the two costs to the position b where SAC is greater than LAC. Hence the addition to total cost ($=MC$) must be larger for the short-run curve than for the long-run curve. Thus $LMC < SMC$ to the right of a.

Since to the left of a, $LMC > SMC$, and to the right of a, $LMC < SMC$, it follows that at a, $LMC = SMC$. If we draw a vertical line from a to the X-axis the point at which it intersects the *SMC* (point A for SAC_1) is a point of the *LMC*.

If we repeat this procedure for all points of tangency of *SRAC* and *LAC* curves to the left of the minimum point of the *LAC*, we obtain points of the section of the *LMC*

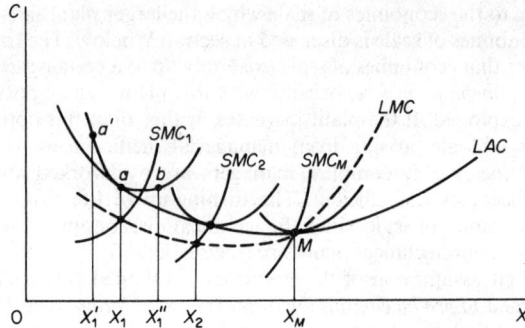

Figure 4.14

which lies below the *LAC*. At the minimum point M the *LMC* intersects the *LAC*. To the right of M the *LMC* lies above the *LAC* curve. At point M we have

$$SAC_M = SMC_M = LAC = LMC$$

There are various mathematical forms which give rise to U-shaped unit cost curves. The simplest total cost function which would incorporate the law of variable proportions is the cubic polynomial

$$C = \underbrace{b_0}_{TC \,=\, TFC \,+} + \underbrace{b_1 X - b_2 X^2 + b_3 X^3}_{TVC}$$

The *AVC* is

$$AVC = \frac{TVC}{X} = b_1 - b_2 X + b_3 X^2$$

The *MC* is

$$MC = \frac{\partial C}{\partial X} = b_1 - 2b_2 X + 3b_3 X^2$$

The *ATC* is

$$\frac{C}{X} = \frac{b_0}{X} + b_1 - b_2 X + b_3 X^2$$

The *TC* curve is roughly S-shaped (figure 4.3), while the *ATC*, the *AVC* and the *MC* are all U-shaped; the *MC* curve intersects the other two curves at their minimum points (figure 4.11).

III. MODERN THEORY OF COSTS

The U-shaped cost curves of the traditional theory have been questioned by various writers both on theoretical *a priori* and on empirical grounds. As early as 1939 George Stigler[1] suggested that the short-run average variable cost has a flat stretch over a range of output which reflects the fact that firms build plants with some flexibility in their

[1] G. Stigler, 'Production and Distribution in the Short Run', *Journal of Political Economy* (1939). Reprinted in *Readings in the Theory of Income Distribution* (American Economic Association) (Blakiston, 1946).

productive capacity. The reasons for this reserve capacity have been discussed in detail by various economists.[1]

The shape of the long-run cost curve has attracted greater attention in economic literature, due probably to the serious policy implications of the economies of large-scale production (see section VII below). Several reasons have been put forward to explain why the long-run cost curve is L-shaped rather than U-shaped.[2] It has been argued that managerial diseconomies can be avoided by the improved methods of modern management science, and even when they appear (at very large scales of output) they are insignificant relative to the technical (production) economies of large plants, so that the total costs per unit of output fall, at least over the scales which have been operated in the real industrial world.

There is growing empirical evidence in support of the above shapes of costs (see section VI below). In view of this accumulating evidence it is surprising to see that several economists are still sceptical,[3] and that even the most recently published microeconomic textbooks[4] are still based on predominantly U-shaped cost curves.[5]

Like the traditional theory, modern microeconomics distinguishes between short-run and long-run costs.

A. SHORT-RUN COSTS IN THE MODERN MICROECONOMIC THEORY

As in the traditional theory, short-run costs are distinguished into average variable costs (AVC) and average fixed costs (AFC).

The average fixed cost

This is the cost of indirect factors, that is, the cost of the physical and personal organisation of the firm. The fixed costs include the costs for:

(a) the salaries and other expenses of administrative staff

(b) the salaries of staff involved directly in the production, but paid on a fixed-term basis

(c) the wear and tear of machinery (standard depreciation allowances)

(d) the expenses for maintenance of buildings

(e) the expenses for the maintenance of land on which the plant is installed and operates.

The 'planning' of the plant (or the firm) consists in deciding the 'size' of these fixed, indirect factors, which determine the size of the plant, because they set limits to its

[1] See, for example, P. W. S. Andrews, *Manufacturing Business* (Macmillan, 1949). Also R. Harrod, *Economic Essays* (Macmillan, 1952); P. J. D. Wiles, *Price Cost and Output* (Blackwell, 1961).

[2] Sargent Florence, *The Logic of British and American Industry* (Routledge & Kegan Paul, 1953). See also P. W. S. Andrews, *Manufacturing Business* (Macmillan, 1949) and P. J. D. Wiles, *Price, Cost and Output* (Blackwell, 1961).

[3] C. A. Smith, 'Survey of Empirical Evidence on Economies of Scale', reprinted in G. C. Archibald (ed.), *Readings in the Theory of the Firm* (Penguin, 1971).

M. Friedman, 'Comment', Universities National Bureau Committee for Economics Research, *Business Concentration and Price Policy* (Princeton University Press, 1955); reprinted in G. C. Archibald (ed.), *Readings in the Theory of the Firm* (Penguin, 1971).

A. Silberston, 'Economies of Scale in Theory and Practice', *Economic Journal* (1972); reprinted in *Readings in Applied Microeconomics*, L. Wagner and N. Valtazzis (eds.) (Oxford University Press, 1973).

[4] A notable exception is K. Lancaster's textbook *Introduction to Modern Microeconomics* (Rand-McNally, 1969).

[5] See C. J. Hawkins, *Theory of the Firm* (Macmillan, 1973).

production. (Direct factors such as labour and raw materials are assumed not to set limits on size; the firm can acquire them easily from the market without any time lag.) The businessman will start his planning with a figure for the level of output which he anticipates selling, and he will choose the size of plant which will allow him to produce this level of output more efficiently and with the maximum flexibility. The plant will have a capacity larger than the 'expected average' level of sales, because the businessman wants to have some *reserve capacity* for various reasons:[1]

The businessman will want to be able to meet seasonal and cyclical fluctuations in his demand. Such fluctuations, cannot always be met efficiently by a stock-inventory policy. Reserve capacity will allow the entrepreneur to work with more shifts and with lower costs than a stock-piling policy.

Reserve capacity will give the businessman greater flexibility for repairs of broken-down machinery without disrupting the smooth flow of the production process.

The entrepreneur will want to have more freedom to increase his output if demand increases. All businessmen hope for growth. In view of anticipated increases in demand the entrepreneur builds some reserve capacity, because he would not like to let all new demand go to his rivals, as this may endanger his future hold on the market. It also gives him some flexibility for minor alterations of his product, in view of changing tastes of customers.

Technology usually makes it necessary to build into the plant some reserve capacity. Some basic types of machinery (e.g. a turbine) may not be technically fully employed when combined with other small types of machines in certain numbers, more of which may not be required, given the specific size of the chosen plant. Also such basic machinery may be difficult to install due to time-lags in the acquisition. The entrepreneurs will thus buy from the beginning such a 'basic' machine which allows the highest flexibility, in view of future growth in demand, even though this is a more expensive alternative now. Furthermore some machinery may be so specialised as to be available only to order, which takes time. In this case such machinery will be bought in excess of the minimum required at present numbers, as a reserve.

Some reserve capacity will always be allowed in the land and buildings, since expansion of operations may be seriously limited if new land or new buildings have to be acquired.

Finally, there will be some reserve capacity on the 'organisational and administrative' level. The administrative staff will be hired at such numbers as to allow some increase in the operations of the firm.

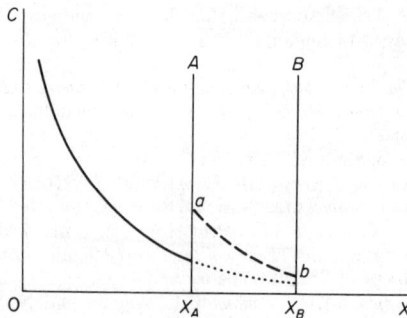

Figure 4.15

[1] See P. W. S. Andrews, *Manufacturing Business* (Macmillan, 1949).

In summary, the businessman will not necessarily choose the plant which will give him *today* the lowest cost, but rather that equipment which will allow him the greatest possible flexibility, for minor alterations of his product or his technique.

Under these conditions the *AFC* curve will be as in figure 4.15. The firm has some 'largest-capacity' units of machinery which set an absolute limit to the short-run expansion of output (boundary *B* in figure 4.15).[1] The firm has also small-unit machinery, which sets a limit to expansion (boundary *A* in figure 4.15). This, however, is not an absolute boundary, because the firm can increase its output in the short run (until the absolute limit *B* is encountered), *either* by paying overtime to direct labour for working longer hours (in this case the *AFC* is shown by the dotted line in figure 4.15), *or* by buying some additional small-unit types of machinery (in this case the *AFC* curve shifts upwards, and starts falling again, as shown by the line *ab* in figure 4.15).

The average variable cost

As in the traditional theory, the average variable cost of modern microeconomics includes the cost of:

(*a*) direct labour which varies with output
(*b*) raw materials
(*c*) running expenses of machinery.

The *SAVC* in modern theory has a saucer-type shape, that is, it is broadly U-shaped but has a flat stretch over a range of output (figure 4.16). The flat stretch corresponds to the built-in-the-plant reserve capacity. Over this stretch the *SAVC* is equal to the *MC*, both being constant per unit of output. To the left of the flat stretch, *MC* lies below the *SAVC*, while to the right of the flat stretch the *MC* rises above the *SAVC*. The falling part of the *SAVC* shows the reduction in costs due to the better utilisation of the fixed factor and the consequent increase in skills and productivity of the variable factor (labour). With better skills the wastes in raw materials are also being reduced and a better utilisation of the whole plant is reached.

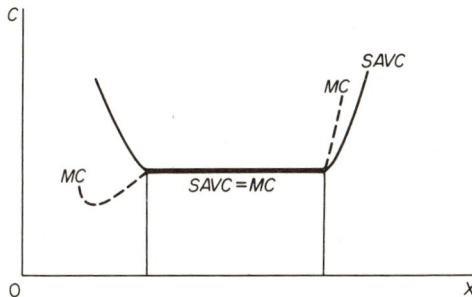

Figure 4.16

The increasing part of the *SAVC* reflects reduction in labour productivity due to the longer hours of work, the increase in cost of labour due to overtime payment (which is higher than the current wage), the wastes in materials and the more frequent breakdown of machinery as the firm operates with overtime or with more shifts.

The innovation of modern microeconomics in this field is the theoretical establishment of a short-run *SAVC* curve with a flat stretch over a certain range of output. The

[1] See Andrews, *Manufacturing Business.*

reserve capacity makes it possible to have constant *SAVC* within a certain *range of output* (figure 4.18). It should be clear that this reserve capacity is planned in order to give the maximum flexibility in the operation of the firm. It is completely different from the *excess capacity* which arises with the U-shaped costs of the traditional theory of the firm. The traditional theory assumes that each plant is designed without any flexibility; it is designed to produce optimally only a single level of output (X_M in figure 4.17). If the firm produces an output X smaller than X_M there is excess (unplanned) capacity, equal to the difference $X_M - X$. This excess capacity is obviously undesirable because it leads to higher unit costs.

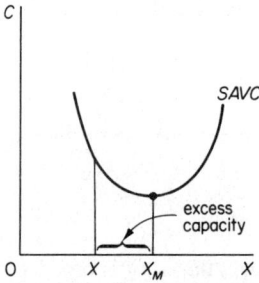
Figure 4.17

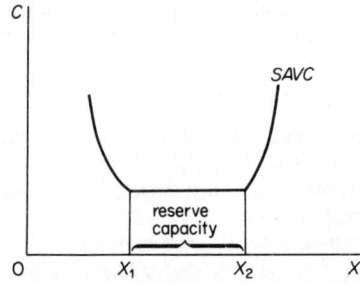
Figure 4.18

In the modern theory of costs the range of output $X_1 X_2$ in figure 4.18 reflects the planned reserve capacity which does not lead to increases in costs. The firm anticipates using its plant sometimes closer to X_1 and at others closer to X_2. On the average the entrepreneur expects to operate his plant within the $X_1 X_2$ range. Usually firms consider that the 'normal' level of utilisation of their plant is somewhere between two-thirds and three-quarters of their capacity, that is, at a point closer to X_2 than to X_1. The level of utilisation of the plant which firms consider as 'normal' is called 'the load factor' of the plant (see p. 121).

The average total cost

The average total cost is obtained by adding the average fixed (inclusive of the normal profit) and the average variable costs at each level of output. The *ATC* is shown in

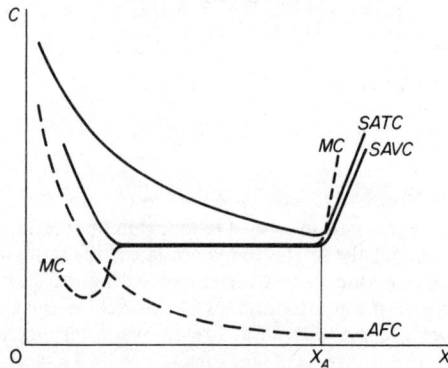
Figure 4.19

figure 4.19. The ATC curve falls continuously up to the level of output (X_2) at which the reserve capacity is exhausted. Beyond that level ATC will start rising. The MC will intersect the average total-cost curve at its minimum point (which occurs to the right of the level of output X_A, at which the flat stretch of the AVC ends).

The composition of the short-run total costs may be schematically presented as follows:

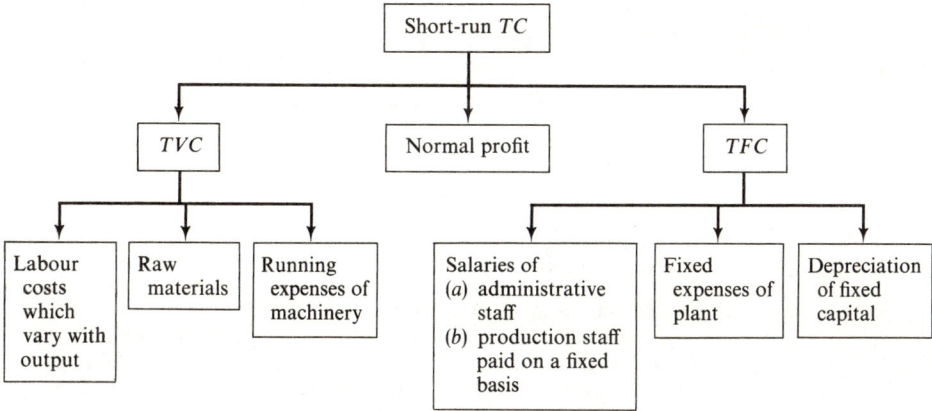

```
                        ┌──────────────┐
                        │  Short-run TC │
                        └──────────────┘
          ┌────────────────────┼────────────────────┐
      ┌───────┐         ┌──────────────┐         ┌───────┐
      │  TVC  │         │ Normal profit │         │  TFC  │
      └───────┘         └──────────────┘         └───────┘
```

| Labour costs which vary with output | Raw materials | Running expenses of machinery | Salaries of (a) administrative staff (b) production staff paid on a fixed basis | Fixed expenses of plant | Depreciation of fixed capital |

Mathematically the cost–output relation may be written in the form

$$C = \underbrace{b_0}_{} + \underbrace{b_1 X}_{}$$
$$TC = TFC + TVC$$

The TC is a straight line with a positive slope over the range of reserve capacity (figure 4.20).

The AFC is a rectangular hyperbola

$$AFC = \frac{b_0}{X}$$

The AVC is a straight line parallel to the output axis

$$AVC = \frac{(b_1 X)}{X} = b_1$$

The ATC is falling over the range of reserve capacity

$$ATC = \frac{b_0}{X} + b_1$$

The MC is a straight line which coincides with the AVC

$$\frac{\partial C}{\partial X} = b_1$$

Thus over the range of reserve capacity we have $MC = AVC = b_1$, while the ATC falls continuously over this range (figure 4.21). Note that the above total-cost function does not extend to the increasing part of costs, that is, it does not apply to ranges of output beyond the reserve capacity of the firm.

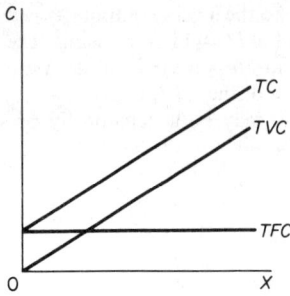

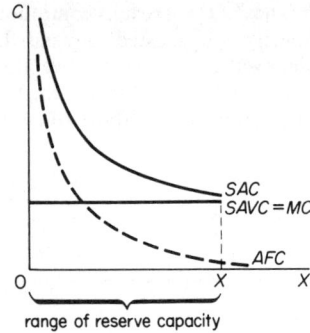

range of reserve capacity

Figure 4.20   Figure 4.21

B. LONG-RUN COSTS IN MODERN MICROECONOMIC THEORY: THE 'L-SHAPED' SCALE CURVE

These are distinguished into *production costs* and *managerial costs*. All costs are variable in the long run and they give rise to a long-run cost curve which is roughly L-shaped. The production costs fall continuously with increases in output. At very large scales of output managerial costs may rise. But the fall in production costs more than offsets the increase in the managerial costs, so that the total *LAC* falls with increases in scale.

Production costs

Production costs fall steeply to begin with and then gradually as the scale of production increases. The L-shape of the production cost curve is explained by the technical economies of large-scale production. Initially these economies are substantial, but after a certain level of output is reached all or most of these economies are attained and the firm is said to have reached the *minimum optimal scale*, given the technology of the industry. If new techniques are invented for larger scales of output, they must be cheaper to operate. But even with the existing known techniques some economies can always be achieved at larger outputs:

    (*a*) economies from further decentralisation and improvement in skills;

    (*b*) lower repairs costs may be attained if the firm reaches a certain size;

    (*c*) the firm, especially if it is multiproduct, may well undertake itself the production of some of the materials or equipment which it needs instead of buying them from other firms.

Managerial costs

In the modern management science for each plant size there is a corresponding organisational-administrative set-up appropriate for the smooth operating of that plant. There are various levels of management, each with its appropriate kind of management technique. Each management technique is applicable to a *range* of output. There are small-scale as well as large-scale organisational techniques. The costs of different techniques of management first fall up to a certain plant size. At very large scales of output managerial costs may rise, but very slowly.

In summary: Production costs fall smoothly at very large scales, while managerial costs may rise only slowly at very large scales. Modern theorists seem to accept that the fall in technical costs more than offsets the probable rise of managerial costs, so that the *LRAC* curve falls smoothly or remains constant at very large scales of output.

We may draw the *LAC* implied by the modern theory of costs as follows. For each short-run period we obtain the *SRAC* which includes production costs, administration costs, other fixed costs and an allowance for normal profit. Assume that we have a technology with four plant sizes, with costs falling as size increases. We said that in business practice it is customary to consider that a plant is used 'normally' when it operates at a level between two-thirds and three-quarters of capacity.[1] Bain writes:

> The plant or firm will have a somewhat fluctuating output, over time, and at a given scale will thus operate at a number of somewhat different output rates. Correspondingly, it will have a certain 'load factor' reflecting the ratio of average actual rate of use to the capacity or best rate of use, and this load factor will generally be smaller than one. In this circumstance, the relevant relationship of unit cost to scale is that which prevails when it is assumed that each alternative scale of plant or firm is operated subject to prevailing or anticipated market fluctuations, and is thus subject to a resultant *typical load factor* on its capacity. The long-run average unit cost of each alternative scale should be calculated on this assumption, and conclusions as to minimum optimal scales and shapes of such curves should be derived accordingly.[2]

Following this procedure, and assuming that the typical load factor of each plant is two-thirds of its full capacity (limit capacity), we may draw the *LAC* curve by joining the points on the *SATC* curves corresponding to the two-thirds of the full capacity of each plant size. If we assume that there is a very large number of available plant sizes the *LAC* curve will be continuous (figure 4.22). The characteristic of this *LAC* curve is that (*a*) it does not turn up at very large scales of output; (*b*) it is not the envelope of the *SATC* curves, but rather intersects them (at the level of output defined by the 'typical load factor' of each plant). If, as some writers believe,[3] the *LAC* falls continuously (though smoothly at very large scales of output), the *LMC* will lie below the *LAC* at all scales (figure 4.23). If there is a *minimum optimal scale of plant* ($\bar{x}$ in figure 4.24) at

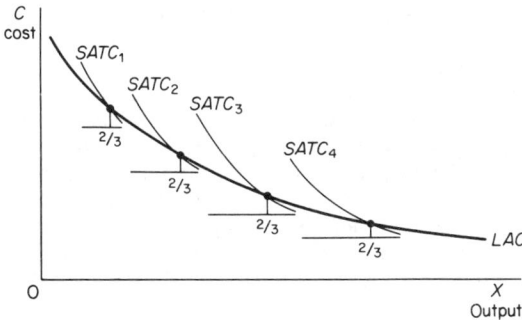

Figure 4.22

[1] See R. W. Clower and J. F. Due, *Microeconomics* (Irwin–Dorsey, 1972) p. 232.
[2] J. S. Bain, *Barriers to New Competition* (Harvard University Press, Cambridge, Mass., 1956) p. 63.
[3] See, for example, Andrews, *Manufacturing Business* (Macmillan, 1949).

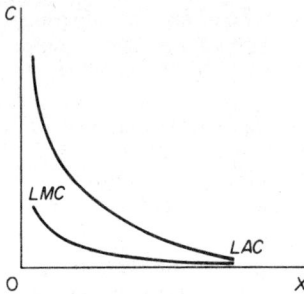

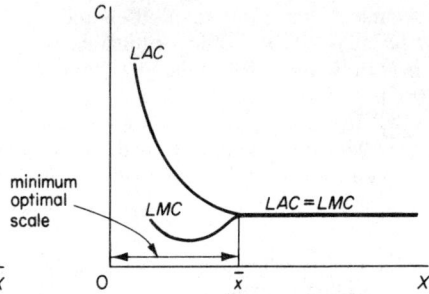

Figure 4.23   Figure 4.24

which all possible scale economies are reaped (as Bain and other writers have suggested), beyond that scale the *LAC* remains constant. In this case the *LMC* lies below
the *LAC* until the minimum optimal scale is reached, and coincides with the *LAC*
beyond that level of output (figure 4.24). The above shapes of costs are more realistic
than the U-shaped costs of traditional theory. As we will see in section VI, most of the
empirical studies on cost have provided evidence which substantiates the hypotheses of
a flat-bottomed *SAVC* and of an L-shaped *LAC*.

IV. ENGINEERING COST CURVES

Engineering costs are derived from engineering production functions.[1] Each productive method is divided into sub-activities corresponding to the various physical-technical
phases of production for the particular commodity. For each phase the quantities of
factors of production are estimated and finally the cost of each phase is calculated on the
basis of the prevailing factor prices. The total cost of the particular method of production
is the sum of the costs of its different phases.

Such calculations are done for all available plant sizes. Production isoquants are
subsequently estimated, and from them, given the factor prices, the short-run and the
long-run cost functions may be derived.

It should be noted that engineering production functions and the cost functions
derived from them refer usually to the production costs and do not include the administrative costs for the operation of any given plant.[2]

Engineering production functions are characterised by a limited number of methods
of production. The production isoquants are kinked (see Chapter 3), reflecting the fact
that factor substitutability is not continuous, but limited. Substitution of factors occurs
directly at the kinks of the isoquants, where one production technique is substituted
for another (figure 4.25). On the straight segments of the production isoquant a combination of the adjacent methods of production is employed. What happens in engineering
production functions along the segments of the isoquants is an indirect substitution of
factors via substitution of processes.

Factors cannot be substituted for each other except by changing the levels at which entire
technical processes are used, because each process uses factors in fixed characteristic ratios.[3]

[1] See H. Chenery, 'Engineering Production Functions', *Quarterly Journal of Economics*
(1949) pp. 507–31.
[2] See section VI below.
[3] See R. Dorfmann, 'Mathematical or Linear Programming', *American Economic Review*
(1953) p. 803.

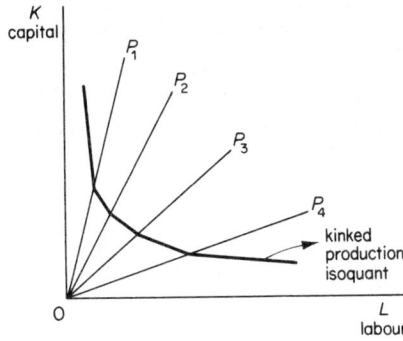

Figure 4.25

Engineering production functions are the basis of linear programming. In this approach process substitution plays a role analogous to that of factor substitution in conventional analysis.

Assume that there are two methods of production, P_1 and P_2, using labour and capital at a fixed ratio, denoted by the slopes of the rays representing the two processes (figure 4.26). With capital fixed at $\bar{K}$ the firm can produce only X_1 (with the one or the other method, depending on the ratio of factor prices, w/r). Part of the capital would remain unused (ab, if P_1 is used, and cd if P_2 is chosen). However, the firm can reach a higher level of production X_2 by a combination of P_1 and P_2, which would allow the full use of $\bar{K}$. Assume that the factor prices are w and r, so that P_1 is chosen initially and output X_1 is produced, with ab of capital unemployed. The firm will be better off by using a combination of the two methods. Thus at point e (where $\bar{K}$ intersects the higher isoquant X_2) all $\bar{K}$ is employed. P_1 and P_2 are used at the levels $0A$ and $0B$ respectively, these levels being determined by drawing parallel lines to P_1 and P_2 through e.[1] A substitution of factors has become indirectly possible (the K/L is defined by the slope of $0e$), although $\bar{K}$ is given and the available technology does not allow substitution of K and L except by change of technique. What happens at e is a substitution of processes: instead of using P_1 or P_2 alone to produce X_2, we achieve the same result (X_2) by using a combination of P_1 and P_2. Actually, given $\bar{K}$ and given the price ratio w/r, the output X_2 is technically

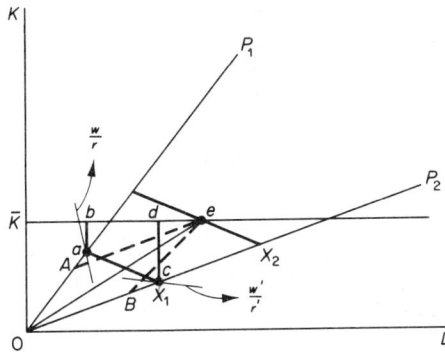

Figure 4.26

[1] See J. Johnston, *Statistical Cost Analysis* (McGraw-Hill, 1960).

impossible to produce by using only P_1, while X_2 is not economically profitable to produce by using only P_2 (given w/r), although with this process the level X_2 is technically possible, since $\bar{K}$ does not limit effectively the production of X_2, when P_2 is employed.

We turn now to the shape of total- and unit-cost curves when there are only a few processes available. The assumptions are that the prices of factors are given and the technology gives rise to kinked isoquants.

A. SHORT-RUN ENGINEERING COSTS

It is assumed that there is a fixed factor of production which requires a minimum outlay, and that there is some reserve capacity in the plant. The total-cost curve under these assumptions will be as in figure 4.27.

For the range $0X_1$ the TC is formed from linear segments, with the slope of each segment constant, but increasing for successive segments. The ends of linear segments correspond to outputs at which one process is replaced by another.

(a) Along each linear segment the slope is the MC. Along the first segment (AB) the $MC = AVC$. For each successive section (that is, for sections BC and CD) the $MC > AVC$. The marginal cost increases step-wise while the AVC increases smoothly, at a decreasing rate.

(b) The AC falls continuously over the range $ABCD$. We said that the AC is the slope of the rays from the origin to any point on the TC curve. The slope of such rays declines as we move from A to B to C to D (figure 4.27).

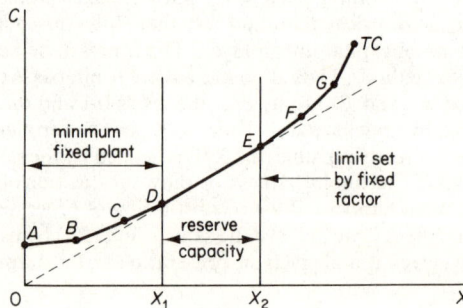

Figure 4.27

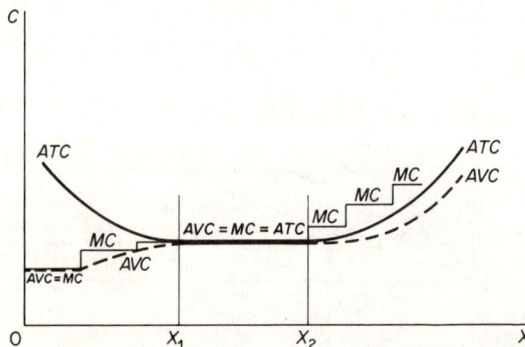

Figure 4.28

Over the range of reserve capacity the slope of total cost is constant. Furthermore this segment of TC lies on a line through the origin, reflecting the fact that only the TVC varies in proportion to output, while the fixed outlay has already been paid at the installation of the plant. The reserve capacity built into the plant allows the firm to operate by increasing only its variable costs proportionally with output. Thus over the reserve capacity segment the AVC, the MC and the ATC are equal and remain constant (between X_1 and X_2 in figure 4.28).

Once all reserve capacity is exhausted, output can be increased by overworking of the plant and paying overtime labour. The total-cost curve consists of linear segments, with each segment having a steeper slope than the previous one. Along each linear segment marginal cost is constant, but the level of marginal cost increases step-wise. The AVC increases continuously, but is lower than the MC. The average total cost increases continuously and lies below the MC but above the AVC.

The short-run engineering-cost curves are shown in figure 4.28.

B. LONG-RUN ENGINEERING COSTS

We said that the engineering costs include generally only the technical cost of production. Thus diseconomies of large scale, which are associated with administration costs, are not encountered here.

There is a minimum optimal size of plant for each production process. The TC, AC and MC are shown in figures 4.29 and 4.30. If we assume that there is a very large

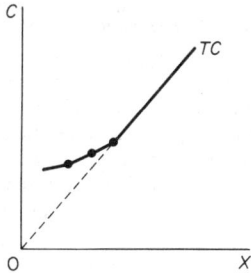

Figure 4.29

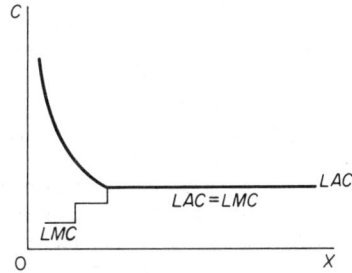

Figure 4.30

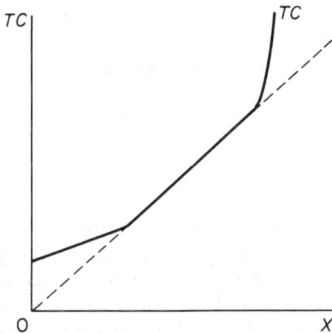

Figure 4.31 Short-run total costs with reserve capacity

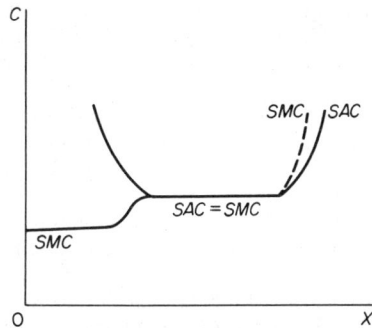

Figure 4.32 Short-run unit costs with reserve capacity

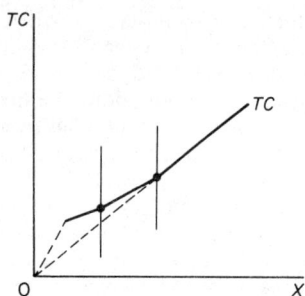

Figure 4.33   Long-run total costs
without diseconomies of scale

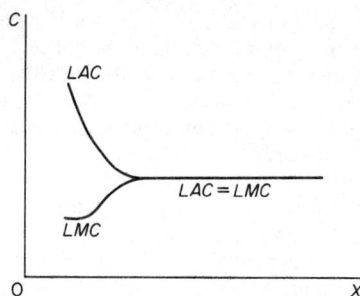

Figure 4.34   Long-run unit costs
without diseconomies of scale

number of processes, the total and unit cost curves become continuous (smooth) but retain broadly the above shapes, provided that there is a minimum fixed outlay and some reserve capacity in the short run (figures 4.31 and 4.32). In the long run the *LAC* will not turn upwards if we are considering only production costs; but if we add the administrative costs and if there are strong managerial diseconomies, the *LAC* will rise at very large scales of output (figures 4.33 and 4.34).

V. THE ANALYSIS OF ECONOMIES OF SCALE

In this section we will discuss in some detail the nature of the internal economies of scale, that is, economies which arise from the firm increasing its plant size.

We will concentrate on the economies which may be achieved within a particular plant. However, economies of scale may also arise from an increase in the *number of plants* of a firm, irrespective of whether the firm continues to produce the same product in the new plants or diversifies. In general, such *inter-plant economies of scale* are of the same nature as the single-plant (intra-plant) economies, although the importance of each type of scale economies may be different with an increase of the scale of operations of the firm via the installation of additional plants.

It is important to stress once more that the scale economies determine the shape of the *LRAC* curve (the 'scale curve' as this is often called), while the position of this curve depends on external economies such as a change in technology (improvement in techniques) and changes of factor prices in the industry or the economy as a whole. Changes in these external economies will result in a shift of the *LRAC*.

Firstly we will present the various types of economies of scale and their causes. Subsequently we will examine the possibility of negative economies (diseconomies) as the plant grows beyond a certain size.

There are various possible classifications of economies of scale. We will adopt the classification which is shown schematically in figure 4.35.

Economies of scale are distinguished into *real economies* and strictly *pecuniary economies* of scale.

Pecuniary economies are economies realised from paying lower prices for the factors used in the production and distribution of the product, due to bulk-buying by the firm as its size increases. Such strictly monetary economies do not imply an actual decrease in the quantity of inputs used but accrue to the firm from lower prices paid for raw materials (bought at a discount due to the large volume of the purchase), lower interest rates (and lower cost of finance in general) as the size of the firm increases, or lower wages and salaries. Lower wages are rare and can result only if the firm becomes so

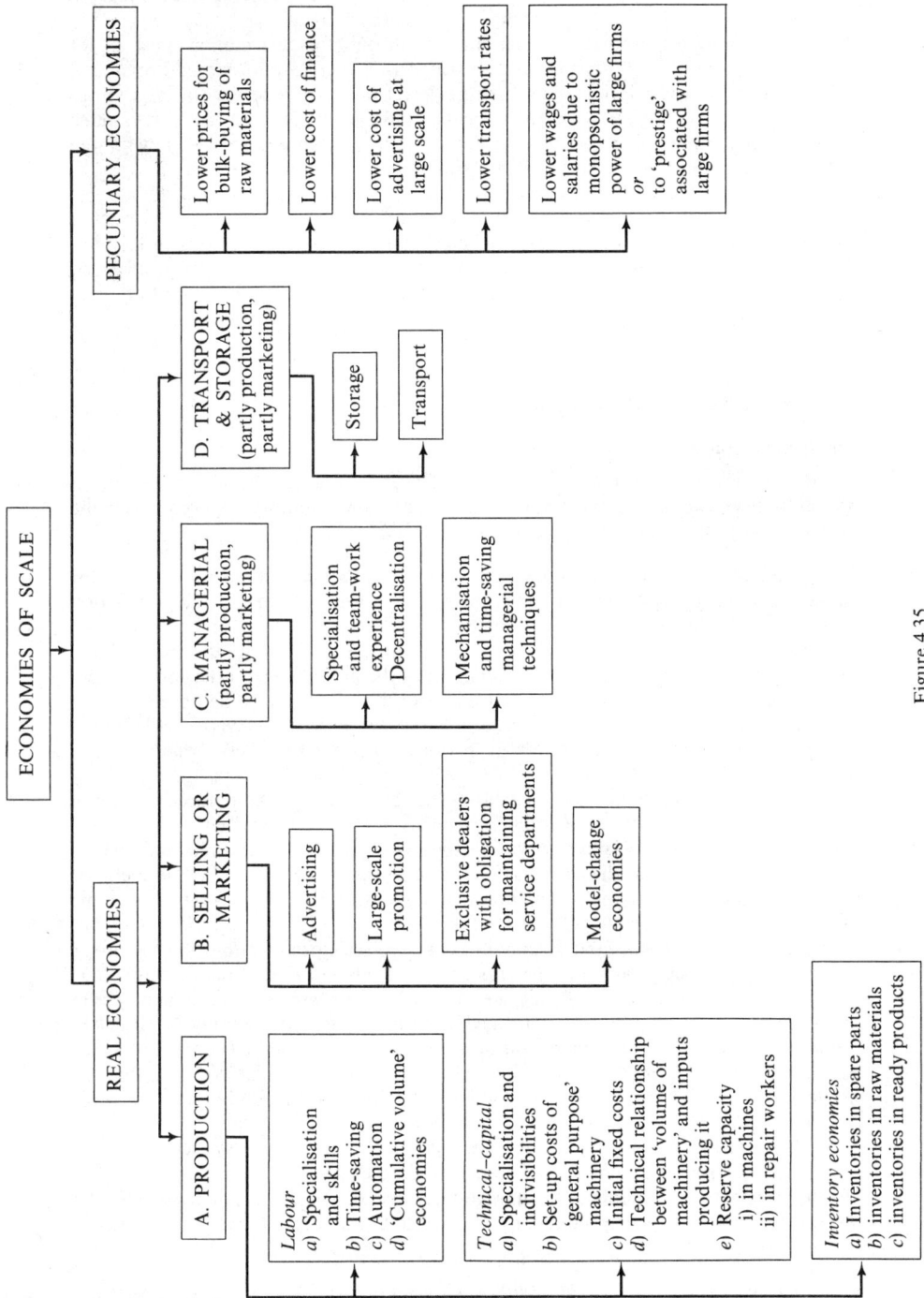

ECONOMIES OF SCALE

REAL ECONOMIES

PECUNIARY ECONOMIES

A. PRODUCTION

Labour
a) Specialisation and skills
b) Time-saving
c) Automation
d) 'Cumulative volume' economies

Technical–capital
a) Specialisation and indivisibilities
b) Set-up costs of 'general purpose' machinery
c) Initial fixed costs
d) Technical relationship between 'volume of machinery' and inputs producing it
e) Reserve capacity
   i) in machines
   ii) in repair workers

Inventory economies
a) Inventories in spare parts
b) inventories in raw materials
c) inventories in ready products

B. SELLING OR MARKETING

Advertising

Large-scale promotion

Exclusive dealers with obligation for maintaining service departments

Model-change economies

C. MANAGERIAL (partly production, partly marketing)

Specialisation and team-work experience
Decentralisation

Mechanisation and time-saving managerial techniques

D. TRANSPORT & STORAGE (partly production, partly marketing)

Storage

Transport

PECUNIARY ECONOMIES

Lower prices for bulk-buying of raw materials

Lower cost of finance

Lower cost of advertising at large scale

Lower transport rates

Lower wages and salaries due to monopsonistic power of large firms *or* to 'prestige' associated with large firms

Figure 4.35

large as to acquire the power of a labour monopsonist or near-monopsonist, as for example some mining companies, and provided that there are no srongly organised labour unions. Lower salaries (and sometimes lower wages) may be paid by larger firms if there is some 'prestige' associated with the employment by such firms. It is often observed that employees prefer to work for a larger firm whose name is known, even if they could earn more by working for a small unknown firm.

Real economies are those associated with a reduction in the physical quantity of inputs, raw materials, various types of labour and various types of capital (fixed or circulating capital). We may distinguish the following main types of real economies: (i) production economies, (ii) selling or marketing economies, (iii) managerial economies, (iv) transport and storage economies. Clearly the last two categories are partly production and partly selling costs. Their presentation in distinct groups facilitates their analysis.

A. REAL ECONOMIES OF SCALE

Production economies of scale

Production economies may arise from the factor 'labour' (labour economies), from the factor fixed capital (technical economies), or from the inventory requirements of the firm (inventory economies or stochastic economies).

Labour economies. Labour economies are achieved as the scale of output increases for several reasons: (*a*) specialisation, (*b*) time-saving, (*c*) automation of the production process, (*d*) 'cumulative volume' economies.

Larger scale allows division of labour and specialisation of the labour force with the result of an improvement of the skills and hence of the productivity of the various types of labour. In a small plant a worker may be assigned three or four different jobs, while in a large plant these jobs are assigned to different workers. This division of labour is not profitable at small scales of output, because the skilled workers would stay unemployed part of the time.

Division of labour, apart from increasing the skills of the labour force, results in saving of the time usually lost in going from one type of work to another.

Finally, the division of labour promotes the invention of tools and machines which facilitate and supplement the workers. Such mechanisation of the production methods in larger plants increases the labour productivity and leads to decreasing costs as the scale of output increases.

A classic example of the labour economies of large-scale production is the motor-car industry. Large-scale production made possible the introduction of the assembly-line, a process which involves a very wide specialisation of the workers, each one of whom performs a single job to which he is assisted by special tools. The assembly-line involves extensive investment in machinery and other equipment and its use is unprofitable for small-scale production. At large scales, however, this method of high automation resulted in huge increases in the productivity of labour and made possible the mass production of motor cars at low costs and prices.

With increasing scale there is a 'cumulative effect' on the skills of technical personnel in particular. Production engineers, foremen and other production employees tend to acquire considerable experience from large-scale operations. This 'cumulative-volume' experience leads to higher productivity and hence to reduced costs at larger levels of output.[1]

[1] See F. M. Scherer, *Industrial Market Structure and Economic Performance* (Rand-McNally, 1970) pp. 72–9.

Technical economies. Technical economies are associated with the 'fixed capital' which includes all types of machinery and other equipment. The main technical economies arise from (*a*) specialisation and indivisibilities of capital, (*b*) set-up costs, (*c*) initial fixed costs, (*d*) technical volume/input relations, (*e*) reserve capacity requirements.

The main technical economies result from the *specialisation* of the capital equipment (and the associated labour) which becomes possible only at large scales of production, and from the *indivisibilities* which are a characteristic of the modern industrial techniques of production. Modern technology usually involves a higher degree of mechanisation for larger scales of output. That is, the production methods become more mechanised (capital intensive) as the scale increases. Mechanisation often implies more specialised capital equipment as well as more investment, a fact that makes the large-scale methods of production have high overhead costs. Of course these methods have lower variable costs, but at low levels of output the high average-fixed costs more than offset the lower labour (and other operating) costs. Once the appropriate scale is reached the highly mechanised and specialised techniques become profitable.

An example will illustrate how specialisation of the plant and technical indivisibilities result in economies of scale.

Assume that there are three methods of producing a certain commodity, a small-scale method (Process *A*) suitable for producing at minimum cost '1 unit' of output, a medium-scale method suitable for producing optimally (i.e., with minimum cost) 100 'units' of output (Process *B*), and a large-scale method suitable for producing 400 'units' of output (Process *C*). The first method uses 1 unit of labour and 1 unit of capital per unit of output. The second method uses 50 units of labour and 50 units of capital, and the third uses 100 units of labour and 100 units of capital. Clearly the labour/capital ratio is the same in all three techniques, but the larger-scale techniques have a higher productivity (as measured by the output per man, X/L) due to the specialisation of labour (direct and managerial) which becomes possible only at the large scales of production. The three techniques are indivisible, that is, the technology is characterised by *indivisibilities* in the sense that each size plant can be duplicated but cannot be halved and retain its higher productivity. Furthermore, all techniques are assumed to have constant returns to scale.[1] The above technology is summarised in table 4.1.

Table 4.1   Technology with indivisibilities (and discontinuities)

Available methods of production	Level of output	L (man-hours)	K (machine hours)	K/L ratio	Average product of labour $AP_L = \frac{X}{L}$	Average product of capital $AP_K = \frac{X}{K}$	Prices of factors (£ per hour)	Total cost (TC)	Average cost (AC)
Process *A* (small plant)	1	1	1	1	1	1	$P_L = 1$	2	2
Process *B* (medium plant)	100	50	50	1	2	2	$P_K = 1$	100	1
Process *C* (large plant)	400	100	100	1	4	4		200	0·5

[1] In particular it is assumed that, although the processes *B* and *C* cannot be used efficiently at a level less than their 'base unit', they can be operated at any higher level, with constant returns to scale. See also K. Lancaster, *Introduction to Modern Microeconomics* (Rand-McNally, 1969) pp. 88–91.

Let us look at the shapes of the *AC* and the *MC* when indivisibilities are present in the technology of a firm. Increasing technical returns to scale (with constant factor prices) in the long run are explained by indivisibilities. It is because the firm cannot continue to reduce all inputs proportionately when output is reduced that long-run average cost is bound to rise with reduction in output. Or, to put it in another way, large-scale plants cannot be halved (or decreased in another ratio) and still remain equally efficient. Assume constant prices of factors, £1 per man hour and £1 per machine hour. The total and average cost for each process are shown in the last two columns of table 4.1 and are plotted in figures 4.36 and 4.37. For each level of output the least-cost process will be chosen. Up to $X = 49$ the small-scale process is the one with the least cost (equal to £2 per unit of output). At $X = 49$ the firm uses 49 man hours and 49 machine hours. The total cost increases proportionally with output, as can be seen from table 4.2. The level of output $X = 50$, if produced with the small-scale process, would cost £100 (50 labour cost + 50 machine cost). However, with the same cost (i.e. by employing the same quantities of factors, $50L$ and $50K$) the firm can produce 100 units of output by adopting the second method of production, thus reducing its average cost to £1 (per unit of output). At any level of output higher than 50 units process *B* has a lower cost than process *A*, and hence for $X > 50$ the firm will switch to process *B*. For any level of output $50 < X < 100$ total cost will be constant (equal to £100) ir-respective of the level of production within these limits, because with $50L$ and $50K$ the firm can produce any output up to 100 units. Clearly the *AC* would fall continuously over the range of output 50 to 100, since total cost remains constant at the level of £100.

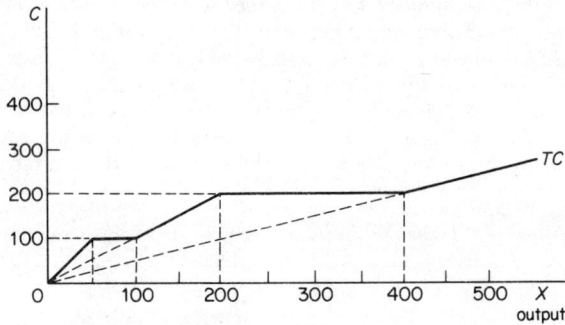

Figure 4.36

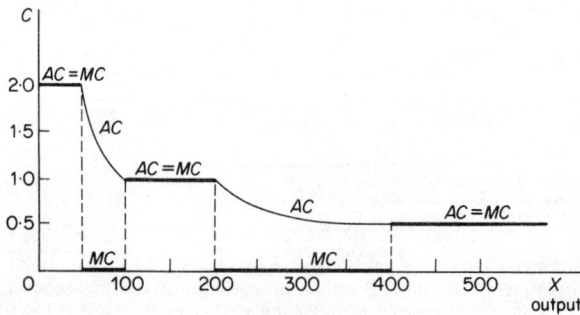

Figure 4.37

Table 4.2   Cost of production with the small plant size *A*

Output with small size plant	Labour (hours)	Capital (hours)	Total cost (TC)	Average cost (AC)
$X = 1$	$L = 1$	$K = 1$	$TC = 2$	$AC = 2$
$X = 2$	$L = 2$	$K = 2$	$TC = 4$	$AC = 2$
$\vdots$	$\vdots$	$\vdots$	$\vdots$	$\vdots$
$X = 49$	$L = 49$	$K = 49$	$TC = 98$	$AC = 2$
$X = 50$	$L = 50$	$K = 50$	$TC = 100$	$AC = 2$

Beyond the level of $X = 100$ total costs will start rising, since more L and more K will be required. However, AC will remain constant at £1 per unit of output (see table 4.3).

The level of output $X = 200$, if produced by process B, would cost £200 and would require $100L$ and $100K$. However, with the same quantities of factors (and presumably the same total cost) the firm could produce 400 units of output by switching to process C. At any level of output higher than 200 units, process C has a lower cost than either of the other processes. Hence it will be chosen by the rational producer. For any level of output $200 < X < 400$ total cost will be constant (equal to £200), with AC falling continuously over this range. Beyond the level of 400 units of output total cost would start rising proportionally with output, since more L and K would be required (for $X > 400$, $L > 100$ and $K > 100$). However, the AC will remain constant (at £0·5 for levels of X greater than 400 units).

Table 4.3   Cost of production of the medium plant size *B*

$X = 50$	$L = 50$	$K = 50$	$TC = 100$	$AC = 2$
$X = 60$	$L = 50$	$K = 50$	$TC = 100$	$AC = 1·66$
$X = 80$	$L = 50$	$K = 50$	$TC = 100$	$AC = 1·25$
$X = 100$	$L = 50$	$K = 50$	$TC = 100$	$AC = 1$
$X = 102$	$L = 51$	$K = 51$	$TC = 102$	$AC = 1$
$X = 104$	$L = 52$	$K = 52$	$TC = 104$	$AC = 1$
$\vdots$	$\vdots$	$\vdots$	$\vdots$	$\vdots$
$X = 198$	$L = 99$	$K = 99$	$TC = 198$	$AC = 1$
$X = 200$	$L = 100$	$K = 100$	$TC = 200$	$AC = 1$

The MC would be equal to the AC over the flat parts of this curve, but would be zero over the falling parts of the AC curve. This is because over these ranges of X (for which AC is falling), total cost remains constant, and hence $MC = 0$.

The AC and MC curves in the case of technological indivisibilities are shown in figures 4.36 and 4.37.

Set-up costs are the costs involved in the preparation (arrangement) of 'multipurpose' machinery for performing a particular job or product. For example in the motor-car industry or in firms producing electrical household equipment the use of 'general-purpose' machines is quite common. One such type of machinery is the metal-stamping press which produces the frames and various components of the final product. The metal stamping press has to be reset any time that a particular part of, say, a car has to be produced. For example, different set-ups are required for producing the doors, the roof, the wings of a car, and each set-up involves considerable time and cost. The larger the scale of output the more a multipurpose machine is left to one set-up (say, stamping doors) and hence resetting becomes less frequent. This is a source of technical economies of large-scale production.

'Initial costs' are usually involved in starting a business or introducing a new product. Research and development expenditures, costs of market exploration, design costs for the product are examples of such costs. Clearly the larger the scale of output, the lower the unit costs of such 'fixed' expenses.

Technical economies of scale also arise from some technical-geometric relationships between particular equipment and the inputs required to produce and install it. These are important in the so-called 'process industries', such as petroleum refining, steam generation, gas transmission, chemical industry, cement industry, glass manufacturing, and iron reduction.[1] The methods of production used in the 'process-industries', includes special equipment, such as storage tanks, reaction chambers, connecting pipes, etc. The material and labour costs of constructing such plants are proportional to the surface area that they occupy. But the volume capacity (which determines the level of output) of a plant increases more than proportionately as the area increases. Hence the technical cost of installing such industrial plants falls as the output (volume) capacity increases, at least up to the point where the equipment becomes so large as to require stronger materials and special constructions in order to make the larger plants safe.

Another source of technical economies are the so-called 'reserve-capacity' economies. Firms always want some reserve capacity in order to avoid disruption of their production flow when breakdown of machinery occurs. A small firm which uses a single large machine will have to keep two such machines if it wants to avoid disruptions from a breakdown. A larger firm which uses several large machines can attain the required 'security' from breakdowns by holding only a proportion of their total numbers as reserve capacity. Similarly the number of workers required for repairs within the firm does not increase proportionately with the size of scale.

Inventory economies. These are sometimes called 'stochastic economies', because the role of inventories is to meet the random changes in the input and the output sides of the operations of the firm.

Stocks of raw materials do increase with scale but not proportionately. Random fluctuations in the supply of such inputs are smoothed out with stocks whose size need change by less than the size of the firm.

The 'reserve-capacity' economies discussed in the previous paragraph are also a type of stochastic economies. The breakdowns in machinery do not increase *pari-passu* with size. If anything the 'cumulative volume' experience of production personnel will tend to reduce the frequency of such breakdowns in larger plants, and require a proportionately smaller amount of reserve machinery and stocks of spare parts.

Similarly on the demand side, random changes in the demand of customers will tend to be smoothed out as the plant size increases. The larger the number of customers the more the random fluctuations of their demands tend to offset peaks and recessions, thus allowing the firm to hold a smaller percentage of its output to meet such random changes.

Selling or marketing economies

Selling economies are associated with the distribution of the product of a firm. The main types of such economies are (*a*) advertising economies, (*b*) other large-scale economies, (*c*) economies from special arrangements with exclusive dealers (representatives, or distributors, wholesalers or retailers), (*d*) model-change economies.

Advertising expenses are not necessary only for a new firm or a new product, but

[1] See F. M. Scherer, *Industrial Market Structure and Economic Performance* (Rand-McNally, 1970).

also for established firms, who need a minimum of advertising in order to keep their name in the minds of actual or potential customers. It is generally agreed that advertising economies do exist at least up to a certain scale of output. Advertising space (in newspapers or magazines) and time (on television or radio) increase less than proportionately with scale, so that advertising costs per unit of output fall with scale. The advertising budget is usually decided on the basis of available funds, profits, similar activities of competitors, rather than on the basis of the output. Thus the larger the output the smaller the advertising cost per unit.

Similar considerations hold for other types of selling activities, such as the salesmen force, the distribution of samples, etc. Such large-scale promotion expenditures increase by less than proportionately with output, at least up to a certain scale.

Large firms can enter exclusive agreements with distributors, who undertake the obligation of maintaining a good service department for the product of the manufacturer. This is usual for the motor-car industry, where the dealers build up garages and keep regular stocks of spare parts for various models. The buyers of durables pay a lot of attention to the availability of spares and of good servicing-shops for the brands they buy.

In modern industry, firms need to change the style of their product quite frequently in order to meet the demands of their customers and the competition of the rival firms. A change in the model or style of the product often involves considerable expenses in research and development, and possibly on new materials and equipment. The spreading of such overheads is lower per unit if the scale of output is large.

Selling activities in general absorb productive resources. There is no general agreement among economists regarding the implications of advertising and other selling activities. Some economists argue that advertising is a waste of resources, since they do not add anything to the already-produced commodity, whose price to the consumer will, as a consequence, be higher.[1] Others argue that advertising is not a waste of resources, but a cost which consumers are willing to pay (in the higher price they are charged) in order to have a wider choice of products. Product differentiation is something that consumers want, hence the selling costs associated with this differentiation are increasing the welfare of the consumers.[2] This argument implicitly assumes that all advertising and other selling activities are truly informative: they provide information to the buyers about the existence and the technical characteristics of the different varieties of a certain product. Whether this is true or not, and the extent to which selling activities are simply manipulative of consumers' tastes, and create fancied differentiation for products technically identical (or almost identical) is a theme highly disputed in economic circles.[3] At this point we are interested not in the nature and the social justification of advertising and other selling activities, but in whether there are 'economies of large-scale promotion', that is, whether the selling cost per unit of output declines with the scale of the plant (or firm). It is generally agreed that such large-scale marketing economies do exist, at least up to a certain size of the plant (or firm). Disagreement exists as to whether the average-selling-cost curve turns upwards at very

---

[1] See, for example, J. K. Galbraith, *The Affluent Society* (Houghton Mifflin, 1958), and idem, *American Capitalism: The Concept of Countervailing Power* (Houghton Mifflin, 1956). Also Joel Dean, *Managerial Economics* (Prentice-Hall, 1951); N. Borden, *The Economic Effects of Advertising* (Irwin, 1942); H. Demetz, 'The Welfare and Empirical Implications of Monopolistic Competition', *Economic Journal* (1964).

[2] E. Chamberlin, *The Theory of Monopolistic Competition* (Harvard University Press, Cambridge, Mass., 1933). Also J. Backman, *Advertising and Competition* (New York University Press, 1967).

[3] For a survey of the literature in this field see P. Doyle, 'Economic Aspects of Advertising: A Survey', *Economic Journal* (1968).

large scales of output (due to diseconomies of selling activities) or whether the unit selling costs fall continuously with scale. Chamberlin[1] argues on the lines of a U-shaped selling-cost curve while Andrews[2] and others support the idea of a continuously-falling selling-cost curve. Given that the technical costs of production fall with scale, the total average-cost curve may eventually turn upwards if selling diseconomies do exist after a certain plant size. Empirical evidence is not conclusive in this respect.[3]

Managerial economies

Managerial costs are partly production costs and partly selling costs, since the managerial team in a firm is concerned with both the production and the distribution activities of the firm. The grouping of managerial costs in a separate category facilitates their analysis and in particular the analysis of possible sources of diseconomies of large-scale plants (see below).

Managerial economies arise for various reasons, the most important being (*a*) specialisation of management, and (*b*) mechanisation of managerial functions.

Large firms make possible the division of managerial tasks. The existence of a production manager and a sales manager, a finance manager, a personnel manager and so on, is common in large firms, while all or most managerial decisions are taken by a single manager (who possibly is also the owner) in a small firm. This division of managerial work increases the experience of managers in their own areas of responsibility and leads to the more efficient working of the firm.

Furthermore the decentralisation of decision-making in large firms has been found very effective in the increase of the efficiency of management. With decentralisation the flow of information within the firm is reduced and thus distortions and delays of this information in the various sections of the firm is to a large extent avoided. Decentralisation of the decision-making process is one of the main means of increasing the efficiency of management in large scale plants and of avoiding managerial diseconomies in still larger plants.

Large firms apply techniques of management involving a high degree of mechanisation, such as telephones, telex machines, television screens and computers. These techniques save time in the decision-making process and speed up the processing of information, as well as increasing its amount and its accuracy.

A problem still disputed in economic theory is whether managerial costs continue to decline at very large scales of output. In the traditional theory of costs, managerial diseconomies were assumed to be the cause of the upward turning of the long-run average-cost curve beyond a certain scale of output. Management, like any other factor of production, is variable in the long run. However, traditional theory postulated that beyond a certain stage increases in management lead to less than proportionate increases in output and thus cause an increase in the long-run unit costs.[4] The decrease in the efficiency of management is usually attributed to two factors. Firstly, loss of

[1] E. Chamberlin, *The Theory of Monopolistic Competition* (1933).

[2] P. W. S. Andrews, *Manufacturing Business* (Macmillan, 1949).

[3] For a summary discussion of advertising and additional references see D. Needham, *Economic Analysis and Industrial Structure* (Holt, Rinehart & Winston, 1969) chap. 5. Also G. Stigler, 'The Economics of Information', *Journal of Political Economy* (1961) pp. 213–25; D. Needham, 'How Much Does it Pay Whom to Advertise', *American Economic Review* (1961) pp. 194–205; G. Stigler, 'Price and Non-Price Competition', *Journal of Political Economy* (1968) pp. 149–54; N. S. Buchanan, 'Advertising Expenditures; a Suggested Treatment', *Journal of Political Economy* (1942); G. Stigler, 'The Economies of Scale', *Journal of Law and Economics* (1958); W. S. Comanor and T. A. Wilson, 'Advertising, Market Structure and Performance', *Review of Economics and Statistics* (1967).

[4] See section II of this chapter.

control of the top management once the firm has surpassed an optimum size. Decisions are delayed in the bureaucracy of large-size firms, where information is often consciously or unconsciously distorted as it passes through the various hierarchical levels, or is stopped for various reasons at some stage. Obviously decisions of the top management will not be optimal if the information on which they are based is inaccurate or comes with time lags, during which crucial changes in the environment of the firm may have taken place. Secondly, the uncertainty (from the market conditions and the reactions of competitors) increases with size and this leads to eventually less efficient decision-making.

These arguments are attacked by other theorists,[1] who argue that managerial diseconomies are not a necessary consequence of the increase in the scale of the plant. The decentralisation of the decision-making process, the mechanisation of various managerial tasks, the improvements in budgeting of the activities of the various departments, the system of regular reports at the different levels of the administrative hierarchy, the use of computers and similar devices for the quick access and processing of information tend to offset the deficiencies of complex organisations, so that managerial diseconomies are not a problem in the modern industrial world.

Other writers[2] argue that at very large scales of output the efficiency of management is somewhat adversely affected by the unavoidable complexity of big organisations, but the increase in costs from the managerial diseconomies is only slight at very large scales of output. And in general such diseconomies are more than offset by the technical-production economies, so that the total long-run average cost curve does not turn upwards at very large scales, but rather has the form of an 'inverse J'.

Returning to the uncertainty problem, there is no general consensus among economists that uncertainty increases with size and leads to eventually increasing costs. It is true that if the firm expands its share continuously in one market only the uncertainty from changes in market conditions increases (for example, a minor change in the market demand will greatly affect the sales of a dominant firm), but the uncertainty from the competitors will tend to be reduced since their share shrinks, and consequently their power will normally be weakened. The balance between these opposite developments cannot be determined on strictly theoretical *a priori* grounds. If one considers the more realistic situation of firms diversifying in various markets, the above arguments are reversed: the market uncertainty is generally reduced for the multiproduct firm by the simple fact that it 'does not put all its eggs in one basket'. On the other hand, the uncertainty from the reaction of competitors may well increase as the firm diversifies, since in this process the firm must anticipate the attitudes of the firms in the new markets in which it enters as well as its rivals in its old markets.[3]

In summary, the controversy among theorists regarding the shape of managerial costs is not as yet settled. The empirical evidence from various studies of costs (see section VI), shows that the total *LAC* curve is L-shaped, but since these studies include all types of costs, their evidence cannot be interpreted as refuting the U-shaped form of the managerial costs alone.

Transport and storage costs

Transport costs are incurred partly on the production side (transportation of raw materials or intermediate products) and partly on the selling side of the firm (transportation of final product to its markets). The same holds for storage costs.

[1] See, for example, P. Sargant Florence, *The Logic of British and American Industry* (University of North Carolina Press, 1953).

[2] See, for example, P. W. S. Andrews, *Manufacturing Business* (Macmillan, 1949).

[3] See F. M. Scherer, *Industrial Market Structure and Economic Performance* (Rand McNally, 1970).

Storage costs will clearly fall with size. The construction of storehouses follows broadly the same rules of geometrical relationships between surface, capacity–volume and inputs, which we discussed in page 132. The storage-cost curve will thus be falling in general but will be scalloped, due to technical indivisibilities and discontinuities. The storing capacity can normally be increased by increasing the number of floors of storehouses, in which case the geometrical input–output relationships clearly do hold. Beyond a certain scale additional storehouses will be required, the construction of which will increase the total cost, but unit costs will normally be lower the larger the output.

The analysis of transport costs is more complicated. The exhaustive examination of transport costs goes beyond the scope of this book. We can, however, give some idea of the problems involved in the treatment of transport costs.

If the firm uses its own transport means (e.g. lorries) transport unit costs would fall up to the point of their full capacity. At larger scales of output it might be possible to use larger vehicles, in which case the unit costs would fall, and the *LAC* of transport would be falling and would have a scalloped form. Beyond the level of output which allows the employment of the largest available means of transport one should normally expect constant unit transport costs by duplicating, etc., of these means as output expands. If the firm uses public transport the unit costs would normally increase with distance. If special freight rates are obtained for larger quantities transported such pecuniary economies might offset the increases from the greater distance.

To the above considerations one should add three relevant aspects of transport: the distance to which the product has to be carried, the importance of transport costs relative to the value of the product, and the possibility of passing the higher transport costs to the buyer.[1]

If the transport costs are negligible relative to the value of the product and if the firm can pass the transport costs to the buyers, the average transport cost will be U-shaped, but will rise slowly with size, so that the effect of the transport costs on the optimal plant size will be negligible. Such a case is shown in figure 4.38. Without taking into account the transport costs the minimum optimal scale of output is X, while the addition of transport costs (*TrAC*), which increase smoothly according to our assumptions, reduce the minimum optimal scale slightly, to X'. However, if the transport costs rise fast with distance and their amount is an important component of the total unit costs (without the firm being able to pass the increases to the buyers), the average unit transport costs will rise rapidly, offsetting possibly other economies of scale and reducing significantly the minimum optimal scale of plant. Such a situation is shown in figure 4.39.

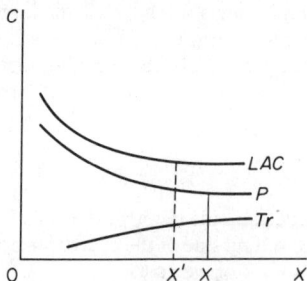

Figure 4.38

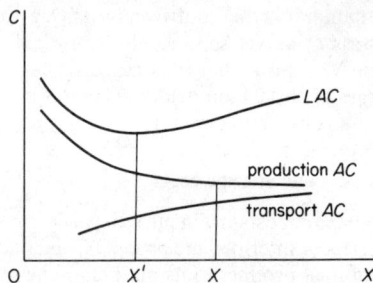

Figure 4.39

[1] See F. M. Scherer, *Industrial Market Structure and Economic Performance* (Rand-McNally, 1970).

B. PECUNIARY ECONOMIES OF SCALE

These are economies accruing to the firm due to discounts that it can obtain due to its large scale operations. The larger firm may achieve:

(*a*) Lower prices of its raw materials, bought at special discounts from its suppliers.

(*b*) Lower cost of external finance. Banks usually offer loans to large corporations at a lower rate of interest and other favourable terms.

(*c*) Lower advertising prices may be granted to larger firms if they advertise at large scales.

(*d*) Transport rates are often lower if the amounts of commodities transported are large.

(*e*) Finally, larger firms may be able to pay lower earnings to their workers if they attain a size which gives them monopsonistic power (for example, extraction industries in some areas), or due to the prestige associated with the employment by a large, well-known firm.

The total average cost is the summation of all costs (of production, marketing, managerial, transport, etc.). As we said in section III, it is generally accepted that the total *LAC* curve falls as the scale of the plant (and of the firm) increases, at least up to a certain plant (or firm) size. Disagreement exists among economists as to whether (*a*) there are diseconomies at very large scales of output (figure 4.40); (*b*) there is a minimum optimum scale of output at which all possible economies have been reaped so that costs remain constant beyond that level (figure 4.41); (*c*) there are economies of scale at all levels of output, although their magnitude becomes small beyond a certain scale ('inverse J' costs, figure 4.42).

The empirical evidence, which will be discussed in section VI, supports the view that there are no diseconomies of scale at large scales of output. The empirical evidence has not, however, established conclusively whether costs remain constant beyond a certain minimum optimum scale, or fall continuously with scale.

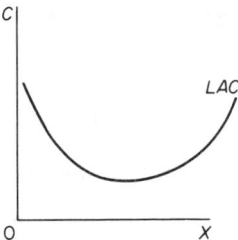

Figure 4.40 Traditional 'envelope' *LAC*

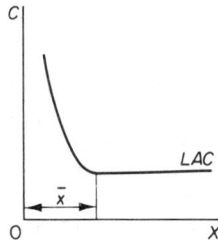

Figure 4.41 L-shaped *LAC*

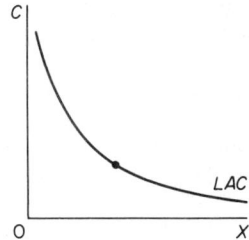

Figure 4.42 Inverse-J *LAC*

VI. EMPIRICAL EVIDENCE ON THE SHAPE OF COSTS

There are various types of empirical cost studies: statistical cost studies, studies based on questionnaires to firms, engineering cost studies, studies based on the 'survivor technique'.

The majority of the empirical cost studies suggest that the U-shaped costs postulated by the traditional theory are not observed in the real world. Two major results emerge predominantly from most studies. Firstly, the short-run *TVC* is best approximated with a straight (positively-sloping) line. This means that the *AVC* and the *MC* are constant over a fairly wide range of output. Secondly, in the long run the average costs fall sharply over low levels of output and subsequently remain practically constant as the scale of output increases. This means that the long-run cost is L-shaped rather than U-shaped. Only in very few cases were diseconomies of scale observed, and these at very high levels of output.

Of course, all the sources of evidence can and have been attacked on various grounds, some justified and others unjustified. However, the fact that so many diverse sources of evidence point in general to the same direction (that is, lead to broadly similar conclusions) regarding the shape of costs in practice, surely suggests that the strictly U-shaped cost curves of traditional theory do not adequately represent reality.

We will examine the different types of cost studies in some detail.

A. STATISTICAL COST STUDIES

Statistical cost studies consist in the application of regression analysis to time series or cross-section data. Time-series data include observations on different magnitudes (output, costs, prices, etc.) of a firm over time. Cross-section data give information on the inputs, costs, outputs and other relevant magnitudes of a group of firms at a given point of time.

In principle one can estimate short-run and long-run cost functions either from time series or from cross-section data.

We may estimate a short-run cost-function *either* from time-series data of a single firm over a period during which the firm has a given plant capacity which it has been utilising at different levels due, for example, to demand fluctuations; *or* a cross-section sample of firms of the same plant capacity, each of them operating at a different level of output for any reason (for example, due to consumers' preferences, market-sharing agreements, etc.). Due to the difficulties in obtaining a cross-section sample of firms fulfilling the above requirements, short-run cost functions are typically estimated from time-series data of a single firm whose plant has remained the same during the period covered by the sample.

We may estimate a long-run cost function *either* from a time-series sample including the cost–output data of a single firm whose scale of operations has been expanding (with the same state of technology); *or* a cross-section sample of firms with different plant sizes, each being operated optimally (at its minimum cost level). Given that over time technology changes, time-series data are not appropriate for the estimation of long-run cost curves. Thus, for long-run statistical cost estimation, cross-sectional analysis is typically used in an attempt to overcome the problem of changing technology, since presumably 'the state of arts' is given at any one point of time.

The procedure adopted in statistical cost studies may be outlined as follows. Once the data are collected and appropriately processed (see below) the researcher typically starts by fitting a linear function to the cost–output observations

$$C = b_1 X_1 + u$$

where C = total variable cost[1]
X = output (measured in physical volume)
u = a random variable which absorbs (mainly) the influence on costs of all the factors which do not appear explicitly in the cost function.[2]

[1] Fixed costs are omitted because they are irrelevant to the shape of the *AVC* and *MC* whose knowledge is crucial for short-run decision-making. Furthermore, the omission of fixed costs avoids the intricate problems of their allocation within the firm.

[2] For a discussion of the meaning of the random variable u in economic relationships see A. Koutsoyiannis, *Theory of Econometrics* (Macmillan, 1973) pp. 48–54.

This function implies that the AVC and the MC are constant at all levels of output

$$MC = \frac{\partial C}{\partial X} = b_1$$

$$AVC = \frac{C}{X} = b_1$$

The researcher next proceeds with introducing in the linear function higher powers of output (X), in an attempt to explore the hypothesis of increasing costs or U-shaped costs. For example, the quadratic cost function

$$C = b_1 X + b_2 X^2 + u$$

implies increasing AVC and MC (with $MC > AVC$) at all levels of output

$$MC = \frac{\partial C}{\partial X} = b_1 + 2b_2 X$$

$$AVC = \frac{C}{X} = b_1 + b_2 X$$

Similarly, the cubic cost function

$$C = b_1 X - b_2 X^2 + b_3 X^3 + u$$

implies U-shaped AVC and MC (with the MC intersecting the AVC curve – from below – at its lowest point)

$$MC = \frac{\partial C}{\partial X} = b_1 - 2b_2 X + 3b_3 X^2$$

$$AVC = \frac{C}{X} = b_1 - b_2 X + b_3 X^2$$

A comprehensive summary and critique of a wide range of statistical cost studies is given by J. Johnston[1] in his classic work. The evidence from most statistical studies is that in the short run the AVC is constant over a considerable range of output, while in the long run the AC is in general L-shaped.

The results of statistical cost studies have been criticised on grounds of their interpretation, data limitations, and omission or inadequate treatment of important explanatory variables (mis-specification of the cost function).

Interpretation problems

The nature of the data. Statistical cost studies are based on accounting data which differ from the opportunity costs ideally required for the estimation of theoretical cost functions. Accounting data do not include several items which constitute costs in the economist's view. For example, profit is not included in the accountant's costs, and the same holds for all imputed costs, which do not involve actual payments. Thus the statistical cost functions, based on *ex post* data (realised accounting data), cannot refute the U-shape of costs of the traditional theory, which show the *ex ante* relationship between cost and output. The statistical results reflect the simple fact that firms in the short run operate within their planned capacity range, and do not go beyond their

[1] J. Johnston, *Statistical Cost Analysis* (McGraw-Hill, 1960).

capacity limits, precisely because they know that beyond these limits costs rise sharply. Similarly, the evidence of L-shaped long-run costs reflects the actual costs up to levels of outputs so far experienced, and the fact that firms do not expand beyond these levels because they believe that at larger scales of output they will be faced with diseconomies of scale (increasing costs).

The length of the time period. Ideally the length of the time period should cover the complete production cycle of the commodity. However, the time period of the accountants does not coincide with the true time period over which the production cycle is completed. Usually the accounting data are aggregate data for two or many production periods, and this aggregation may impart some bias towards linearity of the estimated cost functions.

Coverage of cost studies. Statistical cost studies refer mostly to public companies, which are completely different to companies in the competitive industries. Consequently the evidence cannot be generalised to apply to all industries.

Data deficiencies

Accounting data are not appropriate for estimating theoretical cost functions not only because they are *ex post* (realised) expenditures (and not opportunity costs), but for several additional reasons.

Depreciation expenses. Among the variable costs one should include the user's cost of the capital equipment. Accounting data give full depreciation figures which include not only the user's cost but also the obsolescence (or time) costs of the equipment. Furthermore, in general accountants use the linear depreciation method, while in the real world depreciation and running expenses of fixed capital are non-linear: they increase as the age of the machinery increases.

Allocation of costs. Costs should be correctly allocated to outputs. However, the allocation of semi-fixed costs (which are included in the dependent variable (TVC) of the cost function) are often allocated by accountants to the various products on the basis of some rule of thumb, so that there is not exact correspondence between the output and its reported costs of production.

Cost functions of multiproduct firms. With multiproduct firms one should estimate a separate cost function for each product. However, the required data either are not available or are not accurate due to the usually *ad hoc* allocation of joint costs to the various products. Thus researchers tend to estimate an aggregate cost function for all the products of the firm. Such functions are not reliable because of the 'output index' which is used as the dependent variable. The index of output is a weighted index of the various products, the weights being the average cost of the individual products. Under these conditions what one is really measuring is a 'circular' relation, some sort of identity rather than a causal relationship, since

$$C = f(X)$$

and

$$X = f(AC)$$

so that

$$C = f(AC)$$

Specification of the cost functions

The cost curves assume constant technology and constant prices of inputs. If these factors change the cost curves will shift. Statistical cost studies have been criticised for failing to deal adequately with changes in technology and in factor prices.

Changes in technology. We said that short-run cost curves are typically estimated from time series data of a single firm whose scale of plant has remained constant over the sample period. It is assumed by researchers that the requirement of constant technology is automatically fulfilled from the nature of the time-series data. This, however, may not be true. A firm may report the same plant size, while the physical units of its equipment have been replaced with more advanced pieces of machinery. For example, a textile firm may have kept its capacity constant while having replaced several obsolete manual weaving machines (which have been fully depreciated) with a single automated machine. This replacement constitutes a change in technology which, if not accounted for, will distort the cost–output relationship.

When using a cross-section sample of firms of different sizes for the estimation of the long-run cost curve, it is assumed that the problem of changing technology is solved, since the available methods of production ('state of arts') are known to all firms: technology in a cross-section sample is constant in the sense of common knowledge of the 'state of arts' at any one time. This, however, does not mean that all firms in the cross-section sample use equally advanced methods of production. Some firms use modern while others use obsolete methods of production. Under these conditions the problem of differences in technology is brushed away by researchers, by the convenient assumption that technology (i.e. age of plant) is randomly distributed among firms: some small firms have obsolete technology while others have advanced technology, and the same is assumed to hold for all firm sizes. If this assumption is true, differences in the technology of the firms are absorbed by the random variable u and do not affect the cost–output relation. However, this assumption may not be justified in the real world. Indeed it is conceivable that large firms have lower costs because they have more advanced technology. If this is the case, the estimated long-run cost function does not reflect the theoretical cost–output relationship.

In summary, the cost curves, both short-run and long-run, shift continuously due to improvements in technology and the 'quality' of the factors of production. These shifts have not been accounted for in estimating the cost curves. Hence the estimated statistical functions are in fact obtained from 'joining' points belonging to shifting cost curves, and do not show the theoretical shape of costs.

Changes in factor prices. Cost functions have been criticised for not dealing adequately with the problem of changes of the prices of factors of production.

Time-series data, used in estimating *SR* cost curves, have in fact been deflated. But the price indexes used were not the ideally required ones, and thus the estimates have a bias. Johnston[1] has argued that the bias involved in the adopted deflating procedures does not necessarily invalidate the statistical findings, since it is not at all clear that the bias should be towards linearity of the cost–output relation.

[1] J. Johnston, *Statistical Cost Analysis* (McGraw-Hill, 1960).

Cross-section studies are thought to avoid the problem of price changes, since prices are given at any one time. This is true if the firms included in the sample are in the same location. However, cross-section samples include firms in different locations. If factor prices are different in the various locations they should be introduced explicitly in the function (as an explanatory variable or by an appropriate deflating procedure), unless the price differentials are due to the size of the firms in each location, in which case no adjustment of costs would be required. Usually cross-section studies ignore the problem of price differences, and thus their results may not represent the true cost curve.

Changes in the quality of the product. It is assumed that the product does not change during the sample period. If quality improvements have taken place (and have not been accounted for), the cost–output relation will be biased. Given the difficulties involved in 'measuring' quality differences (over time or between the products of different firms) this problem has largely been ignored in statistical cost analysis.

Specific criticisms of the long-run cost studies

The following (additional) criticisms have been directed against studies of long-run costs.

Friedman argued that the empirical findings from cross-section data of firms are not surprising, since all firms in equilibrium have equal costs (they produce at the minimum point of their *LAC*) irrespective of their size. This argument would be valid if the firms worked in pure competition. However, in manufacturing industries pure competition does not exist (as we will see in Part Two of this book).

Friedman has also argued that all firms' unit costs should actually be the same, irrespective of their size, since all rents are costs to the individual firms. This argument also implies the existence of pure competition and accounting procedures which would include 'rents', and normal profits (as well as monopoly profits) in the costs. Clearly accountants do not include these items in their cost figures. Yet their cost figures show constant cost at large scales of output.

The cross-section data assume (i) that each firm has adjusted its operations so as to produce optimally; (ii) that technology (i.e. age of plant) is randomly distributed among firms: some small firms have old technology, while others have advanced technology, and the same is true for large firms; (iii) that entrepreneurial ability is randomly associated with the various plant sizes. In short, there are too many inter-firm differences which cannot be assumed randomly distributed to different plant sizes. Hence, the measured cost function is not the true cost function of economic theory. This criticism is basically a valid one.

The measured cost function is a 'bogus', fallacious relation which is biased towards linearity. The firms use 'standard costing' procedures which tend to show ficticiously low costs for small firms and high costs for large firms: in the application of standard costing methods small firms tend to use a high 'typical loading factor', while large firms tend to apply a conservative (low) 'typical loading factor'. Thus, the cost data of firms which apply standard costing methods, if used for the estimation of statistical cost functions, will impart a bias towards linearity.

The statistical *LAC* is furthermore fallacious due to the observed fact that usually small firms work below their 'average' capacity, while large firms work above full capacity.

The last two 'regression-fallacy' arguments are valid for many industries for which cost functions have been statistically estimated.

B. STUDIES BASED ON QUESTIONNAIRES

The most known and debated study in this group is the one conducted by Eiteman and Guthrie.[1] The researchers attempted to draw inferences about the shape of the cost curves by the method of questionnaires. Selected firms were presented with various graphs of costs and were asked to state which shape they thought their costs were. Most of the firms reported that their costs would not increase in the long run, while they remain constant over some range of output. This is the same evidence as that provided by the statistical cost functions.

The Eiteman–Guthrie study has been criticised on the grounds that the authors did not ask the appropriate questions and did not interpret their results correctly. In particular it has been argued that businessmen might have interpreted the term 'capacity' to mean 'optimum operating capacity' or 'absolute capacity'.[2]

C. ENGINEERING COST STUDIES

The engineering method is based on the technical relationships between inputs and output levels included in the production function.[3] From available engineering information the researcher decides what are the optimal input combinations for producing any given level of output. These technically-optimal input combinations are multiplied by the prices of inputs (factors of production) to give the cost of the corresponding level of output. The cost function includes the cost of the optimal (least-cost) methods of producing various levels of output.

To illustrate the engineering method we will use L. Cookenboo's study of the costs of operation of crude-oil trunk-lines.[4] The first stage in the engineering method involves the estimation of the production function, that is, the technical relation between inputs and output. In the case of crude-oil trunk-lines output (X) was measured as barrels of crude oil per day. The main inputs in a pipeline system are 'pipe diameter', 'horse-power of pumps', 'number of pumping stations'. Cookenboo estimated from engineering information the production function

$$X = (0{\cdot}01046)^{-1/2{\cdot}735} \cdot H^{0{\cdot}37} \cdot D^{1{\cdot}73}$$

where X = barrels per day (the study was restricted to outputs ranging between 25,000 and 400,000 barrels per day)
   H = horse-power
   D = pipe diameter

The production function is homogeneous of degree 2·1, that is, the returns to scale are approximately equal to 2, implying that an increase in factor inputs by k per cent leads to an increase of output by $2k$ per cent. The input 'number of pumping stations', did not lend itself readily to *a priori* engineering estimation, and Cookenboo used for this input actual (historical) costs obtained from a pipeline company (after adjusting them for

---

[1] W. J. Eiteman and G. E. Guthrie, 'The Shape of the Average Cost Curve', *American Economic Review* (1952) pp. 832–8. The findings of Eiteman and Guthrie have been widely criticised in a series of comments in *American Economic Review* (1953).

[2] See R. W. Clower and J. F. Due, *Microeconomics* (Irwin, 1972) p. 122.

[3] For a discussion of the engineering method see H. Chenery, 'Engineering Production Functions', *Quarterly Journal of Economics* (1949) pp. 507–31.

[4] L. Cookenboo Jr, 'Costs of Operation of Crude Oil Trunk Lines', in *Crude Oil Pipe Lines and Competition in the Oil Industry* (Harvard University Press, 1955); reprinted in H. Townsend (ed.), *Readings in Price Theory* (Penguin, 1971).

abnormal weather conditions prevailing during the construction of the pumping stations).

The production function relating X, H and D will depend on several factors such as the density of the crude oil carried through the pipes, the wall thickness of pipe used, and so forth. Cookenboo estimated his 'engineering production function' for the typical 'Mid-Continent' crude oil,[1] and for wall thickness of $\frac{1}{4}$-inch pipe throughout the length of pipes (allowing 5 per cent terrain variation, and assuming no influence of gravity on flow of crude oil).

The above production function was computed by the use of a hydraulic formula for computing horse-powers for various volumes of liquid flow in pipes (adjusted with appropriate constants for the crude oil of Mid-Continent type). The estimated engineering production function is shown in figure 4.43 (reproduced from Cookenboo's work).

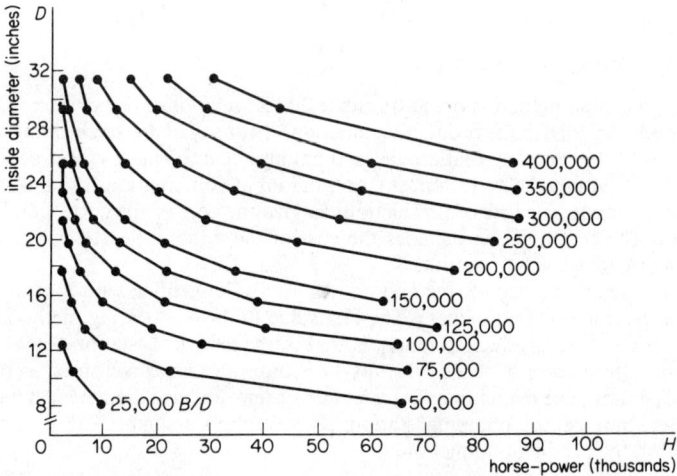

Figure 4.43   Production function for crude-oil trunk pipelines (output measured in barrels per day)

The second stage in the engineering method is the estimation of the cost curves from the technical information provided by the engineering production function. From the production function it is seen that a given level of output can be technically produced with various combinations of the D and H inputs. In order to compute the long-run cost curve Cookenboo proceeded as follows. For each level of output he estimated the total cost of all possible combinations of H and D, and he chose the least expensive of these combinations as the optimum one for that level of output. The long-run cost curve was then formed by the least-cost combinations of inputs for the production of each level of output included in his study.

The total cost (for each level of output) includes three items, the costs of D, the costs of H, and 'other costs':

The costs of pipe diameter (D). These include the cost of raw materials (steel, valves, corrosion protectives, and so forth) and the labour costs of laying 1000 miles of pipe (this being the unit length of piping of $\frac{1}{4}$-inch wall).

---

[1] This crude oil is of 60 SUS viscosity, 34°. API gravity.

The costs of horse-power (H). These are the annual expenditures for electric power, labour and maintenance required to operate the pumping stations. Cookenboo included in this category the initial cost of pumping stations (costs of raw materials and labour costs).

Other costs. These include the initial costs of storing-tank capacity, surveying the right-of-way, damages to terrain crossed, a communications system, and the expenses of a central office force. Cookenboo assumes that these costs are proportional to output (or to the length of pipes), with the exception of the last item (expenses of the central office force), which, however, he considers as unimportant:

> There are no significant per-barrel costs of a pipe line which change with length. The only such costs are those of a central office force; these are inconsequential in relation to total. Hence, it is possible to state that (other) costs per barrel-mile for a 1000 mile trunk line are representative of costs per barrel-mile of any trunk line.

The derived long-run average-cost curve from the engineering production function is shown in figure 4.44 (based on Cookenboo's work).

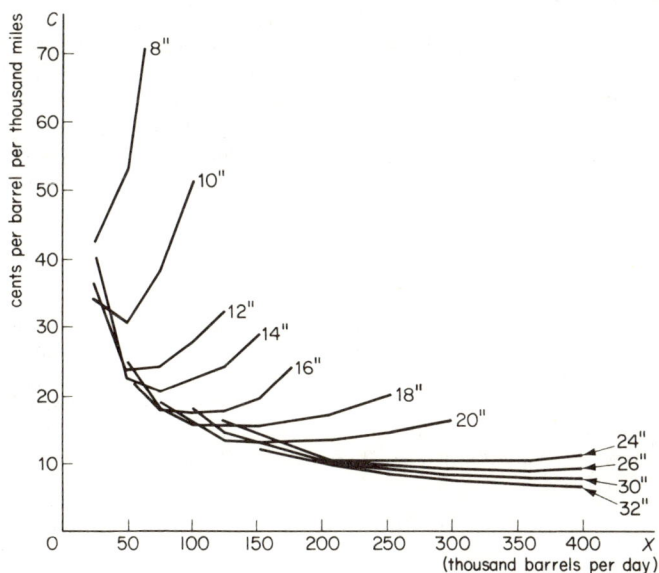

Figure 4.44   Costs per barrel of operating crude-oil trunk pipelines.

From his study Cookenboo concluded that the *LR* costs fall continuously over the range of output covered by his study.

It should be noted that engineering cost studies are mainly concerned with the production costs and pay too little attention to the distribution (selling) and other administrative-managerial expenses. Given their nature, their findings are not surprising and cannot seriously challenge the U-shaped *LR* curve of the traditional theory. The existence of technical economies in large-scale plants has not been questioned. Indeed, by their design large-scale plants have a lower unit cost, otherwise firms would not be interested in switching to such production techniques as their market increased; they would rather prefer to expand by duplicating smaller-size plants with whose operations their labour force (and their administrative staff) is familiar. What has been questioned is the existence of managerial diseconomies at large scales of output. And engineering cost studies are not very well suited for providing decisive evidence about the existence of such diseconomies.

Engineering costs are probably the closest approximation to the economist's *production costs*, since they avoid the problems of changing technology (by concentrating on a given 'state of arts') and of changing factor prices (by using current price quotations furnished by suppliers). Furthermore, by their nature, they provide *ex ante* information about the cost–output relation, as economic theory requires. However, engineering costs give inadequate information about managerial costs and hence are poor approximations to the total *LAC* of economic theory.

Another shortcoming of engineering cost studies is the underestimation of costs of large-scale plants obtained from extension of the results of the studies to levels of output outside their range. Usually engineering cost studies are based on a small-scale pilot plant. Engineers next project the input–output relations derived from the pilot plant to full-scale (large) production plants. It has often been found that the extension of the existing engineering systems to larger ranges of output levels grossly underestimates the costs of full-scale, large-size operations.

Finally, engineering cost studies are applicable to operations which lend themselves readily to engineering analysis. This is the reason why such studies have been found useful in estimating the cost functions of oil-refining, chemical industrial processes, nuclear-power generation. However, the technical laws underlying the transformation of inputs into outputs are not known with the desired detail for most of the manufacturing industry, where, as a consequence, the engineering technique cannot be applied.

D. STATISTICAL PRODUCTION FUNCTIONS

Another source of evidence about the returns to scale are the statistical studies of production functions. Most of these studies show constant returns to scale, from which it is inferred that the costs are constant, at least over certain ranges of scale. Like the statistical cost functions, statistical production functions have been attacked on various grounds. Their discussion goes beyond the scope of this book. The interested reader is referred to A. A. Walters's article: 'Econometric Production and Cost Functions', *Econometrica* (1963).

E. THE 'SURVIVOR TECHNIQUE'

This technique has been developed by George Stigler.[1] It is based on the Darwinian doctrine of the survival of the fittest. The method implies that the firms with the lowest costs will survive through time:

(The basic postulate of the survivor technique) is that competition of different sizes of firms sifts out the more efficient enterprises.

Therefore by examining the development of the size of firms in an industry at different periods of time one can infer what is the shape of costs in that industry. Presumably,

---

[1] G. J. Stigler, 'The Economies of Scale', *The Journal of Law and Economics* (1958) pp. 54–71.

the survivor technique traces out the long-run cost curve, since it examines the development over time of firms operating at different scales of output.

In applying the survivor technique firms or plants in an industry are classified into groups by size, and the share of each group in the market output is calculated over time. If the share of a given group (class) falls, the conclusion is that this size is relatively inefficient, that is, it has high costs (decreasing returns). The criterion for the classification of firms into groups is usually the number of employees or the capacity of firms (as a percentage of the total output of the industry).

To illustrate the application of the survivor technique we present below the results of Stigler's study of the economies of scale of the steel industry of the U.S.A. The firms have been grouped into seven classes according to their percentage market share. From the data shown in table 4.4 Stigler concluded that during the two decades covered by his study there has been a continuous decline in the share of the small and the large firms in the steel industry of the U.S.A. Thus Stigler concluded that the small and the large firms are inefficient (have high costs). The medium-size firms increased or held their market share, so they constitute, according to Stigler, the optimum firm size for the steel industry in the U.S.A.

Table 4.4 Market share of firms of different sizes in the U.S.A. steel industry

Groups (*criterion of classification: per cent of industry capacity*)		*Market share over time: per cent of industry output*		
		1930	*1938*	*1951*
small size	under 0·5	7·16	6·11	4·65
	0·5–1	5·94	5·08	5·37
	1–2·5	13·17	8·30	9·07
medium size	2·5–5	10·64	16·59	22·21
	5·0–10	11·18	14·03	8·12
	10–25	13·24	13·99	16·10
large size	over 25	38·67	35·91	34·50

Source: G. J. Stigler, 'The Economies of Scale', *Journal of Law and Economics* (1958).

These findings suggest that the long-run cost curve of the steel industry has a considerable flat stretch (figure 4.45):

Over a wide range of outputs there is no evidence of net economies or diseconomies of scale.

The survivor technique, although attractive for its simplicity, suffers from serious limitations. Its validity rests on the following assumptions, which are rarely fulfilled in the real world. It assumes that: (*a*) the firms pursue the same objectives; (*b*) the firms operate in similar environments so that they do not have locational (or other) advantages; (*c*) prices of factors and technology are not changing, since such changes might well be expected to lead to changes in the optimum plant size; (*d*) the firms operate in a very competitive market structure, that is, there are no barriers to entry or collusive agreements, since under such conditions inefficient (high-cost) firms would probably survive for long periods of time.

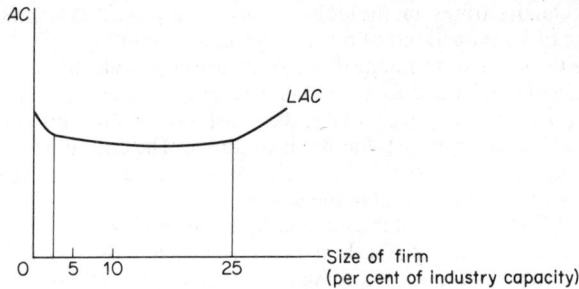

Figure 4.45   Long-run *AC* curve for the steel industry of the U.S.A. as determined by the 'survivor technique'.

Even if conducted with the greatest care and in conditions where the above assumptions are fulfilled, the survivor technique indicates only the broad shape of the long-run cost curve, but does not show the actual magnitude of the economies or diseconomies of scale.

Another shortcoming of the survivor technique is that it cannot explain cases where the size distribution of firms remains constant over time. If the share of the various plant sizes does not change over time, this does not necessarily imply that all scales of plant are equally efficient. The size distribution of firms does not depend only on costs. Changes in technology and factor prices, entry barriers, collusive practices, objectives of firms and other factors as well as costs should be taken into account when analysing the size distribution of firms over time.

VII. THE RELEVANCE OF THE SHAPE OF COSTS IN DECISION-MAKING

Knowledge of the cost functions is very important for optimal decision-making by the firm and the government.

Knowledge of the short-run costs is crucial for pricing and output decisions while the long-run costs provide useful information for planning the growth and investment policies of the firm.

The implications of the L-shaped cost curves for the theory of the firm and for economic theory as a whole have been discussed by various writers.[1] Oliver Williamson[2] and Rowley[3] have examined in detail the effects of economies of scale on the problem of mergers and monopoly. The following examples are chosen as an illustration of the importance of the shape of costs in the theory of the firm.

Costs and price–output decisions

As we will see in the remaining chapters of this book, costs are one of the main determinants of price in all market structures, and in all models pertaining to the explanation of the behaviour of the firm.

[1] See, for example, J. M. Clark, *Competition as a Dynamic Process* (Brookings Institution, 1961); P. Samuelson's article in *Monopolistic Competition Theory: Studies in Impact* (Wiley, 1966); N. Kaldor, 'The Irrelevance of Equilibrium Economics', *Economic Journal* (1972); P. J. D. Wiles, *Price, Cost and Output* (Blackwell, 1961).

[2] O. Williamson, 'Economies as an Antitrust Defense', *American Economic Review* (1968).

[3] C. K. Rowley, *Antitrust and Economic Efficiency* (Macmillan, 1973).

The pure competition model breaks down unless the costs are U-shaped, since otherwise the size of the firm (its optimal output) is indeterminate (see Chapter 5).

In monopolistic competition the shape of the cost curves is of no particular importance; so long as the slope of the marginal cost is smaller than the slope of the marginal revenue curve the size of the firm is determinate. However, costs are one of the determinants of price and output both in the short run and in the long run, since the profit maximising position of the firm is determined by the marginalistic rule $MC = MR$ (see Chapter 8).

Similar considerations hold for the equilibrium of the monopolist, who sets his price at the level defined by the intersection of his MC and MR curves. Thus, the cost curves are entering into the monopolist's price–output decisions explicitly (see Chapter 6).

In oligopolistic markets that operate with collusion, the level of costs is one of the main determinants of the bargaining power of the firms which enter collusive agreements. In cartels the costs of individual firms determine the supply of the industry and the price which will be set in the market, as well as the quota of each firm member, either by marginalistic calculations or by bargaining procedures (see Chapter 10).

In the traditional theory of price leadership the leader will be the firm with the lowest costs. Even if the leader is a large firm, its costs must be low if it is to enforce its leadership on the smaller firms (see Chapter 10).

The average-cost pricing practices (see Chapters 11–12) are based on detailed knowledge of the costs of the firm.

Managerial and behavioural models imply some form of collusion, which, as we said, is based on the cost structure of the firms (see Chapters 15, 16, 17, 18).

Costs and barriers to entry

Costs, either in the form of an absolute cost advantage or in the form of minimum optimal scale of output, have been found the most important determinants of the height of barriers to entry in many industries. Preference barriers may in general be overcome if new firms are prepared to spend an adequate amount of money on research and development as well as on advertising and other selling activities. Such actions, of course, will raise the costs of the new firms and thus put them at a relative cost disadvantage. The lower the costs (at all levels of output) and the larger the minimum optimal scale (that is, the greater the economies of scale) the greater the entry barriers and hence the higher the price that firms in an industry can charge without attracting entry (see Chapters 13 and 14).

Costs and market structure

Costs determine, to a large extent, the market structure. Given the size of the market, the greater the economies of scale, the smaller the number of firms in the industry. Thus, when the economies of large-scale production are important one should expect an oligopolistic market structure to emerge in the long run. If the economies of scale are not important one should in general expect a large number of firms in the industry.

Costs and growth policy of the firm

Given the market size, the direction of growth of a firm is determined basically by cost considerations. If the long-run costs are U-shaped and the firm has exhausted the available economies of scale, further expansion in the same market will most probably take place by building up a new plant. If the firm is faced with a U-shaped scale curve and the market is stagnant, the firm will look for investment in other markets (diversification).

Mergers and take-overs are based (among other things) on cost considerations. Similarly if cost advantages are expected from a vertical integration of the various stages of production, the firm will sooner or later adopt such a policy. Integrated production may also be attractive as a means for preventing entry, since a new firm must enter with a similar integrated production organisation, which requires substantial initial capital outlays.

Costs and the regulation of industry

A detailed knowledge of costs is also essential for the regulation of industry by the government. Regulatory authorities, such as the Monopoly Commission, require detailed information on the costs of the various firms before they decide to split up large firms, to encourage or prohibit mergers, to create a monopoly or dissolve an existing one in order to enhance competition. If there are too many, small firms in an industry in which economies of scale are substantial, the government can justify a policy aiming at the increase in the size of firms. On the other hand, if economies of scale are unimportant and the industry is highly concentrated, the government may decide to adopt policies aiming at the reduction of the size of the firm (for example, by forbidding mergers or breaking up the existing large firms).

The above are some illustrative examples of the importance of cost functions in optimal decision-making.

PART TWO

THEORY OF THE FIRM

SECTION A

PERFECT COMPETITION
MONOPOLY
MONOPOLISTIC COMPETITION

5. Perfect Competition

Perfect competition is a market structure characterised by a complete absence of rivalry among the individual firms. Thus perfect competition in economic theory has a meaning diametrically opposite to the everyday use of this term. In practice businessmen use the word competition as synonymous to rivalry. In theory, perfect competition implies no rivalry among firms.

I. ASSUMPTIONS

The model of *perfect competition* is based on the following assumptions.

Large numbers of sellers and buyers

The industry or market includes a large number of firms (and buyers), so that each individual firm, however large, supplies only a small part of the total quantity offered in the market. The buyers are also numerous so that no monopsonistic power can affect the working of the market. Under these conditions each firm alone cannot affect the price in the market by changing its output.

Product homogeneity

The industry is defined as a group of firms producing a homogeneous product. The technical characteristics of the product as well as the services associated with its sale and delivery are identical. There is no way in which a buyer could differentiate among the products of different firms. If the product were differentiated the firm would have some discretion in setting its price. This is ruled out *ex hypothesi* in perfect competition.

The assumptions of large numbers of sellers and of product homogeneity imply that the individual firm in pure competition is a price-taker: its demand curve is infinitely elastic, indicating that the firm can sell any amount of output at the prevailing market

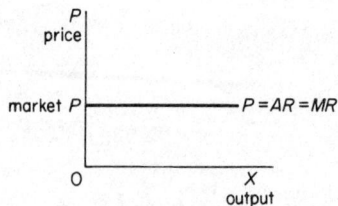

Figure 5.1

price (figure 5.1). The demand curve of the individual firm is also its average revenue and its marginal revenue curve (see page 156).

Free entry and exit of firms

There is no barrier to entry or exit from the industry. Entry or exit may take time, but firms have freedom of movement in and out of the industry. This assumption is supplementary to the assumption of large numbers. If barriers exist the number of firms in the industry may be reduced so that each one of them may acquire power to affect the price in the market.

Profit maximisation

The goal of all firms is profit maximisation. No other goals are pursued.

No government regulation

There is no government intervention in the market (tariffs, subsidies, rationing of production or demand and so on are ruled out).

The above assumptions are sufficient for the firm to be a price-taker and have an infinitely elastic demand curve. The market structure in which the above assumptions are fulfilled is called *pure competition*. It is different from *perfect competition*, which requires the fulfilment of the following additional assumptions.

Perfect mobility of factors of production

The factors of production are free to move from one firm to another throughout the economy. It is also assumed that workers can move between different jobs, which implies that skills can be learned easily. Finally, raw materials and other factors are not monopolised and labour is not unionised. In short, there is perfect competition in the markets of factors of production.

Perfect knowledge

It is assumed that all sellers and buyers have complete knowledge of the conditions of the market. This knowledge refers not only to the prevailing conditions in the current period but in all future periods as well. Information is free and costless. Under these conditions uncertainty about future developments in the market is ruled out.

Under the above assumptions we will examine the equilibrium of the firm and the industry in the short run and in the long run.

II. SHORT-RUN EQUILIBRIUM

In order to determine the equilibrium of the industry we need to derive the market supply. This requires the determination of the supply of the individual firms, since the market supply is the sum of the supply of all the firms in the industry.

A. EQUILIBRIUM OF THE FIRM IN THE SHORT RUN

The firm is in equilibrium when it maximises its profits (Π), defined as the difference between total cost and total revenue:

$$\Pi = TR - TC$$

Given that the normal rate of profit is included in the cost items of the firm, Π is the profit above the normal rate of return on capital and the remuneration for the risk-bearing function of the entrepreneur. The firm is in equilibrium when it produces the output that maximises the difference between total receipts and total costs. The equilibrium of the firm may be shown graphically in two ways. Either by using the TR and TC curves, or the MR and MC curves.

In figure 5.2 we show the total revenue and total cost curves of a firm in a perfectly competitive market. The total-revenue curve is a straight line through the origin, showing that the price is constant at all levels of output. The firm is a price-taker and can sell any amount of output at the going market price, with its TR increasing proportionately with its sales. The slope of the TR curve is the marginal revenue. It is constant and equal to the prevailing market price, since all units are sold at the same price. Thus in pure competition $MR = AR = P$.

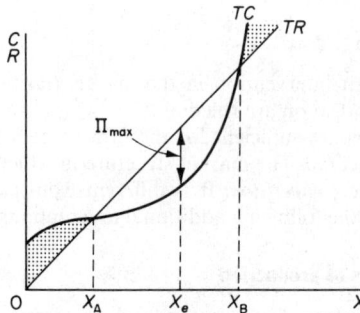

Figure 5.2

The shape of the total-cost curve reflects the U shape of the average-cost curve, that is, the law of variable proportions. The firm maximises its profit at the output X_e, where the distance between the TR and TC curves is the greatest. At lower and higher levels of output total profit is not maximised: at levels smaller than X_A and larger than X_B the firm has losses.

The total-revenue–total-cost approach is awkward to use when firms are combined together in the study of the industry. The alternative approach, which is based on marginal cost and marginal revenue, uses price as an explicit variable, and shows clearly the behavioural rule that leads to profit maximisation.

In figure 5.3 we show the average- and marginal-cost curves of the firm together with its demand curve. We said that the demand curve is also the average revenue curve and

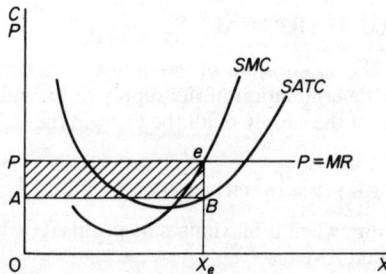

Figure 5.3

the marginal revenue curve of the firm in a perfectly competitive market. The marginal cost cuts the *SATC* at its minimum point. Both curves are U-shaped, reflecting the law of variable proportions which is operative in the short run during which the plant is constant. The firm is in equilibrium (maximises its profit) at the level of output defined by the intersection of the *MC* and the *MR* curves (point *e* in figure 5.3). To the left of *e* profit has not reached its maximum level because each unit of output to the left of X_e brings to the firm a revenue which is greater than its marginal cost. To the right of X_e each additional unit of output costs more than the revenue earned by its sale, so that a loss is made and total profit is reduced. In summary:

(*a*) If *MC* < *MR* total profit has not been maximised and it pays the firm to expand its output.

(*b*) If *MC* > *MR* the level of total profit is being reduced and it pays the firm to cut its production.

(*c*) If *MC* = *MR* short-run profits are maximised.

Thus the first condition for the equilibrium of the firm is that marginal cost be equal to marginal revenue. However, this condition is not sufficient, since it may be fulfilled and yet the firm may not be in equilibrium. In figure 5.4 we observe that the condition

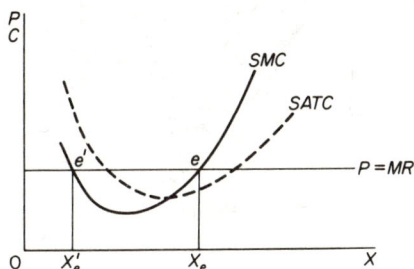

Figure 5.4

MC = *MR* is satisfied at point *e'*, yet clearly the firm is not in equilibrium, since profit is maximized at $X_e > X_{e'}$. The second condition for equilibrium requires that the *MC* be rising at the point of its intersection with the *MR* curve. This means that the *MC* must cut the *MR* curve from below, i.e. the slope of the *MC* must be steeper than the slope of the *MR* curve. In figure 5.4 the slope of *MC* is positive at *e*, while the slope of the *MR* curve is zero at all levels of output. Thus at *e* both conditions for equilibrium are satisfied

(i) *MC* = *MR*

and

(ii) (slope of *MC*) > (slope of *MR*).

It should be noted that the *MC* is always positive, because the firm must spend some money in order to produce an additional unit of output. Thus at equilibrium the *MR* is also positive.

The fact that a firm is in (short-run) equilibrium does not necessarily mean that it makes excess profits. Whether the firm makes excess profits or losses depends on the level of the *ATC* at the short-run equilibrium. If the *ATC* is below the price at equilibrium (figure 5.5) the firm earns excess profits (equal to the area *PABe*). If, however, the *ATC* is above the price (figure 5.6) the firm makes a loss (equal to the area *FPeC*). In the latter case the firm will continue to produce only if it covers its variable costs. Otherwise it will close down, since by discontinuing its operations the firm is better off: it mimimises its losses. The point at which the firm covers its variable costs is called 'the closing-down

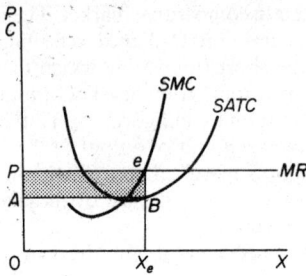

Figure 5.5

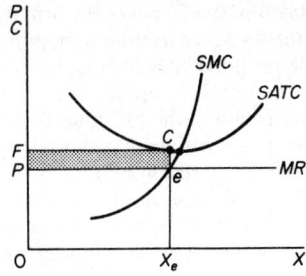

Figure 5.6

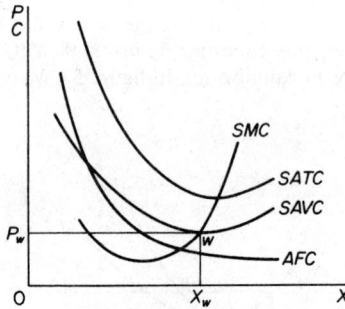

Figure 5.7

point.' In figure 5.7 the closing-down point of the firm is denoted by point w. If price falls below P_w the firm does not cover its variable costs and is better off if it closes down.

Mathematical derivation of the equilibrium of the firm

The firm aims at the maximisation of its profit

$$\Pi = R - C$$

where Π = profit
       R = total revenue
       C = total cost

Clearly $R = f_1(X)$ and $C = f_2(X)$, given the price P.

(a) The first-order condition for the maximisation of a function is that its first derivative (with respect to X in our case) be equal to zero. Differentiating the total-profit function and equating to zero we obtain

$$\frac{\partial \Pi}{\partial X} = \frac{\partial R}{\partial X} - \frac{\partial C}{\partial X} = 0$$

or

$$\frac{\partial R}{\partial X} = \frac{\partial C}{\partial X}$$

The term $\partial R/\partial X$ is the slope of the total revenue curve, that is, the marginal revenue. The term $\partial C/\partial X$ is the slope of the total cost curve, or the marginal cost. Thus the first-order condition for profit maximisation is

$$MR = MC$$

Given that $MC > 0$, MR must also be positive at equilibrium. Since $MR = P$ the first-order condition may be written as $MC = P$.

(b) The second-order condition for a maximum requires that the second derivative of the function be negative (implying that after its highest point the curve turns downwards). The second derivative of the total-profit function is

$$\frac{\partial^2 \Pi}{\partial X^2} = \frac{\partial^2 R}{\partial X^2} - \frac{\partial^2 C}{\partial X^2}$$

This must be negative if the function has been maximised, that is

$$\frac{\partial^2 R}{\partial X^2} - \frac{\partial^2 C}{\partial X^2} < 0$$

which yields the condition

$$\frac{\partial^2 R}{\partial X^2} < \frac{\partial^2 C}{\partial X^2}$$

But $\partial^2 R / \partial X^2$ is the slope of the MR curve and $\partial^2 C / \partial X^2$ is the slope of the MC curve. Hence the second-order condition may verbally be written as follows

(slope of MR) < (slope of MC)

Thus the MC must have a steeper slope than the MR curve or the MC must cut the MR curve from below. In pure competition the slope of the MR curve is zero, hence the second-order condition is simplified as follows

$$0 < \frac{\partial^2 C}{\partial X^2}$$

which reads: the MC curve must have a positive slope, or the MC must be rising.

B. THE SUPPLY CURVE OF THE FIRM AND THE INDUSTRY

The supply curve of the firm may be derived by the points of intersection of its MC curve with successive demand curves. Assume that the market price increases gradually. This causes an upward shift of the demand curve of the firm. Given the positive slope of the MC curve, each higher demand curve cuts the (given) MC curve to a point which lies to the right of the previous intersection. This implies that the quantity supplied by the firm increases as price rises. The firm, given its cost structure, will not supply any quantity (will close down) if the price falls below P_w, because at a lower price the firm does not cover its variable costs (figure 5.8). If we plot the successive points of intersection of MC and the demand curves on a separate graph we observe that the supply curve of the individual firm is identical to its MC curve to the right of the closing-down point w. Below P_w the quantity supplied by the firm is zero. As price rises above P_w the quantity supplied increases. The supply curve of the firm is shown in figure 5.9.

The industry-supply curve is the horizontal summation of the supply curves of the individual firms. It is assumed that the factor prices and the technology are given and that the number of firms is very large. Under these conditions the total quantity supplied in the market at each price is the sum of the quantities supplied by all firms at that price. In figure 5.10 we show the industry supply as a straight line with a positive slope. It should, however, be noted that the particular shape of the market-supply curve depends on the technology and on factor prices, as well as the size distribution of the firms in the industry. All firms are not usually of the same size. The particular size of each firm in perfect competition depends on the entrepreneurial efficiency of the businessman, which is traditionally considered as a random attribute.

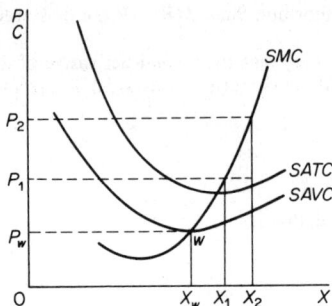

Figure 5.8

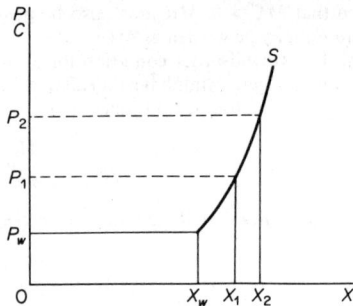

Figure 5.9

C. SHORT-RUN EQUILIBRIUM OF THE INDUSTRY

Given the market demand and the market supply the industry is in equilibrium at that price which *clears the market*, that is at the price at which the quantity demanded is equal to the quantity supplied. In figure 5.10 the industry is in equilibrium at price P, at which the quantity demanded and supplied is $\bar{Q}$. However, this will be a short-run equilibrium, if at the prevailing price firms are making excess profits (figure 5.11) or losses (figure 5.12). In the long run, firms that make losses and cannot readjust their plant will close down. Those that make excess profits will expand their capacity, while excess profits will also attract new firms into the industry. Entry, exit and readjustment of the remaining firms in the industry will lead to a long-run equilibrium in which firms will just be earning normal profits and there will be no entry or exit from the industry.

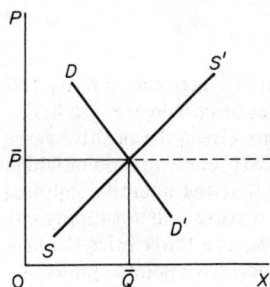

Figure 5.10   Short-run
industry equilibrium

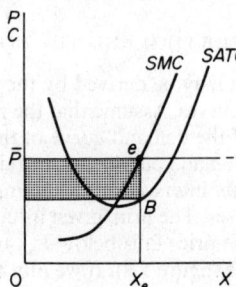

Figure 5.11   Short-run
equilibrium of a firm
(excess profits)

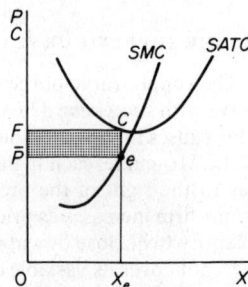

Figure 5.12   Short-run
equilibrium of a firm
(losses)

III. LONG-RUN EQUILIBRIUM

A. EQUILIBRIUM OF THE FIRM IN THE LONG RUN

In the long run firms are in equilibrium when they have adjusted their plant so as to produce at the minimum point of their long-run AC curve, which is tangent (at this point) to the demand curve defined by the market price. In the long run the firms will be earning just normal profits, which are included in the LAC. If they are making excess profits new firms will be attracted in the industry; this will lead to a fall in price (a downward shift in the individual demand curves) and an upward shift of the cost curves due to the increase of the prices of factors as the industry expands. These changes will continue until the *LAC* is tangent to the demand curve defined by the market price. If the firms make losses in the long run they will leave the industry, price will rise and costs may fall as the industry contracts, until the remaining firms in the industry cover their total costs inclusive of the normal rate of profit.

In figure 5.14 we show how firms adjust to their long-run equilibrium position. If the price is P, the firm is making excess profits working with the plant whose cost is denoted by SAC_1. It will therefore have an incentive to build new capacity and it will move along its *LAC*. At the same time new firms will be entering the industry attracted by the excess profits. As the quantity supplied in the market increases (by the increased production of expanding old firms and by the newly established ones) the supply curve in the market will shift to the right and price will fall until it reaches the level of P_1 (in figure 5.13) at which the firms and the industry are in long-run equilibrium. The *LAC* in figure 5.14 is the final-cost curve including any increase in the prices of factors that may have taken place as the industry expanded.

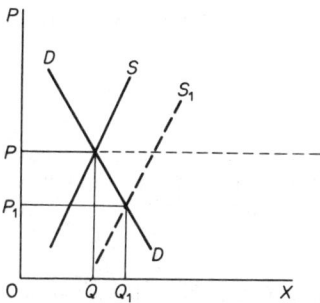

Figure 5.13

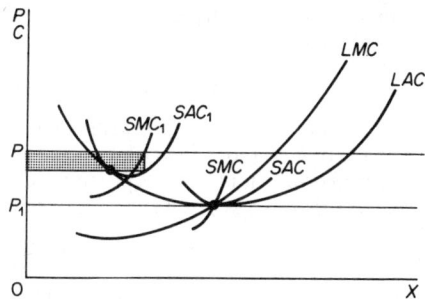

Figure 5.14

The condition for the long-run equilibrium of the firm is that the marginal cost be equal to the price and to the long-run average cost

$$LMC = LAC = P$$

The firm adjusts its plant size so as to produce that level of output at which the *LAC* is the minimum possible, given the technology and the prices of factors of production. At equilibrium the short-run marginal cost is equal to the long-run marginal cost and the short-run average cost is equal to the long-run average cost. Thus, given the above equilibrium condition, we have

$$SMC = LMC = LAC = LMC = P = MR$$

This implies that at the minimum point of the *LAC* the corresponding (short-run) plant is worked at its optimal capacity, so that the minima of the *LAC* and *SAC* coincide. On the other hand, the *LMC* cuts the *LAC* at its minimum point and the *SMC* cuts the *SAC* at its minimum point. Thus at the minimum point of the *LAC* the above equality between short-run and long-run costs is satisfied.

B. EQUILIBRIUM OF THE INDUSTRY IN THE LONG RUN

The industry is in long-run equilibrium when a price is reached at which all firms are in equilibrium (producing at the minimum point of their *LAC* curve and making

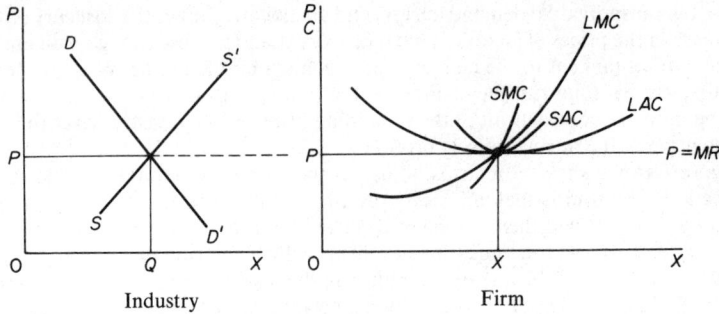

Figure 5.15

just normal profits). Under these conditions there is no further entry or exit of firms in the industry, given the technology and factor prices. The long-run equilibrium of the industry is shown in figure 5.15. At the market price, P, the firms produce at their minimum cost, earning just normal profits. The firm is in equilibrium because at the level of output X

$$LMC = SMC = P = MR$$

This equality ensures that the firm maximises its profit.

At the price P the industry is in equilibrium because profits are normal and all costs are covered so that there is no incentive for entry or exit. That the firms earn just normal profit (neither excess profits nor losses) is shown by the equality

$$LAC = SAC = P$$

which is observed at the minimum point of the LAC curve. With all firms in the industry being in equilibrium and with no entry or exit, the industry supply remains stable, and, given the market demand (DD' in figure 5.15), the price P is a long-run equilibrium price.

Since the price in the market is unique, this implies that all firms in the industry have the same minimum long-run average cost. This, however, does not mean that all firms are of the same size or have the same efficiency, despite the fact that their LAC is the same in equilibrium. The more efficient firms employ more productive factors of production and/or more able managers. These more efficient factors must be remunerated for their higher productivity, otherwise they will be bid off by the new entrants in the industry. In other words, as the price rises in the market the more efficient firms earn a rent which they must pay to their superior resources. Thus rents of more efficient factors become costs for the individual firm, and hence the LAC of the more efficient firms shifts upwards as the market price rises, even if the factor prices for the industry as a whole remain constant as the industry expands. In this situation the LAC of the old, more efficient, firms must be redrawn so as to be tangent at the higher market price. The LMC of the old firms is not affected by the rents accruing to its more productive factors. (It will be shifted only if the prices of factors for the industry in general increase.) Thus the more efficient firms will be in equilibrium, producing that output at which the redrawn LAC is at its minimum (at which point the LAC is cut by the initial LMC given that factor prices remain constant). Under these conditions, with the superior, more productive resources properly costed at their opportunity cost, all firms have the same unit cost in their long-run equilibrium. This is shown in figure 5.16. At the initial price P_0 the second firm was not in the industry as it could not cover its costs at that price. However, at the new price, P_1, firm B enters the industry, making just normal profits. The estab-

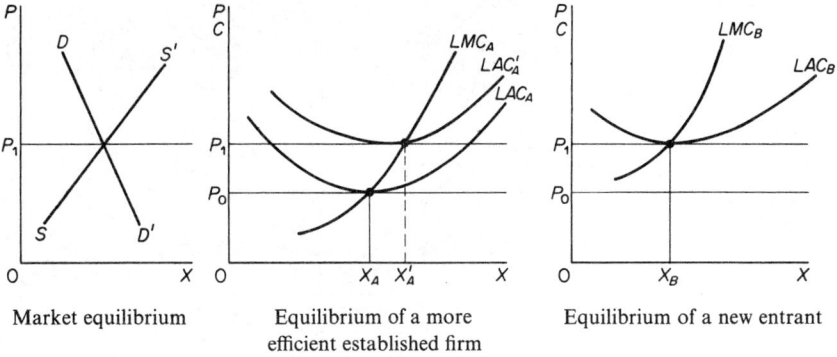

| Market equilibrium | Equilibrium of a more efficient established firm | Equilibrium of a new entrant |

Figure 5.16

lished firm A earns rents which are imputed costs, so that its LAC shifts upwards and it reaches a new long-run equilibrium producing a higher level of output (X'_A).

C. OPTIMAL RESOURCE ALLOCATION

In perfect competition the market mechanism leads to an optimal allocation of resources. The optimality is shown by the following conditions which prevail in the long-run equilibrium of the industry:

(*a*) The output is produced at the minimum feasible cost.

(*b*) Consumers pay the minimum possible price which just covers the marginal cost of the product, that is, price = opportunity cost.

(*c*) Plants are used at full capacity in the long run, so that there is no waste of resources.

(*d*) Firms only earn normal profits.

In the long run these conditions prevail in all markets, so that resources are optimally allocated in the economy as a whole. If we assume for simplicity that there are only two commodities (x and y) produced in the economy we may present the *allocation of the given resources* of the economy with the familiar production-possibility curve. The preferences of the consumers in the economy may be shown by community indifference curves. Given the production-possibility curve and consumers' preferences, perfect competition will lead to the optimal allocation of resources under the following conditions:

Firstly, if the consumers' sovereignty, expressed by the price system (uncontrolled by any government intervention), reflects the correct ranking of preferences of the community.

Secondly, if there are no unexhausted economies of scale in any one industry.

Finally, if resources and technology are given; there is no growth in the economy and no technical progress.

If the above conditions are fulfilled, perfect competition leads to the optimal resource allocation defined by the point of tangency of the given production-possibility curve with the highest possible indifference curve. In figure 5.17 optimal allocation of resources is reached at point e. The economy uses up all the available resources (point e lies *on* the

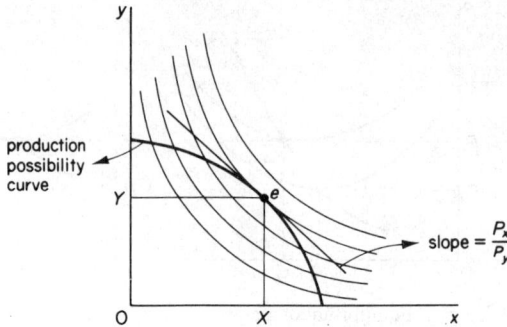

Figure 5.17 Optimal resource allocation in the economy

production-possibility curve) and consumers attain the highest possible welfare, given the available factors of production. The optimal allocation is attained at the prices P_x and P_y at which the levels of output of the two commodities are $0X$ and $0Y$.

IV. DYNAMIC CHANGES AND INDUSTRY EQUILIBRIUM

In this section we will examine the predictions of the perfect competition model in the following situations:

A. A shift in the market demand
B. A shift in the costs following changes in factor prices
C. Imposition of a tax by the government.

A. SHIFT IN THE MARKET DEMAND: CONSTANT-, INCREASING- AND DECREASING-COST INDUSTRIES

Assume that the market demand shifts to the right due to an increase in consumers' income (or to a change in the other determinants of market demand, e.g. increase in total population, etc.). In the short run the supply curve is given. Price will rise (to P' in figure 5.18) and the quantity supplied will increase (from Q to Q' in figure 5.18) by an expansion of the production of the existing firms (from X to X' in figure 5.19), which will be realising excess profits at the higher market price (equal to the area $ABCP'$). In the long run the excess profits made by the established firms will attract new firms into

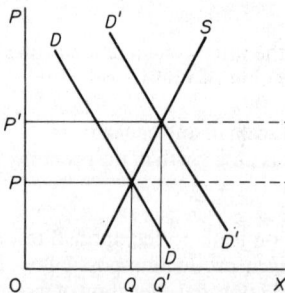

Figure 5.18 Industry

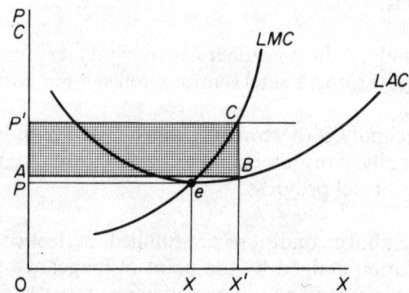

Figure 5.19 Firm

the industry. This influx of firms will shift the market supply to the right and will cause price to fall below the short-run equilibrium level (*P'*). The new equilibrium price may remain above the original level, or it may return to the original level, depending on the size of the shift in the market supply, which reflects the cost conditions of the industry (the change in factor prices as the industry expands).

An industry is a *constant-cost industry* if the prices of factors of production employed by it remain constant as industry output expands. An industry is an *increasing-cost industry* if the prices of factors of production increase as the market expands. An industry is a *decreasing-cost industry* if the prices of factors of production decline as the market expands.

Constant-cost industry

In figure 5.20 we show the case of long-run equilibrium of an industry which grows with constant costs. We start from an initial long-run equilibrium situation where the demand-curve price line of the firm is tangent to the long-run and the short-run average-total-cost curves at their minimum points. Assume that the market demand shifts from *DD'* to $D_1 D'_1$. In the short run price increases to *P'* and the existing firms increase their output, operating their plant above full capacity. The increased quantity is shown by a movement along the market supply *SS'*. This situation, however, cannot persist in the long run because the excess profits attract entry. The resulting increase in the demand of factors of production is assumed not to raise their price, so that the *LAC* curve does not shift upwards. The new firms will produce under the same *LAC* conditions as the already established firms. Entry will continue until the new supply curve $S_1 S'_1$ intersects the shifted-demand curve at the initial price *P*. If the market continues to grow, the industry-demand curve will shift further to the right ($D_2 D'_2$) and the whole process will repeat itself. New firms will enter in the industry and the supply curve will shift to the right until it cuts the new demand curve at the initial price. The long-run industry supply is a straight line (*abc* in figure 5.20) parallel to the quantity-axis at the initial price level.

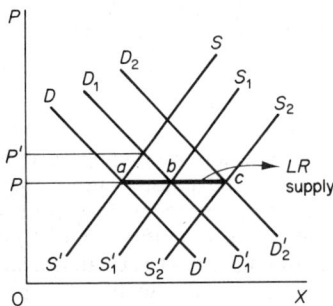

Figure 5.20   Industry

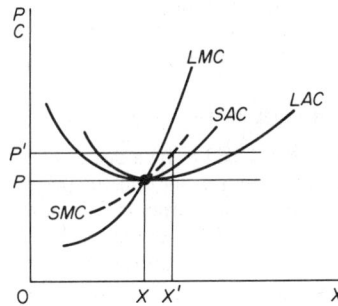

Figure 5.21   Firm

Increasing-cost industry

An industry is said to be an increasing-cost industry if its long-run supply curve has a positive slope, indicating that the prices of factors increase as the industry output expands.

The process of adjustment of the industry supply to the growing market demand under conditions of increasing costs is shown in figure 5.22. As the market demand

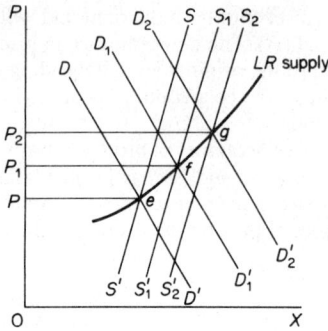

Figure 5.22   Industry

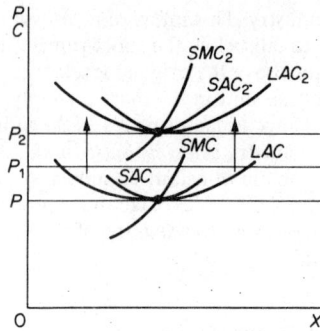

Figure 5.23   Firm

shifts from its initial equilibrium DD' to the new level D_1D_1' price will increase in the short run (to P_1): an increase in the quantity supplied is forthcoming by existing firms working their plant beyond its optimal capacity. Excess profits will attract new firms in the industry. Now, however, we assume that the prices of factors increase as their demand expands.

The LAC of all firms (existing as well as new) shifts upwards, while the LMC shifts to the left with the increasing factor prices. This will tend to shift the industry supply to the left. However, at the same time, the quantity supplied increases as new firms enter the industry and thus the market supply will tend to shift to the right. The latter shift more than offsets the first, so that on balance the supply curve shifts outwards as price increases (otherwise the new firms would work by bidding away resources from the established firms, and industry output would be impossible to expand as required by the increase in the market price). The shift of the supply curve will lead to a fall in price (as compared with the short-run level P_1) if the increase in factor prices permits it. If, however, the increase in factor costs is substantial the new equilibrium price might stay at the short-run level despite the shift in supply. In any case the new market price will be higher than the original level and the long-run supply curve (*efg* in figure 5.22) will be upwards-sloping. In an increasing-cost industry output can expand in the long run only at an increasing supply price.[1]

Decreasing-cost industry

An industry is said to be a decreasing-cost industry if its long-run supply curve has a negative slope, indicating that the prices of factors fall as the industry output expands.

The process of adjustment of the industry supply to the expanding market demand is shown in figure 5.24. As the market demand shifts to the right (from D to D_1) price increases in the short run and entry is attracted. The ensuing increased demand for factors encourages their suppliers to innovate or improve their skills, so that factor costs become in fact lower per unit of output. In these circumstances we speak of *external* (to the industry and to the firm) *economies*[2] (figure 5.24). The decline in factor prices

---

[1] It should be noted that in the new market equilibrium the output (size) of the individual firm may be smaller, greater or equal to the level of output in the original equilibrium, depending on the shift of the cost curves. In figure 5.23 we assumed that the output of the firm is the same as in its original equilibrium. What is certain with increasing cost industries is that the market price, the market output and the number of firms will increase as demand shifts.

[2] Note that *external economies* are different from the internal to the firm *economies of scale*. The latter are under the control of the firm, while external economies are not.

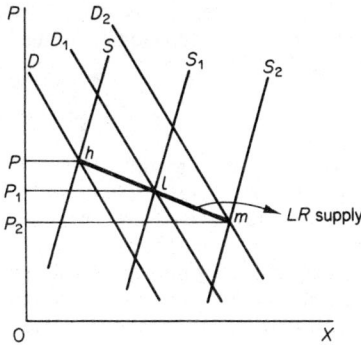

Figure 5.24 Industry

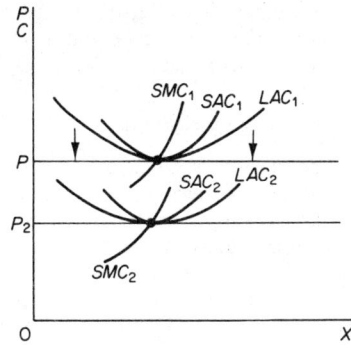

Figure 5.25 Firm

shifts the cost curves of individual firms downward (figure 5.25). The industry supply shifts so far to the right that price in the long run falls below the initial level. The long-run supply curve is the line *hlm* in figure 5.24, which has a negative slope. This implies that if there are strong external economies the industry supply can expand in the long run at a decreasing price.

B. PREDICTIONS OF THE PERFECT COMPETITION MODEL WHEN COSTS CHANGE

The effects of a change in costs depend on whether the change relates to the fixed or the variable costs of the firm.

An increase in the fixed cost

Assume that the rents of the buildings (offices) occupied by a firm are raised. This will result in an upward shift in both the AFC and the ATC curves (figure 5.26). However, the AVC and the MC curves are not affected, since rents are an element of the fixed cost.

Given that the MC curve is the supply curve of the firm, the equilibrium position of the firm (e) is not affected in the short run. Hence the same output will be produced and the market supply and price will not change in the short run.

However, assuming that the firm before the change in costs was in long-run equilibrium earning just normal profits, it will not now cover its higher (shifted) total average costs and will go out of business in the long run. Consequently in the long run the

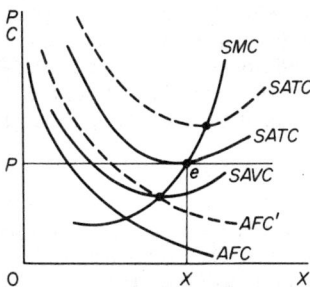

Figure 5.26 Firm

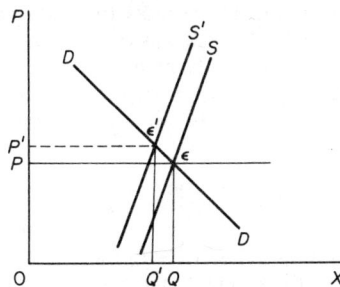

Figure 5.27 Industry

market-supply curve will shift upwards to the left; in the new equilibrium the output will be lower, the price higher, and there will be fewer firms in the industry (if the higher price does not cover the increased costs) (figure 5.27).

An increase in the variable costs

Assume that market wages are increased. This will cause a shift of the AVC the ATC and the MC curves of the firm upwards to the left (figure 5.28). Given that the MC is also the supply curve of the firm, the increase in the variable costs will result in a decrease in the quantity supplied by the firm at the going market price (from x to x' in figure 5.28). Thus, even in the short run, the market-supply curve will shift upwards to the left and, given the market demand, price will rise. In the new market equilibrium the number of firms will be the same but the quantity will be lower and the price higher as compared with the initial equilibrium (figure 5.29).

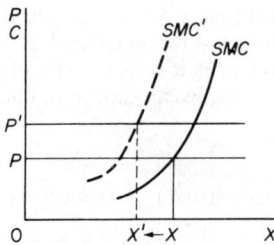

Figure 5.28   Firm   Figure 5.29   Industry

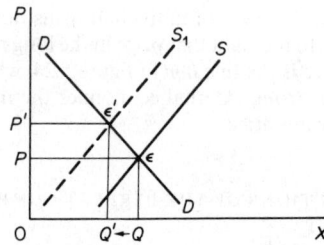

C. EFFECT OF IMPOSITION OF A TAX

We will examine the effects of the imposition by the government of a lump-sum tax, a profits tax, and a specific tax, that is, a tax per unit of output.

Imposition of a lump-sum tax (per period)

The analysis of the effects of a lump-sum tax is the same as in the case of an increase in the fixed cost examined in the previous section, since the lump-sum tax is like a fixed cost to the firm.

Thus in the short run the lump-sum tax will not affect the MC cost curve and the firm will continue to produce the same output as before the imposition of the tax.

However, if the firm was earning just normal profits prior to the tax, it will not be covering its ATC at the going market price and will close down in the long run. Thus in the long run the market-supply curve will shift to the left as firms leave the industry; the output will be lower and the price higher as compared with the pre-tax equilibrium.

Imposition of a profits tax

This tax takes the form of a percentage on the net profit of the firm. The effects of a profits tax are the same with those of a lump-sum tax. The profits tax, while reducing the profits (by adding to the cash expenses of the firm), will not affect its MC. Hence in the short run the equilibrium of the firm and the industry will not change.

However, in the long run, exit of firms will be inevitable if in the pre-tax period firms were earning just normal profits. In the long run the supply in the market would shift to the left and a new equilibrium would be reached with a higher price, a lower quantity produced and a smaller number of firms.

Imposition of a specific sales tax

This takes the form of a given amount of money (e.g. 5p) per unit of output produced. Such a tax clearly affects the *MC* of the firm. The *MC* curve, which is also the supply curve of the firm, will shift upwards to the left, and the amount produced at the going price will be reduced.

The market-supply curve will shift upwards to the left and price will rise. The important question here is by how much will the price increase: will the increase in *P* be smaller, equal, or greater than the specific tax? This is an important question because it relates to who is going to bear the specific sales tax: the consumer-buyer, the firm, or both?

The answer to this question is that the burden of the specific tax that will be borne by the consumer (buyer) depends on the price elasticity of supply, given the market demand. In general, the most elastic the market supply the higher the proportion of the tax that the consumer will bear and the less the burden of the firm from the specific tax.

So long as the market supply has a positive slope the specific tax will be paid partly by the buyer and partly by the firm. The burden to the firm will be smaller the greater the elasticity of supply. In other words, the firms will be able to pass on to the consumer more of the specific tax, the more elastic the market supply. This is illustrated in figures 5.30 and 5.31. The demand curve is identical in both figures and the initial (pre-tax) price is the same, but the supply in figure 5.31 is more elastic. Imposition of a specific tax equal to *ab* raises the price by ΔP in figure 5.30 and by ΔP_1 in figure 5.31. Clearly $\Delta P_1 > \Delta P$, that is, the tax burden to the consumer is greater in the case of a more elastic supply curve (given the market demand).

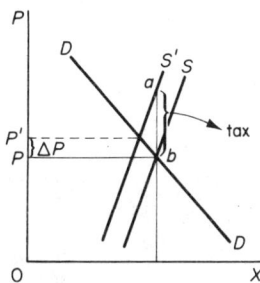

Figure 5.30

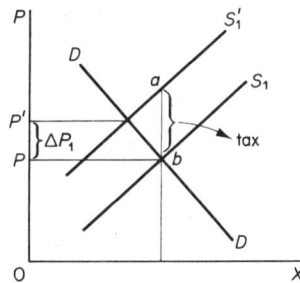

Figure 5.31

In the limiting case of a market-supply curve with infinite elasticity the increase in price is equal to the specific tax and the whole tax burden is borne by the consumer. In figure 5.32 the demand is the same as in figures 5.30 and 5.31, but the supply is parallel to the horizontal axis, showing infinite price elasticity. The imposition of a specific tax equal to *ab* (same as before) leads to an equal increase in the price: $\Delta P_2 = ab$.

If the supply curve has a negative slope (figure 5.33) the imposition of a specific tax results in an increase in the price which is greater than the tax. In figure 5.33 the demand is identical as in the above-examined cases but the supply is negatively sloping (with its

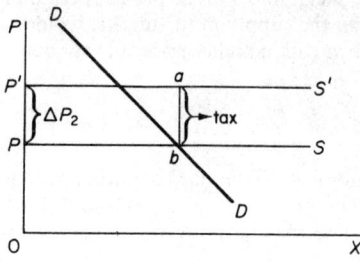

Figure 5.32

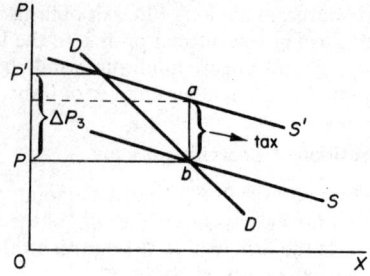

Figure 5.33

slope smaller than the slope of the DD curve). Under these conditions a specific tax of ab leads to an increase in the market price equal to ΔP_3, which is obviously larger than the unit tax.

The analysis of the predictions of the perfect competition model when the environment changes is important. Such analysis will be attempted for other models of the behaviour of the firm. Comparison of the predictions of various models usually shows how to test the different theories and choose between them.

6. Monopoly

I. DEFINITION

Monopoly is a market structure in which there is a single seller, there are no close substitutes for the commodity it produces and there are barriers to entry.

The main causes that lead to monopoly are the following. Firstly, ownership of strategic raw materials, or exclusive knowledge of production techniques. Secondly, patent rights for a product or for a production process. Thirdly, government licensing or the imposition of foreign trade barriers to exclude foreign competitors. Fourthly, the size of the market may be such as not to support more than one plant of optimal size. The technology may be such as to exhibit substantial economies of scale, which require only a single plant, if they are to be fully reaped. For example, in transport, electricity, communications, there are substantial economies which can be realised only at large scales of output. The size of the market may not allow the existence of more than a single large plant. In these conditions it is said that the market creates a 'natural' monopoly, and it is usually the case that the government undertakes the production of the commodity or of the service so as to avoid exploitation of the consumers. This is the case of the public utilities. Fifthly, the existing firm adopts a limit-pricing policy, that is, a pricing policy aiming at the prevention of new entry. Such a pricing policy may be combined with other policies such as heavy advertising or continuous product differentiation, which render entry unattractive. This is the case of monopoly established by creating barriers to new competition.[1]

II. DEMAND AND REVENUE

Since there is a single firm in the industry, the firm's demand curve is the industry-demand curve. This curve is assumed known and has a downward slope (figure 6.1).

We will use a linear demand function for simplicity. We have examined the properties of this form of demand in Chapter 2. They may be summarised as follows:

1. The demand equation, *ceteris paribus*, is

$$X = b_0^* - b_1^* P$$

The clause *ceteris paribus* implies that all the other factors (such as income, tastes, other prices) which affect demand are assumed constant. Changes in these factors will shift the demand curve.

---

[1] See also Chapter 13.

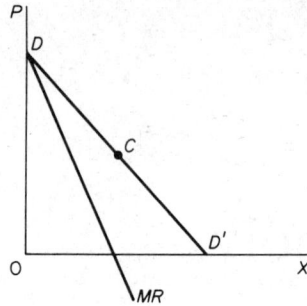

Figure 6.1

2. The slope of the demand curve is

$$\frac{dX}{dP} = -b_1^*$$

3. The price elasticity of demand is

$$e_P = \frac{dX}{dP} \cdot \frac{P}{X} = -b_1^* \cdot \frac{P}{X}$$

That is, elasticity changes at any one point of the demand curve.
(a) At point D the elasticity approaches infinity

$$e_P = -b_1^* \cdot \frac{P}{X} \to \infty$$

(b) At point D' the elasticity is zero

$$e_P = -b_1^* \cdot \frac{P}{X} = -b_1^* \cdot \frac{0}{X} = 0$$

(c) At the mid point C the price elasticity is unity

$$e_P = -1$$

4. The total revenue of the monopolist is

$$R = P \cdot X$$

Solving the demand equation for P we find

$$P = \frac{b_0^*}{b_1^*} - \frac{1}{b_1^*} X \infty$$

Setting $(b_0^*/b_1^*) = b_0$ and $(1/b_1^*) = b_1$ we may rewrite the price equation as

$$P = b_0 - b_1 X$$

Substituting into the revenue equation we find

$$R = PX = (b_0 - b_1 X)X$$

or

$$R = b_0 X - b_1 X^2$$

5. The average revenue is equal to the price:

$$AR = \frac{R}{X} = \frac{PX}{X} = P = b_0 - b_1 X$$

Thus the demand curve is also the AR curve of the monopolist.

6. The marginal revenue is:

$$\frac{dR}{dX} = \frac{d(b_0 X - b_1 X^2)}{dX} = b_0 - 2b_1 X$$

That is, the MR is a straight line with the same intercept as the demand curve, but twice as steep.

The general relation between P and MR is found as follows. Given

$$R = PX$$

$$MR = \frac{dR}{dX} = P\frac{dX}{dX} + X\frac{dP}{dX}$$

or

$$MR = P + X \cdot \frac{dP}{dX}$$

The marginal revenue is at all levels of output smaller than P, given that

$$P = MR - X\frac{dP}{dX}$$

and the term $(X(dP/dX))$ is positive (since the slope of the demand curve $(dP/dX) > 0$). Hence $P > MR$.

Intuitively, since demand is negatively sloping, the firm must lower its price if it is to sell an additional unit. The net change in total revenue, the MR, is the new (lower) price from selling the additional nth unit minus the loss the firm realises from selling all previous units $/n - 1)$ at the lower price:

$$MR_2 = P_2 - (n - 1)(P_1 - P_2)$$

Thus $MR_2 < P_2$, given $(n - 1) > 0$ and $(P_1 - P_2) > 0$

7. The relationship between MR and price elasticity e is

$$MR = P\left(1 - \frac{1}{e}\right)$$

Proof

We established that

$$MR = \frac{dR}{\partial X} = P + X\frac{\partial P}{\partial X}$$

The price elasticity of demand is defined as

$$e_P = -\frac{\partial X}{\partial P} \cdot \frac{P}{X}$$

Inverting this relation we obtain

$$\frac{1}{e} = -\frac{\partial P}{dX} \cdot \frac{X}{P}$$

Solving for dP/dX we find

$$\frac{dP}{dX} = -\frac{1}{e} \cdot \frac{P}{X}$$

Substituting in the expression of the MR we get

$$MR = P + X\left(-\frac{1}{e} \cdot \frac{P}{X}\right)$$

or

$$MR = P\left(1 - \frac{1}{e}\right) \qquad\qquad \text{Q.E.D.}$$

III. COSTS

In the traditional theory of monopoly the shapes of the cost curves are the same as in the theory of pure competition. The AVC, MC and ATC are U-shaped, while the AFC is a rectangular hyperbola. However, the particular shape of the cost curves does not make any difference to the determination of the equilibrium of the firm, provided that the slope of the MC is greater than the slope of the MR curve (see below).

One point should be stressed here. The MC curve is *not* the supply curve of the monopolist, as is the case in pure competition. In monopoly there is no unique relationship between price and the quantity supplied (see below, p. 177).

IV. EQUILIBRIUM OF THE MONOPOLIST

A. SHORT-RUN EQUILIBRIUM

The monopolist maximises his short-run profits if the following two conditions are fulfilled: Firstly, the MC is equal to the MR. Secondly, the slope of MC is greater than the slope of the MR at the point of intersection.

In figure 6.2 the equilibrium of the monopolist is defined by point ε, at which the MC intersects the MR curve from below. Thus both conditions for equilibrium are fulfilled. Price is P_M and the quantity is X_M. The monopolist realises excess profits equal to the shaded area AP_MCB. Note that the price is higher than the MR.

In pure competition the firm is a price-taker, so that its only decision is output determination. The monopolist is faced by two decisions: setting his price and his output. However, given the downward-sloping demand curve, the two decisions are interdependent. The monopolist will either set his price and sell the amount that the market will take at it, or he will produce the output defined by the intersection of MC and MR, which will be sold at the corresponding price, P. The monopolist cannot decide independently both the quantity and the price at which he wants to sell it. The crucial condition for the maximisation of the monopolist's profit is the equality of his MC and the MR, provided that the MC cuts the MR from below.

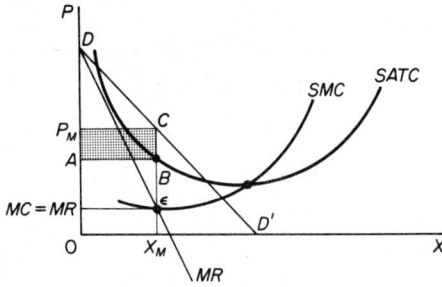

Figure 6.2

Formal derivation of the equilibrium of the monopolist

Given the demand function

$$X = g(P)$$

which may be solved for P

$$P = f_1(X)$$

and given the cost function

$$C = f_2(X)$$

The monopolist aims at the maximisation of his profit

$$\Pi = R - C$$

(a) *The first-order condition for maximum profit* Π

$$\frac{\partial \Pi}{\partial X} = 0$$

$$\frac{\partial \Pi}{\partial X} = \frac{\partial R}{\partial X} - \frac{\partial C}{\partial X} = 0$$

or

$$\frac{\partial R}{\partial X} = \frac{\partial C}{\partial X}$$

that is $MR = MC$

(b) *The second-order condition for maximum profit*

$$\frac{\partial^2 \Pi}{\partial X^2} < 0$$

$$\frac{\partial^2 \Pi}{\partial X^2} = \frac{\partial^2 R}{\partial X^2} - \frac{\partial^2 C}{\partial X^2} < 0$$

or

$$\frac{\partial^2 R}{\partial X^2} < \frac{\partial^2 C}{\partial X^2}$$

that is

$$\begin{bmatrix} \text{slope} \\ \text{of } MR \end{bmatrix} < \begin{bmatrix} \text{slope} \\ \text{of } MC \end{bmatrix}$$

A numerical example

Given the demand curve of the monopolist

$$X = 50 - 0.5P$$

which may be solved for P

$$P = 100 - 2X$$

Given the cost function of the monopolist

$$C = 50 + 40X$$

The goal of the monopolist is to maximise profit

$$\Pi = R - C$$

(i) We first find the MR

$$R = XP = X(100 - 2X)$$
$$R = 100X - 2X^2$$
$$MR = \frac{\partial R}{\partial X} = 100 - 4X$$

(ii) We next find the MC

$$C = 50 + 40X$$
$$MC = \frac{\partial C}{\partial X} = 40$$

(iii) We equate MR and MC

$$MR = MC$$
$$100 - 4X = 40$$
$$X = 15$$

(iv) The monopolist's price is found by substituting $X = 15$ into the demand–price equation

$$P = 100 - 2X = 70$$

(v) The profit is

$$\Pi = R - C = 1050 - 650 = 400$$

This profit is the maximum possible, since the second-order condition is satisfied:
(*a*) from

$$\frac{\partial C}{\partial X} = 40$$

we have

$$\frac{\partial^2 C}{\partial X^2} = 0$$

(b) from

$$\frac{\partial R}{\partial X} = 100 - 4X \qquad \text{we have} \qquad \frac{\partial^2 R}{\partial X^2} = -4$$

Clearly $-4 < 0$.

We may now re-examine the statement that there is no unique supply curve for the monopolist derived from his MC. Given his MC, the same quantity may be offered at different prices depending on the price elasticity of demand. Graphically this is shown in figure 6.3. The quantity X will be sold at price P_1 if demand is D_1, while the same

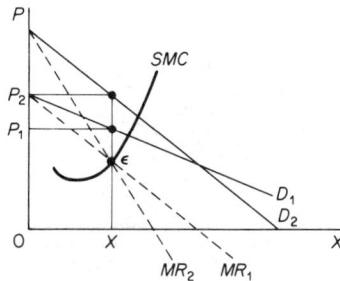

Figure 6.3

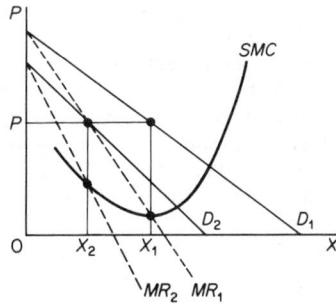

Figure 6.4

quantity X will be sold at price P_2 if demand is D_2. Thus there is no unique relationship between price and quantity. Similarly, given the MC of the monopolist, various quantities may be supplied at any one price, depending on the market demand and the corresponding MR curve. In figure 6.4 we depict such a situation. The cost conditions are represented by the MC curve. Given the costs of the monopolist, he would supply $0X_1$, if the market demand is D_1, while at the same price, P, he would supply only $0X_2$ if the market demand is D_2.

B. LONG-RUN EQUILIBRIUM

In the long run the monopolist has the time to expand his plant, or to use his existing plant at any level which will maximise his profit. With entry blocked, however, it is not necessary for the monopolist to reach an optimal scale (that is, to build up his plant until he reaches the minimum point of the *LAC*). Neither is there any guarantee that he will use his existing plant at optimum capacity. What is certain is that the monopolist will not stay in business if he makes losses in the long run. He will most probably continue to earn supernormal profits even in the long run, given that entry is barred. However, the size of his plant and the degree of utilisation of any given plant size depend entirely on the market demand. He may reach the optimal scale (minimum point of *LAC*) or remain at suboptimal scale (falling part of his *LAC*) or surpass the optimal scale (expand beyond the minimum *LAC*) depending on the market conditions. In figure 6.5 we depict

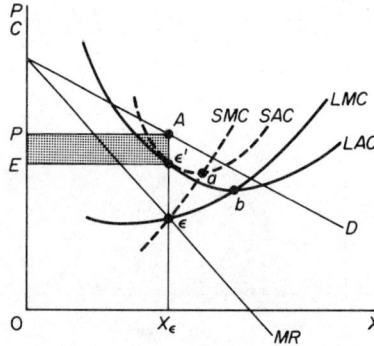

Figure 6.5   Monopolist with suboptimal plant and excess capacity

the case in which the market size does not permit the monopolist to expand to the minimum point of *LAC*. In this case not only is his plant of suboptimal size (in the sense that the full economies of scale are not exhausted) but also the existing plant is under-utilised. This is because to the left of the minimum point of the *LAC* the *SRAC* is tangent to the *LAC* at its falling part, and also because the short-run *MC* must be equal to the *LRMC*. This occurs at ε, while the minimum *LAC* is at *b* and the optimal use of the existing plant is at *a*. Since it is utilised at the level ε', there is excess capacity.

In figure 6.6 we depict the case where the size of the market is so large that the monopolist, in order to maximise his output, must build a plant larger than the optimal and overutilise it. This is because to the right of the minimum point of the *LAC* the *SRAC*

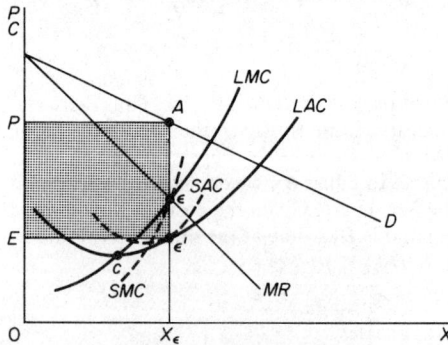

Figure 6.6   Monopolist operating in a large market: his plant is larger than the optimal (*c*) and it is being overutilised (at ε').

and the *LAC* are tangent at a point of their positive slope, and also because the *SRMC* must be equal to the *LAC*. Thus the plant that maximises the monopolist's profits leads to higher costs for two reasons: firstly because it is larger than the optimal size, and secondly because it is overutilised. This is often the case with public utility companies operating at national level.

Finally in figure 6.7 we show the case in which the market size is just large enough to permit the monopolist to build the optimal plant and use it at full capacity.

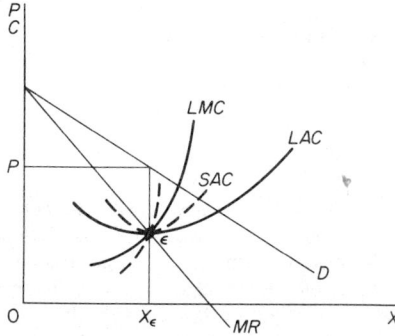

Figure 6.7

It should be clear that which of the above situations will emerge in any particular case depends on the size of the market (given the technology of the monopolist). There is no certainty that in the long run the monopolist will reach the optimal scale, as is the case in a purely competitive market. In monopoly there are no market forces similar to those in pure competition which lead the firms to operate at optimum plant size (and utilise it at its full capacity) in the long run.

V. PREDICTIONS OF THE MONOPOLY MODEL IN DYNAMIC SITUATIONS

In this section we will examine the effects on the monopolist's equilibrium of (*a*) a shift in the market demand, (*b*) a change in costs, (*c*) the imposition of a tax by the government.

A. SHIFT IN THE MARKET DEMAND

We saw in Chapter 5 that an upward shift in the market demand resulted (in the short run) in a new market equilibrium with a higher price and a lower quantity. In a monopoly market this may not be so. An upward shift of the market demand (provided that the new demand does not intersect the initial one) will result in a new market equilibrium in which the quantity produced will be larger, but the price may increase, remain constant or decrease. Let us examine these possibilities.

In the new equilibrium the price may remain constant while the quantity supplied increases. This case is shown in figure 6.8. Assume that the new demand curve is D_2, to the right of D_1. The shift in D will lead to a shift of the MR curve (from MR_1 to MR_2). Given the marginal-cost curve of the monopolist, the new equilibrium position is ε' where the price is the same as before, but the quantity produced is larger ($0X_2 < 0X_1$).

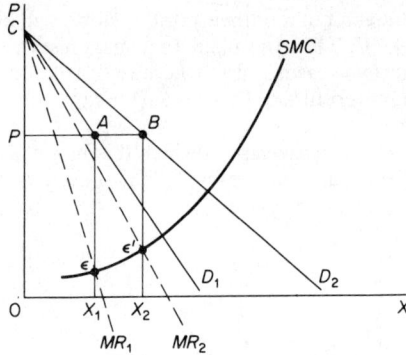

Figure 6.8

In this case the total revenue of the monopolist will increase ($0PBX_2 > 0PAX_1$). Furthermore his profits will be larger, because the monopolist's $SATC$ will be decreasing over the range between X_1 and X_2. This is so because the SMC curve cuts the $SATC$ curve at its minimum point. Thus if at the initial equilibrium the monopolist was earning excess profits (equal to $PKCA$ in figure 6.9), his $SATC$ must have been above his SMC curve, and the $SATC$ must have been declining, since it is impossible for it to start rising before it has been intersected by the SMC curve. Assume that the point of intersection of the $SATC$ and the SMC curves occurs at the level of output X_3. It is clear that at X_2 the $SATC$ is smaller than at the level X_1. Hence the total excess profit of the monopolist increases if the price remains constant while his demand increases ($PK'MB > PKCA$ in figure 6.9.)

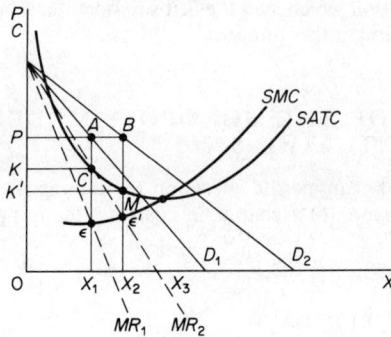

Figure 6.9

In the new equilibrium both the quantity and the price of the monopolist may be greater as compared to the initial equilibrium. This case is shown in figure 6.10. If the demand shifts to D_2 (above D_1) the new equilibrium is ε', at which the price as well as the quantity supplied by the monopolist are greater than at the original equilibrium ε (clearly $P_2 > P_1$, and $0X_2 > 0X_1$).

In the new equilibrium the price may be lower than the initial while the quantity is larger. This is shown in figure 6.11.

If demand shifts to D_2 the quantity in the new equilibrium will be larger ($0X_2 > 0X_1$) and it will be sold at a lower price ($P_2 < P_1$).

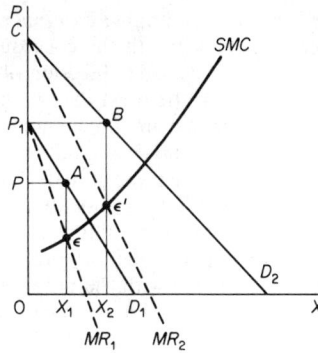

Figure 6.10

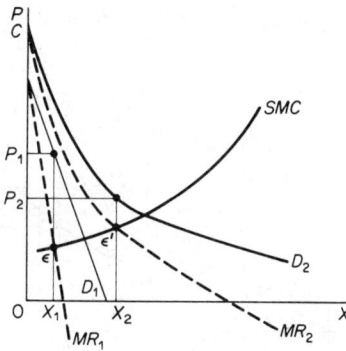

Figure 6.11

It should be clear that the effects of the shift in demand depend on the extent of the shift and on the price elasticity of demand. When demand shifts its elasticity is changing at any one price. If the new demand curve lies above the original and has a substantially greater elasticity (at the original price level), it may be profitable for the monopolist not only to increase his output, but also to sell it at a lower price.

B. AN INCREASE IN THE COSTS OF THE MONOPOLIST

The analysis of the effects of a change in costs of the monopolist is the same as in the case of pure competition.

An increase in fixed costs. If the fixed costs of the monopolist increase, his short-run equilibrium will not be affected, since his demand is given and his *SMC* is not affected by changes in fixed costs. This is the same result as in pure competition.

In the long run also the equilibrium of the monopolist will not be affected so long as the increase in fixed costs are covered by excess profits. If, however, the increase in fixed costs is so substantial as to make the *SATC* shift above the market demand, the monopolist will close down, since at all levels of output he will not be able to cover his total costs.

An increase in the variable costs. If the variable costs increase, the MC curve of the monopolist will shift upwards to the left with the consequence of a reduction in the output and an increase in the price. The same direction of changes are obtained in a pure competition model. The difference between the two markets is that the changes in price and market output will be greater in pure competition. This is due to the fact that the monopolist equates his MC to his MR (and not to price) while the firms in pure competition equate MC to price. The slope of the MR of the monopolist is steeper than the slope of his AR curve, while in pure competition the two curves are the same (MR = AR = P). Consequently the same vertical (upwards) shift of the MC in the two markets results in a smaller decrease in the quantity of the monopolist and hence to a smaller increase in the price as compared with the purely competitive market. This is shown in figures 6.12 and 6.13. In both cases it is assumed that the market demand is the same and the increase in the variable costs shifts the MC curves of the firms identically. Yet the increase in price and the decline in the quantity are more accentuated in the purely competitive market. This leads to the conclusion that price fluctuations and employment changes caused by changes in factor prices will tend to be wider in pure competition than in monopoly (given the market demand).

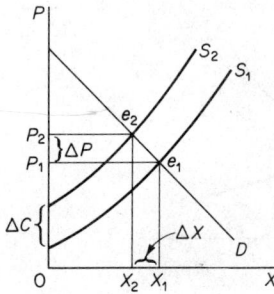

Figure 6.12   Pure competition   Figure 6.13   Monopoly

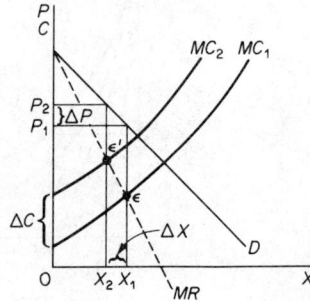

C. IMPOSITION OF A TAX

We will examine the effects on the equilibrium of the monopolist of (a) a lump-sum tax, (b) a profits tax, (c) a specific sales tax.

Imposition of a lump-sum tax (per period). In the case of a monopolist we need not distinguish between the short run and the long run as we did in the purely competitive market because in general the monopolist realises some excess profits both in the short run and in the long run. Under these conditions the imposition of a lump tax will reduce the excess profits of the monopolist because it will increase his total fixed cost. However, the MC curve of the monopolist will not be affected, and hence the equilibrium in the monopoly market will remain the same even in the long run (provided that the lump-sum tax does not exceed the supernormal profits of the monopolist).

Imposition of a profits tax. The effects of taxes on the monopoly profits on the equilibrium of the monopolist are the same as in the case of the lump-sum tax: the profits tax reduces the abnormal (monopoly) profits, but the equilibrium in the market is not affected, so long as the profits tax does not bite into the normal profits of the monopolist, since in this event the monopolist will not be covering his total costs (inclusive of his normal profit) and will close down.

Imposition of a specific sales tax. The effects of a specific tax on the output of the monopolist are broadly the same with those in a purely competitive market.

The imposition of the specific tax will shift the MC curve of the monopolist upwards, which will result in a change of his equilibrium; in the new equilibrium position (ε') the price will be higher and the quantity smaller as compared with the initial equilibrium. This is the same qualitative prediction with the model of pure competition.

The change in the price of the monopolist may be smaller, equal or greater than the specific tax, as in the case of pure competition. However, in the monopoly market we do not distinguish between the short run and the long run, since the conditions of equilibrium are the same in both periods.

Firstly. If the MC of the monopolist has a positive slope, the increase in the price will be smaller than the specific tax, as in the case of pure competition. The monopolist will pass to the consumer part of the specific tax (in figure 6.14 $\Delta P <$ tax).

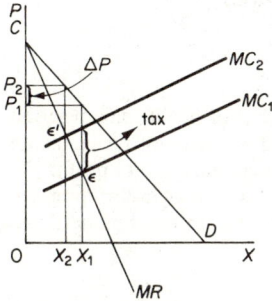
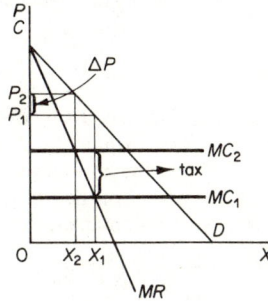

Figure 6.14   Figure 6.15

Secondly. If the MC of the monopolist is horizontal, the monopolist will raise the price, but not by the full amount of the tax, as is the case in pure competition. Even when his MC curve is infinitely elastic, the monopolist will bear some amount of the specific tax (in figure 6.15 $\Delta P <$ tax).

Thirdly. The examination of the conditions under which the monopolist can pass the total tax to the consumer by charging a suitably higher price, or can raise the price more than the amount of the tax, is too complicated to be attempted here. The interested reader is referred to textbooks on public finance and public policy.

VI. COMPARISON OF PURE COMPETITION AND MONOPOLY

When comparing any two models we will be looking at the following aspects.

1. Goals of the firm
2. Assumptions of models regarding:
   (*a*) Product
   (*b*) Number of sellers (and buyers)
   (*c*) Entry conditions
   (*d*) Cost conditions
   (*e*) Degree of knowledge

3. Implications of assumptions for the behaviour of the firm
   (*a*) Shape of demand
   (*b* Atomistic behaviour or interdependence
   (*c*) Policy variables of the firm and main decisions
4. Comparison of basic magnitudes at equilibrium (long-run)
   (*a*) Price (and price elasticity of demand)
   (*b*) Output
   (*c*) Profit
   (*d*) Capacity utilisation (economies of scale)
5. Predictions of the models
   (*a*) Shift in market demand
   (*b*) Shift in costs
   (*c*) Imposition of a tax

Comparing perfect competition and monopoly in the light of the above methodological scheme we derive the following conclusions:

Goals of the firm

In both models the firm has a single goal, that of profit maximisation. Indeed the whole concept of rational behaviour is defined in terms of profit maximisation: the firm is rational when its behaviour aims at the maximisation of profit.

In both models the owner of the firm is also the manager-entrepreneur. There is no separation of ownership and management in these traditional models.

Assumptions

The product is homogeneous in pure competition. In monopoly the product may or may not be homogeneous. The main feature of monopoly is that the total supply of the product is concentrated in a single firm.

In pure competition there is a large number of sellers, so that each one cannot affect the market price by changing his supply. In monopoly there is a single seller in the market.

In pure competition entry (and exit) is free in the sense that there are no barriers to entry. However, in the short run entry is not easy: entry is a long-run phenomenon. In monopoly entry is blockaded by definition.

In both models the cost conditions are such as to give rise to U-shaped cost curves both in the short run and in the long run. The plant is planned to produce a single level of output with minimum cost. There is no flexibility (reserve capacity) in the plant. In the short run the U-shape is due to the inevitable results of the law of eventually diminishing returns of the variable factors (or law of variable proportions). In the long run all factors are variable, but eventually the efficiency of management declines and this causes the *LAC* curve to turn upwards beyond a certain (optimal) scale of output.

Perfect knowledge is assumed in both market structures. Uncertainty is dealt with (in the neoclassical versions of pure competition) by assuming that the firm knows the results of any action up to a probability distribution. Having this knowledge, the firm has a certain time horizon and aims at the maximisation of the present value of its future stream of net profits.

Obtaining information about the present or the future requires some expense. Information or search activity is decided on marginalistic rules, by equating the *MC* of information to its *MR*.

Behavioural rules of the firm

Given the assumptions of large numbers and homogeneous product, the demand curve in pure competition is perfectly elastic, showing that the firm is a price-taker. In monopoly the demand of the firm is also the demand of the industry and hence is negatively sloping.

The only decision (and policy variable) of the firm in pure competition is the determination of its output. There is no room for selling activities, since the firm can sell any amount of output it can produce. Some economists argue that there is no incentive for research and development for the firm in the purely competitive market, since the firm can sell whatever it wishes without such activities. Others argue that the urge for technological research is strong in pure competition, since the firm can increase its profits only by decreasing its costs, something that can be achieved only with research and development in new methods of production. Such arguments are not conclusive, and empirical evidence can hardly be expected to support or refute them, since pure competition does not exist in most economic activities.

The monopolist can determine *either* his output or his *price*, but not both, since once one of these policy variables is decided, the other is simultaneously determined. The monopolist may change the style of his product and/or indulge in research and development activities, especially if there is danger of development of close substitutes in other industries. Under these conditions the monopolist may also undertake heavy advertising and other selling activities. Thus the monopolist has more policy variables at his disposal (product, price, research and development, advertising, etc.). Whether he will make use of these instruments and to what extent, is a matter highly debated in theory and in practice. In general the use of such instruments as product differentiation, advertising, $R \& D$ expenditures, depends on the threat of potential competition from new similar products, or on social and governmental pressures.

In both markets the firm acts *atomistically*, that is, it takes the decisions which will maximise its profit, ignoring the reactions of other firms (in the same or other industries).

In both markets the decisions are taken by applying the *marginalistic rule*

$$MC = MR$$

Both models are basically *static*. Although a distinction is made between the short run and the long run, it is assumed that the long run consists of identical time periods, which are independent: the decisions taken in one period do not affect the profits in other periods. Thus short-run profit maximisation leads to long-run profit maximisation.

Comparison of long-run market equilibrium

Given the cost conditions, in monopoly the level of output will generally be lower and the price higher as compared with pure competition. This is due to the fact that in pure competition the firm produces at optimum cost (minimum point on the *LAC* curve) and earns just normal profit, while the monopolist usually earns abnormal profits even in the long run. Under such conditions price will be higher in monopoly and output lower, as compared with pure competition.

The market elasticity of demand in equilibrium may assume any value in a purely competitive market. In monopoly the price elasticity must be greater than unity in equilibrium, because if $|e| < 1$ the monopolist can increase his revenue by increasing his price.

The firm in pure competition produces at optimum cost in long-run equilibrium, that is, at the minimum point of the *LAC* curve: there are neither unexhausted economies of scale nor diseconomies of large-scale production. In monopoly there is no certainty that the monopolist will produce at minimum long-run costs. He may never reach the lowest point of the *LAC*, or he may overshoot it, depending on the market size.

The supply of a purely competitive firm is uniquely determined: it is its *MC* curve above its intersection with the variable costs of the firm.

In monopoly the supply function is not uniquely determined: the same quantity may be offered at different prices, or the same price may be charged for different quantities, depending on the demand in the market (and given the monopolist's cost structure). Thus the monopolist's *MC* curve is *not* its supply curve.

In pure competition there are no abnormal profits in the long run. In monopoly abnormal profits are usually earned both in the short run and in the long run.

Comparison of predictions

Shift in market demand. In pure competition an increase in market demand will lead to an increase in price and in output in the short run. In the long run the output will be larger, but price may return to its initial level (constant-cost industry), remain above the original level (increasing-cost industry), or fall below the original level (decreasing-cost industry).

In monopoly we do not distinguish between *SR* and *LR*. A shift of the demand above the original level will result in an increase in output, which may be sold at the same, a higher or a lower price, depending on the extent of the shift in the demand and the change in its elasticity.

A shift in costs. An increase in fixed costs in pure competition will not change the firm's output in the short run since *MC* is not affected. In the long run firms will close down if they do not cover their higher total average costs.

The monopolist will not change his output in the short run or in the long run. Only if the increase in fixed costs wipes out the abnormal profits and reduces the normal profit of the monopolist, will he go out of business.

With an increase in variable costs the *MC* is shifted upwards, output is reduced and price increases in both market structures. However, the changes in output and price will be more accentuated in pure competition, *ceteris paribus*.

Imposition of a tax. The imposition of a *lump-tax* in pure competition will not lead to a change in output and price in the short run. However, the shift in the *TFC* will put firms out of business (if they were earning just normal profits in the pre-tax situation), so that market output will decline and price will rise in the long run.

In monopoly a lump-tax will not affect the market equilibrium in the short run or in the long run, so long as the monopolist continues to earn some abnormal profits.

The effects of a *profits tax* are the same (in both markets) as in the case of the imposition of the lump-tax.

In pure competition a specific sales tax will be passed partly on to the consumer so long as the supply curve has a positive slope. The higher the elasticity of supply the more of the tax burden will be shifted to the consumer. If the supply is perfectly elastic, $\Delta P =$ tax and the whole tax is passed to the consumer.

In monopoly the monopolist will bear some of the tax burden even if his *MC* is parallel to the output axis.

VII. THE MULTIPLANT FIRM

In this section we shall examine the case of a monopolist who produces a homogeneous product in different plants. We shall restrict the analysis to two plants for simplicity. However, the analysis may easily be generalised to any number of plants.

Assume that the monopolist operates two plants, A and B, each with a different cost structure (figures 6.16 and 6.17). He has to make two decisions: Firstly, how much output to produce altogether and at what price to sell it so as to maximise profit. Secondly, how to allocate the production of the optimal (profit-maximising) output between the two plants.

The monopolist is assumed to know his market demand (and the corresponding MR curve) and the cost structure of the different plants. The total MC curve of the monopolist may be computed from the horizontal summation of the MC curves of the individual plants

$$MC = MC_1 + MC_2$$

Given the MR and MC curves, the monpolist can define the total output and the price at which it must be sold in order to maximise his profit from the intersection of these two curves (point ε in figure 6.18).

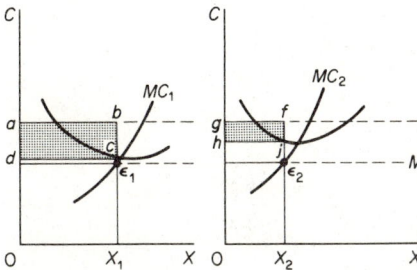

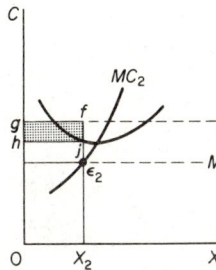

Figure 6.16 Plant A Figure 6.17 Plant B Figure 6.18 Total market

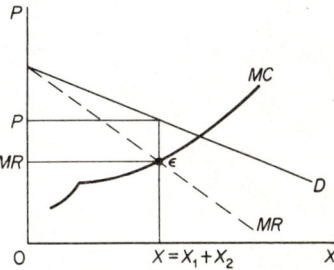

The allocation of production between the plants is decided by the marginalistic rule

$$MC_1 = MC_2 = MR$$

In other words, the monopolist maximises his profit by utilising each plant up to the level at which the marginal costs are equal to each other and to the common marginal revenue. This is because if the MC in one plant, say plant A, is lower than the marginal cost of plant B, the monopolist would increase his profit by increasing the production in A and decreasing it in B, until the condition

$$MC_1 = MC_2 = MR$$

is fulfilled.

Graphically the equilibrium of the multiplant monopolist may be defined as follows. The total profit-maximising output and its price is defined by the intersection of MC and MR curves (point ε in figure 6.18). From the point of intersection we draw a line, parallel to the X axis, until it intersects the individual MC_1 and MC_2 curves of the two plants. At these points the equilibrium condition ($MC = MR = MC_1 = MC_2$) is satisfied. If from these points (ε_1 and ε_2) we draw perpendiculars to the X-axis of figures 6.16 and 6.17, we find the level of output that will be produced in each plant. Clearly $X_1 + X_2$ must be equal to the profit-maximising output X. The total profit is the sum of profits from the products of the two plants. The profit from plant A is the shaded area $abcd$ and the profit from plant B is the shaded area $gfjh$.

Mathematical derivation of the equilibrium of the multiplant monopolist

Given the market demand

$$P = f(X) = f(X_1 + X_2)$$

and the cost structures of the plants

$$C_1 = f_1(X_1)$$
$$C_2 = f_2(X_2)$$

the monopolist aims at the allocation of his production between plant A and plant B so as to maximise his profit

$$\Pi = R - C_1 - C_2$$

The first-order condition for maximum profit requires

$$\frac{\partial \Pi}{\partial X_1} = 0 \quad \text{and} \quad \frac{\partial \Pi}{\partial X_2} = 0$$

(a)
$$\frac{\partial \Pi}{\partial X_1} = \frac{\partial R}{\partial X_1} - \frac{\partial C_1}{\partial X_1} = 0$$

or
$$\frac{\partial R}{\partial X_1} = \frac{\partial C_1}{\partial X_1}$$

i.e.
$$MR_1 = MC_1$$

(b)
$$\frac{\partial \Pi}{\partial X_2} = \frac{\partial R}{\partial X_2} = \frac{\partial C_2}{\partial X_2} = 0$$

or
$$\frac{\partial R}{\partial X_2} = \frac{\partial C_2}{\partial X_2}$$

i.e.
$$MR_2 = MC_1$$

But $MR_1 = MR_2 = MR$ (given that each unit of the homogeneous output will be sold at the same price P and will yield the same marginal revenue, irrespective in which plant the unit has been produced).

Therefore

$$MR = \frac{\partial C_1}{\partial X_1} = MC_1, \quad \text{and} \quad MR = \frac{\partial C_2}{\partial X_2} = MC_2$$

so that
$$MR = MC_1 = MC_2$$

The second-order condition for maximum profit requires

$$\frac{\partial^2 R}{\partial X^2} < \frac{\partial^2 C_1}{\partial X_1^2} \quad \text{and} \quad \frac{\partial^2 R}{\partial X^2} < \frac{\partial^2 C_2}{\partial X_2^2}$$

that is, the MC in each plant must be increasing more rapidly than the (common) MR of the output as a whole.

A numerical example

The monopolist's demand curve is

$$X = 200 - 2P, \quad \text{or} \quad P = 100 - 0 \cdot 5X$$

The costs of the two plants are

$$C_1 = 10X_1 \quad \text{and} \quad C_2 = 0 \cdot 25X_2^2$$

The goal of the monopolist is to maximise profit

$$\Pi = R - C_1 - C_2$$

(1)
$$R = XP = X(100 - 0.5X)$$
$$R = 100X - 0.5X^2$$

$$MR = \frac{\partial R}{\partial X} = 100 - X = 100 - (X_1 + X_2)$$

(2)
$$C_1 = 10X_1$$

$$MC_1 = \frac{\partial C_1}{\partial X_1} = 10$$

and
$$C_2 = 0.25X_2^2$$

$$MC_2 = \frac{\partial C_2}{\partial X_2} = 0.5X_2$$

(3) Equating each MC to the common MR

$$100 - X_1 - X_2 = 10$$
$$100 - X_1 - X_2 = 0.5X_2$$

Solving for X_1 and X_2 we find

$$X_1 = 70 \quad \text{and} \quad X_2 = 20$$

so that the total X is 90 units. This total output will be sold at price P defined by

$$P = 100 - 0.5X = 55$$

The monopolist's profit is

$$\Pi = R - C_1 - C_2$$
$$= 4950 - 10(20) - 0.25(4900)$$
$$\Pi = 3525$$

This is the maximum profit since the second-order condition is fulfilled.

VIII. BILATERAL MONOPOLY

Bilateral monopoly is a market consisting of a single seller (monopolist) and a single buyer (monopsonist). For example, if a single firm produced all the copper in a country and if only one firm used this metal, the copper market would be a bilateral monopoly market. The equilibrium in such a market cannot be determined by the traditional tools of demand and supply. Economic analysis can only define the range within which the price will eventually be settled. The precise level of the price (and output), however, will ultimately be defined by non-economic factors, such as the bargaining power, skill and other strategies of the participant firms. Under conditions of bilateral monopoly economic analysis leads to *indeterminacy* which is finally resolved by exogenous factors.

To illustrate a situation of bilateral monopoly assume that all railway equipment is produced by a single firm and is bought by a single buyer, British Rail. Both firms are assumed to aim at the maximisation of their profit. The equilibrium of the producer–monopolist is defined by the intersection of his marginal revenue and marginal cost curves (point e_1 in figure 6.19). He would maximise his profit if he were to produce X_1 quantity of equipment and sell it at the price P_1.

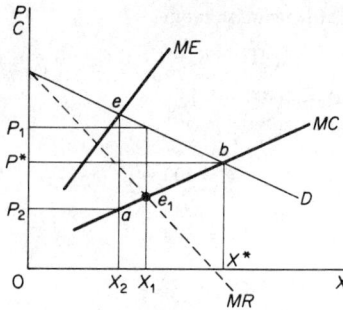

Figure 6.19

However, the producer cannot attain the above profit-maximising position, because he does not sell in a market with many buyers, each of whom would be unable to affect the price by his purchases. The producer–monopolist is selling to a single buyer who can obviously affect the market price by his purchasing decisions.

The buyer is aware of his power, and, being a profit maximiser, he would like to impose his own price terms to the producer. What are the monopsonist's price terms? Clearly the MC curve of the producer represents the supply curve to the buyer: the upward slope of this curve shows that as the monopsonist increases his purchases the price he will have to pay rises. The $MC(=S)$ curve is determined by conditions outside the control of the buyer, and it shows the quantity that the monopolist–seller is willing to supply at various prices. The increase in the expenditure of the buyer (his marginal outlay or marginal expenditure) caused by the increases in his purchases is shown by the curve ME in figure 6.19. In other words, curve ME is the marginal cost of equipment for the monopsonist–buyer (it is a marginal-outlay curve to the total-supply curve MC, with which the buyer is faced). The equipment is an input for the buyer. Thus in order to maximise his profit he would like to purchase additional units of X until his marginal outlay is equal to his price, as determined by the demand curve DD. The equilibrium of the monopsonist is shown by point e in figure 6.19: he would like to purchase X_2 units of equipment at a price P_2, determined by point a on the supply curve $MC(=S)$. However, the monopsonist does not buy from a lot of small firms which would be price-takers (that is, who would accept the price imposed by the single buyer), but from the monopolist, who wants to charge price P_1. Given that the buyer wants to pay P_2 while the seller wants to charge P_1, there is indeterminacy in the market. The two firms will sooner or later start negotiations and will eventually reach an agreement about price, which will be settled somewhere in the range between P_1 and P_2, $(P_2 \leq P \leq P_1)$, depending on the bargaining skill and power of the firms.

It should be obvious that a bilateral monopoly is rare for commodity markets, but is quite common in labour markets, where workers are organised in a union and confront a single employer (for example, the miners' unions and the Coal Board) or firms organised in a trade association.

If a bilateral monopoly emerges in a commodity market the buyer may attempt to buy out the seller–monopolist, thus attaining vertical integration of his production. The consequences of such take-over are interesting. The supply curve $MC(=S)$ becomes the marginal-cost curve of the monopsonist, and hence his equilibrium will be defined by point b in figure 6.19 (where the 'new' marginal-cost curve intersects the price–demand curve DD): output will increase to the level X^* and the marginal cost will be P^*, lower than the price P_1 that the ex-monopolist would like to charge.

The result of the vertical integration in these conditions is an increase in the production of the input, which will lead to an increase in the final product of the ex-monopsonist and a reduction in his price, given that he is faced by a downward-sloping market-demand curve. The examination of the welfare implications of such a situation is beyond the scope of this elementary analysis.

7. Price Discrimination

I. ASSUMPTIONS

Price discrimination exists when the same product is sold at different prices to different buyers. The cost of production is either the same, or it differs but not as much as the difference in the charged prices. The product is basically the same, but it may have slight differences (for example, different binding of the same book; different location of seats in a theatre; different seats in an aircraft or a train). We will concentrate on the typical case of an identical product, produced at the same cost, which is sold at different prices, depending on the preference of the buyers, their income, their location and the ease of availability of substitutes. These factors give rise to demand curves with different elasticities in the various sectors of the market of a firm. It is also common to charge different prices for the same product at different time periods. For example, a new product is often sold at a high price, accessible only to the rich, while subsequently it is sold at lower prices which can be afforded by lower-income consumers.

Although price discrimination is more easily implemented by a monopolist, because he controls the whole supply of a given commodity, this price policy is quite commonly practised by most firms, which charge a different price (give different discounts) to their customers depending on the item they purchase, the length of time they have dealt with the firm–seller, their location and other factors.

The *necessary* conditions, which must be fulfilled for the implementation of price discrimination are the following:

1. The market must be divided into sub-markets with different price elasticities.

2. There must be effective separation of the sub-markets, so that no reselling can take place from a low-price market to a high-price market. This condition shows why price discrimination is easier to apply with commodities like electricity or gas, and services (like services of a doctor, transport, a show), which are 'consumed' by the buyer and cannot be resold.

II. THE MODEL

The reason for a monopolist (or any other firm) to apply price discrimination is to obtain an increase in his total revenue and his profits. By selling the quantity defined by the equation of his *MC* and his *MR* at different prices the monopolist realises a higher total revenue and hence higher profits as compared with the revenues he would receive by charging a uniform price.[1] We will start from the simplest case of a monopolist who sells his product at two different prices.

It is assumed that the monopolist will sell his product in two segregated markets, each of them having a demand curve with different elasticity. In figure 7.1 the demand curve D_1 has a higher price elasticity than D_2 at any given price. The total-demand curve D is found by the horizontal summation of D_1 and D_2. The aggregate marginal revenue (MR) is the horizontal summation of the marginal-revenue curves MR_1 and MR_2. The marginal-cost curve is depicted by the curve MC.

The price-discriminating monopolist has to decide (*a*) the total output that he must produce, (*b*) how much to sell in each market and at what price, so as to maximise his profits.

The total quantity to be produced is defined by the point of intersection of the MC and the aggregate MR curves of the monopolist. In figure 7.1 the two curves intersect at point ε, thus defining a total output OX which must be produced. If the monopolist were to charge a uniform price this would be P, and his total revenue would be $OXAP$.

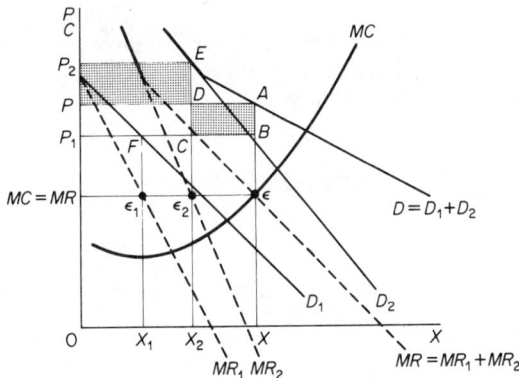

Figure 7.1

His profit would be the difference between this revenue and the cost for producing OX. However, the monopolist can achieve a higher profit by charging different prices in the two markets. The price and the quantity in each market is defined in such a way as to maximise profit in each market. Thus in each market he must equate the marginal revenue with the MC. However, the marginal cost is the same for the whole quantity produced, irrespective of the market in which it is going to be sold. The marginal revenue in each market differs due to the difference in the elasticity of the two demand curves. The profit in each market is maximised by equating MC to the corresponding MR:

In the first market profit is maximised when

$$MR_1 = MC$$

In the second market profit is maximised when

$$MR_2 = MC$$

[1] Although the pursuit of higher profits is the usual reason for price discrimination by a monopolist there are cases where price discrimination simply leads to the realisation of normal profits, or is the only policy which makes feasible the existence of an industry. Such cases will be examined below.

Clearly the total profit is maximised when the monopolist equates the common MC to the individual revenues

$$MC = MR_1 = MR_2$$

If MR in one market were larger, the monopolist would sell more in that market and less in the other, until the above condition was fulfilled. Graphically the determination of the prices and quantities in the two markets is defined as follows.

From the equilibrium point ε we draw a line perpendicular to the price axis. This line cuts the marginal revenue MR_1 at point ε_1 and the marginal revenue MR_2 at point ε_2. Clearly at these points we have the required equality

$$MC = MR_1 = MR_2$$

From ε_1 and ε_2 we drop vertical lines to the quantity axis, and we extend them upwards until they meet the demand curves D_1 and D_2 respectively. These vertical lines define the output and price in each market. Thus in the first market the monopolist will sell $0X_1$ at a price P_1, and in the second market the monopolist will sell $0X_2$ at the price P_2. Clearly $0X_1 + 0X_2 = 0X$.

From figure 7.1 it is obvious that the total revenue from price discrimination is larger than the revenue $0XAP$ which would be received by charging a uniform price P. With price discrimination the total revenue is

$$(P_1)(0X_1) + (P_2)(0X_2) = 0P_1FX_1 + 0P_2EX_2$$

Comparing this revenue with the revenue from the unique price P we find the following:

Revenue from P:

$$R_1 = 0XAP = 0X_2DP + X_2XBC + CBAD \qquad (7.1)$$

Revenue from P_1 and P_2:

$$R_2 = 0X_1FP_1 + 0X_2EP_2$$

But

$$0X_1FP_1 = X_2XBC$$

and

$$0X_2EP_2 = 0X_2DP + PDEP_2$$

Therefore

$$R_2 = X_2XBC + 0X_2DP + PDEP_2 \qquad (7.2)$$

Subtracting (7.1) from (7.2) we find

$$R_2 - R_1 = [X_2XBC + 0X_2DP + PDEP_2] - [0X_2DP + X_2XBC + CBAD]$$
$$= PDEP_2 - CBAD$$

Since $CBAD < PDEP_2$, it is obvious that

$$R_2 > R_1$$

Note that $PDEP_2$ is the additional revenue from selling $0X_2$ at price P_2 which is higher than P, while $CBAD$ is the loss in revenue from selling $0X_1$ at price P_1 which is lower than P. The additional revenue from selling $0X_2$ at a higher price more than offsets the loss of revenue from selling $0X_1$ at a lower price, so that total revenue from price discrimination is larger. Since the cost of producing $0X$ is the same irrespective of the price at which it will be sold, the profits from price discrimination are larger as compared with those that would be obtained from selling all the output at the uniform price P.

The above case has been called *third-degree price discrimination* by the British economist Pigou.[1] The increase in total revenue is achieved by taking away part of the consumers' surplus. To understand this let us concentrate on the demand curve, D (figure 7.2). If the monopolist sold all $0X$ at P he would receive $0XAP$, and the consumers would have a surplus of PAD. Assume now that the monopolist sells $0X_1$ at the price P_1 and the remaining quantity X_1X at the price P. His total revenue will be

$$0X_1CP_1 + X_1XAB = 0XAP + PBCP_1$$

that is, the monopolist has managed to take the part $PBCP_1$ from the consumers' surplus.

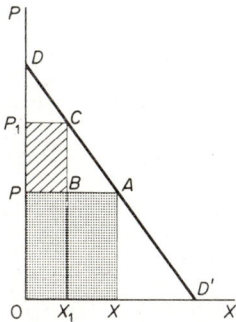

Figure 7.2 Third-degree price discrimination

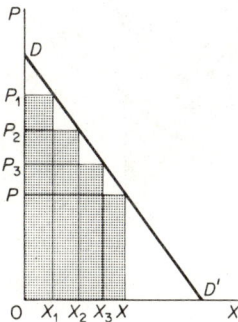

Figure 7.3 Second-degree price discrimination

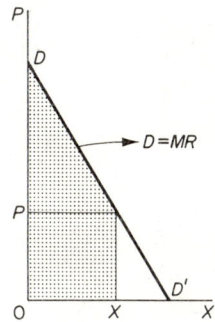

Figure 7.4 First-degree price discrimination

If the monopolist can negotiate and sell at more than two prices (higher than P), for example to sell $0X_1$ at P_1, X_1X_2 at P_2, X_2X_3 at P_3 and X_3X at P, he will receive a still larger part of the consumers' surplus (figure 7.3). This is called a *second-degree price discrimination*.

In the limiting case in which the monopolist can negotiate individually with each buyer and sell each unit of output at its corresponding price as shown from the DD' curve, then he will receive the entire consumers' surplus (figure 7.4). This is known as *first-degree price discrimination* or as 'take-it-or-leave-it' price discrimination, because in negotiating with each buyer the monopolist charges him the maximum price he is willing to pay under threat of denying the selling of any quantity to him: he offers each buyer a 'take-it-or-leave-it' choice. In this case the demand curve also becomes the MR curve of the monopolist.

III. EFFECTS OF PRICE DISCRIMINATION

So long as the price-discriminating monopolist manages to reap part of the consumers' surplus his total revenue and his total profits will be higher, even if he sells the quantity $0X$, which is defined by the intersection of his MC with his (original) aggregate MR curve.

[1] A. C. Pigou, *The Economics of Welfare*, 4th edn. (Macmillan, 1950).

However, the quantity that the discriminating monopolist supplies will be higher than $0X$ if he can charge more than two prices in various sectors of the market, and his total revenue will be higher still. The increase in output is due to the gradual shift of the MR curve upwards and the consequent change of the point of its intersection with the given MC curve. The shift of the MR curve, given that DD' does not change, is due to the fact that the MR (at all levels of output) is higher when price discrimination is being adopted, because the lower price at which the new marginal unit is sold is not the same as for all previously sold units, which have been sold at higher prices via individual negotiations with the buyers. In figure 7.5, if P were uniform, the monopolist would sell

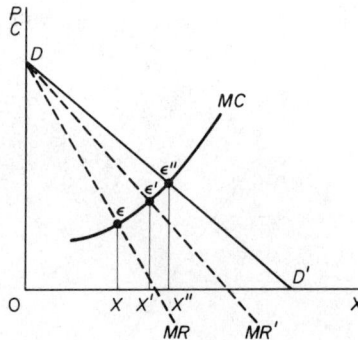

Figure 7.5

$0X$ amount of output. If price discrimination is applied, only the additional units are sold at gradually lower prices, and hence the MR shifts to the position MR'. The new equilibrium position is defined by ε', at which the quantity is $0X' > 0X$. In the limiting case of perfect discrimination the MR will coincide with the DD' curve, since each unit is sold at its own price, the highest price that the buyers are willing to pay on a 'take-it-or-leave-it' basis. The equilibrium will be at ε'', the output will be $0X''$ and the following condition will hold

$$MC = MR = AR = P$$

and the seller will have achieved the maximum increase in his revenue, reaping all consumers' surplus.

*Mathematical derivation of the equilibrium position of the
price-discriminating monopolist*

Given the total demand of the monopolist

$$P = f(X)$$

Assume that the demand curves of the segmented markets are

$$P_1 = f_1(X_1) \quad \text{and} \quad P_2 = f_2(X_2)$$

The cost of the firm is

$$C = f(X) = f(X_1 + X_2)$$

The firm aims at the maximisation of its profit

$$\Pi = R_1 + R_2 - C$$

The first-order condition for profit maximisation requires

$$\frac{\partial \Pi}{\partial X_1} = 0 \quad \text{and} \quad \frac{\partial \Pi}{\partial X_2} = 0$$

(a)
$$\frac{\partial \Pi}{\partial X_1} = \frac{\partial R_1}{\partial X_1} - \frac{\partial C}{\partial X_1} = 0 \quad \text{and} \quad \frac{\partial \Pi}{\partial X_2} = \frac{\partial R_2}{\partial X_2} - \frac{\partial C}{\partial X_2} = 0$$

(b)
$$\frac{\partial R_1}{\partial X_1} = \frac{\partial C}{\partial X_1} \quad \text{or} \quad MR_1 = MC_1; \quad \text{and} \quad \frac{\partial R_2}{\partial X_2} = \frac{\partial C}{\partial X_2} \quad \text{or} \quad MR_2 = MC_2$$

But

$$MC_1 = MC_2 = MC = \frac{dC}{dX}$$

Therefore

$$MC = MR_1 = MR_2$$

The second-order condition for profit maximisation requires

$$\frac{\partial^2 R_1}{\partial X_1^2} < \frac{d^2 C}{dX^2} \quad \text{and} \quad \frac{\partial^2 R_2}{\partial X_2^2} < \frac{d^2 C}{dX^2}$$

That is, the *MR* in each market must be increasing less rapidly than the *MC* for the output as a whole.

A numerical example

We use the same basic equations as in the example of the simple monopolist (p. 176) so as to be able to compare results.
Assume that the total demand is $X = 50 - 5 \cdot 0P$ (or $P = 100 - 2X$).
Assume further that the demand functions of segmented markets are

$$X_1 = 32 - 0 \cdot 4P_1 \quad \text{or} \quad P_1 = 80 - 2 \cdot 5X_1$$
$$X_2 = 18 - 0 \cdot 1P_2 \quad \text{or} \quad P_2 = 180 - 10X_2$$

(Clearly $X_1 + X_2 = X$)
Finally, assume that the cost function is

$$C = 50 + 40X = 50 + 40(X_1 + X_2)$$

The firm aims at the maximisation of its profit

$$\Pi = R_1 + R_2 - C$$

(1)
$$R_1 = X_1 P_1 = X_1(80 - 2 \cdot 5X_1) = 80X_1 - 2 \cdot 5X_1^2$$

$$MR_1 = \frac{\partial R_1}{\partial X_1} = 80 - 5X_1$$

(2)
$$R_2 = X_2 P_2 = X_2(180 - 10X_2) = 180X_2 - 10X_2^2$$

$$MR_2 = \frac{\partial R_2}{\partial X_2} = 180 - 20X_2$$

(3)
$$MC = \frac{\partial C}{\partial X_1} = \frac{\partial C}{\partial X_2} = \frac{\partial C}{\partial X} = 40$$

Setting the MR in each market equal to the common MC we obtain

$$80 - 5X_1 = 40$$
$$180 - 20X_2 = 40$$
$$\begin{rcases} X_1 = 8 \\ X_2 = 7 \end{rcases} X = 15$$

The prices are

$$P_1 = 80 - 2{\cdot}5X_1 = 60$$
$$P_2 = 180 - 10X_2 = 110$$

The profit is

$$\Pi = R_1 + R_2 - C = 500$$

The elasticities are

$$e_1 = \frac{\partial X_1}{\partial P_1} \cdot \frac{P_1}{X_1} = (0{\cdot}4)\tfrac{60}{8} = 3$$

$$e_2 = \frac{\partial X_2}{\partial P_2} \cdot \frac{P_2}{X_2} = (0{\cdot}1)\tfrac{110}{7} = 1{\cdot}57$$

Thus $e_1 > e_2$ and $P_1 < P_2$.

Comparing the above results with those for the example of the simple monopolist we observe that X is the same in both cases but the Π of the discriminating monopolist is larger.

IV. PRICE DISCRIMINATION AND THE PRICE ELASTICITY OF DEMAND

We have established (p. 173) that

$$MR = P\left(1 - \frac{1}{e}\right)$$

In the case of price discrimination we have

$$MR_1 = P_1\left(1 - \frac{1}{e_1}\right)$$

$$MR_2 = P_2\left(1 - \frac{1}{e_2}\right)$$

and

$$MR_1 = MR_2$$

Therefore

$$P_1\left(1 - \frac{1}{e_1}\right) = P_2\left(1 - \frac{1}{e_2}\right)$$

or

$$\frac{P_1}{P_2} = \frac{\left(1 - \dfrac{1}{e_1}\right)}{\left(1 - \dfrac{1}{e_2}\right)}$$

where e_1 = elasticity of D_1
 e_2 = elasticity of D_2

If $e_1 = e_2$ the ratio of prices is equal to unity:

$$\frac{P_1}{P_2} = 1$$

that is, $P_1 = P_2$. This means that when elasticities are the same price discrimination is not possible. The monopolist will charge a uniform price for his product.

If price elasticities differ *price will be higher in the market whose demand is less elastic.* This is obvious from the equality of the *MR*'s

$$P_1\left(1 - \frac{1}{e_1}\right) = P_2\left(1 - \frac{1}{e_2}\right)$$

if $|e_1| > |e_2|$, then

$$\left(1 - \frac{1}{e_1}\right) > \left(1 - \frac{1}{e_2}\right)$$

Thus for the equality of *MR*'s to be fulfilled

$$P_1 < P_2$$

that is, the market with the higher elasticity will have the lower price.

V. PRICE DISCRIMINATION AND THE EXISTENCE OF THE INDUSTRY

In some cases the various sectors of a market may have demand curves which, when added together, give a total market demand which lies at all levels of output below the *LAC* of the firm. Under these circumstances it is clear that production cannot take place at all if a uniform price is charged, no matter how high this price is set (figure 7.6). However, if price discrimination is adopted with a sufficiently high price P_1 charged

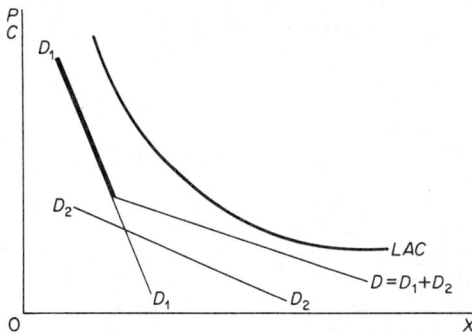

Figure 7.6

for the inelastic sector of the market and a sufficiently low price P_2 set for the elastic section of the market, the total revenue may be sufficient to cover the total costs (and even allow excess profits) so that production can take place. Such a situation is shown in figure 4.7. With quantity $0X_1$ sold at P_1 and quantity $0X_2$ sold at P_2, the total output is $0X$ which brings in a total revenue of $0XA'A$, and an average revenue of $0A$, which is higher than the average cost $0C$, leaving the monopolist an excess profit equal to the shaded area $CC'A'A$. What this implies is that the 'rich' sector of the market subsidises the 'poor' sector, so that production becomes feasible.

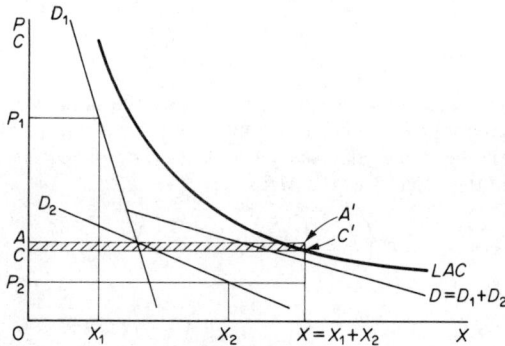

Figure 7.7

For example, assume that the AC takes the following values for the corresponding levels of output:

$$at\ X = 100,\ the\ AC = 30$$
$$at\ X = 400,\ the\ AC = 13$$
$$at\ X = 500,\ the\ AC = 11$$

If the firm can sell to the high-income market 100 units of X at $P_1 = 20$, and to the low-income market 400 units at $P_2 = 10$, the firm's total revenue is

$$R = R_1 + R_2 = X_1P_1 + X_2P_2 = (100)(20) + (400)(10) = 6000$$

and its total cost is

$$TC = (AC) \cdot (X) = (AC) \cdot (X_1 + X_2) = (11) \cdot (500) = 5500$$

Thus, with price discrimination not only does the firm cover its total cost, but also it realises an excess profit of 500 units.

VI. GOVERNMENT-REGULATED MONOPOLY

When the market size is small relative to the optimal size of plant we have the case of 'natural' monopoly, that is a case in which the market cannot support more than one optimally-sized firm, which thus becomes the 'natural' monopolist. Under these circumstances the government may intervene either by itself undertaking the operation of the plant, or by regulating the price (or prices) that the private monopolist is allowed to charge. In both cases the government has to set the price, or the levels of different prices, if price discrimination is adopted.

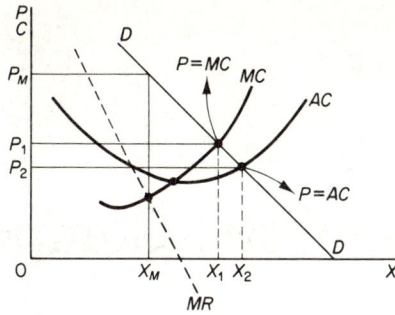

Figure 7.8

The price will be set below the profit-maximising P_M, which corresponds to the intersection of MC and MR, because price P_M would imply excess profits and hence exploitation of the buyers. Two possibilities have been widely discussed both in theory and in practice.

Firstly, the government may set the price at the level of the MC (that is, equate P to MC). This is P_1 in figure 7.8, which would lead to a higher output X_1, but would still allow some excess profits, though less than the monopolist output X_M.

Secondly, the government may set a price equal to the AC. This is P_2, which leads to a still higher output X_2, and covers the total cost inclusive of a 'fair' return on capital as 'normal profit'. Disputes have often occurred over what is the 'fair' return, and what should be the 'capital' on which the 'fair' return, should be applied.

Alternatively, the government may apply a price discrimination scheme. This solution has wide applications in public utilities, like electricity, gas, railways, communications and other government-regulated monopolies. Of course, price discrimination gives rise to serious problems of equity and redistribution of income, and of economic allocation of resources. The discussion of these problems goes beyond the scope of this book.

8. Monopolistic Competition

Up to the early 1920s the classical theory of price included two main models, pure competition and monopoly. Duopoly models were considered as intellectual exercises rather than real-world situations. The general model of economic behaviour from Marshall to Knight[1] was pure competition. In the late 1920s economists became increasingly dissatisfied with the use of pure competition as an analytical model of business behaviour. It was obvious that pure competition could not explain several empirical facts. The assumption of a homogeneous product, in the theory of competition, did not fit the real world. Furthermore advertising and other selling activities, practices widely used by businessmen, could not be explained by pure competition. Finally, firms expanded their output with falling costs, without however growing infinitely large, as the pure competition model would predict in the event of continuously decreasing costs.

It was in particular this last fact of falling costs that produced dissatisfaction and caused a widespread reaction against pure competition theories. The dissatisfaction gave rise to a long series of arguments and the publication of numerous articles which form the 'Great Cost Controversy of the 1920s'. The earliest summary of the Cost Controversy is to be found in Piero Sraffa's article.[2] Sraffa pointed out that the falling-cost dilemma of the classical theory could be resolved theoretically in various ways: by the introduction of a falling-demand curve for the individual firm; by adopting a general equilibrium approach in which shifts of costs induced by external economies of scale (to the firm and the industry) could be adequately incorporated; or by introducing a U-shaped selling-cost curve into the model. Of these solutions Sraffa adopted the first, that is, he argued that a model in which the individual-demand curve is negatively sloping is more operational and theoretically more plausible. The same line was adopted independently by E. Chamberlin[3] and by Joan Robinson,[4] in works both published in 1933. It should be noted that although both writers arrive at the same solution for the firm and market equilibrium, their analytical approach and methodology differ considerably. In this chapter we will develop Chamberlin's model of monopolistic competition (large-group model).

---

[1] F. H. Knight, *Risk, Uncertainty and Profit*, London School Reprints of Scarce Works, No. 16 (1933).
[2] 'The Laws of Returns under Competitive Conditions', *Economic Journal* (1926).
[3] See E. Chamberlin, *Theory of Monopolistic Competition* (Harvard University Press, Cambridge, Mass., 1933).
[4] See J. Robinson, *The Economics of Imperfect Competition* (Macmillan, 1933).

I. ASSUMPTIONS

The basic assumptions of Chamberlin's large-group model are the same as those of pure competition with the exception of the homogeneous product. We may summarise them as follows:

1.　There is a large number of sellers and buyers in the 'group'.
2.　The products of the sellers are differentiated, yet they are close substitutes of one another.
3.　There is free entry and exit of firms in the group.
4.　The goal of the firm is profit maximisation, both in the short run and in the long run.
5.　The prices of factors and technology are given.
6.　The firm is assumed to behave as if it knew its demand and cost curves with certainty.
7.　The long run consists of a number of identical short-run periods, which are assumed to be independent of one another in the sense that decisions in one period do not affect future periods and are not affected by past actions. The optimum decision for any one period is the optimum decision for any other period. Thus, by assumption, maximisation of short-run profits implies maximisation of long-run profits.
8.　Finally Chamberlin makes the 'heroic' assumption that both demand and cost curves for all 'products' are uniform throughout the group. This requires that consumers' preferences be evenly distributed among the different sellers, and that differences between the products be such as not to give rise to differences in costs.[1] Chamberlin makes these assumptions in order to be able to show the equilibrium of the firm and the 'group' on the same diagram. The above 'heroic' assumptions lead to a model which is very restrictive, since it precludes the inclusion in the 'group' of similar products which have different costs of production. Chamberlin himself recognises that the 'heroic' assumptions are unrealistic and he relaxes them at a later stage (see below).

II. COSTS

Chamberlin adopts without much justification the shape of costs of the traditional theory of the firm. The *AVC, MC* and *ATC* curves are all U-shaped implying that there is only a single level of output which can be optimally produced. The particular shape of costs is not important in Chamberlin's model so long as the slope of the *MC* curve is greater than the slope of the *MR* curve (see below).

Chamberlin introduced selling costs in the theory of the firm for the first time. The recognition of product differentiation provides the rationale for the selling expenses incurred by the firm: with advertising and other selling activities the firm seeks to accentuate the difference between its product and the product of other firms in the group; that is, Chamberlin assumes that advertising in general will shift the demand and will make it less elastic by strengthening the preferences of the consumers for the advertised product.

Chamberlin argues that the selling-costs curve is U-shaped, that is, there are economies and diseconomies of advertising as output changes. Initially expansion of output will not require an equiproportional increase in selling costs, and this leads to a fall in the average selling expenditure. However, beyond a certain level of output the firm will have to spend more per unit in order to attract customers from other firms: as output

---

[1] Chamberlin, *Theory of Monopolistic Competition*, pp. 82–3.

expands the firm has to attract customers which are well used to the product of other firms. The U-shaped selling cost, added to the U-shaped production cost, yields a U-shaped ATC curve.

III. PRODUCT DIFFERENTIATION AND THE DEMAND CURVE

Product differentiation as the basis for establishing a downward-falling demand curve was first introduced in economic theory by Sraffa.[1] Yet it was Chamberlin who elaborated the implication of product differentiation for the pricing and output decisions as well as for the selling strategy of the firm. Chamberlin suggested that the demand is determined not only by the price policy of the firm, but also by the style of the product, the services associated with it, and the selling activities of the firm. Thus Chamberlin *introduced two additional policy variables in the theory of the firm*: the *product itself* and *selling activities*. The demand for the product of the individual firm incorporates these dimensions. It shows the quantities demanded for a particular style, associated services, offered with a specific selling strategy. Thus the demand curve will shift if:

(*a*) the style, services, or the selling strategy of the firm changes;
(*b*) competitors change their price, output, services or selling policies;
(*c*) tastes, incomes, prices or selling policies of products from other industries change.

Product differentiation is intended to distinguish the product of one producer from that of the other producers in the industry. It can be *real*, when the inherent characteristics of the products are different, or *fancied*, when the products are basically the same, yet the consumer is persuaded, via advertising or other selling activities, that the products are different. Real differentiation exists when there are differences in the specification of the products or differences in the factor inputs, or the location of the firm, which determines the convenience with which the product is accessible to the consumer, or the services offered by the producer. Fancied differentiation is established by advertising, difference in packaging, difference in design, or simply by brand name, (for example, aspirins made by various manufacturers). Whatever the case, the aim of product differentiation is to make the product unique in the mind of the consumer. Yet differentiation must leave the products closely related if they are to be included in the same 'product group': the products should be close substitutes with high price and cross-elasticities.

The effect of product differentiation is that the producer has some discretion in the determination of the price. He is not a price-taker, but has some degree of monopoly power which he can exploit. However, he faces the keen competition of close substitutes offered by other firms. Hence the discretion over the price is limited. There are elements of monopoly and competition under the above market conditions, hence the name of this model as 'monopolistic competition'. Product differentiation creates brand loyalty of the consumers and gives rise to a negatively sloping demand curve. Product differentiation, finally, provides the rationale of selling expenses. Product changes, advertising and salesmanship are the main means of product differentiation.

IV. THE CONCEPT OF THE 'INDUSTRY' AND 'PRODUCT GROUP'

Product differentiation creates difficulties in the analytical treatment of the industry. Heterogeneous products cannot be added to form the market demand and supply schedules as in the case of homogeneous products.

[1] P. Sraffa, 'The Laws of Returns under Competitive Conditions', *Economic Journal* (1926).

The concept of the industry needs redefinition. Chamberlin uses the concept of 'product group', which includes products which are 'closely related'. The products should be close *technological and economic substitutes*. Technological substitutes are products which can technically cover the same want. For example, all motor cars are technological substitutes in the sense that they provide transport. Economic substitutes are products which cover the same want *and* have similar prices. For example, a Hillman Avenger, and a Morris 1300 can be considered as economic substitutes while a Rolls-Royce and a Mini clearly are not. An operational definition of the 'product group' is that the demand of each single product be highly elastic and that it shifts appreciably when the price of other products in the group changes. In other words, products forming 'the group' or 'industry' should have high price and cross-elasticities. Although this definition may be theoretically plausible and intuitively attractive, it poses further measurement problems. How high should the price and cross-elasticities be? There is no general answer to this question. One has to use subjective judgement in each particular case. (See also Chapter 1, pp. 7–12.)

Summation of the individual demand and cost curves to form the 'industry' demand and supply requires the use of some common denominator. Even so, with product differentiation there is no such thing as a unique price (except under Chamberlin's 'heroic' assumptions, which are discussed below). Product differentiation allows each firm to charge a different price. There will be no unique equilibrium price, but an equilibrium *cluster* of prices, reflecting the preferences of consumers for the products of the various firms in the group. When the market demand shifts or cost conditions change in a way affecting all firms, then the entire cluster of prices will rise or fall simultaneously. This more realistic market situation emerges from Chamberlin's analysis after the relaxation of his 'heroic assumptions'.[1]

V. EQUILIBRIUM OF THE FIRM

Product differentiation gives rise to a negatively sloping demand curve for the product of the individual firm. If the firm increases its price it will lose some but not all of its customers, while if it reduces its price it will increase its sales by attracting some customers from other firms. The individual firm's demand curve is depicted in figure 8.1. Although downward-sloping the demand is highly elastic, because of the assumption of a large number of sellers in the group. Since the firm·is one of a very large number of sellers, if it reduces its price the increase in its sales will produce loss of sales distributed more or less equally over all the other firms, so that each one of them will suffer a negligible loss in customers, not sufficient to induce them to change their own price.

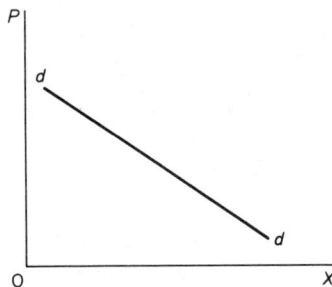

Figure 8.1

[1] See Chamberlin, *Theory of Monopolistic Competition*, pp. 89–92.

Thus the individual demand curve, *dd*, is a *planned sales curve*, drawn on the assumption that the competitors will not react to changes in the particular firm's price. (Of course the *dd* curve is also drawn on the usual *ceteris paribus* assumptions, that tastes, incomes and prices in other industries do not change.)

Chamberlin does not use *MC* and *MR* curves, but they are implicit in his analysis. We will include these curves in our exposition following Joan Robinson, since they facilitate the exposition and the comparison with other market structures.

In the short run the Chamberlinian firm acts like a monopolist. The firm, given its demand and cost curves, maximises its profit by producing the output at which marginal cost is equal to marginal revenue ($MC = MR$).

In order to be able to analyse the equilibrium of the firm and of the industry on the same diagram Chamberlin made two 'heroic assumptions', namely that firms have identical costs, and consumers' preferences are evenly distributed among the different products. That is, although the products are differentiated, all firms have identical demand and cost curves. Under these assumptions the price in the market will be unique. Chamberlin develops three distinct models of equilibrium. In the second model it is assumed that the number of firms in the industry is optimal (no entry or exit) and long-run equilibrium is reached through price adjustments (price competition) of the existing firms. In the first model the existing firms are assumed to be in short-run equilibrium realising abnormal profits; existing firms do not have any incentive to adjust their price, but long-run equilibrium is attained by new entrants who are attracted by the lucrative profit margins. The third model is a combination of the pevious two: long-run equilibrium is achieved through price adjustments of the existing firms and by new firms entering the industry.

Model 1: equilibrium with new firms entering the industry

In this model it is assumed that each firm is in short-run equilibrium, maximising its profits at abnormally high levels. Such a situation is shown in figure 8.2. The firm, having the cost structure depicted by the *SRAC* and the *LMC* curves and faced with the demand curve *dd'*, will set the price P_M which corresponds to the intersection of the *MR* and the *MC* curves. This price yields maximum profits (equal to the area $ABCP_M$).

The firm, being in equilibrium (at *C*), does not have any incentive to change its price. The abnormal profits will, however, attract new competitors into the market. The

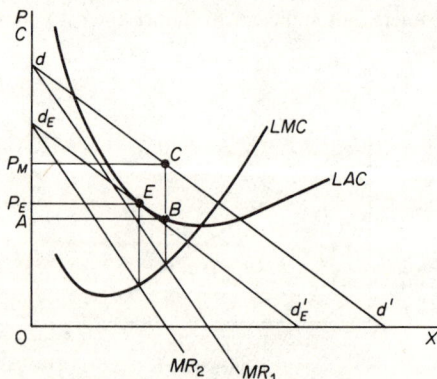

Figure 8.2

result of new entry is a downward shift of the demand curve dd', since the market is shared by a larger number of sellers. Assuming that the cost curves will not shift as entry occurs, each shift to the left of the dd' curve will be followed by a price adjustment as the firm reaches a new equilibrium position, equating the new marginal revenue (on the shifted MR curve) to its marginal cost. The process will continue until the demand is tangent to the average-cost curve, and the excess profits are wiped out. In the final equilibrium of the firm the price will be P_E and the ultimate demand curve $d_E d'_E$. This is an equilibrium position, since price is equal to the average cost. There will be no further entry into the industry, since profits are just normal. The equilibrium is stable, because any firm will lose by either raising or lowering the price P_E.

Model 2: equilibrium with price competition

In this model it is assumed that the number of firms in the industry is that which is compatible with long-run equilibrium, so that neither entry nor exit will take place. But the ruling price in the short run is assumed to be higher than the equilibrium one.

The analysis of this case is done by the introduction of a second demand curve, labelled DD' in figure 8.3, which shows the actual sales of the firm at each price after accounting for the adjustments of the prices of other firms in the group. DD' is sometimes called *actual-sales curve* or *share-of-the-market curve*, since it incorporates the effects of actions of competitors to the price changes by the firm. The DD' curve shows the full effect upon the sales of the firm which results from any change in the price that it charges.

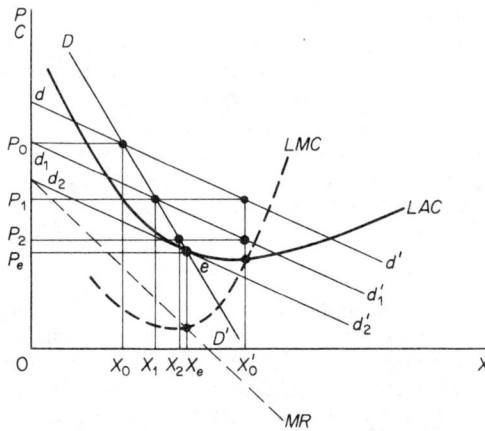

Figure 8.3

DD' is thus the locus of points of shifting dd' curves as competitors, acting simultaneously, change their price. It should be clear that the change in the price does not take place as a deliberate reaction to other firms' reductions, but as an independent action aiming at the profit maximisation of each firm acting independently of the others. The DD' curve shows a constant share of the market, and, as such, it has the same elasticity as the market demand at any one price.[1] Clearly the DD' curve is steeper than dd', because the actual sales from a reduction in P are smaller than expected on the basis of dd' as all firms reduce their price and expand their own sales simultaneously. A movement along DD' shows changes in the actual sales of existing firms as all of them adjust their price

[1] For a proof of this statement see p. 295.

simultaneously and identically, with their share remaining constant. A shift in the DD' is caused by entry of new firms or exit of existing firms from the 'industry' and shows a decline or an increase in the share of the firm.

Assume that the firm is at the non-equilibrium position defined by price P_0 and quantity X_0. The firm, in an attempt to maximise profits, lowers the price at P_1 expecting to sell, on the basis of its individual demand curve, quantity X'_0. This level of sales is not actually realised, because all other firms, faced by the same demand and cost conditions, have the incentive to act in the same way simultaneously. Each one attempts to maximise its own profit, ignoring the reactions of competitors, on the assumption that the effect on the demand of other firms in the group is negligible. Thus all firms, acting independently, reduce their price simultaneously to P_1. As a result the dd' curve shifts downwards $(d_1 d'_1)$ and firm A, instead of selling the expected quantity X'_0, sells actually a smaller quantity X_1 on the shifted-demand curve $d_1 d'_1$ and along the share curve DD'. One might think that the firm would learn to anticipate similar shifts in the future if it decided to reduce its price. However, according to the model, the firm suffers from myopia and does not learn from past experience. It continues to behave on the assumption that its new demand $(d_1 d'_1)$ will not shift further, because the effect of its own decisions on other sellers' demand would be negligible. Thus the firm lowers its price again in an attempt to reach equilibrium, but instead of the expected sales X'_0 the firm achieves actual sales X_2, because all other firms act identically, though independently. The process stops when the dd' curve has shifted so far to the left as to be tangent to the LAC curve. Equilibrium is determined by the tangency of dd' and the LAC curve (point e in figure 8.3). Any further reduction in price will not be attempted since the average cost would not be covered.

In summary, the individual demand curve dd' explains why each firm is led to reduce its price. The DD' curve shows the firm's *actual* sales as the *general downward cut* in price takes place. The dd' curve slides downwards along the DD' curve as prices are lowered, and the adjustment process comes to a stop when the dd' is tangent to the LAC curve. At the point of tangency the DD' curve cuts the dd' curve. Obviously it will pay no one firm to cut the price beyond that point, because its costs of producing the larger output would exceed the price at which this output could be sold in the market.

Model 3: price competition and free entry

Chamberlin suggests that in actual life equilibrium is achieved both by price adjustments of the existing firms and by new entry. Price adjustments are shown along the dd' curve while entry (and exit) cause shifts in the DD' curve. Equilibrium is stable if the dd' curve is tangent to the AC curve and expected sales are equal to actual sales, that is, if *the* DD' *curve cuts the* dd' *curve at the point of its tangency to the* AC *curve*. Let us examine how the equilibrium *tangency solution* is reached (figure 8.4).

It is assumed that profits at point e_1 are abnormal. New firms are attracted until DD shifts to $D'D'$. One might think that e_2 is a long-run equilibrium (with price P and output X) since only normal profits are earned. However, this is not the case, because each entrepreneur thinks that dd is his demand curve, and consequently he believes that if he reduced his price his sales would expand along dd and profits would increase. But each firm has exactly the same incentive and all firms reduce their price. As price is reduced by all firms dd slides down $D'D'$ and each firm realises a loss instead of positive abnormal profits. For example, at position $d'd'$ the firm has reduced its price to P' but, as all firms act similarly, X_1 is produced with a total loss equal to the shaded area $ABP'C$. However, the firm acts on the 'myopia curve' $d'd'$ and so long as this lies above the LAC, it believes that it can obtain positive profits by cutting its price. The loss increases still further as dd slides further down along $D'D'$. One might think that the process would stop when dd becomes tangent to the LAC. This would be so if the firm could

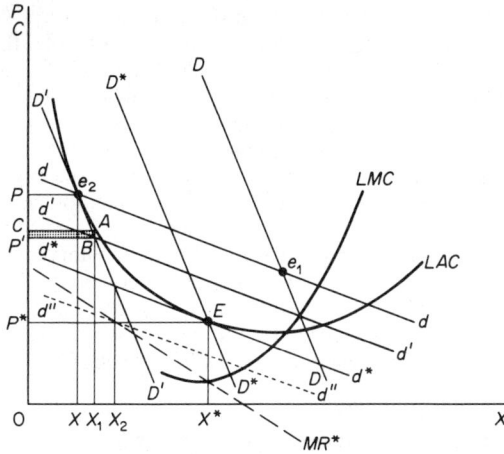

Figure 8.4 Long-run equilibrium

produce X^*. However, there are too many firms in the industry and the share of the firm is only X_2 (on $D'D'$). The firm still on the 'myopia assumption' believes that it can reach X^* if it reduces price to P^*. However, all firms do the same and d^*d^* falls below the LAC with ever-increasing losses. The financially weakest firms will eventually leave the industry first, so that the surviving firms will have a larger share. $D'D'$ moves to the right together with dd. Exit will continue until dd becomes tangent to the AC curve and DD cuts dd at the point of the tangency, E. Equilibrium is then stable at point E with normal profits earned by all firms and no entry or exit taking place. The equilibrium price P^* is unique and each firm has a share equal to $0X^*$.

VI. CRITIQUE OF CHAMBERLIN'S MODEL

Chamberlin's theory has been attacked on several grounds. Some of the criticisms are valid while others do not stand up to a closer examination.

The assumptions of product differentiation and of independent action by the competitors are inconsistent. It is a fact that firms are continuously aware of the actions of competitors whose products are close substitutes of their own product.

It is hard to accept the myopic behaviour of businessmen implied by the model. Surely some firms would learn from past mistakes, and those that did not would be competed out of existence by firms which do take past experience into account in decision-making.

The assumption of product differentiation is also incompatible with the assumption of free entry, especially if the entrants are completely new firms as in Chamberlin's model. A new firm must advertise substantially and adopt intensive selling campaigns in order to make its product known and attract customers from already established firms. Product differentiation and brand loyalty of buyers create a barrier to entry for new firms.

The concept of the industry is destroyed by the recognition of product differentiation. Each firm is an industry in its own right since its product is unique. Heterogeneous products cannot be added to give the industry demand and supply curves. Such summation would be meaningful if the price were unique for the close substitutes constituting the industry. Chamberlin's 'heroic model' is clearly not acceptable as an approximation to the real world in which demands and costs are different among the various firms, giving rise to a cluster of prices rather than a unique price. Of course retention of the concept of industry in economic analysis is very desirable. It is useful to group together close substitutes and analyse their 'demand' and 'supply' conditions. However, one should establish the relationship between the individual demand and cost curves and the market demand and supply curves. This relationship is not established by Chamberlin outside his 'heroic model'. Although he relaxes the 'heroic assumptions' as untenable in the real world, Chamberlin does not examine the implications of this step for his theory. Thus the model of monopolistic competition has been criticised for vagueness of concepts and for being non-operational.

The model assumes a large number of sellers. But it does not define the actual number of firms necessary to justify the myopic disregard of competitors' actions. How many firms should there be in an industry in order to classify it as monopolistically competitive rather than as oligopoly? What is the crucial number that determines whether firms act independently or recognise interdependence? Such problems are not discussed by Chamberlin.

We have mentioned the difficulties in grouping firms in an 'industry'. The model assumes that the products should be close substitutes with high price and high (positive) cross-elasticities. However, this requirement is vague, since it is not clear what is the precise value of elasticities which would be necessary for the classification of products in the same group.

The assumptions of Chamberlin from which he derived the negatively sloping curve have been attacked by Andrews.[1] He argues that Chamberlin's *dd* curve is of questionable analytical use, because it includes only the consumers' demand, and because it implies irrationality of consumers' preferences in the long run. Andrews argues that Chamberlin's demand curve (and any downward-falling demand curve) is applicable only for those rare cases where a firm sells directly to the final consumer, and this only in a short-run analysis. The *dd* curve ignores the demand arising from other manufacturing firms which buy the product as an intermediate commodity to submit it to further processing. It also ignores the bulk of final demand transactions which are carried out by retailers and wholesalers. These type of customers (other manufacturing firms and traders) are themselves profit maximisers and hence, the argument runs, they will not be prepared to pay a higher price for a product sold by other suppliers at a lower price. Therefore the part of demand for the product of a firm arising from other manufacturing firms, retailers and wholesalers cannot give rise to a downward-falling demand curve. This argument is valid for all intermediate commodities, and in particular raw materials. However, for consumer goods, durable and non-durable, as well as for machinery and other equipment, brand names do actually create 'sticky preferences' and 'brand loyalty' of the buyers not only in the short run but also in the long run. It is observed that over long periods of time products that are close substitutes are sold at different prices. For example, soaps and detergents, fabrics, machinery, household durables are sold at a range of prices, which at least partly reflect brand loyalty of the buyers to the particular products. (See also Chapter 2, pp. 63–6.)

The demand of final consumers for the product of the firm sold directly to them can be downward-sloping, Andrews argues, only in the short run. Only for a short period of time will the consumers be prepared to stick to a commodity whose price is higher than that of its close substitutes. Furthermore advertising can create 'sticky preferences' only in the short run. In the long run the consumer will try other less expensive substitutes and, being rational, will turn permanently to them. A downward-falling demand curve in the long run can exist only if consumers are irrational. This argument of Andrews cannot be generally accepted. To begin with, the argument implies a specific definition of

[1] P. W. S. Andrews, *On Competition in Economic Theory* (Macmillan, 1964).

consumers' rationality. A consumer would be irrational if he could identify two identical products and still would pay a higher price for one of them. However, products are or appear different to the consumers. The consumer is rational when he maximises *his* utility. Clearly if by paying the higher price the consumer gets more satisfaction for various reasons (for example, satisfaction from buying from an expensive shop which is fashionable), he cannot be accused of being irrational. The consumer may have all sorts of priorities depending on his tastes, information and time available, and he can only be judged as irrational if he exhibits purchasing patterns inconsistent with his preferences, but not on the nature of his preferences by themselves. Furthermore it is an empirical fact that products having the same (broadly) technical specifications are being sold over several years at different prices, and still they have their own market share although this share may fluctuate over time as new brands are introduced and/or old ones are discontinued. Rational or irrational, the preferences of consumers are such as to give rise to a downward-falling demand curve even in the long run. In particular the demand for durables which involves fairly large expenditures is bound to be based on 'good reputation' and 'information from friends who have tried the products' rather than on minor price differences. It is also true for such products that the buyer may *think* he perceives '*crucial*' differences between rival products – durability, aesthetic appearance, etc. Different buyers will weigh these differently, thus creating their brand loyalties. Only when prices differ considerably would one expect a switch of custom from well-established to new products. In summary, it is an observed fact that for long periods firms producing close substitutes have kept some market share for their individual products despite price differentials. Whether one defines the situation as implying rationality or irrationality on the part of the consumers is irrelevant for the pricing decisions of firms.[1]

It has been argued that Chamberlin's model is indeterminate, due to the effects of product changes and selling activities. Those factors create interdependence of the demand and cost curves of the firm, rendering the equilibrium indeterminate. This argument is not valid. The fact that the cost and demand curves have some common determinants does not necessarily mean that the equilibrium is indeterminate. So long as each of these functions has particular determinants not influencing the other, the demand-and-supply model is identifiable and has a unique solution.

Despite the above criticisms Chamberlin's contribution to the theory of pricing is indisputable.

The most important of these contributions is the introduction of product differentiation and of selling strategy as two additional policy variables in the decision-making process of the firm. These factors are the basis of non-price competition which is the typical form of competition in the real world.

Another contribution is the development of a model which provided a solution, certainly not the only possible or the best, but still a solution, to the dilemma of the falling costs.

The explicit discussion and incorporation of selling activities into price theory is an extremely important step forward in the explanation of the phenomena of the business world. The U-shaped selling-cost curve assumed by Chamberlin may be questioned on theoretical and empirical grounds, but his is the earliest systematic attempt to make an analysis of the selling activities and their influence on the position and shape of the demand of the individual firm.

Another contribution is the introduction of the share-of-the-market-demand curve as a tool of analysis. The combination of *dd* and *DD* gave rise to the 'kinked-demand'

---

[1] It should be noted that the problem discussed in this paragraph probably arises because 'product differentiation' tends to be defined as a *physical* difference *in the product*, whereas it should be defined as any difference, however imaginary or irrational, which the buyer perceives.

curve which has been widely used subsequently as a possible explanation of oligopolistic behaviour (see Chapter 9).

Finally, Chamberlin's attempt to preserve the 'industry' in price theory is important. His assumptions were, as he himself was aware, 'heroic' and unrealistic, but his analysis shows the need for a comprehensive theory of price which will explain the behaviour of the individual firm within an industrial framework. Chamberlin's subsequent abandonment[1] of the 'group' after its heavy criticism by Triffin and others has been rather a drawback in the development of the theory of the firm. (See also Chapter 1.)

VII. COMPARISON WITH PURE COMPETITION

We said that the long-run equilibrium of the firm is defined by the point of tangency of the demand curve to the LAC curve. At this point $MC = MR$ and $AC = P$, but $P > MC$, while in pure competition we have the long-run equilibrium condition $MC = MR = AC = P$.

As a consequence of the different equilibrium conditions price will be higher and output will be lower in monopolistic competition as compared with the perfectly competitive model. Profits, however, will be just normal in the long run in both models. In monopolistic competition there will be too many firms in the industry, each producing an output less than optimal, that is, at a cost higher than the minimum. This is due to the fact that the tangency of AC and demand occurs necessarily at the falling part of the LAC, that is, at a point where LAC has not reached its minimum level. Consequently production costs will be higher than in pure competition. Furthermore, in monopolistic competition firms incur selling costs which are not present in pure competition, and this is another reason for the total cost (and price) to be higher.

Monopolistic competition has been attacked on the grounds that it leads to 'too many, too small' firms, each working with 'excess capacity', as measured by the difference between the 'ideal' output X_F corresponding to the minimum cost level on the LAC curve and the output actually attained in long-run equilibrium X_E (figure 8.5).

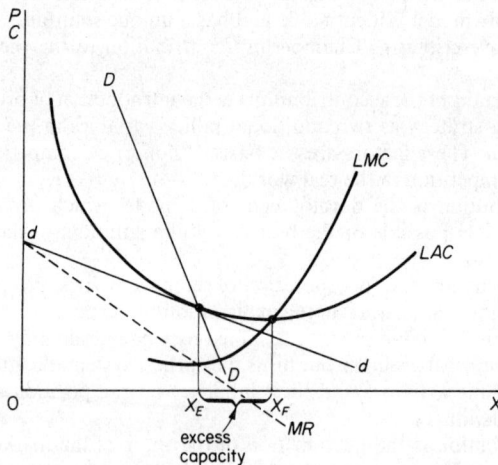

Figure 8.5

[1] E. Chamberlin, 'Monopolistic Competition Revisited', *Economic Journal* (1952).

The term 'excess capacity' is misleading in this case. One should really talk of firms working at suboptimal scales having unexhausted economies of scale. There is a misallocation of resources in the long run because the firm in a monopolistically competitive market does not employ enough of the economy's resources to reach minimum average cost. Chamberlin has argued that the criticism of excess capacity and misallocation of resources is valid only if one assumes that the demand curve of the individual firm is horizontal. Chamberlin argues that if the demand is downward-sloping and firms enter into active price competition while entry is free in the industry, then, Chamberlin argues, X_F cannot be considered as the socially optimal level of output. Consumers desire variety of products: product differentiation reflects the desires of consumers who are willing to pay the higher price in order to have choice among differentiated products. The higher cost, resulting from producing to the left of the minimum average cost, is thus socially acceptable. Consequently the difference between actual output X_E and minimum cost output X_F (figure 8.6) is not a measure of excess

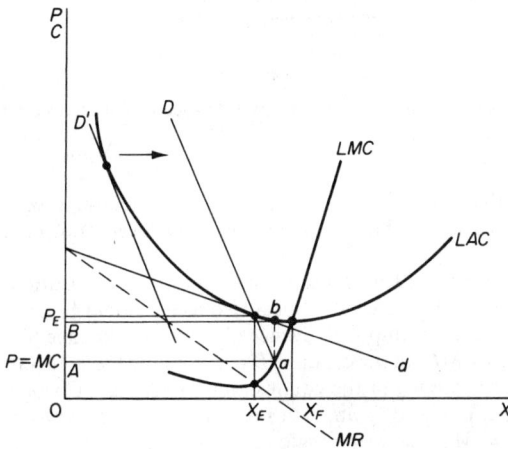

Figure 8.6 Price competition *and* free entry lead to X_E, which is the 'social optimum' (without excess capacity according to Chamberlin)

capacity but rather a measure of the 'social cost' of producing and offering to the consumer greater variety. The output X_E, is a 'sort of ideal' for a market in which product is differentiated.[1] *Chamberlin's argument is based on the assumptions of active price competition and free entry.* Under these circumstances Chamberlin (and later Harrod) argues that the equilibrium output will be very close to the minimum cost output, because firms will be competing along their individual *dd* curves which are very elastic. However if firms avoid price competition and instead enter into non-price competition, there will be excess capacity in each firm and insufficient productive capacity in the industry, that is, unexhausted economies of scale for the firm and the industry. Chamberlin seems to argue that excess capacity (restriction of output) and higher prices are the result of non-price competition coupled with free entry. In this event the firm ignores its *dd* curve (since no price adjustments are made) and concern itself only with its market share. In other words, *DD* becomes the relevant demand curve of the firm. In this event long-run equilibrium is reached only after entry has shifted the *DD* curve to a position

[1] Chamberlin, *Theory of Monopolistic Competition*, p. 94.

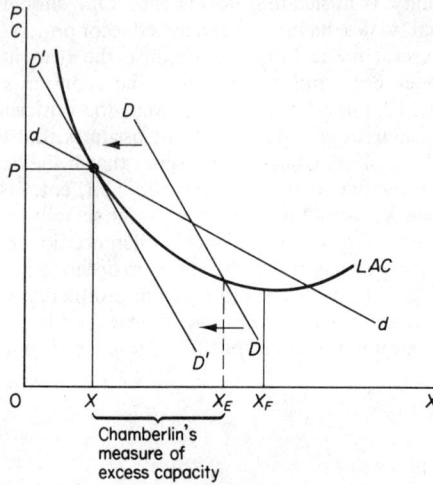

Figure 8.7   Non-price competition and free entry are the causes of excess capacity (according to Chamberlin)

of tangency with the *LAC* curve. According to Chamberlin excess capacity is the difference between X and X_E, the latter being the 'ideal' level of output in a differentiated market (figure 8.7).

From the point of view of social welfare monopolistic competition suffers from the fact that price is higher than the *MC*. Socially output should be increased until price equals *MC*. However, this is impossible since all firms would have to produce at a loss in the long run: the *LRMC* intersects the *DD* curve below the *LAC* (at point *a* in figure 8.6) so that any policy aiming at the equalisation of P and MC would imply a loss of *ab* per unit of output in the long run. Thus if firms were coerced to produce a level of output at which $P = MC$, the firm would close down in the long run. In summary, if the market is monopolistically competitive the output is lower than society would 'ideally' like it to be (that is, price is higher than MC); but the socially desired $P = MC$ cannot be achieved without destroying the whole private enterprise system.

SECTION B

CLASSICAL OLIGOPOLY

9. Non-collusive Oligopoly

In this section we will first present three models of duopoly, which is the limiting case of oligopoly. The common characteristic of these models is that they assume a certain pattern of reaction of competitors in each period and despite the fact that the 'expected' reaction does not in fact materialise, the firms continue to assume that the initial assumption holds. In other words, firms are assumed never to learn from past experience, which makes their behaviour at least naïve (if not stupid).

I. COURNOT'S DUOPOLY MODEL[1]

The earliest duopoly model was developed in 1838 by the French economist Augustin Cournot.

The model may be presented in many ways. The original version is quite limited in that it makes the assumption that the duopolists have identical products and identical costs. Actually Cournot illustrated his model with the example of two firms each owning a spring of mineral water, which is produced at zero costs. We will present briefly this version, and then we will generalise its presentation by using the *reaction curves* approach.

Cournot assumed that there are two firms each owning a mineral well, and operating with zero costs. They sell their output in a market with a straight-line demand curve. Each firm acts on the assumption that its competitor will not change its output, and decides its own output so as to maximise profit.

Assume that firm A is the first to start producing and selling mineral water. It will produce quantity A, at price P where profits are at a maximum (figure 9.1), because at this point $MC = MR = 0$. The elasticity of market demand at this level of output is equal to unity and the total revenue of the firm is a maximum. With zero costs, maximum R implies maximum profits, Π. Now firm B assumes that A will keep its output fixed (at $0A$), and hence considers that its own demand curve is CD'. Clearly firm B will produce half the quantity AD', because (under the Cournot assumption of fixed output of the rival) at this level (AB) of output (and at price P') its revenue and profit is at a maximum. B produces half of the market which has not been supplied by A, that is, B's output is $\frac{1}{4}(=\frac{1}{2} \cdot \frac{1}{2})$ of the total market.

Firm A, faced with this situation, assumes that B will retain his quantity constant in the next period. So he will produce one-half of the market which is not supplied by B. Since B covers one-quarter of the market, A will, in the next period, produce $\frac{1}{2}(1 - \frac{1}{4}) = \frac{1}{2} \cdot \frac{3}{4} = \frac{3}{8}$ of the total market.

[1] A. Cournot, *Rechèrches sur les Principes Mathématiques de la Théorie des Rishesses* (Paris, 1938). Translated by N. T. Bacon, *Researches into the Mathematical Principles of the Theory of Wealth* (Macmillan, 1927).

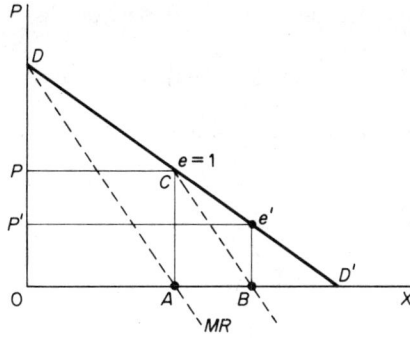

Figure 9.1

Firm B reacts on the Cournot assumption, and will produce one-half of the unsupplied section of the market, i.e. $\frac{1}{2}(1 - \frac{3}{8}) = \frac{5}{16}$.

In the third period firm A will continue to assume that B will not change its quantity, and thus will produce one-half of the remainder of the market, i.e. $\frac{1}{2}(1 - \frac{5}{16})$.

This action-reaction pattern continues, since firms have the naïve behaviour of never learning from past patterns of reaction of their rival. However, eventually an equilibrium will be reached in which each firm produces one-third of the total market. Together they cover two-thirds of the total market. Each firm maximises its profit in each period, but the industry profits are not maximised. That is, the firms would have higher joint profits if they recognised their interdependence, after their failure in forecasting the correct reaction of their rival. Recognition of their interdependence (or open collusion) would lead them to act as 'a monopolist,' producing one-half of the total market output, selling it at the profit-maximising price P, and sharing the market equally, that is, each producing one-quarter of the total market (instead of one-third).

The equilibrium of the Cournot firms may be obtained as follows:

1. The product of firm A in successive periods is

    period 1: $\frac{1}{2}$

    period 2: $\frac{1}{2}(1 - \frac{1}{4}) = \frac{3}{8} = \frac{1}{2} - \frac{1}{8}$

    period 3: $\frac{1}{2}(1 - \frac{5}{16}) = \frac{11}{32} = \frac{1}{2} - \frac{1}{8} - \frac{1}{32}$

    period 4: $\frac{1}{2}(1 - \frac{42}{128}) = \frac{43}{128} = \frac{1}{2} - \frac{1}{8} - \frac{1}{32} - \frac{1}{128}$

We observe that the output of A declines gradually. We may rewrite this expression as follows

$$\begin{bmatrix} \text{Product of } A \\ \text{in equilibrium} \end{bmatrix} = \frac{1}{2} - \frac{1}{8} - \frac{1}{32} - \frac{1}{128} \cdots$$

$$= \frac{1}{2} - [\frac{1}{8} + \frac{1}{8} \cdot \frac{1}{4} + \frac{1}{8} \cdot (\frac{1}{4})^2 + \frac{1}{8}(\frac{1}{4})^3 + \cdots].$$

The expression in parentheses is a declining geometric progression with ratio $r = \frac{1}{4}$. Applying the summation formula for an infinite geometric series

$$\int = \frac{a}{1 - r}$$

(where $\int$ = sum, a = first term of series, r = ratio) we obtain

$$\begin{bmatrix} \text{Product of } A \\ \text{in equilibrium} \end{bmatrix} = \tfrac{1}{2} - \frac{\tfrac{1}{8}}{1 - \tfrac{1}{4}} = \tfrac{1}{2} - \frac{\tfrac{1}{8}}{\tfrac{3}{4}} = \tfrac{1}{2} - \tfrac{4}{24} = \tfrac{8}{24} = \tfrac{1}{3}$$

2. The product of firm B in successive periods is

period 2: $\tfrac{1}{2}(\tfrac{1}{2}) = \tfrac{1}{4}$
period 3: $\tfrac{1}{2}(1 - \tfrac{3}{8}) = \tfrac{5}{16} = \tfrac{1}{4} + \tfrac{1}{16}$
period 3: $\tfrac{1}{2}(1 - \tfrac{11}{32}) = \tfrac{21}{64} = \tfrac{1}{4} + \tfrac{1}{16} + \tfrac{1}{64}$
period 4: $\tfrac{1}{2}(1 - \tfrac{43}{128}) = \tfrac{85}{256} = \tfrac{1}{4} + \tfrac{1}{16} + \tfrac{1}{64} + \tfrac{1}{256}$

We observe that B's output increases, but at a declining rate. We may write

$$\begin{bmatrix} \text{Product of } B \\ \text{in equilibrium} \end{bmatrix} = \tfrac{1}{4} + \tfrac{1}{4} \cdot \tfrac{1}{4} + \tfrac{1}{4}(\tfrac{1}{4})^2 + \tfrac{1}{4}(\tfrac{1}{4})^3 + \cdots$$

Applying the above expression for the summation of a declining geometric series we find

$$\begin{bmatrix} \text{Product of } B \\ \text{in equilibrium} \end{bmatrix} = \frac{\tfrac{1}{4}}{1 - \tfrac{1}{4}} = \frac{\tfrac{1}{4}}{\tfrac{3}{4}} = \tfrac{1}{3}$$

Thus the Cournot solution is stable. Each firm supplies $\tfrac{1}{3}$ of the market, at a common price which is lower than the monopoly price, but above the pure competitive price (which is zero in the Cournot example of costless production). It can be shown that if there are three firms in the industry, each will produce one-quarter of the market and all of them together will supply $\tfrac{3}{4}(=\tfrac{1}{4} \cdot 3)$ of the entire market OD'. And, in general, if there are n firms in the industry each will provide $1/(n + 1)$ of the market, and the industry output will be $n/(n + 1) = 1/(n + 1) \cdot n$. Clearly as more firms are assumed to exist in the industry, the higher the total quantity supplied and hence the lower the price. The larger the number of firms the closer is output and price to the competitive level.

Cournot's model leads to a stable equilibrium. However, his model may be criticised on several accounts:

The behavioural pattern of firms is naïve. Firms do not learn from past miscalculations of competitors' reactions.

Although the quantity produced by the competitors is at each stage assumed constant, a quantity competition emerges which drives P down, towards the competitive level.

The model can be extended to any number of firms. However, it is a 'closed' model, in that entry is not allowed: the number of firms that are assumed in the first period remains the same throughout the adjustment process.

The model does not say how long the adjustment period will be.

The assumption of costless production is unrealistic. However, it can be relaxed without impairing the validity of the model. This is done in the subsequent presentation of the model, based on the *reaction-curves* approach.

The reaction-curves approach is a more powerful method of analysis of oligopolistic markets, because it allows the relaxation of the assumption of identical costs and identical demands. This approach is based on *Stackelberg's indifference-curve analysis*, which introduces the concept of *isoprofit curves* of competitors. We will first establish the shape of the isoprofit curves for substitute commodities, and from these curves we will subsequently derive the reaction curves of the Cournot duopolists.

An isoprofit curve for firm A is the locus of points defined by different levels of output of A and his rival B, which yield to A the same level of profit (figure 9.2).

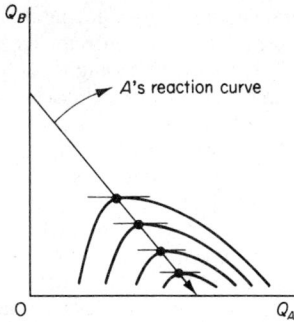
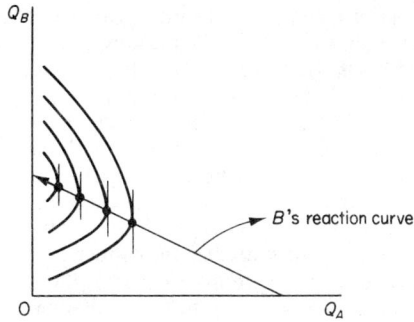

Figure 9.2   Isoprofit map of firm *A*   Figure 9.3   Isoprofit map of firm *B*

Similarly, an isoprofit curve for firm *B* is the locus of points of different levels of output of the two competitors which yield to *B* the same level of profit (figure 9.3).

From the above definitions it should be clear that the isoprofit curves are a type of indifference curves. There is a whole family of isoprofit curves for each firm which have the following properties.

1.   Isoprofit curves for substitute commodities are concave to the axes along which we measure the output of the rival firms. For example, an isoprofit curve of firm *A* is concave to the horizontal axis Q_A. This shape shows how *A* can react to *B*'s output decisions so as to retain a given level of profit. For example, consider the isoprofit curve Π_{A1} in figure 9.4.

Suppose that firm *B* decides to produce the level of output B_1. A line parallel to the horizontal axis through B_1 intersects the isoprofit curve Π_{A1} at points *h* and *g*. This shows that given the output that *B* decides to produce, firm *A* will realise the profit Π_{A1} if it produces either of the two levels of output corresponding to points *h* and *g*, that is, either A_h or A_g. Assume that firm *A* decides to react by producing the higher level A_g. If now firm *B* increases its output (say at the level B_2), firm *A* must decrease its output (at A_f) if it wants to retain its profit at the same level (Π_{A1}). If firm *A* continued to produce A_g while *B* increased its production, the total quantity supplied in the market would depress the price, and hence the profit of firm *A* would decline. Up to a certain point (*e* in figure 9.4) firm *A* must react to increases in *B*'s output by reducing its own production, otherwise the market price would fall and *A*'s profit would decrease. As firm *A* reduces its output, its costs also change, but the net profit ($\Pi = R - C$) remains at the same level (Π_{A1}), because of market elasticity and/or decreasing costs arising from a better utilisation of *A*'s plant.

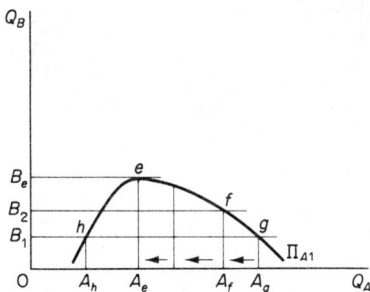
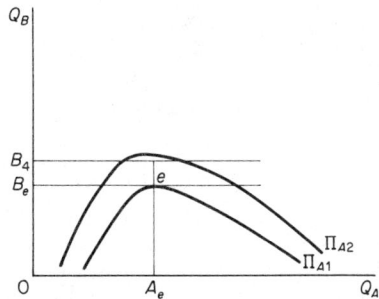

Figure 9.4   Figure 9.5

Consider now point h. If firm A reacts to B's initial decision by producing the lower output A_h, it will clearly earn the same profit Π_{A1}. If firm B decides to increase its output (at the levels B_2, B_3 and so on, up to B_e), firm A will react by increasing its output as well: A's profit·will remain the same despite the resulting fall in the market price, because of market elasticity and/or decrease in its costs due to a better utilisation of its plant.

2.   The farther the isoprofit curves (for substitute commodities) lie from the axes, the lower is the profit. And vice versa, the closer to the quantity-axis an isoprofit curve lies, the higher the profitability of the firm is. Consider figure 9.5. If firm B were to increase its output beyond B_e, firm A would not be able to retain its level of profit. Suppose that firm B decides to produce B_4. Firm A can react in three ways: increase, decrease or retain its output constant (at A_e). If A retains its output constant while B increases its production, the ensuing fall in the market price will result in a reduction in the revenue and in the profits of A, given its costs. If firm A were to increase output beyond A_e, its profit would fall because of inelasticity of demand and/or increasing costs. If firm A were to reduce output below A_e, its profit would fall because of elasticity of demand and/or increasing costs. Thus firm A will earn a lower level of profit, no matter what its reaction, if B increased its output beyond B_e. A line through B_4 parallel to the Q_A-axis lies above Π_{A1}, and will intersect (or will be tangent) to an isoprofit curve which represents a lower profit for firm A. In figure 9.5 the isoprofit curve Π_{A2} represents a lower profit than Π_{A1}. To summarise: for any given output that firm B may produce, there will be a unique level of output for firm A which maximises the latter's profit. This unique profit-maximising level of output will be determined by the point of tangency of the line through the given output of firm B and the lowest attainable isoprofit curve of firm A. In other words, the profit-maximising output of A (for any given quantity of B) is established at the highest point on the lowest attainable isoprofit curve of A.

3.   For firm A, the highest points of successive isoprofit curves lie to the left of each other. If we join the highest points of the isoprofit curves we obtain firm A's *reaction curve*. Thus, the reaction curve of firm A is the locus of points of highest profits that firm A can attain, given the level of output of rival B. It is called 'reaction curve' because it shows how firm A will determine its output as a reaction to B's decision to produce a certain level of output. A's reaction curve is shown in figure 9.6.

B's isoprofit curves are concave to the Q_B axis. Their shape and position are determined by the same factors as the ones underlying firm A's isoprofit curves. The highest point of the isoprofit curves of B lie to the right of each other as we move to curves further away from the Q_B axis. If we join these highest points we obtain B's reaction function (figure 9.7). Each point of the reaction curve shows how much output B must produce in order to maximise its own profit, given the level of output of its rival.

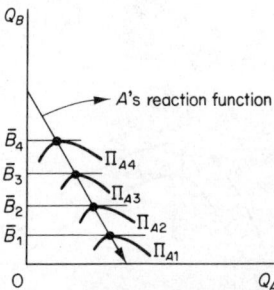

Figure 9.6

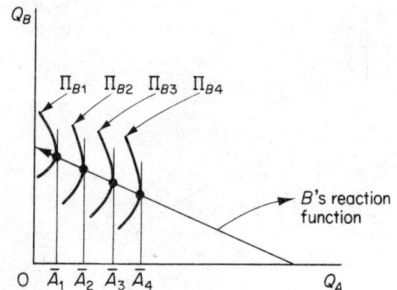

Figure 9.7

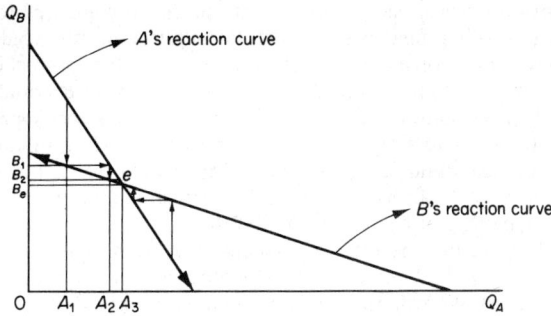

Figure 9.8

Cournot's equilibrium is determined by the intersection of the two reaction curves. It is a stable equilibrium, provided that A's reaction curve is steeper than B's reaction curve. (This condition is satisfied by the assumption we made that the highest points of successive isoprofit curves of A lie to the left of one another, while the highest points of B's isoprofit curves lie to the right of each other.) To see that, let us examine the situation arising from A's decision to produce quantity A_1, lower than the equilibrium quantity A_e (figure 9.8). Firm B will react by producing B_1, given the Cournot assumption that firm A will keep its quantity fixed at A_1. However, A reacts by producing a higher quantity, of A_2, on the assumption that B will stay at the level B_1. Now firm B_1 reacts by reducing its quantity at B_2. This adjustment will continue until point e is reached. The same equilibrium would be reached if we started from a point to the right of e. Thus e is a stable equilibrium.

Note that at point e each firm maximises its own profit, but the industry (joint profit) is not maximised (figure 9.9). This is easily seen by a curve similar to *Edgeworth's contract curve* which traces points of tangency of the two firms' isoprofit curves. Points on the contract curve are optimal in the sense that points *off* this curve imply a lower

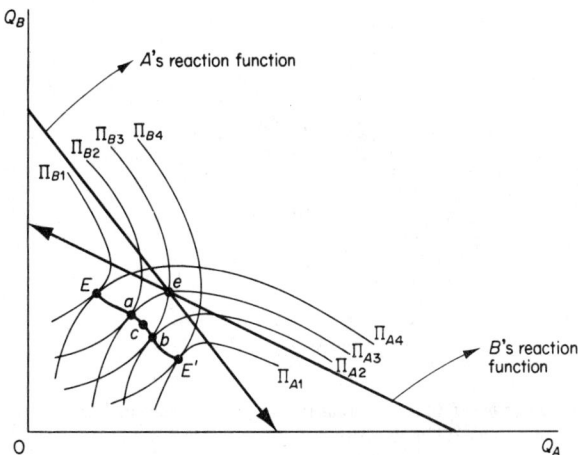

Figure 9.9   *EE'* is the 'Edgeworth's contract curve

profit for one or both firms, that is, less industry profits as compared to points *on* the curve. Point *e* is a suboptimal point, and total industry profits would be higher if firms moved away from it on any point between *a* and *b* on the contract curve: at point *a* firm *A* would continue to have the same profit Π_{A3} while firm *B* would have a higher profit ($\Pi_{B2} > \Pi_{B3}$). At point *b* firm *B* would remain on the same isoprofit curve Π_{B3} while firm *A* would move to a higher isoprofit curve ($\Pi_{A2} > \Pi_{A3}$). Finally at any intermediate point between *a* and *b*, e.g. at *c*, both firms would realise higher profits. The question arises of why the firms choose the suboptimal equilibrium *e*. The answer is that the Cournot pattern of behaviour implies that the firms do not learn from past experience, each expecting the other to remain at a given position. Each firm acts independently, in that it does not know that the other behaves on the same assumption (behaviourial pattern). We will see in a subsequent section how Stackelberg modified this model, by assuming that one or both of the duopolists may be sufficiently alert to recognise that his rival will make the Cournot assumption about his behaviour.

Mathematical derivation of the reaction curves:
A mathematical version of Cournot's model

Assume that the market demand facing the duopolists is

$$X = a* + b*P$$

or

$$P = a + bX \qquad b < 0$$

Given that $X = X_1 + X_2$

$$\frac{\partial X}{\partial X_1} = \frac{\partial X}{\partial X_2} = 1$$

and the *MR*s of the duopolists need not be the same. Actually if the duopolists are of unequal size the one with the larger output will have the smaller *MR*.

Proof:
$$R_i = pX_i$$
$$p = a + b(X_1 + X_2) = f(X_1, X_2)$$

Thus

$$\frac{\partial R_i}{\partial X_i} = p + X_i \frac{\partial P}{\partial X_i}$$

But

$$\frac{\partial P}{\partial X_1} = \frac{\partial P}{\partial X_2} = \frac{\partial P}{\partial X} = b$$

Therefore

$$\frac{\partial R_i}{\partial X_i} = P + X_i \frac{\partial P}{\partial X} = P + (X_i)(b)$$

Given that $P > 0$ while $b < 0$, it is clear that the larger X_i is, the smaller the *MR* will be.
The two duopolists have different costs

$$C_1 = f_1(X_1) \quad \text{and} \quad C_2 = f_2(X_2)$$

The first duopolist maximises his profit by assuming X_2 constant, irrespective of his own decisions, while the second duopolist maximises his profit by assuming that X_1 will remain constant.

The first-order condition for maximum profits of each duopolist is

$$\left.\begin{aligned} \frac{\partial \Pi_1}{\partial X_1} = \frac{\partial R_1}{\partial X_1} - \frac{\partial C_1}{\partial X_1} = 0 \\[2mm] \frac{\partial \Pi_2}{\partial X_2} = \frac{\partial R_2}{\partial X_2} - \frac{\partial C_2}{\partial X_2} = 0 \end{aligned}\right\} \tag{9.1}$$

Rearranging we have

$$\left.\begin{aligned} \frac{\partial R_1}{\partial X_1} = \frac{\partial C_1}{\partial X_1} \\[2mm] \frac{\partial R_2}{\partial X_2} = \frac{\partial C_2}{\partial X_2} \end{aligned}\right\} \tag{9.2}$$

Solving the first equation of (9.2) for X_1 we obtain X_1 as a function of X_2, that is, we obtain the reaction curve of firm A. It expresses the output which A must produce in order to maximise his profit for any given amount X_2 of his rival.

Solving the second equation of (9.2) for X_2 we obtain X_2 as a function of X_1, that is, we obtain the reaction function of firm B.

If we solve the two equations simultaneously we obtain the Cournot equilibrium, the values of X_1 and X_2 which satisfy both equations; this is the point of intersection of the two reaction curves.

The second-order condition for equilibrium requires that

$$\frac{\partial^2 \Pi_i}{\partial X_i^2} = \frac{\partial^2 R_i}{\partial X_i^2} - \frac{\partial^2 C_i}{\partial X_i^2} < 0 \qquad (i = 1, 2)$$

or

$$\frac{\partial^2 R_i}{\partial X_i^2} < \frac{\partial^2 C_i}{\partial X_i^2}$$

Each duopolist's MR must be increasing less rapidly than his MC, that is, the MC must cut the MR from below, for both duopolists.

A numerical example

Assume that the market demand and the costs of the duopolists are

$$P = 100 - 0 \cdot 5(X_1 + X_2)$$
$$C_1 = 5X_1$$
$$C_2 = 0 \cdot 5X_2^2$$

The profits of the duopolists are

(a)
$$\Pi_1 = PX_1 - C_1 = [100 - 0 \cdot 5(X_1 + X_2)]X_1 - 5X_1$$

or

$$\Pi_1 = 100X_1 - 0 \cdot 5X_1^2 - 0 \cdot 5X_1X_2 - 5X_1$$

(b)
$$\Pi_2 = PX_2 - C_2 = [100 - 0 \cdot 5(X_1 + X_2)]X_2 - 0 \cdot 5X_2^2$$

or

$$\Pi_2 = 100X_2 - 0 \cdot 5X_2^2 - 0 \cdot 5X_1X_2 - 0 \cdot 5X_2^2$$

Collecting terms we have

$$\Pi_1 = 95X_1 - 0.5X_1^2 - 0.5X_1X_2$$

and

$$\Pi_2 = 100X_2 - X_2^2 - 0.5X_1X_2$$

For profit maximisation under the Cournot assumption we have

$$\left. \begin{array}{l} \dfrac{\partial \Pi_1}{\partial X_1} = 0 = 95 - X_1 - 0.5X_2 \\[3mm] \dfrac{\partial \Pi_2}{\partial X_2} = 0 = 100 - 2X_2 - 0.5X_1 \end{array} \right\} \qquad (9.3)$$

The reaction functions are

$$X_1 = 95 - 0.5X_2$$
$$X_2 = 50 - 0.25X_1$$

The graphical solution of Cournot's model is found by the intersection of the two reaction curves which are plotted in figure 9.10.

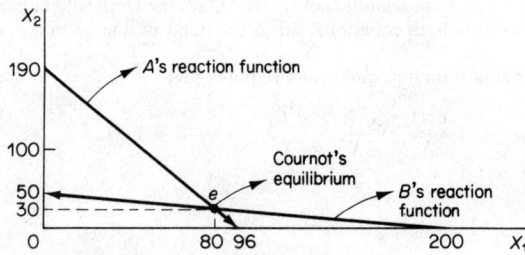

Figure 9.10

Mathematically the solution of system (9.3) yields

$$\left. \begin{array}{l} X_1 = 95 - 0.5X_2 \\ X_2 = 50 - 0.25X_1 \end{array} \right\}$$

$$X_1 = 95 - 0.5(50 - 0.25X_1)$$

or

$$X_1 = 80$$

and

$$X_2 = 50 - 0.25X_1 = 50 - (0.25)(80) = 30$$

Thus total output in the market is

$$X = X_1 + X_2 = 120$$

and the market price

$$P = 100 - 0.5X = 45$$

Note that

$$MR_1 = \frac{\partial R_1}{\partial X_1} = \frac{\partial (PX_1)}{\partial X_1} = P + X_1 \frac{\partial P}{\partial X}$$

$$MR_1 = 45 + 80(-0.5)$$

$$MR_1 = 5$$

while $MR_2 = 45 + 30(-0.5)$

$$MR_2 = 30$$

That is, the firm with the larger output has the smaller marginal revenue. The profits of the duopolists are

$$\Pi_1 = PX_1 - C_1$$
$$\Pi_1 = (45)(80) - 5(80) = 3200$$

and

$$\Pi_2 = PX_2 - C_2$$
$$\Pi_2 = (45)(30) - 0.25(30)^2 = 900$$

The second-order condition is satisfied for both duopolists:

$$\left. \begin{array}{ll} \dfrac{\partial \Pi_1}{\partial X_1} = 95 - X_1 - 0.5X_2 & \dfrac{\partial \Pi_2}{\partial X_2} = 100 - 2X_2 - 0.5X_1 \\[2ex] \dfrac{\partial^2 \Pi_1}{\partial X_1^2} = -1 < 0 & \dfrac{\partial^2 \Pi_2}{\partial X_2^2} = -2 < 0 \end{array} \right\}$$

II. BERTRAND'S DUOPOLY MODEL

Bertrand[1] developed his duopoly model in 1883. His model differs from Cournot's in that he assumes that each firm expects that the rival will keep its price constant, irrespective of its own decision about pricing. Thus each firm is faced by the same *market demand*, and aims at the maximisation of its own profit on the assumption that the price of the competitor will remain constant.

The model may be presented with the analytical tools of the reaction functions of the duopolists. In Bertrand's model the reaction curves are derived from isoprofit maps which are convex to the axes, on which we now measure the prices of the duopolists. Each isoprofit curve for firm A shows the same level of profit which would accrue to A from various levels of prices charged by this firm and its rival. The isoprofit curve for A is convex to its price axis (P_A). This shape shows the fact that firm A must lower its price up to a certain level (point e in figure 9.11) to meet the cutting of price of its competitor, in order to maintain the level of its profits at Π_{A2}. However, after that price level has been reached and if B continues to cut its price, firm A will be unable to retain its profits, even if it keeps its own price unchanged (at P_{Ae}). If, for example, firm B cuts its price at P_B, firm A will find itself at a lower isoprofit curve (Π_{A1}) which shows lower profits. The reduction of profits of A is due to the fall in price, and the increase in output beyond the optimal level of utilisation of the plant with the consequent increase in costs. Clearly the lower the isoprofit curve, the lower the level of profits.

[1] See J. Bertrand, 'Théorie Mathématique de la Richesse Sociale', *Journal des Savants* (Paris, 1883) pp. 499–508.

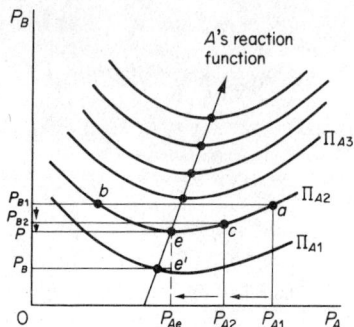

Figure 9.11

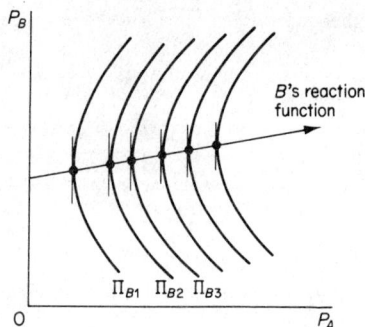

Figure 9.12

To summarise: for any price charged by firm B there will be a unique price of firm A which maximises the latter's profit. This unique profit-maximising price is determined at the lowest point on the highest attainable isoprofit curve of A. The minimum points of the isoprofit curves lie to the right of each other, reflecting the fact that as firm A moves to a higher level of profit, it gains some of the customers of B when the latter increases its price, even if A also raises its price. If we join the lowest points of the successive isoprofit curves we obtain the reaction curve (or conjectural variation) of firm A: this is the locus of points of maximum profits that A can attain by charging a certain price, given the price of its rival.

The reaction curve of firm B may be derived in a similar way, by joining the lowest points of its isoprofit curves (figure 9.12).

Bertrand's model leads to a stable equilibrium, defined by the point of intersection of the two reaction curves (figure 9.13). Point e denotes a stable equilibrium, since any departure from it sets in motion forces which will lead back to point e at which the price charged by A and B are P_{Ae} and P_{Be} respectively. For example, if firm A charges a lower price P_{A1}, firm B will charge P_{B1}, because on the Bertrand assumption, this price will maximise B's profit (given P_{A1}). Firm A will react to this decision of its rival by charging

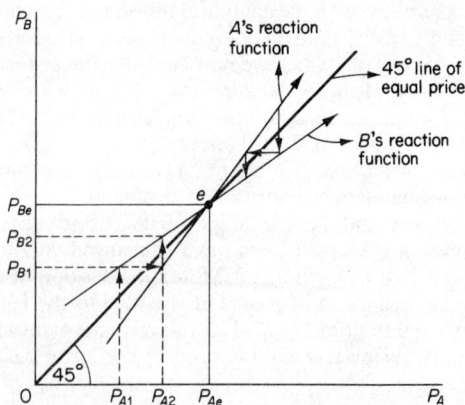

Figure 9.13

a higher price P_{A2}. Firm B will react by increasing its price, and so on, until point e is reached, when the market will be in equilibrium. The same equilibrium will be reached if firms started by charging a price higher than P_{Ae} or P_{Be}: a competitive price cut would take place which would drive both prices down to their equilibrium level P_{Ae} and P_{Be}.

Note that Bertrand's model does not lead to the maximisation of the industry (joint) profit, due to the fact that firms behave naïvely, by always assuming that their rival will keep its price fixed, and they never learn from past experience which showed that the rival did not in fact keep its price constant. The industry profit could be increased if firms recognised their past mistakes and abandoned the Bertrand pattern of behaviour (figure 9.14). If firms moved on any point between c and d on the *Edgeworth contract curve* (which is the locus of points of tangency of the isoprofit curves of the competitors) one or both firms would have higher profits, and hence industry profits would be higher. At point c firm B would retain the same profit (B_6) as at point e, while A would move to a higher profit level (A_9). At point d firm A would have the same profit (A_5) as at the Bertrand equilibrium e, but firm B would move to a higher isoprofit curve (B_{10}). Finally, at any point between c and d (e.g. at f) both firms would realise higher profits (A_7 and B_8) as compared to those attained at Bertrand's solution ($A_7 > A_5$ and $B_8 > B_6$).

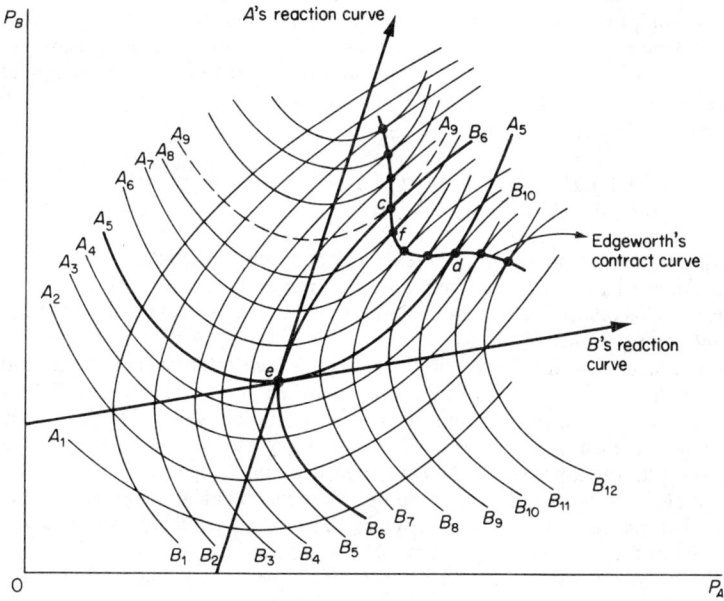

Figure 9.14

Bertrand's model may be criticised on the same grounds as Cournot's model:

The behavioural pattern emerging from Bertrand's assumption is naïve: firms never learn from past experience.

Each firm maximises its own profit, but the industry (joint) profits are not maximised.

The equilibrium price will be the competitive price. (In the example of costless mineral-water production, the price in Bertrand's model would fall to zero. If production is not costless, then price would fall to the level which would cover the costs of the duopolists inclusive of a normal profit.)

The model is 'closed' – does not allow entry.

The interesting feature of both Cournot's and Bertrand's models is that the limit of duopoly is pure competition. Neither model refutes the other. Each is consistent and is based on different behavioural assumptions. We may say that Bertrand's assumption (about the fixity of price of the rival) is more realistic, in view of the observed preoccupation of firms with keeping their prices constant (except in cost inflation situations). Furthermore, Bertrand's model focused attention on price setting as the main decision of the firm. The serious limitations of both models are the naïve behavioural pattern of rivals; the failure to deal with entry; the failure to incorporate other variables in the model, such as advertising and other selling activities, location of the plant, and changes in the product. Product differentiation and selling activities are the two main weapons of non-price competition, which is a main form of competition in the real business world; both models do not define the length of the adjustment process. Although dealing in terms of 'time periods,' their approach is basically static; both models assume that the market demand is known with accuracy; both models are based on individual demand curves which are located by making the convenient assumption of constant reaction curves of the competing firms.

Having discussed the classical duopoly models of Cournot and Bertrand, we proceed with the development of the traditional models of non-collusive oligopoly, which apply to market structures with a few firms conscious of their interdependence. It is worth while pointing out, however, that both Cournot's and Bertrand's models can be extended to markets in which the number of firms is greater than two.

III. CHAMBERLIN'S OLIGOPOLY MODEL
('SMALL-GROUP' MODEL)

Chamberlin's contribution to the theory of oligopoly consists in his suggestion that a stable equilibrium can be reached with the monopoly price being charged by all firms, if firms recognise their interdependence and act so as to maximise the industry profit (monopoly profit).

Chamberlin accepts that if firms do not recognise their interdependence, the industry will reach *either* the Cournot equilibrium, if each firm acts independently on the assumption that the rivals will keep their output constant; *or* the industry will reach the Bertrand equilibrium if each firm acts independently, trying to maximise its own profit on the assumption that the other rivals will keep their price unchanged.

Chamberlin, however, rejects the assumption of independent action by competitors. He says that the firms do in fact recognise their interdependence. Firms are not as naïve as Cournot and Bertrand assume. Firms, when changing their price or output, recognise the *direct* and *indirect* effects of their decisions. The direct effects are those which would occur if competitors were assumed to remain passive (either in the Cournot or in the Bertrand sense). The indirect effects are those which result from the fact that rivals do not in fact remain passive but react to the decisions of the firm which changes its price or output. The recognition of the *full effects* (direct and indirect) of a change in the firm's output (or price) results in a stable industry equilibrium with the monopoly price and monopoly output. Chamberlin assumes that the monopoly solution (with industry or joint profits being maximised) can be achieved without collusion: the entrepreneurs are assumed to be intelligent enough to quickly recognise their interdependence, learn from their past mistakes and adopt the best (for all) position, which is charging the monopoly price. Chamberlin's model can best be understood if presented in a duopoly market. Initially Chamberlin's model is the same as Cournot's. The market demand is a straight line with negative slope, and production is assumed costless for simplicity (figure 9.15). If firm A is the first to start production it will produce the profit-maximising output $0X_M$ and sell it at the monopoly price P_M. Firm B, under the Cournot assumption that the rival A will retain his quantity unchanged, considers that its demand curve is CD and will attempt to maximise its profit by producing one-half of this demand, that is, quantity $X_M B$ (at which B's $MR = MC = 0$). As a consequence the total industry output is $0B$ and the price falls to P. Now firm A realises that its rival does in fact react to its actions, and taking that into account decides to reduce its output to $0A$ which is one-half of $0X_M$ and equal to B's output. The industry output is thus $0X_M$ and price rises to the monopoly level $0P_M$. Firm B realises that this is the best for both of them and so will keep its output the same at $X_M B = AX_M$. Thus, by recognising their interdependence the firms reach the monopoly solution. Under the assumption of our example of equal costs (that is, costs $= 0$) the market will be shared equally between A and B (clearly $0A = AX_M$).

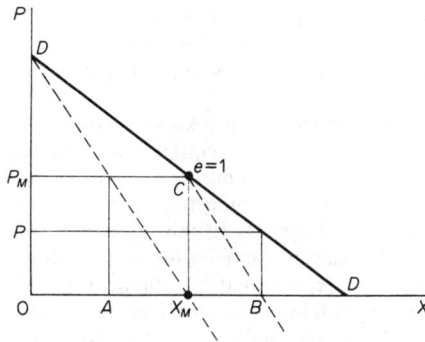

Figure 9.15

Chamberlin's model is an advance over the previous models in that it assumes that the firms are sophisticated enough to realise their interdependence, and that it leads to a stable equilibrium, which is the monopoly solution.

However, joint profit maximisation via non-collusive action implies that firms have a good knowledge of the market-demand curve and that they soon realise their mistakes. That is, they somehow acquire a knowledge of the total-supply curve (i.e. of the individual costs of the rivals) and hence they define the (monopoly) price which is best for the group as a whole. In the next chapter we will examine Fellner's theory of joint profit maximisation and we will see the difficulties which arise and which make it almost impossible to arrive at the monopoly solution even with collusion. Without collusion joint profit maximisation is impossible unless all firms have identical costs and demands.

Chamberlin's small group model suffers also from the defect of ignoring entry. It is a 'closed' model. If entry does occur it is not certain that the stable monopoly solution will ever be reached, unless special assumptions are made concerning the behaviour of the old firms and the new entrant.

It should be noted that althrough the 'kinked-demand curve' appears in Chamberlin's analysis (of both the 'large group' and the 'small group'), he does not use it explicitly as a tool of analysis of the behaviour of the firm. The 'kinked-demand curve model' as an operational oligopoly model was presented by P. Sweezy in 1939. We turn to the examination of this model.

IV. THE 'KINKED-DEMAND' MODEL:
SWEEZY'S NON-COLLUSIVE STABLE EQUILIBRIUM

The kinked-demand curve as a tool of analysis originated from Chamberlin's inter-section of the individual *dd* curve of the firm and its market-share curve *DD'*. However, Chamberlin himself did not use 'kinked-demand' in his analysis.

Hall and Hitch in their famous article 'Price Theory and Business Behaviour'[1] used the kinked-demand curve not as a tool of analysis for the determination of the price and output in oligopolistic markets, but to explain why the price, once determined on the basis of the *average-cost principle*, will remain 'sticky.' That is, Hall and Hitch use the kinked-demand curve in order to explain the 'stickiness' of prices in oligopolistic markets, but not as a tool for the determination of the price itself, which is decided on the average-cost principle (often incorrectly referred to as 'full-cost' principle; see Chapter 12).

However, in the same year (1939), P. Sweezy published an article[2] in which he intro-duced the kinked-demand curve as an operational tool for the determination of the equilibrium in oligopolistic markets. His model, which still holds (surprisingly) an important position as an 'oligopoly theory' in most textbooks, may be presented as follows.

The demand curve of the oligopolist has a kink (at point E in figure 9.16), reflecting the following behavioural pattern. If the entrepreneur reduces his price he expects that his competitors will follow suit, matching the price cut, so that, although the demand in the market increases, the shares of competitors remain unchanged. Thus for price reductions below P (which corresponds to the point of the kink) the share-of-the-market-demand curve is the relevant curve for decision-making.

However, the entrepreneur expects that his competitors will not follow him if he increases his price, so that he will lose a considerable part of his custom. Thus for price increases above P, the relevant demand curve is the section dE of the dd' curve. The

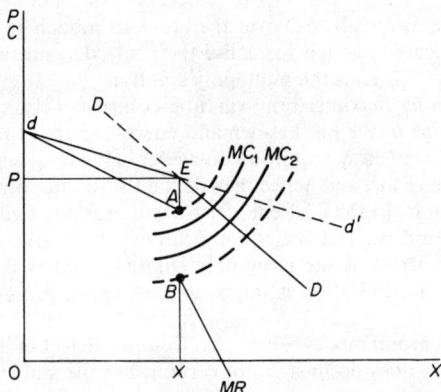

Figure 9.16

[1] R. L. Hall and C. I. Hitch, 'Price Theory and Business Behaviour', *Oxford Economic Papers* (1939) pp. 12–45.
[2] P. Sweezy, 'Demand under Conditions of Oligopoly', *Journal of Political Economy* (1939) pp. 568–737.

upper section of the kinked-demand curve has a higher price elasticity than the lower part. Due to the kink in the demand curve of the oligopolist, his *MR* curve is discontinuous at the level of output corresponding to the kink. The *MR* has two segments: segment *dA* corresponds to the upper part of the demand curve, while the segment from point *B* corresponds to the lower part of the kinked-demand curve.

The equilibrium of the firm is defined by the point of the kink because at any point to the left of the kink *MC* is below the *MR*, while to the right of the kink the *MC* is larger than the *MR*. Thus total profit is maximised at the point of the kink. However, this equilibrium is not necessarily defined by the intersection of the *MC* and the *MR* curve. Indeed in general the *MC* passes somewhere through the discontinuous segment *AB*, and in that sense one might argue that, although marginalistic calculations are behind the 'kink-equilibrium,' the kinked-demand curve is a manifestation of the breakdown of the basic marginalistic rule according to which the price and output level that maximise profit are defined by equating *MC* with *MR*. Intersection of the *MC* with the *MR* segments requires abnormally high or abnormally low costs, which are rather rare in practice. The discontinuity (between *A* and *B*) of the *MR* curve implies that there is a range within which costs may change without affecting the equilibrium *P* and *X* of the firm. In figure 9.16, so long as *MC* passes through the segment *AB*, the firm maximises its profits by producing *P* and *X*. This level of price and output is compatible with a wide range of costs. Thus the kink can explain why price and output will not change despite changes in costs (within the range *AB* defined by the discontinuity of the *MR* curve). The greater the difference of elasticities of the upper and lower parts of the kinked-demand curve, the wider the discontinuity in the *MR* curve, and hence the wider the range of cost conditions compatible with the equilibrium price *P* and output *X*. There is only one case in which a rise in cost will most certainly induce the firm to increase its price when costs rise, despite the fact that the higher costs pass through the discontinuity of the *MR* curve. This occurs when the rise in costs is general (for example, imposition of a sales tax) and affects all firms equally. Under these circumstances the firm will increase its price with the certainty that the others in the industry will follow, since their costs are similarly affected. The point of the kink shifts upwards to the left, and equilibrium is established at a higher price and a lower output (figure 9.17). The firms, via independent action, move closer to the point of joint profit maximisation. Furthermore there is a range through which demand may shift without a change in price although quantity will change. If the demand curve is kinked, a shift in the market demand upwards or downwards will affect the volume of output, but not the level of

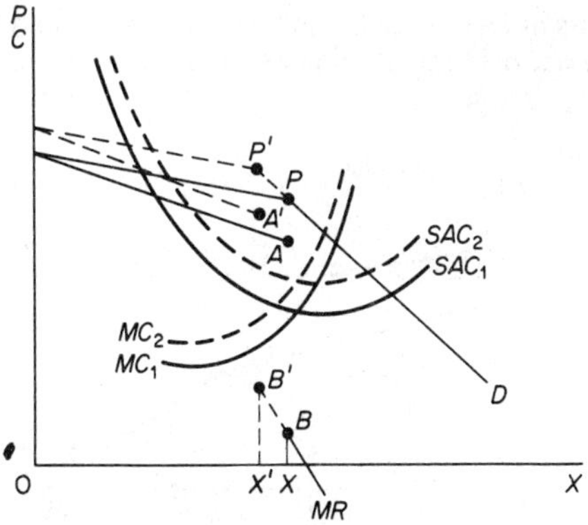

Figure 9.17

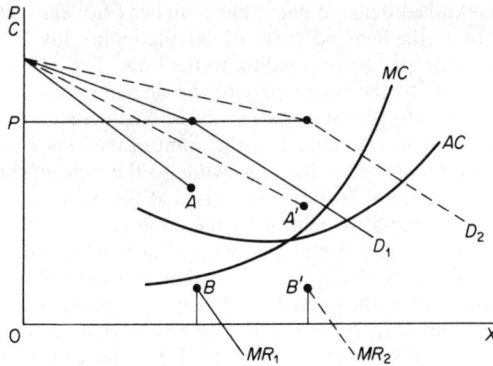

Figure 9.18

price, so long as the cost passes within the range of the discontinuity of the new MR. In this case the shift occurs along the same price line (figure 9.18). As the market expands, the firm will not raise its price, because its (given) cost continues to pass through the discontinuity of the new MR curve and hence there is not incentive to change P, although output will increase.

Prima facie the kinked-demand hypothesis appears attractive. The behavioural pattern implied by the kink seems quite realistic in the highly competitive business world which is dominated by strongly competing oligopolists. However, this model does not explain the price and output decisions of the firms. It does not define the level at which price will be set in order to maximise profits. The kinked-demand curve can explain the 'stickiness' of prices in a situation of changing costs and of high rivalry. The kink is the consequence (manifestation) of the uncertainty of the oligopolists and of their expectations that competitors will match price cuts, but not price increases. However, it does not explain the level of the price at which the kink will occur. In figure 9.19 we depict two kinked-demand curves, with the kink occurring at a different price level. Sweezy's 'theory' cannot define which of the two kinks (that is, which one of the two prices) will materialise. The kinked-demand hypothesis does not explain the height of the kink. Hence, it is not a theory of pricing, but rather a tool for explaining why the price, once determined in one way or another, will tend to remain fixed.

In view of the above criticism, it is indeed surprising that most textbooks of microeconomics still discuss at length the kinked-demand model and present it as the most relevant 'theory' of price determination in oligopolistic markets.

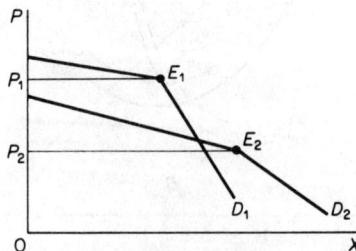

Figure 9.19

V. STACKELBERG'S DUOPOLY MODEL

This model was developed by the German economist Heinrich von Stackelberg[1] and is an extension of Cournot's model. It is assumed, by von Stackelberg, that *one* duopolist is sufficiently sophisticated to recognise that his competitor acts on the Cournot assumption. This recognition allows the sophisticated duopolist to determine the reaction curve of his rival and incorporate it in his own profit function, which he then proceeds to maximise like a monopolist.

Assume that the isoprofit curves and the reaction functions of the duopolists are those depicted in figure 9.20. If firm A is the sophisticated oligopolist, it will assume that its rival will act on the basis of its own reaction curve. This recognition will permit firm A to choose to set its own output at the level which maximises its own profit. This is point a (in figure 9.20) which lies on the lowest possible isoprofit curve of A, denoting the maximum profit A can achieve given B's reaction curve. Firm A, acting as a monopolist (by incorporating B's reaction curve in his profit-maximising computations) will produce X_A, and firm B will react by producing X_B according to its reaction curve. The sophisticated oligopolist becomes in effect the leader, while the naïve rival who acts on the Cournot assumption becomes the follower. Clearly sophistication is rewarding for A because he reaches an isoprofit curve closer to his axis than if he behaved with the same naïveté as his rival. The naïve follower is worse off as compared with the Cournot equilibrium, since with this level of output he reaches an isoprofit curve further away from his axis.

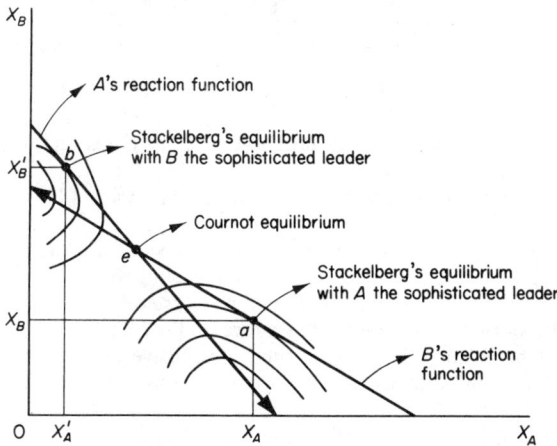

Figure 9.20

If firm B is the sophisticated oligopolist, it will choose to produce X'_B, corresponding to point b on A's reaction curve, because this is the largest profit that B can achieve given his isoprofit map and A's reaction curve. Firm B will now be the leader while firm A becomes the follower. B has a higher profit and the naïve firm A has a lower profit as compared with the Cournot equilibrium.

[1] H. von Stackelberg, *The Theory of the Market Economy*, trans. A. T. Peacock (London, 1952).

In summary, if only one firm is sophisticated, it will emerge as the leader, and a stable equilibrium will emerge, since the naïve firm will act as a follower.

However, if both firms are sophisticated, then both will want to act as leaders, because this action yields a greater profit to them. In this case the market situation becomes unstable. The situation is known as *Stackelberg's disequilibrium* and the effect will *either* be a price war until one of the firms surrenders and agrees to act as follower, *or a collusion* is reached, with both firms abandoning their naïve reaction functions and moving to a point closer to (or on) the Edgeworth contract curve with both of them attaining higher profits. If the final equilibrium lies on the Edgeworth contract curve the industry profits (joint profits) are maximised (figure 9.21).

Von Stackelberg's model has interesting implications.

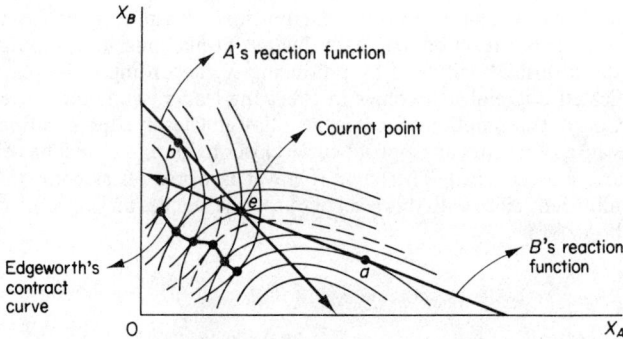

Figure 9.21

It shows clearly that naïve behaviour does not pay. The rivals should recognise their interdependence.

By recognising the other's reactions each duopolist can reach a higher level of profit for himself.

If both firms start recognising their mutual interdependence, each starts worrying about the rival's profits and the rival's reactions. If each ignores the other, a price war will be inevitable, as a result of which both will be worse off.

The model shows that a bargaining procedure and a collusive agreement becomes advantageous to both duopolists. With such a collusive agreement the duopolists may reach a point on the Edgeworth contract curve, thus attaining joint profit maximisation.

It should be noted that Stackelberg's model of sophisticated behaviour is not applicable in a market in which the firms behave on Bertrand's assumption. In a Cournot-type market the sophisticated firm 'bluffs' the rival, by producing a level of output larger than the one that would be produced in the Cournot equilibrium and the naïve rival, sticking to his Cournot behavioural reaction pattern, will be misled and produce less than in the Cournot equilibrium. However, in a Bertrand-type market the sophisticated duopolist can do nothing which would increase his own profit and persuade the other to stop price-cutting. The most he can do is to keep his own price constant, that is, behave exactly as his opponent expects him to behave.[1]

---

[1] See Ira Horowitz, *Decision Making and the Theory of the Firm* (Holt, Rinehart & Winston, 1970) p. 180.

A numerical example of Stackelberg's model

Assume that in a duopoly market the demand function is

$$P = 100 - 0{\cdot}5(X_1 + X_2)$$

and the duopolists' costs are

$$C_1 = 5X_1 \quad \text{and} \quad C_2 = 0{\cdot}5X_2^2$$

The reaction functions are found by taking the partial derivatives of the duopolists' profit functions and equating them to zero:

$$\Pi_1 = PX_1 - C_1 = 95X_1 - 0{\cdot}5X_1^2 - 0{\cdot}5X_1X_2$$
$$\Pi_2 = PX_2 - C_2 = 100X_2 - X_2^2 - 0{\cdot}5X_1X_2$$

The partial derivatives are

$$\frac{\partial\Pi_1}{\partial X_1} = 95 - X_1 - 0{\cdot}5X_2 = 0$$

$$\frac{\partial\Pi_2}{\partial X_2} = 100 - 2X_2 - 0{\cdot}5X_1 = 0$$

The reaction functions are

$$X_1 = 95 - 0{\cdot}5X_2 \rightarrow A\text{'s reaction curve}$$
$$X_2 = 50 - 0{\cdot}25X_1 \rightarrow B\text{'s reaction curve}$$

(1) *Stackelberg's solution with* A *being the sophisticated leader*

Firm *A* will substitute *B*'s reaction function in its own profit equation, which it will then maximise as if it were a monopolist:

$$\Pi_1 = PX_1 - C_1 = 95X_1 - 0{\cdot}5X_1^2 - 0{\cdot}5X_1X_2$$

Substitute $\qquad\qquad\qquad X_2 = 50 - 0{\cdot}25X_1$

Maximise $\qquad\qquad\qquad \Pi_1 = 70X_1 - 0{\cdot}375X_1^2$

(a) First-order condition: $\qquad \dfrac{\partial\Pi_1}{\partial X_1} = 70 - 0{\cdot}75X_1 = 0$

This yields output: $\qquad\qquad X_1 = 93\frac{1}{3}$

and profit: $\qquad\qquad\quad \Pi_1 = 70X_1 - 0{\cdot}375X_1 = 3267$

(b)·The second-order condition for profit maximisation is fulfilled.

Firm *B* would be the follower. It would assume that *A* would produce $93\frac{1}{3}$ units; thus *B* substitutes this amount in its reaction function

$$X_2 = 50 - 0{\cdot}25X_1 = 26\frac{2}{3}$$

and its profit would be

$$\Pi_2 = 100X_2 - X_2^2 - 0{\cdot}5X_1X_2 = 155{\cdot}5$$

(2) *Stackelberg's solution if firm* B *is the sophisticated duopolist*

Firm *B* will substitute *A*'s reaction function in its own profit function, and it will proceed to maximise this profit as a monopolist

$$\Pi_2 = PX_2 - C_2 = 100X_2 - X_2^2 - 0{\cdot}5X_1X_2$$

Substitute $X_1 = 95 - 0{\cdot}5X_2$ (i.e., *A*'s reaction function)

$$\Pi_2 = 52{\cdot}5X_2 - 0{\cdot}75X_2^2$$

(a) The first-order condition for the maximisation of Π_2 requires

$$\frac{\partial \Pi_2}{\partial X_2} = 52.5 - 1.5X_2 = 0$$

which yields output: $X_2 = 35$

and profit: $\Pi_2 = 52.5X_2 - 0.75X_2^2 = 918.75$

(b) The second-order condition for the maximisation of Π_2 is fulfilled.

The follower is now firm A which will act on the Cournot assumption; it will assume that the rival will keep his quantity at $X_2 = 35$, and will find its own output by substituting this quantity in its reaction function.

$$X_1 = 95 - 0.5X_2 = 77.5$$

and its profit is

$$\Pi_1 = 95X_1 - 0.5X_1^2 - 0.5X_1X_2 = 3003$$

(3) *Stackelberg's disequilibrium*

If both entrepreneurs adopt Stackelberg's sophisticated pattern of behaviour, each will examine his profits if he acts as a leader and if he acts as a follower, and will adopt the action that will yield him the greatest profit.

Firm A calculates its profits both as a leader and as a follower:
If A is the leader his profits are 3267
If A is the follower his profits are 3003
Clearly firm A will prefer to act as the leader.

Firm B similarly, calculates its profits as a leader and as a follower:
If B is the leader his profits are 918.75
If B acts as the follower his profits are 155.50
Thus firm B will also choose to act as the leader.[1]

With both firms acting in the sophisticated way implied by Stackelberg's behavioural hypothesis both will want to act as leaders. As they attempt to do so they find that their expectations about the rival are not fulfilled and 'warfare' will start, unless they decide to come to a collusive agreement.

We may now summarise Stackelberg's model. Each duopolist estimates the maximum profit that he would earn (a) if he acted as leader, (b) if he acted as follower, and chooses the behaviour which yields the largest maximum. Four situations may arise: (1) Duopolist A wants to be leader and B wants to be follower. (2) Duopolist B wants to be leader and A wants to be follower. (3) Both firms want to be followers. (4) Both firms desire to be leaders.

In situations (1) and (2) the result is a determinate equilibrium (provided that the first- and second-order conditions for maxima are fulfilled).

If both firms desire to be followers, their expectations do not materialise (since each assumes that the rival will act as a leader), and they must revise them. Two behavioural patterns are possible. If each duopolist recognises that his rival wants also to be a follower, the Cournot equilibrium is reached. Otherwise, one of the rivals must alter his behaviour and act as a leader before equilibrium is attained.

Finally, if both duopolists want to be leaders a disequilibrium arises, whose outcome, according to Stackelberg, is economic warfare. Equilibrium will be reached either by collusion, or after the 'weaker' firm is eliminated or succumbs to the leadership of the other.

---

[1] The numerical example is taken from J. M. Henderson and R. E. Quandt, *Microeconomic Theory* (McGraw-Hill 1958) p. 181.

10. Collusive Oligopoly

One way of avoiding the uncertainty arising from oligopolistic interdependence is to enter into collusive agreements. There are two main types of collusion, cartels and price leadership. Both forms generally imply tacit (secret) agreements, since open collusive action is commonly illegal in most countries at present.

Although direct agreements among the oligopolists are the most obvious examples of collusion, in the modern business world trade associations, professional organisations and similar institutions usually perform many of the activities and achieve in a legal or indirect way the goals of direct collusive agreements. For example, trade associations issue various periodicals with information concerning actual or planned action of members. In this official way firms get the message and act accordingly.

In this chapter we will examine the two formal types of collusion, cartels and price leadership. Both forms have been exhaustively analysed by W. Fellner.[1]

I. CARTELS

We saw that, in the absence of collusion, the monopoly solution in the industry (the solution at which the joint industry profit is maximised) can be achieved under the rare conditions that (a) each firm knows the monopoly price, that is, has a correct knowledge of the market demand and of the costs of all firms, (b) that each firm recognises its interdependence with the others in the industry, (c) all firms have identical costs and identical demands. (Actually condition (c) implies condition (a).)

We will examine two typical forms of cartels: (a) cartels aiming at joint-profit maximisation, that is, maximisation of the industry profit, and (b) cartels aiming at the sharing of the market.

A. CARTELS AIMING AT JOINT-PROFIT MAXIMISATION

Cartels imply direct (although secret) agreements among the competing oligopolist with the aim of reducing the uncertainty arising from their mutual interdependence. In this particular case the aim of the cartel is the maximisation of the industry (joint) profit. The situation is identical with that of a multiplant monopolist who seeks the maximisation of his profit. We concentrate on a homogeneous or pure oligopoly, that is, an oligopoly where all firms produce a homogeneous product. The case of differentiated oligopoly will be examined in a separate section.

The firms appoint a central agency, to which they delegate the authority to decide not only the total quantity and the price at which it must be sold so as to attain maximum

[1] W. Fellner, *Competition Among the Few* (New York, Knopf, 1949).

group profits, but also the allocation of production among the members of the cartel, and the distribution of the maximum joint profit among the participating members. The authority of the central cartel agency is complete. Clearly the central agency will have access to the cost figures of the individual firms, and for the purposes of the present theory we unrealistically suppose that it will calculate the market-demand curve and the corresponding MR curve. From the horizontal summation of the MC curves of individual firms the market MC curve is derived. The central agency, acting as a multi-plant monopolist, will set the price defined by the intersection of the industry MR and MC curves. For simplicity assume that there are only two firms in the cartel. Their cost structure is shown in figures 10.1 and 10.2. From the horizontal summation of the MC curves we obtain the market MC curve. This is implied by the profit-maximisation goal of the cartel: each level of industry output should be produced at the least possible cost. Thus if we add the outputs of A and B that can be produced at the same MC, clearly the resulting total output is the output that can be produced at this common lowest cost. Given the market demand DD (in figure 10.3) the monopoly solution,

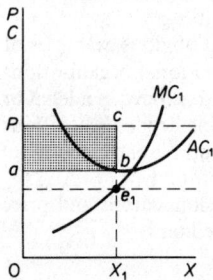 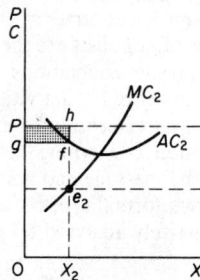 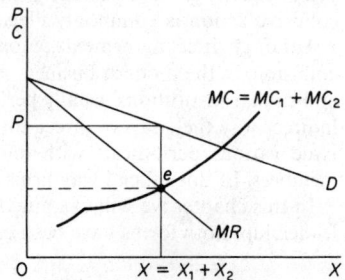

Figure 10.1   Figure 10.2   Figure 10.3

which maximises joint profits, is determined by the intersection of MC and MR (point e in figure 10.3). The total output is X and it will be sold at price P. Now the central agency allocates the production among firm A and firm B as a monopolist would do, that is, by equating the MR to the individual MCs. Thus firm A will produce X_1 and firm B will produce X_2. Note that the firm with the lower costs produces a larger amount of output. However, this does not mean that A will also take the larger share of the attained joint profit. The total industry profit is the sum of the profits from the output of the two firms, denoted by the shaded areas of figures 10.1 and 10.2. The distribution of profits is decided by the central agency of the cartel.

The mathematical presentation of the cartel model which aims at joint profit maximisation is identical to that of the multiplant monopolist. Thus:

$$\text{Maximise} \quad \Pi = \Pi_1 + \Pi_2$$

given

$$P = f(X) = f(X_1 + X_2)$$
$$C_1 = f_1(X_1)$$
$$C_2 = f_2(X_2)$$

We have

$$\Pi_1 = R_1 - C_1$$
$$\Pi_2 = R_2 - C_2$$

Therefore

$$\Pi = R_1 + R_2 - C_1 - C_2 = R - C_1 - C_2$$

and the market marginal revenue is

$$\frac{\partial R}{\partial X} = \frac{\partial R}{\partial X_1} = \frac{\partial R}{\partial X_2}$$

that is, each additional unit will bring the same MR, irrespective of the plant in which it is produced, since all units of X are sold at the same price P.

The first-order condition for maximisation of the joint profit Π requires the allocation of output in such a way that the MC of each firm is the same:

$$\frac{\partial \Pi}{\partial X_1} = \frac{\partial R}{\partial X} - \frac{\partial C_1}{\partial X_1} = 0 \rightarrow \frac{\partial R}{\partial X} = \frac{\partial C_1}{\partial X_1}$$

$$\frac{\partial \Pi}{\partial X_2} = \frac{\partial R}{\partial X} - \frac{\partial C_2}{\partial X_2} = 0 \rightarrow \frac{\partial R}{\partial X} = \frac{\partial C_2}{\partial X_2}$$

or

$$MR = MC_1 = MC_2$$

The second-order condition for maximisation of joint Π requires

$$\frac{\partial^2 R}{\partial X^2} < \frac{\partial^2 C_1}{\partial X_1^2} \quad \text{and} \quad \frac{\partial^2 R}{\partial X^2} < \frac{\partial^2 C_2}{\partial X_2^2}$$

that is, the MC of each firm must be increasing faster than the (common) MR of the output of the cartel as a whole.

These are the same equilibrium conditions as the ones we derived in Chapter 6 for the multiplant monopolist.

Numerical Example

Assume that the market demand is

$$P = 100 - 0 \cdot 5(X) = 100 - 0 \cdot 5(X_1 + X_2) \tag{10.1}$$

and that the two colluding firms have costs given by

$$C_1 = 5X_1, \quad \text{and} \quad C_2 = 0 \cdot 5X_2^2$$

The central agency of the cartel aims at the maximisation of total profit

$$\Pi = \Pi_1 + \Pi_2$$

where

$$\Pi_1 = R_1 - C_1 \quad \text{and} \quad \Pi_2 = R_2 - C_2$$

Thus

$$\Pi = (R_1 + R_2) - C_1 - C_2$$
$$\Pi = P(X_1 + X_2) - C_1 - C_2$$
$$\Pi = [100 - 0 \cdot 5(X_1 + X_2)](X_1 + X_2) - 5X_1 - 0 \cdot 5X_2$$
$$\Pi = 95X_1 - 100X_2 - 0 \cdot 5X_1^2 - X_2^2 - X_1X_2 \tag{10.2}$$

Setting the partial derivatives equal to zero we obtain

$$\frac{\partial \Pi}{\partial X_1} = 85 - X_1 - X_2 = 0$$

$$\frac{\partial \Pi}{\partial X_2} = 100 - X_1 - 2X_2 = 0$$

Solving for X_1 and X_2 we find

$$X_1 = 90 \quad \text{and} \quad X_2 = 5$$

The price is found by substituting in (10.1)

$$P = 100 - 0{\cdot}5(X_1 + X_2) = 52{\cdot}5$$

The joint profit may be obtained by substituting in (10.2)

$$\Pi = 95(90) - 100(5) - 0{\cdot}5(90)^2 - (5)^2 - (90)(5) = 4525$$

Although theoretically the monopoly solution is easy to derive, in practice cartels rarely achieve maximum joint profits. There are several reasons why industry profits cannot be maximised, even with direct cartel collusion.[1]

It should be obvious that equilibrium with joint profit maximisation will be easier to attain and will be in general stable if firms have identical costs and identical demands, conditions that are rarely met in practice. (However, even with identical costs cartels may still be unstable. See below.) Even in these conditions many factors may mitigate against achievement of the joint profit-maximisation goal of the cartel. The main reasons why industry profits may not be maximised may be summarised as follows.

First. Mistakes in the estimation of market demand. Usually the elasticity of market demand is underestimated. Each firm believes that the e of its own demand curve is high due to the existence of perfect (or almost perfect) substitutes made by competitors, while the industry demand is much less elastic. Clearly, mistakes in the estimation of the market demand lead to mistakes in the derivation of the MR and hence to a price which is higher than the monopoly price.

Second. Mistakes in the estimation of MC. The estimation of the market MC, from the summation of individual costs, may involve mistakes, due to incomplete knowledge of the individual MC curves at all levels of output. That is, even if a cartel estimated marginal costs, which is highly improbable, it would probably get them wrong. Such errors lead to an equilibrium which differs from the monopoly solution. There is a strong incentive for the individual members to present low-cost figures to the central agency, since the allocation of output and of profit shares is determined, among others, by the level of costs.

Third. Slow process of cartel negotiations. Cartel agreements take a long time to negotiate due to the differences in size, costs, and markets of the individual firms. During the negotiations each firm is bargaining in order to attain the greatest advantage from the cartel agreement. Thus, even if at the beginning of the negotiations costs and market demand were correctly estimated, by the time agreement is reached market conditions may have changed, thus rendering the initially defined monopoly price obsolete. Cartel agreements with more than about twenty partners are difficult to reach, and break down easily once reached.

Fourth. 'Stickiness' of the negotiated price. Once the agreement about price is reached, its level tends to remain unchanged over long periods, even if market conditions are

[1] See W. Fellner, *Competition Among the Few* (New York, Knopf, 1949).

changing. This price inflexibility (stickiness) is due to the time-consuming process of cartel negotiations and the difficulties and uncertainties about the bargaining of cartel members.

Fifth. The 'bluffing' attitude of some members during the bargaining process. Some firms may attempt to reduce price, to expand their selling activities and in general to achieve a large market share before the final agreement, so as to achieve the maximum advantage from it. However, such activities have only short-run effects and lead to miscalculations of the real monopoly equilibrium price and output.

Sixth. The existence of high-cost firms. If a firm is operating with a cost curve which is higher than the equilibrium MC, clearly this firm should close down if joint profits are to be maximised. (Firm C in figure 10.4 should close down.) However, no firm would join the cartel if it had to close down, even if the other firms agree in allocating to it part of the total profits, because by closing down the firm loses all its customers, and if subsequently the cartel members decide to stop sharing their profits with this member, there is little that he can do about it, since he has to start from scratch in order to attract back his old customers.

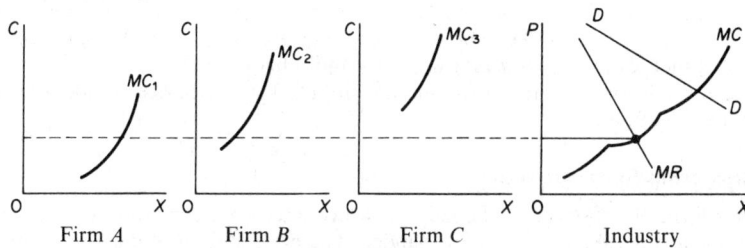

Figure 10.4

Seventh. Fear of government interference. If the monopoly price yields too high profits the cartel members may decide not to charge it, for fear of government interference.

Eighth. The wish to have a good public image. Similarly the members of the cartel may decide not to charge the profit-maximising price if profits are lucrative, if they wish to have the 'good' reputation of charging a 'fair price' and realising 'fair profits'.

Ninth. Fear of entry. One major reason for not charging the profit-maximising price if it yields too high profits is the fear of attracting new firms to the industry. Since there is great uncertainty regarding the behaviour of the new firm, established firms prefer to sacrifice some of their profits in order to prevent entry.

Tenth. Keeping freedom regarding design and selling activities. Even if firms adhere to the price defined by the central agency, they usually keep their freedom in deciding the style of their output and their selling activities. Each firm tries to attain higher sales by better service or intensive selling activities. (This holds in particular for differentiated products. See below.) This attitude leads to increased costs, and hence to a decrease in the monopoly profits.

It is clear that there are too many exceptions to the theory of joint profit maximisation for it to be a satisfactory theory of oligopolistic behaviour.

A note on mergers

The above model of profit-maximising cartel, where output of each member is decided by the central governing body of the cartel on the basis of marginalistic rules, is also applicable to mergers of firms producing the same product. A merger involves the decision of a number of independent firms to form a single corporation. The new firm may act as a cartel: it may decide to change the output quota of each plant so as to maximise the overall profit of its operations. In this process each plant will be allocated a quota defined by the equality of its marginal cost with the common marginal revenue of the corporation created from merger. Under these conditions the difference between a cartel and a merger is only a legal one: while overt cartel agreements are illegal in Britain and in the U.S.A., mergers are generally legal. A merger can be forbidden only if it is proved that its aim is to restrict competition and earn abnormal monopoly profits. However, mergers are usually rationalised on grounds of better utilisation of resources and attainment of economies of scale, and thus are allowed to take place more often than not.

While the above model may be applied to mergers in theory, it is not certain that the implied reallocation of resources and output will actually take place. The analysis of the motives of mergers and their actual operation goes beyond the scope of this book.

B. MARKET-SHARING CARTELS

This form of collusion is more common in practice because it is more popular. The firms agree to share the market, but keep a considerable degree of freedom concerning the style of their output, their selling activities and other decisions.

There are two basic methods for sharing the market: non-price competition and determination of quotas.

Non-price competition agreements

In this form of 'loose' cartel the member firms agree on a common price, at which each of them can sell any quantity demanded. The price is set by bargaining, with the low-cost firms pressing for a lower price and the high-cost firms for a high price. The agreed price must be such as to allow some profits to all members. The firms agree not to sell at a price below the cartel price, but they are free to vary the style of their product and/or their selling activities. In other words, the firms compete on a non-price basis. By keeping their freedom regarding the quality and appearance of their product, as well as advertising and other selling policies, each firm hopes that it can attain a higher share of the market.

This form of cartel is indeed 'loose', in the sense that it is more unstable than the complete cartel aiming at joint profit maximisation. If all firms have the same costs, then the price will be agreed at the monopoly level. However, with cost differences the cartel will be inherently unstable, because the low-cost firms will have a strong incentive to break away from the cartel openly and charge a lower price, or to cheat the other members by secret price concessions to the buyers. However, such cheating will soon be discovered by the other members of the cartel, who will gradually lose their customers. Thus others may split away from the cartel, and a price war and instability may develop until only the fittest low-cost firms survive. Another possibility is that the members of the cartel in conjunction may decide to start a price war until the firm which split off or cheated is driven out of business. Whether this policy will be successful depends on the cost differential (cost advantage) of the splitter relative to the other cartel members as well as on the liquidity position and the ability of obedient members to finance possible losses during the period of the price war.

In figure 10.5 firm B has lower costs than A, and hence B will have the incentive to cut the price below the monopoly level, thus driving the high-cost competitor A out of business.

Even with the same cost structure these cartels are inherently unstable, because if one firm splits away and charges a slightly lower price than the monopoly price P_M while

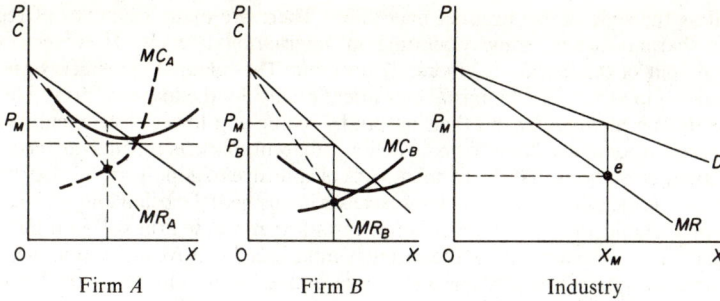

Figure 10.5

the others remain in the cartel, the splitting firm will attract a considerable number of customers from the others: its demand curve will be much more elastic and its profits will be increased. All firms will have the same incentive to leave the cartel, which thus becomes inherently unstable, unless supported by tight legislation. With open collusion being illegal it is not surprising that cartels are usually short-lived.

Sharing of the market by agreement on quotas

The second method for sharing the market is the agreement on quotas, that is, agreement on the quantity that each member may sell at the agreed price (or prices). If all firms have identical costs, the monopoly solution will emerge, with the market being shared equally among member firms. For example, if there are only two firms with identical costs, each firm will sell at the monopoly price one-half of the total quantity demanded in the market at that price. In figure 10.6 the monopoly price is P_M and the quotas which will be agreed are $x_1 = x_2 = \frac{1}{2}X_M$. However, if costs are different, the quotas and shares of the market will differ. Allocation of quota-shares on the basis of costs is again unstable. Shares in the case of cost differentials are decided by bargaining. The final quota of each firm depends on the level of its costs as well as on its bargaining skill. During the bargaining process two main statistical criteria are most often adopted: quotas are decided on the basis of past levels of sales, and/or on the basis of 'productive capacity'. The 'past-period sales' and/or the definition of 'capacity' of the firm depends largely on their bargaining power and skill.

Another popular method of sharing the market is the definition of the region in which each firm is allowed to sell. In this case of geographical sharing of the market the price

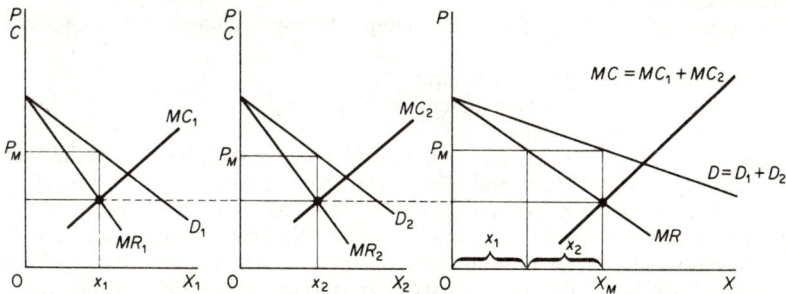

Figure 10.6

as well as the style of the product may differ. There are many examples of regional market-sharing cartels, some operating at international levels. However, even a regional split of the market is inherently unstable. The regional agreements are often violated in practice, either by mistake or intentionally, by the low-cost firms who have always the incentive to expand their output by selling at a lower price openly defined, or by secret price concessions, or by reaching adjacent markets through advertising.

It should be obvious that the cartel models of collusive oligopoly are 'closed' models. If entry is free, the inherent instability of cartels is intensified: the behaviour of the entrant is not predictable with certainty. It is not certain that a new firm will join the cartel. On the contrary, if the profits of the cartel members are lucrative and attract new firms in the industry, the newcomer has a strong incentive not to join the cartel, because in this way his demand curve will be more elastic, and by charging a slightly lower price than the cartel he can secure a considerable share in the market, on the assumption that the cartel members will stick to their agreement. Cartels, being aware of the dangers of entry, will either charge a low price so as to make entry unattractive, or may threaten a price war on the newcomer. If entry occurs and the cartel carries out its threat of price war, the newcomer may still survive, depending on his cost advantage, and his financial strength in withstanding possible losses during the initial period of his establishment, until he reaches the size which will allow him to reap the full 'scale economies' that he has over those enjoyed by existing firms.

II. PRICE LEADERSHIP

Another form of collusion is price leadership. In this form of co-ordinated behaviour of oligopolists one firm sets the price and the others follow it because it is advantageous to them or because they prefer to avoid uncertainty about their competitors' reactions even if this implies departure of the followers from their profit-maximising position. Price leadership is widespread in the business world. It may be practised either by explicit agreement or informally. In nearly all cases price leadership is tacit since open collusive agreements are illegal in most countries.

Price leadership is more widespread than cartels, because it allows the members complete freedom regarding their product and selling activities and thus is more acceptable to the followers than a complete cartel, which requires the surrendering of all freedom of action to the central agency.

If the product is homogeneous and the firms are highly concentrated in a location the price will be identical. However, if the product is differentiated prices will differ, but the direction of their change will be the same, while the same price differentials will broadly be kept.

There are various forms of price leadership. The most common types of leadership are

(a) Price leadership by a low-cost firm.
(b) Price leadership by a large (dominant) firm.
(c) Barometric price leadership.

These are the form of price leadership examined by the traditional theory of leadership as developed by Fellner and others. The characteristic of the traditional price leader is that he sets his price on marginalistic rules, that is, at the level defined by the intersection of his MC and MR curves. For the leader the behavioural rule is $MC = MR$. The other firms are price-takers who will not normally maximise their profit by adopting the price of the leader. If they do, it will be by accident rather than by their own independent decision.

In this chapter we will examine the basic models of the traditional theory of the price leader, the leader who bases his decisions on marginalistic calculations. In subsequent chapters we will examine models of price leadership in which the price leader is a low-cost firm, usually of large size, who sets his price not by equating MC to MR, but in such a way as to prevent entry (see Chapters 13 and 14).

A. THE MODEL OF THE LOW-COST PRICE LEADER

We will illustrate this model with an example of duopoly. It is assumed that there are two firms which produce a homogeneous product at different costs, which clearly must be sold at the same price. The firms may have equal markets (or they may come to an agreement to share the market equally) as in figure 10.7, or they may have unequal markets (or agree to share the market with unequal shares), as in figure 10.8. The important condition for this model is that the firms have unequal costs.

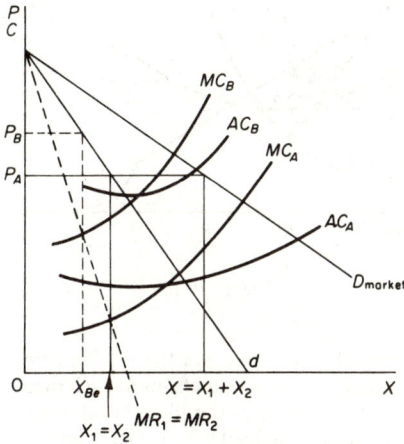

Figure 10.7 Low-cost price leader
Firms with equal market shares

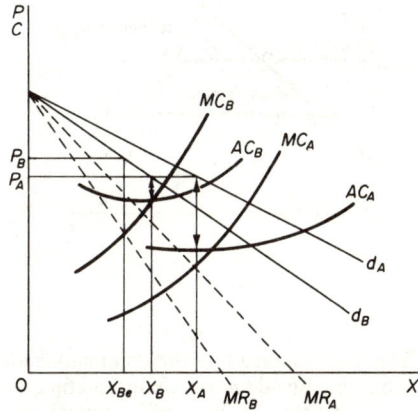

Figure 10.8 Low-cost price leader
Firms with unequal market shares

The firm with the lowest cost will charge a lower price (P_A) and this price will be followed by the high-cost firm, although at this price firm B (the follower) does not maximise its profits. The follower would obtain a higher profit by producing a lower output (X_{Be}) and selling it at a higher price (P_B). However, it prefers to follow the leader, sacrificing some of its profits in order to avoid a price war, which would eliminate it if price fell sufficiently low as not to cover its LAC. It should be stressed that for the leader to maximise his profit price must be retained at the level P_A and he should sell X_A. This implies that the follower must supply a quantity ($0X_B$ in figure 10.8, or $0X_1 = 0X_2$ in figure 10.7) sufficient to maintain the price set by the leader. Although the price-leadership model stresses the fact that the leader sets the price and the follower adopts it, it is clear that the firms must also enter a share-of-the-market agreement, formally or informally, otherwise the follower could adopt the price of the leader but produce a lower quantity than the level required to maintain the price (set by the leader) in the market, and thus push (indirectly, by not producing enough output) the leader to a non-profit-maximising position. In this respect the price follower is not completely passive: he may be coerced to adopt the leader's price, but, unless tied by a quota-share agreement (formal or informal) he can push the leader to a non-maximising position.

B. THE MODEL OF THE DOMINANT-FIRM PRICE LEADER

In this model it is assumed that there is a large dominant firm which has a considerable share of the total market, and some smaller firms, each of them having a small market share. The market demand (*DD* in figure 10.9) is assumed known to the dominant firm.

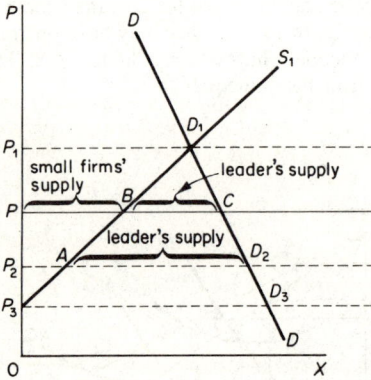

Figure 10.9

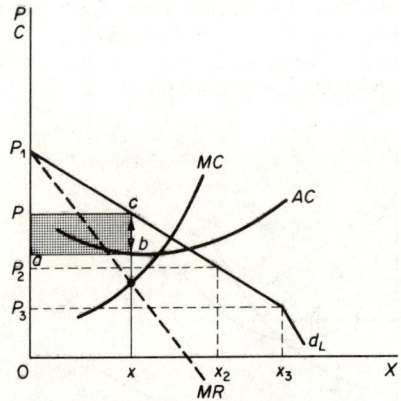

Figure 10.10

It is also assumed that the dominant leader knows the *MC* curves of the smaller firms, which he can add horizontally and find the total supply by the small firms at each price; or at best that he has a fair estimate, from past experience, of the likely total output from this source at various prices. With this knowledge the leader can obtain his own demand curve as follows. At each price the larger firm will be able to supply the section of the total market not supplied by the smaller firms. That is, at each price the demand for the product of the leader will be the difference between total *D* (at that price) and the total S_1. For example, at price P_1 the demand for the product of the leader will be zero, because the total quantity demanded (D_1) is supplied by the smaller firms. As price falls below P_1 the demand for the leader's product increases. At P_2 the total demand is D_2; the part P_2A is supplied by the small firms and the remaining AD_2 is supplied by the leader. At P_3 total demand is D_3 and the total quantity is supplied by the leader since at that price the small firms do not supply any quantity. Below P_3 the market demand coincides with the leader's demand curve.

Having derived his demand curve (d_L in figure 10.10) and given his *MC* curve, the dominant firm will set the price *P* at which his *MR* = *MC* and his output is 0*x*. At price *P* the total market demand is *PC*, and the part *PB* is supplied by the small firms followers while quantity *BC* = 0*x* is supplied by the leader.

The dominant firm leader maximises his profit by equating his *MC* to his *MR*, while the smaller firms are price-takers, and may or may not maximise their profit, depending on their cost structure. It is assumed that the small firms cannot sell more (at each price) than the quantity denoted by S_1. However, if the leader is to maximise his profit, he must make sure that the small firms will not only follow his price, but that they will also produce the right quantity (*PB*, at price *P*). Thus, if there is no tight sharing-the-market agreement, the small firms may produce less output than *PB* and thus force the leader to a nonmaximising position.

C. A CRITIQUE OF THE TRADITIONAL PRICE LEADERSHIP MODELS

The price-leadership model will lead to a stable equilibrium if the leader has the power to make the other firms in the industry follow his price increases or price decreases, and provided that there is some agreement (or other means) for sharing the market, so that the followers produce the 'right' quantity, that is, the quantity which is required to maintain the price set by the leader, with him producing as much as is compatible with this profit-maximising policy (the quantity 0x at which $MC = MR$).

In order to have the power to impose his price the leader must be both a low-cost *and* a large firm. Although two models were developed, one for a low-cost leader and another for a dominant-firm leader, in practice the power of the leader depends both on his costs and his size. If a firm has low costs but is very small compared with the leader, it may not find it possible to survive a price, or advertising or product-design war that the dominant firm may start. On the other hand, if the dominant firm loses its cost advantage, it loses also its power to impose an increase in price, since the smaller firms, having lower costs, will normally not follow it in price increases.

Unless the leader is both a low-cost and a large firm, his demand curve will be kinked: there will be an asymmetry in his power in setting the price. His power will be larger in lowering the price than in increasing it.

A common argument is that in the real world there are many cases in which the initiative for a price change does not come from a large firm, nor from a low-cost firm. There is a frequent case in recessions where a firm depletes its liquid assets faster than his rivals, and starts cutting its price in an attempt to have some 'quick cash'. Thus, the argument runs, the leader loses his initiative in price-setting. I think that this argument plays with semantics: it implies that the leader is the firm that *initiates* the price change. This definition is only partial. A leader is a firm that not only initiates the price change but is able to enforce it in the long run and survive at the price it sets.

A 'desperate' firm which wants some cash and cuts its price to achieve this result quickly, surely cannot be said to be the price leader unless its price cut is justified by some cost advantage and can be maintained in the long run. The price-cutting is the manifestation of the desperate position of the firm rather than an expression of power, which would establish the initiating firm as the leader.

A more valid argument is that the leader will lose its position of leadership if it loses its cost advantage or loses a considerable part of its share of the market for whatever reason. In fact leadership changes frequently in the real world. There is a frequent 'passing to-and-fro' of leadership among the competing oligopolists as a consequence of innovation in their product or processes.

In many cases where there are several firms of similar costs and similar size, it may be difficult to agree who will be the leader, if prestige counts among the competitors. Under such circumstances the leader may be decided by common consent, and may be neither a low-cost nor among the largest firms in the industry. We may then have a case of *barometric price leadership*, the leader being a firm whose price changes are followed by the others for conveniency.

The traditional price leader is assumed to base his price on the marginalistic rule $MC = MR$ and to maximise his profit in each period. However, this behaviour is rather myopic, especially if the profit secured by this policy is lucrative. New firms will then be attracted in the industry, and the leader may in the long run lose his power and position.

Such considerations have led various writers to postulate models of price leadership in which the leader is not a marginalist, short-term profit maximiser, but rather decides the price so as to prevent entry (see Chapters 13 and 14).

The traditional models of price leadership assume either that entry is barred or that the new entrant will follow the leader. This implicitly assumes that the entrant is a new firm with high initial costs, or that it is small and hence will be *de facto* obliged to follow the established leader. These assumptions regarding the entrant are quite unrealistic in the modern business world, where entry often involves an already-established firm in the same or another industry, or the expansion and reorganisation of a taken-over firm (see Chapter 13).

Finally a new entrant may be small initially, but may also have an absolute cost advantage over the established firms. Such a dynamic low-cost firm may gradually increase its share and become the leader.

D. BAROMETRIC PRICE LEADERSHIP

In this model it is formally or informally agreed that all firms will follow (exactly or approximately) the changes of the price of a firm which is considered to have a good knowledge of the prevailing conditions in the market and can forecast better than the others the future developments in the market. In short, the firm chosen as the leader is considered as a barometer, reflecting the changes in economic environment. The barometric firm may be neither a low-cost nor a large firm. Usually it is a firm which from past behaviour has established the reputation of a good forecaster of economic changes. A firm belonging to another industry may also be chosen as the barometric leader. For example, a firm in the steel industry may be agreed as the (barometric) leader for price changes in the motor-car industry. Barometric price leadership may be established for various reasons. Firstly, rivalry between several large firms in an industry may make it impossible to accept one among them as the leader. Secondly, followers avoid the continuous recalculation of costs, as economic conditions change. Thirdly, the barometric firm usually has proved itself as a 'reasonably' good forecaster of changes in cost and demand conditions in the particular industry and the economy as a whole, and by following it the other firms can be 'reasonably' sure that they choose the correct price policy.

A numerical example of the price-leadership models

1. *The low-cost price leader*

It is assumed, for simplicity, that there are only two firms in the industry.
The market demand is defined by the function

$$P = a - b(X) = a - b(X_1 + X_2)$$

where X_1 = output of firm A
X_2 = output of firm B
The firms have different costs, defined by the functions

$$C_1 = f_1(X_1)$$
$$C_2 = f_2(X_2)$$

where $C_1 < C_2$.
The leader will be the low-cost firm A. He assumes that the rival firm will produce an equal amount of output to his own, that is

$$X_1 = X_2$$

With this assumption, the demand function relevant to the leader's decision is

$$P = a - 2b(X_1)$$

The low-cost leader will set the price which maximizes his own profit

$$\Pi_1 = R_1 - C_1 = PX_1 - C_1$$

or

$$\Pi_1 = (a - 2bX_1)X_1 - C_1$$

The first-order condition for the maximisation of Π_1 requires

$$\frac{\partial \Pi_1}{\partial X_1} = \frac{\partial R_1}{\partial X_1} - \frac{\partial C_1}{\partial X_1} = 0$$

or

$$\frac{\partial R_1}{\partial X_1} = \frac{\partial C_1}{\partial X_1}$$

that is, $MR = MC$.

The second-order condition requires

$$\frac{\partial^2 \Pi_1}{\partial X_1^2} < 0$$

or

$$\frac{\partial^2 R_1}{\partial X_1^2} < \frac{\partial^2 C_1}{\partial X_1^2}$$

that is, the marginal cost must rise faster than the marginal revenue; or the MC must cut the MR curve from below.

The solution of this problem yields the price P and output X_1 that the leader must produce in order to maximise his profit. The follower will adopt the same price and will produce (*ex hypothesi*) an equal amount of output ($X_2 = X_1$). Given that $C_2 > C_1$, the follower does not maximise his profit. He would prefer (under the above assumptions) to produce a lower level of output and sell it at a higher price.

A numerical example:

Assume that the market demand is

$$P = 105 - 2 \cdot 5X = 105 - 2.5(X_1 + X_2)$$

The cost functions of the two firms are

$$C_1 = 5X_1$$
$$C_2 = 15X_2$$

The leader will be the low-cost firm A: he will set a price which will maximise his own profit on the assumption that the rival firm will adopt the same price and will produce an equal amount of output. Thus the demand function relevant to the leader's decision is

$$P = 105 - 2 \cdot 5(2X_1) = 105 - 5X_1$$

and his profit function is

$$\Pi_1 = R_1 - C_1 = PX_1 = (105 - 5X_1)X_1 - 5X_1$$

or

$$\Pi_1 = 100X_1 - 5X_1^2$$

From the first-order condition we have

$$\frac{\partial \Pi_1}{\partial X_1} = 100 - 10X_1 = 0$$

which yields

$$X_1 = 10$$

Substituting in the price equation, we find

$$P = 105 - 5X_1 = 55$$

The follower will adopt the same price (55) and will produce an equal level of output ($X_2 = 10$). Note that the profit-maximising output of firm B would be $X_2^* = 9$ units, and he would sell it at $P^* = 60$. This solution is found by maximising firm B's profit function

$$\Pi_2 = R_2 - C_2 = (105 - 5X_2)X_2 - 15X_2$$

2. The dominant-firm leader

This model is also called 'the partial monopoly' model since the large firm acts as a monopolist while the small firms are price-takers and act like the firms in pure competition.

This model is a combination of the theory of pure competition and the theory of monopoly.

(a) The small firms are assumed to accept the prevailing price and adjust their output levels to maximise profit like a perfectly competitive firm.

(b) The dominant firm knows the MC curves of the small firms. By adding these curves horizontally it obtains the supply curve S_1 of the small firms as a function of price. Assume

$$S = 0.2P$$

(c) The dominant firm is assumed to know the market demand

$$D = 50 - 0.3P$$

Thus the dominant firm derives its own demand curve as the difference $X = D - S$ at any one price

$$X = D - S$$
$$X = 50 - 0.3P - 0.2P$$

or

$$P = 100 - 2X$$

(d) The dominant firm maximises its own profit given its total cost function

$$C = 2X$$

Thus

$$\Pi = R - C = PX - 2X$$
$$\Pi = (100 - 2X)X - 2X = 98X - 2X^2$$

$$\frac{\partial \Pi}{\partial X} = 98 - 4X = 0$$

and

$$X = 24.5$$

The leader will set the price

$$P = 100 - 2X = 100 - 2(24.5) = 51$$

At this price the market is in equilibrium. The total quantity demanded is

$$D = 50 - 0.3P = 34.7$$

The total demand of 34·7 units of output (at the price 51 set by the leader) is covered by the leader who produces $X = 24·5$ units and the small firms who produce the remainder

$$S_1 = 0·2P = 0·2(51) = 10·2$$

3. *The market-sharing firm leader*

In this model the product is homogeneous. The firms agree that they are going to share the market in constant proportions:

$$k_1 = \frac{X_1}{X} \quad \text{and} \quad k_2 = \frac{X_2}{X}$$

Given that $X = X_1 + X_2$ we may rewrite the shares

$$k_1 = \frac{X_1}{X_1 + X_2} \quad \text{and} \quad k_2 = \frac{X_2}{X_1 + X_2}$$

Clearly $k_1 + k_2 = 1$, and hence $k_2 = (1 - k_1)$, or $k_1 = (1 - k_2)$. Thus the reaction functions of the two firms are

Firm A	*Firm B*
$k_1(X_1 + X_2) = X_1$	$k_2(X_1 + X_2) = X_2$
$X_1(1 - k_1) = k_1 X_2$	$X_2(1 - k_2) = k_2 X_1$
$X_1 = \dfrac{k_1 X_2}{(1 - k_1)}$	$X_2 = \dfrac{k_2 X_1}{(1 - k_2)}$

Assume that the firms agree that firm A will be the leader. Firm A knows its own demand curve and its own costs:

$$P_1 = 100 - 2X_1 - X_2$$
$$C_1 = 2·5X_1^2$$

The leader will set his price so as to maximise his profit, on the assumption that B will be the follower and will react according to his reaction function $X_2 = k_2 X_1/(1 - k_2)$, adjusting his output whenever the leader changes his, so that the shares remain at the agreed constant levels. Assume that $k_1 = \frac{2}{3}$ and $k_2 = \frac{1}{3}$. Thus $X_2 = X_1/[3(1 - \frac{1}{3})] = 0·5X_1$.

The profit function of the leader is

$$\Pi_1 = R_1 - C_1 = P_1 X_1 - C_1$$
$$\Pi_1 = (100 - 2X_1 - X_2)X_1 - 2·5X_1^2$$

Substituting the reaction function of firm B

$$X_2 = 0·5X_1$$

we obtain the profit function of the leader

$$\Pi_1 = (100 - 2X_1 - 0·5X_1)X_1 - 2·5X^2 = 100X_1 - 5X_1^2$$

For the maximisation of the leader's profit we have

$$\frac{\partial \Pi_1}{\partial X_1} = 100 - 10X_1 = 0$$

$$X_1 = 10$$

The leader will set the profit-maximising price

$$P_1 = 100 - 2X_1 - X_2$$
$$= 100 - 2X_1 - 0·5X_1$$
$$= 100 - 2·5X_1 = 75$$

The leader's profit is

$$\Pi_1 = 100X_1 - 5X_1^2 = 1000 - 500 = 500$$

The quantity which will be produced by the follower is

$$X_2 = 0.5X_1 = 5$$

and he will sell it at the price of the leader $P_1 = 75$. Thus in the sharing-market model of leadership the firms agree on the shares and on who will be the leader. The leader maximises his own profit, by substituting in his profit function the share-reaction curve of the follower. This implies that the leader sets the quantity that maximises his own profit, on the assumption that the follower will adjust his own quantity on the basis of the agreed shares.

III. THE BASING-POINT PRICE SYSTEM

This model is an extension of Hotelling's model of non-collusive pricing by duopolists located in different places.

Basing-point pricing has been adopted often in practice by oligopolists producing a homogeneous product whose transportation costs are relatively high and whose production requires a large plant if the full economies of scale (minimum production costs) are to be realised.

We will examine two varieties of basing-point pricing, the single basing-point system and the multiple basing-point system.

A. THE SINGLE BASING-POINT SYSTEM

In this collusive pricing model the oligopolists agree on a common place as the basing point, and *all* firms quote as their price the production price (mill price) at the basing point, plus transportation cost from the basing point to the place of destination.

Assume that town A is agreed as the basing point for all oligopolists located anywhere. The basing-point production price is AP. Delivered prices increase as the distance from the basing point increases. Assume that the delivered prices change as shown by the curve PT in figure 10.11. These prices are the same for all oligopolists. For example, a firm located in town E will quote the price EG to its local customers, the price DL to

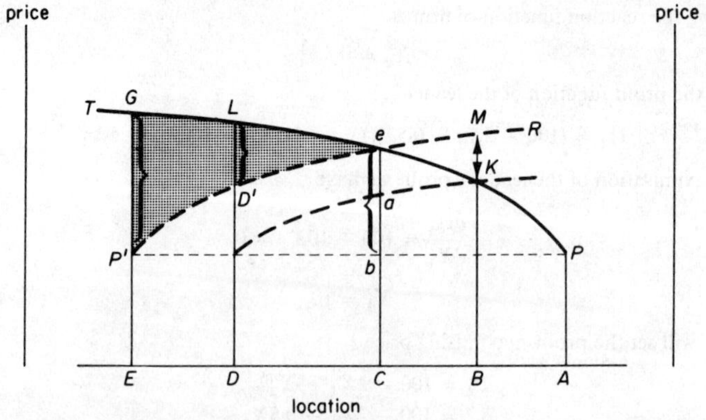

Figure 10.11

customers in town D, and the price BK to buyers located in town B. Clearly if the production price (mill price) is in town E the same as in the basing point A, the firm in E will be realising excess profits by selling to buyers located between E and C. For example, if the firm in E sells to a buyer located in D the firm will be making an excess profit equal to $D'L$ per unit of output, since its freight costs are given by the $P'R$ curve. Such excess profits are called 'phantom freight'. The firm in E may expand its sales beyond point e in the territory-market of firms located at A, if its marginal costs are less than its mill price EP' minus the freight it will have to cover. For example, the firm located at E will find it profitable to sell to buyers at B, if its marginal cost is

$$MC < (EP' - KM)$$

The firm located in the basing point A will be covering all its production and transport costs at all places. Thus the oligopolists may find it profitable to sell in each other's territory-markets. This is known as *cross-hauling*.[1]

B. MULTIPLE BASING-POINT SYSTEM

The excess profits ('phantom freight' gains) realised by firms selling at the basing-point price to buyers located at places where this price is higher than their production costs plus transportation cost, may be reduced under a system of multiple basing-point pricing. In such a system several places are agreed as basing points. The delivered price of all oligopolists will be the same for buyers located in a certain place, and will be the lowest-possible delivered price.

To illustrate the multiple basing-point system assume that location A and location E are both agreed as basing points. The delivered price of firms in location A are those on the curve PT; the delivered prices of firms located in E are those on curve $P'R$ (figure 10.11). Only at the point of intersection of PT and $P'R$ will the delivered price be identical for firms located in A and E. To the left of e the delivered price of firms in A are higher than those of firms located in E; thus for buyers located to the left of e the delivered prices quoted by *all* sellers will be the (lower) prices of curve $P'e$. To the right of point e the delivered prices of firms in A are lower, and these will be quoted by *all* firms to all buyers. In this way the relevant delivered prices for buyers located between E and A are the prices on the segment $P'e$ (of $P'R$) and the segment eP (on PT). A firm located in A will charge the delivered price on $P'e$ to buyers located between E and C, without gaining any 'phantom freight'. If this firm wants to sell to buyers located further than C, it will have to cover itself part of the freight. Only firms in between the basing points will have 'phantom freights', given that they can produce at the same mill price as firms in A or E. For example, a firm located in D will charge the delivered price Ce to buyers located at C, and will receive 'phantom freight' equal to ae. A firm located at C and selling to local customers will receive a greater phantom price (equal to eb) given the two basing-point pricing agreement.

It should be clear that as the number of basing points increases the 'phantom freights' are gradually eliminated. In the limit, if sellers were located next to each other and there were as many basing points as sellers, all would quote the same price $EP' = AP$, which is the lowest of delivered prices of all sellers.

The basing-point system reduces competition. If firms adhere strictly (without secret price concessions and other forms of cheating) to the basing-point pricing agreement, price competition is avoided. Identical prices prevail in all locations, and the share of

[1] See F. M. Scherer, *Industrial Market Structure and Economic Performance* (Rand McNally, 1970) p. 266.

each oligopolist is determined by chance or by non-price competition (advertising, prompt delivery, differentiated product).

Given that open agreements for basing-point pricing are illegal, trade associations and other similar institutions publish detailed data on freights so as to facilitate the member firms to arrive at the same price for buyers in the same location. The firms usually take as a basis the mill price of a tacitly agreed leader who publishes its mill price regularly, and add to this price the freights published by the trade association.

Naturally, there is always the incentive to cheat, and price-chiselling may appear a tentative action. However, in most cases some sort of informal gentlemen's agreement imposes sanctions against firms who are caught not adhering to the basing-point pricing rules.

The basing-point pricing system is sometimes called the 'Pittsburgh-plus' pricing system, because it was widely used by the steel industry in the U.S.A. (with Pittsburgh being the basing point) in the 1920s.

SECTION C

AVERAGE-COST PRICING

11. A Critique of the Neoclassical Theory of the Firm: The Marginalist Controversy

In 1939 there started a gradually mounting dissatisfaction with the traditional neo-classical theory of the firm, its assumptions and its marginalistic behavioural rules.

In England the publication in 1939 of empirical evidence by Hall and Hitch[1] concerning the behaviour of firms in the real world spurred a series of articles and treatises dealing with the weaknesses of traditional theory.

In America a similar discussion started independently. The main participants in the mid- and late-1940s were Lester,[2] Machlup,[3] Oliver,[4] Gordon[5] and Friedman.[6]

In this chapter we will summarise the main arguments against and in defense of the traditional theory of the firm.

I. THE BASIC ASSUMPTIONS OF THE NEOCLASSICAL THEORY

The basic assumptions of the neoclassical theory of the firm may be outlined as follows.

---

[1] R. L. Hall and C. I. Hitch, 'Price Theory and Business Behaviour', *Oxford Economic Papers* (1939) reprinted in P. W. S. Andrews and T. Wilson (eds.), *Oxford Studies in the Price Mechanism* (Oxford University Press, 1952).

[2] R. A. Lester, 'Shortcomings of Marginal Analysis for Wage-Employment Problems', *American Economic Review* (1946).

[3] F. Machlup, 'Marginal Analysis and Empirical Research', *American Economic Review* (1946).

[4] H. M. Oliver, 'Marginal Theory and Business Behaviour', *American Economic Review* (1947).

[5] R. A. Gordon, 'Short-Period Price Determination in Theory and Practice', *American Economic Review* (1948).

[6] M. Friedman, 'The Methodology of Positive Economics', in *Essays in Positive Economics* (University of Chicago Press, 1953).

1. The entrepreneur is also the owner of the firm.
2. The firm has a single goal, that of profit maximisation.
3. This goal is attained by application of the marginalist principle

$$MC = MR$$

4. The world is one of certainty. Full knowledge is assumed about the past performance, the present conditions and the future developments in the environment of the firm. The firm knows with certainty its own demand and cost functions. It learns from past mistakes, in that its experience is incorporated into its continuous appraisal (estimation) of its demand and costs. The costs are U-shaped both in the short and in the long run, implying a single optimum level of output (see Chapter 4).

5. Entry assumptions vary according to the particular model (for example, in monopoly entry is blockaded *ex hypothesi*). The common elements regulating entry in all models of the neoclassical theory of the firm are the following: (*a*) Entry refers to actual entrants in an industry; no account of potential entrants is taken. (*b*) Entry in the short run is practically impossible: entry can take place only in the long run.

6. The firm acts with a certain time-horizon which depends on various factors, such as the rate of technological progress, the capital intensity of the methods of production, the nature and gestation period of the product, etc. The firm aims at the maximisation of its profit over this time-horizon: the goal of the firm is long-run profit maximisation. This is attained by maximising profits in each one period of the time-horizon of the firm, because *the time periods are independent* in the sense that decisions taken in any one period do not affect the behaviour of the firm in other periods. The rule $MC = MR$ is applied in each period, and profits are maximised with this behaviour both in the short run and in the long run.

Let us examine these assumptions in some detail.

The single owner-entrepreneur

The traditional theory of the firm assumes a single owner-entrepreneur. There is no separation between ownership and management. The owner-entrepreneur takes all the decisions. All organisational problems are assumed resolved by payments to the factors employed by the firm.

The entrepreneur is furthermore assumed to have unlimited information, unlimited time at his disposal, and unlimited ability to compare all the possible alternative actions and choose the one that maximises his profit.

This behaviour is described by postulating that the entrepreneur acts with *global rationality*. There are no time, information or other constraints in pursuing the single goal of profit maximisation.

Clearly the above assumptions are unrealistic. In the modern business world the firm is a complex organisation, characterised by the divorce of ownership and management. This gives discretion to the managers to pursue goals other than profit maximisation (see below). Information is not unlimited. Its acquisition involves expenses. Furthermore it is often distorted as it passes through the various hierarchical levels of administration (see Chapter 18). The managers cannot act with the global rationality postulated by the traditional theory, not only because of the limited and/or distorted information, but also because they have neither unlimited time nor unlimited abilities to compare and evaluate all the possible alternative strategies open to them in any particular situation. Such considerations, arising from the complexity of modern enterprises, have been incorporated in the theory of the firm by various writers and have been particularly stressed by the behavioural theories of the firm (see Chapter 18).

The goal of profit maximisation

The attack here was twofold. Firstly, it was argued that firms cannot attain the goal of profit maximisation because they do not have the necessary knowledge, information or ability. Firms do not know with certainty their demand and cost curves, hence they cannot apply the marginalist principle $MC = MR$. This sort of attack will be examined in the next paragraph. Secondly, it was argued that firms, even if they could pursue profit maximisation, do not want to. In particular it has been argued that the firm does not pursue a single goal. There is a multitude of goals, and profit is only one of them.

Several alternative goals have been suggested. We may group them as follows.

Managerialism: maximisation of the managerial utility function. Managerial theories postulate that the divorce of ownership and management allows some discretion to the managers in goal-setting. The managers select such goals which maximise their own utility function. Factors that usually enter the managerial utility function are salaries, prestige, market share, job security, quiet life, and so on.

There is no consensus among the managerial theorists as to how the maximisation of the utility of managers will be attained. Baumol postulated that the managerial utility is maximised when the growth of sales revenue is maximised (see Chapter 15). Marris is more sophisticated. He ingeniously suggests that the managers pursue the maximum 'balanced growth,' that is, the balanced increase of both the sales and the capital assets of the firm. If this is attained, then both the utility of managers *and* of the owners of the firm (shareholders) is maximised (see Chapter 16).

Behaviourism: satisficing behaviour. Some writers have suggested that given the uncertainty in the real world, the lack of accurate information, the limited time and limited ability of managers to process information, and other constraints, firms cannot act with the global rationality implied in the traditional theory of the firm. Indeed uncertainty makes impossible the maximisation of anything. Given these conditions firms do not seek the maximisation of profits, sales, growth or anything else. Instead they exhibit a *satisficing* behaviour: they pursue 'satisfactory profits,' 'satisfactory growth' and so on. This behaviour is considered rational given the uncertainty of the real world. Firms act with *bounded rationality*: firms have constraints in pursuing their goals, set by factors internal and external to the firm (see Chapter 18).

Long-run survival and market-share goals. Some writers[1] have suggested that the primary motive of the entrepreneurs is long-run survival. Thus managers take action which aims at the maximisation of the probability that they will survive over the indefinite future. Still other writers have reported that many firms set as their goal the attainment and retention of a constant market share. It can easily be proved that such policy is compatible with marginalistic behaviour.

Proof

(a) The price elasticity of market demand is defined

$$e_D = \frac{dQ}{dP}\frac{P}{Q}$$

[1] See, for example, K. W. Rothschild, 'Price Theory and Oligopoly', *Economic Journal* (1947) pp. 297–320.

(b) Assume that the firm has a constant share of the market

$$q = k \cdot Q$$

where q = demand for the product of the firm
   k = constant share
   Q = market demand

(c) The price elasticity of the demand of the firm is defined

$$e_q = \frac{dq}{dP} \frac{P}{q}$$

Substituting $q = k \cdot Q$, we obtain

$$e_q = \frac{d(kQ)}{dP} \frac{P}{kQ}$$

Given that k is constant and does not affect the derivative, we may write

$$e_q = k \frac{dQ}{dP} \frac{P}{kQ} = e_Q$$

(d) The market demand is assumed known, and from this the firm can estimate its own demand curve. Given that the firm also knows its costs, it can apply the marginalistic rule $MC = MR$.

Whether this behaviour leads to profit maximisation in the long run is not certain. The firm in this model maximises its profit *given* its desired constant market share. Different target market-shares clearly yield different 'maximum' level of profit. If the firm is a profit maximiser it would choose the maximum maximiorum; that is, the share that yields the highest profit. Thus the goal of constant market share does not necessarily imply maximisation of long-run profits.

Entry-prevention and risk-avoidance. Several writers in recent years have suggested that the goal of the firm is to prevent new entrant firms coming into their market. Firms set the price at such a level as to make entry unattractive (limit-pricing). It is not clearly stated why firms want to prevent entry. Some economists argue that the real goal behind entry prevention is long-run profit maximisation. Others suggest long-run survival or constant market share as the ultimate goal behind limit-pricing. Finally, others have suggested that the firms want to prevent entry as a means of avoiding the risk associated with the unpredictable reactions of new entrants: a firm learns by experience how 'to live' with other existing competitors and can anticipate their reactions to a certain decision of the firm; but the attitude of new entrants is completely uncertain, and by preventing their entry in the market the established firms avoid this uncertainty (see Chapters 13 and 14).

The interesting question is how far can managers deviate from profit maximisation. What is the discretion of managers in goal-setting?

There is no consensus among writers regarding the degree of managerial discretion. The following discussion may illustrate the existing disagreement.

There is some empirical evidence that profits are higher in owner-controlled firms than in firms where management is divorced from ownership.[1] This supports the view

[1] See F. Lanzilotti, 'Pricing Objectives in Large Companies', *American Economic Review* (1958) pp. 921–41, and R. J. Monsen, J. S. Chiu, and D. E. Cooley, 'The Effects of Separation of Ownership and Control on the Performance of the Large Firm', *Quarterly Journal of Economics* (1968) pp. 435–51. See also D. R. Kamerschen, 'The Influence of Ownership and Control on Profit Rates', *American Economic Review* (1968) pp. 432–47. Also J. P. Shelton, 'Allocative Efficiency vs. 'X-Efficiency': Comment', *American Economic Review* (1967) pp. 1252–8.

that managers have at least some discretion in pursuing goals other than profit maxi-misation. However, the evidence is far from conclusive. In any case such empirical findings do not imply that managers have unlimited discretion, or that the goal of profit maximisation is not valid.

The supporters of the profit-maximisation hypothesis resort usually to arguments resembling the Darwinian theory of the survival of the fittest.[1] They argue that in the long run only the profit maximisers survive, because they are the fittest. By maximising profits, the survival argument runs, firms can accumulate financial assets which allow them to grow faster than the non-profit maximisers, whose share gradually shrinks and eventually are eliminated. The economic environment selects the profit maximisers as the fittest and eliminates the rest.

Some supporters of the profit-maximisation hypothesis concede that other goals are actually pursued by firms. But they argue that managers can attain such 'subsidiary' goals easier if they maximise profits.

Those who object to the profit-maximisation goal argue that the 'economic selection' mechanism does not work uninhibited in practice. Firstly, if all firms deviate from profit maximisation, there is no 'fittest' to survive. If, for example, all firms *satisfice*, there is no reason to believe that any one of them has, *ceteris paribus*, a higher probability of surviving. Secondly, in a dynamic world of continuous change in techniques and products, firms can avoid their 'elimination' by differentiation and diversification, so that a firm which deviates from profit maximisation can survive for a long period of time. Thirdly, it has also been suggested that when firms are large and have monopoly power the 'selection process' does not work smoothly because competition is weak in this case.[2] Others, however, argue that the competition is keen among large firms due to the continuous change and the uncertainty of the environment. Under these conditions, even in highly concentrated industries firms cannot deviate from the goal of profit maximisation if they want to survive in the long run.

Such arguments for and against the profit-maximisation hypothesis cannot be resolved on *a priori* grounds, and the empirical evidence regarding the goals of firms is by no means conclusive in one direction or another. What has been found from most empirical studies is that:

(*a*) there is a multiplicity of goals in the modern enterprise;

(*b*) managers have not unlimited discretion in setting their goals. All models accept that there is a minimum profit constraint which limits the other goals of the firm. How high the profit constraint is depends on how strong the competition in the environment of the firm is. If there are barriers to entry (strong preferences, government laws, absolute cost advantage, absolute capital requirements, strong economies of scale) firms can survive in the long run even if they are not profit maximisers.

The treatment of uncertainty in the traditional theory

In the early stages of the theory of the firm it was assumed that the firm had perfect knowledge of its cost and demand functions and of its environment. The theory was not concerned with the way in which this knowledge was acquired. In effect, uncertainty

[1] A. Alchian, 'Uncertainty, Evolution, and Economic Theory', *Journal of Political Economy* (1950) pp. 211–21. Also S. Winter, 'Economic "Natural Selection" and the Theory of the Firm', in *Yale Economic Essays* (1964) pp. 225–72. Also Edith Penrose, 'Biological Analogies in the Theory of the Firm', *American Economic Review* (1952) pp. 804–19.

[2] See C. Kaysen, 'The Corporation: How Much Power? What Scope?', in E. S. Mason (ed.), *The Corporation in Modern Society* (Harvard University Press, Cambridge, Mass., 1960).

was not allowed to influence the decisions of the firm: the firm proceeded to maximise its profits *after* it had acquired the relevant information on costs and revenues. Yet in the real world uncertainty influences the estimation of costs and revenues, and hence the decisions of the firm.

Later it was recognised that firms have no perfect knowledge of their costs, revenues and their environment and they operate in a world of uncertainty. Economists used a probabilistic approach to deal with this uncertainty. They assumed that the firms have perfect knowledge only up to a probability distribution of all possible outcomes. The idea that the profit in any one period was a single-valued magnitude known with certainty by the firm was abandoned. Instead it was assumed that the profit expected from the adoption of any action may assume any value within a certain range of values, each value having an associated probability of being realised. These probabilities are assumed known to the firm subjectively. The decision-maker assigns these subjective probabilities to the possible effects (profits) of each strategy and estimates its mathematical expectation (that is, he assumes that 'the profit' of any action is the sum of the possible profitability values, each multiplied by the corresponding probability.) Having done such computations for all alternative actions, the entrepreneur chooses the action with the highest expected value in each period. These net profitabilities are discounted with a subjective discount rate, and their present value is estimated. The firm then chooses the strategy that maximises the present (discounted) value of the future stream of net profits over its specific time-horizon (which constitutes its long-run operational period).

The above probabilistic treatment of uncertainty, which implies the formulation of definite subjective expectations about the cost, revenues and changes in the environment, has been attacked on several grounds.

Firstly, it has been argued that this procedure requires a lot of knowledge, information and computational ability from entrepreneurs, which they clearly do not possess.

Secondly, the adoption of the decision rule of choosing the alternative which has the highest expected value (expected profit) does not adequately describe the behaviour of firms in the real world. Entrepreneurs' attitudes towards risk plays an important role in actual decision-making. A project with a high expected profit may have a higher risk of bankruptcy as compared to another with a lower expected profit. If the entrepreneur is a risk-avoider he will not choose the projects which have a high risk, even if their expected profitability is high. Unless we know the risk attitudes of entrepreneurs we cannot say what their actual decisions will be by looking only at the expected profitability of the various alternatives.

Thirdly, the length of the time-horizon is also crucial in decision-making. Some firms may prefer a shorter time-horizon, having a high aversion towards the uncertainty of more distant periods. Yet the traditional theory does not deal with the determination of the time-horizon, the long-run period in entrepreneurial life.

Fourthly, additional difficulties arise in the estimating process of future costs and future revenues, implied in the maximisation of the present value of future stream of profits. Choice of a high discount rate implies a short time horizon, while a low discount rate of future profits implies a long time horizon.

Fifthly, conventional theory treats expectations of entrepreneurs (who determine their subjective probabilities) as exogenous to the firm. It does not explain their formation within the firm. Yet expectations are influenced to a great extent by factors internal to the firm. These factors play an important role in the behavioural theories of the firm (see Chapter 18).

In summary. The probabilities of future events are subjectively determined. They are influenced by the time-horizon, the risk attitude and the rate of change of the environment. Thus businessmen's expectations cannot come close to objective reality. Different firms will have different time-horizons, different risk attitude and will form different assessments of uncertain future events. Consequently firms will respond differently to the same (given) conditions of the environment. The interactions among uncertainty, risk-aversion and the time-horizon of the entrepreneurs are not dealt satisfactorily with by the probabilistic approach adopted in the traditional theory of the firm.

The static nature of traditional theory

Time enters into the traditional theory in three respects.[1] Firstly, the distinction between the short and the long run implies time considerations. However, the theory does not really answer the question: how long is the long run in actual decision-making. Secondly, it is assumed that the firm has some time-horizon over which it attempts to maximise its profits. The discounting of future costs and revenues implicit in the long-run profit maximisation clearly involves the time element. But again the length of the time-horizon and its interaction with uncertainty and risk-aversion is not adequately dealt with. Thirdly, the analysis of the timing of demand relative to the production flow implies a period analysis. Considerations of the gestation period of investment and the final product also imply time considerations.

However, the traditional theory is basically static. The time-horizon of the firm consists of *identical* and *independent* time-periods. Decisions are treated as temporally independent, and this is probably the most important shortcoming of the traditional theory. It is clear that decisions are temporally interdependent: decisions taken in any one period are affected by the decisions in past periods, and will in turn influence the future decisions of the firm. This interdependence is ignored by the traditional theory, which postulates that the long-run profits are maximised as the firm maximises its short-run profits in any one period, by equating its marginal cost to its marginal revenue $(MC = MR)$.

Entry considerations

In the traditional theory entry considerations differ, depending on the type of market structure. The common features of the treatment of entry in traditional theory are two: firstly, only actual entry is considered; secondly, entry is assumed to take place only in the long run: it is a long-run phenomenon.

In pure competition entry is free. The same is assumed in the model of monopolistic competition. In both models entry can occur only in the long run.

In monopoly entry is blockaded by definition.

The traditional models of oligopoly are implicit, cryptic or silent so far as entry is concerned.[2] The classical duopoly models are 'closed' models in that they do not allow for entry. These models can be extended to larger numbers of sellers, but the numbers remain unchanged in the final market equilibrium as they were at the initial situation. In the theory of cartels it is implicitly assumed that the entrants, if any, will join the cartel. Without this implicit assumption the inherent instability of cartels becomes even greater. Similar assumptions are made in the traditional price-leadership models: the entrant is assumed to be either a small firm which can be coerced to follow the leader, or is assumed to accept the *status quo* of the established leader.

[1] See Ira Horowitz, *Decision Making and the Theory of the Firm* (Holt, Rinehart & Winston, 1970) p. 332.
[2] See J. Bain, *Barriers to New Competition* (Harvard University Press, Cambridge, Mass., 1956) p. 6.

Potential entry and its effects on decision making are not dealt with in traditional theory.[1]

The marginalist principle

The behavioural rule postulated by the traditional theory in actual decision-making is described by the so-called 'marginalist principle'

$$MC = MR$$

In each period the firm maximises its (short-run) profit by setting its output and price at the level defined by the intersection of the MC and MR curves. Given the temporal independence of decisions, such short-run profit maximisation implies also long-run profit maximisation.

This behavioural rule has been attacked on several grounds. One line of argument is that although the goal of the firm is long-run profit maximisation, this is not necessarily attained by equating the short-run marginal cost ($SRMC$) to the short-run marginal revenue ($SRMR$). Another line of attack centres on the goal of profit maximisation as the single goal of the firm. This has been briefly examined in Section B above, and will be discussed in detail in the various chapters which deal with theories postulating other goals (managerialism, behaviourism, limit-pricing).

In the rest of this chapter we will examine briefly several arguments arising from the above lines of attack. These arguments constitute the essence of what has become known as the 'marginalist controversy.'

II. THE HALL AND HITCH REPORT AND THE 'FULL-COST' PRICING PRINCIPLE

In 1939 Hall and Hitch published some results[2] of research undertaken at Oxford and aiming at the investigation of the decision process of businessmen in relation to government measures.[3] Their study covered 38 firms, out of which 33 were manufacturing firms, 3 were retail trading firms and 2 were building firms. Of the 33 manufacturing firms, 15 produced consumer goods, 4 intermediate products, 7 capital goods, and 7 textiles. The sample was not random, but included firms which may well be expected to belong to 'efficiently managed enterprises'.[3]

The most startling results of the studies of 'The Oxford Economists Research Group' reported by Hall and Hitch were that firms did not attempt to maximise their profits, that they did not use the marginalist rule $MC = MR$, and that oligopoly was the main market structure of the business world. Up to then the theory of monopolistic or imperfect competition of Chamberlin and Joan Robinson had been generally accepted as typical or relevant. The firms were assumed to be able to act atomistically, ignoring their rivals' reactions and pursuing their short-run (and long-run) profit maximisation by equating marginal cost to marginal revenue in each time period. The tangency solution in the long run implied normal profits, but excess capacity (unexhausted

---

[1] See P. W. S. Andrews, *On Competition in Economic Theory* (Macmillan, 1964).

[2] Hall and Hitch, 'Price Theory and Business Behaviour', *Oxford Economic Papers* (1939), reprinted in P. W. S. Andrews and T. Wilson (eds.), *Oxford Studies in the Price Mechanism* (Oxford University Press, 1952).

[3] R. Barback, *The Pricing of Manufactures* (Macmillan, 1964).

economies of scale), which was the main source of criticism of the regime of monopolistic competition. (See Chapter 8.)

Hall and Hitch's findings may be summarised as follows.

Firstly, the firms do not act atomistically. Firms are continuously conscious of the reactions of their competitors. This behaviour, obviously in contradiction to the postulates of monopolistic competition, suggested that oligopoly was much more widespread than had been thought up to that time. Oligopolistic interdependence could not be dealt with within the framework of the traditional theory. Duopoly theory, based on assumptions of constant reaction patterns of competitors, also seemed inadequate to cope with oligopolistic interdependence and the ensuing uncertainty regarding the demand for the product of oligopolistic firms.

Hall and Hitch found that firms do not attempt to maximise short-run profits by applying marginalistic rules ($MC = MR$), but aim at long-run profit maximisation. Firms set their price on the *average-cost principle*.[1] That is, firms do not set their price and output at the levels determined by the intersection of the MC and MR curves, but they set a price to cover the average variable cost, the average fixed cost and a 'normal' profit margin ('usually 10%')

$$P = AVC + AFC + \text{profit margin}$$

The reasons given by Hall and Hitch for the breakdown of marginalism may be summarised as follows. (a) Firms do not know their demand curve nor their marginal costs, hence the application of the marginalist rule ($MC = MR$) is impossible due to lack of relevant information. (b) Firms believed that the 'full-cost price' is the 'right' price, since it allowed a 'fair' profit and covered the costs of production when the plant was 'normally' utilised.

Hall and Hitch reported that firms' main preoccupation is price, and not output as the traditional theory implied. Thus the firms would set their price on the basis of the above average-cost principle and they would sell at that price whatever the market would take.

Although the firms in general would adhere to the average-cost pricing rule, they would be prepared to depart from it if they wanted to secure a big order, or if they thought that they could not set this price without damaging their goodwill and endangering their future position, in view of their rivals charging a lower price.

Finally, it was found that prices of manufacturers were fairly sticky, despite changes in demand and costs. Traditional theory predicted a change in price and output (at least in the short run) in response to changes in demand and costs. This prediction was not observed in the real world, in which 'stickiness' of prices was a general phenomenon. To explain this stickiness of prices Hall and Hitch introduced the Chamberlinian apparatus of the 'kinked' demand curve. The kink implies the following pattern of expected reactions of competitors, witnessed by the firms that were studied. Businessmen held the belief that if they raised their price their competitors would not follow, so that they would lose a considerable number of their customers; while if they cut their price their competitors would follow suit, with the result that their sales would increase by an insignificant amount. The price was set equal to the average cost and the kink would occur at that price. The firms would arrive at this average-cost price independently (without collusion). Firms reported that they did not enter any collusive agreement in order to increase the market price, because of fear of potential entrants who might endanger the long-run position of established firms. Similarly, they did not think that a collusive reduction in the price would be profitable to the 'group', because they believed

---

[1] This principle is often called, although but mistakenly, the *full-cost principle*, due to the use of this terminology by Hall and Hitch.

that the market demand was price inelastic. Furthermore businessmen were aware of the fact that frequent price changes were disliked by their customers. Thus firms prefer to keep their price constant, except in cases of general cost increases which affect all firms and lead to an increase of price by all. The 'kink' in the individual-demand curve, implying that above the given P the demand is very elastic while below P demand is inelastic, provides an explanation of the firms keeping their price constant.

Various writers have interpreted the device of the kinked-demand curve as a 'theory' of oligopolistic behaviour. This view has become so firmly established that the kinked-demand 'theory' has found its place in all textbooks of microeconomics. However, as we saw in Chapter 9, the kinked demand cannot be considered as a theory of pricing and output decisions in oligopolistic markets, since it cannot explain the level of the price, i.e. the location of the kink. In the framework of Hall and Hitch's approach the kinked demand makes sense as a device for explaining the 'stickiness' of the prices, but not their levels. Hall and Hitch suggest that the firms set their price independently of one another on the basis of the average-cost principle. And these prices, once set, tend to be sticky because of the expectations of firms about competitors' reactions to changes in the firm's price, which are such as to create a kink at the level of the average-cost price.

It does not seem that Hall and Hitch have developed a determinate theory of pricing in oligopoly markets, and although they mention several elements relevant to oligopolistic behaviour (long-run profit considerations, goodwill of firms, potential and actual competition and interdependence of firms, average-cost pricing procedures instead of marginalistic computations), they did not combine them into a comprehensive theory of oligopoly. However, their conclusions constituted a serious attack on marginalism. The reported results of the study of their sample suggest the following. Firstly, short-run profit maximisation was rarely stated by businessmen to be their goal. Most firms reported that they aimed at a 'fair' level of profit and that they had also other goals, such as building up their goodwill, being fair to their competitors, etc. Secondly, the demand curve and its price elasticity, on which marginalism so heavily relies, are unknown in practice, because neither consumers preferences nor competitors' reactions are known with certainty. Most firms are oligopolists who are faced with uncertainty concerning their customers and their competitors. Given this uncertain environment the demand schedules cannot be taken as known, hence marginal revenue schedules are unknown to the businessmen. Thirdly, marginal costs are also unknown in multi-product firms, which are typical in the modern business world. Fourthly, even if MC and MR were known, and firms aimed at the maximisation of their (short-run) profits, the adherence to this equality would require continuous changes in the price in view of the continuous changes in costs and demand. Such frequent changes in prices are not desirable, and prices have exhibited considerable stickiness despite changes in short-run costs and demand.[1]

III. GORDON'S ATTACK ON MARGINALISM

In 1948 Gordon[2] joined the marginalist controversy by attacking the assumptions and postulates of the traditional theory of the firm. His line of attack may be summarised as follows.

[1] This finding has been challenged by subsequent empirical studies. See G. J. Stigler, 'The Kinky Oligopoly Demand Curve and Rigid Prices', *Journal of Political Economy* (1947). Also J. L. Simon, 'A Further Test of the Kinky Oligopoly Demand Curve', *American Economic Review*, (1969).

[2] R. A. Gordon, 'Short-Period Price Determination in Theory and Practice', *American Economic Review* (1948).

The real industrial world is extremely complex, with too many variables that determine demand and costs and there are many policy variables which the firm may use in any particular situation (price, product, advertising, diversification, etc.). The determinants of demand and costs vary continuously and marginal adjustments (by equating relevant marginal magnitudes) for all changes simultaneously are beyond the ability of entrepreneurs. Complexity means that firms cannot learn from their past experience, by incorporating such experience in their estimation of demand and costs, because the environment (economic structure) changes continuously, invalidating any extrapolation of the past.

Uncertainty is an additional reason for making marginalist behaviour inapplicable: it makes impossible the accurate knowledge of future demand and cost conditions. A reasonable treatment of uncertainty within a dynamic framework requires information and knowledge about the formation of expectations of businessmen, which is not available (see below). Thus businessmen resort to additional goals apart from profit maximisation) in an attempt to avoid uncertainty. Neither the process of expectation formation nor additional goals can be adequately dealt with by marginal analysis.

Empirical evidence has shown that firms use average-cost pricing widely. The application of the average-cost rule for pricing is the best alternative to marginalism, especially for multiproduct firms, where changes in costs (that is, marginal costs) are practically impossible to estimate for all the products.

In empirical studies firms have been reported to pursue a multitude of goals, like retaining their labour force smoothly employed, acquire goodwill, and so on. It is true that such goals are related to the level of profit, but it is not certain that such additional goals are compatible or competing with the goal of maximisation of profit.

Managers tend to concentrate at any one time on 'local' problems arising in particular sections of the firm and find solutions for such problems without applying marginalistic rules. For example, a frequent breakdown of some part of the productive process will attract the attention of top management to this 'bottleneck'. Local solutions do not necessarily lead to profit maximisation. Thus the average-cost rule, based on some standard normal level of output, is more realistic since it stresses the importance of maintaining production at an adequate level to satisfy the demand rather than maximise profits.

The demand cannot be known or estimated with an adequate degree of accuracy in the long run, due to the continuous change in the economic environment. Under these conditions the adoption of the average-cost rule makes sense since it leads to a price level very similar to all firms, a fact that allows the firms to concentrate on the level of sales at this given price: shifts in demand are much more important to businessmen than the shape (elasticity) of the demand curve.

For marginalist behaviour the demand and cost curves must be objectively known. If one accepts the view that demand and costs are subjectively conceived by businessmen (as Machlup does, see below), then marginalism reduces to a tautology, because any observed behaviour by firms could be presented as aiming at profit maximisation: any action of the firm is compatible with the equality of *subjectively determined MC* and *MR* curves.

Similarly any attempt to build additional goals into cost and revenue functions (by quantifying such goals and evaluating their effects on profits) before proceeding with the marginalist equality leads to tautological predictions. Statements such as 'whatever the firm does is because it aims at maximisation of profits, due account being taken in profitability estimates of any other subsidiary goals' are clearly tautologies since they imply that whatever the firm is observed to do is in its belief that it maximises its profits.

Finally, any attempt to account for expectations by 'doctoring' the demand and cost curves so as to presumably reflect all anticipations of future changes in the environment leads to similar tautological predictions. The equality of MC and MR derived from such 'doctored' demand and cost functions may always be explained in terms of profit maximisation.

Gordon argues that the tautology could be avoided only if one uses a dynamic multi-period analysis. In this approach cost and revenue functions *in each period* (within the entrepreneur's horizon) are postulated, and then the entrepreneur proceeds with the maximisation of the present value of future net revenue (profit). This dynamic approach to the problem of uncertainty, although theoretically plausible, is of little use in practice, because it assumes *given expectations* of entrepreneurs. The entrepreneur must be assumed to have the information and ability to form *definite expectations* about future changes in the economic environment. *Given these expectations*, the entrepreneur can proceed with the maximisation of discounted values of future profitability streams. But expectations are not explained in marginalism, and taking them for given really by-passes the problem of uncertainty instead of solving it.

IV. IN DEFENCE OF MARGINALISM

Four main lines of arguments have been put forward by various writers in defence of the traditional theory of the firm.

The first line of defence is launched in terms of Friedman's methodological issue,[1] that realism of assumptions of a theory is not the main criterion for its acceptance. A theory should be judged not on the basis of the realism of its assumptions but on the basis of its predictions. Friedman says, without providing any conclusive empirical evidence, that the traditional theory of the firm has produced reasonably good predictions, and on this basis it should be judged as being a satisfactory theory. We do not believe that such arguments launched in abstract terms can be taken seriously.

The second line of defence includes empirical studies which provide evidence that firms do in fact apply marginalistic rules in their decision-making. Such studies have been conducted by J. S. Earley,[2] who reported (from a sample of 110 'excellently managed' companies in the U.S.A.) that modern accounting methods provide information on marginal costs and marginal revenues, and this information is actually used by well organised firms in their decision-making.

This evidence is in contradiction to the Hall and Hitch study, which covered 'well organised firms' in the U.K. Furthermore Earley's results cover only 110 large firms which apply modern accounting and management techniques. It may well be that other firms do not have the required information for marginalistic behaviour, or that they do not want to apply marginalistic rules in each period in order to maximise their short-run profits for various reasons (e.g. because this would endanger their long-run profits, or because they want to avoid government intervention, to have a good public image, and so on).[3]

The third line of defence is based on the Darwinian principle of the survival of the fittest. It is argued[4] that the fittest firms are those which maximise their profits, because

---

[1] M. Friedman, 'The Methodology of Positive Economics,' in *Essays in Positive Economics* (University of Chicago Press, 1953).

[2] J. S. Earley, 'Recent Developments in Cost Accounting and the Marginal Analysis', *Journal of Political Economy* (1955), and 'Marginal Policies of Excellently Managed Companies', *American Economic Review* (1956).

[3] See R. Barback, *The Pricing of Manufactures* (Macmillan, 1964) p. 36.

[4] See A. Alchian, 'Uncertainty, Evolution and Economic Theory', *Journal of Political Economy* (1950) pp. 211–21. Also Edith Penrose, 'Biological Analogies in the Theory of the Firm', *American Economic Review* (1952) pp. 804–19.

in this way they can accumulate assets and grow faster than firms which are not profit maximisers. This is a process of 'economic natural elimination of the weaker firms' (defined as the firms which do not maximise profit).

The defects of this line of defence have been examined in section I above. They may be summarised as follows. The process of natural economic selection does not work uninhibited in the modern industrial world, because even firms which are not profit maximisers can adopt various policies (e.g. diversity) which will allow them to survive in the long run. Furthermore one should hardly expect that the fittest firms today will also be the fittest tomorrow, given the continuous change in products and techniques. And of course there would be no fittest if all firms are not profit maximisers but pursue other goals (e.g. if every firm adopts satisficing behaviour).

The fourth line of defence of marginalism attempts to establish in an abstract theoretical way that the assumptions of the marginalist theory are 'fairly realistic'. The main writer who has adopted this line of defence is F. Machlup.[1] His arguments are of three kinds. Firstly, he argues that the empirical evidence against marginalism (e.g. Lester's work, Hall and Hitch's study, etc.) has too many weaknesses and, hence, is not conclusive. Secondly, he argues that the basic assumptions and postulates of marginalism are plausible. Thirdly, he argues that there has been a misunderstanding regarding the purpose of the traditional theory; this theory is a theory of markets, constructed to explain resource allocation via the price mechanism; the theory predicts well the effects on resource allocation of various changes in the environment (shifts in demand, changes in costs, tax changes); hence the traditional theory does well the job for which it has been designed.

Machlup has criticised the studies of Lester, Hall and Hitch and other empirical evidence against marginalism on the following grounds.

There was a lack of communication between businessmen and economic researchers, due to the differences in their terminology. Economists speak in terms of MC, MR and elasticities, concepts with which businessmen are not familiar. Businessmen's statement, that they set price equal to their average cost, is not incompatible with the marginalistic rule $MC = MR$ which is used by economists. The majority of businessmen are not economists and do not know the calculus technique of $MC = MR$ at equilibrium. An economist, however, applying the marginal tools with which he is equipped from his university training will reach the same unique (tangency) solution as the businessman. Thus in these conditions either of the rules

$$P = AC$$

or

$$MC = MR$$

will lead to the same unique price–output combination which maximises profits.

To this criticism Hall and Hitch replied by saying that their questionnaires were followed by intensive interviews with entrepreneurs and managers, during which the economic researchers made sure that the persons being interviewed would understand what they were questioned about.

There are psychological reasons (Machlup argues) explaining businessmen's answers that maximisation of profit was not their goal. A businessman being interviewed wishes to appear as pursuing 'fair' policies, which do not yield maximum (monopoly) profits, but just a 'fair' profit. Furthermore firms were afraid to admit that they were charging the

---

[1] F. Machlup, 'Marginal Analysis and Empirical Research', *American Economic Review* (1946). Also F. Machlup, 'Theories of the Firm: Marginalist, Managerialist, Behavioural', *American Economic Review* (1967).

monopoly price (the price which maximises profits), preferring to state that they set price equal to their AC, since in law average costs are taken as a basis for fair prices.

Firms need not apply calculus continuously, since pricing and output decisions, Machlup argues, become routine. Thus the 'pricing practices' reported by businessmen (that is, the setting of P equal to AVC plus a profit margin) reflects their routine rules applied in decision-making, and are not incompatible with marginalist calculations. This argument of Machlup is not valid, unless he can establish that these pricing routines have originated from marginalistic rules, applied at the initial stages of the working of the firm.[1]

Regarding the attack on the basic assumptions of marginalist theory, Machlup attempted to argue that these assumptions were fairly plausible. He agreed that MC and MR were not objectively known to businessmen. However, he argued that this is not a serious problem, since a *subjective assessment* of these schedules by businessmen is adequate for the application of marginalism. What matters is the *beliefs* of firms as to what their MC and MR are, and not their objective values. Costs and revenues are based on beliefs and hunches of businessmen. Arguing on these lines Machlup failed to see that subjective definitions of MC and MR render marginalism a tautology, since any action of firms may be explained as marginalistic, based on such subjective 'hunches'.

Machlup argued that firms may not understand the concept of demand elasticity, but surely elasticity considerations were implicit in their pricing procedures: the elasticity of demand for the product of any firm, he argues, depends on the availability of substitutes and on the supply elasticity of such substitutes; the best guide to the elasticity of supply of competitors is provided by the firm's own costs, because competitors are expected to have similar costs; thus the elasticity of demand is 'guessed' from the knowledge of the costs of the firm. This argument of Machlup's is valid, but does not, as it stands, provide evidence for the application of marginalism. We will show, however, in Chapter 12 that average-cost pricing implies an estimate of the elasticity of demand if the average variable cost is constant over a certain range (and the empirical evidence from cost studies shows that this shape of AVC is generally found in the real world[2]). Under these conditions average-cost pricing leads to the same equilibrium solution as marginalist behaviour.

Regarding the goals of the firm Machlup argues that the firm has as its (single) goal the maximisation of its long-run profit. This is attained by using long-run cost and long-run demand curves, which incorporate expectations of future conditions and changes in the market environment. Machlup failed to see that this treatment of expectations (which implies 'doctored' demand and cost curves) again reduces marginalism to a tautology, since any observed behaviour can be compatible with profit maximisation, with appropriately constructed cost and demand curves in which future uncertainty is *ex ante* eliminated. (See above, pp. 266–7).

Machlup rejected the suggestion that other goals of the firm can be incorporated in the calculation of the cost and demand curves. He recognised that this treatment of other goals would make any action of the firm compatible with profit maximisation, and this, he accepted, would render profit maximisation a tautology. It is surprising that Machlup recognised the danger of tautology when other goals would be incorporated in long-run cost and demand schedules, yet he did not perceive this danger when he was arguing in terms of cost and revenues being subjective 'hunches', and uncertainty being realistically possible to incorporate into the long-run demand and costs.

From the above discussion it should be clear that the marginalist controversy cannot be considered as resolved. Three main points need stressing:

[1] See R. Barback, *The Pricing of Manufactures* (Macmillan, 1964).
[2] See Chapter 4, pp. 137–46.

Firstly. The application of the marginalistic rule to maximise short-run profits requires that businessmen make continuous adjustment to price as demand and costs change continuously. The observed 'stickiness' of prices in the face of changing conditions of the environment suggest that marginalism is not applied, at least in the short-run.[1,2]

Secondly. Marginalism faces the dilemma of *either* being unrealistic, *or* being in danger of becoming merely tautological if one attempts to incorporate time and uncertainty or additional goals in a single set of appropriately 'doctored' long-run demand and long-run costs schedules.

Thirdly. However, it is not certain that the 'pricing practices' reported by businessmen in the context of various studies are inconsistent with marginalism, or that the average-cost pricing theories, based on this evidence, provide an alternative to the model of marginalism. We will return to this point in the next chapter, in which we present what we hope to be a 'representative' model of average-cost pricing.

[1] G. J. Stigler ('The Kinky-Oligopoly' Demand Curve and Rigid Prices', *Journal of Political Economy* (1947) pp. 432–49) presented evidence contradicting the 'stickiness' of prices, and questioned the validity of the assumption of long-run profit maximisation implied in the kinked-oligopoly model. He studied the price changes of about one hundred firms belonging to oligopolistic markets. He found that there is a negative correlation between the degree of concentration in an industry and the frequency of price changes: the higher the degree of concentration the less frequent the changes in prices are. However, Stigler also found that prices were not rigid, as Hall and Hitch, Sweezy and others had found (or assumed) in their studies. Furthermore, contrary to Sweezy, Stigler argued that the kinked demand curve is incompatible with the goal of profit maximisation. If firms were profit maximisers, they would make adjustments to their prices as soon as their MC changed. The 'kinky' oligopoly model implies that managers adhere to price inflexibility in the face of changing cost conditions. This reflects the risk-aversion of managers to the oligopolistic uncertainty. The kink in the demand curve, Stigler argues, reflects the beliefs of managers about competitors' reactions, and makes the firm deviate from marginal adjustments of prices and hence from profit maximisation.

[2] See also Julian L. Simon, 'A Further Test of the Kinky Oligopoly Demand Curve', *American Economic Review* (1969).

12. A 'Representative' Model of Average-Cost Pricing

Average-cost pricing models have been developed by various writers.[1] Their basic characteristic is the postulate that price is set according to the average-cost principle

$$P = AVC + GPM = AC$$

where AVC = average variable cost
        GPM = gross profit margin

The firm sets a price equal to its total average cost which includes a certain net profit margin. This pricing behaviour is assumed by the writers in this field to be different than the marginalist behaviour of the traditional theory of the firm. We will return to this point in section IV of this chapter, where we attempt to compare the average-cost theories with other theories of the firm.

The various average-cost pricing theories differ in that they postulate different methods of arriving at the estimate of the average cost which will be charged as price. However, these theories have general common characteristics which may be combined in a 'representative model' of average-cost pricing. We first present such a model. We next examine its predictions when dynamic changes take place. Finally we attempt to compare average-cost pricing with other theories of the firm.

I. GOALS OF THE FIRM

In average-cost theories of pricing it is explicitly or implicitly assumed that the goal of the firm is long-run profit maximisation. However, this goal is not attained by maximising profits in each one period within the time horizon of the firm. It is recognised that short-run profit maximisation by equating MC to MR in each period does not lead to profit maximisation in the long run (as the traditional theory postulated), because the individual time periods are not independent: decisions taken in any one period are influenced by decisions in past periods and will affect decisions in future

---

[1] The most important writers in this field are: (a) R. Hall and C. Hitch, 'Price Theory and Business Behaviour', *Oxford Economic Papers* (1939); reprinted in P. W. S. Andrews and T. Wilson (eds.), *Studies in the Price Mechanism* (1952). (b) P. W. S. Andrews, *Manufacturing Business* (Macmillan, 1949). (c) R. Barback, *The Pricing of Manufactures* (Macmillan, 1964). (d) H. R. Edwards, *Competition and Monopoly in the British Soap Industry* (Macmillan, 1964).

points of time. Hence the behavioural rule of equating MC to MR in decision-making is inappropriate for describing businessmen's behaviour. Instead long-run profit-maximisation is attained by equating price to the average cost of the firm (see below).

II. DEMAND AND COST SCHEDULES

For analysing the long-run behaviour of the firm we would require knowledge of its long-run demand and its long-run cost schedules. However, there is great uncertainty regarding these schedules. Tastes in the market change continuously and the reaction of competitors is impossible to predict. Thus firms cannot estimate their future demand. Past experience does not help much in reducing uncertainty, because extrapolation of past conditions in the future is haphazardous given the dynamic changes in the economic structure. Given this uncertainty average-cost pricing theorists reject the demand schedule as a tool of analysis, thus abandoning half of the apparatus of the traditional theory of the firm.

Uncertainty also envelops the long-run costs of the firm. Rapid technological change and changes in factor prices make it impossible to obtain reliable estimates of the long-run cost schedule. Thus in average-cost theories it is assumed that the firm takes its decisions on the basis of its short-run average costs.

It is explicitly or implicitly assumed that the short-run average variable cost has a flat stretch (figure 12.1) which reflects the fact that firms build into their plant some *reserve capacity* which allows them flexibility in their operations.[1] Reserve capacity is required for various reasons: (*a*) To meet seasonal fluctuations in demand. (*b*) To allow a smooth flow of production when break-down of some equipment occurs. (*c*) To meet a growing demand until further expansion of scale is realised. (*d*) To allow some flexibility for minor alterations of the style of the product in view of the changing tastes of customers, and for other reasons.[2]

The average variable cost has a saucer-type shape (figure 12.1). The falling part shows the decrease in cost due to better utilisation of some of the fixed factors up to the capacity of the plant. Over the range of the falling $SAVC$ the SMC is below it.

The increasing part of the $SAVC$ reflects the waste of raw materials, the higher repair costs of machinery and overtime payment to the labour force. When the $SAVC$ is rising the SMC lies above it.

Over the flat stretch of the $SAVC$ the SMC is equal to the average variable cost (the two curves coincide). Pricing is based on the flat stretch of the $SAVC$. At levels of output

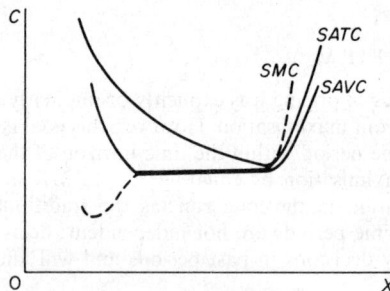

Figure 12.1

---

[1] Note that reserve capacity is built not only in the technical part of production but also into the organisational and administrative staff side.

[2] See Chapter 4, pp. 114–20.

lower than the normal capacity level (that is, the range of output for which the plant has been optimally designed) firms have high costs, yet they do not charge a price to cover these costs because they expect to eventually reach the normal range of output. Similarly, the firms may produce (when there is pressure of demand) on the increasing part of their *AC*, but they will not charge a higher price to cover such costs because they are afraid of losing their goodwill. (If the pressure of demand is revealed to be permanent, firms will install additional equipment, enlarging their plant capacity; see page 276 below.)

III. PRICE DETERMINATION: THE 'MARK-UP' RULE

The price determination involves two distinct stages. First, the firm defines the price that it *would like* to charge (*P*) in order to cover its total costs when its plant is operated within its optimal range of capacity and earn a (subjectively determined level of) 'reasonable' profit. Secondly, the firm compares its estimated price with the level of price at which entry would occur, and sets the price at a level (*P**) which would effectively deter entry. Let us examine this procedure of price determination in some detail.

Subjective estimate of the 'desired' price

The firm uses the 'mark-up' rule

$$P = AVC + GPM$$

The average variable cost (*AVC*) is assumed known to the firm with certainty. The firm concentrates on the straight stretch of the *SAVC* curve which represents normal utilisation of its plant capacity. The firm looks at its *long-run* position and aims at the long-run profit maximisation. However, given the uncertainty in the environment, the firm bases its price on the *short-run AVC*; the firm *believes* that its costs will not increase if it expands its scale (in the long run) and probably they will be lower than in the short run. Thus the short-run *AC* is thought by businessmen to be a good approximation to the long-run average cost.[1]

The gross profit margin will cover the average fixed cost (*AFC*) and yield a normal profit

$$GPM = AFC + NPM$$

where *NPM* = net profit margin. The *AFC* element is determined by dividing the total fixed cost (*TFC*) by a 'planned' or 'budgeted' or 'normal' level of output (*X**). This is a level of output (within the range for which the plant has been set up) which the firm expects to produce and sell with normal utilisation of its plant.[2] Thus

$$AFC = \frac{TFC}{X^*}$$

where *X** = 'planned', or 'budgeted', or 'normal' output.

The net profit margin is assumed to be known to the established firms 'as a matter of experience': it should yield a 'fair' return on capital (so that capital keeps flowing regularly in the industry for investment in the long run) and cover all risks peculiar to the product. For an already-produced commodity, firms have formed a fair view of

---

[1] See Andrews, *Manufacturing Business.*

[2] The 'normal utilisation' of a plant differs for various firms. Usually it varies between 80% and 90% of full capacity. For example, General Motors considers that the normal utilisation of its plant is 80% of its full capacity (see F. M. Scherer, *Industrial Market Structure and Economic Performance* (Rand McNally, 1970)).

what the net profit margin is from their past experience. For a new product the firm is assumed to make a fair judgement about what the *NPM* is 'safe', in the sense of not attracting entrants.

The addition of *AVC*, *AFC* and *NPM* gives an estimate of the 'desired' price, that is, *the price which the firm would wish to charge if it is to cover all its costs (with a normal utilisation of its plant) and make what it thinks to be a normal profit.*

Actual price setting

However, the thus estimated price will not necessarily be charged. The 'desired' or 'standard' price will be taken as the initial basis of the price that will actually be charged (P^*). The level of actual price depends mainly on the threat of potential entry (potential competition). Actual competition by existing firms is resolved by either tacit collusion or by price leadership. Tacit collusion takes various forms. Typically it is realised within trade associations, which publish industry-wide average-cost information by product line. This information then becomes, by the common consent of the firms belonging to the particular trade association the basis of price calculations.[1]

When firms in the industry have widely different costs, pricing on the basis of average costs by each firm independently may result in market instability and price wars. The 'orderly co-ordination' and functioning of the industry is often attained by price leadership. The price leader is among the largest firms with the lowest costs. The less efficient firms will be effectively price-takers. The price leader makes his price calculations according to the average-costing rule earlier described, but will actually charge a price, P^*, which depends

(*a*)   on potential competition

(*b*)   on general economic conditions (booming or depressed business).

Thus, if there are barriers to entry,[2] P^* will be higher than the normal price (P), and the price leader (and possibly other less efficient firms) will be making abnormal profit. However, if the threat of potential entry is strong, the quoted price (P^*) will be equal to the leader's normal price (P), who will be earning just normal profits. Thus the effective (realised) gross profit margin is competitively determined, by the threat of potential entrants.[3]

There is also evidence that the gross profit margin is readjusted when an entrant charges a lower price, and when the general market conditions deviate from the normal: in a sellers' market a higher *GPM* is often charged while in periods of depressed trade the *GPM* is downward readjusted (see below).[4]

Figure 12.2 depicts the determination of price in our 'representative' average-cost pricing model. It should be stressed that the horizontal lines are *not* demand curves, but show the price that would be charged under certain conditions. At this price the firms would be prepared to sell whatever they could produce with their plant capacity. Their sales in any one period is ultimately determined by their 'goodwill'.

In figure 12.2 the *SATC* curve includes the net profit margin which the firms consider normal for the particular product. The price leader, given his cost structure, would normally desire to charge the price P which would cover his *SAVC* and his 'normal gross profit margin' (*ab*). At this price the firm leader would be prepared to sell what the

[1] See F. M. Scherer, *Industrial Market Structure and Economic Performance*, p. 178. Also R. M. Cyert and J. G. March, *A Behavioural Theory of the Firm* (Prentice-Hall, 1963). Also W. Haynes,'Pricing Practices in Small Firms', *Southern Economic Journal* (1964).

[2] See Chapter 13.

[3] The average-cost pricing has a strong link with entry-preventing behaviour (see Chapters 13 and 14).

[4] An example is provided by the pricing behaviour of General Motors during the 1930s.

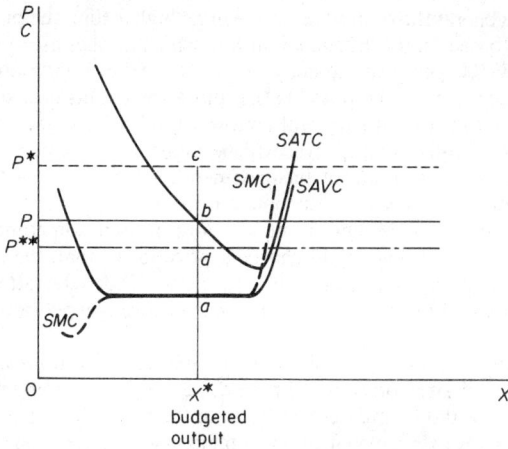

Note ———— denotes the initial desired level of price with a normal gross profit margin (*ab*).
------- denotes the quoted price when there are barriers to entry: the *GPM* is *ac* > *ab*.
—·— denotes the quoted price when there is strong potential competition: the *GPM*
      is *ad* < *ab*.

Figure 12.2

market would take. (It should be noted that *P* is calculated on the assumption that the budgeted output will be *X**.) If barriers to entry exist (or sometimes in persistent booming trade) the leader would charge the price *P** which would yield abnormal profits (at outputs equal or greater than the budgeted output): clearly the effective *GPM* at *P** is *ac* > *ab*. If potential competition (threat of entry) is strong (or sometimes in periods of depressed business) the leader would actually charge the price *P*** (lower than the 'desired' or 'initial-base' price *P*) and at this price his effective *GPM* would be *ad*, which is smaller than the desired one *ab*.

The average-cost pricing model apparently discards demand curves. Price is based on the costs of the firm and in particular on the short-run costs, since the long-run costs are blurred with uncertainty.

If the product is technically homogeneous there will be a unique price in the market in the long run.

However, if products are differentiated (*either* with brand names, or in style and quality) there will be a cluster of prices in the industry, reflecting the differences in costs (if product differentiation is real) or the degree of strength of the preferences of the customers (if differentiation is of the 'fancied' type; see Chapter 8).

IV. COMPARISON WITH PURE COMPETITION IN LONG-RUN EQUILIBRIUM

The average-cost theorists are in general vague in their statements, and this has been the source of strong criticism.[1] This being so, the following comparison can only be tentative.

[1] See, for example, E. A. Robinson, 'The Pricing of Manufactures', *Economic Journal* (1950); A. Silberston, 'The Pricing of Manufacturing Products; A Comment,' *Economic Journal* (1951); G. C. Archibald (ed.), *Readings in the Theory of the Firm*, (Penguin, 1972), Introduction; J. R. Wildsmith, *Managerial Theories of the Firm* (Martin–Robertson, 1973) p. 53.

It seems that in general the desired price P will be higher than the purely competitive price, because P is based on the 'budgeted output' which implies use of the plant (on the average) below its 100 per cent capacity. Thus, if market conditions and potential competition are such as to make possible the quotation of this desired price, we must conclude that output in the industry will be lower (and price higher) than in a purely competitive market. Profits at this level will be higher than in pure competition, reflecting the risk-aversion attitude of businessmen, who, because of this, consider as 'normal profit' a margin higher than the one in pure competition.

However, if the threat of potential entry is strong (and sometimes when market conditions are depressed) firms would charge a price lower than the desired P, which actually might be equal to the purely competitive one. Under the latter conditions the level of output, price and profit would be identical in pure competition and in average-costing theory.

If, however, there are barriers to entry or the market conditions allow charging a price higher than the desired one (P), then the deviation of the long-run equilibrium in average-cost theory would be even greater than in the first case (when P is charged).

If firms persist (on the average) in using their plant at less than its 100 per cent capacity, it is obvious that there will be a certain amount of underutilisation of the plant.

V. PREDICTIONS OF THE AVERAGE-COST PRICING THEORY IN CHANGING MARKET CONDITIONS

Given the nature of average-cost pricing models one should expect prices to be much more sensitive to changes in cost than to changes in demand.

A change in costs

If there is a minor change in costs, firms would tend to absorb it by variation in the quantity or quality of their product. For example, a small increase in factor prices would lead firms to change the appearance of the product (e.g., a new packaging) so as to allow them to reduce the quantity offered at the going price (e.g. sell cigarettes slightly shorter, offer a thinner chocolate bar). Similarly, if there is a minor decrease of factor prices, firms will not disturb the price, being afraid of triggering a price war, but would rather pass the reduction in costs to customers via improved quality or increased quantity at the given price.

However, if the change in costs is substantial, price will be accordingly changed. A substantial fall in costs, originating from fast technical progress in the industry or a fall in factor prices, will result in a decrease in price, otherwise the excess profits would attract entry and endanger the long-run profitability of the existing firms. Similarly, if there is a substantial increase in factor prices all firms in the industry are similarly affected and the price will be raised eventually to cover the increased costs.

Change in demand

If demand increases, in the short run firms will usually prefer to adopt a queueing policy (backlog of demand) rather than increase their prices, because they do not know whether the pressure of demand will last for long and they are afraid to damage their reputation by exploiting a 'temporary sellers' market'. If the increase in demand persists, firms will install new equipment and expand their capacity, thus moving to a new point on their *LRAC*, where the cost per unit of output is not expected to be higher, and may probably be lower. This expectation about the shape of the *LRAC* deters firms from raising their price, lest they should attract entry and damage permanently their goodwill with dissatisfied customers who would shift their purchases to the new entrants if they charged a price lower than the 'exploitative' one of their old suppliers.

If demand declines, in the short run firms would avoid an increase in the price to cover probably higher costs (as they are pushed backwards to levels of output corresponding to the increasing part of their cost curve); such a policy would almost certainly accelerate the decline of sales. In the short run the firm would, while holding its price unchanged, search for the causes of the decline in sales and act accordingly. For example, if the fall in demand is due to change in tastes, the firm will improve or alter its product or diversify. However, under conditions of secular decline in demand weaker firms, faced with decreased liquidity, may be led to the desperate action of price-cutting. This would then be generalised in a competitive price-cutting and a price war, in which the most efficient firms would survive and the market would settle to a new equilibrium.

In summary, average-cost theories predict that prices would tend to be sticky, changing less than marginalism would imply in the face of changing demand.

Imposition of a tax

In average-cost theories the imposition of a corporate tax (lump-sum or profit tax) will affect all firms similarly and hence all firms will raise their price concurrently, thus shifting the tax to the customers.

Similarly the imposition of a specific tax per unit of output would shift the AVC curve upwards and even with the same GPM, price would increase by the full amount of the tax.

The difference between the corporate tax and the specific tax is that in the first case the AFC will shift upwards and the GPM will be accordingly readjusted, while the tax per unit of output shifts upwards the AVC. However, both types of taxes will be passed on to the buyers.

The prediction of the average-cost theories from the imposition of a corporate tax are thus different from the prediction of marginalism. There is empirical evidence that firms do in fact pass (at least partly), on to their customers corporate taxes via increases in their price.[1]

VI. A CRITIQUE OF AVERAGE-COST PRICING

Average-cost pricing practices have been widely supported by empirical studies. It has been found that this pricing practice is adopted by a large number of small and large firms in most industries.[2] This, however, does not establish that average-cost

[1] See R. J. Gordon, 'The Incidence of the Corporation Income Tax in U.S. Manufacturing, 1925–62', *American Economic Review* (1967) pp. 731–58. Also M. Krzyzaniak and R. A. Musgrave, *The Shifting of the Corporation Income Tax* (Johns Hopkins Press, 1963). Also J. G. Cragg *et al.*, 'Empirical Evidence on the Incidence of the Corporation Income Tax', *Journal of Political Economy* (1967) pp. 811–21.

[2] See R. Heflebower, 'Full Costs, Cost Changes and Prices', in *Cost Behaviour and Price Policy*, National Bureau of Economic Research (New York, 1963); P. J. D. Wiles, *Price, Cost and Output* (Blackwell, 1961); J. M. Clark, *Competition as a Dynamic Process* (Brookings Institution, 1961); A Kaplan, J. Dirlam, and R. Lanzilotti, *Pricing in Big Business, A Case Approach* (Brookings Institution, 1958); B. Fog, *Industrial Pricing Policies* (North-Holland, 1960); R. Lanzilotti, 'Pricing Objectives in Large Companies', *American Economic Review* (1958); also 'Pricing Objectives in Large Companies, a Reply', *American Economic Review* (1959); I. F. Pearce, 'A Study in Price Policy', *Economica* (1956); National Bureau of Economic Research, *Cost Behavior and Price Policy* (New York, 1963); National Bureau of Economic Research, *Business Concentration and Price Policy* (Princeton, 1955); W. Haynes, 'Pricing Practices in Small Firms', *Southern Economic Journal* (1964); R. Barback, *The Pricing of Manufactures* (Macmillan, 1964); H. R. Edwards, *Competition and Monopoly in the British Soap Industry* (Oxford University Press, 1964).

pricing is *a theory* different than other theories of the firm. Average-cost pricing practices are compatible with almost all hypotheses pertaining to explain the behaviour of the firm. For example average-costing rules of pricing are compatible with Baumol's sales maximisation hypothesis (see Chapter 15), Cyert and March's satisficing behavioural model (see Chapter 18), with short-run marginalistic profit-maximising behaviour (e.g. in the monopolistic competition models of Chamberlin and Joan Robinson the final tangency equilibrium may be arrived at either by equating MC to MR, or by setting $P = AC$), and with long-run profit maximisation of the sort earlier described. The question then arises whether average-cost pricing is a different theory of the firm, or whether it is a pricing practice (a pricing routine), adopted by firms for various reasons, irrespective of their goals.

It should be clear that the 'mark-up' margin would be different, depending on the goals of the firm, and hence the price level would be different. Thus, unless we know what the goals of the firm are, we cannot say just by looking at its pricing rules of thumb whether it is a sales maximiser, a satisficer, or a firm aiming at the long-run profit maximisation, because all these motivations may be attained by applying an average-cost routine in price setting. However, the empirical evidence regarding the goals of the firm is far from conclusive.[1] What is established from various studies is that: (*a*) The average-cost pricing practice is widely adopted by firms in the modern industrial world. (*b*) The prices are not adjusted as soon as a change in demand or costs takes place, as the narrow marginalistic behaviour (of equating MC to MR) would imply. Thus short-run profit maximisation by applying the marginalistic rule $MC = MR$ in each period within the time-horizon of the firm has been refuted by empirical studies. (*c*) The shifting of corporate taxes to the buyers through price increases is a well-established fact, but this is compatible, with many motivations-goals (e.g. Baumol's theory yields the same qualitative predictions as long-run profit maximisation pursued by equating price to AC). (*d*) In some studies it has been reported that prices have been 'sticky' over long periods over which cost conditions and demand conditions have been changing.[2] This stickiness of prices is incompatible with short-run marginalistic behaviour, but is compatible not only with long-run profit maximisation (based on the average-cost principle) but also with collusive agreements, price-leadership models, etc., and can be explained by a kinked-demand curve which can plausibly be accepted not as a price theory but as describing the beliefs (subjective assessment) of businessmen about the probable behaviour of their rivals. (*e*) It is generally found by empirical studies that firms have a multiplicity of goals, and not the single goal of profit maximisation. This evidence may be interpreted as refuting average-cost pricing as a theory, since this postulates a single goal, that of long-run profit maximisation. The proponents of average-cost pricing theory would, however, resort to 'survival arguments' in support of the long-run profit-maximisation goal. For example, some argue that other goals can be attained more easily if firms maximise profits; others, that there is a mechanism of 'economic selection' analogous to the biological Darwinian law of 'natural selection' which postulates the 'survival of the fittest'. These arguments cannot be resolved on *a priori* grounds. Several counter-arguments have been discussed in Chapter 11.

However, even if one accepted that long-run profit maximisation is the single goal of the firm, average-cost pricing would not be a new theory of the firm, since it can be proved that the same long-run equilibrium solution would be reached if one applied marginal analysis in the long run. We will prove that setting the price on the basis of the

---

[1] See Chapter 11, p. 258.

[2] However, other studies show that prices have not been all that 'sticky'. See, for example, G. J. Stigler, 'The Kinky-Oligopoly Demand Curve and Rigid Prices', *Journal of Political Economy* (1947) pp. 432–49.

average-cost principle involves implicitly the (subjective) estimation of the elasticity of demand in the long-run equilibrium position. In other words, when the firms apply the mark-up rule

$$P = AVC + GPM$$

with the aim of attaining maximum profits in the long run, they implicitly 'guess' at the value of the demand elasticity, provided that the AVC is constant over the relevant range of output (and the empirical evidence from cost studies shows that the AVC is constant over the range of output within which firms operate).[1]

Proof

(1)   The necessary condition for profit maximisation is

$$MC = MR \tag{12.1}$$

(2)   It has been established that

$$MR = P\left(1 - \frac{1}{e}\right) \tag{12.2}$$

(3)   Given that $MC > 0$, MR must be positive for profit maximisation. This implies that profits can be maximised only if $|e| > 1$, since
(a) if $e = 1$, $MR = 0$
(b) if $e < 1$, $MR < 0$
and in both these cases the maximisation procedure breaks down, because the necessary condition (12.1) is violated.
(4)   Over the flat stretch of the AVC we have

$$AVC = MC \tag{12.3}$$

Substituting (12.3) and (12.2) in (12.1) we have

$$AVC = MR$$

and

$$AVC = P\left(1 - \frac{1}{e}\right) = P\left(\frac{e - 1}{e}\right)$$

Solving for P we find

$$P = AVC\left(\frac{e}{e - 1}\right)$$

Given that $|e| > 1$ the term in brackets is always greater than unity. We thus may write

$$\left(\frac{e}{e - 1}\right) = (1 + k)$$

where $k > 0$. Therefore

$$P = AVC(1 + k)$$

[1] See Chapter 4, pp. 137–46.

where k is the gross profit margin. For example, if the firm sets a 20 per cent (of its AVC) as its profit margin we have

$$(1 + k) = 1 + 0.20 = \left(\frac{e}{e - 1}\right)$$

Solving for $|e|$ we find that the elasticity of demand is 6.

Thus setting a gross profit margin is tantamount of estimating the price elasticity of demand and then applying the marginalist analysis.

In summary average-cost pricing reduces to marginalism in a different vocabulary, if the goal of the firm is long-run profit maximisation and the AVC is constant over the range of output which is relevant for pricing. Both these assumptions are explicit in average-cost 'theories' of pricing. Hence average-cost pricing does not provide a new theory of the firm and the claim of average-cost theorists that firms resort to average-cost pricing because they do not know their demand elasticity with certainty in the long run, is not a valid argument, because elasticity considerations are wrapped up in setting the gross profit margin. It is commonly observed that multiproduct firms set a lower mark-up on commodities which have close substitutes, while the mark-up on commodities which have no close substitutes is typically high. These differential mark-ups show that firms know from experience the responsiveness of their customers to the prices of their different products. Although they may not have heard the term 'elasticity', the charging of different mark-ups implies their awareness of the reactions of their customers to their prices, and of course this is exactly what the measure of elasticity is devised for by economists. This behaviour, of setting low mark-ups for products with close substitutes and high mark-ups for commodities with few substitutes, is predicted by the average-cost rule of pricing. Thus this rule reflects implicit considerations of demand elasticities. (See C. Cole, *Microeconomics* (Harcourt, Brace-Jovanovich, 1973) pp. 348–51.)

How then can we explain the wide application of the average-cost pricing practices in the modern business world? Several reasons can be put forward to justify the average-cost routine of pricing.

Firstly, average-cost pricing is easier to apply, because the concepts it involves are familiar to businessmen and accountants, while the concept of elasticity is not perhaps understood by the average businessman.

Secondly, average-cost rules facilitate price-setting in multiproduct firms. In these firms acquisition of information on price elasticities for all products is both difficult and costly. The application of general costing margins to the various products becomes a routine which is easy to apply and yields on the average the target level of profit that the firm sets for its overall operation.

Thirdly, trade associations often publicise information of costs of individual product lines, and sometimes go so far as to develop standard cost accounting methods for their members. Use of such information or standard cost accounting techniques is bound to lead to similar prices (for broadly similar products) and hence to a tacit collusion, which co-ordinates the market mechanism.[1]

Fourthly, even without trade associations, average-cost rules of pricing secure 'orderly working' of the market, in that firms get used to these rules and learn to anticipate fairly accurately the reactions of competitors to changes in the environment.[2]

[1] See W. W. Haynes, 'Pricing Practices in Small Firms' *Southern Economic Journal* (1964) p. 317. Also R. M. Cyert and J. G. March, *A Behavioural Theory of the Firm* (Prentice-Hall, 1963).

[2] See A. Kaplan, J. Dirlam, and R. Lanzillotti, *Pricing in Big Business* (Brookings Institution, 1958).

In conclusion, we can say that average-cost rules of pricing are useful for avoiding uncertainty and to 'co-ordinate' the market. But the evidence of constant *AVC* (over the relevant ranges of output) strips the average-cost 'theory' of its essence as a new theory of long-run profit maximisation different from marginal analysis (applied in the long run as above described). Average-cost pricing practices should thus be interpreted as routine rules-of-thumb, which are adopted in the real world because they are useful as a market co-ordinating device, but cannot explain the motivations–goals and hence the decision-making of firms.[1]

---

[1] A somewhat obscure exposition of average-cost pricing as a market co-ordinating device may be found in Scherer, *Industrial Market Structure and Economic Performance* (Rand McNally, 1970) pp. 173–8.

SECTION D

LIMIT-PRICING (OR ENTRY-PREVENTING PRICING)

13. Bain's Limit-Pricing Theory

I. BAIN'S EARLY MODEL

Bain formulated his 'limit-price' theory in an article published in 1949,[1] several years before his major work *Barriers to New Competition* which was published in 1956. His aim in his early article was to explain why firms over a long period of time were keeping their price at a level of demand where the elasticity was below unity, that is, they did not charge the price which would maximise their revenue.[2] His conclusion was that the traditional theory was unable to explain this empirical fact due to the omission from the pricing decision of an important factor, namely the threat of *potential* entry. Traditional theory was concerned only with actual entry, which resulted in the long-run equilibrium of the firm and the industry (where $P = LAC$). However, the price, Bain argued, did not fall to the level of LAC in the long run because of the existence of barriers to entry, while at the same time price was not set at the level compatible with profit maximisation because of the threat of potential entry. Actually he maintained that price was set at a level above the LAC ($=$ pure competition price) and below the monopoly price (the price where $MC = MR$ and short-run profits are maximised). This behaviour can be explained by assuming that there are barriers to entry, and that the existing firms do not set the monopoly price but the '*limit price*', that is, the highest price which the established firms believe they can charge without inducing entry.

Bain, in his 1949 article, develops two models of price setting in oligopolistic markets.

Assumptions

1. There is a determinate long-run demand curve for industry output, which is unaffected by price adjustments of sellers or by entry. Hence the market marginal revenue curve is determinate. The long-run industry-demand curve shows the expected sales at different prices maintained over long periods.
2. There is effective collusion among the established oligopolists.
3. The established firms can compute a limit price, below which entry will not occur. The level at which the limit price will be set depends (*a*) on the estimation of costs of the potential entrant, (*b*) on the market elasticity of demand (*c*) on the shape and level of the LAC, (*d*) on the size of the market, (*e*) on the number of firms in the industry.

---

[1] J. Bain, 'Oligopoly and Entry-Prevention', *American Economic Review* (1947).
[2] If $e < 1$ then $MR < 0$, given $MR = P(1 - 1/e) < 0$. Hence the first condition for a maximum is violated, given $MC > 0$.

4. Above the limit price, entry is attracted and there is considerable uncertainty concerning the sales of the established firms (post entry).

5. The established firms seek the maximisation of their own long-run profit.

Model A: there is no collusion with the new entrant

Assume that the market demand is $DABD'$ and the corresponding marginal revenue is $Dabm$ (figure 13.1).

Assume further that the limit price (P_L) is correctly calculated (and known both to the existing firms and to the potential entrants). Given P_L, only the part AD' of the demand curve and the section am of the MR are certain for the firms. The part to the left of A, that is, DA is uncertain, because the behaviour of the entrant is not known.

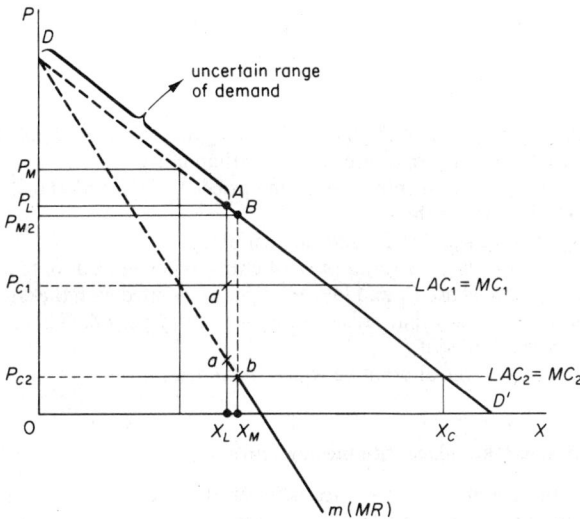

Figure 13.1

Whether the firms will charge the P_L or not depends on the profitability of alternatives open to them, given their costs.

Assume the LAC (which is uniquely determined by the addition of the $LMC = LAC$ of the collusive oligopolists) is LAC_1. In this case two alternatives are possible.

Either to charge the P_L (and realise the profit $P_L AdP_{C1}$ with certainty).

Or to charge the monopoly price, that is, the price that corresponds to the intersection of $LAC_1 = MC_1$ with the MR. This price will be higher than P_L (given LAC_1), but its precise level is uncertain post-entry. Thus the profits in the second alternative are uncertain and must be risk-discounted. The firm will compare the certain profits from charging P_L with the heavily risk-discounted profits from the second 'gamble' alternative, and will choose the price (P_L or P_M) that yields the greatest total profits.

Assume that the LAC is $LAC_2 = MC_2$. In this case the price that maximises profit is P_{M2} (corresponding to the intersection MC_2 and MR over the certain range of the latter). The P_{M2} is lower than P_L. The firm will clearly charge P_{M2} which maximises the profits. In this case the ceiling set by the price P_L is not operative.

The observed fact of setting the price at a level where $e < 1$ is justified by a situation where the limit price is low, cutting the demand curve at a point at which the MR is

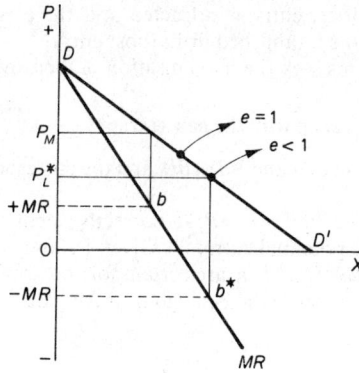

Figure 13.2

negative (figure 13.2). Clearly if the limit price is P_L^* the MR is b^* which is negative and hence the elasticity of demand at price P_L is less than unity.

In summary: given that an entry-preventing price P_L is defined, the alternatives open to the established firms are three:

1. To charge a price *equal to* P_L and prevent entry.
2. To charge a price *below* P_L and prevent entry (this will be adopted if $P_M < P_L$).
3. To charge a price *above* P_L and take the risks associated with the ensuing entry and the indeterminate situation that arises in the post-entry period. (This course of action will be in any case adopted if $P_L < LAC$).

The firm will choose the alternative which maximises profit.

Model B: collusion takes place with the new entrant

With collusion assumed to take place between the established firms and the entrant the conclusions are as before. The model is easier, however. With collusion the whole D curve shifts to the left by the share which is allocated to the new entrant at each price. The new DD'' curve is known with certainty at all its points, as a consequence of the collusion, and so is the corresponding m'' (figure 13.3). Again the alternatives open to the firm are three.

1. *Either* charge P_L and exploit AD' without entry.
2. *Or* charge a price above P_L and attract entry. The firm will eventually move to a point on the share-of-the-market curve DD'', via collusive agreement with the new entrant.
3. *Or* charge the profit-maximising price P_M, if $P_M < P_L$.

Among these alternatives the firm will choose the one that yields maximum profits.

The basic and crucial assumptions of the above analysis are: firstly, that the entrants react on the basis of the current price: they expect the price charged by the established firms to continue in the post-entry period; secondly, that the established firms are aware of the threat of potential entry; thirdly, that the established firms can estimate correctly the limit price. Then three major possibilities exist:

The policy of pricing to maximise industry profit with no entry resulting is adopted when $P_L > P_M$, i.e. the limit price is not operative because by charging the lower P_M price (monopoly price corresponding to $MC = MR$) profits (certain in this case) are maximised.

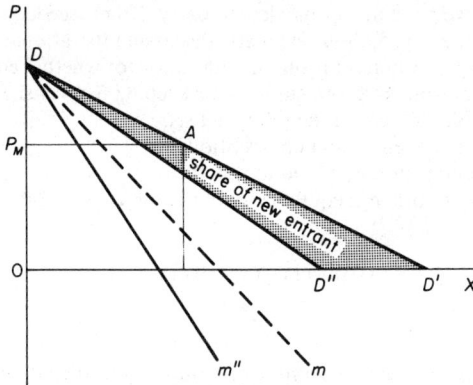

Figure 13.3

Pricing to forestall entry with industry profits not maximised, but the profit of established sellers maximised, is adopted when $P_L < P_M$ and the certain profit accruing by charging P_L is greater than the heavily risk-discounted profit which would accrue if the higher P_M were charged and an uncertain quantity sold.

Pricing to maximise industry profit but with resulting entry. This implies $P_M > P_L$. This action would be chosen if it is more profitable as compared with charging P_L; and necessarily, if $P_L < LAC$.

The first two situations lead to long-run equilibrium of the industry without entry or exit. The third case implies an unstable equilibrium since entry would be taking place.

In all the above cases one should add to the profits of established sellers any transitional profit which the established sellers might gain while raising the price above P_L and before entry became effective.

The new element of Bain's model is the redrawing of the market demand so as to account for the threat of entry. Once the demand is redefined, the model accepts collusion and profit maximisation as valid hypotheses, capable of explaining the policy of setting a price below the monopoly level, that is, below the level that maximises profit. Bain's model is not incompatible with profit maximisation. The limit price will be chosen in favour of monopoly price if the former yields maximum long-run profits. The rationale of adopting an entry-prevention policy is profit maximisation. Whenever such a limit price is adopted it is implied that the firm has done all the relevant calculations of profits of alternative policies and has adopted the limit price because this yields maximum profits.

II. BARRIERS TO NEW COMPETITION

In his book *Barriers to New Competition* (1956) Bain changes the basis of his study. In his 1949 article he tried to explain why the actual price set by oligopolists is below the monopoly price. His answer was that the retention of price below the monopoly level is due to the threat of potential entry. The firms charged the limit price, lower than the monopoly price, because the entry-prevention policy secured maximum long-run profits.

In his book Bain sets out to explain why price is set above the competitive price, that is, the price which is equal to the long-run AC. His conclusion is that the limit price is above the competitive price due to barriers to entry. He proceeded to develop a theory of pricing to prevent entry, without explicitly discussing its rationality, that is, without saying whether this policy aims at profit maximisation, or whether entry-prevention is a goal in itself, for achieving long-run survival, or keeping market share constant.

We will develop Bain's ideas in the following sequence:

1. Bain's concepts of entry and competition.
2. Barriers to entry (in theory and in practice).
3. Bain's theory of pricing: equilibrium of the industry.

A. BAIN'S CONCEPTS OF COMPETITION AND ENTRY

The concept of competition

Bain distinguishes between two types of competition, *actual competition* between established firms, and *potential competition* arising from the potential entry of firms outside the industry. Actual competition is probably of high importance as a regulator of business activity especially in oligopolistic markets. Existing firms act continuously under the feeling of interdependence with their actual competitors. However, the threat of potential entry is also an important determinant of the pricing policies of firms. There is a double form of recognised interdependence: interdependence among established firms, and interdependence between established firms and potential entrants.

In the traditional theory of pure competition and monopolistic competition entry is discussed explicitly.[1] In both models entry is treated as actual entry, whose effects on equilibrium are determinate, and as a long-run phenomenon, in the sense that entry can take place only in the long run. The latter implies that entry comes from completely new firms, starting from scratch. The former implies no consideration of the effects on current price – output decisions of the threat arising from *potential* entrants.

Both models assume that entry is free (in the sense of there being no legal restrictions) and easy in the long run (in the sense that there are no insurmountable barriers to entry).

The consequence of the assumption of free entry in pure competition is that in the long run equilibrium of each firm and of the industry is attained at

$$P = LAC = LMC$$

and costs are at a minimum.

The consequence of the assumption of free entry in a monopolistic market in the long run is that equilibrium is reached with the tangency solution

$$P = LAC \quad \text{and} \quad P > LMC$$

but costs are not at a minimum, because excess capacity is a necessary consequence of the falling demand curve.

In oligopolistic markets, however, conventional theory has in general been inexplicit, cryptic or silent. The naïve oligopoly models of Cournot, Bertrand, Edgeworth and Chamberlin are closed models, not allowing for entry: the number of firms in the model is assumed constant. The models of collusive solutions are also closed models. Cartels are inherently unstable and they break down once entry is allowed, while in the traditional models of price leadership the entrant is usually assumed to be a small firm which follows the leader.

---

[1] In the traditional theory of monopoly entry is explicitly assumed to be barred in both the short and the long run.

Fellner was the first writer to mention that the threat of potential entry is one of the reasons why the collusive oligopolists do not charge the monopoly price.

Entry considerations and their importance in pricing policies appeared fairly recently in the theory of the firm.[1] In this chapter we will examine Bain's contribution to the analysis of entry barriers. In Chapter 14 we will discuss some recent developments in the entry-forestalling theories.

The concept of entry in Bain's theory

Bain considers entry as the establishment of a *new firm* which builds or introduces *new productive capacity* that was not used for production in the industry prior to the establishment of the new firm. Thus for Bain entry involves the setting up of a *new* firm and the *addition of new capacity* in the industry.[2]

Bain explicitly excludes from his entry concept (*a*) the take-over of an existing firm by some other firm, which constitutes change in ownership; (*b*) the expansion of capacity by an established firm; (*c*) cross-entry, that is, entry by a firm already established in another industry, which adds the product of this industry to its line of products.

B. BARRIERS TO ENTRY

Bain introduced the concept of '*the condition of entry*', which he defined as the margin by which established firms can raise their price above the competitive price level *persistently* without attracting entry. Symbolically we have

$$E = \frac{P_L - P_C}{P_C}$$

where E = 'condition of entry'
   P_L = limit price
   P_C = competitive price, that is, price under pure competition in the long run ($P_C = LAC$).

Solving for P_L we find

$$P_L = P_C(1 + E)$$

Thus the condition of entry, E, is in fact the premium accruing to the established firms in an industry from charging a price, P_L, higher than the pure competitive price, P_C, without attracting entry.

[1] Hall and Hitch in their celebrated article 'Price Theory and Business Behaviour', *Oxford Economic Papers* (1939) mentioned potential entry as a determinant of pricing decisions. P. W. S. Andrews (in his *Manufacturing Business*, Macmillan London, 1949) and R. S. Edwards ('Price Formation in Manufacturing Industry and Excess Capacity', in *Oxford Economic Papers*, 1965) describe a pricing behaviour in which the threat of potential competition plays a prominent role. However, their exposition does not lead to a rigorous model of entry-prevention, unambiguously defined, despite the wealth of hypotheses emerging from these authors' works. Thus we did not attempt to present the ideas of these writers in any specific model.

[2] Although Bain mentions (p. 6) that the new firm can enter *either* by building new capacity, *or* by converting for use in this industry plants previously used in another industry, *or* by reactivating old capacity, in his subsequent analysis he concentrates on *new* capacity only. Surely the creation of a 'new legal entity' is typical of a completely new firm, and not of the introduction of a new line of product by an already established firm. Established firms would decide to create a 'new legal entity' only if this was advantageous (e.g. when there are tax advantages). In the modern industrial world this is rather rare. Diversification takes place without the creation of a new legal entity in most cases.

The time period which is implied in the above definition of the 'condition of entry' is 'long enough to encompass a typical range of varying conditions of demand, factor prices, and the like. This period normally might be thought of as 5 to 10 years', Bain argues (*Barriers to New Competition, p. 7*).

Given that Bain concentrates on entry by *new* firms, ignoring cross-entry, as well as the effects of take-overs on pricing behaviour, and of the expansion of capacity by existing firms, entry in his theory is a long-run phenomenon. The lag of entry is an important determinant of the barriers to entry. For example, the establishment of a firm in women's garments may require four months, in cement one to two years, in liquor four to five years. The longer the lag, the less the threat of entry and hence the greater the gap between the limit price P_L and the competitive price P_C.

The lag of entry, that is, the time required for a new firm to be established, depends on various factors which constitute the barriers to entry. Bain distinguishes four main barriers to entry: (1) Product-differentiation barrier, or preference-barrier. (2) Absolute-cost advantage of established firms. (3) Economies of scale. (4) Large initial capital requirements.

One could add to this list the legal barriers to entry which are imposed by law. These, however, are exogenous and if they exist entry is blocked. The firms protected by such legal barriers may charge any price without the fear of attracting new entrants.

We will examine Bain's barriers in some detail and present Bain's main empirical findings on the actual importance of these barriers in the real world.

Product-differentiation barrier

Some aspects of product differentiation were discussed initially by Chamberlin and subsequently by other writers. Traditional theory stressed the following consequences of product differentiation.

Product differentiation gives to the firm a degree of control on the price of its product. Product differentiation is also the reason for advertising and other selling activities, which actually aim at intensifying the differences between a firm's product and the products of competitors. Such expenses clearly affect both the demand and the costs of the firm.

Furthermore, product differentiation results in internal organisational changes of the firm. Thus large firms have to set up special sales departments to organise the promotion and distribution of their products.

Finally product differentiation also has some effect on the concentration of firms and on industry structure.

What was completely neglected in traditional theory was the importance of differentiation for *entry*. The preferences of buyers, attached to various existing brands, clearly create a barrier to the entry of a *new* firm. An entrant is at a disadvantage because he has to make his product known and attract some of the customary buyers of the product of other established firms. To surmount this goodwill or preference barrier a new firm must either offer its product at substantially lower price than the established firms, or do heavier advertising (and other selling activities) or both. Such activities lead to higher costs in the new firm and can formally be analysed on the same lines as the absolute cost advantage barrier, assuming that at all levels of output the new entrant will always have a higher cost. But even if the new firm manages to establish itself and reach a scale and a price–cost position similar to that of the established firms, the losses incurred at the initial stages of establishing goodwill will never be recovered.

Bain, in his monumental study of twenty manufacturing industries has found that the product-differentiation barrier is the most serious barrier to entry. It is more important for the modern differentiated oligopoly which produces branded consumer

commodities and to a smaller degree for those industries that produce branded producers' goods (machinery). The strength of this barrier depends firstly on the size of
advertising and other selling expenses required for establishing goodwill; secondly, on
the durability and complexity of the products; in purchasing durable or complex goods
the buyer relies more on reputation and information from friends who have used the
commodity; to acquire a similar reputation the new firm needs a long time and heavy
promotion expenses. The strength of this barrier depends also on the method of distribution of the commodity; if established firms use 'exclusive arrangements' practices with
wholesale dealers the new entrant is faced with increased difficulties. Finally, this barrier
is influenced by the importance of 'conspicuous consumption'; if established products
have a 'prestige' reputation a new entrant will have increased difficulties in his effort
to establish himself. In particular Bain's empirical findings regarding the preference
barrier may be summarised as follows:

Very important preference barriers were found in five industries (automobiles,
cigarettes, liquor, tractors, typewriters) and in some lines of expensive fountain pens
and heavy farm machinery.

Moderately important preference barriers were detected in four industries (tyres,
soap, petroleum refining, metal containers), and in specific lines of another three
industries (some canned fruit, flour sold branded to consumers, expensive branded
shoes).

In the remaining industries (general canned goods, cement, copper, gypsum products,
simple farm machinery, flour, cheap fountain pens, meat packing, rayon, low-price
shoes, steel) preference barriers were negligible.

These findings are not surprising given the fact that Bain examines the difficulties of
entry by completely *new* firms. However, the importance of the preference-barrier is
greatly diminished if one adopts the view of the typical entrant, which is a firm already
established in an industry (cross-entry or within entry) and already has built up its own
goodwill. Furthermore, product differentiation works also in the opposite direction:
it encourages entry. Given that in the modern industrial world the main weapon of
competition is product innovation, a firm can count on producing and establishing a
new-styled product, if it decides to enter a particular market, by adopting similar
tactics as existing firms.

Absolute cost advantage

Absolute cost advantage may arise from the following situations. (*a*) Skills of expert
management personnel. A completely new firm usually has difficulties in recruiting
trained managerial personnel and ordinarily it has to pay a higher salary in order to
attract managers away from other firms. (*b*) Patents and superior techniques (know-
how) available only to the established firms. (*c*) Control of the supply of key raw materials.
In this event, the entrant must either pay a higher price for the acquisition of such
materials or he will be coerced to use inferior substitutes. In both cases the advantage of
established firms is an indisputable fact, and the cost curve of the entrant will lie above
the cost curve of the established firms at *all* sizes of output (figure 13.4). (*d*) Lower prices
for raw materials due to exclusive arrangements with suppliers or because of bulk-buying
by the (large) established firms. (*e*) Lower cost of capital for the established firms.
A new firm may have to pay a higher interest rate for obtaining the capital required for
its setting up. Established firms have access to some internal financing or to the capital
markets at relatively favourable terms as compared to a new firm. (*f*) Lower cost due
to the vertical integration of the production processes of established firms. If the entrant
is to achieve the same advantageous cost structure, he will have to enter with a fully
integrated productive unit, and the absolute capital requirements for setting up such

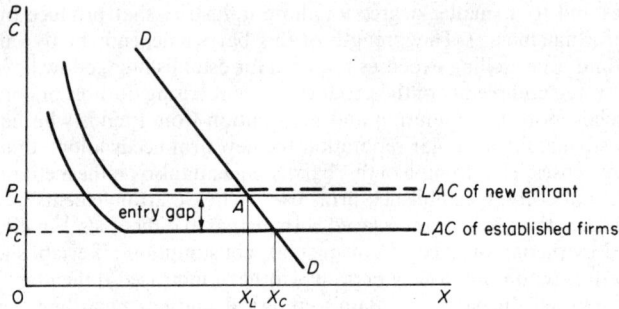

Figure 13.4   Absolute cost advantage barrier

a complex organisation may create an *absolute barrier to entry* (see below), and not merely an absolute cost disadvantage for the entrant.

If any type of absolute cost advantage exists the *LAC* of the entrant will be higher at every scale of production than that of the established firms (figure 13.4).

The entry-preventing price, P_L, will be set at a level just below the cost of the potential new entrant. The entrants demand is *AD*, that is, the part of the market demand to the right of X_L. The section *AD* of the market demand lies below the *LAC* of the entrant and hence entry becomes impossible, since the entrant cannot cover its costs at any level of output. The difference $P_L - P_C$ is called *the entry gap* and shows the amount by which established firms can raise their price above their costs, that is, above the competitive price P_C, without attracting entry. (Recall that the condition of entry is defined as the ratio of the entry gap over the competitive price.) From his empirical studies of twenty manufacturing industries Bain found that in general absolute cost barriers are less important than those arising from product differentiation or from economies of large-scale production. Slight absolute cost barriers commonly result from the difficulty of entrants in acquiring skilled managers and know-how. Ordinarily this barrier to entry would be reflected in 'shake-down losses' for a very limited time, or in slightly higher costs for a few years. Less frequent were barriers from patents or from control of key resources.

Bain found that in four industries (steel, copper, automobiles, petroleum refining) backward integration by the entrant was necessary to avoid a serious absolute cost disadvantage. In two industries (copper, steel) substantial cost barriers were found. These were due to close control of existing resources. Similarly, in the industry of gypsum products absolute-cost-advantage barriers were very important due to patents and secrecy in know-how. In the remaining seventeen industries absolute cost barriers were very slight.

Two points should be stressed with respect to the absolute-cost-advantage barrier. First, the absolute-cost-advantage barrier loses its significance if the entrant is an already-established firm in the same industry (intra-industry entry or within-entry) or in another industry (cross-industry entry or cross-entry). Such firms–entrants have their own trained managerial team, their own know-how, their own sources of supply, easy access to internal and external sources of finance, and will be already vertically integrated if this is advantageous. Patents or ownership of a key resource may still be barriers, but may also be an advantage if the entrants have the patent, or the key resource, or have hit upon an improved method of production. Secondly, if the entrant is a completely *new* firm, it has two advantages over existing firms. A new firm can plan its plant *de novo* (from scratch) and adopt the most up-to-date methods of production, while established firms have some old machinery, which cannot normally be scrapped completely in the short run. In addition, a new firm has absolute freedom to choose the location of its plant and its distribution channels, a choice which is not open to the already established firms (at least in the short run). These factors may significantly reduce or eliminate any other cost advantage that the established firms might enjoy.

Barrier from initial capital requirements

To set up a new business one needs an initial capital outlay, whose amount depends on the technology of the industry in which entry is being considered. One might argue that new firms have difficulties in securing the required initial amount of capital. Banks may be reluctant to finance a new business, and the capital market is almost inaccessible to a new firm which has not built up a reputation. If such a new entrant can secure the capital required, most often he will have to pay a higher interest rate than the established firms, and in this case he will have an absolute cost disadvantage. This, however, may be overcome in the long run if the firm succeeds and reaches the size that has the same costs as the established firms. However, in some cases it may be impossible for a new firm to obtain finance at any interest rate. In this case the initial capital requirement creates an absolute entry barrier, which is more probable if the amount of capital initially required is large.

From his empirical studies Bain found that absolute capital requirements have been important in five industries (steel, automobiles, petroleum refining, tractors, cigarettes), and somewhat less important in another five industries (rayon, liquor, cement, tyres, soap). Bain could not classify three industries (copper, farm machinery, typewriters) due to lack of sufficient information. In the remaining industries Bain did not find any significant barrier raised by absolute capital requirements (meat packing, fountain pens, metal containers, gypsum products, canned goods, flour, shoes).

We should like to point out that Bain's findings are not surprising given his concentration on the entry of *new* firms. Clearly, if the entrant is an already-established firm, it will not have difficulties in securing the finance required for expansion, either from internal funds or from the capital market. Furthermore, the widespread diversification and conglomerate movement facilitates the finance of a new firm or a new venture within the conglomerate: the finance requirements are most often provided by other member-firms of the conglomerate.

Economies of scale[1]

Economies of scale may be *real* (those which reduce the inputs of factors per unit of output) or *pecuniary* (those which result from paying a lower price for the inputs purchased by the firm). The latter do not reduce the quantity of inputs, but rather the money cost of the inputs for the particular firms.

Real economies are technical (resulting from using more efficient large-scale machinery), managerial (resulting from spreading the managerial fixed input over a larger amount of output) and labour economies (arising from the greater specialisation of labour).

---

[1] Bain has studied two types of scale economies, (*a*) single-plant economies, (*b*) multiplant economies. We will not deal with the second type of economies, because the results of Bain's study show that these economies do not affect the conclusions drawn from the single-plant economies.

Pecuniary economies arise from bulk-buying at preferential lower prices; lower transport costs achieved when output is large; and lower advertising and other selling costs per unit of output.[1]

Whatever their nature economies of scale, whenever present, do form an important barrier to entry for new firms.

The analysis of this barrier is not as simple as the previous ones, because the effects of the economies of scale on the level of the limit price depend on the expectations of entrants about the reactions of established firms after entry, as well as on the expectations of the established firms about the behaviour of entrants. Various reaction patterns may arise. Bain cites six possible categories of conjecture by potential entrants.

Firstly. The potential entrant expects that established firms will keep the price constant post-entry.

Secondly. The potential entrant expects that established firms will retain their output constant at the pre-entry level.

Thirdly. The potential entrant expects that established firms will partly reduce their output and will allow the price to fall, but by less than in the previous case.

Fourthly. The potential entrant expects 'retaliation' by the established firms, that is, he expects that existing firms will increase their pre-entry output, thus effecting a greater fall in price than in the second case.

Fifthly. The entrant expects that established firms will substantially reduce their quantity of output so that the price rises above the pre-entry level.

Sixthly. The entrant expects that his entry will be 'unnoticed', because he enters at an insignificantly small scale. Thus he expects that the existing firms will change neither their quantity nor allow a change in the market price.

Bain states that the most probable conjecture is the third one, in which the entrant expects that the existing firms will partly reduce their output and will also allow the market price to fall, thus partly accommodating the entrant. This is an intermediate conjecture between the first and the second cases. Thus Bain concentrates his analysis on the first two 'limiting cases' because in this way the content of the most likely third conjecture 'is best understood by examining the two limiting cases which surround it'. The last three patterns of behaviour are not examined by Bain on the grounds that they are unlikely and unrealistic.

The following set of assumptions and definitions underlies Bain's models:

1. For each industry there exists a *minimum optimal scale of plant*, that is, a minimum plant size at which the economies of scale are fully realised. We will denote the minimum optimal scale by $\bar{x}$.

2. The *LAC* curve is L-shaped. Costs remain constant beyond the minimum optimal scale (figure 13.5).

3. The *LAC* is the same for all firms, the established ones and the potential entrant, since technology is the same for all. The advantage of the established firms is that they have already reached scales of output larger than the minimum optimal $\bar{x}$, while the entrant will have to establish himself gradually, starting perhaps from suboptimal levels of production ($x < \bar{x}$). In this event the entrant must be assumed to expect that he will eventually reach the minimum optimal scale $\bar{x}$, otherwise he would not enter the market.

4. The flat part of the *LAC* curve determines the long-run competitive price, P_C, because price cannot remain below the *LAC* in the long run. Thus $P_C = LAC$ (over the flat part of the long average-cost curve). The output corresponding to the competitive

---

[1] The distinction between real and pecuniary economies is irrelevant for the analysis of the barriers to entry. But it is useful for other purposes and in particular for the welfare implications of these economies. Real economies are socially desirable, while the desirability of pecuniary economies depends on the particular conditions of the industry being examined.

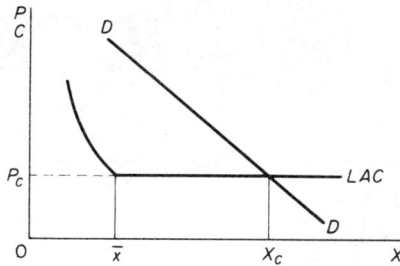

Figure 13.5

price, given the market-demand curve *DD*, is the *competitive market size (or competitive output)*. It will be denoted throughout by X_C.

5. The market-demand curve *DD* is known to all firms, existing and potential entrants. That is, all firms know the price elasticity of the market-demand curve.

6. All firms produce very similar products, so that the price is the same for all competitors (actual and potential). This assumption isolates the scale-barrier from the preference-barrier. If the two co-exist, the one reinforces the other, so that the overall entry-barrier will be stronger.

7. All firms are assumed to have equal market shares. Although this is a simplifying assumption, it is not unrealistic given the earlier assumption of the homogeneity of the products of the firms. It is further assumed that the entrant will capture the same share as the existing firms, that is, the total market is equally shared between the old and the new firms.

8. The share of each firm is a constant proportion of the market demand at all price levels. Thus we may use a share-of-the-market-demand curve for the individual firm, which shows a constant share of the total market at all prices. The share-demand curve, denoted by *d*, has the same price elasticity as the market demand at all price levels.[1]

Under the above set of assumptions we may use the individual *LAC* and *dd* curves to derive the equilibrium of the firm and the industry. In figure 13.6 the two graphs are drawn with different units of measurement for the quantity of output. The right-hand

[1] *Proof*

(a) The price elasticity of the market demand is defined as

$$e = \frac{\partial Q}{\partial P} \cdot \frac{P}{Q}$$

(b) The firm has a constant market share equal to k per cent of the total market demand

$$q = k \cdot Q$$

where q is the individual demand of the firm.

(c) The price elasticity of the individual demand curve is

$$e^* = \frac{\partial q}{\partial P} \cdot \frac{P}{q}$$

Substituting $q = k \cdot Q$ we obtain

$$e^* = \frac{\partial(kQ)}{\partial P} \cdot \frac{P}{(kQ)} = k \frac{\partial Q}{\partial P} \cdot \frac{P}{kQ} = e$$

given that k is a constant and does not affect the derivative (Q.E.D.).

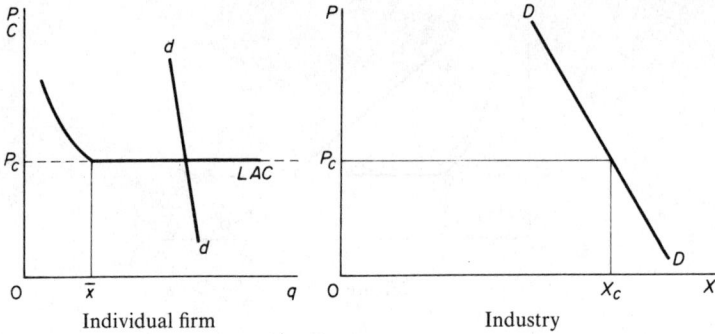

Figure 13.6

figure refers to the industry, with DD the aggregate demand curve and X_C the competitive output at $P_C = LAC$. The left-hand diagram refers to the individual firm.

We may now turn to the examination of Bain's models.

Model A: constant P, at the pre-entry level

The behavioural pattern of this model may be stated as follows. The entrant expects that the established firms will keep their price constant at the pre-entry level (unless the price is undercut by the entrant himself) and allow the entrant to secure any share he can at this price. This implies that, given the market DD curve, the established firms will 'accommodate' the entrant, their market shares being reduced by the amount that the entrant will sell.

The established firms will set the price at a level which will make entry unattractive to outside firms

$$P_L = P_c(1 + E)$$

The premium E by which the limit price will exceed the competitive price depends on four factors: (1) The initial share d of the entrant relative to the minimum optimal scale $\bar{x}$. (2) The number of firms in the industry, N. (3) The steepness of the LAC curve. (4) The elasticity of demand, e.

The share of the entrant, d, *relative to* x̄

If the actual share of the entrant is equal to or greater than the minimum optimal size of plant $\bar{x}$, there is no barrier to entry. The established firms cannot set a price to prevent entry higher than P_C. Given $\bar{x}$, the smaller the share d is, the higher the premium E will be. Thus d and E are negatively related. In figure 13.7 the minimum optimal plant size is $\bar{x}$. If the share-demand curve is d_1 or any other such curve to the right of d_1, there is no price larger than $P_C = LAC$ which would prevent entry. If the share is smaller than $\bar{x}$ there is a scale-barrier and P_L will be larger, the smaller the actual share. For example, the limit price P_{L_3} is higher when the share is d_3, as compared to the level P_{L_2} corresponding to share d_2 (where $d_3 < d_2$).

The number of existing firms in the industry, N

It is assumed that if entry occurs the share of the entrant (and of every other firm) will be smaller than $\bar{x}$. Thus the greater the number of firms in the industry (the more

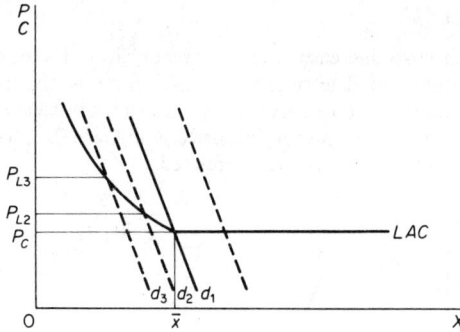

Figure 13.7

'crowded' the industry is) the greater the premium and the higher the entry-preventing price will be. The number of established firms N and the premium E are positively related, because N determines how much smaller than $\bar{x}$ the actual share d will be post-entry. In figure 13.8 we assume the pre-entry share is d_1. If entry occurs the share curve will shift to the left, say to the position d'_1, where the share of all firms will be smaller than $\bar{x}$. The established firms may prevent entry by charging the price P_{L_1} on the assumption that the potential entrant will not be attracted if he is to operate with suboptimal scale of output. If the industry initially was so 'crowded' that established firms had shares d_2 instead of d_1, entry would shift the shares to d'_2, and the entry-preventing price would be higher, P_{L_2}.

One might argue that since by assumption shares are equal and costs are the same, all firms including the entrant, will be equally worse off in the post-entry situation, producing at a suboptimal scale, and under these conditions survival is a matter of financial strength and of chance. This argument implies irrational behaviour of the entrant, since no rational entrepreneur will normally enter a market if he knows that he will not be able to work his plant at optimal capacity. Furthermore, the assumption that the entrant will capture an equal share with the established firms is rather optimistic, since the product of the entrant is new in the market. It is probably more reasonable to expect that the entrant's share will be smaller, at least initially.

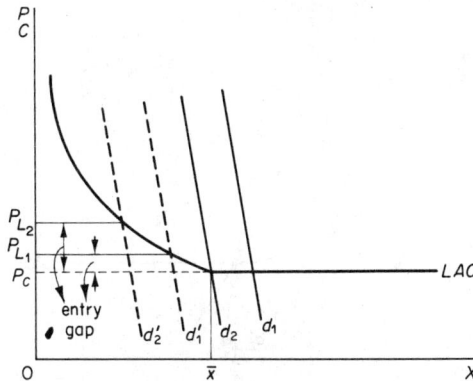

Figure 13.8

The steepness of the LAC

The rate at which costs increase when the plant is used suboptimally is another determinant of the premium. The steeper the *LAC* curve is, the higher the premium. In figure 13.9 we see that if the cost curve is LAC_1 the limit price is P_{L_1}. If the cost curve is steeper (e.g. LAC_2) the entry-preventing price is higher (P_{L_2}). The steepness of the *LAC* curve and the premium are positively related.

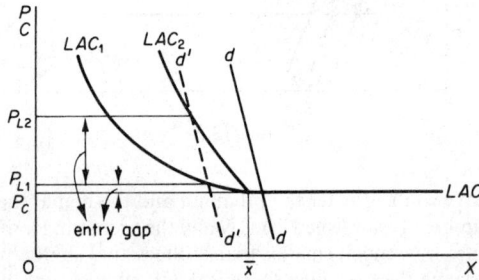

Figure 13.9

The elasticity of the industry demand curve

The elasticity of the market demand is by assumption the same as the elasticity of the individual-share curve. The greater the price elasticity, the higher the premium and the higher the entry-preventing price will be. In figure 13.10 with the pre-entry-share curve d_1 the entry-preventing price will be P_{L_1}. However, with a pre-entry-share curve like d_2, which is more elastic that d_1 the entry-preventing price would be higher, P_{L_2}.

In summary, if the entrant expects the price to remain constant and his actual share is equal to or greater than $\bar{x}$, there is no barrier to entry and the established firms cannot find a price above the minimal cost (P_C) which will exclude entry.

However, if the share is smaller than $\bar{x}$, then there exists a scale-barrier; the limit price will be above the $P_C = LAC$. The amount by which P_L will exceed P_C, that is, the entry gap will be higher the larger the number of firms in the industry, the steeper the *LAC*, the larger the elasticity of market demand and the smaller the share d relative to the minimum optimal plant size $\bar{x}$.

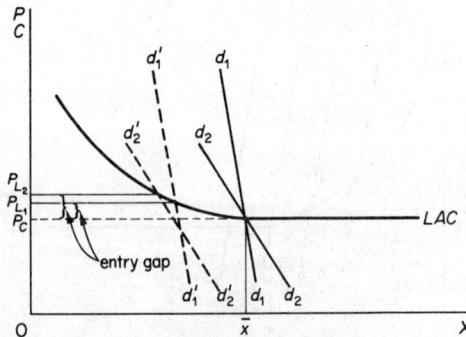

Figure 13.10

Model B: constant quantity Q, at the pre-entry level

The entrant expects that the established firms will retain their output constant, thus permitting industry price to fall as a consequence of such additions to industry output as the entrant is able to make. The established firms keep their output at the pre-entry level and allow the added output of the entrant to lower price accordingly. The existing firms expect that entry will not occur if the price falls below the minimum range of the *LAC* curve. It is also assumed that the entrant will enter at the minimum optimal plant size $\bar{x}$.

Under the above assumptions there is a scale-barrier to entry. The existing firms will charge an entry-preventing price which is above the competitive price

$$P_L = P_C(1 + E)$$

The determinants of the premium by which the limit price will exceed the $P_C(=LAC)$ are: (1) The minimum optimal scale, $\bar{x}$. (2) The size of the market at the competitive price, X_C. (3) The elasticity of market demand. (4) The number of established firms in the industry.

The premium is positively correlated with $\bar{x}$. The larger the minimum optimal scale the higher the price that the existing firms will be able to charge without attracting entry.

The premium is negatively related to the market size, X_C, and the price elasticity of demand, e. Thus the limit price will be higher the smaller X_C and the smaller e.

Finally, the premium is positively related to the number of firms in the industry. The larger the number of existing firms the higher the limit price will be.

The above factors that affect the limit price in this model will be discussed in detail in Chapter 14 within the framework of the Sylos-Labini theory of limit-pricing. (Sylos-Labini concentrated his analysis on the scale-barrier, while Bain examined all major types of barriers to entry). Bain did not use diagrams for this model. We will present relevant graphs for the individual determinants of the limit price in Chapter 14. Here we will show the determination of the limit price assuming given $\bar{x}$, X_C, N, and e.

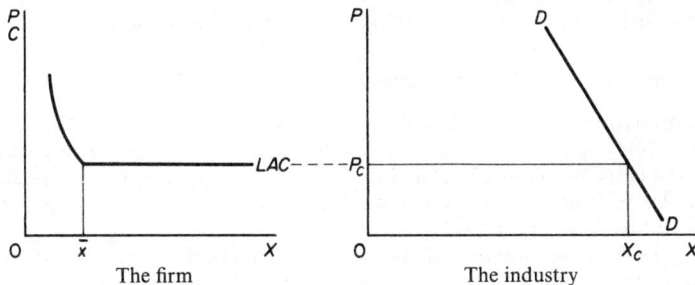

Figure 13.11

In figure 13.11 we show graphs for the individual firm and for the industry. It is more convenient to use the industry graph for the presentation of this model. Given the *LAC* curve and the minimum optimal scale plant $\bar{x}$ we may determine the market size X_C at the competitive price $P_C = LAC$ (figure 13.11).

The limit price is set by determining the total level of output that the existing firms will produce so as to prevent entry. The established firms will produce a quantity X_L such that, if the entrant adds his minimum optimal output $\bar{x}$, the market price will fall

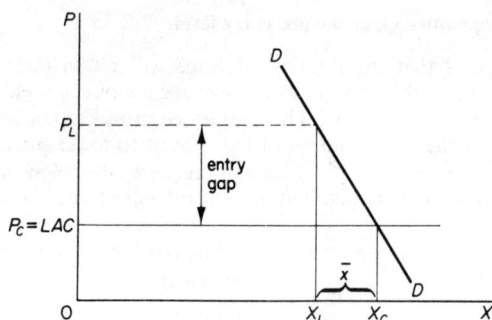

Figure 13.12

(just) below the $LAC = P_C$. Clearly

$$X_L = X_C - \bar{x}$$

Having determined X_L, the limit price P_L is defined simultaneously from the given market-demand curve DD (figure 13.12). The limit price will be higher the larger $\bar{x}$, the larger N, the smaller X_C and the smaller the price elasticity e (see Chapter 14).

Model C: price and output change post-entry

The entrant expects the established firms partly to decrease their quantity and partly to allow the price to fall. In other words the established firms 'accommodate' the entrant only partially. This is the intermediate case between the above two limiting cases. Bain (p. 109) says that this is the more realistic and probable expectation. Existing firms will reduce their output somewhat, but not enough to maintain prices in the face of entry. In this case the entry-barriers resulting from economies of scale alone will lie somewhere between the barriers of the limit-pricing models A and B.

Model D: increase of the pre-entry output

The entrant expects the established firms to increase their output, thus driving price below the LAC until the entrant is closed down. They can subsequently elevate the price to the entry-preventing level and no entry will occur since any potential entrant will have learned the 'retaliation' lesson. Bain does not deal with this case, assuming that its occurrence is very unlikely.

Bain found from his empirical studies that the scale-barriers were important only in three out of the twenty industries that he included in his research: in the automobile, tractor and typewriter industries.

Bain's empirical evidence regarding the importance of scale-barriers to entry may be summarised as follows.

Scale-barriers were very important for two industries (automobiles, typewriters). Substantial barriers (moderately important) were found in seven industries (cement, farm machinery, steel, tractors, rayon, soap, shoes). Scale-barriers were important in seven industries (canned goods, cigarettes, flour, liquor, meat packing, petroleum refining, tyres and tubes). The remaining four industries (copper, gypsum products, fountain pens, metal containers) could not be classified due to insufficient information on the shape of the cost curve of plant sizes.

III. SUMMARY OF BAIN'S EMPIRICAL FINDINGS

Table 13.1 summarises Bain's empirical findings. The notation adopted by Bain for the classification of the twenty industries in his study of the strength of the barriers to entry is the following:

Importance of barrier	*Notation*
Very strong (important) barriers	III
Substantial barriers (moderately important)	II
Unimportant (small) barriers	I
Insignificant barriers	Φ
Not classified	n.a.

In interpreting Bain's findings one should bear in mind that Bain considered the barriers faced by *completely new* firms. This limits seriously the generality of his results. If we take into account that the most typical form of entry is that of an already-established firm which diversifies its production, or integrates vertically, or takes over other firms, or merges with other existing firms, one should expect that Bain's results are not valid in the modern business world. Cross-entry and within-entry practically eliminate the importance of barriers to entry.

IV. INDUSTRY EQUILIBRIUM

In oligopolistic markets each of the few large firms, whether they act collusively or singly, will appraise the barriers to entry, that is the importance of the threat of potential entrants, and will set a price low enough to forestall entry.

If costs are the same for all established firms, they can arrive at the limit price sooner or later by independent action, via trial and error. Collusion is not necessary if costs and efficiency are identical, although with collusive action the limit price will be arrived at quicker and with less danger of 'spoiling the market' by triggering off a price war. However, if efficiencies differ among established firms, the limit price will be set by the most efficient, least-cost, firm.

The threat of potential entry, defined by the strength of barriers to entry, is crucial in pricing decisions. There is a recognised double interdependence between existing firms, and between them and potential entrants. The actual competition is taken into account either by various competitive devices (price, advertising, product style) if costs are similar and efficiencies the same, or via collusion, if costs and efficiencies differ between established firms. Potential competition is dealt with by charging the limit price.

We said that the estimate by the established firms of the strength of barriers is summarised in what Bain calls '*the condition of entry*'. Recall that this is defined as the percentage by which established firms can raise their price above the competitive level (P_C) without attracting entry:

$$E = \frac{P_L - P_c}{P_c}$$

where E = condition of entry
       P_C = competitive price ($= LAC$)
       P_L = limit price

Table 13.1   Summary of relative heights of entry barriers in the U.S. manufacturing industry

Industry	Scale-economies barrier	Product-differentiation barrier	Absolute-cost-advantage barrier	Initial-capital-requirement barrier	Overall barriers
Automobiles	III	III	I	III	III
Canned goods	I	I–II	I	I	I
Cement	I	I	I	II	I
Cigarettes	I	III	I	III	III
Copper	n.a.	I	III	n.a.	II
Farm machinery	II	I–III	I	n.a.	I–II
Flour	I	I–II	I	Φ	I
Fountain pens	n.a.	I–III	I	I	I–III
Gypsum products	n.a.	I	III	I	I
Liquor	I	III	I	II	III
Meat packing	I	I	I	Φ–I	I
Metal containers	n.a.	II	I	I	I
Petroleum refining	I	II	I	III	II
Rayon	II	II	I	III	I–II
Shoes	II	I–II	I	Φ	I
Soap	II	II	I	II	I–II
Steel	II	I	III	III	II
Tractors	II	III	I	III	III
Typewriters	III	III	I	n.a.	III
Tyres and tubes	III	II	I	II	III

Note: The table is based on Bain's book, *Barriers to New Competition* (Harvard University Press, 1956), pp. 90–2, 127–9, 155, 166, 170.

Rearranging the above formula we obtain

$$P_L = P_c(1 + E)$$

In this form we see that the price limiting entry is determined by the competitive price (= the *LAC* of the most efficient firm) and the premium E which is a measure of the barriers to entry.

If entry is easy, barriers are non-existent (or negligible). Thus $E = 0$, and hence

$$P_L = P_c = LAC$$

That is, if barriers are not present the price actually set will be the competitive price, which is equal to the *LAC* of the most efficient firm. If barriers exist $E > 0$ and hence

$$P_L > P_c$$

That is, the firms will be able to charge a price P_L which will be higher than P_c and they will be earning abnormal profits (since $P_L > LAC$), although these may be absorbed by higher selling costs or other inefficiencies which develop gradually if firms are protected behind high barriers from 'outside' competition.

The competitive level of price is equal to the *LAC* of the most efficient firm. The long-run-cost curve is L-shaped: long-run costs are approximately constant as the firm size exceeds the minimum optimal scale. The *LAC* ($= P_c$) includes a normal profit, that is, a normal return to capital, taking also into account any risk particular to the product and process employed by the firm. Thus E is a premium, a margin above the long-run competitive price.

In the real world, firms have differentiated products and different efficiencies. Firms have different demands and different costs. However, the industry concept can be maintained. The 'industry' includes products for which a stable relative price–quality pattern emerges. As Hicks and Samuelson[1] have shown, such a group of products can be treated as one for demand purposes. In practice it has been observed[2] that there are products which can be classified within a 'broad commodity group' which may for all practical purposes be characterised as a distinct 'industry'; because, in fact, there is a tendency for the pattern of production (within such a broad commodity group) to stabilise in settled conditions into a conventional product–pattern with a corresponding conventional price-pattern. Of course, the price–quality pattern will not in fact remain strictly stable, but the degree of stability is adequate to justify the retention of the 'industry' concept and to proceed in analysis on a partial equilibrium approach.

Thus in equilibrium the price is not unique. There is a cluster of prices reflecting the differences in product-quality and costs. Under these conditions the 'condition of entry' (E) may be measured specifically as *the maximum gap* between price and the minimal cost of the most efficient firm(s) at which entry is forestalled:

> The condition of entry (E) is measured by the long-run gap between minimal cost and price which the most favoured firms can reach without attracting entry. (Bain, *Barriers to New Competition*).

> The less efficient firms will be making 'concurrent price elevations'. The entry-gap between price and minimum cost will be the one observed when all established firms elevate their prices concurrently by similar amounts or proportions, maintaining any customary competitive price differentials. (Bain, *Barriers to New Competition*).

[1] J. R. Hicks, *Value and Capital* (Oxford University Press, 1946) pp. 311–12 and P. A. Samuelson, *Foundations of Economic Analysis* (Harvard University Press, Cambridge, Mass., 1947) pp. 141–3.

[2] See, for example, H. R. Edwards, *Competition and Monopoly in the British Soap Industry* (Oxford University Press, 1964) p. 54.

There are many potential entrants. But the one that is crucial for the pricing decision of the established firms is the potential firm with the lowest costs as compared with the other potential entrants. Thus the relevant entrant is the 'most-favoured' entrant in the sense that he has the lowest costs and thus will be the first to enter once the price–cost difference is sufficient to grant him a profitable existence.

In summary, the price is set by the firm which has the lowest cost. This firm acts as the leader, and sets the price at a level adequate to forestall entry. The less efficient firms will be followers. Prices may differ to reflect traditional product differences. But the price-cluster is formed on the basis of the entry-preventing policy of the most-favoured leader-firm.

V. SOME COMMENTS

Bain's contribution to the theory of the firm is important. His 1949 article and his 1956 book contain the elements of an interesting theory of pricing: pricing to prevent entry.

The exposition is tedious and lacks rigour. Nevertheless Bain's work contains seminal ideas on the importance of potential entry in pricing decisions.

Bain's empirical findings have serious limitations due to the narrow definition of entry. Bain concentrates on entry by new firms. He omits cross-entry, take-overs, vertical integration, and addition to capacity by existing firms. All these situations have serious implications for the pricing behaviour of the firm.

Finally, Bain fails to see that product-differentiation and scale economies may enhance the likelihood of entry under certain conditions.

Bain's theory of pricing is basically collusive. The price is set by the firm with the lowest cost, and the less efficient firms are price followers. The leader, however, does not set price to maximise his own short-run profit, as the traditional theory of the price leader postulates, but rather aims at a price which would prevent entry. The rationale of this policy is that by preventing entry long-run profits are maximised.

14. Recent Developments in the Theory of Limit-Pricing

I. THE MODEL OF SYLOS-LABINI

Sylos-Labini[1] developed a model of limit-pricing based on scale-barriers to entry. His model is clumsy, due to its unnecessarily stringent assumptions and the use of arithmetical examples. However, his analysis of the economies-of-scale barrier is more thorough than that of Bain. He highlighted the determinants of the limit price and discussed their implications, thus providing the basis for Modigliani's more general model of entry-preventing pricing.

Sylos-Labini concentrated his analysis on the case of a homogeneous oligopoly whose technology is characterised by technical discontinuities and economies of scale.

Assumptions

1. The market demand is given and has unitary elasticity. The product is homogeneous and will be sold at a unique equilibrium price.

2. The technology consists of three types of plant: a small plant with a capacity of 100 units of output; a medium-size plant with a capacity of 1000 units of output; a large-size plant with a capacity of 8000 units of output. Each firm can expand by multiples of its initial plant size only. That is, a small firm may expand by installing another small plant, a medium firm may expand by setting up a second medium-size plant, and so on. There are economies of scale: cost decreases as the size of the plant increases. However, with this rigid technology we cannot construct a continuous $LRAC$ curve. We have three cost lines, corresponding to the three plant sizes (figure 14.1).

3. The price is set by the price leader who is the largest firm, with the lowest cost (*ex hypothesi*) at a level low enough to prevent entry. The smaller firms are price-takers. Each one individually cannot affect the price. However, collectively they may put pressure on the leader by regulating their output. Thus the largest firm does not have unlimited discretion in setting the price: it must set a price that is acceptable to all the firms in the industry (Sylos-Labini, *Oligopoly and Technical Progress*, p. 39) as well as preventing entry.

[1] P. Sylos-Labini, *Oligopoly and Technical Progress* (Harvard University Press, Cambridge Mass., 1957).

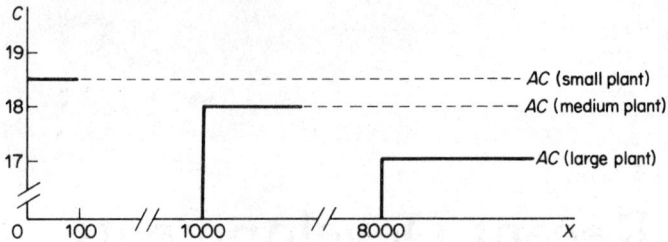

Figure 14.1

4. There is a normal rate of profit in each industry. (Sylos, in his example, assumed that the rate of normal profit is 5 per cent.)

5. The leader is assumed to know the cost structure of all plant sizes, and the market demand.

6. The entrant is assumed to come into the industry with the smallest plant size.

7. The established firms and the entrant behave according to what Modigliani called the 'Sylos's Postulate'. This includes two behavioural rules, one describing the expectations of the established firms and the other the expectations of the entrant. Firstly, the existing firms expect that the potential entrant will not come into the market if he thinks that the price post-entry will fall below his *LAC*. Secondly, the entrant expects that the established firms will continue in the post-entry period to produce the same level of output as pre-entry. Under these assumptions, as entry takes place the market price falls and the whole of the resulting increase in the quantity demanded accrues to the new entrant. Clearly this is the same as Bain's Model *B*.

Sylos does not give any reason for this behavioural pattern. The rationalisation of the Sylos's postulate has been discussed by subsequent writers.[1]

The model

Sylos-Labini presents his model with a numerical example. He starts with the market structure shown in table 14.1 which is assumed to be created at random, and proceeds to examine how equilibrium is attained in this market. The equilibrium at price 20 is not

Table 14.1   Initial market structure

Plant size	Capacity (units of X)	Number of firms	Total output X	Initial price (arbitrary units)	Market demand (value)
Small (X_s)	$X_s = 100$	20	2000	20	40,000
Medium (X_m)	$X_m = 1000$	2	2000	20	40,000
Large (X_l)	$X_l = 8000$	1	8000	20	160,000
Total market		23	12,000		240,000

[1] See H. R. Edwards, *Competition and Monopoly in the British Soap Industry*. Also J. N. Bhagwati, 'Oligopoly Theory, Entry-Prevention and Growth', *Oxford Economic Papers* (1970).

Table 14.2 Cost structure of firms, with the assumed technology

Plant size	Capacity output	TFC	AFC	TVC	AVC	TC	ATC	Profit rate % on ATC	Unit profit	Price	Total revenue
Small firm	100	100	1	1750	17·5	1850	18·5	8·1	1·5	20·0	2000
								5·4	1·0	19·5	1950
								5·0	0·9	**19·4**	1940
Medium firm	1000	2000	2	16,000	16	18,000	18	11·1	2·0	20·0	20,000
								8·3	1·5	19·5	19,500
								7·8	1·4	19·4	19,400
								6·7	1·2	19·2	19,200
								5·0	0·9	**18·9**	18,900
Large firm	8000	24,000	3	112,000	14	136,000	17	17·6	3·0	20·0	160,000
								14·7	2·5	19·5	156,000
								14·1	2·4	19·4	155,200
								12·9	2·2	19·2	153,600
								5·0	0·85	**17·85**	142,800

stable, because the market output is too small and the price is too high, so entry will take place. This is due to the fact that, given the cost structure of the three plants in the industry (see table 14.2), the profits are too high for all firms at the price of 20. From table 14.2 it is apparent that the profit rate of the small firms is 8·1 per cent of the medium firms 11·1 per cent and of the large firms 17·6 per cent. These rates are higher than the minimum profit rate (normal profit) of the industry which is assumed to be 5 per cent. The excess profits will attract entry. Under the above rigid assumptions regarding technology, the possibility of expansion of the existing firms by multiples of their initial plant size and the unitary elasticity of demand, the following results emerge:

No new large firm will enter into the industry. If it did, total sales would rise to 20,000 units and the price would fall to 12, a level lower than the minimum acceptable price to any firm in the industry. From table 14.2 we can see that the minimum acceptable prices for the three plant sizes are 19·4 (for the small plant), 18·9 (for the medium size plant) and 17·85 (for the large scale plant).

Even the entry of a new medium-size firm is precluded given the costs and the demand in the industry. If a medium-size plant were installed sales would increase to 13,000 units, and the price would fall to 18·4, which is not acceptable by the small and the medium-size firms.

However, up to three small firms can enter the market. Their entry would cause sales to rise to 12,300 units and the price to fall to 19·5, which exceeds the minimum acceptable price of all firms. The entry of a fourth small firm would depress the price to 19·3, a level below the minimum acceptable price (of 19·4) of the small firms.

Thus the entry-forestalling price is just above the minimum acceptable level of the smallest, least efficient firms.

The above results regarding the entry conditions under the given cost and demand conditions are shown in table 14.3. The computations are based on the assumption that the demand has unitary elasticity so that the total expenditure is the same (equal to the initial level of 240,000) at all prices.

Table 14.3   Prices and level of output yielding a total expenditure of 240,000

Output X	Price P	Total expenditure $R = XP$ $(e = 1)$
12,000	20·0	240,000
12,100	19·8	240,000
12,200	19·6	240,000
12,300	19·5	240,000
12,400	19·3	240,000
12,500	19·2	240,000
12,770	18·8	240,000
13,000	18·4	240,000
18,000	13·3	240,000
20,000	12·0	240,000

Price determination

We said that the price is set by the largest, most efficient firm. The equilibrium price must be acceptable by all the firms in the industry, and should be at a level which would prevent entry.

Given that firms have different costs, there are as many minimum acceptable prices as plant sizes. For each plant the minimum acceptable price is defined on the average-cost principle

$$P_i = TAC_i(1 + r)$$

where P_i = the minimum acceptable price for the ith plant size
    TAC_i = total average cost for the ith plant size
    r = normal profit rate of the industry

The minimum acceptable price covers the TAC of the plant and the normal (minimum) profit rate of the industry (in Sylos's example $r = 5$ per cent for all plant sizes, that is, the normal profit of the *industry* is 5 per cent).

The price leader is assumed to know the cost structure of all plant sizes and the normal (minimum) profit rate of the industry. Given this information the leader will set the price that is acceptable by the smallest, least efficient firms, and will deter entry.

The price tends to settle at a level immediately above the entry preventing price of the least efficient firms, which it is to the advantage of the largest and most efficient firms to let live....[1]

The price leader, which is the most efficient firm, will set the price at a level acceptable to all existing firms and low enough to forestall entry. Entry takes place with the minimum plant scale which has the highest cost. In Sylos's model, where differential costs are assumed, the price, in order to be a long-run equilibrium one, apart from preventing entry must also be acceptable by the least efficient firms, allowing them to earn at least the normal industry profit given that the most efficient firm (leader) does not find it worth while to eliminate the smaller firms, either because such action is not profitable or because the leader is afraid of attracting government intervention due to high concentration in the industry. Clearly the medium and large-scale firms, having lower costs, will be earning abnormal profits. But small firms will also normally be earning some abnormal profits without attracting entry. Given the market demand at the minimum acceptable price of the smallest least efficient firm (and given that at that price all established firms work their plants to full capacity), the price leader will set the price at such a level, that, if the entrant decides to enter, the market price will fall below his minimum acceptable price (which is the same as the minimum acceptable price of the smallest, least efficient plant size). In figure 14.2 the market demand at the minimum acceptable price P_S of the smallest, least efficient, firm is X. The leader will set the

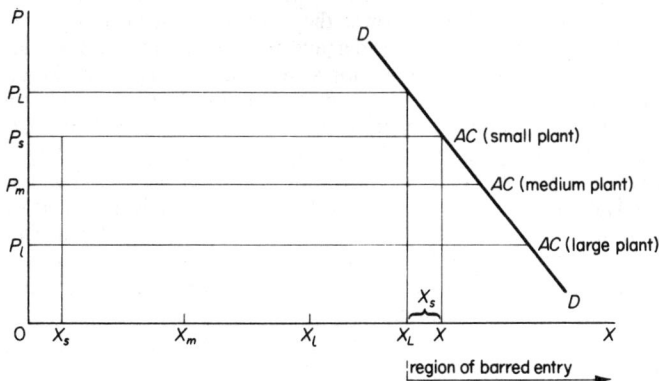

Figure 14.2

[1] P. Sylos-Labini, *Oligopoly and Technical Progress*, p. 50.

limit price $P_L > P_S$. The price P_L corresponds to the level of output $X_L = X - X_S$ and is the equilibrium price because it satisfies the two necessary conditions: it is acceptable by all firms, and it deters entry, because if entry occurs the total output X_L will be increased at the level $X_L + X_S = X$ and the price will fall to (just below) the minimum acceptable price of the entrant, that is, to a level just below P_S. The P_L is indirectly determined by the determination of the total output that the established firms will sell in the market. Given that in the long run price cannot fall below the cost of the least efficient firm, and that the entrant can enter only with the smallest least-efficient plant size, the leader can determine the output X at which all established firms use their plants up to capacity. He next determines the total quantity that the firms will sell in the industry X_L so as to prevent entry. X_L is such that if the entrant comes into the market with the minimum viable size, X_S, the total post-entry output $(X_L + X_S)$ will just exceed X, and hence will drive price down to a level just below the AC of the entrant $(= AC$ of the small least-efficient firms). Given X_L, the limit price P_L is determined from the market-demand curve DD. The entrant will be deterred from entering the market because (under the Sylos's Postulate) he knows that if he enters he will cause the price to fall below his AC. Any output larger than X_L is entry-preventing, while any output smaller than X_L will not prevent entry.

It should be clear that in Sylos's model all firms earn abnormal profits, which are increasing with plant size and there is an upper and a lower limit of the entry-preventing price: the equilibrium price cannot be higher than P_L nor lower than P_S.

In Sylos's model the determinants of the entry-preventing price are:

(1) The absolute size of the market X.
(2) The elasticity of market demand.
(3) The technology of the industry, which defines the available sizes of plant.
(4) The prices of factors of production, which, together with the technology, determine the total average cost of the firms.

The absolute market size. There is a negative relationship between the absolute size of the market and the limit price. The larger the market size the lower the entry prevention price (see below, p. 316).

If there is a dynamic increase in the demand, denoted by a shift to the right of the industry-demand curve, the effect on the price and the structure of the industry depends on the size and the rate of increase.

If the increase in demand is considerable and occurs rapidly, the existing firms, if they want to prevent entry, must lower the price (or set a lower price initially, in anticipation of the developments on the demand side) and build up additional capacity to meet the demand (or have adequate foresight so as to keep a continuous reserve capacity). If the price is high and profits lucrative, and if the established firms cannot build up capacity fast enough to keep up with the rate of growth in demand, then entry from new firms or already established firms in other industries will take place. If we relax the restrictive assumption that the entrant will enter with the smallest optimal plant size, and accept that large firms from other industries manage to enter at a lower cost, some or all of the small firms will be eliminated, and price will fall. Thus a rapid increase in the absolute market size will tend to reduce price and increase the average plant size in the industry, unless the existing firms can keep their shares constant by keeping continuously adequate reserve capacity. This policy, however, may be very costly. Thus in fast-expanding industries entry is amost certain to occur and price will be reduced.

If the growth of demand is slow, the existing firms will most probably be able to meet the increased demand by appropriate reserve capacity and gradual new investment, and the price will not be reduced unless new techniques with lower costs can be adopted for the larger scales of output to which the established firms are gradually led.

The elasticity of market demand.[1] The elasticity of market demand is also negatively related to the limit price. The more elastic the demand is, the lower the price that established firms can charge without attracting entry.

If at the going price there is a *considerable* increase in the elasticity of demand (for price reductions), and if the firms are able to identify clearly this change in the elasticity of demand, the effects on price and on market structure are the same as in the case of a shift in the market demand. The detection of changes in the elasticity is almost impossibly difficult in practice, and the established firms will most probably not count (and plan ahead) on such uncertain changes in *e*. Thus if *e* does in fact change substantially, new large firms (established elsewhere) will enter into the market, since the existing firms will not be able to cope with such change, and the price will fall.

The technology and technical change. The technology determines the minimum viable plant size. In any given 'state of arts,' the larger the minimum viable plant size, the higher will be the limit price. Thus there is a positive relation between the minimum viable plant and the premium included in the limit price (see section II below).

If technology changes (technical progress) and benefits all plant sizes, costs will fall and price will decrease. However, if technical progress is such that only large firms have access to it, the limit price will not change. The large firms will have larger actual profits, but under the assumptions of Sylos's model the price need not change.

If technical progress is associated with product innovation (rather than process innovation) the price in the market will not normally be affected. One should expect an intensification of non-price competition as all firms in the industry will attempt to imitate the innovation.

Sylos seems to imply that technical progress is accessible only to the large firms who can afford large research and development departments. He argues that in the real world the large firms will not have any incentive to lower the price of their commodities despite the reduction in their costs. Under these conditions the large firms will realise higher profits and this will have serious implications for the distribution of income and employment. This argument is elaborated in the second part of Sylos's book. However, we will not deal with these macro-aspects of Sylos's theory.

The prices of factors of production. Changes in factor prices affect all the firms in the industry in the same way. Thus an increase in factor prices will lead to an increase in the costs and the limit price in the industry. Similarly a reduction in factor prices will lead to a decrease in the limit price.

Differentiated oligopoly

Sylos extended his analysis to the case of differentiated oligopoly. Sylos argues that when the products are differentiated the entry-barriers will be stronger than in the case of homogeneous oligopoly due to marketing economies of scale. He seems to accept that advertising unit costs and possibly the cost of raw materials per unit of output are likely to fall as the scale of output increases. Hence the overall cost difference between the smaller and larger plants will be greater as compared to the homogeneous oligopoly case. Product differentiation, therefore, will reinforce the scale-barrier.

Sylos's analysis of differentiated oligopoly lacks the rigour of his model of homogeneous oligopoly. He suggests, however, that he is primarily concerned with the implications of technological discontinuities for price and output, and that product differentiation is one of the main concerns of the 'theoreticians of imperfect competition' to whose analysis Sylos's work is complementary.

[1] Note that Sylos-Labini assumed unitary elasticity of demand in his numerical example, but relaxed this assumption in his subsequent analysis.

Critique of Sylos's theory of limit-pricing

Sylos's model has been severely attacked on several grounds. The criticisms launched against his theory may be classified in two groups: weaknesses due to unrealistic assumptions; and weaknesses due to assumptions which, even if relaxed, do not affect the validity of the model.

The second group comprises the following criticisms. Firstly, Sylos has adopted a methodologically naïve approach, based on numerical examples. Secondly, he has assumed a very rigid technology, with strong discontinuities. Thirdly, he has used a definition of unitary elasticity which is rather confusing. These criticisms, correct as they are, do not impair the basic model. In sections II and III below we will see how Modigliani and Bhagwati relaxed these assumptions and generalised Sylos's model, also giving it a rigorous appearance.

The first group of criticisms concentrates on the plausibility of Sylos's Postulate. It has been argued that the strategy of keeping the pre-entry quantity constant is not the best alternative action open to the established firms:

The Sylos strategy implies a defensive attitude: the existing firms practically give up their initiative in price-setting, since the price will be determined by the quantity which the entrant decides to sell in the market. It may be preferable for the existing firms to retain their control on the price and adopt other actions; for example, increase their pre-entry output. This 'retaliation strategy' will lead to a reduction in price, possibly below the LAC of all firms. Depending, however, on their financial reserves and the length of the time period over which established firms expect the price to remain below their LAC, they may find it profitable in the long run to start a price war and eliminate the entrant. Such elimination tactics have been successfully adopted in several cases. This strategy is particularly attractive since it will serve as a lesson to future potential entrants.

The 'mixed strategy' of partly reducing the pre-entry output and partly allowing the price to fall post-entry seems to have several advantages: some excess profits will still be earned, while the established firms can start an intensive non-price competition which may both eliminate the entrant and discourage further entry. Bain and others have argued that the 'mixed strategy' is the more realistic and more likely in the real world.[1]

Other serious shortcomings of Sylos's model are the following. Firstly, the scale-barriers are not important if the entrant is an already-established firm in the same or in another industry (within-entry and cross-entry). Even for completely new firms economies of scale have not been found to be important barriers in practice (see Chapter 13). Secondly, scale economies may in fact enhance entry if the limit price is very high; a firm may decide to enter despite the initial losses, if the current price yields lucrative profits to the large-scale plants. Thirdly, scale-barriers may be offset by the advantages of a new firm, which can adopt the most up-to-date methods of production and choose its location optimally, given the supply and demand conditions in the market. Fourthly, the rationale of an entry-preventing policy is not given; neither does Sylos discuss explicitly the assumed preference of firms, existing and potential, for the behavioural pattern implied by the Sylos's Postulate. Fifthly, the model is static; it does not examine the long-run implications of the adoption of an entry-preventing policy. As Pashigian has suggested, the rational firm should examine the profitability of all the alternatives open to it. Pashigian argues that in most cases it may be more profitable to charge the monopoly price for a certain (initial) period of time and subsequently charge a limit price or a purely competitive price, depending on the profitability of each alternative

---

[1] Bain, *Barriers to New Competition* (Harvard University Press, Cambridge, Mass.) p. 109.

strategy (see section IV below). Such an analysis is dynamic, since it involves the examination of the time paths of alternative strategies. Sixthly, the model assumes considerable knowledge of the conditions of supply and demand: the price leader is assumed to know the cost structure of all plant sizes, to have estimated accurately the market demand, and to know the minimum (normal) acceptable profit of the industry. The required amount of information is very unlikely to be available in practice.

In general Sylos's contribution lies in the systematic discussion of the most important determinants of the limit price in the case of substantial economies of scale. These factors provided the basic material used by Modigliani and Bhagwati in the development of more general and more rigorous models of limit-pricing.

II. THE MODEL OF FRANCO MODIGLIANI

Franco Modigliani[1] presented a model of limit-pricing which may be considered as a generalisation of Sylos's model.

The assumptions of the model

Modigliani relaxed the restrictive assumptions which underlie Sylos's model, but retained the assumption of scale-barriers and the behavioural pattern of Sylos's Postulate.

Modigliani's assumptions may be stated as follows:

1. The technology is the same for all firms in the industry. There is a minimum optimal plant size ($\bar{x}$) at which the economies of scale are fully reaped. Once the minimum optimal scale is reached the LAC becomes a straight line. Under these conditions the LAC is L-shaped (figure 14.3) and is the same for all firms.

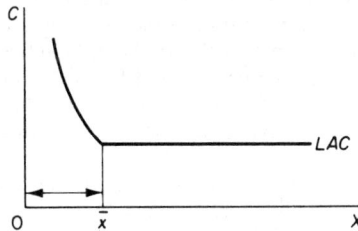

Figure 14.3

2. Entry occurs with the minimum optimal plant size. Entry with suboptimal size is precluded because in the long run it would imply irrational behaviour. There is an implicit assumption regarding entry, namely that entry comes from new firms.

3. The product is homogeneous and the market demand is known. The point of intersection of the given demand curve with a line drawn at the level of the flat section of the LAC determines the competitive output X_C and the competitive price P_C, that is, the price and quantity that would be sold at that price in the long run if the market were purely competitive, given that in the long run equilibrium $LAC = P_C$ (figure 14.4).

4. The price is set by the largest firm in the industry, at such a level as to prevent entry.

[1] F. Modigliani, 'New Developments on the Oligopoly Front', *Journal of Political Economy* (1958).

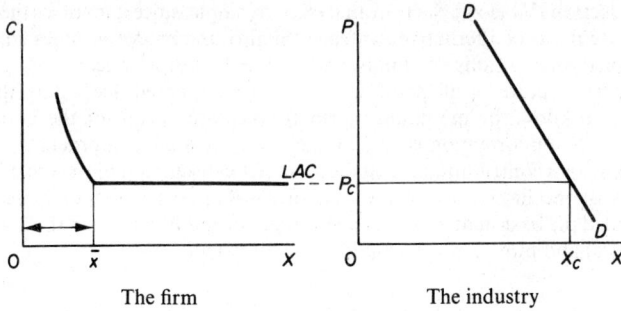

The firm   The industry

Figure 14.4

5. The firms behave according to the Sylos's Postulate. That is, the existing firms expect that the entrant cannot enter with a plant smaller than the minimum optimal scale $\bar{x}$, and that he will not enter if he believes that the price post-entry will fall below the flat segment of the LAC. The entrant expects that the established firms will keep their output constant at the pre-entry level.

The model

Under the above assumptions the equilibrium price P_L will be higher than the $P_C \, (= LAC)$. The established firms will earn abnormal profits due to the scale-barrier which is reflected in the minimum optimal plant size $\bar{x}$.

The main preoccupation of the firms is the determination of price at a level which will not attract entry. The limit price P_L is determined indirectly by determining the total output which will be sold by all firms in the industry. The established firms decide to sell a quantity X_L such that if the entrant comes and offers an additional quantity $\bar{x}$ (the minimum he can produce optimally), the total output in the market will just exceed the competitive output X_C, and the price would fall just below the $P_C = LAC$ level (figure 14.5). Symbolically this behaviour may be stated as follows: the entry-preventing output is X_L, such that $X_L + \bar{x} > X_C$, and the post-entry price falls to $P < P_C$ (where $P_C = LAC$).

Given X_L, the entry-preventing price P_L is simultaneously determined from the given industry-demand curve. Entry will be prevented as long as $X \geq X_L$. If $X < X_L$ entry will occur.

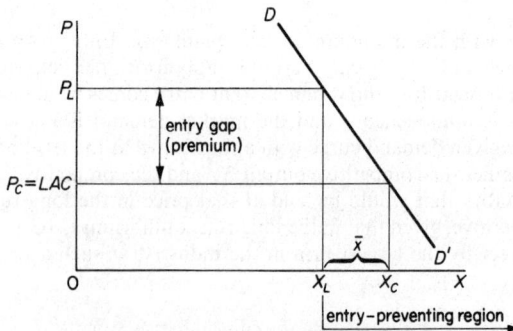

Figure 14.5

In figure 14.5 DD' is the industry-demand curve, $\bar{x}$ is the minimum optimal level of output, $X_L = X_C - \bar{x}$ is the output which the established firms should produce in order to prevent entry, and P_L is the entry-preventing price, defined from the demand curve, given X_L.

The scale-barriers cause P_L to be higher than P_C. The difference $P_L - P_C$ is the *entry gap* or *premium* and defines the amount by which the price can exceed the *LAC* without attracting entry. The determinants of the entry gap and the entry-preventing price are:

(1) The absolute market size X_C
(2) The price elasticity of demand e
(3) The minimum optimal scale $\bar{x}$
(4) The prices of factors of production, which together with the technology determine the *LAC*, and hence the competitive price P_C.

Modigliani reaches the same conclusions as Sylos; namely that there is a determinate equilibrium price P_L, which is positively correlated with $\bar{x}$ and P_C ($=LAC$), and negatively correlated with the absolute market size X_C and the elasticity of demand e. The limit price will be higher, the larger $\bar{x}$, the higher the P_C, the smaller the X_C and the smaller the price elasticity e.

Modigliani combined the above factors ingeniously in the following expression:

$$P_L = P_C\left(1 + \frac{\bar{x}}{X_C \cdot e}\right)$$

Clearly the term $\bar{x}/X_C \cdot e$ corresponds to Bain's condition to entry, E.

Derivation of Modigliani's limit price

The relation between the limit price P_L and the competitive equilibrium price P_C can be stated approximately in terms of the elasticity of demand in the neighbourhood of P_C.

(a) The formula for the price elasticity

$$e = \frac{dX}{X} : \frac{dP}{P}$$

may be expressed approximately in finite differences as follows

$$e = \frac{\Delta X}{X} : \frac{\Delta P}{P}$$

(b) Under Sylos's Postulate all increments in demand will accrue to the entrant, so that

$$\Delta X = \frac{X_C - X_L}{X} = \bar{x}$$

(c) The change in price is $\Delta P = P_L - P_C$
Thus at the neighbourhood of P_C the elasticity is

$$e = \frac{\bar{x}}{X_C} : \frac{P_L - P_C}{P_C}$$

Solving for P_L we obtain

$$P_L = P_C\left\{1 + \frac{\bar{x}}{X_C \cdot e}\right\}$$

Note that the approximation of the price elasticity with finite changes is not satisfactory for large values of

$$\frac{\bar{x}}{X_C} = \frac{X_L - X_C}{X_C}$$

In particular, if the demand curve has constant elasticity, then for large values of $\bar{x}/X_C$ the premium (price rise) will be significantly underestimated. (Modigliani, 'New Developments on the Oligopoly Front', p. 218.)

The determinants of the limit price

From the above expression it is clear that the limit price P_L will be higher the larger the minimum optimal scale of plant $\bar{x}$, the less elastic the demand curve and the smaller the absolute size of the market X_C at the competitive price P_C. The relationship between P_L and each one of the above determinants is graphically shown in figures 14.6, 14.7, and 14.8.

In figure 14.6 we show the relationship between the limit price P_L and the minimum optimal scale of plant $\bar{x}$, for given X_C and e. The larger minimum optimal scale $\bar{x}_2$ allows the established firms to charge a higher limit price P_{L2} without attracting entry.

In figure 14.7 we show the relationship between the limit price P_L and the elasticity of demand e, for given X_C and $\bar{x}$. At P_C the demand curve D_2 is more elastic than D_1.

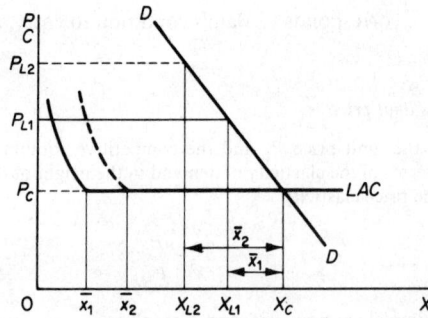

Figure 14.6 $P_L = f(\bar{x})$, given X_C and e. For $\bar{x}_2 > \bar{x}_1$, $P_{L2} > P_{L1}$

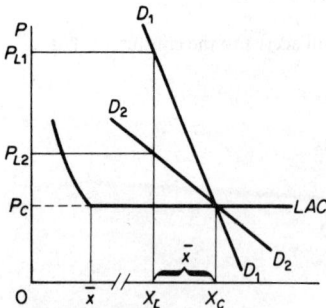

Figure 14.7 $P_L = f(e)$, given X_C and $\bar{x}$. For $e_{D2} > e_{D1}$, $P_{L2} < P_{L1}$

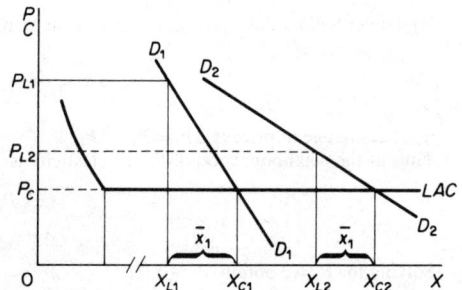

Figure 14.8 $P_L = f(X_C)$, given $\bar{x}$ and e. For $X_{C2} > X_{C1}$, $P_{L2} < P_{L1}$

Consequently the price that the established firms will charge is P_{L2}, lower than P_{L1} which corresponds to the less elastic demand curve D_1.

Finally, in figure 14.8 we show the relationship between P_L and the competitive equilibrium market size X_C, for given $\bar{x}$ and e. The larger the X_C, the lower the limit price.

Dynamic changes in the market

Increase in costs. If costs change, all firms are affected and hence the long-run cost curve will be raised more or less uniformly. This development will lead to a rise in the limit price.

Firms in oligopolistic markets adhere to 'average-cost' pricing, because it facilitates the orderly working of the market mechanism.

> The full-cost pricing (which consists in applying to the new prime cost the original total percentage mark-up) may well represent a very useful rule of thumb in reacting to cost changes affecting the entire industry... In an oligopolistic situation, with its precarious internal equilibrium, there is much to be gained from simple and widely understood rules of thumb, which minimise the danger of behaviour intended to be peaceful and co-operative being misunderstood as predatory or retaliatory. (Modigliani, 'New Developments on the Oligopoly Front'.)

Cyclical variations in demand. Modigliani agrees with Sylos's main conclusions concerning the variations in price and the gross profit mark-up over the various phases of the cycle.

(a) In a recession

The limit price will show a mild tendency to rise. However, the mark-up may not rise due to the costs of idle capacity, which will push the firms to give secret price concessions in their eagerness to secure a larger share of the smaller demand.

(b) During recovery

There will be a tendency for the price to rise, when full capacity is reached. However, large firms may strongly resist this tendency due to fear of potential entry. Instead they will adopt other policies such as allowing a backlog of demand or instituting informal rationing of their deliveries, while at the same time expanding capacity. The mark-up will tend to retrace the sliding path followed in the contraction, and will stabilise at its normal level, corresponding to the normal 'price line' of the large firms. In general the mark-up (on the average) is not likely to change over the cycle appreciably, but one should expect some scatter around this central tendency; prices would tend to show little or no fluctuation over the cycle. Prices would tend to fluctuate only if prime costs change, because such changes would affect all firms.

The above general conclusions are not in agreement with all empirical evidence. In particular, these results are consistent with Stigler's findings,[1] but do not agree with other empirical studies of price flexibility.[2]

The rationalisation of the Sylos's Postulate

Modigliani argues that the behavioural pattern implied by the Sylos Postulate is the most plausible in the real world. His argument is of no general validity, as he does

---

[1] 'The Kinky Oligopoly Demand Curve and Rigid Prices', *Journal of Political Economy* (1947).

[2] Richard Ruggles, 'The Nature of Price Flexibility and Determinants of Relative Price Changes in the Economy', in *Business Concentration and Price Policy* (Princeton University Press, 1955).

concentrate on the comparison of Sylos's Postulate with the optimistic alternative implied by Bain's Model A, namely, that the prospective entrant expects that the established firms will keep the pre-entry price unchanged. Modigliani's argument may be summarised as follows:

The optimistic assumption (on the part of the potential entrant) that existing firms will adopt a strategy of maintaining the pre-entry price, by contracting their output, is a rather foolish expectation. It implies that established firms will allow the entrant to gain any share of the market that he likes, while their own share is accordingly shrinking and their profits are reduced on two accounts: (*a*) price would fall, and at this price they would sell less; (*b*) their costs would rise as they would be gradually driven to the increasing part of their cost curve. Furthermore, such an 'accommodating' behaviour would create a precedent for further potential entrants. Thus the strategy implied by Sylos's Postulate, of the existing firms keeping the pre-entry quantity constant, seems a more realistic assumption for the entrant to make. We have discussed the shortcomings of the Sylos Postulate in section I. To sum up these critisms:

Sylos's strategy implies a defensive attitude, in that the existing firms give up their initiative for price-setting. Price will be virtually set by the entrant, depending on the quantity he decides to sell in the market.

The diametrically opposite strategy of maintaining price is equally unlikely for the reasons given above. However, a *mixed strategy* of partly accommodating the entrant and partly allowing the price to fall seems the most likely in the real world. With this combined action some excess profits will still be earned. Furthermore the established firms can undertake an intensive non-price competition which may make the survival of the entrant difficult and discourage further entry.

There is another strategy which may be more profitable for established firms, namely, existing firms may decide to charge the monopoly price over a certain period and then reduce it to the entry-preventing level, or retain the monopoly price for a longer period and allow the price to fall to the competitive equilibrium level P_C as entry occurs. These alternatives have been explored by Pashigian (see page 320).

Finally, the alternative strategy of increasing the output post-entry may be more advantageous. This behaviour would imply a price war aiming at the elimination of the entrant, since price would fall below the *LAC* (that is, below P_C). The adoption of this strategy depends on the financial reserves of established firms (which define their ability to finance their losses) and on the length of time that they expect the price war to last. If this 'retaliation strategy' is successfully carried out it will serve as a lesson to future prospective entrants.

Thus the Sylos Postulate, although convenient for the determinate equilibrium that it provides, is by no means the best or the most likely behavioural assumption.

The main shortcomings of Modigliani's model may be summarised as follows. Firstly, the model does not determine the individual shares of the firms. Thus the number of firms in the industry is not defined. Secondly, it assumes scale-barriers are important. This implies that Modigliani does not take into account the typical form of entry in the modern business world, namely entry by an already-established firm in the same or in another industry. Thirdly, the rationale of the policy of entry-prevention is not discussed. Fourthly, dynamic aspects arising from growing markets are not considered. Fifthly, although at some point Modigliani states that the 'large firms typically set the pace in the market' and they set the price by applying 'the full-cost rules of thumb,' he does not fully explain how the price is defined, nor does he discuss how the interaction of firms with different costs and different shares leads to a stable market equilibrium. Sixthly, the assumption that the entrant can enter only with the minimum optimal scale is applicable to new firms only. An already-established firm may enter at scales which are profitable for it, although suboptimal for new firms.

III. THE MODEL OF BHAGWATI

Bhagwati[1] extended Modigliani's model in two directions. Firstly, he incorporated two additional determinants of the limit price in Modigliani's expression. Secondly, he introduced a term which renders the limit-price theory dynamic, in the sense that it can predict the changes in the limit price arising from a growing market.

The two factors which Bhagwati introduced into Modigliani's model are the number of firms in the industry and a measure of the switch of customers of established firms to the entrant due to their feeling of dissatisfaction (chagrin) from their exploitation by the suppliers charging them a higher price (before entry occurred).

Regarding the number of firms Bhagwati assumes that, as price falls with entry, some of the new buyers will buy from established firms whose name is known, and some will buy from the entrant. For simplicity Bhagwati assumes that the increment in the market demand is shared equally between the established firms and the entrant:

$$\frac{\Delta X}{N + 1} = \bar{x}$$

or

$$\Delta X = \bar{x}(N + 1)$$

The 'chagrin effect' is a positive elasticity which measures the proportionate decrease in the sales of established firms as the price decreases and dissatisfied customers turn to the new entrant. It is denoted by ε and is of opposite sign to the normal price elasticity e. Thus the relevant elasticity for the determination of the limit price by the established firms is (approximately)

$$[e + \varepsilon(N + 1)] = \frac{\Delta X}{X} : \frac{\Delta P}{P}$$

where

$$\frac{\Delta X}{X} = \frac{\bar{x}(N + 1)}{X_C}$$

and

$$\frac{\Delta P}{P} = \frac{P_L - P_C}{P_C}$$

Substituting and solving for P_L we obtain

$$P_L = P_C \left\{ 1 + \frac{\bar{x}(N + 1)}{X_C[e + \varepsilon(N + 1)]} \right\}$$

Thus apart from $\bar{x}$, X_C and e, the limit price is determined by the number of firms in the industry and the chagrin-elasticity ε:

[1] See J. N. Bhagwati, 'Oligopoly Theory, Entry-Prevention and Growth', *Oxford Economic Papers* (1970).

The premium obtainable in an industry will vary directly with (1) the minimum size of scale of most efficient production $(\bar{x})$ and (2) the number of existing firms (N); and inversely with (1) the size of the total market (X_C), (2) the price-elasticity of industry demand and (3) the extent to which existing buyers will transfer custom to the entrant consequent upon entry. (Bhagwati, 'Oligopoly Theory, Entry-Prevention and Growth'.)

The above expression has been extended to cover dynamic changes in market demand. If demand increases by an amount λ and out of this increase k per cent accrues to the new entrant, the limit price will be defined by

$$
P_L = P_C \left\{ 1 + \frac{\bar{x} - k\lambda}{X_C \left[\dfrac{e}{N+1} + \varepsilon \right]} \right\}
$$

where X_C is now the aggregate demand at the competitive price after growth. The factor k is inversely related to P_L, denoting the fact that entry is easier in an expanding market. The faster the growth in demand the smaller the premium by which P_L will exceed P_C.

The important implication of this formulation is that if $(k\lambda) > \bar{x}$, the prevention of entry is impossible, since P_L must fall below P_C, that is, to a level that does not cover the *LAC*. This cannot be a long-run equilibrium situation. So, the use of price policy to prevent entry becomes an ineffective device. Under these conditions the only entry-preventing policy must be based on other actions such as keeping adequate spare capacity *continuously* so as to keep production at the same pace as demand. This, however, may be a costly and non-profitable policy. Furthermore it requires a good forecasting ability on the part of the entrepreneur. If $(k\lambda) > \bar{x}$, that is, if the market is growing very fast, the existing firms cannot rely on price alone as the appropriate instrument for their entry-forestalling policy. They must look for methods to ensure the maximum appropriation to themselves (rather than to any potential entrant) of the increment of the growing demand. Thus, in dynamic markets, if the firms want to prevent entry they must look for the factors that determine their share and try to operate on those factors that are under their control.

The theoretical problem thus shifts from devising an entry-preventing *price* to a formal analysis of the *non-price* factors which determine the share of the existing firms in the growing market and the ways in which these are within the range of influence of these firms. (Bhagwati, 'Oligopoly Theory, Entry-Prevention and Growth'.)

IV. THE MODEL OF PASHIGIAN

The Sylos–Bain–Modigliani–Bhagwati model postulates that the limit price will be higher than the *LAC* due to the scale-barriers to entry. Thus the firms will be earning abnormal profits without attracting entry. Bhagwati mentions that firms under certain conditions may adopt a mixed strategy, namely charge the monopoly price $(P_M > P_L)$ over a certain period of time and subsequently reduce their price to the level that will prevent entry (P_L). The adoption of this strategy depends on the length of two time periods: the period over which entry will not occur due to various barriers, and the period that is required for the established firms to adjust their pre-entry plant to the post-entry optimum size. If the latter period is longer, then the firms maximise their profits by charging to begin with the limit price, while if the former period is longer, the existing firms will attain higher profits by adopting the above mixed strategy.

Pashigian[1] explored more systematically the implications of the above mixed strategy, by defining the period T at which the firms will switch from the monopoly price to the entry-preventing price (P_L) or to the competitive equilibrium price (P_C), depending on the profitability of each alternative. For simplicity he starts by assuming that there is only one firm in the industry (monopoly). The firm has to decide *whether* and *for how long* it is profitable to charge the monopoly price that maximises its short-run profits. By setting the price at the monopoly level (P_M) entry will occur eventually. Thus the crucial element is the number of periods during which the price will remain above the limit price while entry is taking place. Pashigian concentrates for simplicity on two alternatives open to the firm. He assumes that over a period T the firms will charge the monopoly price and allow entry to occur. The entrants are assumed to collude with the existing firms and sell at the pre-entry price. Thus over the period T the price will be P_M and the quantity supplied X_M (figure 14.9), but it will be produced by a gradually increasing number of firms.

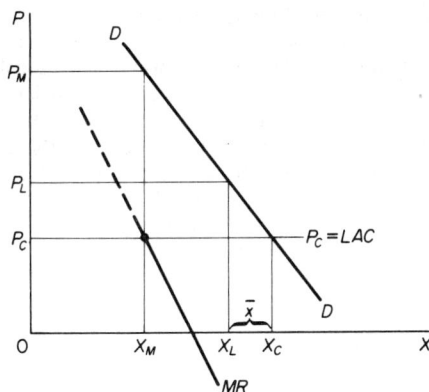

Figure 14.9

The share of the ex-monopolist (to the market and to the monopoly profit) will be decreasing over this period as he will be 'accommodating' the entrants. After period T the originally established firms (the ex-monopolist in Pashigian's model) must choose one of the following two policies: *either* to charge the limit price (P_L) and enjoy thereafter the excess profits that this price allows, *or* to continue over an additional period, TT', to charge the monopoly price and allow further entry to take place until price has eventually fallen to the competitive level P_C, which yields only normal profits. The choice between these two alternatives will be based on the comparison of the discounted flows of profits resulting from these policies. If the ex-monopolist, who is assumed to set the pace in the market, adopts the former policy, his discounted profits will be the area under the thick line in figure 14.10. If he adopts the second strategy his discounted stream of profits will be the area under the dotted curve. The ex-monopolist (leader) will thus compare the shaded areas $BFCG$ and $CKDL$. The former denotes the profits which will be forgone if the firm chooses to continue charging the monopoly price during the time period TT', while the latter area $(CKDL)$ shows the profits which will be earned beyond period T' if the firm chooses to charge the limit price at period T.

[1] B. P. Pashigian, 'Limit Price and the Market Share of the Leading Firm', *Journal of Industrial Economics* (1968).

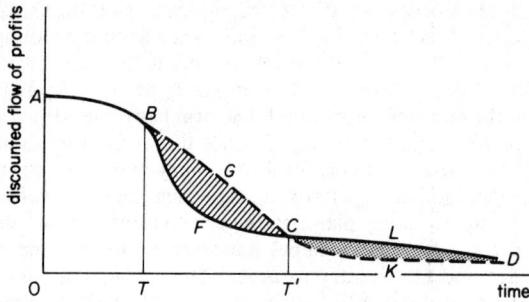

Figure 14.10

If *BFCG* > *CKDL* the firm leader will stick to the monopoly price for a longer period (*TT'*) because this policy maximises his profits. Pashigian's time-period analysis has the advantage of treating time explicitly and of attempting to justify the entry-preventing policy on grounds of maximum profitability. However, the model is based on several assumptions that might be questioned. For example, the model assumes that entry will not take place immediately due to barriers of various forms. Furthermore it assumes that the entrant is a small firm which will be coerced by the dominant established firm(s) to collude and charge the same price.

SECTION E

MANAGERIAL THEORIES
OF THE FIRM

MANAGERIAL THEORIES OF THE FIRM

Managerial theories conceive the firm as a 'coalition' (of managers, workers, stock-holders, suppliers, customers, tax collectors) whose members have conflicting goals that must be reconciled if the firm is to survive. The conflicts are resolved by top management by various methods which will be examined in Chapter 18.

Clearly the most important member of the 'coalition' is top management, because of its power in decision-making (goal-setting, basic decisions on investment and expansion, promotions and appointments of 'key' personnel) and access to information.

The basic characteristic of the 'managerial business' is the divorce of ownership from management. The owners are the shareholders, whose power lies in appointing the board of directors, which in turn appoints the top management.

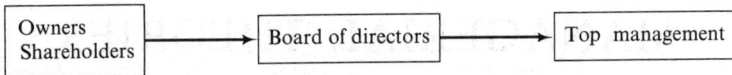

| Owners Shareholders | → | Board of directors | → | Top management |

The shareholders have in fact less power than the above scheme may suggest, because shares are in the hands of a large number of persons or institutions (mainly insurance companies, pension funds, finance companies). Small shareholders rarely attend general meetings. Instead the election of the board of directors is arranged by the existing board, assisted by the appointment of proxies (representatives of shareholders). The system of voting by proxies is well manipulated by the top management, which is often directly represented in the board of directors and can thus influence decisions on further appointments of top managers. Thus the top management tends to be self-perpetuating, provided that the level of profits is 'acceptable' to the body of shareholders, the rate of growth of the firm is 'reasonable' relative to the growth of other firms, and the dividends paid out to shareholders are sufficient to keep them happy and prevent a fall in the prices of shares, which would make the firm attractive to take-over raids.

The divorce of ownership from management permits the top management to deviate from profit maximisation (which maximises the utility to the owners) and pursue goals which maximise their own utility. However, the managers' discretion in defining the goals of the firm is not unlimited. A minimum level of profit is necessary for a dividend policy acceptable to the body of shareholders; for undertaking the investment necessary for a satisfactory operation of the firm; for keeping a good reputation with banks so as to secure adequate finance for current transactions; for avoiding a relative fall in prices of shares on the stock exchange and the risk of a take-over. If these conditions are not satisfied, the top management runs the risk of mass dismissal; their job security is endangered. However, so long as the above conditions are fulfilled, the managers can pursue policies and set goals which maximise their own welfare.

Thus the basic feature of all managerial theories is that the managers maximise their own utility, subject to a minimum profit constraint (which is set at a level adequate to satisfy the above conditions) necessary for the job security of the top managers.

We will present three models of managerialism. Baumol's model of 'sales revenue maximisation'; Marris's model of 'managerial enterprise'; Williamson's model of managerial discretion'.

These models have the same basic assumption, the maximisation of the utility of the managers subject to a minimum profit constraint. They differ (a) in the factors which enter into the managerial utility function, (b) in the key policy variables (instruments) which the managers will use in attaining their goals, (c) in their predictions of the consequences of changes of various parameters of the model.

15. Baumol's Theory of Sales Revenue Maximisation

W. J. Baumol suggested sales revenue maximisation as an alternative goal to profit maximisation.[1] He presented two basic models: the first is a static single-period model, the second is a multi-period dynamic model of growth of sales revenue maximisation. Each model has two versions, one without and one with advertising activities. We will first present these models, examine the predictions of Baumol's theory in various situations, and then discuss the empirical evidence from research directed to the verification of the sales maximisation hypothesis. Finally, we state some criticisms of Baumol's theory.

I. RATIONALISATION OF THE SALES MAXIMISATION HYPOTHESIS

Baumol offers several justifications of sales maximisation as a goal of the firm. The separation of ownership from management, characteristic of the modern firm, gives discretion to the managers to pursue goals which maximise their own utility and deviate from profit maximisation, which is the desirable goal of owners. Given this discretion, Baumol argues that sales maximisation seems the most plausible goal of managers. From his experience as a consultant to large firms Baumol found that managers are preoccupied with maximisation of the sales rather than profits. Several reasons seem to explain this attitude of the top management.

Firstly, there is evidence that salaries and other (slack)[2] earnings of top managers are correlated more closely with sales than with profits. Secondly, the banks and other financial institutions keep a close eye on the sales of firms and are more willing to finance firms with large and growing sales. Thirdly, personnel problems are handled more satisfactorily when sales are growing. The employees at all levels can be given higher earnings and better terms of work in general. Declining sales, on the other hand, will make necessary the reduction of salaries and other payments and perhaps the lay-off of some employees. Such measures create dissatisfaction and uncertainty among personnel at all levels. Fourthly, large sales, growing over time, give prestige to the managers, while large profits go into the pockets of shareholders. Fifthly, managers

---

[1] W. J. Baumol, *Business Behaviour, Value and Growth* (Macmillan, New York, 1959. Revised edn., Harcourt, Brace & World, Inc., 1967).

[2] Slack is defined as payments or other perquisites to the managers above the minimum necessary to retain them in the firm. It is equivalent to the 'economic rent' to factors of production of the traditional theory. (See also Chapter 18.)

prefer a steady performance with 'satisfactory' profits to spectacular profit maximisation projects. If they realise maximum high profits in one period, they might find themselves in trouble in other periods when profits are less than maximum. Sixthly, large, growing sales strengthen the power to adopt competitive tactics, while a low or declining share of the market weakens the competitive position of the firm and its bargaining power *vis-à-vis* its rivals.

The desire for a steady performance with satisfactory profits, coupled with the separation of ownership and management, tend to make the managers reluctant to adopt promising projects which are risky. The top managers become to a certain extent risk-avoiders, and this attitude may act as a curb on economic growth. However, the desire for steady performance has a stabilising effect on economic activity. In general, large firms have research units which develop new ideas of products or techniques of production. The application of these projects is spread over time so as to avoid wide swings in the economic performance of the firm. Baumol seems to imply that the risk-avoidance and the desire for steady growth of the large corporations secure 'orderly markets', in the sense that they have stabilising effects on the economy.

II. INTERDEPENDENCE AND OLIGOPOLISTIC BEHAVIOUR

Although Baumol recognises the interdependence of firms as the main feature of oligopolistic markets, he argues that in 'day-to-day decision-making management often acts explicitly or implicitly on the premise that its decisions will produce no changes in the behaviour of those with whom they are competing . . .'. It is only when the firm makes 'more radical decisions, such as the launching of a major advertising campaign or the introduction of a radically new line of products, [that] management usually does consider the probable competitive response. But often, even in fairly crucial decisions, and almost always in routine policy-making, only the most cursory attention is paid to competitive reactions'.

This attitude towards competitors is attributed by Baumol to several reasons:

The complexity of the internal organisation of large firms renders decision-making a lengthy process: proposals originate from some sections, but final decisions are taken by top management after these proposals have passed through various levels of management and often from different departments. It is a characteristic inherent in the delegation of authority within the firm that each decision-maker will attempt to shift the responsibility on to others. Thus any reaction of competitors is bound to take place after 'a considerable time lag'.

Large organisations work to a 'blue-print' which includes a variety of rules of thumb, which simplify complicated problems such as pricing, size of advertising expenditure, level of inventories. Prices are set by applying a standard mark-up to costs, advertising expenses are determined by setting aside a fixed percentage of total revenues, inventories are determined as a percentage of sales, and so on. Such rules of thumb clearly do not automatically take into account the actions of competitors, and the adaptation of the 'blue-print' of a firm to a new environment takes time.

The desire of top management for a 'quiet life' has led large enterprises to some tacit collusion: firms depend on each other to behave in an 'orderly' way. They expect no 'breach of etiquette' in the established order in the industry as a whole.

However, the above reasons do not imply that businessmen are completely indifferent to actions of competitors. In particular, being sales maximisers and growth seekers, they are very alert to any change in their share of the market. Top management will ignore competitors only to the extent that their actions do not encroach on the firm's market and do not interfere with the desired rate of growth of the sales of the firm.

III. BAUMOL'S STATIC MODELS

The basic assumptions of the static models

1. The time-horizon of a firm is a single period.

2. During this period the firm attempts to maximise its total sales revenue (not physical volume of output) subject to a profit constraint. The firm in these models does not consider what will happen in subsequent periods as a result of the decisions taken in the current period.

3. The minimum profit constraint is exogenously determined by the demands and expectations of the shareholders, the banks and other financial institutions. The firm must realise a minimum level of profits to keep shareholders happy and avoid a fall of the prices of shares on the stock exchange. If profits are below this exogenously determined minimum acceptable level the managers run the risk of being dismissed, since shareholders may sell their shares and take-over raiders may be attracted by a fall of the prices of shares.

4. 'Conventional' cost and revenue functions are assumed. That is, Baumol accepts that cost curves are U-shaped and the demand curve of the firm is downward-sloping. We will examine four models:

    (1) A single-product model, without advertising.
    (2) A single-product model, with advertising.
    (3) A multiproduct model, without advertising.
    (4) A multiproduct model, with selling activities.

Model 1: a single-product model, without advertising

The total-cost and total-revenue curves under the above assumptions are shown in figure 15.1. Total sales revenue is at its maximum level at the highest point of the TR curve, where the price elasticity of demand is unity and the slope of this TR curve (the marginal revenue) is equal to zero.

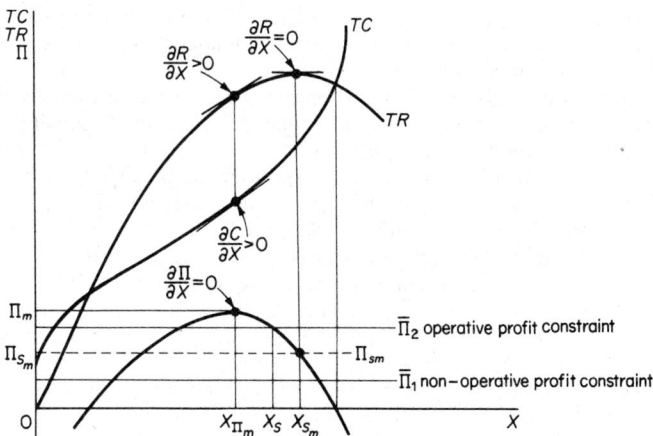

Figure 15.1

Proof

It has been established in Chapter 2 that

$$MR = P\left(1 - \frac{1}{e}\right)$$

At the point of maximum revenue the slope of the total revenue curve is

$$\frac{\partial R}{\partial X} = MR = 0$$

Therefore

$$0 = P\left(1 - \frac{1}{e}\right)$$

Given $P > 0$, we have

$$1 - \frac{1}{e} = 0$$

or

$$e = 1$$

Whether this maximum sales revenue will be realised or not depends on the level of the minimum acceptable level of profit which may act as a constraint to the activity of the firm. If the firm were a profit maximiser, it would produce the level of output $X_{\Pi m}$. However, in Baumol's model the firm is a sales maximiser, but it must also earn a minimum level of profit acceptable to shareholders and to those who finance its operations. If the minimum acceptable level of profit is $\overline{\Pi}_1$, the firm will produce the level of output X_{Sm} which maximises its sales revenue. With this level of output (X_{Sm}) the firm earns profits Π_{Sm}, which are greater than the minimum required to keep the stockholders (and other interested parties) satisfied. Under these circumstances we say that the minimum profit constraint is not operative.

If the minimum acceptable profit is $\overline{\Pi}_2$, the firm will not be able to attain the maximum sales revenue because the profit constraint is operative, and the firm will produce X_S units of output, which are less than at the level X_{Sm}.

In summary: '... two types of equilibria appear to be possible: one in which the profit constraint provides no effective barrier to sales maximisation (X_{Sm} units of output with a minimum acceptable profit of $\overline{\Pi}_1$), and one in which it does (X_S units of output with a minimum acceptable profit of $\overline{\Pi}_2$)'. (W. J. Baumol, *Business Behaviour, Value and Growth* (revised edn, Harcourt, Brace & World, Inc., 1967).) The firm is assumed to be able to pursue an independent price policy, that is, to set its price so as to achieve its goal of sales maximisation (given the profit constraint) without being concerned about the reactions of competitors.

Provided that the profit constraint is operative, the following predictions of Baumol's single-period model (without advertising) emerge:

The sales maximiser will produce a higher level of output as compared to a profit maximiser.

Proof

A profit maximiser produces the output $X_{\Pi m}$ defined by the equilibrium condition $MR = MC$ or

$$\frac{\partial R}{\partial X} = \frac{\partial C}{\partial X}$$

Given that the marginal cost is always positive $(\partial C/\partial X > 0)$ it is obvious that at the level $X_{\Pi m}$ the marginal revenue is also positive $(\partial R/\partial X > 0)$. That is, TR is still increasing at $X_{\Pi m}$, since its slope is still positive. In other words, the maximum of the TR curve (where its slope is $\partial R/\partial X = 0$) occurs to the right of the level of output at which profit is maximised. Hence $X_{Sm} > X_{\Pi m}$.

The sales maximiser sells at a price lower than the profit maximiser. The price at any level of output is the slope of the line through the origin to the relevant point of the total-revenue curve (corresponding to the particular level of output). In figure 15.2 the price of the profit maximiser is

$$P_{\Pi m} = \left[\frac{\text{slope}}{\text{of } 0A}\right] = \frac{R_{\Pi}}{X_{\Pi}}$$

while the price of the sales maximiser is

$$P_{Sm} = \left[\frac{\text{slope}}{\text{of } 0B}\right] = \frac{R_S}{X_S}$$

It is obvious that (slope $0A$) > (slope $0B$), that is, the price of the profit maximiser is higher than the price of the sales maximiser.

The sales maximiser will earn lower profits than the profit maximiser. In figure 15.2 the profit of the sales maximiser is $0\Pi_S$, which is lower than the profit $0\Pi_{\Pi}$ of the profit maximiser.

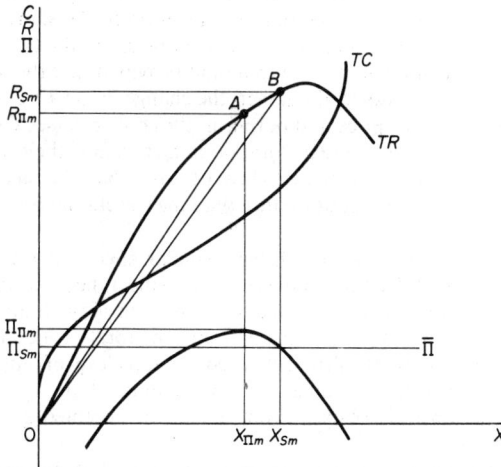

Figure 15.2

The sales maximiser will never choose a level of output at which price elasticity (e) is less than unity, because from the expression

$$MR = P\left(1 - \frac{1}{e}\right)$$

we see that if $|e| < 1$, the $MR < 0$, denoting that TR is declining. The maximum sales revenue will be where $|e| = 1$ (and hence $MR = 0$) and will be earned only if the profit constraint is not operative. If the profit constraint is operative the price elasticity will be greater than unity.

An increase in the fixed costs will affect the equilibrium position of a sales maximiser: he will reduce his level of output and increase his price, since the increase in fixed costs shifts the total-profit curve downwards. Subject to the profit constraint, the sales maximiser will pass the increase in costs to the customers by charging a higher price. This is shown in figure 15.3. The increase in fixed costs shifts the total costs upwards and the total-profits curve downwards (Π'). Subject to the profit constraint $\overline{\Pi}$, the firm will reduce its output (to X'_S) and will increase its price.

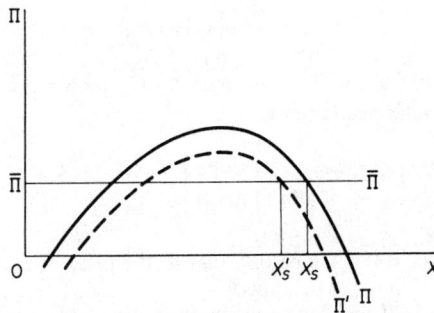

Figure 15.3

This prediction is contrary to the traditional hypothesis of profit maximisation. A profit maximiser will not change his equilibrium position in the short run, since fixed costs do not enter into the determination of the equilibrium of the firm. So long as the fixed costs do not vary with the level of output (and provided that the increase in TFC does not lead the firm to close down altogether) the change in the TFC will not lead the profit maximiser to change his price and output in the short run (see Chapter 6).

Beaumol claims that firms in the real world do in fact change their output and price whenever their overhead costs increase. Thus he says that the sales-maximisation hypothesis has a better predictive performance than the traditional profit-maximisation hypothesis.

The imposition of a lump-sum tax will have similar effects. If the firm is a profit maximiser the imposition of the lump-sum tax will not affect the price and output in the short run: the profit maximiser will bear the whole burden of the lump-tax. If the firm is a sales maximiser, however, the lump-tax will shift the total-profit curve downwards and, given the profit constraint, the firm will be led to cut its level of output and increase its price, thus passing on to the consumer the lump-sum tax. Baumol argues that firms do in fact shift the tax on to the buyers, contrary to the accepted doctrine about the 'unshiftability' of the tax.

The imposition of a specific tax (per unit of output) will shift the profit curve downwards and to the left (figure 15.4). Given $\overline{\Pi}$, the sales maximiser will reduce his output

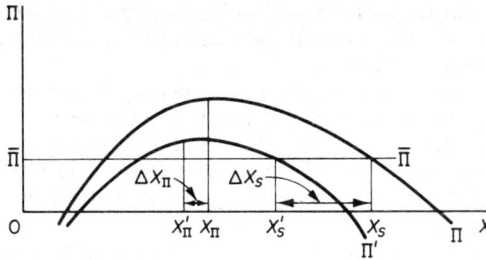

Figure 15.4

from X_S to X_S' and will raise his price, passing the tax to the buyers (at least partly). The profit maximiser will also reduce his output (from X_Π to X_Π') and raise his price. However, the decrease in output will be larger than the decrease of the output of a profit maximiser.

A similar analysis holds for an increase in the variable cost. Both the sales maximiser and the profit maximiser will raise their price and reduce their output. The reduction in output, however, and the increase in price will be more accentuated for the sales maximiser, *ceteris paribus*.

A shift in demand will result in an increase in output and sales revenue but the effects on price are not certain in Baumol's model. Price will depend on the shift of the demand and the cost conditions of the firm. (See below.)

Model 2: a single-product model, with advertising

The assumptions of the model. As in the previous model the goal of the firm is sales revenue maximisation subject to a minimum profit constraint which is exogenously determined. The new element in this model is the introduction of advertising as a major instrument (policy variable) of the firm. Baumol argues that in the real world non-price competition is the typical form of competition in oligopolistic markets. The model presented by Baumol treats explicitly advertising, but other forms of non-price competition (product change, service, quality, etc.) may be analysed on similar lines.

The crucial assumption of the advertising model is that sales revenue increases with advertising expenditure (that is, $\partial R/\partial a > 0$, where a = advertising expenditure). This implies that advertising will always shift the demand curve of the firm to the right and the firm will sell a larger quantity and earn a larger revenue. The price is assumed to remain constant. This, however, is a simplifying assumption which may be relaxed in a more general analysis (Baumol, *Business Behaviour, Value and Growth*, p. 58).[1] Another simplifying assumption is that production costs are independent of advertising. Baumol recognises that this is an unrealistic assumption, since with advertising the physical volume of output increases and the firm might move to a cost structure where production cost is different (increasing or decreasing). But he claims that this assumption is simplifying and can be relaxed without substantially altering the analysis. (In fact

---

[1] An explicit geometric treatment of the interdependence between price and advertising has been presented by R. L. Sandmeyer, 'Baumol's Sales-Maximisation Model: Comment', *American Economic Review* (1964), and has been extended by R. Haveman and G. DeBartolo, 'The Revenue Maximisation Oligopoly Model: Comment', *American Economic Review* (1968) and by M. Kafoglis and R. Bushnell, 'The Revenue-Maximisation Oligopoly Model: Comment', *American Economic Review* (1970). The Haveman–DeBartolo model, as modified by Kafoglis and Bushnell, is presented on pp. 333–5 below.

Baumol relaxes this assumption, as well as the assumption of constant price in the mathematical presentation of his model; see below.) From the above assumptions the following inferences can be drawn.

A firm in an oligopolistic market will prefer to increase its sales by advertising rather than by a cut in price. While an increase in physical volume induced by a price cut may or may not increase the sales revenue, depending on whether demand is elastic or inelastic, an increase in volume brought about by an increase in advertising will always increase sales revenue, since by assumption the marginal revenue of advertising is positive ($\partial R/\partial a > 0$).

With advertising introduced into the model, it is no longer possible to have an equilibrium where the profit constraint is not operative. While with price competition alone it is possible to reach an equilibrium (that is, maximise sales) where $\overline{\Pi}$ is not operative, with non-price competition such an unconstrained equilibrium is impossible. Unlike a price reduction, increased advertising always increases sales revenue. Consequently it will always pay the sales maximiser to increase his advertising expenditure until he is stopped by the profit constraint. Consequently the minimum profit constraint is always operative when advertising (or any other form of non-price competition) is introduced in the model.

The sales maximiser will normally have higher advertising expenditures than a profit maximiser. In any case advertising cannot be less in a sales-maximising model.

Baumol's single-product model with advertising is shown in figure 15.5. Advertising outlay is measured on the horizontal axis and the advertising function is shown as a 45° line. Costs, total revenue and profits are measured on the vertical axis. Production costs are shown as being independent of the level of advertising (curve CC'). If these costs are added to the advertising cost line we obtain the total-cost curve (TC) as a function of advertising outlay. Subtracting the total cost from the total revenue at each level of output we obtain the total-profit curve Π. The interrelationship between output and advertising and in particular the (assumed) positive marginal revenue of advertising permits us to see clearly that an unconstrained sales maximisation is (ordinarily) not possible. If price is such as to enable the firm to sell an output yielding profits above their minimum acceptable level, it will pay the firm to increase advertising and reach a higher level of sales revenue. The advertising outlay of the sales maximiser ($0A_s$) is higher than

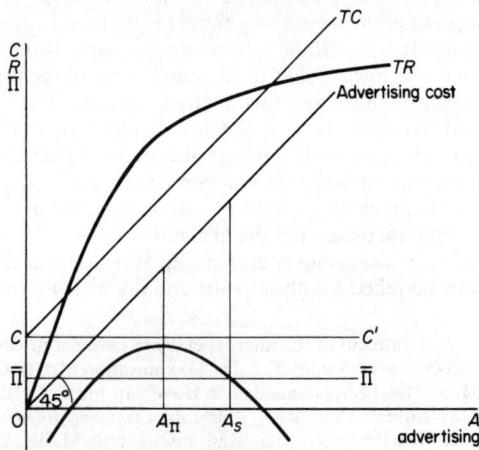

Figure 15.5

that of the profit maximiser ($0A_\Pi$), and the profit constraint ($\overline{\Pi}$) is operative at equilibrium.

It should be stressed that the validity of this model rests on the crucial assumption that advertising always increases sales revenue. Baumol *assumes* that $\partial R/\partial a > 0$, but does not establish the implied positive relation between total revenue and advertising.

In particular Baumol does not examine explicitly the interrelationship between advertising, price, cost of production and level of output.

If total production costs are independent of advertising, (that is, production costs remain constant after advertising takes place) as Baumol assumes, this implies that total output X will remain constant after advertising has taken place; consequently an increase in sales revenue R, given X, can be attained only if P is raised. This case is in fact implied in figure 15.5, reproduced from Baumol's book (p. 59).

However, this is inconsistent with what Baumol states elsewhere (p. 60), that 'unlike a price reduction a *ceteris paribus* rise in advertising expenditure involves no change in the market value of the item sold'. This statement implies clearly that advertising will *not* change the price. Hence Baumol implies that the increase in revenue will be attained from an increase in the volume X. But then production costs will increase, since MC is always positive.

In short, Baumol's graphical representation of his model is inconsistent with his statements. In particular the price implications of a change in advertising are not obvious in Baumol's analysis. Sandmeyer,[1] Haveman and DeBartolo,[2] and Kafoglis and Bushnell[3] have highlighted this deficiency of Baumol's model. They suggested that with advertising expenditures the TR curve will shift and in the new equilibrium revenue will be higher and advertising expenditure will be higher (consistent with Baumol). However, output may be lower and price higher in the new equilibrium, depending on the shift and the elasticity of the demand curve following advertising, as well as on the cost conditions of the firm. This situation has not been explicitly envisaged by Baumol, whose model has been interpreted as implying that all 'excess' profit will be devoted to advertising and that, therefore, the increase in revenue will accrue from an increase in output resulting from the shift of the demand curve following advertising. However, Baumol's mathematical model allows for the possibility of a change in price as well as of advertising and output (see below).

Haveman and DeBartolo have presented a model which they call 'generalised Baumol model'. In their model price, cost, output and advertising expenditure are all free to vary. We will first present graphically their model as modified by M. Kafoglis and R. Bushnell[4] and by C. J. Hawkins.[5] We will next present their model mathematically and will point out that actually their model is identical to Baumol's mathematical presentation of his advertising model.

The cost curves. It is assumed that: (a) Production costs vary proportionally with output. Thus the total production cost function is a straight (positively-sloping) line through the

---

[1] R. L. Sandmeyer, 'Baumol's Sales-Maximisation Model: Comment', *American Economic Review* (1964).

[2] R. Haveman and G. DeBartolo, 'The Revenue-Maximisation Oligopoly Model: Comment', *American Economic Review* (1968) pp. 1355–8.

[3] M. Kafoglis and R. Bushnell, 'The Revenue-Maximisation Oligopoly Model: Comment', *American Economic Review* (1970). Also R. Haveman and G. DeBartolo, 'Reply', *American Economic Review* (1970).

[4] M. Kafoglis and R. Bushnell, 'The Revenue-Maximisation Oligopoly Model: Comment', *American Economic Review* (1970).

[5] C. J. Hawkins, 'The Revenue Maximisation Oligopoly Model: Comment', *American Economic Review* (1970).

origin. (*b*) Advertising expenditure may change but is independent of the level of output. Thus a given level of advertising is presented by a straight line parallel to the X-axis. Higher advertising levels are shown by parallel lines which are further away from the X-axis. (*c*) The minimum profit constraint is exogenously determined and is denoted by a line parallel to the X-axis.

The total cost function is the summation of the production cost (C), the advertising expenditure (A_i) and the minimum profit constraint ($\overline{\Pi}$). Given the production cost function and the minimum profit constraint, a change in advertising (A_i) will generate a family of total-cost curves which will be upward-sloping (with their slope equal to the slope of production cost function). Such a family of total-cost curves is shown in figure 15.6.

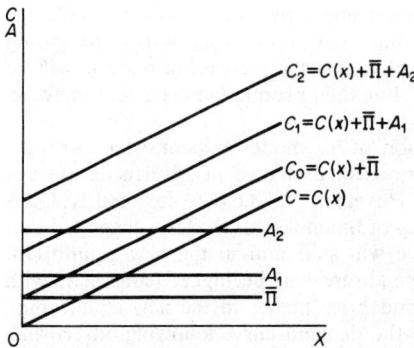

Figure 15.6

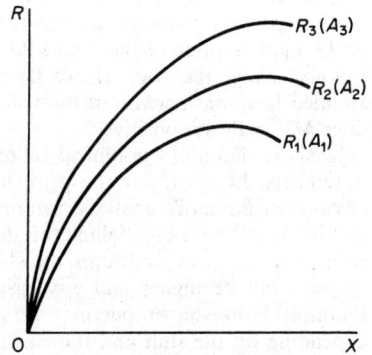

Figure 15.7

The revenue curves. The total-revenue curve has the usual shape, initially increasing but at a decreasing rate, reaching a maximum (where $\partial R/\partial X = 0$), and then decreasing (as $\partial R/\partial X < 0$).

The total-revenue curve shifts upwards as advertising is increased. Thus, by changing advertising we may generate a family of total-revenue curves, each representing the relationship of total revenue to output at different levels of advertising expenditure. Such a family of total-revenue curves is shown in figure 15.7. Curve R_1 is drawn on the assumption that advertising expenditure is A_1. Curve R_2 implies an advertising expenditure of A_2, and so on.

Equilibrium of the firm. If we superimpose figures 15.6 and 15.7 and join the points of intersection of total-cost and total-revenue curves corresponding to the same amount of advertising expenditure, we obtain a curve which is called by Haveman and DeBartolo the '$TC = TR$' curve. It is the dotted curve in figure 15.8. The firm is in equilibrium when it reaches the highest point of this curve. The equilibrium of the firm is at point a^*, with total costs C^*, total revenue R^*, output X^*, advertising A^*, and price equal to $0R^*/0X^*$.

It should be clear that two conditions must be satisfied for equilibrium: Firstly, the firm must operate on some point of the '$TC = TR$' curve. Secondly, $MC > MR$ at equilibrium. Thus at point a_3 the first condition is fulfilled ($C_3 = R_3$) but the second condition is violated, since at a_3 the two curves are tangent, implying $MC = MR$. Thus if the sales maximiser was producing at X_3, he would substitute production expenditure for advertising expenditure (a reallocation of resources from advertising to increased production) until output increased to X^*. In the process of adjustment price would fall,

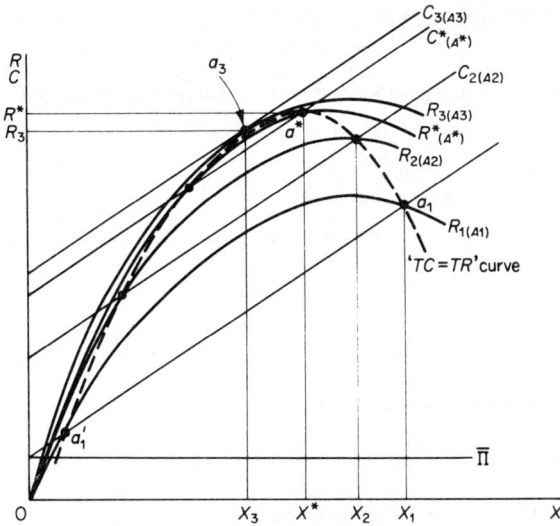

Figure 15.8

but the loss in revenue from this cause would be more than offset by the additional revenue from the increased output sold. In figure 15.8 we see that $R^* > R_3$.

A mathematical presentation of Baumol's Model 2

We define

$$R = f_1(X, a) = \text{total revenue function}$$
$$C = f_2(X) = \text{total production cost function}$$
$$\overline{\Pi} = \text{minimum acceptable profit}$$
$$A(a) = \text{total cost of advertising function}$$

The firm aims at the maximisation of

$$R = f_1(X, a)$$

subject to the minimum profit constraint

$$\Pi = R - C - A \geq \overline{\Pi}$$

It is assumed that

$$\frac{\partial R}{\partial a} > 0, \qquad \frac{\partial C}{\partial X} > 0, \qquad X > 0$$

Baumol's assumption

$$\frac{\partial R}{\partial a} > 0$$

that is, demand shifts always in response to advertising, ensures that the constraint is operative.[1]

---

[1] Alternatively the assumption $\partial R/\partial X > 0$, that is, demand is always elastic ($e > 1$) for any relevant output, would alone ensure that the constraint is operative.

(1) For the constrained firm we have

$$R - C - A = \bar{\Pi}$$

(2) Using the Lagrangian multiplier method we may write the constraint in the form

$$\lambda(R - C - A - \bar{\Pi}) = 0$$

where λ is the Lagrangian multiplier.
(3) We next maximise the Lagrangian expression

$$\Phi = R + \lambda(\Pi - \bar{\Pi})$$

or

$$\Phi = R + \lambda(R - C - A - \bar{\Pi}) \tag{15.1}$$

Given that we choose to write the second term of the Lagrangian form with a positive sign, the value of λ must be positive ($\lambda > 0$).[1]
The necessary conditions for a maximum are

$$\frac{\partial \Phi}{\partial X} \leq 0, \qquad \frac{\partial \Phi}{\partial a} \leq 0, \qquad \frac{\partial \Phi}{\partial \lambda} \geq 0$$

(i) Differentiating (15.1) with respect to X we obtain

$$\frac{\partial \Phi}{\partial X} = \frac{\partial R}{\partial X} + \lambda\left(\frac{\partial R}{\partial X} - \frac{\partial C}{\partial X}\right) \leq 0$$

Given $X > 0$, the above expression holds as an equality. Solving for $\partial C/\partial X$ we obtain

$$\frac{\partial C}{\partial X} = \frac{\lambda + 1}{\lambda} \cdot \frac{\partial R}{\partial X} = \left(1 + \frac{1}{\lambda}\right)\frac{\partial R}{\partial X} \tag{15.2}$$

Given that $\lambda > 0$, it is obvious that

$$\frac{\partial C}{\partial X} > \frac{\partial R}{\partial X} \quad \text{or} \quad MC > MR$$

while for a profit maximiser $MC = MR$. This shows that the output of a sales maximiser will be larger than the output of a profit maximiser.
(ii) Differentiating (15.1) with respect to advertising a we obtain

$$\frac{\partial \Phi}{\partial a} = \frac{\partial R}{\partial a} + \lambda\left(\frac{\partial R}{\partial a} - \frac{\partial A}{\partial a}\right) \leq 0$$

Assuming $a > 0$, the above expression holds as an equality. Solving for $\partial A/\partial a$ we obtain

$$\frac{\partial A}{\partial a} = \left(1 + \frac{1}{\lambda}\right)\frac{\partial R}{\partial a}$$

or

$$\left(\frac{\partial A}{\partial a} \middle/ \frac{\partial R}{\partial a}\right) = \left(1 + \frac{1}{\lambda}\right) \tag{15.3}$$

[1] Baumol writes the Lagrangian form as

$$\Phi = R - \lambda(R - C - A - \bar{\Pi})$$

Hence in his analysis $\lambda < 0$.

while for a profit maximiser

$$\left(\frac{\partial A}{\partial a} \middle/ \frac{\partial R}{\partial a}\right) = 1$$

Thus, given $\lambda > 0$, advertising expenditure will be higher for a sales maximiser.

M. Kafoglis and R. Bushnell have extended Baumol's mathematical presentation as follows.

(1) Expression (15.2) may be written as

$$\left(\frac{\partial C}{\partial X} \middle/ \frac{\partial R}{\partial X}\right) = \left(1 + \frac{1}{\lambda}\right) \tag{15.4}$$

For $a > 0$, expression (15.3) holds. Hence when advertising takes place the following equilibrium condition holds

$$\left(\frac{\partial C}{\partial X} \middle/ \frac{\partial R}{\partial X}\right) = \left(\frac{\partial A}{\partial a} \middle/ \frac{\partial R}{\partial a}\right) = \left(1 + \frac{1}{\lambda}\right) \tag{15.5}$$

This implies that surplus profits will be devoted partly to advertising and partly to increased production.

(2) If we make no assumption about the value of a (advertising), then expression (15.3) becomes

$$\left(\frac{\partial A}{\partial a} \middle/ \frac{\partial R}{\partial a}\right) \geq \left(1 + \frac{1}{\lambda}\right) \tag{15.6}$$

Combining (15.4) and (15.6) we obtain

$$\left(\frac{\partial R}{\partial X} \middle/ \frac{\partial C}{\partial X}\right) \geq \left(\frac{\partial R}{\partial a} \middle/ \frac{\partial A}{\partial a}\right) \tag{15.7}$$

The inequality sign implies that an extra money unit spent on producing additional X adds more to the total revenue than if it were spent on additional advertising. Thus all surplus profit will be spent on increased production and no advertising will take place.

In any case (Kafoglis and Bushnell conclude) price will always be lower and advertising expenditure smaller than when all surplus profit is allocated to advertising.

In conclusion Baumol's mathematical version of his advertising model allows for 'excessive' production expenditure and lower price as well as for the more commonly accepted case of 'excessive' advertising and higher price. In fact Baumol's model is even compatible with strong price competition, which may result in a price lower than the MC. This can be easily seen if in the equilibrium condition

$$MC > MR$$

we substitute

$$MR = P\left(1 - \frac{1}{e}\right)$$

to obtain

$$MC > P\left(1 - \frac{1}{e}\right)$$

With appropriate values of $|e|$ it is possible that[1]

$$MC > P > MR$$

[1] See M. Kafoglis and R. Bushnell, 'The Revenue-Maximisation Oligopoly Model: Comment', *American Economic Review* (1970).

Model 3: multiproduct firm, without advertising

If we assume that the firm has a given amount of resources (and given costs $\bar{C}$) and wants to allocate them among the various commodities it produces so as to maximise sales revenue, it will reach the same equilibrium solution as the profit maximiser, that is, it will produce the same quantities of the various products as if it were a profit maximiser. Formally, the condition for the equilibrium of the multiproduct firm (with given resources and costs) is

$$\frac{\partial R/\partial X_i}{\partial R/\partial X_j} = \frac{\partial C/\partial X_i}{\partial C/\partial X_j}$$

which reads: the firm is in equilibrium when the ratio of the marginal revenue from any two commodities (i and j) is equal to the ratio of their marginal costs.

We may present the above solution graphically, assuming for simplicity that the firm produces two commodities, y and x. The required apparatus has been developed in Chapter 3. It involves the tools of the product transformation curve and of isorevenue curves.

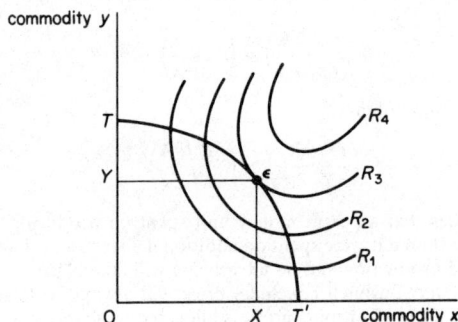

Figure 15.9

The slope of the transformation curve is called the marginal rate of product transformation and is equal to the ratio of the marginal costs of the two commodities:

$$MRT_{y,x} = -\frac{\partial C/\partial X}{\partial C/\partial Y}$$

The product transformation curve is concave to the origin showing the increasing difficulty (increasing cost) of reducing product y and reallocating the resources to the increase of product x.

An isorevenue curve shows the same revenue earned by different combinations of quantities of y and x. The further away from the origin, the higher the total revenue earned. The isorevenue curve has a slope equal to the ratio of the marginal revenues of the two commodities:

$$\begin{bmatrix} \text{Slope of} \\ \text{isorevenue} \\ \text{curve} \end{bmatrix} = \frac{\partial R/\partial X}{\partial R/\partial Y} = \frac{\text{Marginal revenue of } x}{\text{Marginal revenue of } y}$$

The isorevenue curve is drawn convex to the origin, implying a falling demand curve for the two products, and hence a declining marginal revenue for additional units sold.

(If prices were constant, the isorevenue curve would be a straight line with a negative slope, equal to the ratio of the prices of x and y.)

The firm is in equilibrium at point ε where the given product transformation curve is tangent to the highest isorevenue curve. The firm maximises its sales revenue by selling $0X$ of commodity x and $0Y$ of commodity y. This solution is identical with the equilibrium of a profit maximiser (see Chapter 3). There is nothing startling about this, since in both models we assume given resources and costs. The profit maximiser maximises

$$\Pi = R - \bar{C}$$

Clearly, given $\bar{C}$, whatever output combination maximises R also maximises profit Π.

However, if the resources (and costs) are not given and the firm can allocate increased quantities of factors to the production of any product, the profit maximiser will have a different equilibrium product mix than the sales maximiser. This may be shown graphically by using isorevenue and isoprofit curves (figure 15.10). The isorevenue curves have the same convex shape as previously. The isoprofit curves are concave to the origin,

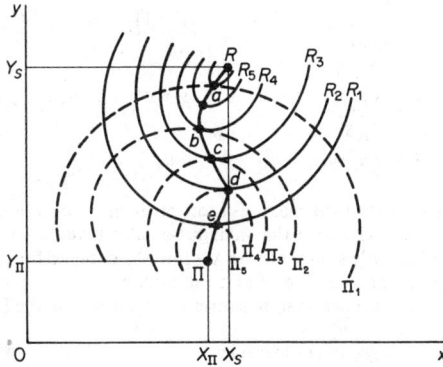

Figure 15.10

showing that the profitability of y and x decreases after a certain level of output, and may even become negative (losses): with a downward-falling demand curve for both commodities, revenues and profits decrease at high levels of output (as well as at low levels of output). Since the products compete for the resources of the firm, the closer to the origin an isoprofit curve is the higher the level of profit it depicts (see Chapter 9). If the minimum profit constraint is Π_1, the equilibrium of the sales maximiser is defined by point a on the isorevenue curve R_6. Similarly, if the minimum acceptable profit is Π_2, the sales-maximising solution is b on curve R_4. In general, the higher the profit constraint the lower is the attainable sales revenue. Point R represents the unconstrained sales-maximisation solution; it is the level of sales where $MR = 0$, and is attained if the profit constraint is not operative, while point Π represents the profit-maximisation solution. Given the shapes of costs and demand curves implied by the isorevenue and the isoprofit curves, output levels of both y and x are higher for a sales maximiser than for a profit maximiser.

In summary, if the resources (and costs) are not given, the multiproduct firm will reach a different product mix, depending on whether it is a profit maximiser or a sales maximiser.

The formal condition of equilibrium of a sales-maximising multiproduct firm may be stated as follows:

$$\frac{\partial R}{\partial X_i} \bigg/ \frac{\partial R}{\partial X_j} = \frac{\partial \Pi}{\partial X_i} \bigg/ \frac{\partial \Pi}{\partial X_j}$$

which reads: the ratio of the marginal revenues of commodities i and j must be equal to the ratio of their marginal profitabilities. That is, the equilibrium of a sales maximiser is defined by a point of tangency of the isorevenue and the isoprofit curves; it will be a point on the curve *Rabcde*.

Model 4: multiproduct model, with advertising

We will develop this model using calculus so as to achieve maximum generality. The firm aims at sales revenue maximisation subject to a minimum profit constraint.
Formally we have:

Maximise $\qquad\qquad\qquad R = f_1(X_i, a_i)$

(where a_i = advertising expenditure on commodity i)

subject to $\qquad\qquad\qquad \Pi = R - C - A = \overline{\Pi}$

where

$$R = \Sigma P_i X_i = P_1 X_1 + P_2 X_2 + \cdots + P_n X_n$$
$$C = f_2(X_1, X_2, \ldots, X_n)$$
$$A = \Sigma a_i = a_1 + a_2 + \cdots + a_n$$

From the solution of this constrained maximisation problem[1] we obtain the levels of output (X_is) and the levels of advertising (a_is) that maximise sales revenue and earn the minimum acceptable profit. We subsequently substitute the X_is into the demand functions of the individual products (which are assumed known) and obtain the prices.

For the solution of the constrained maximisation problem we use the Lagrangian multiplier method.
The 'composite' function (or Lagrangian form) is

$$\phi = R + \lambda(R - C - A - \overline{\Pi}) \qquad\qquad\qquad (15.8)$$

The levels of output $X_1, X_2, \ldots, X_n$ are defined by a set of n equations derived by differentiating (15.8) with respect to X_i. For any two products (X_i and X_j) we have the functions

$$\frac{\partial \phi}{\partial X_i} = \frac{\partial R}{\partial X_i} + \lambda\left(\frac{\partial R}{\partial X_i} - \frac{\partial C}{\partial X_i}\right) = 0$$

$$\frac{\partial \phi}{\partial X_j} = \frac{\partial R}{\partial X_j} + \lambda\left(\frac{\partial R}{\partial X_j} - \frac{\partial C}{\partial X_j}\right) = 0$$

which yield

$$\frac{\partial R}{\partial X_i} \bigg/ \frac{\partial R}{\partial X_j} = \frac{\partial C}{\partial X_i} \bigg/ \frac{\partial C}{\partial X_j}$$

This is the same condition as the one for model 3. Advertising does not alter this condition due to Baumol's assumption that advertising is not a function of output.
The levels of advertising expenses on each product, $a_1, a_2, \ldots, a_n$ are obtained from another

---

[1] It is assumed that the minimum profit constraint is operative.

set of n equations derived by differentiating ϕ with respect to a_i. Thus for any two products $(X_i$ and $X_j)$ we have

$$\frac{\partial \phi}{\partial a_i} = \frac{\partial R}{\partial a_i} + \lambda \left(\frac{\partial R}{\partial a_i} - 1 \right) = 0$$

$$\frac{\partial \phi}{\partial a_j} = \frac{\partial R}{\partial a_j} + \lambda \left(\frac{\partial R}{\partial a_j} - 1 \right) = 0$$

which yield the additional equilibrium condition

$$\frac{\partial R}{\partial a_i} \bigg/ \frac{\partial R}{\partial a_j} = 1$$

or

$$\frac{\partial R}{\partial a_i} = \frac{\partial R}{\partial a_j}$$

This condition states that the marginal revenue of advertising commodity i must be equal to the marginal revenue of advertising commodity j. If this were not so, the firm could increase R by reallocating the total advertising expenditure A among the different products, increasing advertising on those commodities for which the marginal revenue would be higher.

We thus have $2n + 1$ equations to be solved for the n outputs $(X_1, X_2, \ldots, X_n)$, the n advertising expenditures $(a_1, a_2, \ldots, a_n)$ and for the Lagrangian multiplier λ:

$$\frac{\partial R}{\partial X_i} = \frac{\lambda}{1 + \lambda} \frac{\partial C}{\partial X_i} \qquad (i = 1, 2, \ldots, n)$$

$$\frac{\partial R}{\partial a_i} = \frac{\lambda}{1 + \lambda} \qquad (i = 1, 2, \ldots, n)$$

$$R - C - A = \overline{\Pi}$$

We may easily establish that with advertising included in the model the minimum profit constraint will always be operative. That is, the firm will not reach point R on figure 15.10, because it will be stopped at a lower revenue by the profit constraint. To prove this it suffices to show that the marginal revenues of the products are positive at the equilibrium solution, that is

$$\frac{\partial R}{\partial X_i} > 0 \qquad (i = 1, 2, \ldots, n)$$

We established that

$$\frac{\partial R}{\partial X_i} = \frac{\lambda}{1 + \lambda} \frac{\partial C}{\partial X_i} = \left(\frac{\lambda}{\lambda + 1} \right) \left(\frac{\partial C}{\partial X_i} \right) \qquad (15.9)$$

and

$$\frac{\partial R}{\partial a_i} = \frac{\lambda}{\lambda + 1}$$

But the marginal cost is always positive $(\partial C / \partial X_i > 0)$ and by Baumol's assumption the marginal revenue of advertising is positive $(\partial R / \partial a_i > 0)$, so that $\lambda / (\lambda + 1) > 0$. Consequently

$$\frac{\partial R}{\partial X_i} > 0$$

given

$$\frac{\lambda}{\lambda + 1} > 0 \quad \text{and} \quad \frac{\partial C}{\partial X_i} > 0$$

Thus the firm will not be in equilibrium if $\Pi > \bar{\Pi}$, because by increasing its advertising expenditure (and reducing Π) it will attain a higher sales revenue. In other words the profit constraint is always operative.

Furthermore, at equilibrium

$$\frac{\partial C}{\partial X_i} > \frac{\partial R}{\partial X_i}$$

that is, the marginal cost for any one commodity is greater than its marginal revenue. This is derived from expression (15.9) as follows.

$$\frac{\partial R}{\partial X_i} = \left(\frac{\lambda}{\lambda + 1}\right)\left(\frac{\partial C}{\partial X_i}\right)$$

Solving for $\partial C/\partial X_i$ we obtain

$$\frac{\partial C}{\partial X_i} = \left(\frac{\lambda + 1}{\lambda}\right)\left(\frac{\partial R}{\partial X_i}\right) = \left(1 + \frac{1}{\lambda}\right)\frac{\partial R}{\partial X_i}$$

Given $\lambda > 0$, it follows that

$$\frac{\partial C}{\partial X_i} > \frac{\partial R}{\partial X_i}$$

This model can be extended to cover simultaneous changes in advertising and in output when surplus profits are earned.

IV. BAUMOL'S DYNAMIC MODEL

The static single-period model developed in the previous section is only an introduction to the more ambitious multiperiod analysis attempted by Baumol. The most serious weakness of the static model is the short time-horizon of the firm and the treatment of the profit constraint as an exogenously determined magnitude. In the dynamic model the time-horizon is extended and the profit constraint is endogenously determined.

The assumptions of the dynamic model

1. The firm attempts to maximise the rate of growth of sales over its lifetime.
2. Profit is the main means of financing growth of sales, and as such is an instrumental variable whose value is endogenously determined.
3. Demand and costs have the traditional shape: demand is downward-falling and costs are U-shaped.

Profit is not a constraint (as in the static model) but an instrumental variable, a means whereby the top management will achieve its goal of a maximum rate of growth of sales.

Growth may be financed by internal and external sources. However, there are limits to the external sources of finance. Thus profits will be the main source for financing the rate of growth of sales revenue. For simplicity we may actually assume that growth will be entirely financed by profits.

The multiperiod model

We assume that the sales revenue (R) grows at a rate of growth (g) per cent. Over its lifetime the firm will have a stream of revenues

$$R, R(1 + g), R(1 + g)^2, \ldots, R(1 + g)^n$$

The present value of this stream of future revenues is estimated by the usual discount formula

$$R, R\left(\frac{1 + g}{1 + i}\right), R\left(\frac{1 + g}{1 + i}\right)^2, \ldots, R\left(\frac{1 + g}{1 + i}\right)^n$$

where i is the subjective rate of discount of the firm. The latter is exogenously given by the expectations and risk-preferences of the firm, and is higher than any form of market interest rate because it includes subjective assessment of risk.

The total present (discounted) value of all future revenues is

$$S = \sum_{t=0}^{n} R\left(\frac{1 + g}{1 + i}\right)^t \qquad (t = 0, 1, \ldots, n)$$

The firm attempts to maximise the present value of the stream of sales revenue over its lifetime, by choosing appropriate values for the current (initial) level of sales revenue (R) and its growth rate (g). It is obvious that S is positively related to both R and g: the present value of the stream of revenues will be higher for higher R and g values. Thus the firm should choose as large as possible values of R and g.[1]

Given that g is financed (mainly or totally) by the internal profits one might ask whether sales maximisation makes sense as the goal of the firm in a multiperiod analysis. Surely by maximising profits the firm could finance a higher rate of growth. Why then sacrifice current profits in favour of increased current sales? The answer to this question lies in the nature of the relationship between profits (Π), current sales (R), and the rate of growth (g). The growth function is

$$g = f_1(\Pi, R)$$

where R, the current sales revenue, is an instrumental variable, and profits Π are defined by the function

$$\Pi = f_2(R, g, i, C)$$

(where C denotes costs).

The growth function is actually derived from the profit function and is shown in figure 15.11. Expansion of the firm will depend on the current level of profits, because the retained portion of Π is the (primary) source of growth. Consequently the highest attainable growth rate (g) will be at the point of maximum profits. Beyond the level of sales revenue where profits are maximised, that is, beyond $R_{\Pi m}$ in figure 15.11, the growth rate will decline, as profits are declining. In other words, up to point a, which corresponds to the maximum profit level, both the current sales revenue R and its rate of growth g increase simultaneously. Beyond that point, however, current sales revenue continues to increase but the rate of growth declines. Thus beyond $R_{\Pi m}$ sales revenue and growth become competing goals: the firm has to choose between higher current revenue growing at a lower growth rate over time, and lower current sales growing faster over time. Clearly there is an infinite combination of values of g and R that the firm may

---

[1] Note that the firm cannot choose both the maximum g *and* the maximum R simultaneously, due to the nature of the functional relationship between g and R, which is explained below.

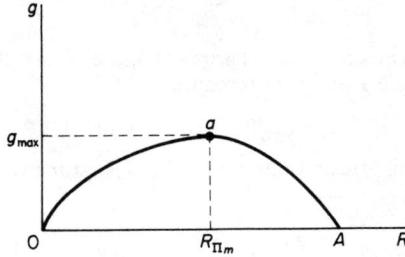

Figure 15.11

choose. Among all possible values the firm will choose the pair of values of g and R that maximise the present value of the future stream of sales S.

To find the equilibrium of the firm we need an additional tool, the *iso-present-value curve*. This curve shows all combinations of g and R that yield the same S. Recall that from the definition of S

$$S = \sum_{t=0}^{n} R\left(\frac{1 + g}{1 + i}\right)^{t}$$

that is, the discounted value of the stream of future revenues is positively related to both g and R and negatively related to the subjective discount rate i. Given i (which is exogenously determined), the simplest relationship that can be postulated between these variables is of a linear form

$$S = b_1 \cdot g + b_2 \cdot R \tag{15.10}$$

where b_1 and b_2 are constant coefficients, which may be estimated from past performance. Solving this equation for g we find

$$g = \frac{1}{b_1} S - \frac{b_2}{b_1} R \tag{15.11}$$

With this equation we may find any iso-present-value curve. For example, assume that the values of the parameters of the S function are

$$b_1 = 250 \quad \text{and} \quad b_2 = 0.5$$

These values, substituted in (15.11), yield

$$g = \frac{1}{250} S - \frac{0.5}{250} R$$

or

$$g = 0.004S - 0.002R \tag{15.12}$$

The iso-present-value curve showing $S = 10$ is found by substituting this value in (15.12) and assigning different values to R. Thus:

$$
\begin{array}{ll}
\text{if } R = 0 & g = 0.4 \\
\text{if } R = 1 & g = 0.038 \\
\text{if } R = 2 & g = 0.036 \\
\text{if } R = 20 & g = 0
\end{array}
$$

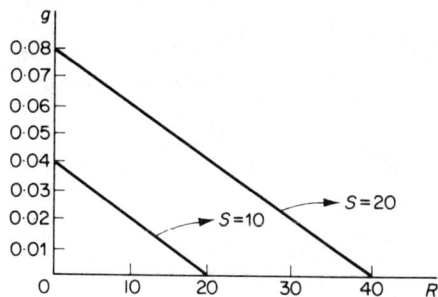

Figure 15.12

Plotting these pairs of g, R values on a graph and joining them with a straight line we obtain the iso-present-value curve $S = 10$ (see figure 15.12). By assigning different values to S and repeating the above process we may obtain a set of S curves. Under our assumptions the iso-present-value curves will be downward-sloping and will be parallel to one another. Their slope is given by the ratio of the coefficients b_1 and b_2 of the S function (that is, slope of $S = b_2/b_1$). Of course the S curves may be non-linear, of any form. The only requirement is that they have a negative slope, and this has been established on *a priori* grounds. Clearly the further away from the origin an iso-present-value curve lies, the higher the discounted stream of revenues it depicts.

The firm will choose the highest possible of the iso-present-value curves. That is, the firm is in equilibrium at the point of tangency of the growth curve ($0aA$) to the highest S curve (point ε in figure 15.13). The point of tangency defines the equilibrium values g^* and R^*, that is, the attainable rate of growth and the level of current sales which maximises the present value of the stream of future revenues (S^* in figure 15.13).

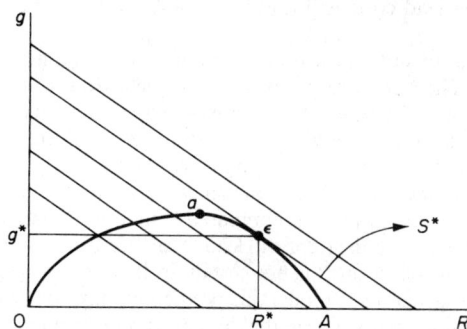

Figure 15.13

The curve $0aA$ depicts the attainable growth rate (g) for any given value of current sales revenue (R). Growth is financed out of current profits, and the growth curve is therefore derived from the profit curve (0Π in figure 15.14). Note that at the origin and at the output level $0B$ total profit is zero and hence the rate of growth is zero). Given R^*, we may determine the equilibrium level of output from the total revenue curve in figure 15.14. The sales maximiser will produce output X^* and will sell it at a price equal to $0R^*/0X^*$. Given the equilibrium output X^* and the profit function, the profit constraint is now endogenously determined at Π^*. In other words, the sales maximiser will require a profit level of Π^* in order to finance the optimal growth rate g^*.

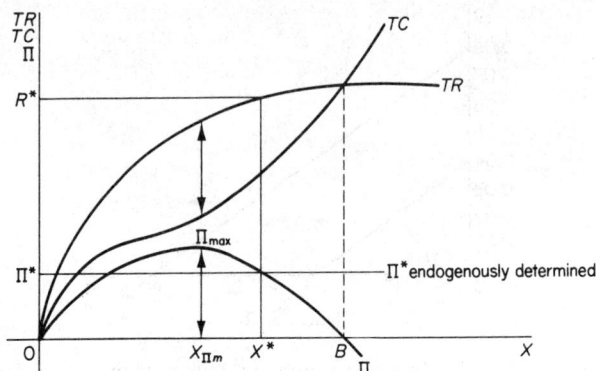

Figure 15.14

The multiperiod model can be modified to allow for an exogenously determined minimum acceptable level of profit, as well as to allow for advertising and other non-price competition activities and for multiproduct activities.

The predictions of the multiperiod model are the same as those of the single-period model:

Output will be higher and price lower for a sales maximiser than for a profit maximiser if advertising is ignored. However, with advertising taking place there may be conditions under which these predictions will be different. (See the Haveman–DeBartolo version of the sales-maximisation model.)

Advertising expenditures will be higher for a sales maximiser, due to the assumption of a monotonic positive relation between sales revenue (R) and advertising expenditure.

An increase in overhead costs will lead to a reduction in output and an increase in price.

The levying of a lump-sum tax will have similar results: an increase in price and a reduction in output. The welfare implications of the behaviour of a sales maximiser are obvious. If the government imposes a lump-sum tax with the aim of redistributing income away from the taxed firm, its goal will not be attained, since the sales maximiser will shift the burden to his customers by charging increased prices.

Imposition of a specific tax will lead the sales maximiser to a larger reduction in output and a larger increase in price as compared with a profit maximiser.

A shift in market demand to the right will lead to an increase in output and an increase in advertising, while the effect on P is not certain in Baumol's model. However, in the Haveman–DeBartolo generalised model this prediction may not be true.

An increase in variable costs will lead the sales maximiser to an increase in price and a reduction in output. These changes will be greater than those of a profit maximiser.

V. EMPIRICAL EVIDENCE

Baumol claims that an increase in overheads, or the imposition of a lump-tax, both lead to an increase in the price charged by firms. This business practice, Baumol argues, provides evidence in support of his theory.

However, the same business behaviour would be appropriate for a firm which sets its price at such a level as to prevent entry. Recall that according to all versions of limit-pricing, a general increase in costs, or the imposition of a tax that affects all firms in the industry in the same way, will induce firms to increase their prices, because they know that everyone will follow the same policy and thus there is no danger of losing market share. In general the behavioural differences between long-run profit maximisation and sales maximisation are so subtle that no conclusive econometric tests can be carried out with the available data, most of which are compatible with various behavioural hypotheses.

Sales maximisation is incompatible with an elasticity of demand of less than unity. Thus one would think that if the estimation of firms' demand functions show $|e| < 1$, this would provide evidence against the sales-maximisation hypothesis.[1] Yet there are so many variables that affect demand over time that econometric studies of individual demand functions become extremely tedious and mostly unreliable. No one has as yet published satisfactory results on individual demand functions.

McGuire, Chiu and Elbing[2] attempted to test Baumol's contention that 'executive salaries appear to be far more closely correlated with the scale of operations of the firm than with profitability'. They chose 45 of the largest 100 industrial corporations in the United States and computed simple correlation coefficients between executive incomes and sales revenue (r_{YR}) and profits ($r_{Y\Pi}$) over the seven-year period 1953–59. Their results suggest that the correlation between executive incomes and sales revenue is stronger than the correlation between executive incomes and profits.

However, the authors recognise the serious limitations of simple correlation analysis, and in particular the fact that correlation does not necessarily imply causation, and they thus accept that their evidence is far from conclusive.

A more comprehensive empirical study was made by M. Hall.[3] He attempted to test the hypothesis implicit in Baumol's theory, that if profits above the minimum constraint are earned, *ceteris paribus*, firms pursue policies (for example, cut prices, and increase advertising and investment) in order to increase their sales revenue. He applied regression analysis to a sample of the largest American corporations, which operate in markets which fulfil the conditions of the sales-maximisation model. For each industry Hall estimated a minimum profit constraint (equal to the five-year mean profit rates for firms in the industry) and he assumed that this is the same for all the firms of his sample belonging to that industry. Hall's regression model is of the general form

$$\Delta S_{ij} = f(\Delta P_{ij}, \Delta D_{ij}, \Delta A_{ij}, V_1, V_2)$$

where ΔS_{ij} = change in sales of the ith firm in the jth industry.
$\quad\quad \Delta P_{ij}$ = deviation of the actual profit from the minimum profit constraint of the ith firm in the jth industry.
$\quad\quad \Delta D_{ij}$ = change in industry demand.
$\quad\quad \Delta A_{ij}$ = change in assets of the ith firm in the jth industry.
$\quad\quad V_1, V_2$ = dummy variables to account for other factors that are common across firms in a given industry.

On *a priori* grounds (that is, if firms were sales maximisers) Hall expected a strong positive relationship between sales revenue changes and the deviation of *actual* from the *desired* profit (that is, the estimated profit constraint), since a positive departure of actual profits from the minimum acceptable level would induce the firms to pursue policies which increase sales revenue. However, his measurements revealed insignificant correlations between these variables, thus providing evidence against Baumol's sales-maximisation hypothesis.

---

[1] Such evidence would support the limit-pricing theories; see Chapter 13.

[2] J. W. McGuire, J. S. Y. Chiu and A. O. Elbing, 'Executive Incomes, Sales, and Profits,' *American Economic Review* (1962).

[3] M. Hall, 'Sales Revenue Maximisation: An Empirical Examination', *Journal of Industrial Economics* (1967).

L. Waverman[1] questioned the empirical findings of Hall on the following main grounds: (a) the influence of exogenous variables, such as changes in demand and prices of factors, had not been adequately taken into account; (b) the estimate of the minimum profit constraint could be questioned on several grounds; (c) the estimation method used by Hall was not appropriate due to errors of measurement of the profits available. Hall in an answer to Waverman[2] accepts that the main defect of his study lies in the method of estimation of the minimum profit constraint, but he points out that this was the best he could do with the available data. This weakness, however, is very important and Waverman seems justified in questioning the results of Hall's study.

Marby and Siders[3] computed correlation coefficients between sales and profits (adjusted for trend) over twelve years (1952–63) for 120 large American Corporations. They argue that zero or negative correlations between sales and profits would support Baumol's hypothesis. Their findings showed positive significant correlations between sales revenue and profits. This result does not necessarily contradict the sales-maximisation hypothesis, since sales and profits are positively correlated in Baumol's model up to the point of maximum profits. The authors, recognising this fact, concentrated on 'reliable' data of twenty-five firms, which, they thought, had been operating at scales of output beyond the levels corresponding to maximum profit. However, even in these cases the correlations between profits and sales were mostly positive. This evidence was interpreted as refuting the sales-maximisation hypothesis.

D. R. Roberts[4] using a cross-section sample of 77 American firms (for the period 1948–50) found that executive earnings are correlated with the size of sales but not with the level of profits. This result provides evidence supporting Baumol's claim that managers have strong reasons to pursue the expansion of sales rather than increase profits.

In summary, we can say that although various studies have been conducted to test Baumol's hypothesis, the empirical evidence is not conclusive in favour of or against the sales-maximisation hypothesis.

VI. SOME COMMENTS

The sales-maximisation hypothesis cannot be tested against competing behavioural hypotheses unless the demand and cost functions of individual firms are measured. However, such data are not disclosed by firms to researchers, and are commonly unknown to the firms.

It has been argued that in the long run the sales-maximisation and the profit-maximisation hypotheses yield identical solutions; because profits attain their normal level in the long-run and the minimum profit constraint will coincide with the maximum attainable ('normal') level of profit. This argument cannot be accepted without any empirical evidence to support it.

The sales-maximisation theory does not show how equilibrium in an industry, in which all firms are sales maximisers, will be attained. The relationship between the firm and the industry is not established by Baumol.

Baumol's hypothesis is based on the implicit assumption that the firm has market

---

[1] L. Waverman, 'Sales Revenue Maximisation: A Note', *Journal of Industrial Economics* (1968).

[2] M. Hall, 'Sales Revenue Maximisation: Reply', *Journal of Industrial Economics* (1969).

[3] B. D. Marby and D. L. Siders, 'An Empirical Test of the Sales Maximisation Hypothesis', *Southern Economic Journal* (1966–7).

[4] D. R. Roberts, *Executive Compensation* (Glencoe, Ill.: Free Press, 1959).

power, that is, it can have control on its price and expansion policies. The firm can take decisions without being affected by competitors' reactions.

Thus Baumol rules out interdependence *ex hypothesi*, and hence his theory cannot explain the core problem of uncertainty in non-collusive oligopoly markets.

The theory cannot explain observed market situations in which price is kept for considerable time periods in the range of inelastic demand.

The theory ignores not only actual competition, but also the threat of potential competition. It fails to see that if a firm encroaches on the share of firms in the same industry or other industries, reactions are bound to set limits to its discretion in expanding sales.

The assumption that the *MR* of advertising is positive ($\partial R / \partial a > 0$) is not justified by Baumol. And casual observation shows that this may not be so.

M. H. Peston[1] ventured the idea that sales maximisation is not incompatible with the goal of long-run profit maximisation. A firm, he argues, may be willing to keep sales at a high level, even though they are unprofitable in the short run, in the hope that eventually (in the long run) the product will become profitable once established in the market.

Such behaviour is common for new products, for which the firm expects no profits or even losses at the initial stage of their introduction. However, firms expect to earn profits once their product becomes known in the market and captures a share at least equal to the minimum optimum scale. This behaviour, however, does not by itself provide a proof that the firm is a sales maximiser or a profit maximiser. After all, in Baumol's model, sales and profits are not competing goals up to the level of output at which profit is maximised. Thus Peston's argument does not seem to invalidate Baumol's theory.

Peston also argued that firms may increase their sales beyond the level at which profit is maximised from sheer ignorance of their demand curve. If the *LRAC* is falling and firms miscalculate their demand, they almost certainly surpass the profit-maximising output. Thus, Peston concludes, if firms are observed to sell too large an output, this does not show their preference for sales over profits, but may well be attributed to ignorance of demand conditions and the eagerness of firms to exploit technological changes which reduce costs at higher scales of output. We think that this argument of Peston's does not contradict the sales-revenue-maximisation hypothesis. Even with falling costs the two goals are complementary over some scales of output but become competing beyond a certain level of output.

J. R. Wildsmith[2] attacks Baumol on 'intuitive' grounds. He argues that the sales-maximisation model has the unacceptable implication that whenever profits above the minimum required level are earned 'managers would derive extra satisfaction from huge outlays on advertising which brought negligible increases in sales and large reductions in profits'. Put in this way the argument seems plausible enough. However, Wildsmith seems to overlook Baumol's statement that although in his model only advertising is explicitly introduced for simplicity, other activities (such as change in the style of the product, increase of staff, increase of perquisites of managers, research and development expenses) may be incorporated in it without altering its basic mechanics. Such activities are often undertaken (as well as additional advertising) when profits above the minimum required level are earned, and presumably they increase the utility of managers. Furthermore the 'generalised Baumol model' allows increases of output as well as increases in advertising when surplus profits are earned (see above, p. 333). Thus Wildsmith's argument does not seem valid.

[1] M. H. Peston, 'On the Sales Maximisation Hypothesis', *Economica* (1959).
[2] J. R. Wildsmith, *Managerial Theories of the Firm* (Martin–Robertson, 1973) p. 61.

Shepherd[1] has suggested that if the demand curve has a steep kink, so that to the right of the kink the MR is negative (figure 15.15), the goals of profit maximisation and sales maximisation would not be competing as Baumol implies, because under these conditions the firm's equilibrium would be at the point of the kink. In other words, the 'kinky' solution would be chosen *both* by a profit maximiser *and* a sales maximiser.

This is easy to understand if we consider that the necessary condition of equilibrium for both types of firms is

$$\frac{\partial R}{\partial X} > 0$$

(provided that the profit constraint is operative). Since at the output corresponding to the kink $MR > 0$, while at any larger output $MR < 0$, it is clear that irrespective of goal (profit maximisation or sales maximisation) the firm will choose to produce the output corresponding to the kink.

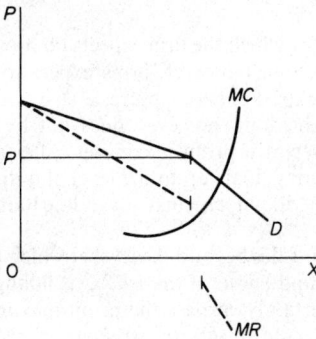   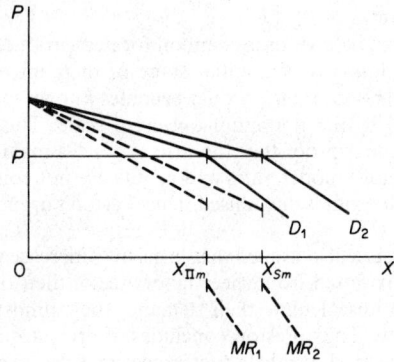

Figure 15.15   Figure 15.16

This argument has been attacked by Hawkins,[2] who argues that Shepherd would be right if price were the only competitive weapon of firms. Given that in the modern oligopolistic industrial world advertising and other non-price weapons (for example, product changes) are the main instruments of competition, Shepherd's argument is not valid. With advertising taking place the kinked-demand curve of a profit maximiser will be closer to the origin than the kinked curve of a sales maximiser, because the latter indulges in heavier advertising expenditures. Thus both types of firms will operate at the kink of their demand curves (if beyond the kink $MR < 0$), but the output of the profit maximiser will be smaller than the output of the sales maximiser, because (at the same price level) the kink of the latter's demand will occur to the right of the kink of the profit maximiser. This situation is shown in figure 15.16, from which it is obvious that $X_{\Pi m} < X_{Sm}$ at the same price, P.

Hawkins suggests that if in fact there is a steep kink in the demand curve Baumol's model is improved, because its predictions (in case of shifts in the demand) become precise. With an accentuated kink, if demand shifts, advertising and output will increase, while price will remain unchanged, *ceteris paribus*, at the level of the kink.

[1] W. G. Shepherd, 'On Sales Maximisation and Oligopoly Behaviour', *Economica* (1962).
[2] C. J. Hawkins, 'On the Sales Revenue Maximisation Hypothesis', *Journal of Industrial Economics* (1970).

Baumol claims that because in his model output will be larger than the output of a profit maximiser, the sales-maximisation hypothesis implies a lower degree of mis-allocation of resources and hence an increase in the welfare of the society. This claim is not necessarily true. The whole argument rests on the shape of the demand and cost curves as well as on the way by which one measures the society's optimal output.

Assume that the cost and revenue curves are as shown in figure 15.17.

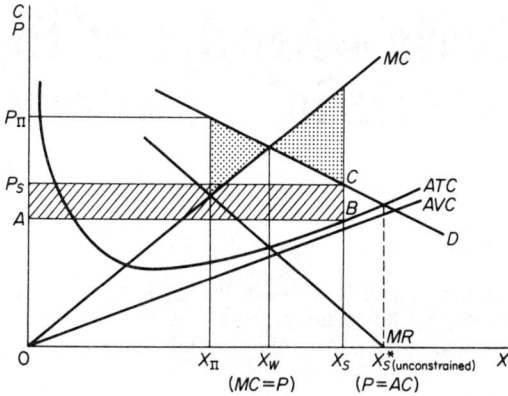

Figure 15.17

A profit maximiser will produce (at $MC = MR$) output X_Π and charge the price P_Π.

An unconstrained sales maximiser would produce X_S^* (where $MR = 0$). If he is constrained to have a maximum profit equal (say,) to the shaded area $P_S CBA$, the sales maximiser will produce X_S and sell it at P_S.

Clearly $X_S > X_\Pi$ and $P_s < P_\Pi$. Profits also will be higher for the profit maximiser.

The question is: will the society be better off with a sales maximiser?

If the optimal output for the society is X_w (defined by $P = MC$), the sales maximiser's output under the above conditions will be further away from the optimum output than the profit maximiser's output. In this case the misallocation of resources (if measured as a departure of P from MC) will be greater for the sales maximiser.

However, if the society's optimum is X_S^* (where $P = ATC$ inclusive of a normal profit), then the sales maximiser is preferable to a profit maximiser.

Thus Baumol's claim, that his solution is preferable from the society's welfare point of view, is not necessarily valid.[1]

---

[1] This topic is discussed in more detail by J. R. Wildsmith, *Managerial Theories of the Firm* (Martin–Robertson) pp. 58–60.

16. Marris's Model of the Managerial Enterprise

I. GOALS OF THE FIRM

The goal of the firm in Marris's model[1] is the maximisation of the *balanced* rate of growth of the firm, that is, the maximisation of the rate of growth of demand for the products of the firm, and of the growth of its capital supply:

Maximise $g = g_D = g_C$

where g = balanced growth rate
   g_D = growth of demand for the products of the firm
   g_C = growth of the supply of capital

In pursuing this maximum balanced growth rate the firm has two constraints. Firstly, a constraint set by the available managerial team and its skills. Secondly, a financial constraint, set by the desire of managers to achieve maximum job security. These constraints are analysed in a subsequent section.

The rationalisation of this goal is that by jointly maximising the rate of growth of demand and capital the managers achieve maximisation of their own utility as well as of the utility of the owners–shareholders.

It is usually argued by managerial theorists that the division of ownership and management allows the managers to set goals which do not necessarily coincide with those of owners. The utility function of managers includes variables such as salaries, status, power and job security, while the utility function of owners includes variables such as profits, size of output, size of capital, share of the market and public image. Thus managers want to maximise their own utility

$$U_M = f(\text{salaries, power, status, job security})$$

while the owners seek the maximisation of their utility

$$U_0 = f^*(\text{profits, capital, output, market share, public esteem}).$$

Marris argues that the difference between the goals of managers and the goals of the owners is not so wide as other managerial theories claim, because most of the variables appearing in both functions are strongly correlated with a single variable: the *size* of the firm (see below). There are various measures (indicators) of size: capital, output,

---

[1] R. Marris, 'A Model of the Managerial Enterprise,' *Quarterly Journal of Economics* (1963). Also R. Marris, *Theory of 'Managerial' Capitalism* (Macmillan, 1964).

revenue, market share, and there is no consensus about which of these measures is the best. However, Marris limits his model to situations of *steady rate of growth* over time during which most of the relevant economic magnitudes change simultaneously, so that 'maximising the long-run growth rate of any indicator can reasonably be assumed equivalent to maximising the long-run rate of most others.' (Marris, 'A Model of the Managerial Enterprise'.)

Furthermore, Marris argues that the managers do not maximise the absolute *size* of the firm (however measured), but the *rate of growth* (=change of the size) of the firm. The size and the rate of growth are not necessarily equivalent from the point of view of managerial utility. If they were equivalent we would observe a high mobility of managers between firms: the managers would be indifferent in choosing between being employed and promoted within the same growing firm (enjoying higher salaries, power and prestige), and moving from a smaller firm to a larger firm where they would eventually have the same earnings and status. In the real world the mobility of managers is low. Various studies provide evidence that managers prefer to be promoted within the same growing organisation rather than move to a larger one, where the environment might be hostile to the 'newcomer' and where he would have to give considerable time and effort to 'learn' the mechanism of the new organisation. Hence managers aim at the maximisation of the *rate of growth* rather than the absolute size of the firm.

Marris argues that since growth happens to be compatible with the interests of the shareholders in general, the goal of maximisation of the growth rate (however measured) seems *a priori* plausible. There is no need to distinguish between the rate of growth of demand (which maximises the U of managers) and the rate of growth of capital supply (which maximises the U of owners) since in equilibrium these growth rates are equal.

From Marris's discussion it follows that the utility function of owners can be written as follows

$$U \text{ owners} = f^*(g_C)$$

where g_C = rate of growth of capital.

It is not clear why owners should prefer growth to profits, unless g_C and profits are positively related. At the end of his article Marris argues in fact that g_C and Π are not always positively related. Under certain circumstances g_C and Π become competing goals (see p. 364 below). Furthermore from Marris's discussion of the nature of the variables of the managerial utility function it seems that he implicitly assumes that salaries, status and power of managers are strongly correlated with the growth of demand for the products of the firm: managers will enjoy higher salaries and will have more prestige the faster the rate of growth of demand. Therefore the managerial utility function may be written as follows

$$U_M = f(g_D, s)$$

where g_D = rate of growth of demand for the products of the firm
s = a measure of job security.

Marris, following Penrose, argues that there is a constraint to g_D set by the decision-making capacity of the managerial team. Furthermore Marris suggests that 's' can be measured by a weighted average of three crucial ratios, the liquidity ratio, the leverage–debt ratio and the profit-retention ratio, which reflect the financial policy of the firm. As a first approximation Marris treats 's' as an exogenously determined constraint by assuming that there is a saturation level for job security: above the saturation level the marginal utility from an increase in 's' (job security) is zero, while below the saturation level the marginal utility from an increase in 's' is infinite. With this assumption the managerial utility function becomes

$$U_M = f(g_D)\bar{s}$$

where $\bar{s}$ is the security constraint.

Thus in the initial model there are two constraints – the managerial team constraint and the job security constraint – reflected in a financial constraint. We will examine these constraints in some detail.

II. CONSTRAINTS

The managerial constraint

Marris adopts Penrose's thesis of the existence of a definite limit on the rate of efficient managerial expansion. At any one time period the capacity of the top management is given: there is a ceiling to the growth of the firm set by the capacity of its managerial team. The managerial capacity can be increased by hiring new managers, but there is a definite limit to the rate at which management can expand and remain competent (efficient). Penrose's theory is that decision-making and the planning of the operations of the firm are the result of teamwork requiring the co-operation of all managers. Co-ordination and co-operation require experience. A new manager requires time before he is fully ready to join the teamwork necessary for the efficient functioning of the organisation. Thus, although the 'managerial ceiling' is receding gradually, the process cannot be speeded up.

Similarly, the 'research and development' (R & D) department sets a limit to the rate of growth of the firm. This department is the source of new ideas and new products, which affect the growth of demand for the products of the firm. The work in the R & D department is 'teamwork' and as such it cannot be expanded quickly, simply by hiring more personnel for this section: new scientists and designers require time before they can efficiently contribute to the teamwork of the R & D department.

The managerial constraint and the R & D capacity of the firm set limits both to the rate of growth of demand (g_D) and the rate of growth of capital supply (g_C). (See section III below.)

The job security constraint

We said that the managers want job security; they attach (not surprisingly) a definite disutility to the risk of being dismissed. The desire of managers for security is reflected in their preference for service contracts, generous pension schemes, and their dislike for policies which endanger their position by increasing the risk of their dismissal by the owners (that is, the shareholders or the directors they appoint). Marris suggests that job security is attained by adopting a prudent financial policy. The risk of dismissal of managers arises if their policies lead the firm towards financial failure (bankruptcy) or render the firm attractive to take-over raiders. In the first case the shareholders may decide to replace the old management in the hope that by appointing new management the firm will be run more successfully. In the second case, if the take-over raid is successful, the new owners may well decide to replace the old management.

The risk of dismissal is largely avoided by: (*a*) Non-involvement with risky investments. The managers choose projects which guarantee a steady performance, rather than risky ventures which may be highly profitable, if successful, but will endanger the managers' position if they fail. Thus the managers become risk-avoiders. (*b*) Choosing a 'prudent financial policy'. The latter consists of determining optimal levels for three crucial financial ratios, the leverage (or debt ratio), the liquidity ratio, and the retention ratio.

The *leverage* or *debt ratio* is defined as the ratio of debt to the gross value of total assets of the firm

$$\begin{bmatrix} \text{Leverage} \\ \text{or} \\ \text{Debt ratio} \end{bmatrix} = \frac{\text{Value of debts}}{\text{Total assets}} = \frac{D}{A}$$

The managers do not want excessive borrowing because the firm may become insolvent and be proclaimed bankrupt, due to demands for interest payments and repayment of loans, notwithstanding the good prospects that the firm may have.

The *liquidity ratio* is defined as the ratio of liquid assets to the total gross assets of the firm

$$\begin{bmatrix} \text{Liquidity} \\ \text{ratio} \end{bmatrix} = \frac{\text{Liquid assets}}{\text{Total assets}} = \frac{L}{A}$$

Liquidity policy is very important. Too low a liquidity ratio increases the risk of insolvency and bankruptcy. On the other hand, too high a liquidity ratio makes the firm attractive to take-over raids, because the raiders think that they can utilise the excessive liquid assets to promote the operations of their enterprises. Thus the managers have to choose an *optimal* liquidity ratio: neither too high nor dangerously low. In his model, however, Marris assumes without much justification, that the firm operates in the region where there is a positive relation between liquidity and security: an increase in liquidity increases security.

The *retention ratio* is defined as the ratio of retained profits (net of interest on debt) to total profits

$$[\text{Retention ratio}] = \frac{\text{Retained profits}}{\text{Total profits}} = \frac{\Pi_R}{\Pi}$$

Retained profits are, according to Marris, the most important source of finance for the growth of capital (see section III below). However, the firm is not free to retain as much profits as it might wish, because distributed profits must be adequate to satisfy the shareholders and avoid a fall in the price of shares which would render the firm attractive to take-over raiders. If distributed profits are low the existing shareholders may decide to replace the top management. If the low profits lead to a fall in the price of shares, a take-over raid may be successful and the position of managers is thus endangered.

The three financial ratios are combined (subjectively by the managers) into a single parameter $\bar{a}$ which is called the '*financial security constraint*'. This is exogenously determined, by the risk attitude of the top management. Marris does not explain the process by which $\bar{a}$ is determined. It is stated that it is not a simple average of the three ratios, but rather a weighted average, the weights depending on the subjective decisions of managers.

Two points should be stressed regarding the overall financial constraint $\bar{a}$.

Firstly. Let

$$a_1 = \text{liquidity ratio} = \frac{L}{A}$$

$$a_2 = \text{leverage ratio} = \frac{D}{A}$$

$$a_3 = \text{retention ratio} = \frac{\Pi_R}{\Pi}$$

Marris postulates that the overall $\bar{a}$ is negatively related to a_1, and positively to a_2 and a_3. That is, $\bar{a}$ increases if *either* the liquidity is reduced, *or* the debt ratio is raised by increasing external finance (loans), *or* the proportion of retained profits is increased. Similarly, $\bar{a}$ declines if the managers increase the liquidity of the firm, or reduce the proportion of external finance (D/A), or reduce the proportion of retained profits (that is, increase the distributed profits), or a combination of all three.

Secondly. Marris implicitly assumes that there is a negative relation between 'job security' (s) and the financial constraint $\bar{a}$: if $\bar{a}$ increases (by either reducing a_1 or increasing a_2 or increasing a_3) clearly the position of the firm becomes more vulnerable to bankruptcy and/or to take-over raids, and consequently the job security of managers is reduced. Thus a high value of $\bar{a}$ implies that the managers are risk-takers, while a low value of $\bar{a}$ shows that managers are risk-avoiders.

The financial security constraint sets a limit to the rate of growth of the capital supply, g_C, in Marris model (see below).

III. THE MODEL: EQUILIBRIUM OF THE FIRM

The managers aim at the maximisation of their own utility, which is a function of the growth of demand for the products of the firm (given the security constraint)

$$U_{\text{managers}} = f(g_D)^1$$

The owners–shareholders aim at the maximisation of their own utility which Marris assumes to be a function of the rate of growth of the capital supply (and not of profits, as the traditional theory postulated)

$$U_{\text{owners}} = f^*(g_C)$$

The firm is in equilibrium when the maximum *balanced-growth rate* is attained, that is, the condition for equilibrium is

$$g_D = g_C = g^* \text{ maximum}$$

The first stage in the solution of the model is to derive the 'demand' and 'supply' functions, that is, to determine the factors that determine g_D and g_C.

Marris establishes that the factors that determine g_D and g_C can be expressed in terms of two variables, the diversification rate, d, and the average profit margin, m.

The instrumental variables

The firm will first determine (subjectively) its financial policy, that is, the value of the financial constraint $\bar{a}$, and subsequently it will choose the rate of diversification d, and the profit margin m, which maximise the balanced-growth rate g^*.

The following are policy variables in the Marris model:

Firstly, $\bar{a}$ implies freedom of choice of the financial policy of the firm. As we shall see in section IV, the firm can affect its rate of growth by changing its three security ratios (leverage, liquidity, dividend policies).

Secondly, the firm can choose its diversification rate, d, either by a change in the style of its existing range of products, or by expanding the range of its products.

Thirdly, in Marris's model *price is given* by the oligopolistic structure of the industry.

---

[1] At this stage it is assumed that there is a saturation level of utility from security, so that s becomes a constraint. At a later stage this assumption is relaxed and a general managerial utility function is used in which U_M increases as both g_D and s increase.

Hence price is not actually a policy variable of the firm. The determination of the price in the market is very briefly mentioned in Marris's article. He argues that eventually a price structure will develop in which the market shares are stabilised. This equilibrium will be arrived at *either* by tacit collusion, *or* after a period of war during which price competition, advertising, product variation or all three weapons are used. The length of time involved and the level of price and the number of firms which will remain in business is uncertain, due to 'imperfect knowledge of the competitors' strength, determination, and skill', and from the unpredictability of games containing chance moves. From this line of argument it seems that Marris is not concerned with price determination in oligo-polistic markets, but rather takes it for granted that a price structure will eventually develop. Thus Marris seems to treat price as a parameter (given) rather than as a policy variable at the discretion of the firm. Similarly, Marris assumes that production costs are given.

Fourthly, the firm can choose the level of its advertising, A, and of its research and development activities, R & D. Since the price, P, and the production costs, C, are given, then it is obvious that a higher A and/or R & D expenditures will imply a lower average profit margin and, vice versa, a low level of A and/or R & D implies a higher average profit rate. Implicit in Marris's model is the average-cost pricing rule

$$\bar{P} = \bar{C} + A + (R \& D) + m$$

where $\bar{P}$ = price, given from the market
$\bar{C}$ = production costs, assumed given
A = advertising and other selling expenses
R & D = research and development expenses
m = average profit margin

Clearly m is the residual

$$m = \bar{P} - \bar{C} - (A) - (R \& D)$$

Given $\bar{P}$ and $\bar{C}$, m is negatively correlated with the level of advertising and R & D ex-penditures. Thus m is used as a proxy for the policy variables A and R & D.

In summary, all the policy variables are combined into three instruments:

$\bar{a}$, the financial security coefficient
d, the rate of diversification
m, the average profit margin

The next step is to define the variables that determine the rate of growth of demand, g_D, and the rate of growth of supply, g_C, and express these rates in terms of the policy variables, $\bar{a}$, d and m.

The rate of growth of the demand: g_D

It is assumed that the firm grows by diversification. Growth by merger or take-over is excluded from this model.

The rate of growth of demand for the products of the firm depends on the diversific-ation rate, d, and the percentage of successful new products, k, that is,

$$g_D = f_1(d, k)$$

where d = the diversification rate, defined as the number of new products introduced per time period, and k = the proportion of successful new products.

Diversification may take two forms. Firstly, the firm may introduce a completely new product, which has no close substitutes, which creates *new demand* and thus competes with other products for the income of the consumer. (Marris seems to narrow his analysis to firms producing consumers' goods.) This Marris calls *differentiated diversification*, and is considered the most important form in which the firm seeks to grow, since there is no danger of encroaching on the market of competitors and hence provoking retaliation. Secondly, the firm may introduce a product which is a substitute for similar commodities already produced by existing competitors. This is called *imitative diversification*, and is almost certain to induce competitors' reactions. Given the uncertainty regarding the reactions of competitors the firm prefers to diversify with new products. The greater d, the higher the rate of growth of demand.

The proportion of successful new products, k, depends on the rate of diversification d, on their price, the advertising expenses, and the R & D expenditure, as well as on the intrinsic value of the products:

$$k = f_3(d, P, A, \text{R \& D, intrinsic value})$$

Regarding the intrinsic value of the new product Marris seems to adopt Galbraith's[1] and Penrose's[2] thesis (rather far-fetched)[3] that a firm can sell almost anything to the consumers by an appropriately organised selling campaign, even against consumers' resistance. He implicitly combines intrinsic value with price, that is, price is associated with a given intrinsic value. Price is assumed to have reached equilibrium in some way or another. Thus price is taken as given, despite the fact that the product is new.

k depends on the advertising, A, the R & D expenditures and on d. The higher A and/or R & D, the higher the proportion of successful new products and vice versa. Marris uses m, the average profit margin as a proxy for these two policy variables. Given that m is negatively related to A and R & D, the proportion of successful new products is also negatively correlated with the average profit margin.

Finally, k depends on d, the rate of new products introduced in each period: if too many new products are introduced too fast, the proportion of fails increases. Thus, although the rate of growth of demand, g_D, is positively correlated with the diversification rate (d), g_D increases at a decreasing rate as d increases, due to the rate of introduction of new products outrunning the capacity of the personnel involved in the development and the marketing of the products. There is an optimal rate of flow of 'new ideas' from the R & D department of the firm. If the research team is pressed to speed up the development process of new products there is no time to 'research' the product and/or its marketability adequately. Furthermore, top management becomes overworked when the rate of introduction of new products is high, and the proportion of unsuccessful products is bound to increase.

In summary

$$g_D = f_1(d, m)$$

$$\frac{\partial g_D}{\partial d} > 0 \text{ (but declining)}$$

$$\frac{\partial g_D}{\partial m} < 0$$

The g_D function is shown in figures 16.1 and 16.2.

[1] See J. K. Galbraith, *The New Industrial State* (Houghton, Mifflin, 1967).

[2] See E. Penrose, *The Theory of the Growth of the Firm* (Blackwell, 1959).

[3] See H. Townsend, 'Competition and Big Business', in T. M. Rybczynski (ed)., *A New Era in Competition* (Blackwell, 1973).

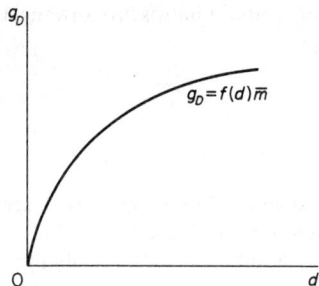

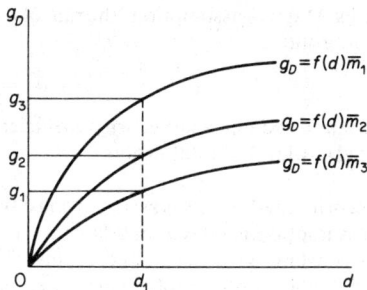

Figure 16.1 $g_D = f(d)$ given m Figure 16.2 $g_D = f(d, m)$

The average rate of profit is constant along any g_D curve. But the curve shifts downwards as m increases ($\bar{m}_1 < \bar{m}_2 < \bar{m}_3$). This is due to the negative relationship between g_D and m. With a given rate of diversification (for example, at d_1 in figure 16.2) and given the price of the products, the lower m, the larger the A and/or the R & D expenses, and hence the larger the proportion of successful products and the higher the growth of demand ($g_3 > g_2 > g_1$). Of course the monotonic positive relationship between d and A (and R & D), which is implied by Galbraith's and Penrose's hypothesis and is adopted by Marris, is highly questionable on *a priori* and empirical grounds.[1]

The rate of growth of capital supply: g_C

It is assumed that the shareholder–owners aim at the maximisation of the rate of growth of the corporate capital, which is taken as a measure of the size of the firm. Corporate capital is defined as the sum of fixed assets, inventories, short-term assets and cash reserves. It is not stated why the shareholders prefer growth to profits in periods during which growth is not steady.

The rate of growth is financed from internal and external sources. The source of internal finance for growth is profits. External finance may be obtained by the issue of new bonds or from bank loans. The optimal relation between external and internal finance is still strongly disputed in economic literature.[2]

Marris takes the position that the main source of finance for growth is profits, on the following grounds. Firstly, the issue of new shares as a means of obtaining funds is, for prestige and other reasons, not often used by an established firm. Secondly, external finance is limited by the security attitude of managers, that is, from their desire to avoid mass dismissal. Financial security is achieved by setting an upper limit to the debt/assets ratio (leverage) and a lower limit to the liquidity ratio in the long run.

Although profits are the main source of finance for growth, the top management cannot retain as much profits as it would like. There is an upper limit to the 'retention ratio' set by the desire of managers to distribute a satisfactory dividend, which will keep shareholders happy and avoid a fall in the prices of shares. Otherwise the selling of shares, or a successful take-over raid, would endanger the position of managers.

The three security ratios are subjectively determined by the managers through the security parameter $\bar{a}$, which is a determinant of the retained profits, and hence a determinant of the rate of growth of capital.

[1] See H. Townsend, 'Competition and Big Business'.
[2] J. Meyer and E. Kuh, *The Investment Decision* (Harvard University Press, Cambridge, Mass., 1957).

Under Marris's assumptions the rate of growth of capital supply is proportional to the level of profits

$$g_C = \bar{a}(\Pi)$$

where $\bar{a}$ = the financial security coefficient
         Π = level of total profits

The security coefficient $\bar{a}$ is assumed constant and exogenously determined in this model. This assumption is relaxed at a later stage. It should be stressed, however, that so long as $\bar{a}$ is constant, growth, g_C, and profits, Π, are *not* competing goals, but are positively related: higher profits imply higher rate of growth.

The next step is to express g_C in terms of the policy variables d and m.

The level of total profits depends on the average rate of profit, m, and on the efficiency of the performance of the firm as reflected by its overall capital output ratio, K/X:

$$\Pi = f_4\left(m, \frac{K}{X}\right)$$

It is intuitively obvious that Π and m are positively correlated (an increase in the average profit margin results in an increase in the total profits)

$$\frac{\partial \Pi}{\partial m} > 0$$

The relationship between Π and the capital/output ratio is more complicated. The capital/output ratio is claimed to be a measure of efficiency of the activity of the firm, given its human and capital resources. The overall K/X ratio is not a simple arithmetic average of the capital/output ratios of the individual products of the firm, but is a function of the diversification rate d

$$(\bar{K}/X) = f_5(d)$$

Given $\bar{K}$, the relation between X and d is up to a certain level of d positive, reaches a maximum, and subsequently output declines with further increases in the number of new products: the overall output increases initially with d due to a better utilisation of the team in the R & D department as well as of the skills of the existing managerial team. Output reaches a maximum when the d is at its optimum level allowing the optimal use of the managerial team and the R & D personnel. Beyond that point, the total output X decreases with further increases in d, and the efficiency of the firm falls: the R & D personnel are overworked and the decision-making process becomes inefficient, as there is not enough time allowed for the development of new products or for the study of their marketability. Hence the success rate for new products falls and efficiency declines.

Substituting for K/X in the profit function we obtain

$$\Pi = f_4(m, d)$$

The relationship between Π and d is initially positive, reaches a maximum, and then declines as d is further accelerated.

We next substitute Π in the g_C function

$$g_C = \bar{a}.[f_4(m, d)]$$

The rate of growth of capital is determined by three factors: the financial policies of the managers, the average rate of profit and the diversification rate.

Marris assumes in his initial model that $\bar{a}$ is a constant parameter exogenously determined by the risk-attitude of managers, while there is a positive relation between g_C and m

$$\frac{\partial g_C}{\partial m} > 0$$

The relationship between g_C and d is not monotonic. The rate of growth of capital, g_C, is positively correlated with d up to the point of optimal use of the R & D personnel and the team of managers; but g_C is negatively correlated with d beyond that point: a higher d implies hastening up of the diversification process $\longrightarrow$ inefficient decisions $\longrightarrow$ fall in the overall profit level $\longrightarrow$ low availability of internal finance and consequently a lower rate of growth g_C.

The relation between g_C and d, keeping $\bar{a}$ and m constant, is shown in figure 16.3. If we allow both d and m to change, while keeping $\bar{a}$ constant, we obtain a family of $g_C = f_2 (d, m)$ curves (figure 16.4). The average profit rate is depicted as a shift factor of the $g_C = f(d)$ curve. The higher the average profit rate, the further from the origin the g_C curves will be ($m_1 < m_2 < m_3$). These curves are drawn under the assumption that $\bar{a}$ is constant. (The effects of a change in $\bar{a}$ are discussed in section IV below.)

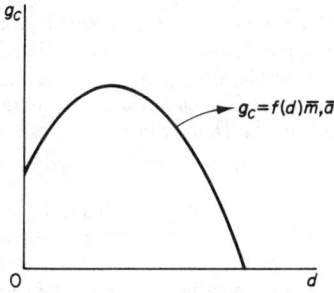

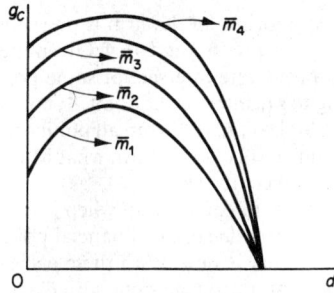

Figure 16.3 $g_C = f(d)$, given $\bar{m}$ and $\bar{a}$ Figure 16.4 $g_C = f(d, m)$, given $\bar{a}$

Summarising the above arguments, we may present Marris's model in its complete form as follows.

$g_D = f_1(m, d)$	(demand-growth equation)
$\Pi = f_4(m, d)$	(profit equation)
$g_C = \bar{a}.[f_4(m, d)]$	(supply-of-capital equation)
$\bar{a} \leq a^*$	(security constraint)
$g_D = g_C$	(balanced-growth equilibrium condition)

$\bar{a}$ is exogenously determined by the risk-attitude of managers. The level of profit Π is endogenously determined. The variables m and d are the policy instruments. Given the balanced-growth equilibrium condition, we have in fact one equation in two unknowns (m and d, given $\bar{a}$)

$$f_1(m, d) = \bar{a}.[f_4(m, d)]$$

Equilibrium of the firm

Clearly the model cannot be solved (is underidentified), unless one of the variables m or d is subjectively determined by the managers. Once the managers define $\bar{a}$ and one of the other two policy variables, the equilibrium rate of growth can be determined.

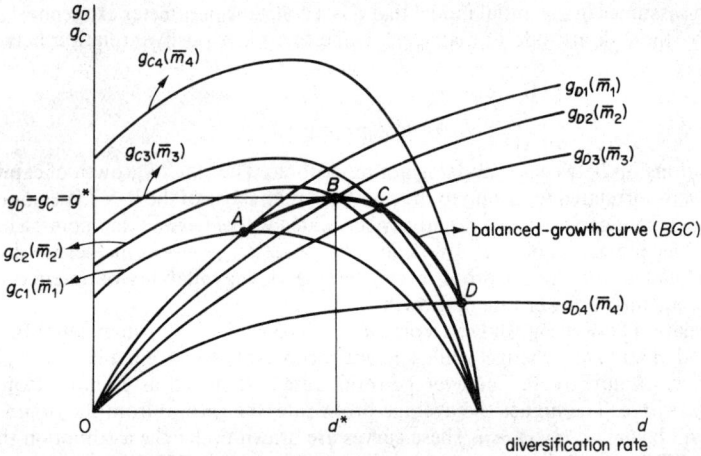

Figure 16.5

The equilibrium of the firm is presented graphically in figure 16.5, formed by superimposing figures 16.2 and 16.4. Given their shapes, the g_D and g_C curves associated with a given profit rate intersect at some point. For example, the g_D and g_C curves corresponding to m_1 intersect at point A; the g_D and g_C curves associated with m_2 intersect at point B, and so on. If we join all points of intersection of g_D and g_C curves corresponding to the same level of m we form what Marris calls the *balanced-growth curve* (*BGC*), given the financial coefficient $\bar{a}$.

The firm is in equilibrium when it reaches the highest point on the balanced-growth curve. The firm decides its financial policy, denoted by $\bar{a}$. It next chooses subjectively a value for either m or d. With these decisions taken, the firm can find its maximum balanced-growth rate, consistent with $\bar{a}$ and with the chosen value of one of the other two policy variables. In figure 16.5 the *BGC* corresponding to $\bar{a}$ is *ABCD*. The balanced-growth rate g^* is defined by the highest point B of this *BGC*. This g^* rate is compatible with a unique pair of values of the policy variables, m^* and d^*. If the firm chooses d^*, then m^* is simultaneously determined; alternatively, if the firm chooses m^*, then d^* is simultaneously determined from the function

$$g^* = f_1(m^*, d^*) = \bar{a} \cdot [f_4(m^*, d^*)]$$

Substituting m^* and d^* in the profit function

$$\Pi = \bar{a}[f_4(m, d)]$$

we find the level of profit, Π^*, required to finance the balanced-growth rate, g^*. Thus profit is endogenously determined in Marris's model. Furthermore, growth and profit are *not* competing goals (so long as $\bar{a}$ is constant). From the g_C function

$$g_C = \bar{a} \cdot (\Pi)$$

it is obvious that higher profit implies higher growth rate. However, if the financial coefficient $\bar{a}$ is allowed to vary, then profits and growth become competing goals (see below).[1]

---

[1] If the endogenously determined profit Π^* is very low and is not adequate to satisfy the demands of the shareholders (for dividends), the managers will have to reduce the retention ratio, that is, reduce the $\bar{a}$ coefficient. The model will then be solved again with the new (smaller) $\bar{a}$. The solution will yield a lower growth rate, but a higher profit level Π. See section IV.

The question is: does the *BGC* have a maximum? Marris argues that so long as either (or both) of the g_C or g_D curves flattens out or bends, there will always be a maximum point on the *BGC* curve. Furthermore, depending on the shape of the g_C and the g_D curves, the *BGC* may be *platykurtic*, that is, have a flat stretch which indicates that there are several optimal solutions: the $g*$ may be achieved by a large number of combinations of the values of the policy variables m and d (given $\bar{a}$ is already chosen). It is only if the g_C curve is parallel to the d-axis ($g_C = f(m)$ but $g_C \neq f(d)$) *and* the g_D curves are straight upwards-sloping curves (implying that $g_D = f(d, m)$, but $k \neq f(d)$ and hence the g_D curve does not flatten out) that the *BGC* increases continuously, never reaching a maximum. This situation is, however, improbable given the capacity for efficient decision making of the managerial team and the capacity for well-explored new products of the R & D department of the firm.

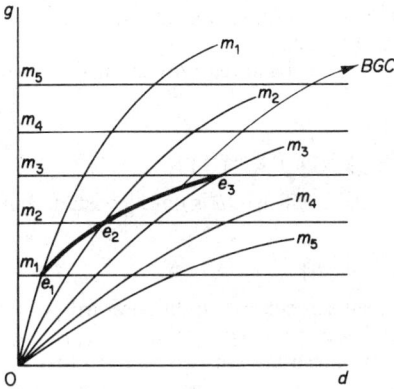

$$g_D = f_1(d, m)$$
$$g_C \neq f(d)$$
$$g_C = f(m)$$

Figure 16.6

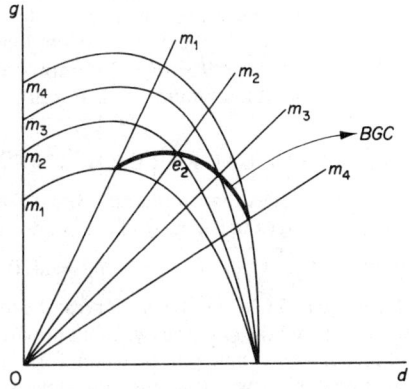

$$g_D = f(d, m)$$
(with $\partial g_D / \partial d$ constant)
$$g_C = f(d, m)$$

Figure 16.7

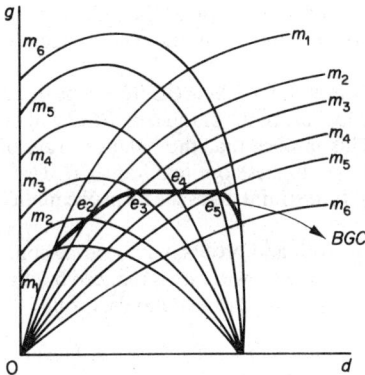

$$g_D = f(m, d)$$
$$g_C = f(m, d)$$

Figure 16.8

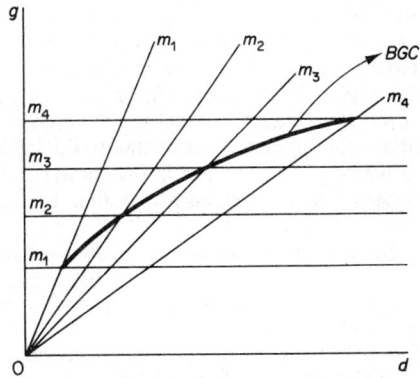

$$g_D = f(m, d), \quad \frac{\partial g_D}{\partial d} \text{ constant}$$

$$g_D \neq f(d), \quad g_C = f(m)$$

Figure 16.9

These cases are graphically shown in figures 16.6–16.9. Figure 16.6 depicts the case where $g_C \neq f(d)$, while $g_D = f(d, m)$. The g_C curve becomes parallel to the d-axis, showing that g_C does not vary as d increases. The g_C curve shifts upwards (parallel to itself) as the average profit margin increases, given that g_C and m are positively related. The balanced-growth curve has a maximum defined by the curvature of the $g_D = f(m, d)$ function (the maximum g occurs at point e_3 in figure 16.6).

Figure 16.7 depicts the case where $g_D = f_1(m, d)$, and $g_C = f_2(d, m)$. But the curve g_D becomes a straight line through the origin, showing that g_D has a constant slope irrespective of changes in the diversification rate. The g_D curve (line) shifts downwards towards the x-axis as m increases. The balanced-growth curve has still a maximum (e_2) due to the curvature of the g_C function.

Figure 16.8 shows a *platykurtic* balanced-growth curve: the g_D and g_C functions have several points of intersection (due to their shapes) that lie on a straight line. The flat part of the balanced-growth curve implies that the same optimal (maximum) g^* may be achieved by a very large number of combinations of m and d.

Finally figure 16.9 shows the improbable case of a balanced-growth curve which never reaches a maximum (explosive growth).

IV. MAXIMUM RATE OF GROWTH AND PROFITS

Marris argues that in the real world the financial coefficient $\bar{a}$ is not a constant, but varies. Changes in $\bar{a}$ clearly affect g_C, given

$$g_C = \bar{a}(\Pi) = \bar{a}[f_4(m, d)]$$

A change in $\bar{a}$ will shift the g_C curves: if $\bar{a}$ increases the g_C curves will shift upwards, while if $\bar{a}$ is reduced the g_C curves will shift downwards. The new set of g_C intersects the given set of g_D curves[1] at new points, which form a new balanced-growth curve. Given that the relationship between g_C and $\bar{a}$ is positive ($\partial g_D / \partial \bar{a} > 0$), an increase in $\bar{a}$ leads to an increase in the rate of growth. An increase in $\bar{a}$ will occur if one or more of the three security ratios changes as follows: $\bar{a}$ is higher if the liquidity ratio (a_1) is lowered; or if the debt ratio (a_2) is increased; or if the retention ratio (a_3) is increased. This is due to the fact that $\bar{a}$ is positively related to a_2 and a_3, but negatively related to a_1 (see p. 355 above). Clearly an increase in $\bar{a}$, however realised, implies a less 'prudent', more risky policy of the managers, since a decrease in the liquidity ratio, or an increase in the indebtedness or an increase in the retained profits (which implies a reduction in the paid dividends) reduces the job security of the managers.

Graphically an increase in $\bar{a}$ is shown by an upwards shift of the BGC (to the position $A'B'C'D'$ in figure 16.10). Given the g_D curves, the highest point of the new BGC will be above the highest point of the original BGC.[2] This implies that the balanced rate of growth g cannot be maximised unless $\bar{a}$ assumes its highest optimal value a^*. Consequently in equilibrium $\bar{a} = a^*$, that is, the financial constraint takes the form of equality at equilibrium.

Marris next argues that if $\bar{a}$ is allowed to vary, growth and profits may become competing goals. If $\bar{a}$ is lowered below its optimum value a^* the growth rate is reduced but the profit level, Π, may be raised.[3] A lower value of $\bar{a}$ (given the d rate) denotes a shift to a

---

[1] A change in $\bar{a}$ is assumed not to affect the g_D curves, since $\bar{a}$ does not enter the g_D function. This assumption of Marris's could be challenged on several grounds.

[2] See Marris, 'A Model of the Managerial Enterprise', p. 204.

[3] This result holds always for this particular model (see Marris, 'A Model of the Managerial Enterprise', p. 204). In general, however, the results of a fall in $\bar{a}$ are complex because the new position involves not only a higher m, but also a possibly different d and hence a different K/X ratio.

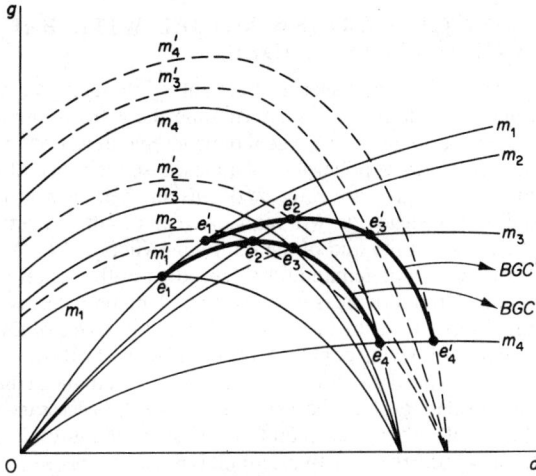

Figure 16.10

lower balanced-growth curve, which implies the intersection of g_D and g_C curves corresponding to a higher m, and hence a higher Π, since Π is a positive function of m (figure 16.11). Thus, although when $\bar{a}$ is held constant, maximising the growth rate implies maximising profit (g and Π are not competing goals), when $\bar{a}$ is allowed to vary, growth and profits become competing goals: if $\bar{a}$ is treated as a variable, the firm cannot maximise both the rate of growth *and* profit. This explains that under some circumstances managers' objectives (for higher g) and stockholders' objectives (for higher Π) may conflict. It should, however, be clear that $\bar{a}$ cannot be increased beyond a certain value,

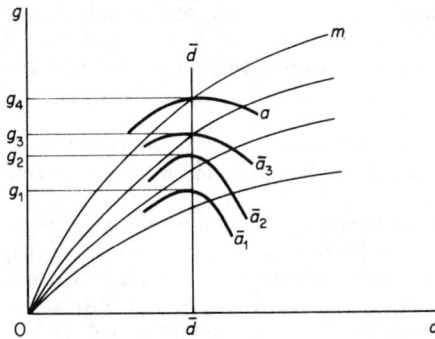

Figure 16.11 $\bar{a}_1 < \bar{a}_2 < \bar{a}_3 < \bar{a}_4$

determined by the minimum profit requirements of the shareholders; otherwise the job security of managers decreases dangerously. If the solution of the model does not yield Π adequate to satisfy the stockholders, $\bar{a}$ will be reduced (via, for example, a lowering of the retention ratio), until the maximum obtainable balanced-growth rate is consistent with a level of profit that is satisfactory. This implies that managers seek to maximise the growth rate subject to a minimum profit constraint.[1]

[1] See Marris, 'A Model of the Managerial Enterprise', p. 205.

V. COMPARISON OF MARRIS'S MODEL WITH BAUMOL'S SALES MAXIMISATION MODEL

Both models belong to the 'managerialist school' of thought, which accepts as an axiom that managers have discretion in determining the goals of the firm. Given this discretion, the managers deviate from the goal of profit maximisation (which maximises the utility of owners) and pursue policies, which maximise their own utility.

In Baumol's model managers are interested only in their own utility. In Marris's model under conditions of steady growth managers can attain contemporaneously the maximisation of their own utility and of the utility of owners.

In both models the growth of demand for the product of the firm is maximised (subject to some constraints). Baumol measures growth of demand in terms of the change in sales revenue, while Marris measures growth of demand in terms of the diversification rate, that is, the number of new products introduced by the firm per period of time.

In Baumol's model the rate of growth of capital is of interest to the managers implicitly: in order to maximise sales revenue the firm must have the necessary equipment, the acquisition of which will be financed mainly from internal sources (retained profits). However, in Baumol's model the growth of capital is not a goal *per se*. In Marris's model the growth of capital is an explicit goal of the firm, aiming at the maximisation of the utility of owners.

In both models profit is endogenously determined. Both Baumol and Marris assume that retained profits are the main source for financing growth (of sales or of the firm in general). Thus, from the solution of their models, they determine not only the optimal rate of growth, but also the level of profit required to finance this growth. In both models exogenous demands for a minimum profit level (for dividends) can be incorporated without affecting the basic mechanics of the optimal solution.

It is interesting to examine whether profit and growth are competing goals in these two models at their equilibrium solution.

In Baumol's dynamic multiperiod analysis, growth and profits are always competing goals in equilibrium. Recall that the tangency solution in Baumol's model occurs always on the negatively sloping part of the growth curve: in equilibrium, the g^* that maximises the present value of the stream of sales revenue is lower than the maximum rate of growth, which corresponds to the peak level of profit (highest point of the growth function $g = f(\Pi, R)$).

In Marris's model of steady balanced growth, profits and growth are non-competing goals so long as the financial policy (reflected in $\bar{a}$) is kept constant (is treated as a parameter).

However, in the real world managers do not treat $\bar{a}$ as a constant. In fact the financial ratios are important policy instruments at the disposal of managers. If managers are growth-seekers, they will favour a financial policy which increases $\bar{a}$ and growth, at the expense of profits. Recall that $\bar{a}$ is positively related to growth, but inversely related to profits. Thus in the modern 'managerial capitalism' a conflict of goals between managers (seeking high growth) and owners–shareholders (seeking higher dividends) may often be observed, unless one *assumes* that owners do *prefer growth* to profits.[1] Of course there is a limit to the desire of managers for growth, set by their desire for job security: beyond a certain stage growth and security are competing goals.

We will next compare the instrumental variables and their use in each of the two models.

---

[1] This may be the case if the taxation of dividends is high, while the taxation of capital gains is low. Under these conditions (and provided that shareholders are few and belong to high income brackets) owners may prefer growth in the expectation of capital gains from an increase (eventually) of the prices of shares, if the assets of the firm are growing.

Price

Both models assume a given price structure, which is arrived at in some way not explicitly discussed. Baumol's model *assumes* a known downward-sloping demand curve, from which total revenue is presumably derived. Marris states that price determination is not his main concern. He implies that the price structure will emerge either after a period of economic warfare (price war, advertising war, and/or product-change war), or by collusion in the form of trade associations or price leadership. Thus in both models price is a parameter rather than a policy variable. The problem of oligopolistic interdependence is not satisfactorily dealt with in non-collusive markets. It seems that these models are applicable to large firms which have considerable monopoly power so as to afford to ignore their competitors' reactions, or that the price is given historically, or determined collusively.

In both models average-cost pricing practices are implicitly or explicitly assumed, as a device for the 'orderly' co-ordination of the market.

The level of output

The level of output is an important policy variable in both models. Baumol treats firms as 'output-makers' rather than 'price-makers'. The level of output is determined by the optimal revenue value (R^*), and by advertising, given the market price.

In Marris's model the level of output is not explicitly determined. From his model the level of diversification (d) is determined. It is not explained how from d the firm will reach decisions about the optimal output levels (product-mix).

Advertising and R & D expenditures

The advertising expenses play a prominent role in Baumol's model. Their level is determined directly from the solution of his model. Baumol does not examine the implications of R & D expenses.

In Marris's model advertising is not treated explicitly. Its effects are reflected in the profit margin m. Since, however, m absorbs both the effects of A and R & D expenditures, the level of each one of these activities is not uniquely determined.

Financial policy

Financial policy is explicitly treated in Marris's model, in which it plays a crucial role. It is explicitly shown how manipulation of the financial instruments can affect the rate of growth and the profits of the firm.

Baumol does not deal explicitly with the financial policy of the firm. However, financial policy considerations are implicit in his model, when he discusses the minimum profit constraint for internal and external purposes.

The predictions of both models regarding changes in demand, costs and taxes are similar as will be seen from the following section.

VI. COMPARISON OF MARRIS'S FIRM WITH A PROFIT MAXIMISER

The imposition of either a unit profit tax or a lump tax will lead to a reduction in the level of total profit Π. A growth maximiser will react to a profits tax by reducing his growth rate, reducing his output and raising his price. A profit maximiser will not react to a profits tax in the short run.

An increase in fixed cost will not affect the equilibrium of a profit maximiser in the short run. A growth maximiser, faced with an increase in fixed costs, will react by reducing his output and his rate of growth.

The advertising (A) and the research and development (R & D) expenditures will be higher for a growth maximiser than for a profit maximiser.

There will be slack payments[1] to the administrative staff, while slack is zero for a profit maximiser.

The profits of a growth maximiser are smaller than the profits of a profit maximiser.

In the profit-maximisation model Π and g are always positively correlated, while in Marris's model this positive correlation will be observed only (i) if $\bar{a}$ is constant and is set equal to its optimal value a^*, or (ii) if a^* is the same for all firms in the market (while firms are heterogeneous in respect of efficiency). If, however, $\bar{a} < a^*$, or if firms do not have the same a^*, then g and Π may not be correlated at all, or may even be negatively correlated. Thus, the observed negative correlation coefficient between g and Π, in several applied studies, could be explained by firms having different a^*, or setting $\bar{a} < a^*$ (that is, not pursuing a growth-maximising policy).

VII. A CRITIQUE OF MARRIS'S MODEL

Marris's main contribution is the incorporation of the financial policies of the firm into the decision-making process of the firm. This is done by introducing the financial coefficient $\bar{a} = a^*$ in the model as an additional policy variable. However, not much is said regarding the actual value of this coefficient. The determination of $\bar{a}$ is exogenous to the model, reflecting the subjective risk attitudes of managers. Surely $\bar{a}$ is at least partly endogenous. Some exogenous influences are imposed from the demands of shareholders, but the risk attitude of managers is affected by the past performance of the firm. If in the past the firm has launched a series of successful new products, and if the profit margin has been increasing, the managers will tend to be more adventurous and take more risks.

Marris's model is ingenious in that it postulates a solution which maximises the utility of both the managers and the owners. However, whether the balanced-growth solution will maximise the utility functions of managers *and* owners, depends on the assumption that all factors appearing in these functions are correlated with *size and rate of growth*. This may be so in periods of steady growth, but need not be true for recessions or 'tight' markets. Even in conditions of steady growth it is questionable whether the goals of managers and owners can be reconciled.

The model can deal with the observed fact of multiplicity of goals. Furthermore it shows that growth and profits are competing goals in the real world. The model implies that both managers and owners perceive that the firm cannot simultaneously achieve maximum growth and maximum profits, and that owners do in fact prefer the maximisation of the rate of growth, sacrificing some profits. Marris does not justify the preference of owners for capital growth over maximisation of profits.

The maximum g^* depends on the value of a^*, which is exogenously determined. It is reasonable to argue that the divorce of ownership and management turns the managers into risk-avoiders. Top management seeks a 'steady performance' rather than the adoption of promising but risky projects. This fact is reflected in setting a value to a^* which does not in fact lead to the maximisation of the rate of growth in the long run.

Marris assumes given production costs and a price structure whose determination is not explained. Oligopolistic interdependence is not satisfactorily dealt within Marris's model. Really Marris brushes aside the mechanism by which prices are determined. This

---

[1] Slack payments are payments to the factors of production over and above the price required to keep them in their present employment (see Chapter 18).

is a serious shortcoming of the model, in view of Marris's assumption that the growth of the firm is achieved mainly via the introduction of *new* products, which will (sooner rather than later) be imitated by competitors.

The assumption that continuous growth is possible by creating new markets, that is, by developing 'products whose sales grow at the expense of total demand in the economy at large', is highly questionable. It is based on Galbraith's and Penrose's theory that a firm can sell anything to the consumers (via an appropriately organised marketing campaign) even against consumers' resistance. The firm surely does not have unlimited influence on the consumer. After all, if one or two new products prove unsuccessful, it is highly unlikely that the consumer will be willing to try other new products of the firm, launched after the earlier failures.[1]

Even if the assumption of 'differentiated diversification' is accepted, Marris's model is applicable basically to those firms which produce consumers' goods. The model is not appropriate for analysing the behaviour of manufacturing businesses or traders.

There are five policy weapons in Marris's model; price (P), the product (represented by d), advertising (A), research and development (R & D), and the financial variable a^*. However, P and a^* are exogenously given, and A and R & D are combined in a single variable, the average profit margin, m. Ultimately the firm is free to decide only one of the policy variables, m or d, but not both. Determination of the one, defines the other simultaneously.

The lumping together of A and R & D expenses is a serious shortcoming of the model, since the effectiveness of these two weapons is not the same in any given period.

Marris accepts that the firm prefers to grow with new products which have no close substitutes, because in this way the firm does not encroach on the markets of competitors and hence does not run the danger of retaliatory reactions. We think that there are two weaknesses in this argument. Firstly, Marris argues at another point that successful new products are eventually imitated. Successful new products thus 'shelter' the firm from competition only in the short run, since in the long run this shelter is eroded by imitation. Secondly, this behaviour creates interdependence of oligopolistic firms. Even if prices are assumed as given, competition takes the form of new products. This sort of interdependence is not analysed by Marris.

Marris's model relies heavily on the restrictive assumption that firms have their own research and development department. Actually most firms do not have such departments but rely on imitation of the inventions of other firms, or, when this is not successful, they pay royalty for using a patented invention.

Marris argues that 'the firms which most successfully maximise growth will in the long run increase their share of total economic activity'. This implies that concentration should increase over time if firms are growth maximisers. There is some empirical evidence which shows an increase in concentration in many industries. This, however, does not necessarily support Marris's theory. Actually most of the observed change in concentration has been achieved by mergers, which are excluded from Marris's model. An increase in concentration may be due to factors other than the desire of firms to maximise growth.

The welfare implications of Marris's model are not obvious. One might reasonably argue that if all firms compete with new products, serious misallocation of resources may arise from excessive advertising or wasteful use of research and development resources. Furthermore, the risk-avoidance of managers may affect the growth of the economy as a whole. Growth may be retarded by not exploiting some new project because of their high risk. However, one could also argue that the welfare of consumers will increase, since they will have a wider choice between continuously increasing number of products.

[1] See H. Townsend, 'Competition and Big Business', in T. M. Rybczynski (ed.), *A New Era in Competition* (Blackwell, 1973).

In general the basic weaknesses of managerial theories are the following: (1) They fail to explain oligopolistic interdependence in noncollusive markets. Not only is price interdependence ruled out *ex hypothesi*, but the interdependence created by non-price competition is not analysed. The timing of launching of a new product, or of a new advertising campaign, or of a new research project, is crucial in oligopolistic markets. Yet the 'imitative process' in all these forms of competition is not analysed. (2) The assumption that the firm has unlimited power to create *new needs* of the consumers via advertising and other selling activities seems rather far fetched. (3) The managerial models, while explicitly or implicitly assuming continuous diversification, seem to narrow the scope of economic analysis to a 'micro–micro' level: these theories seem to be suitable for the analysis of the behaviour of individual large firms, while the observed direction of diversification clearly indicates the need for a more general approach. (4) The managerial models do not explian how price is determined in the market. They imply that firms pay much more attention to their output than to the price at which it will be sold. There are only vague hints about a price structure which may be arrived at in many ways (for example, with collusion, price leadership, or after some period of price war, advertising war, and/or product war).

17. O. Williamson's Model of Managerial Discretion

I. THE MANAGERIAL UTILITY FUNCTION

Williamson[1] argues that managers have discretion in pursuing policies which maximise their own utility rather than attempting the maximisation of profits which maximises the utility of owner–shareholders. Profit acts as a constraint to this managerial behaviour, in that the financial market and the shareholders require a minimum profit to be paid out in the form of dividends, otherwise the job security of managers is endangered.

The managerial utility function includes such variables as salary, security, power, status, prestige, professional excellence. Of these variables only the first (salary) is measurable. The others are non-pecuniary and if they are to be operational they must be expressed in terms of other variables with which they are connected and which are measurable. This is attained by the concept of *expense preference*, which is defined as the satisfaction which managers derive from certain types of expenditures. In particular, staff expenditures on emoluments (slack payments), and funds available for discretionary investment give to managers a positive satisfaction (utility), because these expenditures are a source of security and reflect the power, status, prestige and professional achievement of managers.

Staff increases are to a certain extent equivalent to promotion, since they increase the range of activity and control of managers over resources. Being the head of a large staff is a symbol of power, status and prestige, as well as a measure of professional success, because a progressive and increasing staff implies successful expansion of the particular activity for which a manager is responsible within a firm.

Managers' prestige, power and status are to a large extent reflected in the amount of *emoluments* or *slack* they receive in the form of expense accounts, luxurious offices, company cars, etc. Emoluments are economic rents accruing to the managers; they have zero productivity in that, if removed, they would not cause the managers to leave the firm and seek employment elsewhere. They are discretionary expenditures which are made possible because of the strategic position that managers have in the running of the business. Emoluments are probably less attractive than salary payments since there are certain restrictions in the way in which they may be spent. However, they may have tax advantages (since they are tax deductible) and furthermore they are less visible

[1] This chapter is based on O. Williamson's article 'Managerial Discretion and Business Behaviour', *American Economic Review* (1963). The article has been reprinted in M. Gilbert (ed.), *The Modern Business Enterprise* (Penguin, 1973).

remunerations to the managers than salary, and hence are less likely to attract the attentions and cause dissatisfaction of the shareholders or the labour force of the firm.

Finally the status and power of managers is associated with the discretion they have in undertaking investments beyond those required for the normal operation of the firm. These minimum investment requirements are included in the minimum profit constraint together with the amount of profits required for a satisfactory dividend policy. Discretionary investment expenditure gives satisfaction to the managers because it allows them to materialise their personal favourite projects. This is an obvious measure of self-fulfilment for managers and top executives.

Staff expenditures, emoluments and discretionary investment expenses are measurable in money terms and will be used as proxy-variables to replace the non-operational concepts (power, status, prestige, professional excellence) appearing in the managerial utility function. Thus the utility function of the managers may be written in the form

$$U = f_1(S, M, I_D)$$

where S = staff expenditure, including managerial salaries (administrative and selling expenditure)
   M = managerial emoluments
   I_D = discretionary investment

II. BASIC RELATIONS AND DEFINITIONS

The demand of the firm

It is assumed that the firm has a known downward-sloping demand curve, defined by the function

$$X = f^*(P, S, \varepsilon)$$

or

$$P = f_2(X, S, \varepsilon)$$

where X = output
   P = price
   S = staff expenditure
   ε = the condition of the environment (a demand-shift parameter reflecting autonomous changes in demand)

It is assumed that the demand is negatively related to price, but positively related to staff expenditure and to the shift factor ε. Thus

$$\frac{\partial P}{\partial X} < 0; \qquad \frac{\partial P}{\partial S} > 0; \qquad \frac{\partial P}{\partial \varepsilon} > 0$$

An increase in staff expenditure is assumed to cause a shift in the demand curve upwards and thus allow the charging of a higher price. The same holds for any other change in the environment (ε, for example an increase in income) which shifts upwards the demand curve of the firm.

The production cost

The total production cost (C) is assumed to be an increasing function of output

$$C = f_3(X)$$

where

$$\frac{\partial C}{\partial X} > 0$$

Actual profit Π

The actual profit is revenue from sales (R), less the production costs (C), and less the staff expenditure (S)

$$\Pi = R - C - S$$

Reported profit Π_R

This is the profit reported to the tax authorities. It is the actual profit less the managerial emoluments (M) which are tax deductible

$$\Pi_R = \Pi - M = R - C - S - M$$

Minimum profit Π_0

This is the amount of profits (after tax) which is required for an acceptable dividend policy by the shareholders. If shareholders do not receive some profit they will be inclined to sell their shares or to vote for a change in the top management. Both actions obviously reduce the job security of managers. Hence they will make sure to have a minimum profit Π_0 adequate to keep shareholders satisfied. For this the reported profits must be at least as high as the minimum profit requirement plus the tax that must be paid to the government

$$\Pi_R \geq \Pi_0 + T$$

where T = tax
The tax function is of the form

$$T = \overline{T} + t \cdot \Pi_R$$

where t = marginal tax rate (or unit profit tax)
$\overline{T}$ = a lump sum tax

Discretionary investment = I_D

Discretionary investment is the amount left from the reported profit, after substracting the minimum profit (Π_0) and the tax (T)

$$I_D = \Pi_R - \Pi_0 - T$$

Discretionary profit = Π_D

This is the amount of profit left after subtracting from the actual profit (Π) the minimum profit requirement (Π_0) and the tax (T)

$$\Pi_D = \Pi - \Pi_0 - T$$

III. THE MODEL

A. A SIMPLIFIED MODEL OF MANAGERIAL DISCRETION

We will present the model in two stages to simplify the exposition. In the first stage we assume that there are no managerial emoluments ($M = 0$), so that the actual profit is the reported profit for tax purposes.

The simplified model may be stated formally as follows

maximise $\qquad\qquad\qquad\qquad U = f(S, I_D)$

subject to $\qquad\qquad\qquad\qquad \Pi \geq \Pi_0 + T$

Since there are no emoluments, discretionary investment absorbs all the discretionary profit. Thus we may write the managerial utility function as

$$U = f[S, (\Pi - \Pi_0 - T)]$$

For simplicity we may assume that there is no lump-sum tax so that $T = t\Pi$. Thus the managerial utility function becomes

$$U = f[S, (1 - t)\Pi - \Pi_0]$$

where $(1 - t)\Pi - \Pi_0 = \Pi_D$ is the discretionary profit.

The graphical presentation of the equilibrium of the firm in Williamson's model requires the construction of the indifference curves map of managers, and the curve showing the relationship between the two variables appearing in the utility function, S and Π_D.

The indifference curves of managers will be drawn on a graph on whose axes we measure staff expenditure (S) and discretionary profit (Π_D). Each indifference curve shows combinations of S and Π_D which give the same satisfaction to the managers. It is assumed that the indifference curves of managers are of the usual shape: they are convex to the origin implying diminishing marginal rate of substitution of staff expenditure and discretionary profit (figure 17.1). It is further assumed that the indifference curves do not intersect the axes. This assumption restricts the choice of managers to positive levels of both staff expenditures and discretionary profits,[1] implying that the firm will

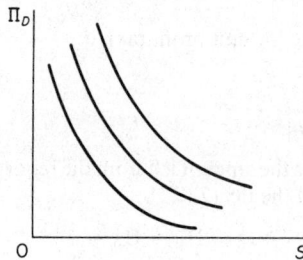

Figure 17.1

[1] This means that the model in this version excludes *corner solutions*, such as points *a, b, c,* etc., (in figure 17.2), where Π_D would be zero in the final equilibrium of the firm.

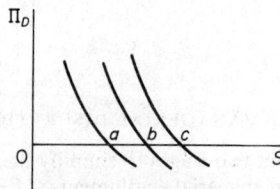

Figure 17.2

choose values of Π_D and S 'that will yield positive utility with respect to each component of its utility function'.

The relationship between S, staff expenditure, and Π_D, discretionary profit, is determined by the profit function

$$\Pi = f(X) = f(P, S, \varepsilon)$$

since t and Π_0 are exogenously given (by the tax laws and the demand for dividends of shareholders). Assuming that output is chosen optimally (according to the marginalistic rule $MC = MR$) and that the market environment is given (ε), the relationship between Π_D and S is shown in figure 17.3.

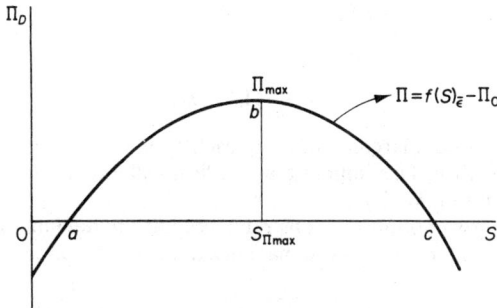

Figure 17.3

At the initial stages of production and up to the level of output where profits reach their maximum level (point b in figure 17.3) both discretionary profits and staff expenditures increase. However, if production exceeds this level, profits will start declining, but staff expenditures continue to increase. If these expenditures exceed point c, the minimum profit constraint is not satisfied and hence points to the right of c (and to the left of a) are not feasible solutions. It should be clear from the above discussion that the drawn profit curve does not include the minimum profit requirement Π_0.

An alternative way of showing the minimum acceptable profit would be to draw the profit function $\Pi = f(S)_{\bar{P}, \bar{\varepsilon}}$ and show Π_0 as in Baumol's model, by a straight line parallel to the S-axis. The advantage of subtracting Π_0 from each level of actual profit (Π) is that we can reduce the constrained maximisation problem into an unconstrained one.

The equilibrium of the firm is determined by the point of tangency of the profit–staff curve with the highest possible managerial indifference curve (point e in figure 17.4).

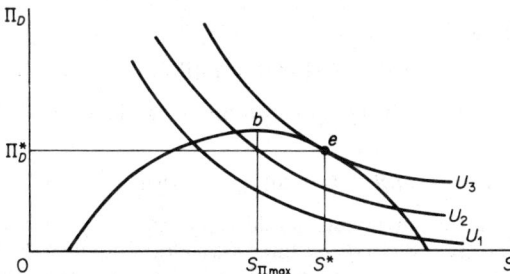

Figure 17.4

Given that the indifference curves have a negative slope, it follows that the equilibrium solution will be always on the falling section of the profit–staff curve. This shows the preference of managers for staff expenditure: in Williamson's model the staff expenditure (S^*) will be greater than that of a profit maximiser ($S_{\Pi_{max}}$). Furthermore, Williamson's model implies higher output, lower price and lower level of profit than the profit-maximisation model.

The above predictions will be better understood after the presentation of the general model of managerial discretion.

B. THE GENERAL MODEL OF MANAGERIAL DISCRETION

Formally the model may be stated as follows

Maximise $\qquad\qquad\qquad U = f(S, M, \Pi_R - \Pi_0 - T)$

subject to $\qquad\qquad\qquad \Pi_R \geq \Pi_0 + T$

It is assumed that the marginal utility of each component of the utility function is diminishing but positive. This implies that the firm will always choose positive values for these components (S, M, I_D).

With the above assumption the constraint becomes redundant, and we may treat the problem as one of straightforward maximisation.

Substituting

$$\Pi_R = \Pi - M = R - C - S - M$$

and

$$T = \bar{T} + t(R - C - S - M)$$

we obtain

$$U = f[S, M, \{(1 - t)(R - C - S - M) - \Pi_0\}]$$

We may also substitute M as follows. Define ρ as the ratio of retained to actual profit

$$\rho = \frac{\Pi_R}{\Pi}$$

so that $\Pi_R = \Pi \cdot \rho$.

Substituting this expression in the definition of retained profit and rearranging we obtain

$$\Pi_R = \Pi - M = \Pi \cdot \rho$$

Solving for M we find

$$M = (1 - \rho)\Pi = (1 - \rho)(R - C - S)$$

where $(1 - \rho)$ is the proportion of profits absorbed by emoluments. Thus the managerial utility function becomes

$$U = f[S, \{(1 - \rho)(R - C - S)\}, \{\rho(1 - t)(R - C - S) - \Pi_0\}] \qquad (17.1)$$

The tax rate t, and the minimum profit requirement Π_0 are given exogenously. Hence the utility function depends on three variables: output X, staff expenditure S, and the proportion ρ. These are the policy variables of the firm: the managers will choose such values for X, S and ρ so as to maximise U.

In the maximisation procedure we will denote the first partial derivatives of U with respect to S, M and I_D by U_1, U_2 and U_3 respectively, that is

$$\frac{\partial U}{\partial S} = U_1 \qquad \frac{\partial U}{\partial M} = U_2 \qquad \frac{\partial U}{\partial I_D} = U_3$$

The first-order conditions for a maximum require that the first partial derivatives be equal to zero. (Note that the second-order conditions are satisfied by the assumption of diminishing but positive marginal utilities of the three components of the managerial utility function.)

In the maximisation procedure we will use the total differential of the managerial utility function

$$dU = U_1 \cdot (dS) + U_2 \cdot (dM) + U_3(dI_D) \tag{17.2}$$

where $\quad M = (1 - \rho)(R - C - S)$
$\quad\quad I_D = \rho(1 - t)(R - C - S) - \Pi_0$

Equating the partial derivatives of the managerial utility function to zero, taking into account the total differential (17.2), we obtain

$$\frac{\partial U}{\partial X} = U_2\left[(1 - \rho)\left(\frac{\partial R}{\partial X} - \frac{\partial C}{\partial X}\right)\right] + U_3\left[\rho(1 - t)\left(\frac{\partial R}{\partial X} - \frac{\partial C}{\partial X}\right)\right] = 0 \tag{17.3}$$

$$\frac{\partial U}{\partial S} = U_1 + U_2\left[(1 - \rho)\left(\frac{\partial R}{\partial S} - 1\right)\right] + U_3\left[\rho(1 - t)\left(\frac{\partial R}{\partial S} - 1\right)\right] = 0 \tag{17.4}$$

$$\frac{\partial U}{\partial \rho} = U_2[(-1)(R - C - S)] + U_3[(1 - t)(R - C - S)] = 0 \tag{17.5}$$

From equation (17.3) we obtain

$$\left(\frac{\partial R}{\partial X} - \frac{\partial C}{\partial X}\right)[U_2(1 - \rho) + U_3(\rho)(1 - t)] = 0 \tag{17.6}$$

The only way for this equation to be satisfied is

$$\frac{\partial R}{\partial X} - \frac{\partial C}{\partial X} = 0 \quad \text{or} \quad \frac{\partial R}{\partial X} = \frac{\partial C}{\partial X} \tag{17.7}$$

given that all the elements in the second expression of the left-hand side of (17.6) are positive by assumption. Thus from the partial derivative of the managerial utility function with respect to X we conclude that in Williamson's model the firm makes its production decision in the conventional way by equating marginal production cost to marginal revenue.

From equation (17.4), solving for $\partial R/\partial S$, we obtain

$$\frac{\partial R}{\partial S} = 1 - \frac{U_1}{U_2(1 - \rho) + U_3(\rho)(1 - t)} \tag{17.8}$$

Given that by assumption all the elements appearing in the fraction are positive, it follows that

$$\frac{\partial R}{\partial S} < 1$$

This finding implies that at equilibrium the mangerial firm will employ administrative staff beyond the optimal level (that is, beyond the point where the marginal cost of staff is equal to its marginal revenue). Thus there is a tendency for the managerial firm to overspend on staff, to employ more administrative staff than a profit-maximising firm.

From equation (17.5) we obtain

$$(R - C - S)[-U_2 + U_3(1 - t)] = 0$$

For this equation to be satisfied the second factor must be equal to zero (since $(R - C - S) > 0$), that is,

$$-U_2 + U_3(1 - t) = 0$$

or

$$U_2 = (1 - t)U_3 \qquad (17.9)$$

This finding shows that in Williamson's model some amount of profit will be absorbed as emoluments, the amount depending on the tax rate: the higher t the smaller U_2/U_3, the smaller the marginal rate of substitution of emoluments for discretionary investment, and the more will be spent on M and the less on discretionary investment.

Given that the marginal utilities have known values (subjectively determined by the managers' preferences), the simultaneous solution of (17.7), (17.8) and (17.9) yields the equilibrium values of the policy variables X (output), S (staff expenditure), and ρ (the factor that determines the proportion of Π absorbed as slack payments to managers).

IV. IMPLICATIONS OF THE MODEL

The implications of this model will become clear if we compare it with the model of a profit maximiser.

For the profit maximiser

$$\Pi = R - C - S$$

and

$$\Pi_R = \Pi$$

that is $\rho = 1$. The profit maximiser will choose the values of X and S that maximise his profit

$$\Pi = R - C - S$$

From the first-order conditions we have

(a)
$$\frac{\partial \Pi}{\partial X} = \frac{\partial R}{\partial X} - \frac{\partial C}{\partial X} = 0 \quad \text{or} \quad \frac{\partial R}{\partial X} = \frac{\partial C}{\partial X} \qquad (17.10)$$

(b)
$$\frac{\partial \Pi}{\partial S} = \frac{\partial R}{\partial S} - 1 = 0 \quad \text{or} \quad \frac{\partial R}{\partial S} = 1 \qquad (17.11)$$

The equilibrium conditions of the two models may now be easily compared (table 17.1).

There will be no slack payments to managers or discretionary investment if a firm is a profit maximiser, while both $M > 0$ and $I_D > 0$ in Williamson's model.

The expenditure on staff will be larger in Williamson's model

$$S_W > S_{\Pi_{max}}$$

since the profit maximiser will spend on staff up to the point at which an additional unit expenditure on staff will bring to the firm a revenue equal to unity (MC on staff $= MR$ from staff), while the utility-maximising managers will employ staff beyond that point. This follows from the second-equilibrium condition ($\partial R/\partial S < 1$ and $\partial R/\partial S = 1$ for Williamson's firm and the profit maximiser respectively).

Although the first condition for equilibrium is the same in both models ($MR = MC$), no definite prediction can be drawn about the level of output. In general the optimal X will not be the same in the two models, given that output depends on S, staff expenditures, and these will be larger in Williamson's model. One might draw the inference (from $S_W > S_{\Pi_{max}}$) that $X_W > X_{\Pi_{max}}$, but this is not necessarily true. The result of increased staff expenditures on the level of output depends on the particular relationship between X and S in the two models.

Table 17.1

	Williamson	Profit-maximiser
Equilibrium conditions	$\dfrac{\partial R}{\partial X} = \dfrac{\partial C}{\partial X}$	$\dfrac{\partial R}{\partial X} = \dfrac{\partial C}{\partial X}$
	$\dfrac{\partial R}{\partial S} < 1$	$\dfrac{\partial R}{\partial S} = 1$
	$\rho < 1$	$\rho = 1$
Differences of M, S, I_D at equilibrium	$M > 0$ $S > 0$ $I_D > 0$	$M = 0$ $S = 0$ $I_D = 0$

In summary, staff expenditure, managerial slack and discretionary investment spending will be larger for a firm that maximises utility than for a firm that maximises profits. However, no general conclusion can be drawn regarding the level of output in the two models. (*Note*: Williamson's model yields identical results to those of a profit-maximising model if $\rho = 1$ and the marginal utility for staff (U_1) is zero. Thus Williamson's model includes the profit-maximising firm as a special case).

V. COMPARATIVE STATIC PROPERTIES

We may compare further the two models by examining their predictions about the changes of the policy variables (the reaction of firms) when some change in the environment takes place. We will examine the effects on the levels of the policy variables (X, S, ρ) of a shift in demand (change in the shift factor ε), a change in the profit tax rate, t, and of the imposition of a lump-tax $\bar{T}$ to the firm. We will examine only the directions of these changes.

A shift in the market demand

This may be denoted by a change in the shift factor ε, appearing in the demand function. The effects of such a shift on X, S and ρ in the two models are shown (without proof) below:

Williamson's firm: $\quad\dfrac{\partial X}{\partial \varepsilon} > 0 \qquad \dfrac{\partial S}{\partial \varepsilon} > 0 \qquad \dfrac{\partial \rho}{\partial \varepsilon} > 0$

Profit maximiser: $\quad\dfrac{\partial X}{\partial \varepsilon} > 0 \qquad \dfrac{\partial S}{\partial \varepsilon} > 0 \qquad \dfrac{\partial \rho}{\partial \varepsilon} = 0$

A shift in demand will increase output X, and staff expenditure S, in both models. The two models give identical predictions of the direction of changes in X and S, so that by observing only changes in these variables in response to a shift in demand we cannot tell whether the firm is a utility-maximiser or a profit-maximiser. The two models cannot be verified by simply looking at what happens to X and S as demand changes. However, an upward shift in demand, while not affecting ρ in a classical model, will lead to a reduction in ρ if the firm is utility-maximising. A shift in demand will increase slack payments faster than the increase in the actual profits (Williamson argues). Thus an increase in slack payments in booms, and a decrease of slack in recessions, suggest that the firm is of the Williamson type rather than a profit maximiser.

An increase in the profit tax rate t

The effects of this change on X, S and ρ are summarised below:

Williamson's firm: $\quad\dfrac{\partial X}{\partial t} > 0 \qquad \dfrac{\partial S}{\partial t} > 0 \qquad \dfrac{\partial \rho}{\partial t} < 0$

Profit maximiser: $\quad\dfrac{\partial X}{\partial t} = 0 \qquad \dfrac{\partial S}{\partial t} = 0 \qquad \dfrac{\partial \rho}{\partial t} = 0$

An increase in the profit tax rate will not change the equilibrium X and S of a profit-maximising firm. A profit-maximising firm cannot avoid the burden of an increase in the profit tax rate by changing its output (or its price) or its staff expenditure, unless the burden is so high as to lead the firm to close down.

A utility-maximising firm, on the other hand, will be able to avoid part of the tax burden by increasing its staff expenditure and its slack payments, and reporting a lower level of profit for taxation.[1]

Effects of the imposition of a lump-tax T

The effects on output, staff expenditure and on slack payments are summarised below:

Williamson's firm: $\quad\dfrac{\partial X}{\partial T} < 0 \qquad \dfrac{\partial S}{\partial T} < 0 \qquad \dfrac{\partial \rho}{\partial T} > 0$

Profit maximiser: $\quad\dfrac{\partial X}{\partial T} = 0 \qquad \dfrac{\partial S}{\partial T} = 0 \qquad \dfrac{\partial \rho}{\partial T} = 0$

[1] Actually the effects of a change in the profits tax rate is not unambiguous. It can be shown that these effects on the firm's decisions can be decomposed into a substitution effect, which is always positive, and an income effect which is negative. Thus the net effect depends on its two components. Williamson argues that in most cases the substitution effect will more than offset the income effect, so that the responses of the firm to a change in t will most often be as above outlined. For a detailed analysis of this response see J. R. Wildsmith, *Managerial Theories of the Firm* (Martin–Robertson, 1972) pp. 77–8.

The imposition of a lump-tax will not change the short-run equilibrium X and S of a profit-maximising firm, which cannot avoid the burden of T (unless it is so heavy as to make it more profitable to close down). On the other hand, the imposition of T leads a utility maximiser to a reduction of his output, reduction of his staff expenditure and reduction of the slack payments. (The decrease in X will occur as a result of a shift downwards of the demand curve, due to the cut in staff expenditure.)

Change in fixed costs

Since a lump-sum tax is similar in its impact on the firm's activities to an increase in its fixed costs, we may infer from the above analysis that an increase in the fixed costs will not affect the short-run equilibrium X and S of a profit maximiser (unless he is driven out of business completely), while it will lead to a change in the level of output, the staff expenditure and the slack payments of a utility maximiser.

VI. EMPIRICAL EVIDENCE

Williamson conducted several tests of his model. We will discuss briefly his 'principal-firm analysis' and we will summarise the evidence he presented from several case studies.

Principal-firm analysis

Williamson attempted to test the hypothesis that managerial discretion influences the expenditures for which managers have a strong expense preference (staff expenditure, emoluments, discretionary investment). He applied ordinary least squares to the model

$$X_i = a_0 \cdot S_i^{a_1} \cdot C_i^{a_2} \cdot H_i^{a_3} \cdot B_i^{a_4} \cdot u_i$$

where X_i = compensation of the top executive of the ith firm
        S_i = staff expenditure (administrative, general and selling expense)
        C_i = concentration ratio in the industry where the ith firm belongs
        H_i = height of the barriers to entry in the industry
        B_i = composition of the board of the ith firm (proportional representation of
              the management in the board)
        u_i = random variable

He fitted the above model to cross-section samples for the years 1953, 1957 and 1961. Each sample included the two largest (principal) firms (ranked according to sales) from twenty-six industries. The samples were not random, but included the large firms for which the managerial model is thought to be more appropriate.

Surprisingly enough the dependent variable is only a small fraction of staff expenditure, not any one or all of the expenses for which managers have a definite preference. Williamson argues that the remuneration of the top executive is determined within a carefully designed scale for the salaries of the rest of the managerial group. 'Payments between executive levels are carefully scaled so that the factors which influence compensation of the top executive can be presumed to affect the level of staff compensation generally.' (Williamson, 'Managerial Discretion and Business Behaviour').

Even more questionable is the use of S, staff expenditure, as a determinant of the remuneration of the top executive. Williamson uses S as a proxy for the 'compensation which the top executive would receive strictly on a profit-maximising basis', on the grounds that staff expenditure reflects the size of personnel over which the top executive has responsibility. This may be so, but the logic for including the profit-maximising remuneration as a determinant of the actual compensation of the top executive does not seem clear to us, given the hypothesis being tested. If anything, staff expenditure, S, is probably the most important element in the discretionary expenses of managers, and, hence, should be the dependent rather than an explanatory variable.

The concentration ratio, C_i, and the height of the barriers to entry, H_i, are used as measures of opportunities for managerial discretion. Williamson argues that the higher the concentration (the fewer the firms in an industry) and the stronger the barriers to entry, the greater the power of managers for discretionary spending. Williamson, anticipating the criticism that C_i and H_i are another measure of 'size', estimated the correlation coefficient between sales and C_i, and sales and height of barriers to entry. He found the values of these correlations sufficiently low (-0.13 and -0.14) for the firms included in his samples, and he thus concluded that C_i and H_i are not proxies for size. However, he found that the correlation between sales and S ('staff expense') was considerable (0.75). Yet, he does not comment on the implications of this correlation for his estimated regression.

Another criticism might be the simultaneous use of C_i and H_i as measures of the opportunities of discretion for managers. Why is neither of these measures adequate for capturing the effect of 'opportunity for managerial discretion'? Williamson does not answer this question; hence one might suspect that the combined use of C_i and H_i was chosen in order to improve the statistical fit, rather than on grounds of theoretical importance of these variables in explaining the dependent variable.

Williamson, anticipating the criticism that C_i and H_i are a measure of profitability, estimated several equations in which profits were included either in combination with C_i and H_i, or replacing them. From his statistical findings he concluded that profits give a worse fit to his data. We should think that the evaluation of the regression findings on the basis of statistical results alone is not adequate for concluding that C_i and H_i are not in fact a proxy for profits.

The variable B_i, proportionate representation of management on the board, is used by Williamson as a measure of the 'desire of managers to act free from outside interference', that is, free from the interference of owner–shareholders. The greater the number of managers on the board, the greater the 'desire' of management for discretionary action. It seems to us that the distinction between the 'desire of managers' and the 'opportunity of managers' for discretionary behaviour cannot be disentangled and measured independently by the three variables C_i, H_i and B_i. Obviously one can argue that the greater the representation of management on the board, the greater (not only their desire but also) their opportunity for discretionary action. Thus, we should think that C_i, H_i and B_i are largely overlapping measures of the same factor: the degree of discretion that managers have in the allocation of resources in the firm.

In summary, the causality implied by staff, S, plus the fact that S and sales are highly correlated, that H_i and C_i may reflect profitability, that C_i, H_i and B_i may measure (at least partly) the same factor, cast serious doubt on the suitability of the fitted model for testing the hypothesis of managerial discretion.

Evidence from field studies

Williamson conducted several case studies from which he infers that his model is better suited for the explanation of some real-world phenomena, such as:

1. Increase in S and M in booms, and drastic cut of these expenditures in recessions.
2. Reaction of firms to taxation changes.
3. Changes of the level of X, S and M in response to changes in the fixed costs of the firm.

4. Drastic cuts in staff expenditure by newly appointed top management, without affecting the productivity of the firm.

5. Allocation of 'fixed overheads' of multiplant-multiactivity corporations to their different plants and activities so as to obtain the effects of a lump-tax (that is reduction of inefficient plants and activities).

Such phenomena, Williamson argues, while incompatible with a profit-maximising behaviour, can be explained by his model of 'rational managerial behaviour'.

We think that the available evidence is not enough for the verification of the theory. The above arguments of Williamson rest on an implicit '*ceteris paribus*' clause, which is not at all sure to be fulfilled in dynamic situations, such as shifts in demand and costs in booms and recessions.

Furthermore, Williamson's model fails to deal with the core problem of oligopolistic interdependence and of strong oligopolistic rivalry. Williamson's model is applicable in markets where rivalry is not strong (for example, in an oligopolistic market where there is some form of collusion), or for firms who have some advantage over their rivals (for example, patents, superior know-how). However, in the long run such advantages which shelter a firm from competition are usually weakened, and competition is enhanced. When rivalry is strong a profit-maximising model may be more appropriate, unless some form of collusive agreement is achieved and firms adhere to it.

SECTION F

BEHAVIOURAL THEORY
OF THE FIRM

18. The Behavioural Model of Cyert and March

The behavioural theories of the firm started developing in the early 1950s. Some of the seminal work may be traced in Simon's article 'A Behavioural Model of Rational Choice', published in the *Quarterly Journal of Economics* in 1955. The theory has subsequently been elaborated by Cyert and March, with whose names it has been connected to this day. The writers founded their theory on four case studies and two 'laboratory'-experimental studies.

We will develop the model of Cyert and March in the following sequence:

1. The firm as a coalition of groups with conflicting interests.
2. Process of formation of demand-goals of the different groups within the firm.
3. Definition of the goals of the firm by the top management. *Satisficing* behaviour of the firm.
4. Means for the resolution of the conflicting demands and interests of the various groups of the firm-coalition.
5. The process of decision-making for the implementation of the goals set by the management.
6. The environment of the firm and the treatment of uncertainty in the behavioural theory.
7. A simple model of behaviourism.
8. Comparison of the behavioural theory with the traditional theory of the firm.
9. Summary and conclusions.

I. THE FIRM AS A COALITION OF GROUPS WITH CONFLICTING GOALS

The behavioural theory of the firm, as developed by Cyert and March, focuses on the decision-making process of the 'large multiproduct firm under uncertainty in an imperfect market'. Cyert and March deal with the large corporate managerial business in which ownership is divorced from management. Their theory originated from the concern about the organisational problems which the internal structure of such firms creates and from the need to investigate their effect on the decision-making process in these large organisations. Such internal organisational factors may well explain the difference in the reactions of firms to the same external stimuli, that is, to the same change in their economic environment.

The assumptions underlying the behavioural theories about the complex nature of the firm introduces an element of realism into the theory of the firm. The firm is not treated as a single-goal single-decision unit, as in the traditional theory, but as a multi-goal, multidecision organisational coalition. The firm is conceived as a coalition of different groups which are connected with its activity in various ways: managers, workers, shareholders, customers, suppliers, bankers, tax inspectors and so on. Each group has its own set of *goals or demands*. For example, workers want high wages, good pension schemes, good conditions of work. The managers want high salaries, power, prestige. The shareholders want high profits, growing capital and market size. The customers want low prices and good quality and service. The suppliers want steady contracts for the materials they sell to the firm, and so on. The most important groups, however, within the framework of the behavioural theories are those most directly and actively connected with the firm, namely the managers, the workers and the shareholders.

Our next step is to examine the process by which the demand-goals of the different groups are formed.

II. THE PROCESS OF GOAL-FORMATION: THE CONCEPT OF THE 'ASPIRATION LEVEL'

The behavioural theory recognises explicitly that there exists a basic dichotomy in the firm. On the one side there are the individual members of the coalition-firm, and on the other side there is the organisation-coalition called 'the firm'. The consequence of this dichotomy is a conflict of goals: individuals may have (and usually have) different goals to those of the organisation–firm.

The purpose of the behavioural theory is to determine the key variables in the decision-making process in the firm. It is not interested in the goals of the firm as such, but rather in their origin and the decision process which leads to their formation. Cyert and March argue that the goals of the firm depend on (are determined by) the demands of the members of the coalition, while the demands of these members are determined by various factors, such as the aspirations of the members, their success in the past in pursuing their demands (past achievement), their expectations, the achievements of other groups in the same or other firms, the information available to them and so on.

Each member or group of the coalition–firm has a multiplicity of demands on the organisation–firm, often conflicting with the demands of other members and with the overall goals of the firm. The demands of each group are too many and not all of them can be satisfied in any one period, given the limited amount of resources available to the firm. Thus, in any particular period the various members (or groups) present to the top management only a part of their demands, the ones that they consider as more important, while keeping the others for later periods.

The demands of the different groups are competing for the given resources of the firm, and there is a continuous conflict. Conflict is unavoidable in any coalition whose members compete for the given resources of the firm. The different groups bargain continuously to achieve their demands.

There is a strong relation between demands and past achievement. Demands take the form of *aspiration levels*. Demands change continuously, depending on past achievement and on changes in the firm and its environment. In any one period the demands which will actually be presented by any particular group to the top management depend on past achievement of demands previously pursued by the particular group, on the achievement of other groups in the same firm, on the achievement of similar groups in other firms, on past aspiration levels, on expectations, and on available information.

Cyert and March argue that the relationship between demands-aspirations and past achievement depends on actual and expected changes in the performance of the firm and changes in its environment: Firstly, in a 'steady situation', with no growth or dynamic changes in the environment, aspirations (demands) and past achievement tend to become equal. Secondly, in a dynamic situation with growth, aspiration levels (demands) lag behind achievement. This time-lag is crucial to the behavioural theory. During this time lag the firm is able to accumulate 'surpluses' or 'excess-profits', which may be used as a means of resolution of the conflict in the firm and which act as a stabiliser of the firm's activity in a changing environment (see below, section IV). Thirdly, in a period of decline of the activity of the firm, demands are larger than past achievements, because the aspiration levels of the members of the coalition adjust downwards slowly.

This process of demand and aspiration-level formation renders the behavioural theory dynamic: the aspiration levels-demands at any time t depend on the previous history of the firm, that is, on previous levels of achievement and previous aspiration levels. (See H. A. Simon, 'A Behavioural Model of Rational Choice', *Quarterly Journal of Economics*, 1955, p. 113.)

In summary, the demands of the various groups of the coalition-firm change continuously over time. Given the resources of the firm in any one period, not all demands which confront the top management can be satisfied. Hence there is a continuous bargaining process between the various members of the coalition–firm and inevitable conflict.

The top management has several tasks: to set the goals of the firm, which often are in conflict with the demands of the various groups; to resolve the conflict between the various groups; to reconcile as far as possible the conflict in goals of the firm and of its individual groups, to take decisions in order to implement the set goals.

III. GOALS OF THE FIRM: SATISFICING BEHAVIOUR

The goals of the firm are set ultimately by the top management. There are five main goals of the firm: (*a*) Production goal. (*b*) Inventory goal. (*c*) Sales goal. (*d*) Share-of-the-market goal. (*e*) Profit goal.

The production goal originates from the production department. The main goal of the production manager is the smooth running of the production process. Production should be distributed evenly over time, irrespective of possible seasonal fluctuations of demand, so as to avoid excess capacity and lay-off of workers at some periods, and overworking the plant and resorting to rush recruitment of workers at other times, with the consequence of higher costs, due to excess capacity and dismissal payments or too frequent breakdowns of machinery and wastes of raw materials in period of 'rush' production.

The inventory goal originates mainly from the inventory department, if such a department exists, or from the sales and production departments. The sales department wants an adequate stock of output for the customers, while the production department requires adequate stocks of raw materials and other items necessary for a smooth flow of the output process.

The sales goal and possibly the share-of-the-market goal originate from the sales department. The same department will also normally set the 'sales strategy,' that is, decide on the advertising campaigns, the market research programmes, and so on.

The profit goal is set by the top management so as to satisfy the demands of shareholders and the expectations of bankers and other finance institutions; and also to create funds with which they can accomplish their own goals and projects, or satisfy the other goals of the firm.

What we said earlier about the dynamic changes in the goals of individuals or groups, holds also for the goals of the firm: these goals change over time depending on the past history of the firm (past aspiration levels relative to past attainments), as well as on the conditions of the external environment and on the changes of aspirations of groups *within* the organisation.

The number of goals of the firm may be increased, but the decision-making process becomes increasingly complex. The efficiency of decision-making decreases as the number of goals increases. The law of diminishing returns holds for managerial work as for all other types of labour.

The goals of the firm are ultimately decided by the top management, through continuous bargaining between the groups of the coalition. In the process of goal formation the top management attempts to satisfy as many as possible of the demands with which it is confronted by the various members of the coalition.

Some of the above goals may be desirable to (and consequently acceptable by) all members of the coalition. For example, the sales goal is directly desirable to the sales manager and his department, to the top management and most probably to the shareholders. But this goal is also indirectly desirable to all the other members of the coalition, since all groups know that unless the firm sells whatever it produces no one will be able to attain his own individual goals. Other goals are desirable to only some of the groups. For example, profits are the concern of the shareholders and the top management, but not of the employees in lower administrative levels or of the workers 'on the floor.' The conflicts arising in the process of goal-setting at the level of top management are resolved by various means which are examined in section IV below.

The goals of the firm, like the goals of the individual members or particular groups of the coalition, take the form of aspiration levels rather than strict maximising constraints. The firm in the behavioural theories seeks to *satisfice*, that is, to attain a 'satisfactory' overall performance, as defined by the set aspiration goals, rather than maximise profits, sales or other magnitudes. The firm is a *satisficing* organisation rather than a *maximising* entrepreneur. The top management, responsible for the coordination of the activities of the various members of the firm, wishes to attain a 'satisfactory' level of production, to attain a 'satisfactory' share of the market, to earn a 'satisfactory' level of profit, to divert a 'satisfactory' percentage of their total receipts to research and development or to advertising, to acquire a 'satisfactory' public image, and so on. However, it is not clear in the behavioural theories what is a satisfactory and what is an unsatisfactory attainment.

Some objectives may even take the form of sheer wishful thinking, that is, they are unquantifiable goals, of a non-operational form; for example, the goal of 'serving best the public', or 'keeping a good public image', or 'being progressive and pioneering', and so on. Such goals do not necessarily lead to specific actions. However, they may indirectly affect other goals in that they may lead to appointment of personnel or other policy commitments. What is important about such goals is that they may be used as an excuse by the top management for justifying particular projects or expenses, given that such goals are consistent with virtually any other set of goals of particular members or groups of the coalition.

Cyert and March argue that *satisficing* behaviour is *rational* given the limitations, internal and external, within which the operation of the firm is confined. Simon introduced the concept of *'bounded rationality'* to justify the satisficing behaviour of the large corporate firms. The goals, irrespective of where they originate, are finally decided by the top management and approved, normally, by the board of directors. They take the form of aspiration levels, and, if attained, the performance of the firm is considered as *'satisfactory'*. The goals–targets do not normally take the form of maximisation of the relevant magnitudes. The firm is not a maximising but rather a *satisficing organisation*.

This behaviour is characterised by Simon[1] as a behaviour of 'limited' or 'bounded' rationality, as opposed to 'global' rationality of the entrepreneur–firm of the traditional theory. Traditional theory conceived of the entrepreneur as a person with unlimited and costless information, unlimited computational ability and with unlimited time at his disposal. Such a rational entrepreneur could afford the luxury of pursuing maximisation of his profit by comparing diligently *all* possible alternative actions facing him at any one time. 'Global' rationality implies that the firm has a clearly defined ordering of preferences for the various goals, each of which has been set after the scrutiny of all possible alternatives, and has been assigned a definite weight, possibly in terms of probabilities. The behavioural theory recognises explicitly the fact that in the modern real world the entrepreneurial work is executed by the group of top management. These are people with limited time at their disposal, have limited and imperfect information and limited computational ability. Hence it is impossible for them to examine all possible alternatives open to them and choose the one that maximises profits (or anything else). Instead they examine only a small number of alternatives and choose the 'best' given their limited time, information and computational abilities. Thus the top management (the firm) acts with 'bounded' rationality.

It should be obvious that the behaviourists redefine rationality. Traditional theory defined the rational firm as the firm that maximises profit (short-run and long-run). The behaviourist school is the only theory that postulates a *satisficing behaviour of the firm*, which is *rational* given the limited information and limited computational abilities of the managers.

IV. MEANS FOR THE RESOLUTION OF THE CONFLICT

We said that the demands of the individual members or groups as well as the goals of the firm take the form of aspiration levels, and are continuously changing in response to past achievement, expectations and changes within the firm and its environment. Given the limited resources of the firm in any one period, and the impossibility of satisfying all demands, conflict is inevitable. There is a continuous struggle and bargaining process as the various groups compete for the given resources of the firm.

Under these conditions one might think that the activity and performance of the firm would be highly unstable. This is not, however, the case. The conflict and bargaining process between the competing groups do not lead to chaotic unstable situations. Both the goals and the functioning of the firm show remarkable stability. There are various reasons for the observed stability of the goals of the various groups and of the firm. The various members or groups have limited time to bargain, and hence they do not examine all possible alternative actions open to them at any particular time. Furthermore the groups are constrained to act according to some initially agreed goals. Their behaviour is enforced by some general self-controlling devices such as the budget-share and its use by the various groups. There are penalties for not spending the budget-share and equally severe penalties for overshooting it. An unfilled position in a department in one period is likely to be taken away and allocated to another department. Past performance in spending the budget-share creates a precedent. The firm 'learns' by its past mistakes, it is an adaptive organisation with a 'memory' of its past performance. The behaviour, goals and decisions are based largely on past history, that is, past bargaining attainments become precedents for present bargaining, goal-setting and decision-making. Finally, there is delegation of functions in the firm, which limits the discretion of various members or groups of the coalition, thus reducing the sources of

---

[1] H. A. Simon, 'A Behavioural Model of Rational Choice', *Quarterly Journal of Economics* (1955) pp. 99–118.

probable conflict. For these reasons objectives (of members, groups and the firm) exhibit much greater stability than would be expected in view of the conflict and the continuous bargaining process within the firm.

Apart from the budget and the delegation of authority, the smooth functioning of the firm is secured by various means which the top management uses to resolve the conflict within the firm. The most important means for the resolution of the conflict are money payments, side payments (which take the form of policy commitments), slack payments, sequential attention to the demands of the individual members or groups, and de-centralisation of decision-making (delegating authority for action within given limits).

Money payments

Money payments are a major means for satisfying the demands of the various groups of the coalition–firm. In the traditional theory of the firm, money payments are the only means for achieving the goals of the firm: the entrepreneur (being synonymous with the firm) resolves all demands by money payments, that is, by paying to the factors their market prices. Thus, in traditional theory, there is no conflict between the owner–entrepreneur and the firm, and all the demands of the owners of factors of production are satisfied by money payments. In the behavioural theory of the firm payments of market prices to the owners of factors of production are not adequate for resolving the conflicting demands. A large part of demands is satisfied by money payments: workers and employees are getting their wages and salaries; shareholders get their dividends, and so on. However, there are other means necessary for the resolution of the conflicting demands.

Side payments – policy commitments

Policy commitments absorb part of the resources of the firm and are in this sense payments to the factors of production. For example, the top management, in order to keep a good scientist in its research department, apart from paying him his salary (opportunity cost), must allocate certain funds for the development and conduct of the research plans (projects) of the scientist. These funds are money payments which, of course, do not go into the pocket of the scientist. They form a *side payment* for him, in the sense that they satisfy part of his demands which are associated with his research interests. Thus side payments mostly take the form of policy commitments by the top management and are a means for satisfying some demands of the groups within the firm.

'Slack' payments

Slack is defined as payments to the various groups of the coalition over and above those required for the efficient working of the firm.

'Organisational slack consists in payments to members of the coalition in excess of what is required to maintain the organisation.' (R. M. Cyert and J. G. March, *A Behavioural Theory of the Firm*, Prentice-Hall, 1963.)

Slack may be 'earned' by all groups of the coalition. For example, workers may be paid wages higher than what is required to keep them in the firm; managers may be paid higher salaries or have other perquisites (luxurious offices, limousines, expense-accounts); shareholders may be paid higher dividends than the minimum required to satisfy their demands, customers may be given discounts which are not necessary to keep them tied to the firm.

In the long run demands of groups adjust to actual payments of *the firm* and of other *similar firms*. Thus in the long run coalition demands are analogous to the factor prices of the conventional theory. However, in the short run there is a difference between demands and payments. In periods of growth the difference is positive and this difference is what Cyert and March call *slack payments*. It is due to the rather slow process of adjustment of demands to actual payments to the managers and other groups of the coalition. Thus 'slack is typically not zero'.

In managerial economics only one type of slack is discussed, namely the slack payments to the managers, while the other types of slack are usually assumed to be zero. Cyert and March, while recognising that other kinds of slack may be non-zero, still maintain that the most important form of slack is the *managerial slack*. As said, this may take the form of higher salaries or other perquisites that the firm provides to the top management.

The existence of slack has a *stabilising effect on the performance of the firm*. It allows the firm to pursue its goals and have a steady performance in a changing environment. That is, slack allows the firm to ignore to a large extent changes in its environment: in a period of 'bad business' the firm cuts the slack payments, thus achieving a reduction in its costs, which makes it possible for the firm not to make other major downward readjustments in its aspiration levels. Similarly in periods of flourishing business slack payments increase, that is, part of the realised profits is absorbed in costs and hence profits appear as less than they would otherwise be so that there is less room for an excessively optimistic upward adjustment of other aspiration levels. Thus aspiration levels and the activity of the firm are more stable in a widely fluctuating environment, due to the built-in stabiliser, the slack. Without slack and the resulting adjustment of costs the activity of the firm would be much more unstable, because the only way to adjust to changing environment would be a readjustment of aspiration levels of the firm. With slack the adjustment of the firm to the changing external conditions becomes easier: slack acts as a buffer to the changes of the environment and thus it explains the smooth functioning of the firm.

Cyert and March offer the stabilising role of slack as the explanation of the 'orderly' function of the firm. Yet they themselves state that this 'role' is played by slack 'automatically.' Slack is created autonomously because of the time-lag in the adjustment (upwards) of aspirations to achievement, and acts as an autonomous built-in stabiliser, without the top management consciously using slack as a means for the stabilisation of the firm.

The hypothesis set by Cyert and March about the stabilising effect of the slack can be tested empirically by observing the behaviour of costs in bad and good business periods.

Sequential attention to demands

One of the most important ways used by top management for the resolution of conflict is sequential attention to the demands of the various groups. The top management, depending on the urgency of the different demands, attaches priority and satisfies first the demands that seem more important in any one period, while postponing the demands of other members for future periods. If in a period the production process needs renewal, the demands of the production manager will be given priority. If, however, a competitor launches a new product or a big selling campaign, the top management will allocate more funds to the sales department, giving a lower priority to other demands.

Decentralisation of decision-making

Conflict is partly avoided if the decision area of each member or group is well defined. The top management organises departments and sections to which definite assignments and authority are delegated. Of course there will always be areas in which common action of managers will be required and conflict may arise, but in setting the plan of the organisation the top management tries to minimise these areas of conflict.

V. THE PROCESS OF DECISION-MAKING

The goals of the firm, as set by the top management and approved by the board of directors, have to be implemented by decisions. Decisions are taken at various levels of administration (or hierarchy). We will distinguish two levels of decision-making: decisions at the level of top management and decisions at lower levels of administration.

The decision-making process at the level of top management

Given the goals of the firm and the resources available, the allocation of these resources to the various departments is decided by the top management and is implemented by the budget. Each department is allocated a certain proportion of the budget, the share of the budget depending mainly on the bargaining power and skill of the head of each department. The bargaining power is to a large extent determined by the past performance of the particular department, how well it has attained its targets as set by the top management, how well the department's work was internally co-ordinated, how efficiently the past budget of this department was used up. The bargaining skill, while affected by past achievement, is basically an inherent attribute of the various managers and executives, of education and experience. The heads of sections present demands to the top management and by bargaining they attempt to secure as large as possible a share of the firm's total budget. Their ability in deciding which projects (demands), and at what time to present them to the top management, is crucial.

This process determines *the internal allocation of most of the resources*. Of course the top management always retains some funds for allocation at its own discretion at any point of time to the best of its judgement and ability.

The top management examines and decides on the propositions (projects) presented to it by the managers. We said in section III that the top management, given the limits of time, information and its computational abilities, behaves in a 'limited' rational way. It examines any one project on its own merits, by comparing it perhaps with one or two other alternatives aiming at the solution of the same target-problem. No comparison of all possible alternatives is ever attempted. The top management does not seek information on all possible alternatives since this information is not costless. Whenever a problem is detected a few alternatives are roughly screened and examined. No detailed cost–benefit studies are normally undertaken. Two crude criteria are set for the evaluation of any particular proposal. The first is a *budgetary (financial) criterion*: are there funds available for the realisation of the proposed project? The second is an '*improvement criterion*': does the project being proposed improve the existing situation beyond doubt? If these two criteria are satisfied the top management may approve the project without further considering whether there exist other alternative solutions superior to the one proposed.

In the above decision process, information is required to facilitate the decision-makers. *Information activity is problematic* in the behavioural theories. That is, a search is made whenever a problem is identified. Information flow is not costless, as the traditional theory of the firm assumed. Furthermore a search is not made on marginalistic rules, as the neoclassical theory postulated. Economists have eventually recognised that information is not costless, but they have treated the information search as another resource-absorbing activity, which is undertaken and carried out up to the point at which the marginal cost of the information flow is equated to the marginal benefit which would accrue to the firm from the acquisition of the information. Cyert and March, following Simon, postulate that search is not undertaken on such marginalistic rules, but is directed to the particular area in which some problem appears. Decision-making in general reflects heavily a response of the management to local problems of pressing needs. For example, if sales are dropping, search will be concentrated on the sales department to find out the causes of the shrinking market share and find methods for sales promotion. If frequent breakdowns in the production flow occur, search will be directed to the production side of the firm and information will be obtained as to the causes of the breakdowns in order to find the 'best' possible remedial action. Search is undertaken when and where a problem arises.

Information determines demands of the groups, which, in turn, determine the setting of goals by the top management. Information also affects expectations and hence demands and goals. Thus the role of the flow of information is very important in internal resource allocation. As the search for information is conducted and the results flow from the several sections of the firm, the information is affected by what is known as '*position bias*'. This bias originates from the desire of the various managers for security and power in the organisation. Production managers tend to give high estimates of costs, so as to be 'on the safe side': if costs *ex post* are lower than the *ex ante* estimate the position of the production manager is 'favourable' as compared with the situation in which realised costs exceed estimated costs. Sales managers tend to give conservative estimates of expected sales for similar reasons and considerations. In general, staff in the production section tend to acquire an 'upward bias' for costs, but presumably a 'downward bias' for output, while staff related to the sales section tend to give a 'downward bias' for sales, but an 'upward bias' for sales costs, which is reflected in their conservative forecasts. This 'position bias' affects information, expectations, demands and ultimately the goals of the firm. Furthermore, the flow of information from one section or member to another is far from perfect. Information may be withheld or distorted as it passes through different sections of the organisation.

In summary; the decisions at the level of top management are not taken on a complete and exhaustive examination of all possible (not even of all known) alternatives, nor are they based on detailed cost–benefit studies, or application of marginalistic rules. Rather the top management undertakes a quick screening of the most promising alternatives and then directs more search for further information on the 'best' of these solutions.

Four points are stressed by the behavioural theories regarding the search activity: search is problem oriented, it is not costless, it may be biased due to 'position bias', and its flow within the organisation is not always smooth. The final decision on any particular project is based normally on two simple evaluation criteria, a '*financial*' and an '*improvement*' criterion.

Decisions at lower levels of management (administration)

The decision process at lower levels of administration involves various degrees of freedom of action. Once the budget-shares are allocated, each manager has normally considerable discretion in spending the funds allocated to his department. The routine sales strategy may be decided by the sales manager and his subordinates; the organisation of labour 'on the floor' is decided by the production manager, and so on. However, all the routine, day-to-day decisions are simplified by delegation of authority within each section and by simple rules which form the 'blue-print' of the organisation. For example, to facilitate the calculations involved in costing and pricing the 'blue-print' may include a directive-rule to the relevant department, that the price will be set at the level defined by the average direct cost plus a certain gross profit margin (for example, 10 per cent on the direct cost). This is the rule of 'average cost pricing,' which helps employees in their computations, but does not allow them any initiative in deciding the final level of price. Final price decisions are the concern of the top management, which takes into account various factors (see below). These decisions are subsequently 'translated' into simple rules-of-thumb which, when applied at the lower level of administration, result in a price 'range' which is consistent with the decision of the top management. Similarly the 'blue-print' may include the rule-of-thumb that costs should be increased by, say, 5 per cent if over two or three successive periods the target profit has been attained or overshot (in order to cover probably increased slack payments).

The administrative staff at lower levels of the hierarchy 'learn' by experience, and are helped by such 'blue-print' rules in making their decisions. The execution of the budget in each period provides invaluable experience. The staff 'learn' by the mistakes and successes of the past. The whole firm is *an adaptively rational system*. Measures which failed in the past are unlikely to be adopted again, while measures which worked successfully are likely to be adopted again. The top management has the budget and the balance sheet of each section and uses these as controlling devices for the lower levels, on top of various other 'policing' techniques (for example, employment of supervisors).

VI. UNCERTAINTY AND THE ENVIRONMENT OF THE FIRM

Cyert and March distinguish two types of uncertainty: market uncertainty and uncertainty of competitors' reactions. Market uncertainty refers to possible changes in customers' preferences or changes in the techniques of production. This form of uncertainty is inherent in any market structure. It can partly be avoided by search activity and information-gathering, but it cannot be avoided completely. Given the market uncertainty the managerial firm avoids long-term planning and works within a short time-horizon. The behavioural theory postulates that the firm considers only the short-run and chooses to ignore the long-run consequences of short-run decisions.

The uncertainty arising from competitors' actions and reactions, that is, from oligopolistic interdependence, is brushed aside by this theory by assuming that existing firms have arrived at some form of *tacit collusion*. The various forms of trade associations, clubs and the issue of various 'informative' bulletins or other publications provide a means by which firms give out information concerning their prices or future outlays of various kinds, expecting every other competitor to do the same. This sort of *modus vivendi* is called a 'negotiated environment' by Cyert and March. The firm is assumed to 'negotiate' in some way or another with its competitors so as to avoid uncertainty. Thus the core problem of oligopolistic markets, that of competitors' interdependence, is 'solved' by assuming collusive action of the firms.

In general the theory pays too little attention to the environment and its effect on the goal-formation process and the pricing and output decisions at the level of top management. It examines internal resource allocation, assuming collusion with competitors. It says nothing about the threat of potential entry which is crucial in the present world of mergers and continuous diversification. The environment is taken as given and as such is practically ignored in the analysis of the behaviour of the firm. This ignoring of the environment is apparent in the model that follows, which is used by Cyert and March as an illustration of the workings of their theory. The rules by which demand and costs are estimated, the rules for investment decisions and other crucial steps in the analysis are too mechanical. The decision process as presented by this theory has very serious implications for resource allocation in the firms and in the economy as a whole. The short-run horizon postulated in one part of the theory is incompatible with investment decisions, which by their nature involve long-run considerations and hence must take into account expected future demand and competitors' reactions. We will discuss these shortcomings of the theory again in the last section of this chapter.

VII. A SIMPLE MODEL OF BEHAVIOURISM

In this section we briefly present the simple model used by Cyert and March as an illustration of the decision-making process within the modern large corporation.

The model refers to the case of a duopoly. The decision process involves the determination of the output which is homogeneous, so that a single price will ultimately prevail in the market. Of course, each firm, in deciding its output automatically induces price changes in the market. However, when both firms finally decide their outputs, price will be determined by the market. No changes in inventories are allowed in this model. The steps may be outlined as follows (K. J. Cohen and R. M. Cyert, *Theory of the Firm*, Prentice-Hall, 1965):

1. *Forecast of competitors' reactions.* The forecast is basically a straightforward extrapolation of the past observed reactions of competitors.

2. *Forecast of firm's demand.* This is based on an estimate of the demand function from past observations. Future demand is thus an extrapolation of the past sales of the firm.

3. *Estimation of costs.* The cost in the current period is assumed to be the same as in the past period. However, if the profit goal has been achieved over the past two periods, average unit costs are increased by a certain percentage to allow for slack payments.

4. *Specification of goals of the firm.* These are aspiration levels. In this model profit is the only goal of the firm. The aspiration level of profits is some average of the profits of past periods.

5. *Evaluation of results by comparing them to the goals.* From the information obtained in steps 1–3 we obtain a solution, i.e. an estimate of the level of output, price, cost and profits. These are compared to the target level of profits. If the goals are satisfied by this solution the firm adopts it. If the profit and other goals are not achieved the firm proceeds to step 6.

6. *If goals are not attained the firm re-examines the estimate of its costs.* Re-examination starts with costs because this variable is under the direct control of the firm. It usually involves a cut in slack and other expenses.

7. *Evaluation of the new solution by comparing it to goals.* If the new solution with the downward-adjusted costs leads to the target profits it is adopted. If not, the firm proceeds to step 8.

8. *If goals are not attained the firm re-examines the estimate of its demand.* The re-examination consists in considering possible changes in the sales strategy (more market research, more advertising, more salesmen, etc). The result is an upward adjustment of the initial estimate of demand.

9. *Evaluation of the new solution by comparing it to goals.* If the new solution with the revised costs and demand estimates attains the target profits, it is adopted. If not, the firm proceeds to step 10.

10. *If goals are not met the firm readjusts downwards its aspiration levels.* If with the revision of costs (in step 6) and of demand (in step 9) the goals are not attainable, the firm readjusts downwards its aspiration levels.

The firm has multiple goals (although only one explicitly appears in the above model), which take the form of aspiration levels: the firm is a satisficer rather than a maximiser. The goals change over time depending on past attainments, aspirations, demands of groups, and expectations. The criterion of choice for goal-setting is that the alternative selected meets the demands (goals) of the coalition.

The firm adopts the procedure of sequential consideration of alternatives. The first satisfactory alternative evoked is accepted. Where an existing policy satisfies the goals there is little search for alternatives. When failure occurs search is intensified.

The organisation seeks to avoid uncertainty. The market-originated uncertainty is avoided by undertaking information searches, by avoiding long-term planning, by following 'regular procedures' and a policy of reacting to feedback information rather than of forecasting the environment. The competitor-originated uncertainty is avoided by creating a 'negotiated' environment, that is, by some sort of collusive behaviour.

The organisation uses standard *operating procedures* such as task-performance rules, continuous records and reports, information-building rules, planning devices, budgeting, investment planning, and longer-run planning. It also uses *'blue-print' rules-of-thumb* (on-costing pricing rules, slack-absorbed-in-cost rules, equipment-expansion rules). But the operating procedures and 'blue-print' rules aim at implementing the goals, that is, helping the lower hierarchical levels to act in a way which is consistent with the goals set by the top management.

On the above-outlined process of decision-making we note the following: Firstly, the 'forecasts' of competitors' reactions and of the demand are really an extrapolation of *past* experience. No allowance is made for *future* uncertainty. Secondly, the estimates of costs and the rules for their upward or downward adjustment are mechanical and do not show the implications of such adjustments. Readjusting costs without looking at the cost structure of competitors, actual and potential, is too short-sighted a policy. Thirdly, there is an implication for investment decisions which is not shown in the above outline. Investment decisions are connected with costs and with the degree of utilisation of the equipment. Regarding costs, it is assumed that the average direct cost is constant when the plant is used at between 10 per cent and 90 per cent of full capacity. (This implies that the average variable cost curve has a flat stretch over the 10 per cent to the 90 per cent range of the plant capacity.)[1] The decision rule with regard to investment runs as follows: if over three consecutive periods the plant is used to its full capacity, investment should increase by 20 per cent. Again this rule has dangerous implications for resource allocation. If the firm extrapolates in the future its past performance, without considering possible changes in the environment in the future, serious mis-allocations may occur. Unless the equipment is short-lived any mechanical rules for investment decisions which do not take into consideration the future are 'irrational' from the point of view of the firm, no matter what its goals are, and most probably wasteful for the economy as a whole, given the now rapid rate of technological progress. Fourthly, the adjustment of the aspiration levels, if all other adjustments of costs and demand forecasts fail, is perhaps the most serious defect of the theory. The postulate of 'satisficing behaviour' loses its meaning, since almost any performance, by continuous downward readjustment of goals, can be considered as 'satisfactory'. The behaviourist school postulates that by the downward revision of the goals to lower 'satisficing' levels whenever the initial targets are not attained 'the firm does the best under the circumstances'. Surely this behaviour renders any judgement on the performance of

---

[1] This is scarcely credible; but the figures are not essential to the argument.

the firm impossible, since the 'satisficing' criterion changes continuously, thus becoming non-operational.

VIII. A COMPARISON WITH THE TRADITIONAL THEORY

The behavioural theory differs in almost all its aspects from the traditional theory of the firm.

The firm in the behavioural theory is conceived as a coalition of groups with largely conflicting interests. There is a dichotomy between ownership and management. There is also a dichotomy between individual members and the firm–organisation. The consequence of these dichotomies is conflict between the different members of the coalition.

The traditional theory conceives the firm as synonymous with the entrepreneur. The owner–businessman is at the same time the manager of the firm. The 'members' of the firm are the entrepreneur and the owners of the factors of production, whose demands are satisfied via money payments. Consequently there is no conflict since the entrepreneur pays to the factors of production in his employment their market prices (opportunity cost).

The firm of the traditional theory has a single goal, that of profit maximisation. The behavioural theory recognises that the modern corporate business has a multiplicity of goals. The goals are ultimately set by the top management through a continuous process of bargaining. These goals take the form of aspiration levels rather than strict maximising constraints. Attainment of the aspiration level 'satisfices' the firm: the contemporary firm's behaviour is satisficing rather than maximising. The firm seeks levels of profits, sales, rate of growth (and similar magnitudes) that are 'satisfactory', not maxima.

The behavioural theory is the only theory that postulates *satisficing* behaviour as opposed to the *maximising* behaviour of other theories. Satisficing is considered as rational, given the limited information, time, and computational abilities of the top management. Thus the behavioural theory redefines rationality: it introduces the concept of 'bounded' or 'limited' rationality, as opposed to the 'global' rationality of the traditional theory of the firm.

The traditional theory of the firm initially assumed that in deciding the allocation of resources (within the firm) the entrepreneur equates marginal revenue to opportunity cost. This behaviour implicitly assumes global rationality, that is, *perfect knowledge* of all alternatives, *examination of all possible* alternatives and *certainty* about future returns. Later theorists recognised uncertainty as a fact of the real business world and introduced a probabilistic approach to the above decision rule for the allocation of internal resources. The entrepreneur was assumed to be able to assign definite probabilities to future returns and he equated *expected returns* with opportunity costs. Furthermore, later theorists recognised the fact that the entrepreneur has limited knowledge, limited information, which is not costless, but is acquired at a cost. The allocation of resources to search activity (activity aiming at acquisition of information) was assumed to be decided by comparing expected profitability of the information with its cost. That is, search activity was treated by the traditional theory as an activity, like all the other activities of the firm, which absorbs resources and hence must be judged on marginalistic rules like the other activities.

In general, traditional theory (earlier and later versions) postulated that the decisions about resource allocation are taken by comparing marginal (expected) return to marginal cost. The probabilistic approach was attacked and other theories were developed to cope with uncertainty. The most important of these theories is the *theory of games*, which, however, has not as yet been generally accepted. (See Chapter 19.)

Cyert and March criticised the probabilistic–marginalistic behaviour of the traditional theory on the following grounds. Firstly, the traditional theory assumed continuous competition among all alternative resource uses. In the actual world we observe local problem-solving rather than general planning for all activities of the firm simultaneously. Secondly, the traditional theory treats 'search' as another investment decision, that is, in terms of calculable returns and costs. In reality, it has been observed that search is problem-oriented and is not decided on marginalistic rules. Thirdly, traditional theory assumes substantial computational ability of the firm: projects are decided after screening of *all* alternatives on the basis of detailed calculations of all direct and indirect benefits and costs. Reality suggests that firms are of limited computational ability and do not make decisions on the basis of detailed studies or marginalistic rules. Fourthly, the traditional theory treats expectations as exogenously determined. In reality expectations are to a large extent endogenous, being affected by various internal factors, for example, the desires–aspirations of various groups, the information available and its flow through the various sections of the firm, and from past attainments of the various groups and of the firm–organisation as a whole.

In the traditional theory there is no conflict of goals between the organisation and its individual members. In the behavioural theory conflict among the various members of the coalition is inevitable. It is never fully resolved at any one time. There is rather a continuous process of bargaining between members and the organisation, and the conflict is quasi-resolved in any one period by money payments, slack adjustment, policy commitments, delegation of authority (decentralisation of the decision-making activity), and by sequential attention to the conflicting demands. Such means permit the firm to make decisions with inconsistent goals, and within a continuously changing internal and external environment.

Unlike the traditional theory, Cyert and March distinguish two sources of uncertainty: uncertainty arising from changes in market conditions (tastes, products and methods of production), and uncertainty arising from competitors' behaviour. Market-originated uncertainty is avoided, according to the behavioural school, partly by search activity, partly by maintaining R & D departments, and partly by concentrating on short-term planning. Contrary to the traditional theory, Cyert and March postulate that the short run is much more important than the long run.

> In particular, so long as the environment of the firm is unstable (and unpredictably unstable) the heart of the theory must be the process of short-run, adaptive reactions.

It seems to us, however, that unless the long-run goals are defined, any short-run description of the behaviour of the firm cannot attain the degree of generality expected from a theory of the firm. Regarding the competitor-originated uncertainty, Cyert and March accept that firms act within a 'negotiated environment', that is, firms adopt business practices of a collusive nature. Thus, the behavioural theory is not applicable to non-collusive oligopolistic markets.

In the behavioural theory the instruments which the firm uses in the decision-making process are the same as those of the traditional theory: output, price, and sales strategy (the latter including all activities of non-price competition, such as advertising, salesmanship, service, quality). The difference lies in the way by which the values of these policy variables are determined. In the traditional theory the firm chooses such values of the policy variables which will result in the maximisation of the long-run profits. In the behavioural theory the policies adopted should lead to the 'satisficing' level of sales, profits, growth and so on.

Cyert and March postulate that the firm is an adaptive organisation: it learns from its experience. It is not from the beginning a rational institution in the traditional sense of 'global' rationality. In the long run the firm may tend towards the 'omniscient rationality' of profit maximisation, but in the short run there is an adaptive process of learning: there are mistakes, trials and errors. The firm has a memory and learns through its past experience.

It seems strange to us that despite this 'adaptive learning process' the firm does not ever seem to acquire the ability for long-run planning. The behavioural theory is basically a short-run theory. The determination of the values of the instrumental variables (output, price, sales strategy) does not adequately take into account the environment: past performance and past conditions of the environment are crudely extrapolated into the future.

IX. CRITIQUE

The behavioural theory has contributed to the development of the theory of the firm in several respects. Its main contributions are: firstly, the insight into the process of goal-formation and the internal resource allocation, and secondly, the systematic analysis of the stabilising role of 'slack' on the activity of the firm.

The behavioural theory deals with the allocation of resources within the firm, and the decision-making processes, an aspect neglected in the traditional theory. In the latter the firm was assumed to react to the all-powerful environment. The behaviourist school assumes that the firm has some discretion, and does not necessarily take the constraints of the environment as definite and impossible to change. The traditional theory stressed the role of the market (price) mechanism for the allocation of resources *between* the various sectors of the economy, while the behavioural theory examines the mechanism of the resource allocation *within* the firm. Clearly the two theories are complementary rather than substitutes. Actually various theorists have attempted to incorporate the behavioural aspects of Cyert and March's theory into their own models.[1]

Cyert and March's definition of 'slack' shows that this concept is equivalent to the 'economic rent' of factors of production of the traditional theory of the firm. The contribution of the behavioural school lies in the analysis of the stabilising role of 'slack' on the activity of the firm. Changes in slack payments in periods of booming and depressed business enables the firm to maintain its aspiration levels despite the changing environment.

It should be pointed out that Cyert and March deal only with one form of slack, the managerial slack. Slack payments accruing to other members of the firm–coalition and their short-run and long-run implications for the performance of the firm are not examined.

The behavioural theory has, however, serious shortcomings.

The behavioural theories basically provide a simulation approach to the complexity of the mechanism of the modern multigoal, multiproduct corporation. Simulation, however, is a predictive technique. It does not explain the behaviour of the firm; it predicts the behaviour without providing an explanation of any particular action of the firm.

The behavioural theories do not deal with industry equilibrium. They do not explain the interdependence and interaction of firms, nor the way in which the interrelationship of firms leads to an equilibrium of output and price at the industry level. Thus the conditions for the attainment of a stable equilibrium in the industry are not determined.

No account is given of conditions of entry or of the effects on the behaviour of established firms of a threat by potential entrants.

---

[1] See, for example, R. Marris, 'A Model of the Managerial Enterprise', *Quarterly Journal of Economics* (1963).

The behavioural theory, although dealing realistically with the search activity of the firm (in the sense that search is considered as problem-oriented), cannot explain the dynamic aspects of invention and innovation, which are by their nature long-run activities with long-run implications.

The 'plasticity' (readjustment) of the aspiration levels downwards whenever the set targets are not attained deprives the theory of objective criteria for the evaluation of 'satisfactory' performance. To judge whether the performance of a firm is satisfactory one should have a 'constant measuring-rod', that is, a well-defined set of (long-run) goals. If goals are readjusted downward whenever their attainment has not been achieved, how are we to judge the performance of the firm? The 'measuring-rod' behaves like an elastic ruler that stretches and shrinks, depending on the attainment or not of the aspiration (goals) initially set.

No exact predictions can be derived from the postulates of the behavioural theory. The acceptance of satisficing behaviour renders practically the theory into a tautological structure: whatever the firms are observed to do can be rationalised on the lines of satisficing.

The behavioural theory implies a short-sighted behaviour of firms. Surely the uncertainty of the market cannot be avoided by short-term planning. Most decisions require a long-term view of the environment.

The behavioural theory resolves the chore problem of oligopolistic interdependence by accepting tacit collusion of the firms in the industry. This solution is unstable, especially when entry takes place, a situation brushed aside by the behavioural theorists.

Cyert and March based their theory on four actual case studies and two experimental studies conducted with hypothetical firms. It is obvious that the theory is founded on too few case studies for it to be possible to show that it has the generality appropriate to a theory of the firm. However, the part that describes the decision-making process and the allocation of resources in large complex organisations could be incorporated in, and hence enrich, other theories of the firm.

SECTION G

THEORY OF GAMES
LINEAR PROGRAMMING

19. Theory of Games

The interdependence of firms in oligopolistic markets and the inherent uncertainty about competitors' reactions to any course of action adopted by a firm cannot be analysed effectively by the traditional tools of economic theory.

Economists have developed collusive models, limit-pricing models, managerial models, and behavioural models, but these do not provide a general theory of oligopoly in the sense that none of these models could fully explain the decision-making process of oligopolists.

A different approach to the study of the oligopoly problem is provided by the theory of games. The first systematic attempt in this field is von Neumann's and Morgenstern's *Theory of Games and Economic Behaviour*, published in 1944. Since that time numerous economists have developed models of oligopolistic behaviour based on the theory of games. Perhaps the most prominent proponent of the games-theory approach is Martin Shubik,[1] who seems to believe that the only hope for the development of a general theory of oligopoly is the games theory. Despite such enthusiasts the games-theory approach has not yet provided results which could lead to a general theory of oligopoly. The main contribution of this approach is that it can use high-speed computers to conduct experiments of oligopolistic behaviour. Such controlled experiments cannot be conducted in the real business world. Thus the computerised study of oligopolistic behaviour is an extremely useful tool which might lead to generalisations about the decision-making process of oligopolists in real-world situations, and thus provide the basis for a theory of oligopoly. This development, however, is still in its infancy, and has not as yet gained much acclaim by the majority of economists.

In this chapter we provide an elementary exposition of the simplest models of games theory.

I. SOME DEFINITIONS

The firm has various *instruments* or *policy variables* with which it can pursue its goals. The most important are the price, quantity and style of its products, advertising and other selling activities, research and development expenditures, channels for selling the product(s), and changes in the number of products (discontinuation of an old product or introduction of new ones).

A *strategy* is a specific course of action with clearly defined values for the policy variables. For example, a strategy may consist of setting a price of £3·95, spending £2000 on advertising, making a change in the packaging of the product, and selling it in

---

[1] M. Shubik, *Strategy and Market Structure* (John Wiley, 1959). Also M. Shubik, 'A Curmudgeon's Guide to Microeconomics', *Journal of Economic Literature* (1971).

supermarkets. Another strategy may involve leaving the price unchanged, spending £1000 on advertising, devoting £2000 to research on a new product, and so on. To each of these strategies a competitor may react in different ways, that is, by adopting different strategies. He may decide to adopt the same or a different course of action than the one adopted by the other firm. Thus each firm has various strategies open to it, and in any particular case it will adopt the one that will seem most advantageous under the circumstances.

The *payoff* of a strategy is the 'net gain' it will bring to the firm for any given counter-strategy of the competitor(s). This gain is measured in terms of the goal(s) of the firm. For example, if the goal of the firm is to maximise its profit, the payoffs of a strategy will be measured in terms of profit levels that it yields; if the goal is maximisation of the market share, the payoffs will be measured as the actual shares that the strategy will secure to the firm adopting it.

The *payoff matrix* of a firm is a table showing the payoffs accruing to this firm as a result of each possible combination of strategies adopted by it and by its rival(s). For example, assume that there are two firms in the industry. Firm I has to choose among five strategies $(A_1, A_2, \ldots, A_5)$ and Firm II can react by adopting any one of six strategies open to it $(B_1, B_2, \ldots, B_6)$. Thus to each strategy of Firm I there are six possible counter-strategies of Firm II, and similarly to each strategy of Firm II there are five counter-strategies of the rival Firm I. Thus the payoff matrix of each firm will include $5 \times 6 = 30$ payoffs, corresponding to the results of each possible combination of strategies selected by both rivals.

Let us denote each payoff G_{ij}, where i refers to the strategy adopted by Firm I and j to the counter-strategy adopted by Firm II. Thus for the above example the payoff matrix for Firm I will be of the general form of table 19.1. If Firm I adopts strategy A_1 and its rival reacts by adopting among the strategies open to it B_5, the payoff (gain) of Firm I will be G_{15}. If Firm I chooses strategy A_4 and its rival reacts with strategy B_6, the payoff of Firm I will be G_{46}, and so on.

In the theory of games the firms in oligopolistic markets are treated as players in a chess game: to each movement by one player the other may choose among several counter-movements. The counter-movements of rivals are probable but not certain.

Table 19.1 Payoff matrix of Firm I

		Firm II's strategies					
		B_1	B_2	B_3	B_4	B_5	B_6
Firm I's strategies	A_1	G_{11}	G_{12}	G_{13}	G_{14}	G_{15}	G_{16}
	A_2	G_{21}	G_{22}	G_{23}	G_{24}	G_{25}	G_{26}
	A_3	G_{31}	G_{32}	G_{33}	G_{34}	G_{35}	G_{36}
	A_4	G_{41}	G_{42}	G_{43}	G_{44}	G_{45}	G_{46}
	A_5	G_{51}	G_{52}	G_{53}	G_{54}	G_{55}	G_{56}

Yet it is possible to choose a strategy which (under certain conditions) will maximise the firm's expected 'gain', after making due allowance for the effects of rivals' probable reactions.

II. TWO-PERSON ZERO-SUM GAME

A. CERTAINTY MODEL

The simplest model is a duopoly market in which each duopolist attempts to maximise his market share. Given this goal, whatever a firm gains (by increasing its share of the market) the other firm loses (because of the decrease in its share). Thus any gain of one rival is offset by the loss of the other, and the net gain sums up to zero. Hence the name 'zero-sum game'.

The assumptions of the model are:

1. The firms have a given, well-defined goal. In our particular example the goal is maximisation of the market share.

2. Each firm knows the strategies open to it and to its rival, or concentrates on the most important of these strategies.

3. Each firm knows with certainty the payoffs of all combinations of the strategies being considered. This implies that the firm knows its total revenue, total costs and total profit from each combination of strategies.

4. The actions chosen by the duopolists do not affect the total size of the market.

5. Each firm chooses its strategy 'expecting the worst from its rival', that is, each firm acts in the most conservative way, expecting that the rival will choose the best possible counter-strategy open to him. This behaviour is defined as 'rational'.

6. In the zero-sum game there is no incentive for collusion, given assumption 4, since the goals of the firms are diametrically opposed.

In order to find the equilibrium solution we need information on the payoff matrix of the two firms. In our example the payoffs will be shares of the market resulting from the adoption of any two strategies by the rivals. Assume that Firm I has four strategies open to it and Firm II has five strategies. The payoff matrices of the duopolists are shown in tables 19.2 and 19.3.

Table 19.2   Payoff matrix of Firm I

	Firm II's strategies				
	B_1	B_2	B_3	B_4	B_5
A_1	(0·10)	0·20	0·15	0·30	0·25
A_2	0·40	(0·30)	0·50	0·55	0·45
A_3	0·35	0·25	(0·20)	0·40	0·50
A_4	0·25	(0·15)	0·35	0·60	0·20

Firm I's strategies

Table 19.3   Payoff matrix of Firm II

		Firm II's strategies				
		B_1	B_2	B_3	B_4	B_5
Firm I's strategies	A_1	0·90	0·80	0·85	0·70	0·75
	A_2	0·60	0·70	0·50	0·45	0·55
	A_3	0·65	0·75	0·80	0·60	0·50
	A_4	0·75	0·85	0·65	0·40	0·80

Clearly the sum of the payoffs in corresponding cells of the two payoff tables add up to unity, since the numbers in these cells are shares, and the total market is shared between the two firms. In general, in the two-person zero-sum game we need not write both payoff matrices because of the nature of the game: the goals are opposing, and, in our example, the payoff table of Firm I contains indirectly information about the payoff of Firm II. Still we start by showing both tables, and then we show how the equilibrium solution can be found from only the first payoff matrix.

Choice of strategy by Firm I

Firm I examines the outcomes of each strategy open to it. That is, Firm I examines each row of its payoff matrix and finds the most favourable outcome of the corresponding strategy, because the firm expects the rival to adopt the most advantageous action open to him. This is the behavioural rule implied by assumption 5 of this model. Thus:

If Firm I adopts strategy A_1, the worst outcome that it may expect is a share of 0·10 (which will be realised if the rival Firm II adopts its most favourable strategy B_1).

If Firm I adopts strategy A_2, the worst outcome will be a share of 0·30 (if the rival adopts the best action for him, B_2).

If Firm I adopts strategy A_3, the worst outcome will be a share of 0·20 (if Firm II chooses the best open alternative, B_3).

If Firm I adopts strategy A_4, the worst outcome will be a share of 0·15 (which would be realised by action B_2 of Firm II).

Among all these *minima* (that is, among the above worst outcomes) Firm I chooses the *maximum*, the 'best of the worst'. This is called a *maximin strategy*, because the firm chooses the maximum among the minima. In our example the maximin strategy of Firm I is A_2, that is, the strategy which yields a share of 0·30.

Choice of strategy by Firm II

Firm II behaves in exactly the same way. The only difference is that Firm II examines the *columns* of its payoff table, because these columns include the results–payoffs of each of the strategies open to Firm II. For each strategy, that is, for each column, Firm II finds the worst outcome (on the assumption that the rival will choose the best),

Table 19.4   Combined payoff matrix

		Firm II's strategies (minimax behaviour)				
		B_1	B_2	B_3	B_4	B_5
Firm I's strategies (maximin behaviour)	A_1	(0·10)	0·20	0·15	0·30	0·25
	A_2	0·40	(0·30)	0·50	0·55	0·45
	A_3	0·35	0·25	(0·20)	0·40	0·50
	A_4	0·25	(0·15)	0·35	0·60	0·20

and among these worst outcomes Firm II chooses the best. Thus, if Firm II uses its own payoff table, its behaviour is a maximin behaviour identical to the behaviour of Firm I.

However, as we said earlier, in the zero-sum game only one payoff matrix is adequate for the equilibrium solution. In our example the first payoff table will be used not only by Firm I but also by Firm II. Thus concentrating on the first payoff table we may re-state the decision-making process of Firm II as follows. Firm II examines the columns of the (first) payoff matrix because these columns contain the information about the payoffs of its strategies. For each column-strategy Firm II finds the maximum payoff (of Firm I) because this is the worst situation the firm (II) will face if it adopts the strategy correponding to that column. Thus for strategy B_1 the worst outcome (for Firm II) is 0·40; for strategy B_2 the worst outcome is 0·30; for strategy B_3 the worst outcome is 0·50; for strategy B_4 the worst result is 0·60; for strategy B_5 the worst result is 0·50. Among these maxima of each column-strategy Firm II will choose the strategy with minimum value. Thus the strategy of Firm II is a *minimax* strategy, since it involves the choice of a minimum among the maxima payoffs. (Table 19.4.)

It should be stressed that although different terms are used for the choice of the two firms (maximin behaviour of Firm I, minimax behaviour of Firm II), the behavioural rule for both firms is the same: each firm expects the worst from its rival.

In our example the equilibrium solution is strategy A_2 for Firm I and B_2 for Firm II. This solution yields shares 0·30 for Firm I and 0·70 for Firm II. It is an equilibrium solution because it is the preferred one by both firms. This solution is called the '*saddle point*', and the preferred strategies A_2 and B_2 are called '*dominant strategies*'.

It should be clear that there exists no such equilibrium (saddle) solution if there is no payoff which is preferred by both firms simultaneously. Under certain mathematical conditions other solutions and strategy choices can be determined. The analysis of the resulting *mixed strategies* requires a sophisticated exposition of utility theory and random selection which is beyond the scope of this book.

B. UNCERTAINTY MODEL

The assumption that each firm knows with certainty the exact value of the payoff of each strategy is unrealistic. The most probable situation in the real business world is that the firm, by adopting a certain strategy, may expect a range of results for each counter-strategy of the rival, each result with an associated probability. Thus the payoff matrix is constructed so as to include the *expected value* of each payoff. The expected value is the sum of the products of the possible outcomes of a pair of strategies (adopted by the two firms) each multiplied by its probability:

$$E(G_{ij}) = g_{1i}P_1 + g_{2i}P_2 + \cdots + g_{ni}P_n$$

$$= \sum_{s=1}^{n} g_{si}P_s$$

where g_{si} = the *s*th of the *n* possible outcomes of strategy *i* of Firm I (given that Firm II has chosen strategy *j*)

P_s = the probability of the *s*th outcome of strategy *i*

For example, assume that Firm I chooses strategy A_1 and Firm II reacts with strategy B_1. This pair of simultaneous strategies may yield the shares for Firm I each with a certain probability, shown in the second column of table 19.5. Thus the expected payoff of the pair of strategies A_1 and B_1 is

$$E(G_{11}) = (0.00)(0.00) + (0.05)(0.05) + (0.15)(0.05) + \cdots + (0.95)(0.02) + (1)(0)$$
$$= 0.458$$

Table 19.5

Possible shares of Firm I for the pair of strategies A$_1$, B$_1$	Probability of each share
0·00	0·00
0·05	0·05
0·15	0·05
0·25	0·10
0·35	0·15
0·45	0·25
0·55	0·20
0·65	0·10
0·75	0·05
0·85	0·03
0·95	0·02
1·00	0·00
	$\Sigma P_i = 1$

In a similar way we find the expected payoff of all combinations of strategies. Given the matrix of expected payoffs, the behavioural pattern of the firms is the same as in the certainty model.
That is:
Firm I adopts the *maximin strategy*. It finds for *each row* the minimum expected payoff, and among these minima the firm chooses the one with the highest value (the maximum among the minima).
Firm II adopts the *minimax strategy*. It finds for *each column* the maximum expected payoff, and among these maxima Firm II chooses the one with the smallest value (the minimum among the maxima).

Although the uncertainty zero-sum game seems simple, its assumptions are quite stringent:

1. The firms maximise their expected payoffs.

2. The zero-sum game assumes that both firms assign the same probability to each pair of payoffs; they make the same judgement. This implies that the firms must have the same information and the same objective criteria with which to evaluate the probabilities of the different payoffs. Otherwise the probability distribution of the payoffs will not be objective.

3. The firms maximise their total utility, and the utility of each payoff is proportional to the value assumed by the payoff.

The above assumptions are clearly strong and unrealistic. Furthermore, the basic condition of the zero-sum game, that the 'gain' of one firm is equal to the 'loss' of the other, is rarely met in the real business world. Usually the 'gains' are not 'offset' by equal 'losses'. Only in the case of a share goal, and in the rare case of extinction tactics, do we have a zero-sum game. In most cases we have a non-zero-sum game.

III. NON-ZERO-SUM GAME

We will illustrate this model with a duopolistic market in which the firms aim at the maximisation of their profit. Their products are close substitutes so that if their prices differ the firm with the lower price will supply the largest part of the market. It is assumed that the firms will use price as their instrumental variable. For simplicity we assume that each firm can charge two prices (either £3 or £5), that is, there are two strategies open to each competitor. Each firm has a different cost structure and the market size is affected by the rivals' combined action. Under these conditions the payoff matrix of each firm is expressed in terms of levels of profit, and the gains of one rival need not be (and in our example are not) equal to the losses of the other. The payoff matrices of the two firms are shown below in tables 19.6 and 19.7, and are subsequently combined in a single table. (Table 19.8.)

Table 19.6   Firm I's payoff matrix
(level of profits of I)

		Firm II's strategies	
		$P = 5$	$P = 3$
Firm I's strategies	$P = 5$	$\Pi_A = 90$	$\Pi_A = 50$
	$P = 3$	$\Pi_A = 150$	$\Pi_A = 80$

Table 19.7   Firm II's payoff matrix
(levels of profit of II)

		Firm II's strategies	
		$P_B = 5$	$P_B = 3$
Firm I's strategies	$P_A = 5$	$\Pi_B = 110$	$\Pi_B = 120$
	$P_A = 3$	$\Pi_B = 60$	$\Pi_B = 100$

Table 19.8   Combined payoff matrix

		Firm II's strategies			
		$P_B = 5$		$P_B = 3$	
Firm I's strategies	$P_A = 5$	$\Pi_A = 90$ ⋮ $\Pi_B = 110$ Joint $\Pi = 200$		$\Pi_A = 50$ ⋮ $\Pi_B = 120$ Joint $\Pi = 170$	
	$P_A = 3$	$\Pi_A = 150$ ⋮ $\Pi_B = 60$ Joint $\Pi = 210$		$\Pi_A = 80$ ⋮ $\Pi_B = 100$ Joint $\Pi = 180$	

The behavioural rule is the same for both firms: each expects the worst from the rival. The choice of Firm I is a *maximin strategy*. If Firm I sets the price of £5 the minimum gain is £50; if it sets $P = 3$ its minimum profit is £80. Among these two minima the firm chooses the maximum, that is, the preferred strategy by Firm I is $P = 3$.

The choice of Firm II is also a *maximin strategy*. If Firm II charges a price of £5 the worst it can expect is a profit of £60; if it charges a price of £3 the minimum level of profit is £100. Among these minima the firm will choose the maximum, that is, Firm II will choose the price of £3.

Under these circumstances there is a unique equilibrium price (£3) which will be adopted by both firms. Thus the strategy $P = £3$ is a *dominant strategy*. Yet with this strategy both firms are in a worse situation as compared to the alternative strategy $P = 5$, since both realise a lower profit. And of course the industry (joint) profit is not maximised. The conservative maximin strategy is not the optimal solution in this case. If the firms colluded and both charged the higher price of £5 the joint profit and their individual profits would be higher ($90 > 80, 110 > 100$, and $200 > 180$). Thus while the maximin strategy provides an optimal solution in the zero-sum game, this may not be so in the variable-sum game.

Many other oligopolistic actions may be analysed with the above apparatus of the theory of games. For example, advertising campaigns, change in style or diversification, research and development expenditures may be examined by the principles of the games theory. In most real-world cases we see that firms choose strategies which do not maximise their profits: advertising or new-product rivalry often lead to excessive increases in costs of all firms in the industry. Such situations may be explained by the conservative behaviour of maximin strategies.

In many oligopolistic situations firms seem to avoid the unfavourable outcomes predicted by the maximin–minimax behaviour of the theory of games. Several reasons have been offered for these cases. Firstly, the duration of rivalry. If rivalry has been continuous for a considerable time-period the rivals 'learn' to predict the reactions of each other and this leads to the avoidance of moves which, from well-established past patterns, have proved disadvantageous to all parties. Secondly, the stability of tastes and processes. Firms are more likely to avoid mutually damaging actions in a market where demand does not change and technological progress is slow. On the other hand, in markets with frequent changes of tastes it is almost certain that firms will adopt maximin strategies despite their mutually unfavourable results. Thirdly, the existence of common sources of information and communication between rivals. If the rivals lack information it is most natural to fear the worst (maximin assumption) from the competitors and reach suboptimal solutions. Fourthly, time-lags are important in deciding which strategy to adopt. If the imitation of an action (for example, a new product, a new process) is easy the firms will recognise that they have little to gain and much to lose by aggressive action and hence will adopt maximin strategies, which are by their nature conservative. If, however, an action cannot easily or quickly be imitated the firms will tend to abandon maximin attitudes and adopt actions which lead to more favourable positions for themselves, instead of expecting the worst from their rivals, for the simple reason that the rivals cannot quickly adopt the most advantageous action.

In summary: games theory has not provided a general theory of oligopolistic behaviour. However, the games-theory approach has been able to explain some real-world situations. It has helped in showing that there are strong incentives for collusion in several oligopolistic situations. Perhaps the most important contribution of this theory is that it has led to controlled experiments in the study of firms' behaviour. By expressing the alternatives open to a firm and its rivals in the form of payoff matrices it has made possible the examination of an increasing number of alternatives with controlled experiments based on the use of high-speed computers. Playing 'monopoly games' with computers has been a fashionable tendency in many American universities. Such 'controlled' studies have provided insight into various aspects of the decision-making process of individuals in uncertain situations similar to those facing the firms in the real world. Yet games theory is still a long way from providing a comprehensive theory of oligopolistic behaviour.

IV. THE PRISONER'S DILEMMA: A DIGRESSION

We saw that in most cases of variable-sum games the maximin–minimax behaviour leads the rivals to suboptimal solutions, that is, to situations worse than they need be. These examples and their suboptimal solutions are a special case of the general group of problems which are known as *Prisoner's Dilemma Games*. A brief exposition of the original prisoner's dilemma might help the understanding of the behaviour of firms faced by uncertainty about their rivals' action.

Two criminals are arrested after committing a big bank robbery. However, the evidence is not adequate to make the robbery charge stand unless one or both criminals confess. Each suspect is interrogated in isolation from his companion so that no communication is possible between them. The District Attorney promises no punishment for the suspect who confesses and a heavy sentence of, say, twenty years' imprisonment for the other party. If both suspects do not confess, both will go free. If both confess, they will get the sentence prescribed by the law for the crime of robbery, for example ten years' imprisonment. Thus each suspect has two 'strategies' open to himself, to confess or not to confess, and is faced with the dilemma: to confess (and go free if the other does not confess, or get the ten-year sentence) or not to confess (and go free if the other does not confess, or get the heavy twenty-year sentence if he is betrayed by the other suspect). The payoff matrix of the two prisoners is shown in table 19.9. Given the lack of communication between the suspects and the uncertainty as to the 'loyalty' of the other prisoner, each one of them prefers to adopt the second strategy, that is, to

Table 19.9

		Prisoner B's strategies			
		No confession		Confession	
Prisoner A's strategies	No confession	A 0	B 0	A 20	B 0
	Confession	A 0	B 20	A 10	B 10

confess, so that both get a ten-year sentence. Clearly this is a worse situation as compared with the adoption of the 'no confession' strategy by both robbers. The 'dominant' strategy, which implies the rule 'expect the worst from the other(s)' (the maximin assumption) leads to a worse position than the robbers need be in! If communication were possible, or if from past experience the fellows had learned to trust each other, they would both plead 'not guilty' and would go free, thus maximising their 'gains'.

The drawing of analogies concerning the conditions of uncertainty facing the firms in oligopolistic markets is straightforward.

20. Linear Programming

I. GENERAL NOTES

Linear programming is a recently devised technique for providing specific numerical solutions of problems which earlier could be solved only in vague qualitative terms by using the apparatus of the general theory of the firm. Linear programming has thus helped to bridge the gap between abstract economic theory and managerial decision-making in practice. The use of linear programming is expanding fast due to the use of computers which can quickly solve complex problems involving the optimal use of many resources which are given to the firm in any particular time and thus set constraints on the firm's choice.

Linear programming can be considered as providing an operational method for dealing with economic relationships, which involve discontinuities. It is a specific approach within the general framework of economic theory.

The main similarities and differences between traditional economic analysis and linear programming may be outlined as follows. Both approaches show how economic agents (consumers or producers) reach optimal choices, how they do their planning or programming in order to attain maximum utility, maximum profit, minimum cost, etc. Neither economic theory nor linear programming say anything about the implementation of the optimal plan or solution. They simply derive the optimal solution in any particular situation. In that sense both approaches are *ex ante* methods aiming at helping the economic units to find the solution that attains their goal (utility maximisation, profit maximisation, cost minimisation) given their resources (income or factor inputs) at any particular time. However, in economic theory the optimal solution is usually shown in qualitative abstract terms, diagrams, or general mathematical symbols, while linear programming yields specific numerical solutions to the particular optimisation problems. Another difference between economic analysis and linear programming is that the relationships of economic theory are usually non-linear, depicted by curves (not straight lines), while in linear programming all relationships between the variables involved are assumed to be linear. Methods of non-linear programming have recently been developed, but their exposition involves sophisticated mathematics and will not be attempted here. In this chapter we will give an introductory exposition of the linear programming technique.

We will illustrate the use of linear programming by a simple example of a firm which has a given quantity of three factors of production with which it can produce two commodities, x and y. The problem of the firm, given its resources, is to choose the optimal product mix which maximises the firm's profit.

II. STATEMENT OF THE LINEAR PROGRAMMING PROBLEM

Assume that a firm has the following quantities of factors of production

$$L = \quad 400 \text{ units of labour} \quad \text{(hours)}$$
$$K = \quad 300 \text{ units of capital} \quad \text{(machine hours)}$$
$$S = 1000 \text{ units of land} \quad \text{(square feet)}$$

The firm can produce either commodity x or commodity y with the following available processes (activities)

	Activity A_1 *for* x	*Activity* A_2 *for* y
Labour	$l_x = 4$	$l_y = 1$
Capital	$k_x = 1$	$k_y = 1$
Land	$s_x = 2$	$s_y = 5$

In words, the production of one unit of x requires 4 hours of labour, 1 machine hour and 2 square feet of land. Similarly, the production of one unit of y requires 1 hour of labour, 1 machine hour and 5 square feet of land.

Commodity x yields a unit profit of £2, and commodity y yields a unit profit of £1. The goal of the firm is to choose the optimal product mix, that is, the mix that maximises its total profit.

The total profit function may be written as follows

$$Z = 2X + 1Y$$

where Z = total profit
X = quantity of commodity x (or level of Activity A_1)
Y = quantity of commodity y (or level of Activity A_2)

2 and 1 are the unit profits of the two commodities. The total profit function is called the *objective function*, because it expresses the objective of the firm, which in our particular example is the maximisation of profit. In general, the objective function is the function which represents the goals of the economic agent.

The firm, in pursuing the maximisation of its objective function, has several constraints. We distinguish two groups of constraints, *technical* (or *functional*) *constraints*, and *non-negativity constraints*. The technical constraints are set by the state of technology and the availability of factors of production. There are as many technical constraints as the factors of production. They express the fact that the quantities of factors which will be absorbed in the production of the commodities cannot exceed the available quantities of these factors. Thus the technological constraints take the form of inequalities. In our example the technical constraints are the following three

$$4X + 1Y \leq \quad 400$$
$$1X + 1Y \leq \quad 300$$
$$2X + 5Y \leq 1000$$

where X and Y are the levels of commodities x and y (levels of utilisation of activities A_1 and A_2) and the integers on the left-hand side are the technical coefficients of production, that is, the factor inputs required for the production of one unit of the products x and y. The figures on the right-hand side are the resources that the firm has at its disposition. These inequality constraints state that the levels of X and Y in the optimal product mix should not require more than the available quantities of the three resources.

The non-negativity constraints express the necessity that the levels of production of the commodities cannot be negative, since negative quantities do not make sense in economics. The level of production of any one commodity can either be zero or positive

$$X \geq 0$$
$$Y \geq 0$$

Given the above information, the linear programming problem may formally be stated as follows:

Maximise $Z = 2X + 1Y$ (objective function)

Subject to $4X + 1Y \leq\ \ \ 400$
                          $1X + 1Y \leq\ \ \ 300$ $\Big\}$ technical constraints $\Big\}$
                          $2X + 5Y \leq 1000$

                          $X \geq 0$
                          $Y \geq 0$ $\Big\}$ non-negativity constraints $\Big\}$

Note that all the constraints take the form of inequalities. Thus the system cannot be solved with the usual methods of solution of simultaneous equations. The linear programming technique has been designed to deal with the solution of problems involving inequalities. Its basic approach is that of iteration: the optimal solution is defined by examining the set of possible alternative solutions and eliminating gradually the suboptimal ones until the optimal is reached (see section IV below).

III. GRAPHICAL SOLUTION OF THE LINEAR PROGRAMMING PROBLEM

The graphical solution is simple when the problem can be presented on two-dimensional diagrams, as in our simple example. When there are more than two variables the graphical solution becomes extremely complicated or impossible to draw. In this case the algebraic solution presented in the next section (the simplex method) should be used.

The graphical solution involves two steps. Firstly, the graphical determination of the region of feasible solutions. Secondly, the graphical presentation of the objective function.

A. GRAPHICAL DETERMINATION OF THE REGION OF FEASIBLE SOLUTIONS

A solution is called feasible when it satisfies all the constraints.

The non-negativity constraints in our example are shown graphically by the area of the positive quadrant of the usual orthogonal co-ordinate system (figure 20.1). Points on the horizontal axis denote that the production of y is zero, while the production of x is positive. That is, on the x-axis $X \geq 0$ and $Y = 0$. Similarly, points on the y-axis denote that there is no production of x, while the production of y is positive. That is, on the y-axis $X = 0$ and $Y \geq 0$. Clearly points lying inside the two axes imply some production of both commodities ($X > 0$ and $Y > 0$). The shaded area in figure 20.1 and its boundaries (denoted by the two axes) represent the region in which the non-negativity constraints are satisfied.

The complete determination of the region of feasible solutions requires in addition the determination of the boundaries or limits set by the technical (functional) constraints, that is, the availability of the factors of production and the given state of technology.

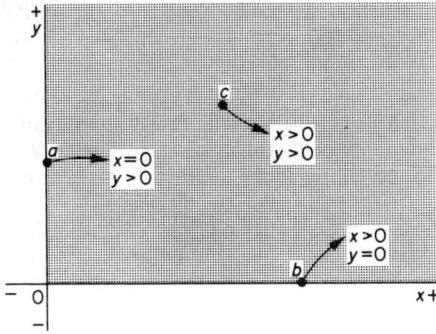

Figure 20.1

Boundary set by the factor 'labour'. This is defined by a straight line whose slope is the ratio of the labour inputs in the production of the two commodities. Thus if we denote the boundary set by labour with the letter L, we have

$$\begin{bmatrix} \text{Slope of} \\ \text{boundary } L \end{bmatrix} = \text{slope of } AB = \frac{\text{input of } L \text{ in } x}{\text{input of } L \text{ in } y} = \frac{4}{1} = \frac{l_x}{l_y}$$

We may find the boundary L as follows. If all the available labour is used in the production of y, the maximum quantity which can be produced of this commodity is

$$0A = \frac{L}{l_y} = \frac{400}{1} = 400$$

If all the available labour is used in producing x the maximum quantity of this commodity is

$$0B = \frac{L}{l_x} = \frac{400}{4} = 100$$

These maximum levels of production are denoted by points A and B in figure 20.2. If we join points A and B with a straight line we form the boundary set by the factor L (labour). The slope of this boundary is

$$\text{Slope of } AB = \frac{0A}{0B} = \frac{L/l_y}{L/l_x} = \frac{400/1}{400/4} = \frac{4}{1} = \frac{\text{input of } L \text{ in } x}{\text{input of } L \text{ in } y}$$

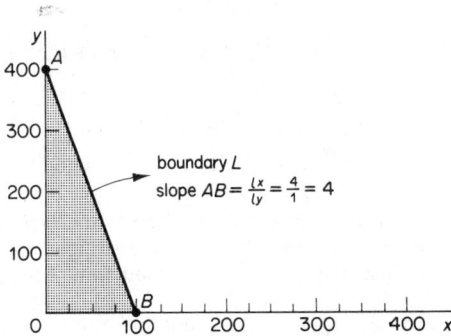

Figure 20.2   Boundary of factor 'labour'

The feasible region of production of x and y defined by the availability of labour (L) is the shaded area $0AB$ in figure 20.2.

Boundary set by the factor 'capital'. In a similar way we may derive the boundary (or limit) set to the production possibilities of the firm by the available quantity of the factor capital (K). The boundary of K will be a straight line (CD in figure 20.3) whose slope is the ratio of the capital inputs in the production of the two commodities

$$\begin{bmatrix} \text{Slope of} \\ \text{boundary } K \end{bmatrix} = \text{slope of } CD = \frac{\text{input of } K \text{ in } x}{\text{input of } K \text{ in } y} = \frac{k_x}{k_y} = \frac{1}{1} = 1$$

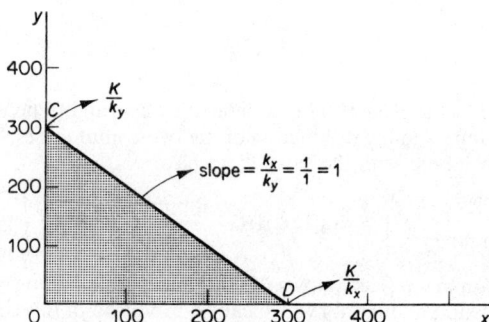

Figure 20.3   Boundary of capital K

In our example the boundary of capital can be determined as follows. If the firm uses all the available units of K in the production of y, the maximum quantity of this commodity is

$$0C = \frac{K}{k_y} = \frac{300}{1} = 300$$

If the firm uses all its K in the production of x, the maximum quantity of this commodity is

$$0D = \frac{K}{k_x} = \frac{300}{1} = 300$$

If we join the points C and D we form the boundary set by the factor K. The slope of this boundary is

$$\text{Slope of } CD = \frac{0C}{0D} = \frac{K/k_y}{K/k_x} = \frac{300/1}{300/1} = \frac{k_x}{k_y} = \frac{\text{input of } K \text{ in } x}{\text{input of } K \text{ in } y}$$

Boundary set by the factor 'land'. The boundary of the factor 'land' (S) is determined in the same way as the previous two boundaries. It is a straight line (EF in figure 20.4) whose slope is the ratio of the land inputs in the production of the two commodities

$$\begin{bmatrix} \text{Slope of} \\ \text{boundary } S \end{bmatrix} = \text{slope of } EF = \frac{\text{input of } S \text{ in } x}{\text{input of } S \text{ in } y} = \frac{s_x}{s_y} = \frac{2}{5}$$

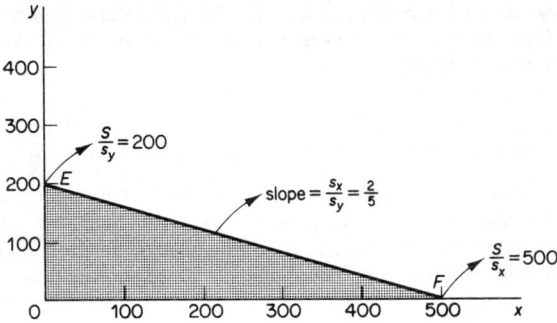

Figure 20.4 Boundary of the factor 'land'

In our example the boundary of the factor 'land' is defined as follows. If the firm uses all the available units of S in producing y, the maximum quantity of this commodity is

$$OE = \frac{S}{s_y} = \frac{1000}{5} = 200$$

If all the units of S are used in producing x, the maximum quantity of this commodity is

$$OF = \frac{S}{s_x} = \frac{1000}{2} = 500$$

If we join the points E and F we form the boundary for the factor 'land' which has the slope

$$\text{slope of } EF = \frac{OE}{OF} = \frac{S/s_y}{S/s_x} = \frac{1000/5}{1000/2} = \frac{2}{5} = \frac{s_x}{s_y}$$

The region of feasible solutions of the firm is determined graphically if we super-impose the three diagrams showing the boundary-constraints set to the production possibilities of the firm by all the factors of production simultaneously. In figure 20.5 the region of feasible solutions is shown by the area $OEGB$ in which all the inequality constraints (technical and non-negativity constraints) are satisfied. Only combinations of x and y lying in this area and on its boundaries are feasible, given the availability

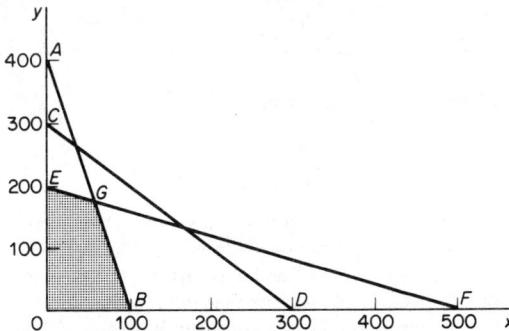

Figure 20.5 Region of feasible solutions

of factors and the state of technology. Of all the feasible solutions only the ones lying on the frontier *EGB* are technically efficient. Thus the optimal solution must be one of the points on the frontier (*EGB*).

B. GRAPHICAL DETERMINATION OF THE OBJECTIVE FUNCTION

We said that among all the feasible solutions the firm will choose the one that maximises its objective function, that is, the product mix which yields the maximum profit. The objective function in our example may be presented graphically by isoprofit lines. We may construct an isoprofit line by solving the objective function for *Y*. Thus the profit function

$$Z = 2X + 1Y = \pi_x X + \pi_y Y$$

solved for *Y* yields

$$Y = \frac{1}{\pi_y} Z - \frac{\pi_x}{\pi_y} X$$

Clearly the slope of this isoprofit line is

$$\frac{\partial Y}{\partial X} = -\frac{\pi_x}{\pi_y} = \frac{\text{unit profit of } x}{\text{unit profit of } y} = \frac{2}{1} = 2$$

By assigning various values to the level of total profit (*Z*) we can compute the whole family of isoprofit lines (isoprofit map, figure 20.6). These lines have a negative slope and are parallel, given that the unit profits of the two commodities are assumed constant. The further away from the origin an iosprofit line is the greater the total profit it denotes.

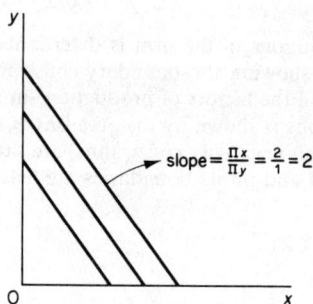

Figure 20.6   Isoprofit map, with $\pi_x = 2$ and $\pi_y = 1$

C. DETERMINATION OF THE OPTIMAL SOLUTION

The optimal solution is found by the point of tangency of the frontier of the region of feasible solutions to the highest possible isoprofit curve. The optimal solution will be a point on the frontier of the region of all feasible solutions, because any point inside this region lies on a lower isoprofit line. It is clear that the optimal solution depends on the slope of the isoprofit lines, that is, on the ratio of the unit profits of the two commodities. In our example the optimal solution is point *G* in figure 20.7.

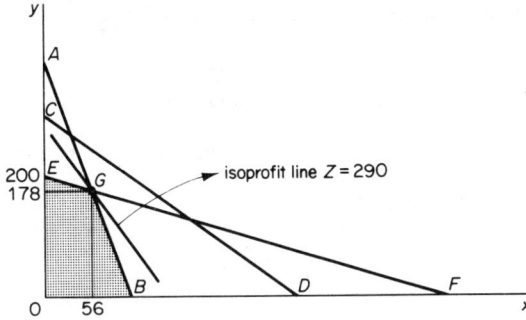

Figure 20.7 Optimal solution

At this point the product mix is 178 units of y and 56 units of x, and the maximum profit amounts to £290, as can be verified from the profit function

$$Z = 2X + 1Y = 2(56) + 1(178) = 290$$

If the slope of the isoprofit line is equal to the slope of any one of the boundary lines which define the region of the feasible solutions, there is no unique optimal solution to the linear programming problem. For example, if $\pi_x/\pi_y = l_x/l_y$ ($=$ slope of AB which is the boundary for the factor 'labour' all the points on the segment GB will be optimal solutions. Similarly, if $\pi_x/\pi_y = s_x/s_y$ ($=$ slope of EF which is the boundary for the factor 'land') all the points on the segment EG of the production-possibility frontier will be optimal solutions. From the above discussion it should be obvious that a unique optimal solution exists if the slope of the line representing the objective function has a value lying within the range set by the slopes of the boundary lines which denote the technical restrictions of the linear programming problem.

We may generalise the above procedure for the determination of the optimal solution as follows.

Step 1. Write the technical inequalities in the form of equalities and solve them for Y

$$l_1X + l_2Y = L$$
$$k_1X + k_2Y = K$$
$$s_1X + s_2Y = S$$

Solving these equations for Y we obtain the equations of the three boundary lines:
The equation of boundary L is

$$Y = \frac{1}{l_2}L - \frac{l_1}{l_2}X$$

The slope of the L boundary is

$$\frac{\partial Y}{\partial X} = -\frac{l_1}{l_2}$$

We may draw the L boundary by assigning various values to X and plotting the resulting points on a graph. (The value of L is given.)
The equation of the boundary K is

$$Y = \frac{1}{k_2}K - \frac{k_1}{k_2}X$$

The slope of the K boundary is

$$\frac{\partial Y}{\partial X} = -\frac{k_1}{k_2}$$

We may draw the K boundary by assigning various values to X (given the value of K) and plotting the resulting points on a graph.

The equation of the boundary S is

$$Y = \frac{1}{s_2} S - \frac{s_1}{s_2} X$$

The slope of the S boundary is

$$\frac{\partial Y}{\partial X} = -\frac{s_1}{s_2}$$

We may draw the S boundary by assigning different values to X (given the quantity of S) and plotting the resulting points on a graph.

Step 2. Determine the region of feasible solutions. This is the area within all the boundaries set by the technical restrictions. Only the parts of the areas below the individual boundary lines that coincide, when the various graphs (of Step 1) are combined, do satisfy all the constraints.

Step 3. Define the isoprofit lines by solving the profit equation for Y

$$Z = \pi_1 X + \pi_2 Y$$

$$Y = \frac{\pi_1}{\pi_2} Z - \frac{\pi_1}{\pi_2} X$$

The slope of the isoprofit line is

$$\frac{\partial Y}{\partial X} = -\frac{\pi_1}{\pi_2}$$

The set of isoprofit lines can be drawn by assigning different values to Z and to X.

Step 4. Define the optimal solution by comparing the slope of the isoprofit line with the slopes of the boundary lines that define the region of feasible solutions. Since all lines have negative slopes we can ignore their signs when doing the comparison. In our example only two boundary lines define the region of feasible solutions. (The factor K does not set any limit to the choice of the firm, given the other factors L and S.) The slopes of the boundary lines are

(*a*) Slope of boundary L: $\dfrac{l_1}{l_2} = \dfrac{4}{1} = 4$

(*b*) Slope of boundary S: $\dfrac{k_1}{k_2} = \dfrac{2}{5}$

The slope of the isoprofit line is

$$\frac{\pi_1}{\pi_2} = \frac{2}{1} = 2$$

Given that

$$\frac{s_1}{s_2} < \frac{\pi_1}{\pi_2} < \frac{l_1}{l_2}$$

$$\frac{2}{5} < 2 < \frac{4}{1}$$

we conclude that there is a unique solution, and that this optimal solution is defined by the intersection of the two boundary lines that define the region of feasible solutions.

IV. THE SIMPLEX METHOD

When the variables whose values must be determined from the linear programming method are more than two, the graphical solution is difficult or impossible because we need multidimensional diagrams. The following iterative method for reaching the optimal solution, which is called the *simplex method*, may be used.

We will illustrate the simplex method by using the following example.

Assume that a firm can produce five commodities, $x_1, x_2, \ldots, x_5$, with three factors of production F_1, F_2, F_3. The available quantities of factors are

$$F_1 = 100 \text{ units of labour}$$
$$F_2 = 80 \text{ units of capital}$$
$$F_3 = 150 \text{ units of land}$$

The known methods of production (processes or activities) for each product are

	A_1 *activity for* x_1	A_2 *activity for* x_2	A_3 *activity for* x_3	A_4 *activity for* x_4	A_5 *activity for* x_5
F_1	$l_1 = 2$	$l_2 = 2$	$l_3 = 1$	$l_4 = 2$	$l_5 = 2$
F_2	$k_1 = 2$	$k_2 = 0$	$k_3 = 1$	$k_4 = 1$	$k_5 = 2$
F_3	$s_1 = 0$	$s_2 = 1$	$s_3 = 2$	$s_4 = 1$	$s_4 = 2$

The unit profits of the five commodities are

$$\pi_1 = 2 \qquad \pi_2 = 2 \qquad \pi_3 = 3 \qquad \pi_4 = 4 \qquad \pi_5 = 6$$

The firm wants to choose the product mix that maximises its total profit Z. Let us denote the levels of production of the five commodities by the capital X letter with the appropriate subscript. With the above information we can state the linear programming problem formally as follows.

Maximise $\qquad Z = \pi_1 X_1 + \pi_2 X_2 + \pi_3 X_3 + \pi_4 X_4 + \pi_5 X_5$

subject to $\qquad l_1 X_1 + l_2 X_2 + l_3 X_3 + l_4 X_4 + l_5 X_5 \le F_1$
$\qquad\qquad\quad k_1 X_1 + k_2 X_2 + k_3 X_3 + k_4 X_4 + k_5 X_5 \le F_2$
$\qquad\qquad\quad s_1 X_1 + s_2 X_2 + s_3 X_3 + s_4 X_4 + s_5 X_5 \le F_3$

$\qquad\qquad X_1 \ge 0, X_2 \ge 0, X_3 \ge 0, X_4 \ge 0, X_5 \ge 0$

Substituting the technical information of our example we

Maximise $\qquad Z = 2X_1 + 2X_2 + 3X_3 + 4X_4 + 6X_5$

subject to $\qquad 2X_1 + 2X_2 + 1X_3 + 2X_4 + 2X_5 \leq 100$

$\qquad\qquad\quad 2X_1 + 0X_2 + 1X_3 + 1X_4 + 2X_5 \leq 80$

$\qquad\qquad\quad 0X_1 + 1X_2 + 2X_3 + 1X_4 + 2X_5 \leq 150$

To overcome the difficulties created by the inequalities in the constraints we transform the technical constraints into equalities by introducing into each one of them a variable, called the '*slack variable*', which will show the unutilised units of the corresponding factor of production. Clearly there will be as many slack variables as there are factors of production. It is assumed that unutilised factors have zero profitability (neither profit nor loss). With the introduction of the slack variables the constraints become

$$l_1 X_1 + l_2 X_2 + l_3 X_3 + l_4 X_4 + l_5 X_5 + S_1 = F_1$$
$$k_1 X_1 + k_2 X_2 + k_3 X_3 + k_4 X_4 + k_5 X_5 + S_2 = F_2$$
$$s_1 X_1 + s_2 X_2 + s_3 X_3 + s_4 X_4 + s_5 X_5 + S_3 = F_3$$

With the technological data of our example the constraints are

$$2X_1 + 2X_2 + 1X_3 + 2X_4 + 2X_5 + S_1 = 100$$
$$2X_1 + 0X_2 + 1X_3 + 1X_4 + 2X_5 + S_2 = 80$$
$$0X_1 + 1X_2 + 2X_3 + 1X_4 + 2X_5 + S_3 = 150$$

A. THE ITERATIVE PROCEDURE

Iteration I

We start from any one feasible solution, find its profitability and consider whether it yields maximum profit as compared with other feasible solutions. The levels of output and of unused factors in any one solution form a *basis*. The easiest way to begin the iterations is to start from the basis that shows zero production, that is, it includes the three slack activities with values equal to the available quantities of the three factors of production, since with no production all the factors are unutilised. Thus the initial solution (Basis I) is the origin, where all levels of output are zero

$$X_1 = X_2 = X_3 = X_4 = X_5 = 0$$

and all inputs are unemployed, so that

$$S_1 = F_1 = 100$$
$$S_2 = F_2 = 80$$
$$S_3 = F_3 = 150$$

This is a feasible solution, because all the constraints are satisfied. Clearly it is not optimal, since profits are zero if there is no production.

$$Z = 2(0) + 2(0) + 3(0) + 4(0) + 6(0) + 0(S_1) + 0(S_2) + 0(S_3) = 0$$

Before we proceed to find a better feasible solution we will present the first solution (Basis I) in a table (table 20.1).

Table 20.1 Iteration I

Activities			A_1 $\pi_1 = 2$	A_2 $\pi_2 = 2$	A_3 $\pi_3 = 3$	A_4 $\pi_4 = 4$	A_5 $\pi_5 = 6$	S_1 $\pi_6 = 0$	S_2 $\pi_7 = 0$	S_3 $\pi_8 = 0$
Basis I	Activities	Levels of Activities								
	S_1	$F_1 = 100$	$l_1 = 2$	$l_2 = 2$	$l_3 = 1$	$l_4 = 2$	$l_5 = 2$	1	0	0
	S_2	$F_2 = 80$	$k_1 = 2$	$k_2 = 0$	$k_3 = 1$	$k_4 = 1$	$k_5 = 2$	0	1	0
	S_3	$F_3 = 150$	$s_1 = 0$	$s_2 = 1$	$s_3 = 2$	$s_4 = 1$	$s_5 = 2$	0	0	1
Profits		Total profit $Z = 0$	-2	-2	-3	-4	-6	0	0	0

In the first column we show the activities that are included in the solution (Basis), which is being examined, and their levels of utilisation. Basis I includes the slack activities S_1, S_2, S_3, and their levels of utilisation are equal to the unused factors of production, 100 units of F_1, 80 units of F_2 and 150 units of F_3.

In the columns of the five productive activities we insert the inputs of the three factors of production which are required for the production of one unit of the corresponding commodities.

In the columns of the slack activities we insert unity for the corresponding factor of production, and zero for all other factors.

In the last row of the table we insert the total profit (Z) of the Basis and the unit profits of the activities with a negative sign. This row (which we will call the 'profitability row') is crucial in the iterative procedure of the simplex method, because it shows which is the most profitable activity which should be introduced in the next iteration. When all the elements in this row become positive or zero we stop the iterations. Positive elements in the 'profitability row' suggest that the introduction of the corresponding activities in the Basis will lead to a decrease in the total profit. Zero elements in the 'profitability row' (in the columns of the productive activities $A_1, \ldots, A_5$) imply that there are other optimal solutions which yield the same total profit. Thus when the elements of the 'profitability row' (of the columns of the productive activities) are either positive or zero we stop (usually) the iterations since an optimal solution has been reached.

Iteration II

We must find the *incoming activity* and the *outgoing activity*, that is the activity which we must introduce in the Basis and the one that will be replaced.

As incoming activity we choose the one with the highest unit profit, that is, the activity with the largest negative element in the 'profitability row'. In our example the most profitable activity is A_5.

The outgoing activity is found by dividing each activity level in the first Basis (F_1, F_2, and F_3 in our example) by the relevant input coefficient of the incoming activity, and choosing to replace the activity of the old Basis for which the ratio is the smallest. In our example we have

$$\frac{F_1}{l_5} = \frac{100}{2} = 50, \qquad \frac{F_2}{k_5} = \frac{80}{2} = 40, \qquad \frac{F_3}{s_5} = \frac{150}{2} = 75$$

The smallest ratio is F_2/k_5, hence the outgoing activity is S_2. The new Basis will include the activities S_1, A_5 and S_3. We replace the slack activity whose ratio is the smallest, because the corresponding resource will be the first to be exhausted as we expand the production of commodity x_5 (produced by the incoming activity).

Our next step is to find the elements of the new iteration table. The following steps are involved in this process.

1. We define *the pivot element*, which is the element at the intersection of the incoming and the outgoing activities. In our example the pivot element is 2, at the intersection of A_5 and S_2.

2. We find the elements of *the pivot row*, that is, the row that will be occupied by the incoming activity, taking the place of the outgoing activity. The elements of the pivot row are found by dividing the elements of the original row (of the outgoing activity) by the pivot element (2 in our example). The elements of the pivot row are the elements of the incoming activity (A_5) in the new iteration table. In our example the elements of the pivot row are

$$\frac{80}{2} = 40, \quad \frac{2}{2} = 1, \quad \frac{0}{2} = 0, \quad \frac{1}{2}, \quad \frac{1}{2}, \quad \frac{2}{2} = 1, \quad \frac{0}{2} = 0, \quad \frac{1}{2}, \quad \frac{0}{2} = 0$$

3. Any other element in the second iteration table b_i is found by subtracting from the corresponding original element a_i (in the first iteration table) the product of the element of the pivot row which is in the same column as a_i multiplied by the element of the incoming activity which is in the same row as a_i. The computations are shown in table 20.2. The crucial data required at this stage are the elements of the pivot row $(b_{10}, b_{11}, \ldots, b_{18})$ and the elements of the column of the outgoing activity $(a_6 = 2, a_{15} = 2, a_{24} = 2)$. The elements of the first and third rows of the second iteration table are

$$b_1 = a_1 - (40)(2) = 100 - 80 = 20$$
$$b_2 = a_2 - (1)(2) = 2 - 2 = 0$$
$$b_3 = a_3 - (0)(2) = 2 - 0 = 2$$
$$b_4 = a_4 - (\tfrac{1}{2})(2) = 1 - 1 = 0$$
$$b_5 = a_5 - (\tfrac{1}{2})(2) = 2 - 1 = 1$$
$$b_6 = a_6 - (1)(2) = 2 - 2 = 0$$
$$b_7 = a_7 - (0)(2) = 1 - 0 = 1$$
$$b_8 = a_8 - (\tfrac{1}{2})(2) = 0 - 1 = -1$$
$$b_9 = a_9 - (0)(2) = 0 - 0 = 0$$
$$b_{19} = a_{19} - (40)(2) = 150 - 80 = 70$$
$$b_{20} = a_{20} - (1)(2) = 0 - 2 = -2$$
$$b_{21} = a_{21} - (0)(2) = 1 - 0 = 1$$
$$b_{22} = a_{22} - (\tfrac{1}{2})(2) = 2 - 1 = 1$$
$$b_{23} = a_{23} - (\tfrac{1}{2})(2) = 1 - 1 = 0$$
$$b_{24} = a_{24} - (1)(2) = 2 - 2 = 0$$
$$b_{25} = a_{25} - (0)(2) = 0 - 0 = 0$$
$$b_{26} = a_{26} - (\tfrac{1}{2})(2) = 0 - 1 = -1$$
$$b_{27} = a_{27} - (0)(2) = 1 - 0 = 1$$

4. The total profit of the new solution (Z_{II}) is found by multiplying the levels of the activities in this Basis by their unit profits

$$Z_{II} = \pi_6(S_1) + \pi_5(A_5) + \pi_8(S_3) = (20)(0) + (40)(6) + (70)(0) = 240$$

5. The elements of the 'profitability row' are estimated in the same way as the other elements of the second iteration table. That is, from the initial 'profitability elements' we subtract the product of the element of the pivot row (which is in the same column as $\pi_{i,1}$) times the 'profitability element' of the incoming activity:

$$\pi_{1,II} = \pi_{1,I} - (1)(-6) = -2 + 6 = 4$$
$$\pi_{2,II} = \pi_{2,I} - (0)(-6) = -2 - 0 = -2$$
$$\pi_{3,II} = \pi_{3,I} - (\tfrac{1}{2})(-6) = -3 + 3 = 0$$
$$\pi_{4,II} = \pi_{4,I} - (\tfrac{1}{2})(-6) = -4 + 3 = -1$$
$$\pi_{5,II} = \pi_{5,I} - (1)(-6) = -6 + 6 = 0$$
$$\pi_{6,II} = \pi_{6,I} - (0)(-6) = 0 + 0 = 0$$
$$\pi_{7,II} = \pi_{7,I} - (\tfrac{1}{2})(-6) = 0 + 3 = 3$$
$$\pi_{8,II} = \pi_{8,I} - (0)(-6) = 0 + 0 = 0$$

We have now completed the computation of the elements of the second iteration. The results are shown in table 20.3.

Table 20.2

'Pivot row' →

b_1	b_2	b_3	b_4	b_5	b_6 $a_6 = 2$ ←	b_7	b_8	b_9
$b_{10} = 40$	$b_{11} = 1$	$b_{12} = 0$	$b_{13} = \frac{1}{2}$	$b_{14} = \frac{1}{2}$	$b_{15} = 1$ $a_{15} = 2$	$b_{16} = 0$	$b_{17} = \frac{1}{2}$	$b_{18} = 0$
b_{19}	b_{20}	b_{21}	b_{22}	b_{23}	b_{24} $a_{24} = 2$	b_{25}	b_{26}	b_{27}
Z_{II}	$\pi_{1,\text{II}}$	$\pi_{2,\text{II}}$	$\pi_{3,\text{II}}$	$\pi_{4,\text{II}}$	$\pi_{5,\text{II}}$ $\pi_{5,1} = 6$	$\pi_{6,\text{II}}$	$\pi_{7,\text{II}}$	$\pi_{8,\text{II}}$

Table 20.3   Iteration II

Activities	Basis II	Levels of Activities	A_1 $\pi_1 = 2$	A_2 $\pi_2 = 2$	A_3 $\pi_3 = 3$	A_4 $\pi_4 = 4$	A_5 $\pi_5 = 6$	S_1 $\pi_6 = 0$	S_2 $\pi_7 = 0$	S_3 $\pi_8 = 0$
	Activities									
	S_1	20	0	2	0	1	0	1	-1	0
	A_5	40	1	0	$\frac{1}{2}$	$\frac{1}{2}$	1	0	$\frac{1}{2}$	0
	S_3	70	-2	1	1	0	0	0	-1	1
'Profitability'	Total profit $Z_{II} = 240$		4	-2	0	-1	0	0	3	0

It is clear that the second Basis

$$S_1 = 20 \qquad A_5 = 40 \qquad S_3 = 70$$

is better than the initial solution, since it yields a total profit of 240 monetary units. However, so long as negative elements appear in the last row of the iteration table, we can further improve our solution (increase profits) by introducing into the basis the activity which has the largest negative 'profitability element'. In our example activity A_2 which produces commodity x_2 will be the incoming activity in the new solution (Basis III). The outgoing activity is determined in the same way as in the previous iteration. That is, we divide the slack activities in Basis II by the corresponding elements in the column of the incoming activity (A_2) and we drop out the activity with the smallest ratio. In our example we have

$$\tfrac{20}{2} = 10 \qquad \text{and} \qquad \tfrac{70}{1} = 70$$

Since $(20/2) < (70/1)$ the outgoing activity at this iteration is S_1. (Table 20.4.)

Before we proceed with the computations of the third iteration it is useful to indicate the implications of the *simplex criterion*. This criterion serves in defining whether the optimal solution has been reached, or whether a further improvement can be achieved by additional iterations.

The *simplex criterion* may be summarised in the following propositions.

If one or more elements in the 'profitability row' are negative, further improvement of the solution is possible, and the iterations should continue, unless all the elements of the incoming activity are positive or zero. In this case we infer that the problem has no solution or it has not been correctly stated.

If all the elements in the 'profitability row' are positive or zero, the Basis in this table is an optimal solution, and further iterations are (usually) not required.

The inclusion in the Basis of activities with positive 'profitability elements' reduces the total profit of the firm, and hence such activities should not be considered as a means for improving the solution.

If some of the productive activities have zero 'profitability elements' in the final table, there is more than one optimal solution. If we introduce in the Basis an activity with zero 'profitability', the total profit is not affected.

Iteration III

The last row of the second iteration table contains negative elements and hence the solution can be improved. The incoming activity is the one with the greatest negative 'profitability element' $(A_2$ in our example), and the outgoing activity is S_1 which has the smallest ratio $(S_1/2 = $ level of S_1 in Basis II divided by the corresponding element of the column of the incoming activity).

Having defined the incoming and the outgoing activities, we repeat the computations of the second iteration.

1. The pivot element is 2, defined by the intersection of the incoming and the outgoing activities.

2. The elements of the 'pivot row' are defined by the division of the elements of the outgoing activity into the pivot element. They are

$$\tfrac{20}{2} = 10, \quad \tfrac{0}{2} = 0, \quad \tfrac{2}{2} = 1, \quad \tfrac{0}{2} = 0, \quad \tfrac{1}{2}, \quad \tfrac{0}{2} = 0, \quad \tfrac{1}{2}, \quad -\tfrac{1}{2}, \quad \tfrac{0}{2} = 0$$

3. The remaining elements (c_i) of the third iteration table are found by subtracting from the corresponding elements of the second iteration table (b_i) the product of the element of the 'pivot row' (which is in the same column as b_i) times the element of the

Table 20.4

	$c_1 = 10$	$c_2 = 0$	$\downarrow$ $c_3 = 1$ $b_3 = 2$	$c_4 = 0$	$c_5 = \frac{1}{2}$	$c_6 = 0$	$c_7 = \frac{1}{2}$	$c_8 = -\frac{1}{2}$	$c_9 = 0$
'Pivot row' $\rightarrow$	c_{10}	c_{11}	c_{12} $b_{12} = 0$	c_{13}	c_{14}	c_{15}	c_{16}	c_{17}	c_{18}
	c_{19}	c_{20}	c_{21} $b_{21} = 1$	c_{22}	c_{23}	c_{24}	c_{25}	c_{26}	c_{27}
	Z_{III}	$\pi_{1,\mathrm{III}}$	$\pi_{2,\mathrm{III}}$	$\pi_{3,\mathrm{III}}$	$\pi_{4,\mathrm{III}}$	$\pi_{5,\mathrm{III}}$	$\pi_{6,\mathrm{III}}$	$\pi_{7,\mathrm{III}}$	$\pi_{8,\mathrm{III}}$

incoming activity (which is in the same row as b_i). The values of the elements of the third iteration are:

$$
\begin{array}{ll}
c_{10} = 40 & c_{19} = 60 \\
c_{11} = 0 & c_{20} = -2 \\
c_{12} = 0 & c_{21} = 0 \\
c_{13} = \frac{1}{2} & c_{22} = 1 \\
c_{14} = \frac{1}{2} & c_{23} = -\frac{1}{2} \\
c_{15} = 1 & c_{24} = 0 \\
c_{16} = 0 & c_{25} = -\frac{1}{2} \\
c_{17} = \frac{1}{2} & c_{26} = -\frac{1}{2} \\
c_{18} = 0 & c_{27} = 1
\end{array}
$$

4. The total profit of the Basis III is found by adding the products of the levels of the activities included in this basis times their corresponding unit profits (as given in the objective function)

$$Z_{III} = (10)(2) + (40)(6) + (60)(0) = 260$$

This is higher than the profit of the previous solution ($Z_{II} = 240$).

5. The elements of the 'profitability row' of the third iteration are computed as in the second iteration:

$$
\begin{aligned}
\pi_{1,III} &= \pi_{1,II} - (0)(-2) = 4 - 0 = 4 \\
\pi_{2,III} &= \pi_{2,II} - (1)(-2) = -2 + 2 = 0 \\
\pi_{3,III} &= \pi_{3,II} - (0)(-2) = 0 - 0 = 0 \\
\pi_{4,III} &= \pi_{4,II} - (\tfrac{1}{2})(-2) = -1 + 1 = 0 \\
\pi_{5,III} &= \pi_{5,II} - (0)(-2) = 0 - 0 = 0 \\
\pi_{6,III} &= \pi_{6,II} - (\tfrac{1}{2})(-2) = 0 + 1 = 1 \\
\pi_{7,III} &= \pi_{7,II} - (-\tfrac{1}{2})(-2) = 3 - 1 = 2 \\
\pi_{8,III} &= \pi_{8,II} - (0)(-2) = 0 - 0 = 0
\end{aligned}
$$

Thus we have completed the computations of the elements of the third Basis. The results are shown in table 20.5.

Using the propositions of the *simplex criterion* we observe the following.

All the elements in the last row ('profitability row') are either positive or zero. This implies that this table contains an optimal solution. The activities of this Basis are:

$$
\begin{aligned}
A_2 &= 10 \text{ units of commodity } x_2 \\
A_5 &= 40 \text{ units of commodity } x_5 \\
S_3 &= 60 \text{ units of unutilised factor } F_3
\end{aligned}
$$

The total profit of this optimal solution is 260 monetary units.

Given that there are zeros in the last row (and in the columns of the productive activities), we infer that the above solution is not unique. That is, there are other optimal solutions (which include the productive activities with zero 'profitability elements'). These alternative optimal solutions of course yield the same total profit. Since we have found an optimal solution we will not proceed with further iterations. However, there are cases in which the location of additional optimal solutions might be useful.[1]

---

[1] See, for example, R. Dorfan, P. Samuelson and R. Solow, *Linear Programming and Economic Analysis* (McGraw-Hill, 1958).

Table 20.5   Iteration III

Activities			A_1 $\pi_1 = 2$	A_2 $\pi_2 = 2$	A_3 $\pi_3 = 3$	A_4 $\pi_4 = 4$	A_5 $\pi_5 = 6$	S_1 $\pi_6 = 0$	S_2 $\pi_7 = 0$	S_3 $\pi_8 = 0$
	Basis III									
	Activities	Levels of Activities								
	A_2	10	0	1	0	$\frac{1}{2}$	0	$\frac{1}{2}$	$-\frac{1}{2}$	0
	A_5	40	1	0	$\frac{1}{2}$	$\frac{1}{2}$	1	0	$\frac{1}{2}$	0
	S_3	60	-2	0	1	$-\frac{1}{2}$	0	$-\frac{1}{2}$	$-\frac{1}{2}$	1
'Profitability'	Total profit $Z_{III} = 260$		4	0	0	0	0	1	2	0

V. THE DUAL PROBLEM AND SHADOW PRICES

The basic problem whose solution is attempted by the linear programming technique is called the *primal problem*. To each primal problem corresponds a *dual problem*, which yields additional information to the decision-maker. The nature of the dual problem depends on the primal problem. If the primal problem is a maximisation problem, its dual is a minimisation problem. Similarly, if the primal is a minimisation problem its dual is a maximisation problem.

The detailed examination of the dual problem is beyond the scope of this book. We will concentrate here on the dual problem of our earlier example of profit maximisation. The dual problem in this case is one of cost minimisation, and from its solution we derive the *shadow prices* of the factors of production used by the firm. The dual problem may be solved independently from its primal by a similar procedure to the one described above. However, the values obtained from the solution of the dual are also obtained as a by-product from the last iteration of the primal, which yields the optimal solution. In our example the shadow prices of the three factors of production are the elements appearing in the last three cells of the 'profitability row' of table 20.5. If the optimal solution contains a slack activity showing that some quantity of the corresponding factor remains unemployed, this factor has a shadow price equal to zero. If the factors are fully employed, their shadow prices are positive. In our example the shadow prices of the factor labour (F_1) and the factor capital (F_2), which are fully employed in the optimal solution, appear as positive and equal to 1 and 2 monetary units respectively. The shadow price of the factor land (F_3) is zero, because this factor is not fully employed in the optimal solution.

The shadow prices of the factors are the *imputed costs* or *opportunity costs* of the factors for the particular firm. As such they are crucial indicators for the expansion of the firm. They show which factors are bottlenecks to the further expansion of the firm, since these factors will appear with a positive shadow price (opportunity cost) in the optimal solution. Furthermore the shadow prices of the resources can be compared with their market prices and help the entrepreneur decide whether it is profitable to hire additional units of these factors. The shadow price of a factor denotes by how much the profit of the firm will be increased if the firm employs an additional unit of this factor. In our example we see that if the firm hired an additional unit of labour its profits would increase by 1 monetary unit. Similarly, if the firm employed an additional unit of capital its profit would rise by 2 monetary units. But in order to hire additional units of L and/or K the firm would have to pay their market price (wage or rent of capital). Thus, if the shadow price of· a factor is larger than its market price, it would pay the firm to increase its employment of that factor, since the firm's net profit would increase. Obviously the shadow prices, whose values are estimated from the linear programming technique, are of great practical importance to the firm.

21. Concluding Remarks

The business world is extremely complex and neo-classical microeconomic theory has proved inadequate to cope with this complexity. The nostalgia of many economists for theoretical models yielding precise equilibria is understandable; but economic analysis cannot be limited to models which describe the behaviour of monolithic firms run by owner-managers acting with omniscience and reaching decisions (aimed at the single goal of profit maximisation) with rationality possible in a world of perfect knowledge and certainty. The neo-classical model is too unrealistic for it to claim general acceptance. Contemporary theorists have not yet managed to develop a single model of the firm having the scope and precise results of the neo-classical model. Instead we have a *constellation* of models, all in a state of flux: models such as those of the 'full-cost' school, 'entry-forestalling' school, 'managerial' school, 'behavioural' school, and 'games-theory' school are being constantly revised, refined, tested and re-evaluated in an attempt to reach acceptable degrees of realism and predictive accuracy.

These models explore various aspects of the decision-making process of the firm that cannot be ignored in any realistic description of how the economic system works. Recent developments have drawn attention to the multiplicity of goals of modern large enterprises (objectives of managers, shareholders and workers) and stress the fact that multiple decisions have to be taken within single planning periods. Pricing decisions, which were the main concern of neo-classical theory, are only one aspect of the behaviour of the firm. These decisions are interlinked with others, such as the improvement of existing and the introduction of new products, the level of advertising expenses (and other sales efforts), the rate and direction of the growth of the firm (diversification, vertical integration, mergers and investment decisions), and the tactics towards actual and potential competition. All these aspects of the competitive behaviour must be examined simultaneously, for concentration on one aspect only (such as price policy) gives a partial picture.

In all models one can find elements of realism, contributing to the improvement of our knowledge of the decision-making process of the firms of the real world. Given the intricacies of the internal organisation of the firms (internal constraints), and the continuous change in the economic environment (external constraints), the advances achieved in micro-theory are impressive.

Whether from such fermentation of hypotheses and models a single general theory of oligopoly will emerge is questionable. There are various reasons for this scepticism. The shifts in demand, technological advance, organisational complexity and peculiarities of large firms, and the increasing concentration of productive activity in the hands of a few hundred giant multiproduct multinational firms, render reality too complex for it to be adequately described and explained by a single general model. To these complexities must be added the difficulties in securing reliable information on crucial variables, the increasing government activity in the private sector, the creation of 'blocks' at the international level, and so on, which change the economic system continuously. The number of variables that theories have to embody is extremely large.

It is hoped, however, that from the accumulation of inductive evidence, and the refinement of the tools and methods of testing hypotheses, the relevant ingredients of the plethora of existing models will be welded into a coherent general framework, flexible enough to permit the construction of specialised models to suit the purpose of the particular decision-maker.

Select Bibliography

CHAPTER 1 INTRODUCTION

Section I

1. Buchanan, J. M., 'Ceteris Paribus: Some Notes on Methodology', *Southern Economic Journal* (1958) pp. 259–70.
2. Friedman, M., 'The Methodology of Positive Economics', in *Essays in Positive Economics* (University of Chicago Press, 1953).
3. Gordon, D. F., 'Operational Propositions in Economic Theory', *Journal of Political Economy* (1955) pp. 150–61.
4. Hutchinson, T. W., 'Professor Machlup on Verification in Economics', *Southern Economic Journal* (1956) pp. 476–83.
5. Koopmans, T. C., 'Measurement Without Theory', *Review of Economics and Statistics* (1947) pp. 161–72.
6. Lange, O., 'The Scope and Method of Economics,' *Review of Economic Studies* (1945–6) pp. 19–32.
7. Leontief, W. W., 'Implicit Theorising: A Methodological Criticism of the Neo-Cambridge School', *Quarterly Journal of Economics* (1937) pp. 337–51.
8. Machlup, F., 'The Problems of Verification in Economics', *Southern Economic Journal* (1955) pp. 1–21.
9. Melitz, T., 'Friedman and Machlup on the Significance of Testing Economic Assumptions', *Journal of Political Economy* (1965).
10. Nagel, E., 'Assumptions in Economic Theory,' *American Economic Review* (1963) pp. 211–19.
11. Robbins, L., *An Essay on the Nature and Significance of Economic Science* (Macmillan, 1935).
12. Samuelson, P. A., *Foundations of Economic Analysis* (Harvard University Press, 1947).
13. Samuelson, P. A., 'Economic Theory and Mathematics: An Appraisal', *American Economic Review* (1952) pp. 56–66.

Section II

1. Bain, J. S., 'Chamberlin's Impact on Microeconomic Theory', in *Monopolistic Competition Theory: Studies in Impact*, ed. R. E. Kuenne (Wiley, 1967). Reprinted in *Readings in Price Theory*, ed. H. Townsend (Penguin, 1971).

2. Bishop, R. L., 'Elasticities, Cross-Elasticities and Market Relationships', *American Economic Review* (1952). Comments by W. Fellner and E. H. Chamberlin, and reply by Bishop, *American Economic Review* (1953) pp. 898–924. Comment by R. Heiser, and reply by Bishop, *American Economic Review* (1955) pp. 373–86.
3. Bishop, R. L., 'Market Classification Again', *Southern Economic Journal* (1961).
4. Chamberlin, E. H., *Towards a More General Theory of Value* (New York: Oxford University Press, 1957) pp. 84–91.
5. Heertje, A., 'Market Classification Systems in Theory', *Southern Economic Journal* (1960).
6. Pfouts, R. W., and C. E. Ferguson, 'Market Classification Systems in Theory and Policy', *Southern Economic Journal* (1959).
7. Pfouts, R. W., and C. E. Ferguson, 'Conjectural Behaviour Classification of Oligopoly Situations', *Southern Economic Journal* (1960).
8. Pfouts, R. W., and C. E. Ferguson, 'Theory, Operationalism, and Policy: A Further Note on Market Classification', *Southern Economic Journal* (1961).

SECTION III

1. Andrews, P. W. S., 'Industrial Analysis in Economics', in *Oxford Studies in the Price Mechanism*, ed. T. Wilson and P. W. S. Andrews (Oxford University Press, 1951).
2. Andrews, P. W. S., *On Competition in Economic Theory* (Macmillan, 1964).
3. Chamberlin, E. H., *The Theory of Monopolistic Competition* (Harvard University Press, 1933).
4. Chamberlin, E. H., 'Monopolistic Competition Re-examined', *Economica* (1951).
5. Kaldor, N., 'Market Imperfection and Excess Capacity', *Economica* (1935).
6. Robinson, Joan, *The Economics of Imperfect Competition* (Macmillan, 1933).
7. Robinson, Joan, 'Imperfect Competition Revisited', *Economic Journal* (1953).
8. Triffin, R., *Monopolistic Competition and General Equilibrium Theory* (Harvard University Press, 1939).

CHAPTER 2 THEORY OF DEMAND

1. Alchian, A. A:, 'The Meaning of Utility Measurement', *American Economic Review* (1953) pp. 26–50. Reprinted in *Readings in Price Theory*, ed. H. Townsend (Penguin, 1971).
2. Andrews, P. W. S., *Manufacturing Business* (Macmillan, 1949).
3. Baumol, W. J., 'The Neumann–Morgenstern Utility Index: An Ordinalist View', *Journal of Political Economy* (1951) pp. 61–6.
4. Baumol, W. J., 'The Cardinal Utility which is Ordinal', *Economic Journal* (1958) pp. 665–72.
5. Ferguson, C. E., 'An Essay on Cardinal Utility', *Southern Economic Journal* (1958) pp. 11–23.
6. Friedman, M., and L. J. Savage, 'The Utility Analysis of Choices Involving Risk', *Journal of Political Economy* (1948) pp. 279–304.
7. Galbraith, J. K., 'Consumer Behaviour and the Dependence Effect', in *Selected Readings in Microeconomics*, ed. E. Mansfield (Norton, 1971).
8. Green, H., *Consumer Theory* (Penguin, 1972).

9. Hayek, F. A., 'The Non Sequitur of the Dependence Effect', *Southern Economic Journal* (1961).

10. Houthakker, H. S., and L. D. Taylor, *Consumer Demand in the United States* (Harvard University Press, 1966).

11. Knight, F. H., 'Realism and Relevance in the Theory of Demand', *Journal of Political Economy* (1944) pp. 289–318.

12. Koutsoyiannis, A., 'Demand Functions for Tobacco', *Manchester School* (1963). Reprinted in *Readings in Applied Economics*, ed. L. Wagner and N. Valtazis (Clarendon Press, Oxford, 1973).

13. Leibenstein, H., 'Bandwagon, Snob and Veblen Effects in the Theory of Consumers' Demand', *Quarterly Journal of Economics* (1950) pp. 183–207.

14. Machlup, F., 'Professor Hicks' Revision of Demand Theory', *American Economic Review* (1957) pp. 119–35.

15. Marshall, A., *Principles of Economics* (Macmillan, 1920).

16. Mishan, E. J., 'Theories of Consumer's Behaviour, A Cynical View', *Economica*, 1961. Reprinted in *Readings in Microeconomics*, ed. D. R. Kamerschen (Wiley, 1969).

17. Samuelson, P., *Foundations of Economic Analysis* (Harvard University Press, 1947)

18. Samuelson, P., 'Consumption Theory in Terms of Revealed Preference', *Economica* (1948) pp. 243–53.

19. Stone, R., *Consumer Demand in the U.K.* (Cambridge University Press, 1954).

20. Stone, R., 'Linear Expenditure Systems and Demand Analysis', *Economic Journal* (1954).

21. Townsend, H., 'Competition and Big Business' in *A New Era in Competition*, ed. T. M. Rybczynski, (Blackwell, 1971).

CHAPTER 3   THEORY OF PRODUCTION

1. Cassels, J., 'On the Law of Variable Proportions', in American Economic Association, *Readings in the Theory of Income Distribution* (1946).

2. Chamberlin, E. H., 'Proportionality, Divisibility, and Economies of Scale', *Quarterly Journal of Economics* (1948) pp. 229–62.

3. Cobb, C. W., and P. H. Douglas, 'A Theory of Production', *American Economic Review* (supplement) (1928) pp. 139–65.

4. Cookenboo, L., Jr., 'Production and Cost Functions for Oil Pine Lines', in *Readings in Price Theory*, ed. H. Townsend (Penguin, 1971).

5. Dorfman, 'Mathematical or Linear Programming: A Nonmathematical Exposition', *American Economic Review* (1953) pp. 797–825.

6. Eckaus, R. S., 'The Factor Proportions Problem in Underdeveloped Areas', *American Economic Review* (1955) pp. 539–65.

7. Enke, S., 'Some Economic Aspects of Fissionable Material', *Quarterly Journal of Economics* (1954) pp. 217–32.

8. Hicks, J. R., *Value and Capital*, 2nd edn (Oxford University Press, 1946) pp. 78–98.

9. Kossentos, K., 'Production Functions for the U.K. Manufacturing Industry' (unpublished M.A. dissertation, 1973, University of Lancaster).

10. Leibenstein, H., 'The Proportionality Controversy and the Theory of Production', *Quarterly Journal of Economics* (1955) pp. 619–25.

11. Mishan, E. J., and G. H. Borts, 'Exploring the Uneconomic Region of the Production Function', *Review of Economic Studies* (1962) pp. 300–12.

12. Moroney, J. R., 'Cobb–Douglas Production Functions and Returns to Scale in U.S. Manufacturing Industry', *Western Economic Journal* (1967) pp. 39–51.
13. Robinson, Joan, 'The Production Function', *Economic Journal*, (1955) pp. 67–71.
14. Samuelson, P. A., *Foundations of Economic Analysis* (Harvard University Press, 1947) pp. 57–76.
15. Samuelson, P. A., 'Parable and Realism in Capital Theory: The Surrogate Production Function', *Review of Economic Studies* (1962) pp. 193–206.
16. Seeber, N. C., 'On the Classification of Inventions', *Southern Economic Journal* (1962) pp. 365–71.
17. Shephard, R. W., *Cost and Production Functions* (Princeton University Press, 1953).
18. Solow, R. M., 'Substitution and Fixed Proportions in the Theory of Capital', *Review of Economic Studies* (1962) pp. 207–18.
19. Stigler, G. J., 'The Division of Labour is Limited by the Extent of the Market', *Journal of Political Economy* (1951) pp. 185–93.
20. Tangri, O. P., 'Omissions in the Treatment of the Law of Variable Proportions', *American Economic Review* (1966) pp. 484–92. Reprinted in *Readings in Price Theory*, ed. H. Townsend (Penguin, 1971).

CHAPTER 4 THEORY OF COSTS

1. Andrews, P. W. S., *Manufacturing Business* (Macmillan, 1949).
2. Apel, H., 'Marginal Cost Controversy and its Implications', *American Economic Review* (1948).
3. Brumberg, R., 'Ceteris Paribus for Supply Curves', *Economic Journal* (1953).
4. Cookenboo, L., Jr, 'Production and Cost Functions for Oil Pipe Lines', in *Readings in Price Theory*, ed. H. Townsend (Penguin, 1971).
5. Friedman, Milton, 'Theory and Measurement of Long-Run Costs', in *Readings in the Theory of the Firm*, ed. G. C. Archibald (Penguin, 1971).
6. Haldi, J., and D. Whitcomb, 'Economies of Scale in Industrial Plants', *Journal of Political Economy* (1967).
7. Hart, P. E., 'The Size and Growth of Firms', *Economica* (1962).
8. Johnston, J., *Statistical Cost Analysis* (Wiley, 1960).
9. Kaldor, N., 'The Irrelevance of Equilibrium Economics', *Economic Journal* (1972).
10. Leibenstein, H., 'Allocative Efficiency vs. "X-efficiency",' *American Economic Review* (1966).
11. Moore, F. T., 'Economies of Scale: Some Statistical Evidence', *Quarterly Journal of Economics* (1959).
12. Rowley, C. K., *Antitrust and Economic Efficiency* (Macmillan, 1973).
13. Saving, T. R., 'Estimation of Optimum Size of Plant by the Survivor Technique', *Quarterly Journal of Economics* (1961).
14. Shepherd, W. G., 'What Does the Survivor Technique Show About Economies of Scale?', *Southern Economic Journal* (1967).
15. Silberston, A., 'Economies of Scale in Theory and Practice', *Economic Journal* (1972) (supplement). Reprinted in *Readings in Applied Economics*, ed. L. Wagner and N. Valtazis (Clarendon Press, Oxford, 1974).

16. Smith, C. A., 'Empirical Evidence on Economies of Scale', in *Readings in the Theory of the Firm*, ed. G. C. Archibald (Penguin, 1971).
17. Stigler, G. J., 'Production and Distribution in the Short Run', *Journal of Political Economy* (1939). Reprinted in American Economic Association, *Readings in the Theory of Income Distribution* (1946).
18. Stigler, G. J., 'The Economies of Scale', *Journal of Law and Economics* (1958).
19. Walters, A. A., 'Production and Cost Functions: An Econometric Survey', *Econometrica* (1963).
20. Weiss, L. W., 'The Survivor Technique and the Extent of Suboptimal Capacity', *Journal of Political Economy* (1964).
21. Wiles, P. J. D., *Price, Cost and Output* (Blackwell, 1961).
22. Williamson, O. E., 'Hierarchical Control and Optimum Firm Size', *Journal of Political Economy* (1967).
23. Williamson, O. E., 'Economies as an Antitrust Defense', *American Economic Review* (1968).

CHAPTER 5   PERFECT COMPETITION

1. Andrews, P. W. S., 'Industrial Analysis in Economics', in *Studies in the Price Mechanism*, ed. T. Wilson and P. W. S. Andrews (Oxford University Press, 1951).
2. Blaug, M., *Economic Theory in Retrospect* (Irwin, 1970).
3. Clark, J. M., 'Toward a Concept of Workable Competition', *American Economic Review* (1940).
4. Galbraith, J. K., *The Affluent Society* (Mifflin, 1958).
5. Hendry, J. B., 'The Bituminous Coal Industry', in *The Structure of American Industry*, ed. W. Adams (Macmillan, 1961).
6. Knight, Frank H., *Risk, Uncertainty and Profit* (London School Reprints of Scarce Works, No. 16, 1933).
7. Machlup, F., *Economics of Sellers' Competition* (Johns Hopkins Press, Baltimore, 1952).
8. McNulty, P. J., 'A Note on the History of Perfect Competition', *Journal of Political Economy* (1967) pp. 395–9.
9. McNulty, P. J., 'Economic Theory and the Meaning of Competition', *Quarterly Journal of Economics* (1968) pp. 639–56.
10. Marshall, Alfred, *Principles of Economics* (Macmillan, 1926).
11. Robinson, Joan, 'What is Perfect Competition?', *Quarterly Journal of Economics* (1934) pp. 104–20.
12. Rothenberg, G., 'Consumers' Sovereignty Revisited and the Hospitality of Freedom of Choice', *American Economic Review* (1962).
13. Shackle, G. L. S., *The Years of High Theory* (Cambridge University Press, 1967).
14. Schumpeter, J. A., *Capitalism, Socialism and Democracy* (Harper, 1942).
15. Scitovsky, Tibor, 'On the Principle of Consumers' Sovereignty', *American Economic Review* (1962).
16. Stigler, G. J., 'Perfect Competition, Historically Contemplated', *Journal of Political Economy* (1957) pp. 1–17.
17. Sosnick, S., 'A Critique of Concepts of Workable Competition', *Journal of Political Economy* (1957).

CHAPTER 6   MONOPOLY

1. Blaug, M., *Economic Theory in Retrospect* (Irwin, 1970).
2. Galbraith, J. K., *American Capitalism: The Concept of Countervailing Power* (Mifflin, 1952).
3. Haberger, A. C., 'Monopoly and Resource Allocation', *American Economic Review* (1954).
4. Leibenstein, H., 'Allocative Efficiency vs. "X-Efficiency",' *American Economic Review* (1966).
5. Lerner, Abba P., 'The Concept of Monopoly and the Measurement of Monopoly Power', *Review of Economic Studies* (1943) pp. 157–75.
6. McGee, J. S., 'Predatory Price Cutting: The Standard Oil (New Jersey) Case', *Journal of Law and Economics* (1958).
7. Markham, J. W., 'Market Structure, Business Conduct, and Innovation', *American Economic Review* (1965) pp. 323–32.
8. Marshall, Alfred, *Principles of Economics* (Macmillan, 1926).
9. Schumpeter, J. A., *Capitalism, Socialism, and Democracy* (Harper, 1942).
10. Schwartzman, D., 'The Effect of Monopoly on Price', *Journal of Political Economy* (1959).
11. Schwartzman, D., 'The Burden of Monopoly', *Journal of Political Economy* (1960).
12. Shackle, G. L. S., *The Years of High Theory* (Cambridge University Press, 1967).
13. Stigler, G. J., 'The Statistics of Monopoly and Merger', *Journal of Political Economy* (1956) pp. 33–40.
14. Tullock, G., 'The Welfare Costs of Tariffs, Monopolies, and Theft', *Western Economic Journal* (1967).
15. Weldon, J. C., 'The Multi-Product Firm', *Canadian Journal of Economics and Political Science* (1948) pp. 176–90.

CHAPTER 7   PRICE DISCRIMINATION

1. Cassady, R., Jr, 'Techniques and Purposes of Price Discrimination', *Journal of Marketing* (1946) pp. 135–50.
2. Clemens, E. W., 'Price Discrimination and the Multi-product Firm', *Review of Economic Studies* (1951) pp. 1–11.
3. Dean, Joel, *Managerial Economics* (Prentice-Hall, 1951).
4. Edwards, C. D., *The Price Discrimination Law* (Brookings Institution, 1959).
5. Edwards, E. O., 'The Analysis of Output Under Discrimination', *Econometrica* (1950) pp. 163–72.
6. Enke, S., 'Some Notes on Price Discrimination', *Canadian Journal of Economics and Political Science* (1964) pp. 95–109.
7. Kessel, R. A., 'Price Discrimination in Medicine', *Journal of Law and Economics* (1958) pp. 20–59.
8. Machlup, Fritz, 'Characteristics and Types of Price Discrimination', in the National Bureau of Economic Research conference report, *Business Concentration and Price Policy* (Princeton University Press, 1955).
9. Pigou, A. C., *The Economics of Welfare* (Macmillan, 1920).

10. Robinson, Joan, *The Economics of Imperfect Competition* (Macmillan, 1933).
11. Simkin, C. G. F., 'Some Aspects and Generalisations of the Theory of Discrimination', *Review of Economic Studies* (1948–9).
12. Wright, J. F., 'Some Reflections on the Place of Discrimination in the Theory of Monopolistic Competition', *Oxford Economic Papers* (1965) pp. 175–87.

CHAPTER 8   MONOPOLISTIC COMPETITION

1. Abbott, L., *Quality and Competition* (Columbia University Press, 1955).
2. Andrews, P. W. S., *On Competition in Economic Theory* (Macmillan, 1964).
3. Archibald, G. C., 'Chamberlin versus Chicago', *Review of Economic Studies* (1961). Reprinted in *Readings in the Theory of the Firm*, ed. G. C. Archibald (Penguin, 1971).
4. Bain, J. S., 'Chamberlin's Impact on Microeconomic Theory', in *Monopolistic Competition Theory: Studies in Impact. Essays in Honour of E. H. Chamberlin*, ed. R. E. Kuenne (Wiley, 1966), Reprinted in *Readings in Price Theory*, ed. H. Townsend (Penguin, 1971).
5. Bishop, R. L., 'The Theory of Monopolistic Competition after Thirty Years: The Impact on General Theory', *American Economic Review* (1964). Reprinted in *Readings in Microeconomics*, ed. D. R. Kamerschen (Wiley, 1969).
6. Buchanan, N. S., 'Advertising Expenditures: A Suggested Treatment', *Journal of Political Economy*, (1942). Reprinted in *Readings in Microeconomics*, ed. W. Breit and H. M. Hochman (Holt, Rinehart & Winston, 1967).
7. Chamberlin, E. H., *The Theory of Monopolistic Competition* (Harvard University Press, 1933).
8. Chamberlin, E. H., 'Monopolistic Competition Re-examined', *Economica* (1951).
9. Demetz, H., 'The Nature of Equilibrium in Monopolistic Competition', *Journal of Political Economy* (1959).
10. Demetz, H., 'The Welfare and Empirical Implications of Monopolistic Competition', *Economic Journal* (1964).
11. Harrod, R. F., 'Theory of Imperfect Competition Revised', *Economic Essays* (Harcourt-Brace, 1952).
12. Hicks, J. R., 'The Process of Imperfect Competition', *Oxford Economic Papers* (1954) pp. 41–54.
13. Robinson, Joan, *The Economics of Imperfect Competition* (Macmillan, 1933).
14. Robinson, Joan, 'Imperfect Competition Revisited', *Economic Journal* (1953).
15. Samuelson, P. A., 'The Monopolistic Competition Revolution', in *Monopolistic Competition Theory: Studies in Impact. Essays in Honour of E. H. Chamberlin*, ed. R. E. Kuenne (Wiley, 1966).
16. Sraffa, P., 'The Laws of Returns under Competitive Conditions', *Economic Journal* (1926). Reprinted in American Economic Association, *Readings in Price Theory* (1946).
17. Stigler, G. J., 'Monopolistic Competition in Retrospect', in *Five Lectures on Economic Problems* (Longmans, Green, 1949).
18. Telser, L. G., 'Monopolistic Competition: Any Impact Yet?, *Journal of Political Economy* (1968).
19. Triffin, R., *Monopolistic Competition and General Equilibrium* (Harvard University Press, 1939).

CHAPTER 9   NON-COLLUSIVE OLIGOPOLY

1. Bishop, R. L., 'Duopoly: Collusion or Warfare?', *American Economic Review* (1960) pp. 933–61.
2. Fellner, W., *Competition among the Few* (Knopf, 1949).
3. Hall, R. L., and C. J. Hitch, 'Price Theory and Business Behaviour', *Oxford Economic Papers* (1939).
4. Hamburger, W., 'Conscious Parallelism and the Kinky Oligopoly Demand Curve', *American Economic Review, Papers and Proceedings* (1967).
5. Primeaux, R., and Bomball, K., 'A Re-examination of the Kinky Oligopoly Demand Curve', *Journal of Political Economy* (1974).
6. Rothschild, K. W., 'Price Theory and Oligopoly', *Economic Journal* (1947) pp. 299–320.
7. Simon, J. L., 'A Further Test of the Kinky Oligopoly Demand Curve', *American Economic Review* (1969).
8. Stackelberg, H. von, *The Theory of the Market Economy* (Hodge, 1952).
9. Stigler, G. J., 'The Kinky Oligopoly Demand Curve and Rigid Prices', *Journal of Political Economy* (1947). Reprinted in *Readings in the Theory of the Firm*, ed. G. C. Archibald (Penguin 1972).
10. Stigler, G. J., 'Notes on a Theory of Duopoly', *Journal of Political Economy* (1940) pp. 521–41.
11. Sweezy, P. M., 'Demand Under Conditions of Oligopoly', *Journal of Political Economy* (1939) pp. 568–73.

CHAPTER 10   COLLUSIVE OLIGOPOLY

1. Adams, W. (ed.), *The Structure of the American Industry* (Macmillan, New York, 1961).
2. Andrews, P. W. S., *On Competition in Economic Theory* (Macmillan 1964).
3. Bain, J. S., 'Price Leaders, Barometers and Kinks', *Journal of Business* (1960).
4. Colberg, M. R., Forbush, D. R., and Whittaker, G. R., *Business Economics: Principles and Cases* (Irwin, 1964).
5. Fellner, W., *Competition Among the Few* (Knopf, 1949).
6. Fellner, W., 'Collusion and its Limits under Oligopoly', *American Economic Review, Papers and Proceedings* (1950).
7. Gordon, R. A., *Business Leadership in the Large Corporation* (California University Press, 1961).
8. Kaplan, A. D. A., Dirlam J. B., and Lanzillotti R. F., *Pricing in Big Business* (Brookings Institution, 1958).
9. Lanzillotti, R. F., 'Competitive Price Leadership: A Critique of Price Leadership Models', *Review of Economics and Statistics* (1957) pp. 55–64.
10. Markham, J. W., 'The Nature and Significance of Price Leadership', *American Economic Review* (1951).
11. Nicholls, W. H., 'Market-Sharing in the Packing Industry', *Journal of Farm Economics* (1940) pp. 225–40.
12. Nutter, G. W., 'Duopoly, Oligopoly and Emerging Competition', *Southern Economic Journal* (1964).

13. Oxenfeldt, A., 'Professor Markham on Price Leadership', *American Economic Review* (1952).
14. Patinkin, D., 'Multiple-Plant Firms, Cartels, and Imperfect Competition', *Quarterly Journal of Economics* (1947) pp. 173–205.
15. Stigler, G. J., 'A Theory of Oligopoly', *Journal of Political Economy* (1964).
16. Stigler, G. J., 'The Dominant Firm and the Inverted Umbrella', *Journal of Law and Economics* (1965).
17. Worcester, D. A., 'Why Dominant Firms Decline', *Journal of Political Economy* (1957).

CHAPTER 11   A CRITIQUE OF THE NEOCLASSICAL
THEORY OF THE FIRM

1. Alchian, A., 'Uncertainty, Evolution, and Economic Theory', *Journal of Political Economy* (1950) pp. 211–21.
2. Alchian, A., 'The Basis of Some Recent Advances in the Theory of Management of the Firm', *Journal of Industrial Economics* (1965) pp. 30–41.
3. Baldwin, L., 'The Motives of Managers, Environmental Restraints and the Theory of Managerial Enterprise', *Quarterly Journal of Economics* (1964).
4. Barback, R., *The Pricing of Manufactures* (Macmillan, 1964).
5. Baumol, W. J., 'Models of Economic Competition', in *Readings in Price Theory*, ed. H. Townsend (Penguin, 1971).
6. Bodenhorn, D., 'A Note on the Theory of the Firm', *Journal of Business* (1959) pp. 164–74.
7. Cooper, W. W., 'Theory of the Firm: Some Suggestions for Revision', *American Economic Review* (1949) pp. 1204–22.
8. Earley, J. S., 'Marginal Policies of "Excellently Managed" Companies', *American Economic Review* (1956).
9. Gordon, R. A., 'Short-Period Price Determination in Theory and Practice', *American Economic Review* (1948).
10. Greenhut, M. L., 'A General Theory of Maximum Profits', *Southern Economic Journal* (1962) pp. 278–85.
11. Hall, R. L., and C. J. Hitch, 'Price Theory and Business Behaviour', *Oxford Economic Papers* (1939). Reprinted in *Studies in the Price Mechanism*, ed. T. Wilson and P. W. S. Andrews (Oxford University Press, 1951).
12. Horowitz, I., 'The Advance of the Theory of the Firm: One Step Forward, One Step Back', *Quarterly Review of Economics and Business* (1967) pp. 53–64.
13. Kamerschen, D. R., 'The Influence of Ownership and Control on Profit Rates', *American Economic Review* (1967) pp. 1252–8.
14. Kaysen, C. 'The Corporation: How Much Power? What Scope?' in *The Corporation in Modern Society*, ed. E. S. Mason (1960).
15. Koplin, H. T., 'The Profit Maximisation Assumption', *Oxford Economic Papers* (1963) pp. 130–9.
16. Lanzillotti, R. F., 'Pricing Objectives in Large Companies', *American Economic Review* (1958).
17. Machlup, F., 'Marginal Analysis and Empirical Research', *American Economic Review* (1946).
18. Machlup, F., 'Theories of the Firm: Marginalist, Managerialist, Behavioural', *American Economic Review* (1967).

19. Margolis, J., 'The Analysis of the Firm: Rationalism, Conventionalism, and Behaviourism', *Journal of Business* (1958) pp. 187–99.
20. Monsen, R. J., *et al.*, 'The Effects of Separation of Ownership and Control on the Performance of the Large Firm', *Quarterly Journal of Economics* (1968) pp. 435–51.
21. Oliver, H. M., 'Marginal Theory and Business Behaviour', *American Economic Review* (1947).
22. Papandreou, A., 'Some Basic Problems in the Theory of the Firm', in *A Survey of Contemporary Economics*, ed. B. F. Haley (Irwin, 1952).
23. Penrose, Edith, 'Biological Analogies in the Theory of the Firm', *American Economic Review* (1952) pp. 804–19.
24. Reder, M. W., 'A Reconsideration of the Marginal Productivity Theory', *Journal of Political Economy* (1947) pp. 450–8.
25. Rothschild, K., 'Price Theory and Oligopoly', *Economic Journal* (1947), pp. 297–320.
26. Scitovsky, Tibor, 'A Note on Profit Maximisation and its Implications', *Review of Economic Studies* (1943–4). Reprinted in American Economic Association, *Readings in Price Theory* (Allen & Unwin, 1953).
27. Simon, H. A., 'A Behavioural Model of Rational Choice', *Quarterly Journal of Economics* (1952) pp. 99–118.
28. Simon, H. A., 'New Developments in the Theory of the Firm', *American Economic Review* (1962) pp. 1–15.
29. Winter, S., 'Economic "Natural Selection" and the Theory of the Firm', *Yale Economic Essays* (1964) pp. 225–72.

CHAPTER 12 A 'REPRESENTATIVE' MODEL OF AVERAGE-COST PRICING

1. Adelman, M. A., 'Steel, Administered Prices and Inflation', *Quarterly Journal of Economics* (1961).
2. Andrews, P. W. S., *Manufacturing Business* (Macmillan, 1949).
3. Barback, R., *The Pricing of Manufactures* (Macmillan, 1964).
4. Baumol, W. J., and Quandt, R. E., 'Rules-of-thumb and Optimally Imperfect Decisions', *American Economic Review* (1964).
5. Edwards, H. R., 'Price Formation in Manufacturing Industry', *Oxford Economic Papers* (1965).
6. Eichken, M., 'A Theory of the Determination of the Mark-up in Oligopoly', *Economic Journal* (1974).
7. Fellner, W., 'Average-Cost Pricing and the Theory of Uncertainty', *Journal of Political Economy* (1948).
8. Ferguson, C. E., 'Static Models of Average-Cost Pricing', *Southern Economic Journal* (1957) pp. 272–84.
9. Fog, B., *Industrial Pricing Policies* (North-Holland, 1960).
10. Hall, R. L., and C. J. Hitch, 'Price Theory and Business Behaviour', *Oxford Economic Papers* (1939). Reprinted in *Studies in the Price Mechanism*, ed. T. Wilson and P. W. S. Andrews (Oxford University Press, 1951).
11. Hawkins, C. J., *Theory of the Firm* (Macmillan, 1973).
12. Haynes, W. W., 'Pricing Practices in Small Firms', *Southern Economic Journal* (1964).

13. Heflebower, R. B., 'Full Costs, Cost Changes and Prices', in National Bureau of Economic Research, *Cost Behaviour and Price Policy* (New York, 1963).
14. Kaplan, A. D. H., Dirlam, J. B., and Lanzillotti, R. F., *Pricing in Big Business* (Washington, D.C.: The Brookings Institution, 1958).
15. Lanzillotti, R. F., 'Pricing Objectives in Large Companies', *American Economic Review* (1958).
16. Pearce, I. F., 'A Study in Price Policy', *Economica* (1956).
17. Tarshis, L., 'Rule-of-Thumb Pricing Can Be Rational', in *Price Theory in Action*, ed. D. S. Watson (Houghton Mifflin, 1969).

CHAPTER 13   BAIN'S LIMIT-PRICING THEORY

1. Bain, J. S., 'A Note on Pricing in Monopoly and Oligopoly', *American Economic Review* (1949).
2. Bain, J. S., 'Economies of Scale, Concentration, and the Condition of Entry in Twenty Manufacturing Industries', *American Economic Review* (1954).
3. Bain, J. S., *Barriers to New Competition* (Harvard University Press, 1956).
4. Bain, J. S., *Essays on Price Theory and Industrial Organisation* (Little, Brown, 1972).
5. Comanor, W. S., and T. A. Wilson, 'Advertising, Market Structure and Performance', *Review of Economics and Statistics* (1967).
6. Hines, H. H., 'Effectiveness of "Entry" by Already Established Firms', *Quarterly Journal of Economics* (1957).
7. Edwards, H. R., *Competition and Monopoly in the British Soap Industry* (Oxford University Press 1962).
8. Mann, H. M., 'Seller Concentration, Barriers to Entry and Rates of Return in Thirty Industries, 1950–1960', *Review of Economics and Statistics* (1966).
9. Telser, L., 'Advertising and Competition', *Journal of Political Economy* (1964).
10. Wenders, J. T., 'Entry and Monopoly Pricing', *Journal of Political Economy* (1967).
11. Williamson, O. E., 'Selling Expense as a Barrier to Entry', *Quarterly Journal of Economics* (1963).

CHAPTER 14   RECENT DEVELOPMENTS IN THE THEORY OF LIMIT-PRICING

1. Baron, D., 'Limit Pricing, Potential Entry and Barriers to Entry', *American Economic Review* (1973) pp. 666–75.
2. Bhagwati, J. N., 'Oligopoly Theory, Entry Prevention and Growth', *Oxford Economic Papers* (1970).
3. Eichken, H., 'A Theory of the Determination of the Mark-up in Oligopoly', *Economic Journal* (1974).
4. Fisher, F., 'New Developments on the Oligopoly Front, Cournot and the Bain–Sylos Analysis', *Journal of Political Economy* (1959).
5. George, K. D., 'Concentration, Barriers to Entry and Rates of Return', *Review of Economics and Statistics* (1968).
6. Kamien, M. I., and N. L. Schwartz,' Limit Pricing and Uncertain Entry,' *Econometrica* (1971).

7. Kamien, M. I., and N. L. Schwartz,' Uncertain Entry and Excess Capacity', *American Economic Review* (1972).
8. Mann, M., Haas, B., and Walgreen, A., 'Entry and Oligopoly Theory: Comment', *Journal of Political Economy* (1965).
9. Mann, M., 'Sellers' Concentration, Barriers to Entry and Rates of Return', *Review of Economics and Statistics* (1966).
10. Modigliani, F., 'New Developments on the Oligopoly Front', *Journal of Political Economy* (1958). Reprinted in *Readings in the Theory of the Firm*, ed. G. C. Archibald (Penguin, 1971).
11. Osborne, D. K., 'The Role of Entry in Oligopoly Theory', *Journal of Political Economy* (1964).
12. Pashigian, P., 'Limit Pricing and the Market Share of the Leading Firm', *Journal of Industrial Economics* (1968).
13. Shepherd, W. G., 'Entry as a Substitute for Regulation', *American Economic Review*, Papers and Proceedings (1973).
14. Sylos-Labini, P., *Oligopoly and Technical Progress* (Harvard University Press, 1962).
15. Wenders, J. T., 'Entry and Monopoly Pricing', *Journal of Political Economy* (1967).
16. Wenders, J. T., 'Collusion and Entry', *Journal of Political Economy* (1971).

CHAPTER 15   BAUMOL'S THEORY OF SALES REVENUE MAXIMISATION

1. Baumol, W. J., *Business Behaviour, Value and Growth* (Harcourt & Brace, 1962).
2. Baumol, W. J., 'Models of Economic Competition', in *Readings in Price Theory*, ed. H. Townsend (Penguin, 1971).
3. Hall, M., 'Sales Maximisation, An Empirical Examination', *Journal of Industrial Economics* (1967).
4. Haveman, A., and DeBartolo, K., 'The Revenue Maximisation Oligopoly Model', *American Economic Review* (1968).
5. Hawkins, C. J., 'On the Sales Revenue Maximisation Hypothesis', *Journal of Industrial Economics* (1970).
6. Hawkins, C. J., 'The Revenue Maximisation Oligopoly Model: Comment', *American Economic Review* (1970).
7. Kafoglis, M., and R. Bushnell, 'The Revenue Maximisation Oligopoly Model: Comment', *American Economic Review* (1970).
8. Lewellen, W. G., and B. Huntsman, 'Managerial Pay and Corporate Performance', *American Economic Review* (1970).
9. McGuire *et al.*, 'Executive Incomes, Sales and Profits', *American Economic Review* (1962).
10. Marby, D. B., and D. L. Siders, 'An Empirical Test of the Sales Maximisation Hypothesis', *Southern Economic Journal* (1967).
11. Peston, M. H., 'On the Sales Maximisation Hypothesis', *Economica* (1959).
12. Rosenberg, R., 'Profit Constrained Revenue Maximisation: Note', *American Economic Review* (1971).
13. Shepherd, W. G., 'On Sales Maximising and Oligopoly Behaviour', *Economica* (1962).
14. Smythl, D., 'Sales Maximisation and Managerial Effort: Note', *American Economic Review* (1969).
15. Williamson, J., 'Profit, Growth and Sales Maximisation', *Economica* (1966).

CHAPTER 16 MARRIS'S MODEL OF THE
MANAGERIAL ENTERPRISE

1. Baumol, W. J., 'On the Theory of Expansion of the Firm, *American Economic Review* (1962).
2. Kuehn, D. A., 'Stock Market Valuation and Acquisitions: An Empirical Test of One Component of Managerial Utility', *Journal of Industrial Economics* (1969).
3. Marris, R., 'A Model of the Managerial Enterprise', *Quarterly Journal of Economics* (1963).
4. Marris, R., *The Economic Theory of 'Managerial' Capitalism* (Macmillan, 1964).
5. Marris, R., and A. Woods (eds), *The Corporate Economy* (Macmillan, 1971).
6. Massey, R. T., 'Executive Motivations, Earnings and Consequent Equity Performance', *Journal of Political Economy* (1971).
7. Monsen, R. J., *et al.*, 'The Effect of Separation of Ownership and Control on the Performance of the Large Firm', *Quarterly Journal of Economics* (1968).
8. Penrose, Edith, *The Theory of the Growth of the Firm* (Blackwell, 1959).
9. Singh, A., and G. Whittington, *Growth, Profitability and Valuation* (Cambridge University Press, 1968).
10. Williamson, J. H., 'Profit, Growth and Sales Maximisation', *Economica* (1966).

CHAPTER 17 O. WILIAMSON'S MODEL OF
MANAGERIAL DISCRETION

1. Encarnacion, J., 'Constraints and the Firm's Utility Function', *Review of Economic Studies* (1964) pp. 113–20.
2. Ferguson, C. E., 'The Theory of Multidimensional Utility Analysis in Relation to Multiple-Goal-Business Behaviour: A Synthesis', *Southern Economic Journal* (1965) pp. 169–75.
3. Simon, H. A., 'New Developments in the Theory of the Firm', *American Economic Review, Papers and Proceedings* (1962) pp. 1–15.
4. Williamson, O. E., 'Managerial Discretion and Business Behaviour', *American Economic Review* (1963).
5. Williamson, O. E., *The Economics of Discretionary Behaviour* (Prentice-Hall, 1964).
6. Williamson, O. E., *Corporate Control and Business Behaviour* (Prentice-Hall, 1970).

CHAPTER 18 THE BEHAVIOURAL MODEL OF
CYERT AND MARCH

1. Baumol, W. J., 'Models of Economic Competition', in *Readings in Price Theory*, ed. H. Townsend (Penguin 1971).
2. Baumol, W. J., and M. Stewart, 'On the Behavioural Theory of the Firm', in *The Corporate Economy*, eds. R. Marris and A. Wood (Macmillan 1971).
3. Cyert, R. M., and M. I. Kamien, 'Behavioural Rules and the Theory of the Firm', in *Prices: Issues in Theory, Practice, and Public Policy*, ed. A. Phillips and O. E. Williamson (Pennsylvania University Press, 1967).

4. Cyert, R. M., and J. G. March, *A Behavioural Theory of the Firm* (Prentice-Hall, 1963).
5. McGuire, J. W., *Theories of Business Behaviour* (Prentice-Hall, 1964).
6. Machlup, F., 'Theories of the Firm: Marginalist, Behavioural, Managerial', *American Economic Review* (1967).
7. Margolis, J., 'The Analysis of the Firm: Rationalism, Conventionalism and Behaviourism', *Journal of Business*, (1958).
8. Monsen, R. J., and A. Downs, 'A Theory of Large Managerial Firms', *Journal of Political Economy* (1965).
9. Simon, H. A., 'A Behavioural Model of Rational Choice', *Quarterly Journal of Economics* (1952) pp. 99–118.
10. Simon, H. A., 'Theories of Decision-Making in Economics and Behavioural Science', *American Economic Review* (1959).
11. Simon, H. A., 'On the Concept of Organisational Goal', *Administrative Science Quarterly* (1964). Reprinted in *Business Strategy*, ed. H. I. Ansoff (Penguin, 1969).

CHAPTER 19   THEORY OF GAMES

1. Baumol, W. J., 'Models of Economic Competition', in *Readings in Price Theory*, ed. H. Townsend (Penguin, 1971).
2. Flood, M. M., 'On Game-Learning Theory and Some Decision-Making Experiments', in *Decision Processes*, ed. R. M. Thrall *et al.* (Wiley 1954).
3. Fouraker, L. E., and S. Siegel, *Bargaining Behaviour* (McGraw-Hill, 1963).
4. Lave, L. B., 'An Empirical Approach to the Prisoners' Dilemma Game', *Quarterly Journal of Economics* (1962) pp. 424–36.
5. Luce, R. D., and H. Raiffa, *Games and Decisions* (Wiley, 1957).
6. Marschack, J., 'Elements for a Theory of Teams', *Management Science* (1955).
7. Neumann, J. von. and O. Morgenstern, *Theory of Games and Economic Behaviour* (Princeton University Press, 1944).
8. Nutter, G. W., 'Duopoly, Oligopoly, and Emerging Competition', *Southern Economic Journal* (1964) pp. 342–52.
9. Shubik, M., 'The Uses of Game Theory in Management Science', *Management Science*, 1955. Reprinted in *Selected Readings in Microeconomics*, ed. E. Mansfield (Norton 1971).
10. Shubik, M., *Strategy and Market Structure* (Wiley, 1959).

CHAPTER 20   LINEAR PROGRAMMING

1. Charnes, A., Cooper, W. W., and A. Henderson, *An Introduction to Linear Programming* (Wiley, 1953).
2. Charnes, A., *et al.*, 'Linear Programming and Profit Preferences Scheduling for a Manufacturing Firm', *Journal of Operations Research Society of America* (1953) pp. 114–29.
3. Dorfman, R., *Application of Linear Programming to the Theory of the Firm* (California University Press, 1951).
4. Dorfman, R., Samuelson, P. A., and Solow, R. M., *Linear Programming and Economic Analysis* (McGraw-Hill, 1958).

5. Dorfman, R. 'Mathematical or "Linear" Programming: A Nonmathematical Exposition', *American Economic Review* (1953). Reprinted in *Readings in the Theory of the Firm*, ed. G. C. Archibald (Penguin, 1972).
6. Henderson, J. M., and R. E. Quandt, *Microeconomic Theory*, 2nd edn (McGraw-Hill, 1968).
7. Koopmans, T. C. (ed.), *Activity Analysis of Production and Allocation* (Wiley, 1951).

CHAPTER 21   CONCLUDING REMARKS

1. Baumol, W. J., 'Models of Economic Competition', in *Readings in the Price Theory*, ed. H. Townsend (Penguin, 1971).
2. Heflebower, R. B., 'Towards a Theory of Industrial Markets and Prices', *American Economic Review* (1954).
3. Machlup, F., 'Theories of the Firm: Marginalist, Behavioural, Managerial', *American Economic Review* (1967).
4. Shackle, G. L. S., *Expectation, Enterprise and Profit: The Theory of the Firm* (Allen & Unwin, 1970).
5. Shubik, M., 'A Curmudgeon's Guide to Microeconomics', *Journal of Economic Literature* (1971).
6. Silberston, A., 'Price Behaviour of Firms', *Economic Journal* (1970) (a survey article).

Subject Index

abnormal profit   156–61, 174–8
absolute cost advantage as a barrier to entry   291–93
activity, productive   65, 415. *See also* process
advertising
  and nonprice competition   203–4, 369
  and sales maximisation   331–5, 340–2
advertising economies of scale   132–5
allocation, optimal of resources   163–4
arc elasticity of demand   48–9
aspiration level   387–8
assumptions
  of neoclassical model   257–70
  role of   3–4
  validity of   3–4, 267–70
attack on marginalism   256–70
average-cost curves   107–10
  economies of scale   126–37
  engineering   122–6
  in modern theory   114–19
  in traditional theory   106–14
  relation between short-run and long-run   111–14
average-cost pricing   271–81. *See also* full-cost pricing
average fixed cost   107–8, 115–17
average product of a factor of production   75
average total cost   107–11, 118–20
average variable cost
  in modern theory   117–18
  in traditional theory   107–11
axioms
  of diminishing marginal rate of substitution   28
  of diminishing marginal utility   14
  of revealed preference   17

Bain's model of limit-pricing   284–304
barometric price leadership   248–9
barriers to entry   287–322
  absolute capital requirements   293
  absolute cost advantage   291–3
  legal   290
  preference barrier   290–1
  scale barrier   290–300, 305–22
basic feasible solution (linear programming)   424
basing-point pricing   252–4
Baumol's sales maximisation model   325–51
  dynamic multiperiod model   342–6
  empirical evidence   346–8
  static models   327–42
behavioural theory of firm   386–401
Bertrand's duopoly model   225–8
Bhagwati's model of limit-pricing   319–20
bilateral monopoly   189–91
bounded rationality   258, 389–90
brand loyalty   61–6
break-even point   157–8
budget constraint   20–1
budget equation   22
budget line   21–22
  effect of change in income on,   24–6
budgeted output   274–5. *See also* target output

capital requirements as a barrier to entry   293
cardinal utility   14–17
cartels
  and collusion   237–54
  and profit maximisation   237–42
  geographical quotas   243–4

instability   242, 244
market-sharing   242–4
Chamberlin's
   'large-group' model   202–14
   'small-group' model   228–9
changes in industry equilibrium   164–70,
   179–83, 276–7
choice of optimal factor proportions   86–
   93
classification of firms into industries   8–
   12
classification of markets   4–7
Cobb–Douglas production function   75–
   6, 78, 97–9
collusion. *See also* cartels
   in modern theory   274–80, 302–4, 308–
      10, 357, 395
   in traditional theory   237–54
commodity classification   20, 27
commodity space   18, 100
comparison with perfect competition
   monopolistic competition   212–14
   monopoly   183–6
   average-cost pricing   275–80
comparison with profit maximiser
   growth maximiser (Marris)   367–8
   managerial utility maximising (William-
      son)   379–81
   sales revenue maximiser (Baumol)
      327–31
   satisficing (Cyert and March)   398–400
competition
   actual *v.* potential   262–63, 274–6, 288–
      9, 305–6
   large firms   326, 357
   monopolistic   202–214
   nonprice   61–6, 203–4, 369
   perfect   154–70
   potential   262–3, 274–6, 288–9, 305–6
compensating variation in income   25, 29
complementary factors of production
   68–9
complementary goods   20, 27
   classification by cross-elasticity   27
   classification by substitution effect   27
concept of 'bounded rationality'   258,
   389–90
concept of entry (in Bain's model)   289
concept of 'global rationality'   258, 389–
   90
concept of 'industry'   7–12
constant cost industries   164–5

constant–elasticity   demand   functions
   53–5
constant elasticity of substitution of inputs
   74–7
constant returns to scale   79
consumer behaviour. *See also* consumer
   demand
   assumptions in   14–15, 17, 28–9
   indifference-curves analysis   17–28
   revealed-preference theory   28–32
consumer demand. *See also* consumer
   behaviour
   and market demand   44–5
   choice between leisure and income
      35–6
   'habit-creation' principle   56
   index numbers   40
   indifference-curves analysis   17–28
   inferior goods   24–5
   revealed-preference theory   28–32
   'stock adjustment' principle   56
   substitution and income effects   25–6
consumer equilibrium   15, 18–24, 29
consumer sovereignty   163
consumers' surplus   32–5
contract curve (Edgeworth's)
   in consumer theory   38–9
   in oligopoly   221, 227
   in production theory   99–100
cost functions
   derivation from production functions
      95–9
cost constraint   88–9
'cost controversy'   202. *See also* Sraffa
cost minimisation   91–2
cost-of-living indexes   40–4
costs
   engineering   122–6
   in modern theory   114–22
   in traditional theory   105–14
costs   105–50
   average-marginal relationship   110–11
   ex ante and *ex post*   111, 139–40
   average total   107–10, 118–20
   long-run
      average   111–13, 120–2
      marginal   113–14, 115–20
   managerial   120, 134
   production   120, 128–31
   set-up   131–32
   short-run
      average total   107–11, 118–20

average fixed   107–8, 115–17
average variable   107–11, 117–18
costs as basis for pricing practices   273–5
costs, empirical evidence on
  engineering cost studies   143–6
  questionnaires   143
  statistical cost studies   138–42
  'survivor' technique   146–8
Cournot's duopoly model   216–25
critique of neoclassical theory of firm
  256–70
cross-elasticity of demand   49
cross-hauling   253
Cyert and March's behavioural theory
  386–401

decreasing returns to scale   81, 112–13
defence of marginalism   267–70. See also
  Machlup
demand
  ceteris paribus clause   45, 63
  consumer   16, 24–7, 29
  determinants of   45
  elasticity concepts   46–9
  firm   60–6
  market   44–60
  recent developments in theory of
    53–60
  and revenue   50–3
  shifts in   164, 179
  Slutsky's theorem   24
demand curves
  consumer   16, 24–7, 29
  kinked   230–2
  market   44–60
  monopolistic competition   61–3, 204
  monopoly   61, 171
  oligopoly   63
  perfect competition   154
  and revenue   50–3
demand functions
  dynamic versions   55–60
  with constant elasticity   53–5
  with distributed lags   55–8
demand systems (linear expenditure)   58–
  60
differentiation of product
  as a barrier to entry   290–1
  in monopolistic competition   204
  in Marris's model   357–8
diminishing returns, law of   82–3
diseconomies of scale   81, 112–13

discretion of managers in goal-setting
  258–60, 324
discretionary profits   373
discriminatory pricing   192–201
disequilibrium, von Stackelberg's   233–6
discontinuities   129–131
distributed lag models in demand analysis
  55–8
  'habit creation' principle   56
  Nerlove's 'stock adjustment' principle
    56
dominant firm leader   246–7
dual problem (linear programming)   434
duopoly
  Bertrand's model   225–8
  Cournot's model   216–25
  Chamberlin's 'small group'   228–9
  von Stackelberg's model   233–6

economic efficiency   68, 86–8, 91–4.
    See also least-cost combination of
    inputs
economic models   3–4
economic region of production   71–3
economies of scale
  as a barrier to entry   293–300, 305–22
  managerial   134–35
  pecuniary   137
  production   128–32
  selling   132–4
  transport   135–6
Edgeworth box diagram   38–40, 99–100
Edgeworth contract curve   38–9, 99–100,
  221, 227
efficiency, technical   67–8
elasticity of demand   46–9
  arc   48–9
  cross   6–7, 49
  income   49
  marginal revenue and   52
  price   46–9
  price discrimination and   198–9
  total revenue and   52–3
elasticity of substitution   74–6
empirical evidence on costs   137–48
  engineering cost studies   143–6
  questionnaires   143
  statistical cost studies   138–42
  'survivor' technique   146–8
Engel's law   49
engineering cost curves   122–6
engineering cost studies   143–6

envelope curve   111–14
entry   262, 284–322
  actual   262
  potential   274, 275, 284–322
entry barriers   284–322. *See also* barriers
    to entry
  absolute capital requirements   293
  absolute cost advantage   291–3
  legal   290
  preference barrier   290–1
  scale barrier   293–300, 305–22
entry-preventing pricing   284–321. *See
    also* limit-pricing
  Bain's models   284–304
  Bhagwati's model   319–20
  Sylos–Labini's model   305–13
  Modigliani's model   313–18
  Pashigian's model   320–2
equilibrium
  consumer   15, 18–24, 29
  firm   86–94
  monopolistic competition   205–9
  monopoly   174–7, 177–9
  perfect competition   155–9, 160–3
excess capacity   117–18, 212=14
exchange, theory of   38–40
expansion path   92–4
expected value   409
expenditure systems (linear)   58–60
external economies and diseconomies
    106

factor intensity   69, 76
factor substitution   68–69, 73–6
fair profit   264, 268
feasible region   416–23
feasible solution   422
firm
  cost functions   105–50
  demand curves   60–6
  equilibrium of   84–94
firms, classification of   8–12
first-degree price discrimination   195
fixed costs   107–8, 115–17
fixed inputs   82–3, 93
fixed technological coefficients   68, 415
fixed technology   105
full-cost pricing   263–5, 271–81
full-cost principle   263–5
function, objective   415
functions
  cost   105–50

demand   45, 53–8
  homogeneous of degree one   77
  homogeneous of degree zero   54
  production   67–104
free-entry
  monopolistic competition   203, 209
  pure competition, 155

game theory   404–13
  expected value   409
  maximin strategy   407
  minimax strategy   408
  non-zero sum games   410–12
  payoff matrix   405
  prisoner's dilemma   412–13
  probability elements   409
  saddle-point   408
  strategies in   404, 408, 409
  zero-sum games   406–10
geographical quotas   243–4
Giffen good   26
global rationality   257–8, 389–90
goals of firms   258–60, 324
Gordon's attack on marginalism   265–7
government food subsidy   36–8
government-regulated monopoly   200–1
graphical solution of the linear program-
    ming problem   416–23
group
  Chamberlin's 'large group' model
      228–9
  Chamberlin's 'small group' model
      202–14
  concept of 'product group'   204–5
growth
  balanced of firms (Marris's model)
      356–67
  of sales revenue (Baumol's model)
      342–8

'habit-creation' principle   56
Hall and Hitch study   263–5. *See also*
    full-cost pricing
Hicks–Allen indifference curves analysis
    14–47
homogeneous demand function   54
homogeneous product   154, 204
homogeneous production function   77–
    83
Houthakker and Taylor's 'habit-creation'
    principle   56–8
hypothesis of profit maximisation   258–
    60

hypothesis of sales revenue maximisation 325–51

imperfect competition, *see* monopolistic competition
income, choice between leisure and 35–6
income, subsistence 60
income-compensated demand curves 25, 29
income effect
  inferior goods 24–5
  normal goods 24–6
income elasticity of demand 49
increasing-cost industries 165–6
increasing returns to scale 80–1, 128–37. *See also* economies of scale
index numbers
  indifference-curve analysis 40–4
indifference curves 17–44
  applications 35–44
  consumers' surplus 32–5
  convexity of 19–20
  marginal rate of substitution 18
  properties 19–20
  revealed-preference 29–32
indifference maps 18
individual demand curves
  consumer 16, 24–7, 29
  firm 60–6
indivisibilities 129–32
industry
  concept of 7–12
  constant-cost 165
  decreasing-cost 166–7
  equilibrium
    monopolistic competition 205–9
    monopoly 174–9
    perfect competition 155–63
  increasing-cost 165–6
industry profit maximisation 221, 227, 229, 237–42. *See also* joint profit maximisation
inferior goods 24–5
information
  in traditional theory 257, 393–4
  in behavioural theory 393–4
input–output isoquant 68
inputs
  elasticity of substitution 74–6
  intensity of 69, 76
  optimal combination of 86–94
  returns to 71–2

intermediate goods
  demand of 63–6
investment, discretionary 373
isocline 78–9
isocost curves 87–8
isoprofit curves 218–21, 225–7
isoquants 68–9
isorevenue curves 102–3, 338–9

joint products 99–104, 338–42
joint profit maximisation 221, 227, 229, 237–42

kinked-demand curve 230–2, 350
knowledge
  'global' *v.* 'bounded' rationality 257, 261, 388–90
  in neoclassical theory 257, 261
  perfect competition 155

labour–leisure trade-off 35–6
Lagrangian method 22–3
Lagrangian multipliers, 22, 336, 340
lags in demand functions 55–8. *See also* distributed lag models
'large-group' model, Chamberlin's 202–14
Laspèyres index 41
least-cost combination of inputs 86–94
leisure, choice between income and 35–6
limit-pricing 284–321. *See also* entry-preventing pricing
  Bain's models 284–304
  Bhagwati's model 319–20
  Modigliani's model 313–18
  Pashigian's model 320–2
  Sylos-Labini's model 305–13
linear demand function 45
linear expenditure systems 58–60
linear programming 414–34
  constraints 415
  dual problem 434
  graphical solution 416–23
  objective function 415–23
  simplex method 423–33
  slack variables 424
long-run
  average cost 111–14, 120–2
  and entry 155, 262, 289
  marginal cost 113–14, 121–2
long-run equilibrium
  monopolistic competition 205–9

monopoly 177–9
multiplant firm 186–9
perfect competition 160–4
long-run industry supply
constant-cost industry 165
decreasing-cost industry 165–6
increasing-cost industry 166–7

Machlup's defence of marginalism 268–70
managerial costs 113, 120–1
managerial enterprise 352
managerial theories 324–83
managerial discretion model (Williamson) 371–83
managerial diseconomies 113
managerial utility function 371–6
managerialism 258
managerial economies of scale 134–5
marginal cost 108–11, 113, 117, 121–2
marginal product of factors 71–3
marginal rate of substitution 18
axiom of diminishing 17
consumer behaviour 17–28
marginal rate of technical substitution 73
classification of technological progress 85–6
marginal revenue 50
and elasticity 52
and total revenue 52–3
marginal utility 14, 16
axiom of diminishing 14
'marginalist controversy' 256–270
marginalist principle 263
'mark-up' rule 273–5
market demand 45–60
determinants 45
elasticities of 46–9
recent developments in the theory of 53–60
market equilibrium
monopolistic competition 205–12
monopoly 174–9
perfect competition 160–3
market-sharing cartels 242–44
markets, classification of 4–7
Marris's model of the managerial enterprise 352–70
mathematical expectation 409
maximin strategy
maximisation of profits, *see* profit maximisation

maximising output for given cost 88–90
measurable utility 14–17. *See also* cardinal utility
mergers, a note on 241–2
minimax strategy 408
minimising cost for given output 91–2
minimum optimal scale 294
and barriers to entry 293–300, 305–20
models, economic 3–4
Modigliani's model of limit-pricing 313–18
money illusion 54–5
money income
budget line 20
monopolistic competition 202–14. *See also* Chamberlin's 'large group' model
assumptions 203
comparison with pure competition 212–14
equilibrium 205–12
excess capacity 212–14
nonprice competition 202–4
product differentiation 204
two demand curves 207
monopoly 171–91
bilateral 189–91
comparison with pure competition 183–6
costs 174
definition 171
demand 171–4
equilibrium 174–9
government-regulated 200–1
multiplant firm 186–9
natural 171
predictions in dynamic situations 179–83
and price discrimination 192–8
supply 177
monopsonist 189
multiplant firm 186–9
multiproduct firm 99–104

natural monopoly 171
natural selection 260, 267. *See also* goals of the firm
Nerlove's 'stock adjustment' principle and demand analysis 56–7
no-money-illusion, assumption of 54
nonprice competition
product differentiation 204, 369
selling activities 204, 331–5, 340–2

normal goods
  income effect   24–6
  price effect   24–7
normal profit, 156, 273

objective function   415–23
objectives of firms, *see* goals of firms
oligopoly   215–413
  average-cost pricing   271–81
  behavioural theory   386–401
  Bertrand's duopoly model   225–8
  Baumol's sales-revenue maximisation
    model   325–51
  cartels   237–44
  Chamberlin's 'small-group' model
    228–9
  collusive   237–54
  Cournot's model   216–25
  games theory   404–13
  kinked-demand curve   230–2
  limit-pricing   284–321
    Bain's models   284–304
    Bhagwati's model   319–20
    Modigliani's model   313–18
    Pashigian's model   320–2
    Sylos–Labini's model   305–13
  Marris's model of the managerial enter-
    prise   352–70
  noncollusive   216–36
  price leadership   244–52
  Stackelberg's model   233–6
  Sweezy's model   230–2
  Williamson's model of managerial dis-
    cretion   371–83
optimal combination of inputs   86–94
optimal expansion path   92–4
optimal resource allocation   163–64
optimal scale   293–300, 305–22
ordinal utility   17, 28
organisational complexity of firms   386–
  90
organisational slack   391–2

Paasche index   43
partial equilibrium   xi
Pashigian's limit-pricing model   320–2
payoff matrix   405
Penrose's hypothesis of growth of the
  firm   358
perfect competition   154–70
  assumptions   154–5
  demand curve for firm   154

homogeneous product   154
large numbers   154
long-run equilibrium
  of firm   155–9
  of industry   161–3
optimal allocation of resources   163–4
perfect knowledge   155
short-run equilibrium
  of firm   155–9
  of industry   160
perfect knowledge   257, 260–1, 393–4
physical product of factors
  average   75
  curves   70–2
  and law of returns to scale   76–82
  and law of variable proportions   82–3
  marginal   70–3
point elasticity of demand   46–8
  graphical measurement   46–7
potential competition   262–3, 274–6,
  288–9, 305–6
prediction *v.* analysis   3
preference, and utility   28
preference barrier to entry   290–1
price
  monopolistic competition   205–9
  limiting entry   284–322
  monopoly   174–7
  shadow (linear programming)   434
price, stickiness of   230–232, 263–5
  Hall and Hitch's study   263–5
  Stigler's study   270
price change   24–6
  income effect   25–6
  substitution effect   25–6
price competition
  absence of
    Hall and Hitch's study   263–5
    Stigler's study   270
price-consumption line   24
price cross-elasticity of demand   49
price discrimination   192–201
price elasticity of demand   46–8
  arc   48–9
  graphical measurement of   46–7
  and marginal revenue   52
  point   46–8
  and total revenue   52–3
price-fixing cartel agreements   237–42
price leadership
  average-cost pricing   274–5
  barometric   248–9
  dominant firm leader   246–8

limit-pricing   303, 308–39
low-cost leader   245–6
Stackelberg's disequilibrium   233–6
price stability and kinked demand   230–2
price-taker   154, 274, 309
pricing practices   263–5, 271–81, 326, 394
pricing rules of thumb   271–81, 326, 394
primal problem (linear programming)
   434
prisoner's dilemma   412–13
product curves
   different amounts of fixed input   70
   isoquants   68–9
   marginal   70–3
product differentiation   204, 357–8
   as a barrier to entry   290–1
product expansion path   92–4
product group   7–12, 204–5
   monopolistic competition   204–5
product lines   78–9
product substitution
   marginal rate of   18–21
product transformation curve   99–102
production
   and cost functions   95–9
   changes in factor prices   92–3
   cost of   120
   economic region of   71–3
   economies of scale   128–32
   equilibrium of   86–94
   expansion path   92–4
   factor substitution   68, 72–6
   fixed factor proportions   67–9
   flows   70
   isocost line   87
   isoquants   68–9
   long-run optimal expansion path   92–3
   marginal rate of technical substitution
      73, 75
   maximise output for given cost   88–90
   method of   67. *See also* process *and*
      activity
   minimise cost for given output   91–92
   of multiproduct firm   99–104
   one fixed factor   70, 93–4
   one variable factor   70, 93–4
   optimal combination of factors   92–3
   returns to scale, law of   76–82
   short-run optimal expansion path   93
   technological progress   85–6
   theory of   67–104
   variable proportions, law of   82–3

production function
   average products   75
   continuous   69–70
   Cobb–Douglas   75–6, 78, 97–9
   and cost functions   95–9
   diminishing marginal returns   82–3
   homogeneous   77, 79, 80
   linear homogeneous   77
   marginal products   70–3
   non-homogeneous   77, 80, 82–3
production-possibility curve   99–102. *See*
      also product transformation curve
production process   67. *See also* activity
profit constraint   327, 365
profit maximisation
   average-cost approach   268, 271–81
   cartels and joint profit maximisation
      237–42
   critique of the hypothesis of   256–70
   long-run   160–1, 258–60, 262
   marginal revenue – marginal cost
      approach   156–7, 173–7
   multiplant firm   186–9
   multiproduct firm   99–104
   price discrimination   192–201
   short-run   156–9, 258–60, 262
   total revenue–total cost approach
      155–6
pure *v.* perfect competition   155

quality differentiation, *see* product differ-
      entiation
quotas and cartels   243–4

ranking of preferences   17, 28
rate of growth
   of firm (Marris's model)   352–70
   of sales revenue (Baumol's model)
      342–51
rate of product transformation   18–24
rate of technical substitution   73–4
rationality
   'bounded'   258, 389–90
   of consumers   14, 17, 28, 64, 210–11
   of firms   258–60, 325–6
   'global'   257, 258, 389–90
reaction curves   218–36
regulated monopoly   200–1
representative model of average-cost
      pricing   271–81
returns to scale   76–82
returns to a variable factor   82–3

revealed preference 28–32
revenue curves
  average 173
  and elasticity 52–3
  marginal 50, 173–4
  total 50, 156, 171–4
revenue maximisation
  Baumol's model of 325–51
ridge lines 72–3
risk and uncertainty 260–2
risk-avoidance 259
rivalry *v.* competition 5, 154
rules of thumb in pricing 271–81, 326, 394. *See also* average-cost pricing

saddle-point (games theory) 408
sales revenue maximisation 325–51
  Baumol's dynamic model 342–51
  Baumol's static models 325–42
satisfaction 14. *See also* utility
satisficing goals of the firm 258, 388–90
satisficing *v.* maximising 388–90
scale barriers to entry 293–300, 305–22
scale economies 126–37
  managerial 134–5
  pecuniary 137
  production 128–32
  real 128–36
  selling 132–4
  storage 135–6
  transport 135–6
scale of plant, minimum optimal 293–300, 305–22
second-degree price discrimination 195
selling costs 203–4, 331–7
selling economies of scale 132–5
separation of ownership and control 258, 324–5, 353
shadow prices (linear programming) 434
short-run
  cost curves 107–11, 115–18
  equilibrium
    monopolistic competition 205–9
    monopoly 174–9
    perfect competition 156–63
    profit maximisation 258, 263
    supply of firm 159–60
simplex criterion (linear programming) 430
simplex method (linear programming) 423–33

slack payments 371, 391–2
slack variables (linear programming) 424
Slutsky's theorem 24
'small-group' model, Chamberlin's 228–9
Sraffa and the 'Cost Controversy' 202
stability
  and Cournot behaviour 216–25
  von Stackelberg's disequilibrium 233–6
statistical cost studies 138–42
stock-adjustment principle 56. *See also* Nerlove
strategy 404–5
  maximin 407
  minimax 408
subjective probabilities 260–2, 266–7, 409
subsidy, food 37–8
subsistence income 60
substitute commodities 20, 27
substitute factors of production 68
substitution effect 25
substitution elasticity 74–6
supernumerary income 60
supply
  equality with demand 160, 161–3
  of a firm 159–60
  of an industry 164–7
    constant-cost industry 165
    decreasing-cost industry 166–7
    increasing-cost industry 165–6
  of the monopolist 177
  of the pure competitor 159–60
surplus, consumers' 32–5
survival of the fittest 260, 267. *See also* natural selection
survivor technique 146–8
Sylos's postulate 305–313, 313–318
Sweezy's kinked-demand model 130–2

tangency solution
  monopolistic competition 208–9
target ouput 274–5. *See also* budgeted output
tastes as a determinant of demand 45, 62–5, 210
taxation effects on equilibrium of firm
  lump-sum tax 168, 330, 380, 182
  profits tax 168, 182, 330, 380
  specific sales tax 169, 183, 277, 330

technical economies of scale   129–32.
    See also indivisibilities
technique of production, *see* activity *and*
    process
technological progress   85–6
    capital deepening   85
    labour deepening   85
    neutral   86
technology of firm   67
third-degree price discrimination   192–5
time and uncertainty   260–2
time dimensions
    short run defined   105
    long run defined   105
trade-off between income and leisure
    35–6
transformation curve, product   99–102.
    See also production-possibility curve
transitivity (in consumer theory)   17, 28
    indifference-curves analysis   17
    revealed-preference   28
transport economies of scale   135–6
total costs   107–9
total revenue   50–3
    and demand   50–3
    and elasticity   52–3
total variable costs   107–9
two-person zero-sum game   406–10

uncertainty and risk
    in behavioural theory   395
    in managerial theories   326, 357
    in neoclassical model   260–2
unitary price elasticity   47–8
utility
    additive   15, 59
    cardinal   14–16
    ordinal   17–28
    managerial   324, 352–3, 371–6
    marginal   15–16
    of shareholders   234, 352–3

variable costs   107–22
variable factors of production   69–74
variable proportions, law of   82–3

welfare maximisation
    and perfect competition   163–4
Williamson's model of managerial dis-
    cretion   371–83
work–leisure trade-off   35–6

zero elasticity of demand   48
zero homogeneity of the demand function
    54. *See also* no-money illusion
zero-sum games   406–10